bear in mind this sacred

the majority is in all cases to

must be reasonable; that the

rights, which equal law must

would be oppression.

Th Jefferson

THE CONSENT

OF THE

GOVERNED

THE CONSENT

OF THE

GOVERNED

John C. Livingston

A N D

Robert G. Thompson

ASSOCIATE PROFESSORS OF GOVERNMENT

SACRAMENTO STATE COLLEGE

The Macmillan Company, New York
Collier-Macmillan Limited, London

Library of Congress catalog card number: 63-9234

The Macmillan Company, New York
Collier-Macmillan Canada, Ltd., Toronto, Ontario
DIVISIONS OF THE CROWELL-COLLIER PUBLISHING COMPANY

Printed in the United States of America

DESIGNED BY GUY FLEMING

To Our Orphaned & Indulgent
Families
Who, We Hope, Will Want
Us Back

ETHEL	PAMELA
CLEVE	STEPHANIE
MICHAEL	STANLEY
REBECCA	STEVE
GEORGE	

PREFACE

EVERY BOOK REFLECTS its author's judgments about what is important and what is not of very great moment. Ours is no exception, but the specific judgments we have made differ radically from those reflected in most books on American government and politics. We have sought to provide students with some basic understanding of the theoretical questions and alternatives which make descriptive materials meaningful and permit the student to define for himself his role as a citizen.

Every book also reflects its author's answers to the questions he thinks are important. The tradition of textbook writing, however, dictates that one must make a great effort to avoid or conceal these biases. We have scandalously ignored this tradition, and it will be a very dull scholar indeed who fails to discern our unreconstructed majoritarian leanings, our skepticism about the politics of group accommodation, or our unconcealed distress over professional manipulation of political preferences.

We do not mean to apologize for our biases, but we hope those who do not share them will find that this book raises the right questions, however misguided the answers. Also we believe we have presented alternative positions accurately and fairly. Where we have failed, we put our faith in the critical attitudes of students and (here we know we are on sound ground) of our colleagues. Undoubtedly, there are errors both of interpretation and of fact. For both the unavoidable and the avoidable kind, each of us happily accords responsibility to the other.

We have had the critical and mechanical help of many people in the process of preparing the manuscript. To all of them we extend our gratitude.

J. C. L. and R. G. T.

C O N T E N T S

1   THE CRISIS OF DEMOCRATIC POLITICS   1

The Communist Challenge and the Internal Crisis. / Internal Sources of Political Crisis. / Government and Politics: Arena of Conflict. / Some Attractive but False Solutions. / Democracy and Communism: An Alternative View. / Authoritarianism and the Open Society.

2   THE CONFLICT OF DEMOCRATIC THEORIES   34

The Decline of Majority Rule. / The Growth of "Minorities Rule." / Descriptive and Normative Theory. / The Theory of Liberal Democracy. / The Assumptions of Liberalism. / Conservative Theories of Democracy.

THE CONSTITUTION: DEMOCRATIC BATTLEGROUND [*Checks and*   63
Balances and Federalism]

The Constitution: Democracy or Republic? / Constitutionalism: Liberal and Conservative. / Four Constitutional Principles. / Separation of Powers and Checks and Balances. / Federalism.

4   THE CONSTITUTION: DEMOCRATIC BATTLEGROUND [*Limited*   98
Government and Judicial Supremacy]

Limited Government. / Governmental Power and Individual Liberty. / Authority and Liberty: An American Consensus? / Civil Rights and Liberties: Continuing Debate. / Judicial Supremacy.

5   THE POLITICS OF MASS SOCIETY   126

The Growth of Mass Society. / Intellectual Changes. / Social Changes: The Growth of "Bigness;" The Growth of the Mass Media and Advertising; The Growth of Anomy. / The Politics of Mass Democracy: A Summary.

6   DEMOCRACY AS MINORITY RULE   149

Calhoun and the Concurrent Majority. / Concurrent Majority in the American Tradition. / The Modern Theory of Minorities Rule. / The Group Basis of Politics. / The Challenge of Minorities Rule to Traditional Democratic Theory.

7   PARTIES, PRESSURE GROUPS, AND PUBLIC RELATIONS   172

Parties and Pressure Groups: Instruments of Democratic Politics. / American Parties: Tweedledee and Tweedledum? / The Nature of the Pressure System. / The Decline of the Political "Boss." / The Rise of Public Relations. / Politicians, People, and Political Power.

8   CITIZENSHIP AND VOTING BEHAVIOR   208

The Mass Electorate: Democratic Theory and Reality. / The Voter: Interested or Apathetic? / The Vote: Reasoned Choice or Conditioned Response? / The Vote: Public Interest or Private Benefits? / The Impact of Suburbia. / The Voter and the Crisis in Democratic Theory. / The Case for the Irrational Voter. / The Case for Traditional Democratic Theory.

9   LEGISLATORS AND THEIR ENVIRONMENT   241

The Role of the Legislator. / Laws and Men. / The Difficulty of Evaluating Legislatures. / What Is a Legislator? / The Legislative Environment. / Legislators and Lobbyists. / Political Parties and the Legislator. / The Dilemmas of a Legislator. / The Legislator and *his Constituents. / The Legislator: Conscience or Compromise? / Who are the Legislators? / The "Club."*

10 LEGISLATIVE ORGANIZATION AND PROCEDURES   268

Bicameralism. / Legislative Districts. / The Necessity for Legislative Procedure. / Party Control of the Legislature. / Legislative Leadership and Organization. / The Committee System and Legislation. / Brokerage Politics and Committees. / Floor Action and Debate. / The Legislative Process and Responsible Government.

11 THE PRESIDENT AND HIS ADMINISTRATION   302

The Presidency: The Office and the Man. / The President as Spokesman for a Public Interest. / The President as Chief Executive. / Presidential Policy and the Men Who Make it. / Presidential Leadership and the Separation of Powers. / The President and Foreign Policy. / The President as Chief Foreign Policy Maker.

12 BUREAUCRACY AND THE PUBLIC INTEREST   327

The Bureaucratic Wilderness. / Government Corporations. / Independent Regulatory Commissions. / The Problem of Bureaucracy. / Public Relations as an Administrative Tool. / Bureaucracy and the Public Interest.

13 COURTS AND THE RULE OF LAW   354

Law and Society. / Freedom and the Law. / Law in a Democracy. / The Nature of the Judicial Process. / Sources of American Legal Principles. / The Role of the Courts in American Government. / The Court Structure in the United States.

14 THE COURTS IN AMERICAN POLITICS   377

The Court as Moral Guardian. / The Court as Guarantor of Due Process. / The Supreme Court as Oracle: "Equal Protection of the Law." / The Supreme Court as Umpire: Freedom Versus National Security. / The Judicial Process as Brokerage. / The Judicial Process and Majority Rule.

15 THE NEW AGENDA OF DEMOCRATIC POLITICS   411

Unfinished Business of the Old Order. / The New Problems of Politics. / The Challenge of Foreign Policy. / Democracy and the Warfare State. / Democracy and Foreign Policy. / Democracy and the Consent of the Governed. / The Crisis in Citizenship. / The Responsibilities of Citizenship.

APPENDIX: *The Constitution of the United States*   424
INDEX   451

I

THE CRISIS OF
DEMOCRATIC
POLITICS

THE COMMUNIST CHALLENGE AND THE
INTERNAL CRISIS

We LIVE IN A PERIOD of political crisis or, perhaps more accurately, political crises. For our political system is threatened by two sorts of fundamental challenges. The most obvious, hence the most readily understood, is the external challenge of an aggressive, well-organized international communist movement and the accompanying internal, subversive threat of an organized communist conspiracy. The other is a crisis of which many Americans are only dimly or vaguely aware; yet, it is as fundamental, far-reaching, and serious as the challenge of communism. This is an internal crisis in the politics and the theory of democratic government. If the world had never heard of Karl Marx, or if tomorrow every Communist in the world should somehow disappear, a major threat to democratic governments would be removed; however, other internal sources of difficulty and perplexity would remain.

The external and internal crises of democracy are related, but they are related in some curious ways. For example, because communism is a

1

threat from outside, it has produced tremendous pressures toward uniformity and conformity at home. Confronted by a common enemy we
tend to assume that we are united by a common creed, that our own
political institutions are in a state of flourishing good health, and that no
fundamental issues in the meaning of our political ideals confront us. These
tendencies are apparent in recent efforts to invoke the "American Way of
Life" as a symbol of our common allegiance and values. The irony of these
efforts is this: If it were, in fact, true that Americans were in fundamental
agreement about their political system and its underlying values, if there
were no clear indications of basic ideological disagreement or of wide
gaps between theory and practice, then these contrived efforts to dramatize our political harmony would be unnecessary. But, as we shall see, there
are such indications of basic disagreements. The result is that the invocation
of "Americanism" promotes ambiguity about what that symbol means and
glosses over issues that need to be understood and debated. The external
challenge of communism, which might have spurred efforts to deal with
internal problems, has promoted an opposite effect.

INTERNAL SOURCES OF POLITICAL CRISIS

THE INTERNAL CRISIS of democratic politics cannot be defined in a sentence or paragraph. Indeed, one evidence that the crisis is both genuine
and fundamental is lack of an agreement on how it is to be defined. Not
only is there disagreement on solutions but also on what the problem is.
At issue is the question of what model or ideal we ought to have in mind
in analyzing and evaluating the actual conduct of political life. What does
democracy mean? How should we expect democratic politics to operate?

The Gulf Between Theory and Practice

In the most general sense, the models of democratic theory which
historically have given both direction and justification to democratic politics were inherited from the eighteenth century. The current crisis in
democratic societies is rooted in two developments.

First, there are striking gaps between model and reality, between the
norms and values to which our allegiance to traditional democratic theory
commits us and the actual processes of American politics. For example,
we still profess ourselves to be committed to the idea of a public interest,
a conception of the general or common welfare which it is the function
of our political system to seek out and implement. Yet, the most obtru-
sive characteristics of our actual politics are that the struggle for power

is dominated by special interest groups—each bent on advancing its own particular claims—and that actual policies tend to be compromises of these partial claims. Similarly, our normative ideals define the ballot box as the supreme institution of democracy and require that the citizen cast his vote knowledgeably and independently. But, in recent years, rapid growth of techniques of psychological manipulation and the application of the methods and morality of advertising to political campaigns have seemed to turn the electorate into a mass market for the "public images" created by professional public relations men.

The second source of the internal crisis in democratic politics is that assumptions about the nature of man and society on which our inherited ideas of democracy rest have been widely challenged or repudiated in recent years. The eighteenth-century view of human nature saw man as essentially a rational, infinitely improvable political animal who could be trusted to govern himself. The growth of psychology as a scientific discipline has led many to conclude that a more realistic definition of political man must start from more soberly pessimistic assumptions that take into account the dominant role of irrationality and selfishness in human behavior. In both secular and religious terms, recent years have been characterized by a "rediscovery of sin." Many have been led to the conclusion that the role reserved to "the people" in traditional democratic thought was based on a tragically and ruinously over-optimistic view of human motivations and capabilities.

Similarly, the dominant eighteenth-century view of society saw it as a mechanical collection of individuals and viewed government, accordingly, as a device for registering the free, spontaneous, and uncoerced decisions of atomistic individuals. The growth of sociology and cultural anthropology has led to an increased recognition of the role of language, culture, group life, status and social class in shaping the expectations, desires, and personalities of individuals. These and other reappraisals of our inherited assumptions have led to challenges to the validity and adequacy of the assumptions on which democratic politics has been based.

Some Challenging Diagnoses of the Crisis

If these changes are as real and as profound as we believe them to be, then any genuine understanding of American government requires much more than familiarity with the structure and processes of the political system and awareness of the traditional symbols of the democratic creed. A more difficult task is required: present political institutions and practices need to be examined in the light of traditional democratic theory and current challenges to it. This is necessarily a philosophical as well as a narrowly descriptive and "scientific" undertaking. The material in this text is selected and organized to facilitate this effort.

The first step, however, is to recognize that we are not justified in taking either the good health of American political institutions or the adequacy of inherited democratic ideals for granted. We must at least attend to the critical analyses of American public life that serious, informed, and patriotic men are currently making. The number and variety of diagnoses that have appeared in recent years attest to the gravity of our political disorders. Some examples of these critical analyses are described briefly below. None of them is trivial, and each represents a position that has many knowledgeable adherents, although not perhaps in precisely the form stated here.

The list is representative but by no means exhaustive. Although we have grossly condensed and simplified the arguments, they will suggest the fundamental character of the issues that must engage our attention and the diversity of points of view from which these issues can be approached. Note, for example, that some of these diagnoses start from a rejection of traditional democratic ideology and from a satisfaction with the current state of democratic practice in America. Others find some traditional pattern of values still adequate and locate the problem in the view that current practices are no longer guided by these traditional ideals.

1. Perhaps the most challenging and disturbing analysis of modern society lies in the view that recent developments in Western democracies reflect a total cultural crisis. In this view, the basic assumptions and values which have sustained democratic societies in the past are no longer operative. The basic belief in a moral order, discoverable through reason or religion (from which such values as human dignity, progress, reform, or individualism might be derived and defended), has been irretrievably shaken by the specters of the concentration camp and nuclear terror. So also has the possibility of believing that the cumulative growth of science and technology is inherently beneficent. An age which promised unlimited and almost inevitable progress ushered in the possibilities of almost unlimited inhumanity and brutality.

At the same time that science was alienating man from nature, secularism was making him a stranger to God, and the forces of industrialism and urbanism were depriving him of a sense of identity and making him a stranger to himself. The result, these critics argue, has been the elimination of all possibility of reliable guides to human conduct and all traditional restraints on human selfishness and inhumanity. Individual, social, and political life are without a rudder and a norm.

One of the spokesmen for this "small but growing critical minority" has drawn up a bill of particulars under the following five headings.[1] First, we are convinced as a nation "that a multitude of material goods, standardized, furiously and expensively advertised by appeals to greed and vanity, will in themselves make life worth the living." Second, our culture seems to be based on the conviction "that animal appetites are mighty and to be sacrificed unto if we would enjoy a satisfactory existence; and the chief of all the appetites is sex." "Our culture, in the third place, seems based upon a conviction that to be comfortable is utterly indispensable if man is to fulfill his destiny. It occurs only to exceptional people that the whole cult of comfort is petty, ignoble, unworthy of human nature, absurd." The fourth root of our cultural malaise is "a ridiculous notion that whether a man be good or bad, wise or foolish, matters less than that he should conform to pattern. The pattern to which we are expected to conform is that set by the overgrown and depersonalized megalopolis." Finally, "our crowd-mindedness renders us suggestible, manipulatable, easy meat for almost any propagandist who is willing to flatter, to encourage animality, to promise ease and opulence with a minimum of labor expended to get them, and freedom from responsibility."

Applied directly to politics, this diagnosis leads to the conclusion that democracy operated effectively only in an intellectual climate characterized by a consensus on certain fundamental truths. Specifically, democratic political institutions were built on the belief in "natural law" and "natural rights." The growth of secularism, relativism, and skepticism has undermined the capacity to believe in any sort of "higher law" which stands above men's customs and desires. As a consequence, the symbols of democracy have tended to become empty words which no longer serve as criteria for justifying and judging its political institutions. There no longer exists that common belief in the ultimate "truths" of a "public philosophy" which serves both to unite the citizens of a body politic and to guide and restrain men's passions in the struggle for political power.

One variation of this diagnosis holds that the democratic ideal of equality is the root of the problem. Under its sway the masses have come to political power. Culturally, "the revolt of the masses" is a revolt against competence and excellence, an acid which dissolves all traditional and civilized standards of human conduct.[2] Where the tastes and judgments of the masses become the arbiters of public life the result is the standardization of taste and judgment at the lowest common denominator and conformity to the average of attitudes and opinions. Politically, the ascendancy of the masses means a glorification of the capabilities of the average man which, if allowed to continue, will result in the paralysis of political life.

[1]Bernard Iddings Bell, *Crowd Culture* (Chicago: Regnery, 1956), pp. 22-24.
[2]José Ortega y Gasset, *The Revolt of the Masses* (New York: Mentor, 1950).

It distorts the role that the masses of "the people" are qualified to play, assigning them tasks of initiating and judging policies which are beyond their experience, wisdom, or interest.

Competent government requires governors who can "assert a public interest against private inclination and against what is easy and popular. If they are to do their duty, they must often swim against the tides of private feeling."[3] Mass opinion has come to dominate democratic government, and the result is "a morbid derangement of the true functions of power."[4]   Politicians must truckle to the current crop of popular prejudices, and the vital role of leadership on which any political system depends cannot be performed.

2. A different group of critics holds that our difficulties lie not in the traditional democratic dogmas but in their corruption. In this view, political democracy can work effectively only if citizens act out the role traditionally required of them; that is, they are to give serious attention and study to public problems, seeking to act politically on behalf of what they conceive to be in the best interest of the entire community. In practice, however, voters tend to behave not as citizens but as private persons, seeing politics as a device for promoting their private and special interests against those of other individuals and groups. The result is an electorate that can be manipulated by appeals to private desires, rather than a "public" to which reasoned arguments about public policy can be addressed.

The argument here is that "the failures of democracy are due not to the sovereignty accorded to the electorate, but to the frustration of that sovereignty by power groups and elites greedy to retain their privileged status." The weak politician, seeking only to get or to hold office, does not really truckle to a mass electorate so much as he yields to "a press campaign, to a lobby, to a party caucus, to a financial backer, or even to experts."[5]

In this analysis, the problem is not the natural perversity of the average man but the absence of an organization of political power which would make possible effective leadership and a responsible electorate. The dominance of interest groups and of the techniques of psychological manipulation robs the citizen of his role as governor and makes a mockery of the ideal of government by the consent of the governed. That ideal has meaning only where consent is freely and independently given by citizens. Under modern conditions of advertising and manipulation, it has

[3]Walter Lippmann, The Public Philosophy (New York: Mentor, 1955), p. 15.
[4]Ibid., p. 19.
[5]Richard Crossman, The Charm of Politics (New York: Harper, 1959), p. 126. See also C. Wright Mills, The Power Elite (New York: Oxford University Press, 1956).

become possible to talk of the "engineering of consent" by an elite of experts and professional politicians. Consent which is thus "engineered" is difficult to distinguish in any fundamental way from the "consent" which supports nondemocratic governments. The manipulated voter has become the normal voter, and the government he supports can hardly be said to rest on his consent in any meaningful sense of that word.

3. A third approach to the problems of democracy stresses the complexity of the issues which face modern governments and the necessarily dominant role of experts in resolving them. These critics ask how the average citizen can be expected to acquire the information or carry through the analysis which would permit him to respond intelligently to questions concerning farm policy, tariff policy, or the requirements of national defense. Particularly is this true of foreign policy where, since World War II, the major political issues are to be found.

In foreign policy, the pressures toward bipartisanism and the necessity for secrecy and executive discretion have further undermined the processes of responsible government. The "garrison state" cannot be a democratic state. Power must increasingly gravitate into the hands of a political-military-industrial elite whose decisions are made without the publicity and the open competition of alternatives which democracy requires. Even if these requirements were met, the complexity of the issues would put them beyond the competence of ordinary citizens.

4. The preceding analyses vary in their diagnoses of the causes and cures of our political ailments, but they share the conclusion that the body politic is in the acute state of a serious illness. Many others, however, contest this conclusion and argue that the political system is healthy and flourishing. In their view, the difficulties lie in the mistaken expectations of the critics, not in the performance of the system. These expectations, in turn, reflect a major fallacy in traditional democratic ideology. This is especially true of those critics who lament the absence from politics of a public interest which, in the traditional doctrine, it was the task of political decisions to express.

In American politics, pressure groups—the vehicles of private interests—are stronger and better organized than political parties, which are the alleged vehicles of a public interest. What the critics do not understand is that the concept of a public interest was always a myth; in reality, there are only a variety of partial interests and conflicting desires. The organization of these interests and the accommodation of their rival claims in ways satisfactory to all is the function of democratic politics.

The essence of democracy, on these premises, is the process by which the conflicting claims of rival interests in society are compromised into a solution agreeable to all of them. This task is performed exceedingly well by American political institutions. But the delicate system of balancing group interests is threatened by moral purists who deplore the fact that principles are absent from politics and by democratic ideologists who invoke time-worn dogma to argue that a majority has a right to prevail over minorities. A majority cannot govern because a majority rarely, if ever, exists. The political problem is to establish balance among the organized minorities.

These have been oversimplified presentations of complex and sophisticated efforts to analyze the problems of modern democracy. Our purpose has been to illustrate some of the perspectives from which the crisis in democratic politics has been approached.

In the contrasts among these perspectives, some fundamental questions are raised which were not entertained seriously by any significant number of observers even a generation ago. For example: Does democracy require a consensus on basic principles which American society now lacks? Are the phenomena of mass society—mediocrity, conformity, alienation, manipulation—the inevitable results of the democratic ideal of equality? Is democratic politics characterized by a default of leadership? Does the ideal of equality require politicians to truckle to popular prejudice, to sacrifice their consciences and the role of leadership to the whims and selfish interests of their constituents?

Does the "retreat from politics" in recent years reflect the apathy, ignorance, and selfishness of the "average" man? Have the issues of politics become so complex that even the interested and informed layman cannot be expected to judge them intelligently? Are elections and popular participation destined to become a facade behind which power inevitably gravitates into the hands of the experts? Where the consent of mass audiences is engineered by professional experts and where elections become "personality contests," what does it mean to say that citizens are ruled by their own consent?

In an age of total war, can a nation forced to gird itself continuously for the possibility of war remain democratic? Ought we to be concerned or alarmed over the fact that political decisions most often reflect compromises agreeable to the major organized groups in American society? Ought democracy to be defined as a process of accommodating the conflicting aims of private interest groups or as a process of defining and applying public goals and principles? If the latter, how is this process to be embodied in political institutions?

These are difficult questions, and they are fundamental. They force the conclusion that the way out of the crisis is through the most searching and critical reappraisal of fundamental beliefs and practices of our political life. Even if communism did not exist, we should have this task before us; the fact that communism does exist gives it urgency and importance. Any positive progress to combat the communist challenge requires that we be more clearly aware of what it is that defines our own common aspirations and inspires our public life.

GOVERNMENT AND POLITICS:
ARENA OF CONFLICT

As SOME OF THE DIAGNOSES described above suggest, the changes in and the challenges to American life are economic and broadly social and cultural, as well as political and governmental. Though we shall not avoid these broader considerations entirely, our concern is with American government and politics.

The Nature of Politics

The boundaries of this area may be roughly drawn as follows: all those situations in which the interests, desires, or values of individuals and groups conflict. Politics includes the techniques and strategies by which the parties carry on the contest and the means by which these conflicts are mediated or resolved.

Defined in this way politics is not confined to the arena of government. It can be seen in the conflicts that occur in families, churches, corporations, labor unions, fraternities, universities—indeed, in virtually every sort of social organization. Wherever there is conflict, there is politics.

The Framework of Government

We are concerned, however, with that particular sphere of politics wherein public policies viewed as affecting the entire community are brought into being or modified. These are the processes which operate through the institutions of government. The central institutions of government include legislatures, courts, executive officers, and administrative agencies. In addition, there is a range of other agencies whose central purposes are related more or less closely to the desire to influence government in ways seen as desirable by their members: pressure groups, political parties, the mass media of communications. Our concern is with the way the struggle to create public policies involves all these institutions in complex interrelationships.

The line between the "private" (or internal) politics of a fraternity, labor union, or corporation and the "public" politics of governmental policy-making is never fixed. What starts out as a private dispute—the conflict between labor and management within the corporation, for example—may be transferred to the public arena at whatever time it may come to be viewed as involving the political interest of the entire community. When this happens, the sphere of the conflict is extended and the political techniques employed come to be those that are relevant to influencing the governmental process. Sometimes, this occurs because it is seen by one or several of the parties to a private conflict as an effective strategy for getting their way. Sometimes, it is the result of third parties insisting successfully that the conflict involves a public interest that cannot be protected in the accommodations worked out by private interests. However it occurs, when a dispute is put into the governmental arena, its resolution becomes a matter of public policy to be embodied in law and administrative rulings which contain the coercive power of the community and are applicable to all.

The Motivations and Techniques of Politics

The political struggle is complicated by the fact that influence on public policy may be sought for different reasons and stem from different motivations. Some of the participants are dominantly motivated by the desire for personal fame, opportunists who seek the ascendancy of personal prestige, power, and fortune that success in the political struggle brings. Others are dominantly concerned in representing the economic interests of a particular group and seeking primarily to achieve the differential advantages over competing groups that are rewards of success in the struggle. Still others are dominantly motivated by an ideology or social philosophy—a commitment to principles they conceive to be necessary to social justice or on which they define the public interest.

The distinction between these motivations is, of course, an analytical one. No one could pretend that those engaged in politics could be neatly fitted into one of the three categories. In almost every political actor there is a mixture of opportunism, interest, and principle. Much the same thing is true of the techniques used by those engaged in the political struggle. The range of possible techniques is wide: force, threats of force, bribery, duplicity, manipulation, martyrdom, reasoned argument, appeals to authority, appeals to shared values. And here, no more than in the realm of motivation, is purity to be expected in democratic politics. A bewildering variety of motivations and techniques greets the close observer of any democratic political system. Depending on his point of view, the panorama may be taken as a sign of robust good health, or of frightening corruption, or as merely interesting.

The *pattern* of motivation and technique—the relative importance and influence of each of the ingredients—is not the same in all political systems, however. Nor are the differences the result of chance. Which motivations are likely to predominate, and which techniques are likely to be most often employed and most effective, will depend on two sets of considerations—one broadly cultural, and the other political and ideological.

The cultural set of influences stems from a people's deeply ingrained habit patterns and customary ways of looking at things. In a culture characterized by a high regard for tradition and a relatively stable system of social class and status, for example, appeals to traditional values and symbols are likely to be the most effective and common technique. In a situation, more like our own, where change is itself a highly regarded value, there are likely to be fewer restrictions on the range of permissible and effective techniques.

Just as cultural characteristics influence techniques, so do they also help to shape political motivations. For example, a society in which status-striving is a cardinal virtue, and successful pursuit of personal material goals the recognized cultural standard of individual success, can be expected to exhibit a pattern of political motivations in which opportunism and interest are dominant. There are those, as one of the diagnoses described above made clear, who see exactly this cultural situation as the root of the problems in American politics. They argue, in effect, that a culture whose values prompt it to rely on the slogan, "Drive Safely: The Life You Save May Be Your Own," to minimize what others have called "murder on the highways" is a culture that is quite likely to produce a pathological oversupply of opportunism and interest-seeking in its politics. Whether or not one agrees with their conclusion that the supply is pathological, they are correct in pointing to the influence of cultural considerations in producing the interest group dominance that characterizes American politics.

The other major set of influences was designated as political-ideological. Every political ideology, (or philosophy, if you prefer), furnishes answers to a variety of fundamental political questions. The question with which we are mainly concerned here is this: How is the conflict of interests and opinions in society to be resolved? The answer given by a political ideology to this question will influence the pattern taken by political motivations and techniques in the political order in which that ideology is effective. We will be in a position to see why and how this influence operates after we have considered the general problem of the resolution of political conflict.

The Resolution of Political Conflict

There are, of course, many different ways of resolving disputes in society. When the interests or goals of two parties conflict the solution may be provided, for example, by the rule of the stronger, by the verdict of an elite, by majority decision, by bargaining and compromise, or by invoking established and traditional rules which prescribe the rights and obligations of the competing parties.

What makes this a fundamental problem is that it is impossible that all those with a claim should be treated equally in the resolution of any conflict. Any conceivable solution of the conflict will favor some individuals or groups over others. Indeed, it is difficult to see what we could mean by "equal treatment" in conflict situations. What solution to the problem of minimum wages, for example, would treat labor, management, stockholders, and consumers equally? Even if theoretically there were such a solution, it is not likely that it could be achieved since the parties to the conflict, each convinced of the merits of his position, would employ all the political techniques at his disposal to secure his point of view.

The problem, then, is to discover a process for resolving conflicts which will provide justice to all the parties. In a very important sense this is the fundamental political problem. Every answer to this question—whether a decision by an aristocracy of birth, by an elite of brains or wealth, by a numerical majority, or by compromise among the interests themselves—rests on certain assumptions about the nature of man and of society and about the role and limitations of reason in human life. We shall have much to say on these matters in the chapters that follow. Here, we wish only to emphasize that the philosophical assumptions of every such theory of politics lead to certain conclusions about which human motivations will be dominant and which political techniques are to be considered legitimate. The theory of majority rule, for reasons that will be made clear in the next chapter if they are not already, assumes the dominance of conflicts of principle and program and specifies reasoned argument as the norm for political techniques. The theory of compromise, on the other hand, makes no such demands on human nature and puts a premium on the techniques appropriate to a bargaining situation.

When political conflicts become public and are brought to the governmental arena, the participants become subject to the norms or standards embodied in the ideology that underlies a society's political system. This ideology prescribes and justifies some basic process for making public decisions. The legitimate roles of the political participants—citizens, politicians, interest groups, political parties, administrators, and judges—will depend on, and be defined by, the particular conflict-resolving process sanctioned by the prevailing ideology.

Politics and Power

Politics, it is clear, is concerned with power, with the exercise of discretion over the behavior of others and the ability to shape common policies and decisions binding on others in accordance with one's own desires. Politics is power because it is the struggle to shape or control the decision-making process. Because politics always implies conflict, competition and struggle, there are those who would define politics in such a way that it becomes coextensive with the struggle for power. Politics, in the title of a well-known book that helped to develop and popularize this point of view, is the study of "who gets what, when, how."[6]

Such a view, we believe, neglects or minimizes an equally important aspect of political struggle. This is the problem of legitimacy which characterizes every political situation. Victory in the political struggle carries with it control over, or a disproportionate share in, the making of decisions which favor some individuals or groups over others and yet will be binding on all. But why should those who do not fare well in the struggle, or lose out altogether, abide by the decisions that are made? The proposition that power is its own justification—that "might makes right"—has been advanced by a few philosophers, but it is not a conclusion that any society or nation has ever accepted. In every political system the means by which conflicts are adjusted and power struggles resolved are held to result, not in the rule of might, but in the supremacy of reason, truth, or justice. Every political order seeks to translate power into legitimate authority. The claim to legitimacy may be more or less rational but it is always an effort to make moral obligation, not fear or force, the basis of obedience to law.

Politics and Legitimacy

Those who argue for an approach to politics that concentrates exclusively on the "reality" of power seek to avoid the problem of legitimacy as being a matter of "values" and therefore beyond the reach of objective, rational inquiry.

Our own premises reject this view. Beneath the reality of competing individuals, group interests, and philosophical principles in every political system is a normative "model" of how the system *ought* to operate. This model justifies some particular method of resolving disputes as conferring legitimate authority, rather than mere power, on those who make the decisions and on the conflict-resolving methods that are employed. At the root of the current predicament lies uncertainty and controversy over what model is appropriate to democracy. What does democracy mean as a way of resolving conflict? What techniques in the struggle for power does it render legitimate? What motivations does it idealize and seek to make into norms of conduct for its citizens? And what methods does it make punishable when they are used?

[6]Harold D. Lasswell, *Politics; Who Gets What, When, How?* (New York: Whittlesey House, 1936).

The actual conduct of American politics presents a bewildering variety of rapidly changing political techniques and processes. More than ever it is necessary that attention be directed to the problem of legitimacy. How are the facts of American political life to be analyzed and evaluated? What model are we to have in mind as we seek to appraise the state of health of our political order? Is American politics moving in the direction of a new sort of tyranny of public opinion and rule of mediocrity? Or are we moving in the direction of a new system of universal toleration and compromise that means a more effective and beneficent democracy? This view, along with the preceding ones, has its equally serious spokesmen.

These divergent judgments are not mainly a matter of disagreement about the facts of American politics. They reflect also more fundamental disagreements over what democracy means as a normative model for resolving disputes and over what political processes are desirable and legitimate within the limits of this model. If the citizen is to participate in what are now the important issues of democratic politics, so must he concern himself with the basic philosophical alternatives about which the scholars are contesting. At the very least, the citizen needs to know enough about the crisis which has prompted the dispute to avoid oversimplified and misleading popular remedies to which he is continuously exposed.

SOME ATTRACTIVE BUT FALSE SOLUTIONS

Efforts to find an easy way out of our difficulties have produced several fallacies that becloud the more searching analysis that is necessary. We shall discuss some of the recent efforts to find a simple, ready-made answer to the problem of deciding what is the American political philosophy and of drawing clear distinctions between democracy and communism. The list is not exhaustive; we have selected current efforts to define democracy which seem particularly widespread because of their deceptive simplicity.

Democracy as "the American Credo"

It is sometimes asserted, and often implied, that we can resolve the issues which confront us by an appeal to history. Basically, this is the proposition that there is, historically, an "American democratic creed"— unambiguously clear, concise, consistent over the years; capable of being set down in a series of simple, straightforward articles of faith; and susceptible of direct application to current conditions. Even though it is true that no understanding of our current predicament and alternatives is possible without a knowledge of our political past, it is equally true that the past itself provides no direct answers to the issues of the present. This is particularly true of people like ourselves, whose past is democratic, because a democratic tradition by its nature cannot be reduced to any clear, monolithic, and authoritative body of beliefs.

The men who made the "democratic revolution" in the eighteenth century were, it is true, united by their opposition to the systems of monarchy, aristocracy, and feudalism and by their positive commitment to the ideals of liberty and equality. But the validity of these ideals was never quite as self-evident, nor was their meaning as clear and unambiguous, as the revolutionaries sometimes proclaimed them to be. Indeed, the subsequent history of democracy has been, in substantial measure, a continuing and sometimes heated controversy over their meaning.

As weapons for assaulting the established political, economic, and social orders, they had a sharp enough cutting edge. Liberty was the basis of man's claim to be free from arbitrary restraints imposed by tradition or by other men and his right to be bound only by the exercise of authority to which he had given his consent. Equality meant equal access to careers and opportunities on the basis of individual merit and without reference to conditions of birth or ancestry. Applied directly to political life, equality meant equal rights to participation in choosing one's governors and to protection against arbitrary enforcement of the laws. But while liberty and equality provided powerful levers for razing the structures of monarchy and aristocracy, they left open many fundamental questions about how the new society was to be organized.

The political symbols of the American tradition have provided only a framework for controversy over their meaning. From the beginning, the American Revolution settled only one question: the political destinies of Americans were in the future to be decided by Americans. It did not determine what the character of the political settlement was to be. The Revolution was, in one of its aspects, a social movement. Fought under the banners of the liberal democratic slogans and ideas of men like Thomas Paine, Patrick Henry, Thomas Jefferson, and Samuel Adams, it was more than a struggle for independence or the "rights of Englishmen." It was also a claim to the natural rights of man and popular government. It was an opening round in the struggle for "the age of the common man." Thomas Paine, who forged the ideas that carried men through the bitter days at Valley Forge, was the spokesman for the ideas of thoroughgoing majoritarian democracy. It was inevitable, therefore, that the new governments established after the Revolution should reflect these ideas in large measure.

But if some of the leading figures of the Revolution were committed to the proposition that the only safe basis for controlling political power is to make it directly responsible to the people through majority vote, not all of them were so minded. Others had something less than full faith in the capacities of common men to govern themselves and to safeguard liberty and justice. In some cases their pessimism approached an open contempt. Even Jefferson admitted that the people may not always be the wisest guardians of their own liberties, but he insisted that they are always the "safest" repository of human rights. John Adams argued that, far from being adequate caretakers of liberty, the masses of the people "are no guardians at all."

Moreover, even such confirmed democrats as Jefferson, Paine, John Taylor of Caroline, Richard Henry Lee, and Benjamin Franklin did not equate the voice of the people with the voice of God: they did not believe that popular control of government and popular choice of public policy would automatically result in the best selections to exercise power responsibly. Depending on their estimates of human nature, their views ranged from Paine's optimistic conclusion that "when public matters are open to debate, and the public judgment free, it will not decide wrong, unless it decides too hastily" to the somewhat more pessimistic views of James Madison that constitutional restraints on the human tendencies toward selfishness and passion are necessary. Among those of the Founding Fathers less enamored of democracy, conclusions ranged all the way to Hamilton's extreme view that "the people seldom judge or determine right."

Even the more optimistic democrats recognized that democracy was an experiment, and that its success hinged on the possibilities of surmounting certain inherent tendencies and dangers. From these considerations, we may conclude that it is highly misleading to think of the Founding Fathers as a homogeneous group who agreed on the fundamentals of political theory and whose only problem was to translate their common premises into political institutions. They were, in fact, in fundamental disagreement about such basic matters as human nature, the nature of society, and the role of property in political power. These disagreements in assumptions were reflected in debates over such matters as whether there is a natural aristocracy whose legitimate role in society and government needs to be protected from popular meddling; what sorts of restraints need be put on the actions of popular majorities; how much power should be vested in the national government; what the proper basis of the right to vote should be; whether the courts should have the right to declare acts of the legislature unconstitutional; whether freedom is compatible with the conditions of an industrial, urban society or whether it requires the rural, independent, agrarian way of life.

Disagreement also extended to the basic ideals themselves. For example, the doctrine of the consent of the governed, as it was expressed in the Declaration of Independence by Jefferson, calls for the direct accountability of governors to the governed. It implies that this accountability is to be enforced through the process of reasoned debate of issues and direct popular vote. But in *The Federalist* (No. 35), Alexander Hamilton argues that the Constitution embodied a quite different theory of the consent of the governed. To him, individuals consent to a government, not primarily by a vote which holds their representatives responsible to their wishes and desires, but by having their economic interests represented by those who are the natural representatives of the economic classes to which they belong.

Thus he held that all those who make their living through manufacturing or commerce are represented by the merchant, who is "their natural patron and friend"; "their interests can be more effectively promoted by the merchant than by themselves." Similarly, the interests of everyone engaged in agriculture "from the wealthiest landlord down to the poorest tenant" will be best protected by the representation of large landholders in government. This theory of consent differs radically from Jefferson's.

There have been other influential Americans who have argued still other positions on this question. In the modern world, the whole problem of "consent," we have already noted, has taken on new dimensions in the light of mass advertising and mass manipulation.

The same sort of analysis holds for the other symbols of the democratic creed. In one sense or another, all democrats have believed in equality, but the variety of meanings given this term is almost as great as the number of men who have been concerned with it. Obviously, men are not equal in such matters as ability, talent, energy, or any other human attribute, and no serious political philosopher has ever held that they were. In what sense, then, are they equal? And in what respects should they be treated equally? Obviously, every organized society involves inequality, hierarchy and differential status, power and prestige. Which *in*equalities, then, are justified and which are arbitrary, illegitimate, or unjustified?

These are the kinds of questions which arise when men try to formulate meaning for the ideal of equality. Men should be treated equally "apart from relevant differences"—on this proposition, all democrats would agree.[7] But what differences are to be considered as relevant? On this question American democrats have disagreed. Are differences in the capacities of men to acquire property the important ones which should be reflected in social inequalities? Some of the Founding Fathers thought

[7] See J. Roland Pennock, *Liberal Democracy: Its Merits and Prospects* (New York: Holt, Rinehart & Winston, 1950), pp. 82-86.

so and argued accordingly for equality of economic opportunity and the right of the economically more successful to rule those who were least successful. Or is it more important that men be free to develop to the fullest their intellectual and moral capacities? Others were equally convinced that this was the case, and argued accordingly for equality of opportunity in this area.

This issue came to focus in the formative period of American political life in the debate over property qualifications on the right to vote. "It is the first time in my life that I have ever heard of a government which was to divorce property from power," lamented John Randolph in the Virginia Constitutional Convention of 1829-30, when it was proposed to eliminate property qualifications on the right of suffrage. Not the protection of property, but the "cultivation of the human mind," is the proper object of government and society, argued James Wilson in the Federal Convention. These are diametrically opposed views, and the fundamental cleavage was rooted in radically different interpretations of the meaning of equality.

This analysis barely scratches the surface of the problem of defining equality and ignores the many other conflicting interpretations of the meaning and implications of the term. We wish only to suggest here that the vitality of the concept, and its role in the American tradition, are to be understood primarily in terms of the conflict over its meaning. Short of an effort to understand this controversy, the concept of equality tells us virtually nothing about the American tradition.

These underlying disagreements extended even to the question of how political conflicts were to be resolved in order to safeguard and promote liberty and justice. For conservative democrats like John Adams, majority rule produced not legitimate authority, but the tyrannical power of numbers. For liberal democrats like Jefferson, the majority will was the only source of legitimacy. The most significant characteristic of the formative period of American government is to be found, not in the documents that express the ways in which these conflicts were resolved, but in the debates over the meaning of these documents that express the differences, conflicts, and cleavages out of which American government was forged.

In the exchange of letters in which Jefferson and John Adams explored their disagreements over the last twenty years of their lives; in the spirited debate between Adams and John Taylor, the architect of Jeffersonian democracy, over the meaning of the Constitution; in Paine's attack on the principles of Edmund Burke's British conservatism; in the struggle over the adoption of the Constitution through the debates in the national and state constitutional conventions—here is revealed the most significant fact about the American political heritage. *It is a heritage of controversy, even about the meaning of the heritage itself.* For this reason, it is a democratic heritage. And for the same reason, there is no justification for the currently popular practice of drawing up lists of concepts which are alleged to sum up the ingredients of the "American way." Such lists are not likely to be very meaningful. Where it is implied that the American political tradition furnishes substantive agreement on their meaning, the implication is historically false. And where the impression is conveyed that the present day democrat need only commit to memory what are almost inevitably platitudes and recite them in a litany, the tendency is positively fatal to democratic citizenship. The moral is clear: beware the easy appeal to articles of the "American democratic creed" which require neither historical study nor serious reflection on rival interpretations of their meaning.

Democracy as Religious Faith

A second prescription often offered follows from the proposition that religious (or Judeo-Christian or, sometimes, Christian) faith is the only sound foundation for democratic values. (The other side of this proposition is often put in the redundant charge that the most significant characteristic of communism is its "Godless atheism".)

It is of course clear that religion—specifically the Hebraic-Christian religious tradition, and more specifically still, Christianity—has played a major formative role in the development of Western civilization and Western-type democracy. Surely no understanding of our cultural and political history is possible without an accounting of the vital role played by religious belief. But this is not at all equivalent to saying that democracy requires and rests on religious belief. However tempting it may be, it is not legitimate to argue that since the communist creed is atheistic and defines religion as "the opiate of the masses," the democratic concept of human dignity must rest on religion and require a belief in God.[8]

The dangers and consequences of this identification of democracy with religious belief were illustrated in the very beginnings of the democratic movement. One of the most influential of its philosophers was the

[8]We refer to the facile and superficial pleas of superpatriotic groups and some editorial writers. There are, on the other hand, some penetrating and thoughtful men who argue, from one or another religious point of view, that some particular religious insight is necessary to the democratic spirit and outlook. Among these are Jacques Maritain, *Man and the State* (Chicago: University of Chicago Press, 1951); John H. Hallowell, *The Moral Foundation of Democracy* (Chicago: University of Chicago Press, 1954); and Reinhold Niebuhr, in any of his stimulating books. The important point is that none of these men conclude that believers have a right to force their views on, or to deny full citizenship and civil liberties to, nonbelievers.

Englishman John Locke. He wrote to justify the "Glorious Revolution" of 1688, which established the fact that the King was not above the law and was to be responsible to the Parliament. His ideas on natural rights and representative government became, in Jefferson's phrase, "the commonsense of mankind" and exerted a profound influence on American democrats. But in his defense of freedom, in his essay "On Toleration," Locke applied the premise that religious belief is necessary to morality, and therefore to responsible citizenship. His conclusion was that atheists are to be excluded from the regime of religious toleration in democratic societies.

Locke's argument graphically illustrates the consequences of insisting that religious belief is necessary to democratic citizenship. He formulated his conclusions broadly enough to encompass all or most religious beliefs (he would also exclude Catholics from the regime of toleration on grounds that they owed loyalty to a foreign power). Within this framework, governments should not interfere with the individual's freedom of choice. Yet, a significant group of other alternatives—atheism, agnosticism, or humanism, for example—could legitimately be foreclosed. Specifically, a modern Socrates, Thomas Paine, Justice Holmes, or Clarence Darrow would be read out of democratic society.

The tendency of modern Americans to adopt Locke's argument is revealed in the current way of speaking of "freedom of religious belief" as a basic tenet of American democracy. What this clearly implies is the existence of a variety of established and respectable religious faiths, and the right of the individual to freedom of choice in deciding among them. This is a quite different meaning of freedom of conscience in this area from, for example, Jefferson's statement in that landmark of religious liberty, the Act for Establishing Religious Freedom in Virginia (1786). That act did not provide for the freedom of men to make a choice between alternative institutionalized modes of worship or even for their freedom to "worship God in their own ways." It provided, rather, in carefully chosen words, "that all men shall be free to profess, and by argument to maintain, their opinions in matters of religion." An atheist, an agnostic, or a humanist has "opinions in matters of religion" which this way of stating the matter protects. But these are positions that are outside the framework of religious beliefs.

Jefferson, in the Declaration of Independence, formulated an alternative to Locke in these words: "We hold these truths to be self-evident: that all men are created equal; that they are endowed by their Creator with certain unalienable rights. . . ." The intent of these words was not to insist on belief in a Creator, but to indicate that men who believed these rights to be derived from God were included in a consensus with those who believed them to be self-evident or derived from nature or reason.

The consensus itself was on the *rights* of men to seek liberty and happiness in their own ways and for themselves. The insistence on one orthodox view of the source of these rights would have operated to limit the exercise of the rights themselves. To argue that religion is one source of democratic values is one thing; to assert that it is the only source, and thereby to read all nonbelievers out of the society of democratic men, is another.

In addition, the identification of democracy with religion or with Christianity encounters considerable difficulty in explaining how Periclean Athens and modern-day Israel meet the other democratic tests while Christian Spain does not. Finally, it is hardly realistic and certainly parochial to imagine that the picture of the Cold War as a conflict between "atheistic communism" and "Christian democracy" is likely to make much sense to the uncommitted peoples of Asia and Africa. It can lead even to the observation, found in a prominent American official's statement, that the Arabs and Jews could solve their conflicts if they would only sit down and talk things over in a "Christian spirit."

Perhaps we can get a clearer view of this question by examining the attitudes of communist Russia to religion. In February of 1918, about three months after the Communists had taken power in the Soviet Union, a decree was issued with this provision: "Every citizen may profess any religion or none at all. Any legal disabilities connected with the profession of any religion or none are abolished." In its separation of church and state and its assertion of freedom of belief and expression, this decree parallels the Virginia Statute of Religious Freedom. But as the Communists cemented their control of the Soviet State, as rival political parties were made illegal, and as the leaders of the party established themselves as the official interpreters of the meaning of socialist doctrine, there were changes in Soviet policy.

The Marxist interpretation of religion as a device to offer the workers "pie-in-the-sky-bye-and-bye," and thus take their minds off their troubles here and now, led to official efforts to eliminate religious belief and religious congregations. The new political reality was reflected in the Soviet Constitution of 1936. That document still provided for freedom of religious *belief*, but freedom "of propaganda" (that is, freedom of expression) was reserved exclusively for antireligious views. Unlike some other provisions of the Soviet Constitution, this one generally has been reflected in political practice. Americans would not be fooled by a pretense of guaranteeing freedom of belief while providing that only certain views are entitled to be expressed. Obviously there is no genuine freedom for the religious point of view under these conditions. What we need to ask ourselves is whether identifying democracy with religion does not put nonreligious views under the same disabilities and restraints.

The heart of the problem seems to be that both people who are atheists because they are Communists and people who assume that democracy requires religion share a common assumption: a society, as a society, must choose between atheism and religion. From the point of view of this assumption, anyone who argues for the "open society" must appear as a camouflaged proponent of, or at least a dupe of, the dreaded position of the enemy. Thus, a Communist reading this chapter will dismiss it as a concealed plea for religion; and some American readers doubtless will interpret it as a skillfully concealed defense of communism or of atheism.

"Religion (atheism) is the creed of capitalism (communism); who except a capitalist (communist) sympathizer, would defend equality for the religious (atheists)." The words may be interchanged; the argument is the same. What it fails to recognize is that there is another possibility, a position which holds that the basis for political loyalty need not and ought not to contain any commitment whatever on the question of religion, except the commitment to the fullest possible freedom of belief and expression. It may be, as some have argued, that men are so constituted that such a society will not satisfy the emotional need for common substantive symbols or the moral restraints for behavior that only final truths can provide. Certainly, the position must be recognized as a possibility that is logically at odds with the positions of both Communists and advocates of religion-based democracy. In our view, it is the only meaningful alternative to authoritarianism, whether justified in the name of religion or of atheism.

Democracy as Capitalism

A third, and common, analysis holds that a capitalist economic system is the fundamental requirement for democratic government. This proposition, like the one that links democracy with religion, suffers the defects of its origin. Usually, it is a result of the effort to define democracy as the negative of the attributes of communism. Thus, if communism means public ownership and socialist planning, democracy requires, therefore, a free enterprise economy.

Like the religious argument, this one is parochial and rooted in one aspect of the American experience. Capitalism, like religion, *is* an important part of our tradition, but that tradition includes other opposing elements as well. And there are other countries in whose democratic traditions anticapitalism has played the dominant role. Certainly, there are many examples of noncommunist, socialist movements whose loyalty to political democracy cannot be questioned. We can hardly afford to sweep under the rug the British, Scandinavian, Western European, Indian, and many other socialist parties, nor ought we to presume to read them out of democratic politics. (For those who join the religious and economic arguments, the difficulties are compounded by the fact that in many democratic nations there are Christian Socialist parties!)

Moreover, for most of the uncommitted peoples of the world, capitalism is, for valid historical reasons, identified with colonialism and white supremacy. So far as the appeal of democracy to these peoples is concerned, to link it necessarily with capitalism could give it the kiss of death. What is more, the democratic socialism of other democratic nations has often been the main bulwark against communism. The Communists themselves recognize this and tend to regard the noncommunist socialists as their major enemies.

The phrases "capitalistic democracy" and "democratic capitalism" are themselves fairly new to American history, having become current only in the period since World War II. During most of the American tradition, the spokesmen for the idea of democracy have been opposed to industrial capitalism. Jefferson, for example, was convinced that democracy required the economic climate of an agrarian society of small independent landholders. The rise of industrial capitalism met with constant attack from the camp of those democratic reformers who saw in it a threat to the independence and the fraternity that, in their view, democracy required. Again, it is one thing to argue that capitalism—at least the modified kind of "mixed economy" that currently prevails in the United States—is compatible with democracy; it is quite another to argue that capitalism is the *only* economic system compatible with democracy.

This problem of the relation of political democracy to forms of economic organization is a complicated one. Most often those who talk of "capitalist democracy" are exceedingly vague about what is meant by capitalism. The growth of the giant corporation and of oligopolistic competition among the giants, the accompanying growth of labor bureaucracy, the shift in emphasis from production to sales and service, the central role of human relations in modern industry, the economic controls and stimulation inherent in the garrison state—these and other developments make the old capitalist shibboleths of *laissez-faire*, competition, the law of supply and demand, and the sovereign consumer largely irrelevant. The result is that the plea for a necessary connection between democracy and capitalism is bound to be an ambiguous one. Such ambiguity serves broadly to put the *status quo* beyond the reach of public criticism. It is a doctrine even more inimical to the democratic requirement of open debate than it would be if its proponents were clear about what they meant by capitalism. For in that event, because their doctrine would refer to a specific set of ideals and institutions, it could more effectively be challenged by rival *ideas*. But where, as seems to be the case, what is being defended is simply "whatever we now have," ideas and ideals will appear as irrelevant or—worse yet—dangerous to morale and social harmony.

This atmosphere is already reflected in the experience, for example, of two economists who recently wrote a book attacking the current tendencies toward capitalistic giantism and monopoly from the point of view of the traditional ideals of a competitive, *laissez-faire* capitalism. Their experience led them to conclude that the response from defenders of present-day capitalism would be to hint darkly at the possibilities of subversion, for, they will ask, "is not this praise of competition and condemnation of monopoly a subtle and devious attempt to undermine the very foundations of American productivity, and thus to deliver us helpless into the hands of our enemies?"[9] Thus, in the kind of climate generated by a public commitment to capitalism as a vague referent for efficiency and prosperity, any ideological attack on the *status quo*, even a very conservative appeal to the historic meaning of capitalism itself, may appear as vaguely subversive and out of order. The result may be not simply to declare specific ideas and principles dangerous but also—the far more corrosive tendency—to regard *all* ideas as irrelevant.

Democracy as American Constitutionalism

The fourth solution holds that democracy depends on the specific constitutional forms which it has taken in the United States. Specifically, the American governmental forms that are often identified with democracy include the institutions of federalism (that is, the constitutional division of powers between the central or federal government and state governments), separation of powers with checks and balances, and judicial supremacy (that is, the right of a court to declare an act of the legislature void if it is contrary to a written constitution). But Great Britain does not have a federal form of government or a system of checks and balances or a written constitution with a supreme court to interpret it. Indeed, these institutions are quite rare among the world's democracies and often have been present in Latin American governments that would be difficult to characterize as democracies.

We will examine these constitutional principles of American government in greater detail in a subsequent chapter. Here we need only note that in the case of federalism, the American solution was related to distinctive American conditions (the heterogeneity of Colonial life and the firmness of emotional attachments to state governments). In the case of checks and balances, there have been continual sharp disagreements over the meaning of the principle and its ultimate accomplishment. Judicial supremacy has been a matter of continuing controversy in American history,

[9]Walter Adams and Horace M. Gray, *Monopoly in America* (New York: Macmillan, 1955), p. 6.

numbering among its opponents Presidents Jefferson, Jackson, and Franklin Roosevelt, as well as current Southern segregationists. Moreover, in every case, the meaning and influence of these principles have been so thoroughly transformed over the course of American history that it may be seriously misleading to speak of them as fixed principles at all.

It is difficult to avoid the conclusion that none of the specific political arrangements of American government is essential to democracy. Whatever it is, democracy refers to deeper, more profound political realities than can be encompassed in specific constitutional forms.

DEMOCRACY AND COMMUNISM: AN ALTERNATIVE VIEW

THE POPULAR, but in our view fallacious, arguments discussed above have the effect of identifying democracy with some specific conclusions and institutions. Their effect and often, one suspects, their intent are to deal with opposing opinions, not by argument and discussion but by labeling them subversive of truths which have come to be regarded as sacred and unquestionable. Because these truths are, in some sense, the opposite of communist dogma they are presumed to be "democratic."

There is another point of view, however, in which the meaning of democracy and its opposition to communism are to be found in its characteristics of diversity, openness, and controversy. In this view, the most significant characteristics of communist governments are their authoritarian (or dictatorial) nature and their totalitarian tendencies. Democratic governments, on the contrary, are seen to rest on the concepts of the "open society" and pluralism. A closer look at these distinctions may serve as a starting point to clarify both the essential features of democracy and the nature of the communist challenge.

Authoritarianism and the Open Society

Earlier we noted that the American political tradition is one of controversy, and that this controversy has extended even to the meaning of the basic symbols of democracy. We argued, too, that the pressing necessity in current American life is for a renewal of such fundamental public discussion and debate. This is the most important sense in which democratic societies are open societies. This openness to criticism and debate of even its most basic institutions and ideals gives rise to both the secret and the underlying dilemma of democracy: It is the only system of government in which *the fundamental meaning of the system itself is open to inquiry and debate.*

Every system of government allows some room for criticism and argu-ment. Every pattern of political organization leaves some alternatives open to individuals. There are areas of public debate and there are options left open to individuals in even the most authoritarian governments. The ques-tion of centralization or decentralization of the instruments of economic planning, for example, has been the subject of public debate in the Soviet Union. At times, the question of consumer goods versus capital goods production has also been a fairly open one. The "thaw" in Soviet culture after Stalin's death broadened the area of permissible discussion in literature and the arts, biology, and—for a time and to some extent—in the areas of economic and political belief.

But the appearance of these small gaps in the fabric of orthodoxy and conformity do not mean that Soviet society is on its way to becoming an open society. In the first place, the authoritarian character of the regime is revealed in the fact that the areas left open to public debate and the options available to individuals are themselves determined by the authori-tative decisions of an elite. Among other things, this means that the boundaries of permissible public initiative and controversy vary, a fact likely to dampen the enthusiasm of citizens for seizing such opportunities as may, at a given time, be available. What it is permissible to think and say today may next week become subversive "obstructionism."

(Something of a parallel nature occurred in the United States after World War II when political activities considered legitimate in the 1930's came to be retroactively labeled subversive. Although never on anything like the level of conformity in totalitarian countries, one effect was to dis-courage people from any political involvement which might, at some time in the future, be publicly labeled subversive. The safe course in the cir-cumstances was not to join anything or take any position on controversial matters.)

Secondly, in the Soviet Union, as in all authoritarian societies, the official ideology is itself always beyond criticism; the fundamentals of the political order which it establishes and justifies are never open to public debate. In communist regimes, the validity of the materialist view of reality, the role of class struggle as the dynamic of history, and the truth of atheism may not be publicly challenged. Nor may the basic alloca-tion of political power and the arrangements for making political decisions. The meaning and proper interpretation of the ideology remain matters for authoritative pronouncement by an elite which is presumed to have access to truth not available to ordinary citizens.

In a democracy, by contrast, the meaning of democracy itself—plus the assumptions appropriate to it, and the political processes and institu-tions needed to implement it—remain open questions. There can be no permanent agreement because there is no authoritative source of dogma with an official corps of interpreters to whom matters can be referred when people disagree. The significance of this is clarified if we recognize that in theory Communists are committed to all the symbols Western-style democracies claim for their own. Communists believe in liberty, in equality, in human dignity, even in government by consent. How, then, do our conceptions of these values differ from theirs? The meaning of the terms in communist ideology is not difficult to discover. When Communists talk about the communist regimes of the world as the "people's democracies," they are neither lying nor dissimulating. They are rather giving voice to the communist doctrine of consent.

Communist regimes are the only ones, in their view, that rest on the consent of the governed. Obviously, they do not mean that those who wield political power in the regimes are held to account to the freely expressed desires and values of those over whom power is exercised. What they do mean is that government is carried on to promote the *real interests* of the people, and that it gives the people what they really want as distinct from what they may sometimes, when they slip into deviationist errors of one sort or another, think they want. What people really want is to be determined not by asking them but by referring to the laws by which material forces objectively shape the course of history. The existence of "objective historical laws" is a premise of the regime which is beyond the reach of public debate. The meaning of these laws in the context of a particular period of history is to be determined by the "vanguard of the proletariat"—the Communist Party and, in particular, the party elite. Thus are "objective historical laws" transformed into political dogma.

The same analysis applies to all the other symbols of democracy that are retained in communist ideology. Equality means "from each according to his abilities; to each according to his needs." This is an article of faith laid down in the sacred scripture of the movement as the principle of a perfect socialist society. What does this mean in a society that has not reached the classless Utopia of complete socialism? This, like all fundamental doctrinal questions, is to be referred to the elite of the movement for their authoritative pronouncement in the light of their ability to align public policy with the historical laws of which only their understanding is perfect.

The Open Society and the Dilemma of Democracy

We stated at the beginning of this section that if the concept of the open society is the key to the secret of democracy, it is also the source of a democratic dilemma. The nature of this dilemma is clarified by considering some of the concepts developed by anthropologists in their analyses of comparative cultures.[10]

Many anthropologists use the term "cultural universals" to describe those basic beliefs that hold a society together by giving the lives of its members a common meaning and significance. These beliefs are the central source of cultural conformity; they are shared by all, or nearly all, adult members of the society; and their acceptance is a condition for full acceptance and participation in the social life of the community. Cultural universals are to be contrasted with alternatives—that is, the existence of optional patterns of belief and behavior available to individuals and groups within the culture. Universals and alternatives are related inversely to each other: when a particular aspect of behavior is governed by a universal belief, alternatives cease in that area. For example, if monogamy is a cultural universal, the option of plural marriages is not available. It is not available in the sense that ordinarily its practice would be met with social disapproval and punishment. In a deeper sense than that, the universals are so thoroughly "internalized" in the process of growing up that plural marriage would ordinarily seem so "unnatural" as not to be regarded as a possibility.

Now if the argument we have made about the open character of even the most fundamental questions in a democracy is valid, does this imply that there are no universals in a democratic society? If not, what are they? How are they distinguished from the universals of authoritarian societies? These questions are important when noting the conclusion of virtually all human culture students that society rests fundamentally on the existence of shared attitudes, beliefs, and values. Unless people perceive the world in substantially the same way, unless they evaluate human actions similarly, society is impossible. Unless the activities of the individual have some larger meaning in the shared purposes of others, the "cement" that holds societies together is missing. What is the cement in the democratic social fabric?

As our earlier analysis has suggested, we would argue that there are no *substantive* universals in democracies, no specific beliefs that make particular kinds of behavior or institutions necessary to democracy. There are, however, commitments to certain *procedural* universals which must be taken to be fundamentally necessary to democratic society. These are the "absolutes," if the term is to be used at all, of democratic society.

The procedural universals of democracy are summed up in the traditional freedoms: freedom of conscience and of belief, freedom of speech

[10]The concepts we employ were developed by Ralph Linton in *The Study of Man* (New York: Appleton-Century-Crofts, 1936), pp. 272 ff.

and press, freedom of association, freedom from arbitrary acts of government officials. These freedoms define the conditions of the open society. Freedom of belief and freedom of expression are the means by which any attempt to authoritatively enforce the acceptance of substantive conclusions or to insist on the finality of any institution may be challenged. Their purpose is to make possible endless controversy about such matters. They are the bulwark against all forms of authoritarianism.

Procedural freedoms clearly imply some common values. Freedom of inquiry and criticism implies the obligation for individuals to carry on the quest for truth and justice. Freedom of speech implies the obligation to speak honestly, while incorporating the faith that speech is a means to rational truth. Freedom of conscience implies the responsibility for integrity in one's beliefs and the obligation to submit one's conclusions to public criticism. In turn, the right of criticism imposes the obligation to deal fairly and honestly with opposing views. Again, Jefferson summed up the kind of bonds that supply the cement in this society in his conclusion that "integrity of views, more than their soundness, is the basis of mutual esteem."

These universals embody the procedures and attitudes that are necessary to the human quest for truth and justice in social life. The dilemma of democracy is rooted in the fact that the quest is never consummated, at least for the society as a whole. Democracy implies that not the Truth, but the unending quest for it, will make a society free. Of course, life compels the individual in his quest to arrive at some conclusions. It is obviously demanding much of human nature for men to refrain from imposing their beliefs on their fellows, and to value the processes of inquiry more highly than their own conclusions.

Although this is a formidable condition, it is clearly not an unattainable one. Something like this bound Athenian citizens together and was the basis for Athenian patriotism. And the same ties were important in binding together American statesmen of the formative period. To be sure, no democratic heaven was ever achieved in which significant numbers of men stuck consistently to Socrates' cardinal principle that it is only the "examined life" that is worth living. Socrates, after all, drank hemlock for his reward. The first session of the Congress under the Constitution reached an impasse in which all business was suspended because of the bitterness generated by the conflict over the funding of the national debt. Just eight years after the Constitution was adopted, the Alien and Sedition Acts were passed making it a crime publicly to criticize elected officials. When the Jeffersonians sought to repeal them in 1800, business in the United States Senate came to a halt as the Federalists drowned out their opponents' arguments by scraping their feet on the chamber floor. We must be wary, then, of over-idealizing the Founding Fathers. And yet, the entire tradition of

American democracy reflects the vitality of the notion that all substantive questions in a democracy are open questions.

At the same time, this doctrine has been under constant attack from one direction or another. Jeffersonian liberals identified democracy with a rural, agrarian way of life and insisted that commercial and industrial activities were fundamentally incompatible with necessary democratic virtues. After the Civil War there were other efforts to identify the democratic creed with unlimited industrial competition and the "survival of the fittest."

Thus, whereas the ideal of democracy requires that all universals be procedural rather than substantive, and that all questions (including the meaning of democracy itself) be at least potentially open ones, there are always forces in every society working in the opposite direction. There is a tendency to identify prevailing and orthodox beliefs with democracy. In addition, there are tendencies in every society to rewrite the past to make it accord with currently fashionable prejudices.

These practices of freezing presently respectable conclusions into absolutes and of translating tradition into substantively unifying myths pose constant challenges to the openness of a democratic society. The "solutions" examined earlier will be recognized as important examples of current tendencies in this direction. The effort to identify religion, or capitalism, or specific constitutional principles with democracy is the effort to make these into universals of American society. To the extent that it succeeds, the range of alternatives in these areas is restricted, and the meaning of freedom of conscience and of speech as democratic universals is limited. Free thought and free speech are in constant competition with all other claimants to a place in the universals of a democratic society.

As noted earlier, and in the examples we cited, the ever-present tendency in society to direct present conclusions and institutions into absolutes has been encouraged and stimulated in recent years by the challenge of communism. Ironically, the effort to distinguish democracy from communism through substantive universals opposite to those of the communists moves us, in a fundamental sense, closer to the communist system. This relationship is illustrated in Figure 1.

One qualification to the ideal of the open society needs to be made: it is neither necessary nor likely (nor, from the point of view of social stability, desirable) that *all* matters *will* be in dispute at all times. It is only necessary that they be potentially open. Thus, for a time in the period after the Civil War unregulated private enterprise served as a largely unchallenged framework for the growth of the American economy. There were, however, protest movements among farmers and industrial workers. Toward the end of the century, the growth of monopoly and unscrupulous treatment of consumers led to the beginnings of regulatory legislation.

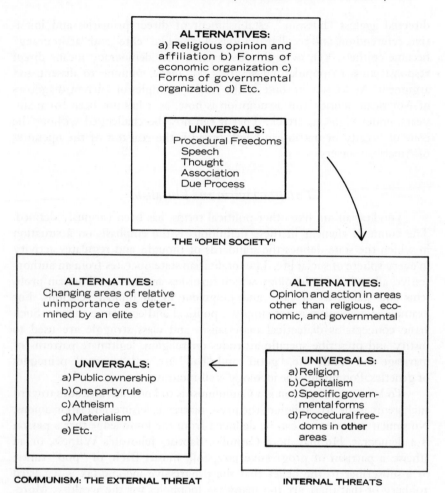

ALTERNATIVES:
a) Religious opinion and affiliation b) Forms of economic organization c) Forms of governmental organization d) Etc.

UNIVERSALS:
Procedural Freedoms
Speech
Thought
Association
Due Process

THE "OPEN SOCIETY"

ALTERNATIVES:
Changing areas of relative unimportance as determined by an elite

UNIVERSALS:
a) Public ownership
b) One party rule
c) Atheism
d) Materialism
e) Etc.

COMMUNISM: THE EXTERNAL THREAT

ALTERNATIVES:
Opinion and action in areas other than religious, economic, and governmental

UNIVERSALS:
a) Religion
b) Capitalism
c) Specific governmental forms
d) Procedural freedoms in **other** areas

INTERNAL THREATS

FIGURE 1.

Efforts were made—in the press, the pulpit, and the Supreme Court—to identify the absolute rights of private property with Americanism and democracy in order to put reform movements, including the organization of labor unions, beyond the pale of legitimate protest. The efforts failed; the right to dissent and to propose reforms in this area prevailed.

Further, in the realm of political ideas, this century saw an unlimited faith develop in the political capabilities of "the people." This idea became, except for a few unpopular conservative critics, an unchallenged and unexamined premise of political debate. On this basis, the cure for the ills of democracy was held to be more democracy. The application of the premise to politics took the form of the extension of the franchise, movements directed against "bossism," establishment of direct primaries and initia-tive, referendum, and recall provisions. Terms like "elite" and "aristocracy" became epithets. Yet, even this assumption that democracy means direct responsiveness to popular wishes was not made immune to dissent and argument. As we saw in some of the earlier examples of current diagnoses of American politics, this assumption is now, as it has not been for many years, under vigorous attack. That it can now be challenged without the issue of loyalty or patriotism being raised is the real test of the openness of American society.

Totalitarianism and Pluralism

Totalitarianism, like other political terms, has been variously defined. The common element in these definitions is the emphasis on a situation in which the state defines the standards of thought and regulates activity in every sphere of social life. The totalitarian state operates from an author-itative, all-embracing ideology which furnishes answers to all human prob-lems and standards of taste and judgment in all human relations. For example, communism is not simply a political and economic theory. Such basic concepts as dialectical materialism and class struggle are used to justify and prescribe specific attitudes on religion, legitimate patterns of marriage and family life, "good" and "bad" art, and "correct" principles of genetics. Potentially, the ideology is all-inclusive.

To know that a person is a Communist is to know his attitudes toward such items as the arts, religion, the press, marriage, leisure, and labor unions. No similar information can be deduced from the knowledge that a person is a democrat. He may be a Catholic, Baptist, Jehovah's Witness, or an atheist; a partisan of progressive jazz, folk music, Bach, or "pop" tunes; or a subscriber to the belief that the progressive income tax is legalized robbery or that there are too many tax loopholes for the wealthy. More-over, he may belong to organizations to advance his varying interests and opinions. And the purposes of these organizations are not required to answer to the demands of an official, all-inclusive ideology.

In this contrast with totalitarianism, the meaning of political pluralism becomes clear: a society in which government does not prescribe the interests or opinions of its citizens and in which, therefore, forms of group life may flourish at the initiative and discretion of citizens.

It is obvious that the procedural freedoms are the condition for a pluralist society. Freedoms of thought and speech are the roots from which the spontaneity and initiative of citizens spring. In addition, without free-dom to associate with others to promote common interests, and without freedom from arbitrary actions of government, intellectual freedom could never be reflected in social and political reality.

The ideal of the open, pluralistic society does not itself offer an answer to most of the basic issues of politics. Pluralism insures the existence of an ever-changing variety of groups of citizens with clashing interests and opinions, all seeking to influence governmental decisions. The central problem of politics, as we argued earlier, is how these conflicts are to be resolved. Pluralism rules out any solution that would make group organization answer to an official ideology. Within this limitation, however, there remain several conflicting models which seek to justify mutually contradictory processes of resolving group conflict and rivalry. The following chapters examine some of these models and seek to clarify the assumptions they embody, the solutions they offer, and the issues over which they contest. Only so, is it possible to get to the heart of the crisis in democratic politics and, at the same time, to acquire the intellectual tools necessary for systematic and critical understanding of the present state of American politics.

2

THE CONFLICT OF
DEMOCRATIC
THEORIES

"IT DID NOT COME EASILY to one who, like myself, had known the soft air of the world before the wars to recognize and acknowledge the sickness of the Western liberal democracies," laments Walter Lippmann. "Yet," he adds, "as we were being drawn into the second of the great wars, there was no denying, it seemed to me, that there is a deep disorder in our society which comes not from the machinations of our enemies and from the adversities of the human condition but from within ourselves."[1]

As the preceding chapter suggested, Mr. Lippmann's is not an isolated voice. In one way or another, Lippmann's fellow "new conservatives," liberals, socialists, and men of other political tendencies echo his complaint. Indeed, most close observers of modern democracies, including and perhaps especially those in the United States, have concluded that something akin to a revolution in the practices and values of democratic government has been in process. In the view of an eminent British historian and

[1] Lippmann, The Public Philosophy, p. 12.

political scientist, we have reached the point where "to speak today of the defense of democracy as if we were defending something which we knew and had possessed for many decades or many centuries is self-deception and sham."[2] The politics we now have is not what democracy meant in the past; it is, in many respects, essentially new, and many of the values and slogans inherited from the past are no longer relevant to our current political institutions. Perhaps these assertions are most dramatically clarified by pointing out that in the American political folklore, democracy and majority rule have been nearly synonymous terms.

THE DECLINE OF MAJORITY RULE

THE DECLARATION OF INDEPENDENCE asserts that all governments derive their just powers from the consent of the governed, and consent has generally been taken to be expressed through the voice of a majority. "The will of the majority," said Jefferson in his celebrated First Inaugural Address, "is in all cases to prevail . . . ." Democracy, said Lincoln, means a government "of the people, by the people, for the people." And how are the people to speak except through the voice of a majority? In our political rhetoric the ideal of majority rule has become almost an unchallenged and unchallengeable premise. Yet, it would be misleading to describe the actual conduct of current American politics as a process of majority rule.

In denying that ours is a politics of majority rule, we do not mean to refer to those obstructions in the constitutional and political scene that make it possible for a minority to frustrate the expression of majority will. Of course, there are such obstructions, and most Americans are familiar with how they work. The electoral college system makes possible the election of a minority president. The federal principle, in its provision for equality of representation by states in the Senate, leads to over-representation of such minority sectional interests as those of the South. The lines of Congressional districts are drawn by state legislatures which are themselves typically dominated by rural areas. The result is that districts are "gerrymandered" so that representatives of rural districts occupy more seats in the House of Representatives than the numbers of their constituents would entitle them to. Seniority as a basis for committee assignments and chairmanships in Congress may give representatives of safe, "one-party" constituencies a political influence exceeding the strength to which they would be entitled on numerical grounds. The Senate rules, especially, give any minority wide powers of obstructing the will of a majority in that body.

It is also true that the turnout of American voters in elections is

[2]E. H. Carr, *The New Society* (Boston: Beacon, 1957), p. 76.

notoriously low, with the result that ballots cast for the winning candidate rarely represent a majority of those eligible to vote. For example, the average turnout of eligible voters in presidential elections in the last forty years has been only 53.6 per cent. No President in this period has even come close to receiving the votes of a majority of citizens eligible to vote.

The effect of these features of American government is to frustrate sometimes the will of a simple majority (50 per cent plus 1) and to necessitate an extraordinary majority to secure a desired policy or program. It is relatively easy to arouse public concern and debate over the electoral college, the seniority system, and the other devices responsible for this state of affairs. But, if all the limitations on the voice of a simple majority were eliminated, it is still not likely that the result would be a politics of majority rule. The underlying obstructions to majority rule are deeper, more informal, more subtle, and less widely understood.

American politics is not organized or conducted in a manner designed to discover the will of a majority on public issues. The politician tends not to conceive his role as representing a majority, or a minority, view of public policy; rather, he sees his function as that of satisfying the many organized minorities that have made claims on the legislature. In the broadest sense, the principle of majority rule is not the model or the ideal which American politics tends to reflect—however much the layman, and even the politician, may continue to pay lip service to it.

Most Americans are aware that the ideal of majority rule has not been universally accepted in American history. Many of the framers of the Constitution were opposed to majority rule because they saw it as a device through which the property interests of a minority might be unjustly attacked. The Constitution itself was seen by some of its framers as a design to curb and restrain the political power of majorities. But these men, in the opinion of many modern Americans, were not believers in democracy. Most of their "undemocratic" mistakes were rectified by the majoritarian reforms of the Jeffersonians and the Jacksonians, the War Between the States, and the constitutional amendments that provided for civil liberties, universal suffrage, and the direct election of Senators. Thus we have been tempted to see American political history as the progressive and triumphant realization of the principle of majority rule (with the corollary principle of freedom for the minority to seek to become a majority). If the tendency of American politics leads actually in a quite different direction, and if the political model that most adequately describes actual political processes is a fundamentally different one, then surely some basic questions are raised which demand our attention as citizens.

What, then, *is* the central characteristic and tendency of American political institutions? Despite the remaining bulwarks against majority action, it is clearly not a matter of minority rule; there is no obvious elite of birth, property, or position in whose hands the power to govern lies.[3] Here is, perhaps, the big source of current confusion about the nature of our political life. Traditionally—in fact, ever since Aristotle—governments have been classified in terms of whether "the one, the few, or the many" determine public policy. The alternatives have appeared to be minority or majority rule. Lincoln stated clearly the case for this view in his First Inaugural Address:

> A majority held in restraint by constitutional checks and limitations, and always changing easily with deliberate changes of popular opinions and sentiments, is the only true sovereign of a free people. Whoever rejects it does of necessity fly to anarchy or to despotism. Unanimity is impossible. The rule of a minority, as a permanent arrangement, is wholly inadmissible; so that, rejecting the majority principle, anarchy or despotism in some form is all that is left.

The Growth of "Minorities Rule"

Students of the politics of modern democracies find the categories of majority and minority rule inadequate to describe political realities. The key to a more adequate descriptive model created in recent years is the concept of minori*ties* rule. This term describes the situation in which public policies are the result of opinions and interests of neither a majority nor a minority, but rather arise through compromise of the interests of varied organized and vocal minorities. This model differs fundamentally from the traditional descriptions of democratic politics. Indeed, it starts from different assumptions about the nature of man, politics, human knowledge, and social values. On the basis of these assumptions, it envisions a different solution to the fundamental political problem of resolving conflicts in society. It implies a radically altered conception of the nature of public opinion; the role and obligations of citizenship; the relation between politicians and the electorate; the function and responsibilities of the democratic politician; and of the legislative, administrative, and judicial processes.

Descriptive and Normative Theory

The development of these, and other, new concepts represents a reaction to a widening gap between the rhetoric of democracy—the

[3] There are those who argue that there is, in practice, a ruling elite. Perhaps the best case for this view is Mills, *The Power Elite*.

traditional folklore, values, and symbols used to justify democratic institutions—and the actual politics of democratic societies. This gap raises
two sets of questions that must be dealt with by anyone seeking to understand American politics. First, what are the characteristics of American
politics? How are they to be adequately described? How are they related
to the traditional American political faith and ideals?

These questions are all *factual* or *descriptive*. Answers will be found
through the analysis of the workings of American political institutions
and processes: the interaction in the policy-making process of legislators,
executives, political parties, interest groups, judges, bureaucrats, and voters.
These relationships, in turn, can only be adequately described by reference
to the underlying philosophical, cultural, and economic changes that provide the social context in which politics operates.

A second set of questions are those that ask, in one way or another,
how democratic political institutions *ought* to operate. These are normative or *value* questions. What model ought we to have in mind—what
criteria ought we to use—for evaluating democratic political realities?
What assumptions about the nature of man and the nature of politics ought
we to make in defining an ideal model of how democratic politics ought
to operate? Answers to these questions require two kinds of inquiry:
(1) The major alternative theories of democracy need to be examined,
and the assumptions made in each of them need to be clarified; and (2)
what the implications of each of these alternatives are (that is, what
specific consequences follow from embracing them) must be ascertained.

There are no final or authoritative answers to any of these questions—
either the factual or the value ones. It is unfortunate, but nevertheless
true, that facts do not "speak for themselves." They are discovered by men,
and the means men employ are the concepts that human imagination
devises for dealing with the world. Thus, even our "factual" knowledge
is ordered and made intelligible by abstractions: for example, power, law,
politics, legislation, lobby, majority rule, public opinion, compromise, and
bureaucracy. The point is that our factual knowledge is always mediated
by our human and abstract ideas about reality. Theory never can be held
to restate or exactly mirror reality. If it could, it would lose that quality
of corrigibility and tentativeness that uniquely distinguishes the method
of science. This means that efforts to describe and explain political reality
must always be tentative, and that different conceptual schemes are available. Even in attempting to describe "what is" the student of politics
must choose from among alternative descriptive concepts.

This is even more true in the area of "what ought to be." The value-
laden question of what we ought to mean by democracy is a question for
which there are no final answers; yet, it is not a question on which "one
answer is as good as another." Certainly an answer that is given in the

largest possible awareness of what the alternative positions are, an answer that is explicit about its assumptions and argues for their plausibility, an answer that takes account of its consequences and implications is better than one which does not meet these tests. Here, too, the student of politics must think for himself, and in the process he is entitled to his own considered opinion; he is not entitled to cling to prejudices that have not met the tests of critical inquiry and argument.

THE THEORY OF LIBERAL DEMOCRACY

IN RECENT YEARS, the American democratic tradition has been dominated by the theory of majority rule. The idea that a majority should have its way is not a self-evident proposition. It is, rather, a doctrine that claimed to solve the problem of political power. It claimed to provide a way of subordinating the struggle for power to the reasoning capacities of large numbers of men, and of insuring that justice prevails over the claims of rival individuals and groups. It was, as are most theories of government, an effort to substitute right for might in the public affairs of a community.

The Problem of Majority Rule

The problem for any theory of majority rule is well delineated in Thomas Nixon Carver's comment: "There are few things more democratic than a lynching bee, where everybody is satisfied except a small and insignificant minority of one."[4] A. Lawrence Lowell formulated even more clearly the problems and the meaning of the doctrine of majority rule:

> If two highwaymen meet a belated traveller on a dark road and propose to relieve him of his watch and wallet, it would clearly be an abuse of terms to say that in the assemblage on that lonely spot there was a public opinion in favor of a redistribution of property. Nor would it make any difference, for this purpose, whether there were two highwaymen and one traveller, or one robber and two victims. The absurdity in such a case of speaking about the duty of the minority to submit to the verdict of public opinion is self-evident; and it is not due to the fact that the three men on the road form part of a larger community, or that they are subject to the jurisdiction of a common government. The expression would be quite as inappropriate if no organized state existed; on a savage island, for example, where two cannibals were eager to devour one

[4]Quoted in Arthur A. Ekirch, *The Decline of American Liberalism* (New York: Longmans, Green, 1955), p. 220.

ship-wrecked mariner. In short the three men in each of the cases supposed do not form a community that is capable of a public opinion on the question involved.[5]

Majority rule as a theory of government requires, as Lowell suggests, something more than a mere counting of noses. There is no magic in the figure 50 per cent plus 1, which confers a right to impose a decision on a minority. Neither is there any obvious reason why the minority should feel an obligation to accept the right of the majority to have its way. For this reason, the central problem in majoritarian theory has always been the problem of majority tyranny—the problem of defining the conditions under which a group of persons constitutes, in Lowell's terms, a "community," and in which the voice of the majority can be held to be legitimate authority rather than raw power. As Lowell went on to argue, "A majority is not enough and unanimity is not required, but the opinion must be such that while the minority may not share it, they feel bound, by conviction not by fear, to accept it . . . ."[6]

The Tyranny of "Factions"

The nature of this problem has never been more clearly expounded than by James Madison, often called the "Father of the Constitution," in his defense of that document in the justly famous The Federalist (No. 10). The problem for Madison and most of his contemporaries was how to protect "the public good" which tends to be disregarded "in the conflicts of rival parties." It is the problem of avoiding tyranny, whether of "the one, the few, or the many." The basic question, of course, is what constitutes tyranny. Madison's answer—an answer shared by most of his contemporaries—was that tyranny means rule by "factions."

The two sources of the factious spirit that continuously threatens democratic politics, Madison argued, are "interest" and "passion." These are really different ways of describing the two threats to democracy with which the philosophers of democratic Athens had been concerned: the dangers of classes and masses. Of the two, the "most common and durable source of factions," according to Madison, is interest expressed through the economic classes that result from "the various and unequal distribution of property." In the early years of the new government the forces of economic faction, as Madison had described them, made their presence known and threatened to swallow up all other considerations in the shaping of public policy.

[5]A. Lawrence Lowell, Public Opinion and Popular Government (New York: Longmans, Green, 1913), pp. 2-3.
[6]Ibid., p. 15.

By 1828, interest group factions were powerful enough in the national government to dominate almost completely the shaping of tariff policy. Silas Wright described how the Tariff Act of 1828, which he successfully steered through the House of Representatives, was drafted: The duties on "all kinds of woolen cloth" were raised to meet the demands of the woolen manufacturers as "high as our own friends in Pennsylvania, Kentucky, and Ohio would vote them"; the duties on molasses were increased in order to get Western farmers "to go for the woolens" increases; duties on hemp, lead, and flax were raised just high enough to secure the support of those interests; "and the duty on iron was the '*sine qua non* with Pennsylvania.' "[7]

The Tariff of Abominations, as it came to be called, illustrated both the economic factions that Madison had discussed and the difficulty of regulating them satisfactorily. Most of the pressure groups in modern society fit Madison's category, and their influence on public policy can hardly be said to have diminished.

The second source of faction Madison located in the fallibility of man's reason and its tendency to be corrupted by his emotions and passions. Here again the danger was not long in expressing itself. The first two great political parties, the Jeffersonian Democrats and the Federalists, had been founded on alternative political principles, but by 1827 the "Era of Good Feelings" had in considerable measure dissolved the significance of the old party alignment. In that year in New York State, traditional party loyalties were almost completely disrupted by the all-consuming emotions of a movement directed against Freemasons. One contemporary observer commented: "I have seen many sharp political and social contests in my day, but viewed in some aspects, I think the Anti-masonic feuds excelled them all."[8] Again, both Madison's diagnosis of the problem and the difficulty of solving it were confirmed.

The control of factions that express these tendencies in human nature is the central problem of democracies, and it is rendered difficult and never permanently soluble by the fact that factions breed on freedom. Freedom in society implies the right of men to organize in order to press on government their private claims; freedom implies pluralism—the existence in society of a diversity of relatively autonomous private associations dedicated to the pursuit of the interests and opinions of their members. The political problem of free societies is how to structure a system of government so that public decisions reflect "rules of justice" and protect human rights rather than simply mirror the power positions of "rival

[7]Robert V. Remini, *Martin Van Buren and the Making of the Democratic Party* (New York: Columbia University Press, 1959), p. 176.
[8]*Ibid.*, p. 156.

parties"; that is, how to control the influence of factions so that the "public councils" are directed to considerations of justice and the public welfare. Faction is the form taken in free societies of the general problem of distinguishing right from might. The problem is the same one Lowell posed later: a society whose politics is dominated by "faction" is more like the scene on the highway than a political "community."

Madison argued that there are two fundamental safeguards against factious politics. The first is the "republican principle" (the principle of representation), which has two effects: (1) By making representatives ultimately responsible to their constituents, it prevents minority tyranny; and (2) it may "refine and enlarge the public views, by passing them through the medium of a chosen body of citizens, whose wisdom may best discern the true interests of their country, and whose patriotism and love of justice will be least likely to sacrifice it to temporary or partial considerations."

Since, in popular governments, these officials must be elected, it is possible that they will win election by making factious appeals to "local prejudices" and passions. This is rendered less likely by the second safeguard: the size of the territory over which a republican government can be extended. In general, he argued, the more extensive the territory and population, and the greater the number of interests, the less likelihood of one of them becoming a majority or of any group of them acting together on the basis of interests.

THE ASSUMPTIONS OF LIBERALISM

THE SOLUTION TO THE PROBLEM developed by spokesmen for majority rule, both European and American, differed from that proposed by Madison in the The Federalist (No. 10). Majoritarian theory, as it was developed by such liberal democrats as Jefferson, Paine, John Taylor, and Samuel Adams, was built around three more or less clearly developed assumptions, the purpose of which was to resolve the problem of faction and majority tyranny. These assumptions can be put in the form of assertions: (1) Decisions about right and wrong are matters of individual conscience, and the cultivation of the individual's rational and moral capacities is the highest purpose of man and society; (2) individuals have certain natural rights which have a validity independent of government and particular societies, and upon which no government is entitled to encroach; and (3) where there is conflict, and action has to be taken in the name of society, rational discussion of the public interest is the only legitimate method for reaching a decision.

The Doctrine of Individualism

Government, Jefferson argued, ought to be responsible to the will of those over whom it is exercised, and it can be safely entrusted to them because man is rational, "endowed by nature with rights," and capable of acting as a responsible moral agent. This is obviously an optimistic view of human nature—so optimistic that it is likely to sound naïve, if not disingenuously quaint, to modern man with his knowledge of the forces of human irrationality and egotism. But Jefferson was not so naïve; he was well aware that men are also self-seeking and that power corrupts. With Samuel Adams and others, he knew that "power is intoxicating; and men legally vested with it too often discover a disposition to make an ill use of it and an unwillingness to part with it."[9]

The motivation to use political power for personal ends is "avarice and ambition," a phrase which recurs constantly in the writings of the liberals of Jefferson's generation, and which expresses the same source of faction as the interest that Madison defined as the problem of free government. "Where avarice and ambition beat up for recruits," said John Taylor, "too many are prone to enlist,"[10] and "it is the thirst of avarice and ambition for wealth and power that we have to withstand."[11]

Nor were these men blind to the danger that political man in the mass could be manipulated by appeals to his emotions rather than to his reason and his ideals. They knew what John Adams, their chief conservative opponent, meant when he warned of the dangers of a majoritarian democracy:

> Every passion and prejudice of every voter will be applied to; every flattery and menace, every trick and bribe that can be bestowed, and will be accepted, will be used; and what is horrible to think of, that candidate or that agent who has fewest scruples; who will propagate lies and slanders with most confidence and secrecy; who will wheedle, flatter and cajole; who will debauch the people by threats, feasts and diversions with the least hesitation, and bribe with the most impudent front, which can consist with hypocritical concealment, will draw in tools and worm out enemies the fastest; unsullied honor, sterling integrity, real virtue, will stand a very unequal chance. When vice, folly, impudence and knavery have

[9]Harry Alonzo Cushing (ed.), *The Writings of Samuel Adams* (New York: G. P. Putnam's Sons, 1904-1908), Vol. IV, p. 214.

[10]John Taylor, *Inquiry into the Principles and Policy of the Government of the United States* (New Haven: Yale University Press, 1950), p. 71.

[11]*Ibid.*, p. 124.

carried the election one year, they will acquire in the course of it, fresh influence and power to succeed the next.[12]

These men understood the danger that, in Taylor's words, "the popularity of parties or individuals" will "free law from a strict examination at the tribunal of moral principles" and that, when this happens, despotism will destroy free institutions.

Unlike Adams, they did not believe that these results were inevitable in governments controlled by popular majorities, and they were optimistic about the possibility of avoiding them. But, clearly, they did not assume that the individual is always rational and always makes responsible choices.

Nor did their faith in individualism rest on the doctrine that man's "natural" condition is individual rather than social. American liberal thought is strikingly free of Lockean speculation about man living in a "state of nature" before society or government existed, or of a "social contract" by which men came together as individuals voluntarily to form a society and a government as contracts between free and independent individuals. Jefferson wrote that "man has no right in opposition to his social duties," and "man was destined for society," and finally that "questions of natural right are triable by their conformity with the moral sense and reason of man."[13]

Joel Barlow went even further to argue: "The fact is that there is no such state [of nature] antecedent to the social, that can be supposed to have existed, unless it be a perfect solitude of one person only; and if there could, it must have been an unnatural state. The only state of nature is a state of society . . . ."[14]

If Jeffersonians did not assume either a pre-social individual with natural rights or socialized individuals who are always rational and responsible moral agents, what did their doctrine of individualism amount to? In the first place, they did assume that moral choice is real and meaningful, that man's fate will depend on the choices he makes, and that man is *capable* of making responsible, reasoned choices. The idea that human behavior is determined, that the subjective feeling of free choice is an illusion, is a very old one. Its most common form was the doctrine of Divine predestination. In that form it constituted an obstacle to the development of democracy. For example, in the American tradition the rigorous determinism of Calvinist thought was embodied in American Puritanism where it waged war with the growing democratic sentiment that men are free agents,

[12]Charles Francis Adams (ed.), *The Works of John Adams* (Boston: Charles C. Little and James Brown, 1850-1856), Vol. VI, p. 275.
[13]John Dewey, *Thomas Jefferson* (New York: Longmans, Green, 1940), p. 16.
[14]Quoted in Martin Ray Adams, *Studies in the Literary Backgrounds of English Radicalism* (Lancaster: Franklin and Marshall College Studies, 1947), p. 47.

capable of making choices to affect the course of their individual and collective destinies. The growth of democracy in America occurred within the framework of Puritanism and represented the triumph of the Yankee sense of individual autonomy and control over the Calvinist creed of human depravity and compulsion; it was the victory of "a feeling of mastery over a sense of mystery."

Secondly, their doctrine of individualism is not so much a description of man as a statement of a moral preference. They did not assume rationality; they *preferred* it. They regarded the searching, questing individual human mind as the source of the dignity of mankind. Man's capacities for reason and choice among conflicting values they viewed as his highest qualities, the cultivation of which is the noblest object of society and government. Politically liberal thinkers regarded a representative democracy as a superior form of government because of its commitment to the freedom and cultivation of the human mind.

They were espousing an ideal *for* individuals, an ideal clearly expressed in a later historian's description of Philip Freneau, a crusading Jeffersonian editor: "He had no vanity, no ambition for place or power, and no fear of either. He wore no man's collar and he was no man's man. He was a law unto himself."[15] But if independence was one aspect of the ideal individual, moral responsibility was equally important. Man has a right to make his own choices, to determine for himself what kind of life is worth living, and to arrive at his own conclusion about the ways existing social conditions needed to be modified. He has a corresponding responsibility to develop for himself his intellectual and moral capacities.

They were insisting that individualism must not and need not be allowed to degenerate into self-centered egotism, that the free society requires men able, in the language of Joel Barlow, to participate in politics as "moral associates." This is the same proposition that underlies the description of Athenian democracy in Pericles' celebrated funeral oration: "We do not allow absorption in our own affairs to interfere with participation in the City's: we yield to none in independence of spirit and complete self-reliance, but we regard him who holds aloof from public affairs as useless."

The fundamental assumption about man implicit in this view was expressed by the Puritan democrat, John Wise, in his assertion that "man is not so wedded to his own interest but that he can make the common good the mark of his aim."[16] This assumes that every person must judge

---

[15]Claude G. Bowers, *Jefferson and Hamilton* (Boston: Houghton Mifflin, 1925), p. 160.
[16]John Wise, *A Vindication of the Government of New England Churches* (1717). Reprinted in *The People Shall Judge* (Chicago: University of Chicago Press, 1949), Vol. I, p. 32.

for himself what is offered to him as a citizen, and that he is potentially at least capable of judging with reference to broader considerations than his own immediate, or even long-range, selfish interests.

Thus defined, individualism was a demand that every person was entitled to be considered and consulted as an individual rather than as a member of a differentiated class or an undifferentiated mass. Applied to political processes, it was a demand that public policies emerge from the reasoned judgments of individuals. At the same time, since the mind is capable of "infinite improvability," change is a permanent condition of society, and society must be continuously adapted to conform to the conclusions of human thought. Democracy was conceived as a process which facilitates the constant re-examination of social institutions by human reason. This assumes that reason can play a somewhat autonomous role in human affairs, enabling man to transcend the determining conditions imposed by the external environment and his own internal drives and desires, and to seek to act in the public interest. Man, in short, can transcend to some extent his own mechanistic psychological drives and the customs, mores, and traditions of his society.

The Doctrine of Natural Rights

If society is to be constantly examined and modified, individuals must have some basis for criticism and evaluation other than existing institutions and the values inherent in them. Otherwise, every existing institution is self-validating and immune to rational attack. It is for this reason that the concept of a "higher law" is an important part of our heritage. The claim to some sort of objective basis for social values has taken a variety of forms: the "conscience" of the individual, God, nature, experience, and history have all been regarded at one time or another as sources of criteria available to individuals on the basis of which the *status quo* might be defended or attacked. In every case, what is claimed is the possibility of going outside the mores and beliefs embodied in the *status quo* in order to assert that existing conditions are morally justified or ought to be modified.

The typical form of the belief in "higher law" in the history of American liberalism has been the assertion of the existence of certain inalienable rights of man—rights which inhere in the individual and have their source outside the prescriptions of any particular society or government. The doctrine of natural rights was thus the major weapon employed to limit the exercise of political power. It served as a moral justification of the right of men to be governed only with their own consent. It was the basis of attacks on tyranny, monarchy, aristocracy, and slavery.

The doctrine of natural rights, like the theory of individualism generally, has a naïve ring to modern ears—probably because it too is often associated with the idea of individual rights in a pre-social state of nature or held, as in the Declaration of Independence, to be a self-evident truth. The idea appears to be both abstruse and metaphysical, two qualities not generally held in high regard in modern America. But it was not necessarily either. The European authors who most influenced American political theory, with the possible exception of some phrases in Locke, did not consider the state of nature as an historical condition in the remote past. It was, rather, an analytical concept designed to shed light on the present. The content of natural rights was not derived from abstract speculation about pre-historic "noble savages," but from the conditions of men living in society.

The primary natural rights were generally held to be those liberties discussed in the first chapter—the procedural freedoms necessary to the development of the individual as a rational being and a responsible moral agent. Freedoms of conscience, speech, and writing—these were the bedrock of man's natural rights. They were held to be natural not in the sense that they are immediately self-evident or retained by men when they entered into an historical compact to form society, but in the sense that they are derived from man's nature; that is, they are necessary to the cultivation, and, hopefully, the fulfillment of his highest qualities. They are natural in the sense that they stand on more fundamental ground and have a higher priority of value than the specific beliefs and institutions of any particular society. John Taylor's defense of these natural rights was most stalwart:

> Man's thoughts, suffered to flow, furnish the purest streams of human happiness. Dam'd up by law, they stagnate, putrify, and poison. To his characteristic qualities of speaking and writing, all man's social discoveries and improvements are owing. *Qualities which distinguish him from the brute creation, must be natural rights*; and those which are the parents of social order, must be useful and beneficial. Why should governments declare war against them?[17]

To be sure, those rights they held to be absolute, and they believed that the First Amendment to the Constitution, in providing that "Congress shall make *no* law . . .," had put them completely beyond the reach of political interference. As Jefferson said, in his *Notes on Virginia*, only "the acts of the body" and never "the operations of the mind" should be "subject to the coercion of the laws."

To argue that the rights of conscience, speech, and press are absolute is to argue that all other specific rights and obligations—all social and political institutions—are tentative and open to critical inquiry. This is the significance of natural rights. The appeal to "nature" is simply the

---

[17]Taylor, *Inquiry*, p. 413.

effort of liberal thought to examine all traditional institutions; "to bring them before the bar of reason to justify themselves."[18]

The chief functional significance of natural rights, particularly freedom to inquire, was to deny that any particular form of government or form of social inequality could be justified as being natural. As the Reverend John Wise, who had developed the theory of natural rights in Puritan New England, expressed it: "There is no particular form of civil government described in God's word; neither does nature prompt it."[19] All social institutions, he held, are the product of "human and rational combinations"; hence, all alike are open to human criticism and change. The final faith of this position is Jefferson's statement in the *Notes on Virginia*: "It is error alone which needs the support of government. Truth can stand by itself."

The Doctrine of the Public Interest

"What is called a 'Republic,'" said Thomas Paine, "is not any *particular form* of Government." It is, rather, a matter of the "object for which a government ought to be instituted, and on which it is to be employed: *res publica*, 'the public affairs,' or 'the public good' . . . ." This defines what "ought to be the character and business of government." Any government, Paine concluded, which "does not act on the principle of a *republic*, or in other words, that does not make the *res publica* its whole and sole object, is not a good government."[20]

This assertion that the public interest or the common good is not only a meaningful goal but the only legitimate goal of politics is at the heart of liberal democratic theory. Like most other concepts its meaning becomes clear only in the light of what it is intended to exclude. As R. M. MacIver points out: "Ever since the founding of the Republic there has been controversy between those who, like Jefferson, regarded democracy as sustained by the sense of common interest and those who, like Hamilton and Madison, tended to regard it as resting essentially on the compromise of particular interests."[21]

The concept of the public interest, then, implies the quest for standards of justice and "the good of all" which can be used as criteria for judging the legitimacy and the relative validity of the claims made on government by factious minorities. The assertion of a public interest is another way of stating the faith that men can control the struggle for power and wealth

[18]Morris R. Cohen, *American Thought: A Critical Sketch* (New York: The Free Press of Glencoe, 1954), p. 124.
[19]Wise, *Vindication*, p. 31
[20]Thomas Paine, *The Rights of Man* (New York: E. P. Dutton, 1951), p. 174.
[21]R. M. MacIver, *The Ramparts We Guard* (New York: Macmillan, 1950), p. 79.

by subordinating it to the higher interests and values of the whole of society. The architects of liberal democracy insisted that all human institutions and all private claims on government answer to the public interest as this is conceived by reasoned debate and majority vote.

The concept of the public interest was a response to the problem of faction. This problem, as Madison made clear, arises in any political system in which the assumptions of individualism and natural rights operate. For if individuals have a natural right to liberty and to the pursuit of happiness as they define it, there can be no external political authority which can coerce them into not pursuing the private, egoistic drives of "avarice and ambition." But the pursuit of private interest at the expense of (or not shared by) others can establish no claim to legitimacy. The clash of private interests in politics, unless it is mediated by general principles of the public interest, turns a political society into Lowell's scene on the highway—indeed, it becomes impossible to distinguish the highwaymen from the travellers.

What does the public interest mean? There are obvious perils in the concept for every authoritarian regime is supported by an idea of the "general will" or the "real interests" of the whole society. If it is assumed that the real interests of all men are ultimately in accord, and that this common interest is knowable, the practical conclusion would seem to be a single political party to embody and translate into reality the interest of all. For this reason it has sometimes been argued that the concept leads logically to political authoritarianism.

In their development of the concept of a public interest, the spokesmen for majority rule sought to avoid both the anarchistic consequences of individualism and natural rights and the totalitarian consequences of the doctrine that there is a final, ultimate, universal good that transcends individual opinions of what is good. The public interest is not something that can be known finally or ultimately. It does not stand above opinions. It is, rather, a quest for principles carried on by the process of rational discourse. Its particular content at any given time is to be clarified with reference to the political questions at issue. But if the public interest can only be arrived at by the opinions of men, it is necessary that men in their political activity concern themselves with questions which transcend their own immediate and personal interest. It is necessary that men have opinions about the public interest rather than simply desires about their private interests. The purpose of democratic politics is a continuing debate of, and temporary definitions of, the goals of public policy. The debate is a continuing one because the progress of the human mind assumes that human reason is fallible, but corrigible. The debate is meaningful because conflicting views of the public interest can be put to the test of reasoned discussion.

The Defense of Majority Rule

Jefferson insisted that "the will of the majority is in all cases to prevail." He went on to argue that this will "to be rightful must be reasonable." It must have resulted from an appeal to a reasoned view of the public interest, or else it can have no moral justification. If the voice of the majority expresses simply the interests or the emotions of the majority, there can be no claim that its authority over the minority is legitimate. In fact, under these conditions the majority has no right to rule, *even on the assumptions of liberalism.* For, as one conservative member of the Virginia Constitutional Convention of 1829-30 argued, the assumptions of individualism and natural rights posit an *equality* of rights among individuals. "But the right of a majority to rule, necessarily implies a right to impose restraints, in some form or other" on the minority—that is, to deprive a minority of some of its equal rights.[22]

This dilemma can only be resolved if it can be argued that the rule of the majority is the rule of reason. This does not imply the notion that the majority is always right and can do no wrong. It only implies that the majority has resulted from an appeal to reason and not to interest or passion. The minority has an obligation to accept the decisions of the majority, so long as it is a majority, not because the majority is right but because the *process* of majority rule permits the minority to appeal rationally from the majority decision—indeed, to make itself a majority by shedding the light of reason rather than the heat of passion on the prevailing opinion.

At the basis of the theory of majority rule is the idea of responsible government. From one point of view, those who govern are to be responsible to the majority. Yet, in a broader context, responsibility means more than this. It requires that the political process be organized so that the making of public policy is responsible to a majority opinion that is derived from reasoned debate. In the final analysis, both majority and minority owe their allegiance to this. This is the basis of the liberal community that makes it possible to argue that majority rule is not armed robbery, that it is a device for subordinating power to reason and moral purpose. The theory of responsible government developed on these foundations implies several things that need better understanding.

MAJORITY RULE AND MINORITY RIGHTS

First, the theory implies that certain minority rights are inviolable. Often it is alleged that there is a conflict between majority rule and minority rights. In one important sense this is impossible. Majority rule requires

[22]Quoted in Alpheus Thomas Mason, *Free Government in the Making* (New York: Oxford University Press, 1949), p. 418.

that the minority be guaranteed those freedoms which make effective opposition possible. If the minority is denied freedom to think, to speak, or to write on matters of public policy, the system of majority rule itself is abrogated, and it is no longer possible to speak of the government as rule by a majority. The only majority which has a right to rule is one which is the product of free and open debate. In the absence of civil liberties and organized public debate, there is no way of asserting that the numerical majority is a legitimate majority, or that it would continue to be a majority if conditions of open controversy existed. The majority, in these circumstances, has lost its right to rule. The minority by definition believes the majority to be in error. The claim on its allegiance is a claim in behalf of the process by which majorities and minorities are formed.

However, what is often meant by minority rights is not the procedural guarantees of the rights of access to the channels of public criticism and debate, but substantive rights and privileges—particularly property rights—that may be threatened by majority action. The question is complicated by the fact that many of the early liberal democrats regarded property as a natural right, which removed it from legitimate majority control. But when they did so, they were assuming either agrarian property or property rights in a system of *laissez-faire*. In both cases, property could be regarded as an inviolable individual right because it was assumed that ownership did not carry with it any power of discretion over the behavior of others.

The objective of property rights was complete individual independence. The farmer on the frontier, or the individual enterprise in an economy ruled by the law of supply and demand, could be viewed as being engaged in a struggle with nature, not with other men. Success in the struggle was deemed dependent on individual qualities of energy, resourcefulness, and ability, and one man's success seemed to have no connection at all with another man's chances.

With the growth of an interdependent economy, industrialism, and urbanization these conditions no longer held. The theory of the natural right of property was carried over and used as the basis of the argument that efforts by a majority to regulate and modify property relations were instances of tyrannical invasion of minority rights. But where rights have come to mean power, the argument for their inviolability can no longer be maintained. To argue that a majority has no right to modify existing relationships of property as power is to argue that the majority has no right at all, and that every minority has a vested right to maintain every privilege it has been able to come by.

It is still true, however, that within the theory of liberal democracy there are limitations on the right of a majority to modify and restructure the pattern of legal rights and privileges. The basic principle, again, is that it be done as a consequence of debate over a *public interest*. A majority which is factious—that is, organized on the basis of an appeal to emotion or on the basis of a private interest or a coalition of private interests—can make no claim that its authority over recalcitrant minorities is legitimate. A majority of debtors organized to reduce the interest rate, a rural majority organized to push a farm program, or a coalition of private interests organized to promote some accommodation of their interests are impossible to distinguish from Lowell's highwaymen. Where voters are organized as classes or as masses, from this point of view, there can be no legitimate authority, and the minority may be expected to continue its allegiance to the system only so long as effective possibilities of revolt are not open to it.

THE ORGANIZATION OF POLITICAL POWER

A second principle of majoritarianism requires that the location of political power be clear and recognized. This seems an obvious enough requirement, but in the history of American political life it has not been. In fact, democratic theory has often been confused by widespread acceptance of the idea that democracy means the absence of any kind of power relations in society. Partly, this has been due to the influence of the agrarian dream of complete individual independence. Partly, it has been due to the myth of New England style "town-meeting democracy" in which citizens gathered together, talked freely, and voted on public policies without professional politicians, organized political parties, bureaucracies, or other instruments of organized political power.

The suspicion of political parties shared by the Founding Fathers stemmed from this myth—myth, because in all likelihood such a political arrangement never existed. Organizations like Sam Adams' "caucus club" in Boston operated behind the scenes of the town meeting in order to agree on issues to be emphasized, to formulate proposals, and to plan strategy. But beyond the myth itself, the early democrats saw political parties and other instruments of organized political power as devices which would magnify the influence of faction by providing a framework for interest group coalitions or a device for the manipulation of the masses. From the beginning, some of the Jeffersonians recognized that responsible majority rule implies an organization of political power—power through which the issues can be framed and alternative solutions proposed. Joel Barlow said: "It has been concluded, and very justly, that *pure democracy*, or the immediate autocracy of the people, is unfit for a great state: it might be added that it is unfit for the smallest state imaginable, even a little town."[23]

[23]*The Political Writings of Joel Barlow* (New York: Mott and Lyon, 1796), p. 54.

By 1796, Jefferson himself saw that responsible majoritarianism required the organization of political power through political parties.[24]

For by then, it had become obvious that the alternative to the organization of responsibility was unorganized irresponsibility. If there were no parties organized on party principles and proposing programs to deal with public issues, there would be "cliques and clacques," personal followings, and the domination of politics by interests, sections, and individuals. But the dream of democracy as a "power-less" Utopia in which public action flows freely and automatically from the independent decisions of autonomous individuals continued to play an important role in American society. It still does.

One of the consequences of this myth has been that, in American life generally, the basic condition for the continued exercise of power has been the ability on the part of men of power to deny that they have any. The union leader, the corporation executive, and the politician all tend to be skilled in the techniques of persuasively creating the impression that "there's nobody here but us folks." Thus the union leader claims to be the "voice of the rank and file"; the congressman, the "spokesman for his constituency." There is a profound difference between these claims and, for example, the position that a union leader or a congressman stands for principles and policies that are supported by a *majority* of his constituents as against other views of a minority. The point is that the basic requirement for holding him responsible is a recognition that he *has power*— that is, he makes decisions that affect the lives of his constituents and his decisions are not the only possible ones that might be made.

The myth of a power-free society has had other consequences incompatible with responsible majority rule. Negatively, it has kept Americans from being concerned about the absence of effective, cohesive, strong political parties—a matter we will explore in detail later. Positively, the consequences are even more far-reaching. It has contributed to the growth of nonpartisanship, the worship of the independent voter, the idea that a bipartisan approach to major social issues is the democratic way, the widespread aversion to "politicians," and the yearning for "statesmen" who will rise above party strife to "speak for everyone."

What all these attitudes neglect is the fact that the politics of majority rule is the politics of controversy over the public interest. This process of reasoned debate requires political organization; it requires politicians and parties which struggle for and wield power. For only if power can be identified can it be held responsible. The purpose of democratic politics is not to eliminate power but to hold it accountable.

[24]Noble E. Cunningham, Jr., *The Jeffersonian Republicans* (Chapel Hill: University of North Carolina Press, 1957), p. 109.

Failure to recognize this has resulted in still another, and more serious, consequence for American politics. Americans have tended to put an inordinate amount of emphasis on the formal structure and machinery of government, and on constitutional guarantees against the abuse of power. The assumptions seem to have been that effective protection against possible abuses automatically guarantees responsibility, and that responsibility is simply a matter of insuring regular elections, honestly counted ballots, and a "government of law." But if the people, expressing their will through majority vote, are to hold politicians accountable, the voter must have alternatives. If the vote is to express reasoned convictions, it must issue from an organized debate of alternatives. Failure to recognize this has prevented Americans from more effectively institutionalizing a necessary element in majority rule: "the loyal opposition." The concept of a "loyal opposition," expressing as it does the necessity and the vital role of controversy in the *system*, is an indispensable element in majoritarian politics. However democratic any political structure may appear, and however carefully abuses of power may be restrained, no political process can provide for responsibility in the majoritarian sense which does not produce a continuing, organized, and effective opposition.

THE POLITICS OF PRINCIPLE

In the third place, in addition to organization of the contest for political power, the theory of majority rule requires that the contestants for public office stand above the strife and rivalry of private interests, that they stand on principles of the public good and apply those principles to current issues and programs. This does not imply that parties and politicians need be rigidly ideological nor that society need be divided into rival ideological camps with a broad no-man's land between them. Nor does it require the Utopian condition that private interests exert no influence on the definition of party principles or that all politicians be principled. What is necessary is that there be significantly different alternatives, and that debate of principles and programs play a significant role in the struggle and remain the *ideal* of the process. This is necessary because voters can only hold politicians responsible if the latter stand for something. Only if the politician has made some commitments and promises is it possible to hold him to account for delivering or to retire him if the voters prefer other goals than those he has promised. As the early American liberals understood, the alternative to a politics of principle and issues is the politics of personality and manipulation.

Here again there has been considerable confusion in American attitudes on this question, reflected most sharply perhaps in the self-congratulatory remark that "I vote for the man, not the party." In terms of the model we are considering, there is no way to hold the man responsible except by voting for his principles rather than for *him*.

More serious is the widespread notion that the most democratic politician is the one who listens most closely to, and responds most readily to, the demands and desires of his constituents. The idea is an old one, though it has been more vocally expressed, perhaps, in the period since the advent of public-opinion polling. On its face, the notion that the representative is simply the agent of those who elected him has a very democratic ring to it. But it is incompatible with the model of majority rule! Paradoxically, the concept of the role of the representative that is required for the liberal doctrine of responsible government was most clearly expressed by Edmund Burke, an eighteenth-century British philosopher who was, perhaps, the most eminent spokesman for conservatism. Burke told his Bristol constituents in 1774 that their representative's "unbiased opinion, his mature judgment, his enlightened conscience, he ought not to sacrifice to you, to any man, or to any set of men living." In Burke's view a representative should act on his own conscientious principles, whether or not this happened at a given time and on a given question to correspond with the desires or will of his constituents.

Although Burke built a conservative philosophy of democracy on this principle, the principle itself is not necessarily a conservative one. In fact, the liberal system of majority rule cannot operate otherwise. Unless the representative has a set of principles which he is unwilling to sacrifice to public opinion, even at the high and unpleasant cost of defeat, he cannot stand for anything for which he can be held responsible. The question is whether he is held accountable at periodic intervals to majority vote at the conclusion of an electoral process in which he has defended his principles, and his record in applying them, against alternative principles and proposals. A contest among candidates all of whom promise to do what the majority wants would provide no means for society to debate what a majority ought to want. As Burke went on to say, "If government were a matter of will upon any side, yours, without question, ought to be superior." But if government were a matter of will, or interest, or unreflective desires, then there is no basis for the imposition of a majority will on a minority.

The image of the democratic politician as a public-opinion poller, with his ear to the ground and his nose to the wind, has grown out of a corruption of liberal doctrine that substituted the desires of the public for their reasoned judgment, and a compromise of private interests for controversy over the public interest. In recent decades, Thurman Arnold reminds us, democracy "ceased being a creed. It simply became a name for a type of organization controlled by voters." It "changed from a creed to a word describing a political fact . . . ."[25]

---

[25]Thurman Arnold, *The Folklore of Capitalism* (New Haven: Yale University Press, 1937), p. 41.

This development has gone a long way toward removing the values that gave the liberal faith its historic meaning. The main tendency of recent American politics has been in the direction of processes which substitute compromises and accommodations of the rival claims of private interest groups for reasoned debate of the public interest. As we shall see later, a widely held theory of democracy has been developed which argues that these developments are healthy and sound. At this point, what is necessary is to recognize that majority rule, as it was defined and defended in liberal democratic theory, is incompatible with the theory of democracy as compromise in a system of minorities rule.

CONSERVATIVE THEORIES OF DEMOCRACY

THE FOUNDING FATHERS were not all liberals. The authors of *The Federalist* (No. 27) noted that "man is very much a creature of habit" and held that the solid basis of any government must be, at least for the masses of men, habitual obedience and reverence for the existing mechanisms of government rather than the appeal to reason implied in the liberal position. The Constitution would become a genuine instrument of government, *Federalist* No. 49 argued, when it had acquired "that veneration which time bestows on everything, and without which perhaps the wisest and freest governments would not possess the requisite stability." It concluded that even "the most rational government will not find it a superfluous advantage to have the prejudices of the community on its side."

In arguing thus, conservatives were contesting the liberal's optimistic view of human nature and his faith in reason. On the specific point at issue here, Paine had stated clearly the liberal assumptions:

As to the prejudices which men have from education and habit, in favour of any particular form or system of Government, those prejudices have yet to stand the test of reason and reflection .... We have but a defective idea of what prejudice is. It might be said that until men think for themselves the whole is prejudice, and not opinion: For that only is opinion which is the result of reason and reflection.[26]

For Paine, democracy was government founded on opinion (that is, on reason and reflection) rather than on habit and prejudice. But there were then, and there have been ever since, many Americans who have been convinced that the liberal faith in human rationality is fatal not only to human freedom but to any stable form of government whatever. Gen-

[26]Paine, *The Rights of Man*, p. 148.

erally we can identify this conviction as the starting point of conservative theories of democracy.

Conservative theories of democracy start from a more pessimistic view of human nature and insist that the rational capacities of the individual are an inadequate basis for society or government. Human reason is too fallible, rare, and capricious an instrument to rely on for the control of the lust for power, particularly power for selfish purposes. Conservatives have sought a solution in various ways: in the traditions of responsibility and service that should govern the behavior of an aristocracy; in the restraints of deeply entrenched traditional values and norms enshrined in social myths and engrained in human habit; in the truths of religion; or in delicately contrived equilibria of the forces struggling in society for power.

Whatever their positive solutions to the political problem, conservatives tend to agree in their diagnosis. Specifically, conservatives challenge the validity of liberal theory at three major points.

The Role of Irrationality in Political Behavior

As we have already suggested, the conservative is likely to hold that the liberal theory of democracy puts too high a premium on intellectual values. It overestimates the power of reason and the rational capacities of individuals in its emphasis on the procedural values necessary to inquiry and debate, and it minimizes the importance of irrational and nonrational forces in human behavior. Liberalism is, perhaps, a philosophy that is adequate for a small minority of men; it is after all an "egghead" philosophy, and a world full of "eggheads," even if it were desirable, is outside the potentialities of human nature.

In all societies everywhere, say the conservatives, most men live by habit and tradition, and when this is not so their behavior is motivated by their interests (usually economic) rather than by their intellects. Indeed, most conservatives have held that reason can play only a very limited role in human affairs. Sometimes, as with the eighteenth-century British philosopher, David Hume, conservatives have argued that reason cannot be invoked to settle political disputes because, in the nature of things, reason is a servant of the passions: "Reason is, and ought only to be, the slave of the passions, and can never pretend to any other office than to serve and obey them." In this view, reason can only claim to enable man to decide rationally on the most efficient means for achieving his desires. If this be the case, then the liberal appeal to reason to resolve the conflicting interests and desires of individuals and groups in society is meaningless. Something other than reason—whether tradition, balance, or Providence—will be necessary to control the struggle for power and prevent tyranny.

Other conservatives have not accepted Hume's conclusion that reason is *logically* limited to telling man how to achieve his emotional desires, rather than to controlling or directing them. But, even when they have admitted the logical possibility that reason may control desire, they have argued, with John Adams, that while "all may have some affection for the public," it is equally true that "there are few who love the public better than themselves." It would be sheer folly, under the circumstances, to expect that rule by a majority could reflect a reasoned view of the public interest rather than the passions and interests of a majority.

The Need for Community

The second major conservative argument is that a society that is committed to the liberal theory of democracy must fail to enlist the necessary support of its citizens. Men require something more than a commitment to a reasoned quest of a public interest to hold them together. In order to give purpose to their lives and institutions, they require the emotional satisfactions derived from membership in a community whose bonds are rooted in history and full of spiritual and moral meaning. The symbols of government—the flag, the pledge of allegiance, the patriotic holidays, the national myths and rituals, and national shrines and memorials—must stand for something more than a mere framework for variety or a set of rules that permit the game to go on. They must be pregnant with emotional meaning; they must provide a sense of community, of shared values and common purposes. A nation is not a debating society, and the effort to make it one fails because it does not fulfill the emotional and spiritual needs of individuals to belong to a larger community which shares a common faith. The failure of a liberal society to provide this produces the mediocrity and conformity of mass society, rather than the free and enlightened individuals that liberals had expected to produce. In the final analysis, the tensions, frustrations, and essential meaninglessness produced by the failure of liberal politics may even produce citizens ripe for the emotional appeals of mass movements led by a man on horseback.

The Need for Hierarchy

Thirdly, the conservative sees in the liberal's faith in the rationality of the common man and the liberal doctrine of equality a fatal attack on the prescription and hierarchy that are necessary to social order and justice. The liberal's emphasis on natural rights would destroy the concepts of duty and obligation. The invitation to all men to subject all social ideals and institutions to critical scrutiny would destroy the necessary reverence for existing instruments of government. The ideal of equality of participation in politics would undermine the foundations of service and responsibility which a natural aristocracy must supply. Conservatives have always tended to believe that, in every society of men, there are "the better sort," the "middling sort," and the "poorer sort."[27]

A decently ordered society requires that the natural inequalities among men be recognized and that the naturally superior be protected from the envy and the ambitions of their inferiors. Perhaps more important, only a social aristocracy, composed of the naturally superior, can serve as the guardians of the traditional faith and symbols of government, thus making change a process of gradual adaptation which maintains continuity with the past and responsibility toward the future. Only such an aristocracy can effectuate Burke's notion of society not as a contract between living individuals, but between "the dead, the living, and those yet unborn."

At the same time, the conservative's argument for the necessity of an aristocracy must not be confused with an elite or authoritarian position. The conservative is no more willing to entrust his aristocracy with unrestrained political power than he is to defer to the masses. The aristocrat is cut from the same human cloth as everyone else; he is no less susceptible to abusing power in the service of his own avarice and ambition. As John Adams said, men "are all of the same clay." While an aristocracy may have "more knowledge and sagacity, derived from education, and more advantages for acquiring wisdom and virtue," still, when it comes to "usurping other's rights," they are "equally guilty." Adams' conclusion is the essence of the conservative position, "No wise man will trust either with an opportunity...."

For American conservatives there were unique problems. They had inherited a revolution that was essentially liberal in its goals and aspirations. There was no inherited system of class or status. And the frontier presented its vast resources of free land. All of these were circumstances that seemed to play into the hands of the liberals. In that situation, the conservatives focused their attention on the problem of faction as it was developed by Madison. What they sought was a solution which would avoid factious politics and, in particular, the attacks of a factious majority on the property rights of a minority. Simultaneously, it had to be a solution that would do as little violence as possible to the principle of republican government which operated to restrain minorities.

The republican principle would prevent minorities from oppressing a majority, but additional safeguards were needed to frustrate the schemes of an "interested and over-bearing majority." They were necessary as barriers, not only against the "schemes of economic injustice" which the majority of the poorer people might perpetrate, but also against the companion danger of a majority dominated by mass emotion. For in the view

[27]Clinton Rossiter, *Conservatism in America* (New York: Knopf, 1955), p. 81.

of the conservatives, every majority would be the product either of economic interests or of emotions engineered by popular leaders who rise to power by playing on the frustrations, jealousies, animosities, and fears of the manipulatable masses. Class interests and mass emotions must be restrained and controlled. The liberal faith in reason, and the liberal creed of freedom and equality, will corrode and destroy the restraints of tradition, habit, aristocracy, and reverence which alone can furnish the necessary restraints. Popular participation in governments is necessary, but if tyranny is to be avoided the power drives of minorities must be pitted against the power of the masses.

Through all of the conservative attitudes runs the emphasis on the necessity of government as a device for controlling the factious tendencies in all men. Liberals have wanted the people to control the government; conservatives have insisted that government must be arranged to control the evil in people. Liberals have had faith that popular participation in democratic government serves to make men less self-centered and more rational; conservatives have rejected the idea that man's nature could be reformed through politics. Majoritarian democracy, conservatives were convinced, could lead only to "democratic convulsion." This ought not be interpreted to mean that they were opposed to popular government as such, or to civil liberties. They were, in fact, often eloquent spokesmen for as much of popular control of government and as much of civil liberties as might be, in their view, compatible with the restraint of man's innate will to power and self-seeking and his natural susceptibility to demogogic appeals. But their assumptions about human nature made them skeptical about how much was possible. They were convinced that a government neither could, nor should, be made to rest on the freely formed opinions of men, particularly common men. This conviction rested on the view that men do not have opinions; they have only desires, appetites, and interests. This doctrine of the radical and permanent depravity of man produced, in the minds of conservatives, an open distrust of the procedures of free public discussion as the *basic principle* of government, even though it remained for most of them a cherished principle and a positive good.

A Conservative Solution: The Theory of Balance

Conservatism starts with a sober and pessimistic appraisal of human nature, with a commitment to natural inequality and a natural aristocracy, and with an insistence on the necessity for community. On these assumptions, the sources of faction are rooted in the nature of man; interest and passion will ever be the springs of human conduct in politics. The crucial question on these assumptions becomes the question of majority tyranny.

The solution to the danger of majority tyranny is to establish a government which makes majority rule impossible.

Perhaps the most consistent and systematic of the early American conservatives was John Adams. He approached the problems of government from the fundamental assumption that society is inevitably and naturally organized into classes—the aristocracy and the common people— and that every class of men has "waged everlasting war against the common rights of man": "so has human nature, in every shape and combination, and so it ever will." The aristocracy, of course, is always in a minority. Since it is rooted in the natural inequalities among men, it is entitled to a higher position in society. But because aristocrats, like all men, are selfish and corrupt by nature, they cannot be trusted to rule without restraints. Because an aristocracy is motivated by pride, it would use the power of government artificially to increase its wealth and prestige. The result would be minority tyranny. But the pride of the nobility is matched by the "vulgar malignity and popular envy" of the masses. If the majority of the common people were allowed to rule, the result would be factious government directed to taking from the few what rightfully belongs to them. The result would be majority tyranny.[28]

Adams' answer to the problem of majority tyranny was to make it impossible for the majority to rule. At the same time, minority rule was equally tyrannical. The solution: Government should be so contrived as to establish and maintain a balance between the interests of the major classes of society, with a neutral arbiter to maintain that balance. This system is what Adams meant by "a government of laws, and not of men." Every effort to establish just and orderly government, he held, "has been found to be no better than committing the lamb to the custody of the wolf, except that one which is called a *balance of power*."[29] In a carefully contrived constitution, itself the result of reason, the basic laws which maintain equilibrium between the social classes would rule and tyranny would be avoided. Here again, there is much confusion in subsequent use of the term "a government of laws." In Adams' sense—a government in which the laws rather than men would rule—it is certainly not a doctrine on which all or most Americans have agreed. In another sense (to be explored presently), it is.

Again, the fact that American conservatives lived in a new society limited the alternatives open to them. There was no established, responsible aristocracy. Nor was there an American tradition to which appeal could be made. The device which seemed capable of restraining the potential evil in all men was that of setting power against power, of devising a constitution so that the efforts of every class of men to invade the rights of others would be neutralized. Professor Sheldon Wolin has aptly summarized the solution of early American conservatives to the problem of political power: "The aim of a political organization was not to educate men, but to deploy them; not to alter their moral character, but to arrange institutions in such a manner that human drives would cancel each other or, without conscious intent, be deflected towards the common good."[30]

In the next two chapters, we will examine how this conservative purpose was elaborated into a system of government in the development of the American Constitution. At the same time, we will be concerned to explore the reaction of liberals to the constitutional arrangements, and how the Constitution became a framework for the continued conflict of liberal and conservative approaches to the problems of politics in a free society.

With respect to this way of approaching the historical background of American democratic ideas, a disclaimer and two words of caution need to be added. We have deliberately centered our attention on the philosophical problems involved in democratic theory and on the major efforts to develop theoretical solutions. We do not pretend to have accounted historically for the form that these particular solutions have taken.

The two warnings follow: (1) American democratic ideas have generally developed in response to practical issues of policy. To extract the ideas from the context of political controversy in which they developed, as we have done generally, involves limitations which need to be kept in mind. (2) Political theories do not, in historical fact, fall anywhere so neatly into categories as we have implied. Oversimplification need not mean serious distortion, however. The best insurance against this is a constant alertness to the fact that the real world of ideas is more complex than can be fitted into any neat categories.

[30]Sheldon S. Wolin, *Politics and Vision* (Boston: Little, Brown, 1960), p. 389.

3

THE CONSTITUTION: DEMOCRATIC BATTLEGROUND

[Checks and Balances and Federalism]

THE CONSTITUTION: DEMOCRACY OR REPUBLIC?

PERIODICALLY IN AMERICAN HISTORY, as the forces of liberal democracy have come gradually to prevail over the minds of Americans there have been loud and strident protests that it was not a democracy, but a republic, which was established by the Constitution in 1789. Most recently organizations of the radical right, like the John Birch Society, have echoed this complaint. Democracy, the founder of the Birch Society has repeatedly insisted, is the worst of all possible forms of government. That organization's campaign to impeach Chief Justice Earl Warren rested largely on the charge that the Chief Justice "has taken the lead in converting this country to democracy."[1] It may be that, as one editorial writer put it, "Anybody who starts out to fight Communism in America by calling democracy 'mob rule' can assure himself of a future filled with futility."[2]

[1] Robert Welch, quoted in a mimeographed report by Attorney General Stanley Mosk to Governor Brown of California, July 7, 1961, p. 2.
[2] Arthur Caylor in the San Francisco *News-Call Bulletin,* quoted in Attorney General Mosk's report (See footnote 1 above).

A good historical case can be made for the Far Right's position. The democracy against which these groups contend is the liberal model of majoritarian government. The framers of the Constitution did not intend to establish an "elective despotism," and they were no friends of liberal democracy. Most of them would, in fact, have found the Birch Society's position on democracy to be the essence of good political sense, however mad and dangerous they might have regarded them for some of their other positions. (For example, the absurd assertions that those who support fluoridation of water, mental health programs, federal aid to education, or the United Nations are all part of the communist conspiracy.)

Those who framed the Constitution did, indeed, intend to establish a republic, one purpose of which was to render majoritarian democracy impossible. It was not simply that they wanted the will of a majority to be expressed through representatives rather than directly; on this point, there was general agreement. The Jeffersonians were in accord with Madison's view, expressed in *The Federalist* (No. 10), that "the public voice, pronounced by the representatives of the people" may well be "more consonant to the public good" than if pronounced directly. The framers of the Constitution wanted a government in which the majority would not rule either directly or indirectly. They were conservatives in the sense in which that term was defined in the preceding chapter. They regarded majority rule as no safeguard at all against the danger of faction.

The device which promised to curb majorities, and at the same time to prevent minority rule, was a carefully contrived Constitution. To that end the men at Philadelphia turned their attentions and their considerable talents.

As we noted earlier, there were other leading Americans whose political philosophy was majoritarian. If the Constitutional Convention was dominantly a conservative gathering (and it was), it was still true that the document had to be ratified by the qualified voters in the states. Here the liberal democrats could bring the full force of their influence to bear.

CONSTITUTIONALISM: LIBERAL
AND CONSERVATIVE

How, THEN, could a Constitution and a system of government be built out of disagreement? There are two general answers to this question: (1) While they disagreed about solutions, liberals and conservatives were in agreement that some form of government was necessary to preserve the independence of the new nation in a hostile world. (2) The principles of the new Constitution were sometimes ambiguous, so that the question of their legitimate meaning remained in doubt.

The Necessity for a Written Constitution

Liberals and conservatives agreed that a written Constitution was necessary, although for different reasons. From the conservative point of view, only a set of restraints on the will to power of all groups could succeed in pitting power against power, thus insuring a system of "balanced liberty." And these restraints could only be permanently effective if a written document put them on a level above the strategies of the contestants in the day-to-day political struggle. For the liberals, the necessity for a written Constitution followed from their commitment to the principles of representation and majority rule. If the people were not to govern directly, there must be constitutional restraints on the powers of their representatives to curb the natural temptation of officials to abuse their power and exceed their commissions from the people. At the same time, the majority principle required that the civil liberties necessary to its operation be spelled out in a basic document that would underscore their fundamental priority.

The Ambiguity of the Constitutional Settlement

The solutions worked out in the constitutional debate which became the basis for government in the new nation were ambiguous. In some cases (the federal compromise between large and small states and the three-fifths compromise between free and slave states), they were clearly compromises which sacrificed the purity of the principles of all the contestants. In other more important cases, wherein they were not compromises but the elaboration of conservative principles, the meaning of the principles was not at all clear, so that the "intentions" of the Founders has been a matter of dispute ever since. As a consequence, men of radically different principles could all claim that the Constitution was sufficiently in accord with their philosophies to be tolerable. Even those who opposed its adoption—and it was adopted by only a narrow majority of a small percentage of the citizenry—found it tolerable enough to forestall rebellion.

In this chapter, we will examine the basic principles of American Constitutionalism, the meaning of these principles as seen from the perspectives of traditional liberal and conservative political philosophies, and the character of the continuing debate over their proper interpretation.

FOUR CONSTITUTIONAL PRINCIPLES

THE FOUR BASIC PRINCIPLES of government established by the Constitution are those with which every American is familiar, however unclear he may be about their intent and their consequences: the separation of powers and checks and balances, federalism, limited government, and judicial supremacy. Since the principles themselves, as they are developed in the Constitution to shape the structure of American government, should already be familiar, we confine ourselves here to a brief review of their content and a more extended analysis of their meaning.

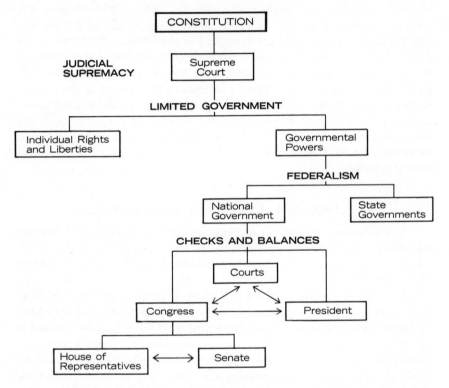

FIGURE 2. Four basic principles of American constitutionalism.

Separation of Powers and Checks and Balances

The principle that the powers of government should be separated and put in the care of different persons was not, of course, an American invention. The development of the rule of law as a limit on the power of the King in England had implied, as it inherently does, the development of an independent judiciary which makes it possible for citizens to bring suit in the courts against governmental officials for exceeding their authority. Before Montesquieu, with whose name the principle is ordinarily associated, John Locke had noted that "it may be too great temptation to human frailty, apt to grasp at power, for the same persons who have the power of making laws to have also in their hands the power to execute them." The Founding Fathers were familiar with both Montesquieu and Locke, and they were practiced in the arts of government under a system of separation of powers since both the Colonial governments and most of the states after independence had practiced it. As a principle it was widely accepted, though the question of its meaning and purpose was in dispute.

The principle itself is not explicitly stated in the Constitution; it is, rather, implied in the structure of government which was erected. The first three Articles define the exercise of legislative, executive and judicial powers, respectively:

> All legislative powers herein granted shall be vested in a Congress of the United States, which shall consist of a Senate and House of Representatives.
>
> The executive power shall be vested in a President of the United States of America.
>
> The judicial power of the United States shall be vested in one Supreme Court, and in such inferior courts as the Congress may from time to time ordain and establish.

The basic principle underlying this system is clear. In Madison's words, "the accumulation of all powers, legislative, executive, and judiciary in the same hands" must be prevented if tyranny is to be avoided. But this does not mean, as it is often interpreted and as the wording of the Constitution quoted above seems to imply, that *only* legislators are to exercise legislative power, the President executive power, and the courts judicial power. In any such arrangement, if it could be instituted, no effective government at all would be possible, for the executive might refuse to enforce laws passed by the Congress or the decisions of the courts. Effective government under these conditions would tend to make the legislative power supreme, for the power to formulate and modify basic policy must take precedence over the powers to administer it and to interpret it. This is clearly not what the Founding Fathers were after; indeed, many of them saw the Constitution as a means of remedying the defects of some of the state governments in which the legislature had become pre-eminent.

The key to the constitutional system is not the principle of separation of powers but the principle of checks and balances. The principle of checks and balances implies that there be an intermixture of powers which will permit the several branches of government to check one another, and particularly, establish checks on the legislative power. The only way in which the President and the courts can put checks on the legislature is to provide for them to share in the legislative power. Again, in Madison's words, "the great security against a gradual concentration of the several powers in the same department consists in giving to those who administer each department the necessary constitutional means and personal motives to resist encroachment on the others."

The President shares in the legislative power by virtue of his right to veto legislation but Congress may, by two-thirds vote, still have its way. The Senate has the power to refuse to confirm the President's nominations of persons to fill executive and judicial offices, or to approve treaties negotiated by the executive. Congress may decline to appropriate funds for any executive agency. The courts, in their power to decide the constitutionality of acts of Congress, are exercising legislative power. Congress may initiate amendments to the Constitution to overcome a judicial veto. More commonly, the President with the consent of the Senate may make appointments to the Supreme Court as vacancies occur which will have the effect of modifying future court decisions. Or, as President Roosevelt unsuccessfully proposed in 1937, Congress and the President may enlarge the size of the Court in order to reverse the Court's decisions. Although this last technique is clearly within the range of constitutional possibilities, it failed because it still seemed to most Americans to violate the principle that each branch of government should be in a position to defend its own prerogatives.

In addition to these mutual checks which the three branches may bring to bear on one another, Congress itself is divided into two houses—the principle of bicameralism—and each house has an absolute veto on the other. But this still does not exhaust the ramifications of the principle. Additional mutual checks are provided for by the fact that the different branches of government have different modes of election and hold office for terms of different length. The House of Representatives was popularly elected for a two-year term; the Senate elected by the state legislatures for staggered six-year terms; the President elected by the electoral college for a four-year term; and the judges appointed by the President, with the concurrence of the Senate, for life during good behavior.

Finally, the principle of federalism (that is, the constitutional division of powers between the national and state governments) may also be considered as an internal check on the powers of government. Federalism probably reflected a necessary compromise between those who favored strong national government and those who were sympathetic to, and jealous of, the rights of the states, much more than it did a conscious effort to elaborate the system of checks and balances. Yet, in *The Federalist* (No. 51), it is defended as a "double security . . . to the rights of the people. The different governments will control each other at the same time that each will be controlled by itself."

Why this elaborate scheme of intermingling governmental power among the several branches, yet leaving each in a position to maintain and defend its own prerogatives? What was its purpose? Here we have a per-

TO PROVIDE "...security against a gradual encroachment of the several powers in the same department..." (Madison):

SEPARATION OF POWERS:

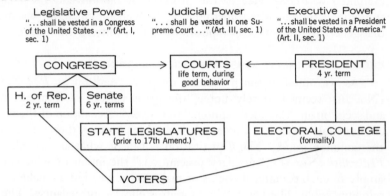

Legislative Power
"...shall be vested in a Congress of the United States..." (Art. I, sec. 1)

Judicial Power
"...shall be vested in one Supreme Court..." (Art. III, sec. 1)

Executive Power
"...shall be vested in a President of the United States of America." (Art. II, sec. 1)

BUT, to give "...to those who administer each department the necessary constitutional means and personal motives to resist encroachment on the others":

CHECKS AND BALANCES

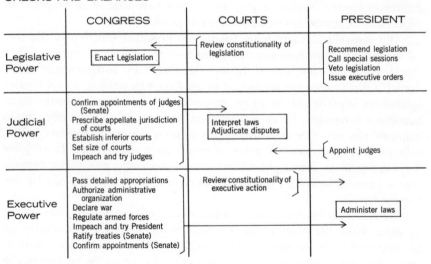

	CONGRESS	COURTS	PRESIDENT
Legislative Power	Enact Legislation	Review constitutionality of legislation	Recommend legislation Call special sessions Veto legislation Issue executive orders
Judicial Power	Confirm appointments of judges (Senate) Prescribe appellate jurisdiction of courts Establish inferior courts Set size of courts Impeach and try judges	Interpret laws Adjudicate disputes	Appoint judges
Executive Power	Pass detailed appropriations Authorize administrative organization Declare war Regulate armed forces Impeach and try President Ratify treaties (Senate) Confirm appointments (Senate)	Review constitutionality of executive action	Administer laws

FIGURE 3.

fect illustration of the way in which the ambiguity of a principle made agreement on it possible. For the principle itself was almost universally accepted. As the authors of *The Federalist* said, "The separate and distinct exercise of the different powers of government ... to a certain extent is admitted on all hands to be essential to the preservation of liberty." The purpose and meaning of the principle were widely disputed. The grounds of the dispute were the conflicting assumptions which we have already examined with reference to the problem of faction and the danger of tyranny. Although it is something of an oversimplification, we may say that generally there were two positions and two interpretations in conflict.

CHECKS AND BALANCES AS A CONSERVATIVE DOCTRINE

As we noted in the preceding chapter, Madison in *The Federalist* (No. 10), seemed to rely upon "the great variety of interests, parties, and sects" in an "extended republic" to prevent "a coalition of the majority of the whole society . . . on any other principles than those of justice and the common good." The Constitution is full of what are called, in *The Federalist* (No. 51), "auxiliary precautions" the intent of which was not simply to curb tyrannical abuses of majority power but to make majority rule impossible. The key to this system is checks and balances. The voice of a majority might find expression in the popularly elected House of Representatives (although property qualifications on the suffrage were counted on even here to keep the completely indigent and those without property from having a direct voice). The House was to be checked by an indirectly elected Senate, sitting for longer terms, who were expected to reflect a more aristocratic and conservative point of view.

To conservatives like John Adams, the President was to play the role of impartial umpire between the interests of the masses as represented in the House and the interests of the natural aristocracy as represented in the Senate. Other conservatives looked to the Court to serve as a final barrier against an impassioned majority. In order to prevent a minority from becoming tyrannical, "a dependence on the people" is necessary, but a majority can never be depended upon to treat minorities equitably. The solution to the problem of power is to divide it and balance it. As John Taylor, foremost liberal polemicist, almost sneeringly put it, the conservative panacea was ". . . doctor Balance, venerable with the rest of antiquity . . ."[3]

Jefferson, in his *Notes on Virginia*, raised the question of what was to be done when the several departments, "being perfectly coordinate by the terms of their common commission," should come into disagreement about the limits of their powers or when one poached on the powers of the others. His answer, consistent with the liberal majoritarian position, was "an appeal to the people themselves, who, as the grantors of the commission, can alone declare its true meaning, and enforce its observance." For conservatives this was no appeal at all, since, as Madison argued in *The*

[3]Taylor, *Inquiry*, p. 61.

Federalist (No. 49), the legislature as the department closest to the people is likely to emerge victorious. Even if, through unusual circumstances,

> . . .the public decision might be less swayed by prepossessions in favor of the legislative party . . . still it could never be expected to turn on the true merits of the question. It would inevitably be connected with the spirit of pre-existing parties, or of parties springing out of the question itself. . . . The *passions*, therefore, not the *reason*, of the public would sit in judgment. But it is the reason of the public, alone, that ought to control and regulate the government. The passions ought to be controlled and regulated by the government.

The reason of the people, this argument suggests, is never to be found in the voice of a majority. Instead, it is embodied in the great object of "maintaining the constitutional equilibrium of the government," which is the only safeguard against the peculiar liability of popular governments to majority tyranny.

THE LIBERAL PRESCRIPTION: DIVIDED POWER AND POPULAR SOVEREIGNTY

Majoritarians were also in favor of a system of checks and balances. Indeed, they saw it as a necessary means to insure majority rule as well as a precaution to be certain that the voice of a majority would be the voice of reason rather than passion. Where they controlled state governments, they had often set up a plural executive to be such a safeguard. Always this was done within the framework of legislative supremacy, in order to preserve the majority principle. They were unwilling to concede that the dangers of majority tyranny could legitimately be averted by making it impossible for the majority to rule. The reason of the people was still to be expressed only in the vote of the people, not in virtual representation or a constitutional equilibrium. They were careful to distinguish their theory of the division of power from those conservative theories which sought the guarantees of freedom in a balancing of class interests or social forces. Thus John Taylor argued:

> Mr. Adams considers our division of power, as the same principle with his balance of orders. We consider these principles as opposite and inimical. Power is divided by our policy, that the people may maintain their sovereignty; by the system of orders, to destroy the sovereignty of the people. Our principle of division is used, to reduce power to that degree of temperature, which may make it a blessing and not a curse. . . .[4]

For the liberal, the checks and balances system was an insurance against

---

[4] *Ibid.*, p. 356.

men of power exceeding their commissions from the people. Taylor was explicit: "We do not balance power against power. It is our policy to reduce it by division, in order to preserve the political power of the people, by forebearing to excite the ambition and avarice of individuals."[5]

In addition to ensuring that political power was responsible to the people, the separation of powers served as a check on factious majorities by encouraging adequate deliberation of public issues. The liberal case for it on these grounds was put most convincingly by John L. O'Sullivan, a liberal journalist, in an issue of the *Democratic Review* of 1837:

> We are opposed to all self-styled "wholesome restraints" on the free action of the popular opinion and will, other than those which have for their sole object the prevention of precipitate legislation. This latter object is to be attained by the expedient of the division of power, and by causing all legislation to pass through the ordeal of successive forms; to be sifted through the discussions of coordinate legislative branches with mutual suspensive veto powers. Yet all should be dependent with equal directness and promptness on the influence of public opinion; the popular will should be equally the animating and moving spirit of them all.[6]

Much of the subsequent discussion of the system of checks and balances has centered around its function in providing a cooling-off device which would permit the taking of an appeal "from the people drunk to the people sober." Here again, what looks at first glance like a basic agreement between liberals and conservatives turns out, on closer analysis, to conceal fundamental differences. Hamilton put the conservative case for the delaying function of checks and balances in *The Federalist* (No. 71):

> It is a just observation, that the people commonly intend the public good. This often applies to their very errors. . . . when occasions present themselves, in which the interests of the people are at variance with their inclinations it is the duty of the persons whom they have appointed to be the guardians of those interests, to withstand the temporary delusion in order to give them time and opportunity for more cool and sedate reflection.

In interpreting Hamilton's position, we must not lose sight of the warning that George Mason had given to the other members of the Convention: "Notwithstanding the oppression and injustice experienced among us from democracy, the genius of the people is in favor of it, and the genius of the people must be consulted." On other occasions, Hamilton had described the people as a "great beast." He clearly did not believe

[5]*Ibid.*, p. 171.
[6]Quoted in Mason, *Free Government In the Making*, p. 447.

that popular delusions would always be temporary. More fundamentally, as the quotation from *The Federalist* (No. 71) makes clear, the real interests of the people are to be defined by their guardians, not directly by public opinion itself.

For the liberal, the distinction between the interests of the people and their inclinations was to be defined by reasoned appeals to the people. For the conservative, the public good must be protected by balance and by a "successive filtration of power" through indirect election which creates guardians of the people's real interests. Time for full reflection and consideration does not constitute a sobriety test for public opinion in this view. Either sobriety is impossible and the best society can do is pit a drunken majority against drunken minorities (which tended to be Madison's position), or a guiding aristocracy must be trusted to tell the majority when it is sober (which tended to be Hamilton's position). Both of these positions are conservative, and they are to be distinguished from the liberal policy of preventing "precipitate legislation" within a framework in which public opinion remains the only permissible court of appeal. Here, as elsewhere in the constitutional framework, agreement was possible because to a considerable extent liberals and conservatives were agreeing to the same words but to different interpretations of their meaning.

Liberals, for their part, failed to some extent to appraise seriously enough the threat posed to their position by the conservative principle of balance. They did so because, while they insisted that majorities must rule, they did not want them to do much ruling. Generally, liberals were the spokesmen for an agrarianism that required an economic policy of *laissez-faire*. They tended to oppose the development of industrialism and urbanization; they found the virtues of individual independence and autonomy to be uniquely related to an agrarian, frontier environment; and, under these conditions, they saw little need for government to do very much. For many of them, even government construction of internal improvements, like roads and canals, was an unjustified interference with individual initiative and independence.

Given these limitations on public policy, even a conservative theory of checks and balances seemed not to pose a major threat. If the functions of government were to be limited to the maintenance of order and the conduct of foreign affairs, and if all else was to be left to the initiative of self-sufficient individuals, it was reasonable to assume that the major threat to the responsible exercise of power was the danger of public officials exceeding their commissions. In a world in which there were no corporations, no large cities, and no networks of mass communication and transportation, it was reasonable to assume that the major problem in making government responsible was to provide safeguards to its potential abuse. Especially was it reasonable to a generation in revolt against too much government and arbitrary governmental intervention in the affairs of individuals.

Under the changed conditions of industrialization and urbanization, where there are private corporations with more wealth and more employees than many of the state governments, and where public opinion requires government to engage in a myriad of activities ranging from social security and unemployment insurance to basic research in science and resource conservation, the conservatives' constitutional equilibrium posed a more obvious and serious threat to the liberal's commitment to majority rule. It was inevitable, therefore, not only that the earlier conflict over the meaning of checks and balances was to continue but that the rift was to widen and the issues to be more sharply posed.

CHECKS AND BALANCES: HISTORICAL DEVELOPMENT

The principle of checks and balances was from the first, and has remained, ambiguous. The actual constitutional arrangements intended to implement it have been rather drastically modified, sometimes by constitutional amendment, but more often by interpretation, usage, and the growth of extra-constitutional political mechanisms. Mainly, these changes have reflected the liberal, at the expense of the conservative, view of the purpose of separation of powers. As liberalism adopted a more positive attitude toward the role of government, particularly in economic affairs, the constitutional restraints on majority action seemed to liberals more oppressive and indefensible. Changes in constitutional provisions and usage designed to make majority rule possible were matched by the reliance of conservatives less and less on the whole system of checks and balances and more on the position of the courts for the protection of minorities. The changes in the American political system that have played the most direct and important role in undermining the conservative principle of checks and balances may be described as follows:

1. *The rise of political parties.* From the beginning, effective liberal government required that there be some means of cutting across the separation of powers—that is, some means of raising the same issues of public policy in all the branches of government so that all were equally responsive to popular will. The political instrument that almost immediately arose to provide continuity and cohesiveness to public policy and the framework for public debate was the political party. Parties were formed to put the same political philosophy and political organization in control of all public offices. Not provided for in the Constitution, they arose as the means by which coherent principles and programs could compete for temporary control of the government. As such, competitive political parties were a powerful weapon of majoritarian democracy which could be em-

ployed to destroy the foundations of the conservative constitutional edifice.

2. *Constitutional changes to make the several agencies directly responsible.* The conservative doctrine of balance, as we have noted, relied in part on indirect election, in part on Madison's "successive filtration" of the popular will. Liberal reforms, written into constitutional amendments, have all but eliminated this conservative safeguard. The Twelfth Amendment, and the custom which binds electors to vote for the presidential and vice-presidential candidates who have secured the largest number of popular votes in their states, have made the President a popularly elected official. (It is, of course still possible for a President to be elected by a minority.) The Seventeenth Amendment made Senators directly elected.

Whereas, for the most part, O'Sullivan's liberal plea that all the branches of government should be "equally dependent on the popular will" has been realized, the same is not true of his argument that this should be so "with equal promptness." We do have, then, the possibility of a President representing one party and a Congress the other, or the two houses of Congress in the control of different parties. Proposals for constitutional reform to remedy this defect (from the liberal viewpoint) have often been made, but not successfully. They continue to operate as a potent deterrent to responsible party government, in the liberal sense.

3. *Changes in usage and practice that facilitate majority rule.* There are, in this category, three developments that have contributed to undermining the constitutional equilibrium: judicial self-restraint after 1937, the growth in the power of the Presidency, and the development of regulatory commissions.

We will examine the role of the Supreme Court in the system of checks and balances in the next chapter. Now we need only note that the Court came to be the major check on majority government and, after the Civil War, the conservative bulwark against majority attacks on the property rights of minorities. The Court's continued reluctance, since 1937, to set aside statutes as unconstitutional in areas other than civil liberties and civil rights has meant the decline of another conservative safeguard.

Secondly, the tremendous growth in the power of the Presidency, to be examined in detail later, saw the emergence of that office as a potential spokesman for a national majority, and made it possible for campaigns which involve nation-wide issues to be fought along nation-wide lines. At the same time the growth of the President's role as national legislative leader, with strong Presidents able to exert considerable leadership in the legislative process, cuts across the separation of powers between those two branches in the interest of a popularly supported legislative program. (At the same time, of course, the wide acceptance of the principle of separation of powers itself set important limits on the powers of the

President, as Franklin D. Roosevelt discovered when he sought unsuccessfully to "purge" Congressmen who had opposed or been lukewarm to his
program.)

The third development to be considered here is the rise of the regula-
tive administrative agency. This device, unknown to the Constitution, was
the major means used by Congress to implement programs designed to regulate various aspects of the economy in response to the demands of national
majorities. Beginning with the Interstate Commerce Commission in 1887,
the independent regulatory commission became the institutional device
most often used to enforce the public interest in such areas of the economy
as the control of monopoly and trade practices (Federal Trade Commission, 1914), the quality of foods and drugs (Pure Food and Drug Administration, 1906), the sale of corporate securities (Securities and Exchange
Commission, 1934), the interstate distribution of electric power and natural
gas (Federal Power Commission, 1920), the uses of radio and television
media (Federal Communications Commission, 1934), and others.

At the same time, the states instituted similar commissions to regulate
in the public interest a range of intrastate activities, including recent fair
employment practices commissions designed to insure the public interest
in equality of economic opportunity regardless of race. In every case,
these agencies resulted from public discussion of what were taken to be
public issues, and in most cases the decision to institute them can be
construed as a majority decision enforced on a recalcitrant minority—
indeed, on a minority which usually claimed that its liberties were being
abrogated by a tyrannical majority.

The most important fact about these new agencies of government was
that they cut across the constitutional system of checks and balances. They
were established by Congress to regulate various aspects of economic
activity, functions which represented a response to new problems posed by
industrialization but which Congress was not itself equipped to carry out.
In establishing the commissions, Congress made them independent of the
rest of the executive establishment: the commissioners who head these
agencies may not be removed by the President except for causes prescribed
by Congress; the decisions of the commission are not reviewed and may
not be vetoed by the President. At the same time, the commissions themselves exercise legislative, executive, and judicial powers. Under a broad
congressional statement of public policy, the commissions develop administrative rules and regulations in their areas which have the force of
law; they are themselves charged with the responsibility of applying and
administering the law and the regulations; and in the course of discharging these obligations, they prosecute offenders, hear cases, and
hand down decisions. It is on these grounds that their functions have been

referred to as quasi-legislative and quasi-judicial. Congress, of course, may terminate any of these agencies at any time or change its functions, and the decisions of the agency are reviewable on issues of law in the regular courts. But the important thing for our purposes here is that the functions of the agencies cut across the traditional separation of powers, and that they developed as applications of a view of the public interest supported by a popular majority.

The constitutional restraints on majority rule embodied in the doctrine of checks and balances have been, in large measure, circumvented and nullified by the developments we have discussed: the popular election of senators and reform in the electoral college, the rise of political parties, the self-imposed restraint of the Supreme Court after 1937, the supremacy of national government over the states, the growth of the governmental commission, and the increase in the power of the Presidency.

The remarkable fact is that these reforms have not succeeded in producing the political system that Jefferson and subsequent liberal reformers envisioned, and it seems very doubtful that the modification of the remaining constitutional barriers (differential terms of office) would transform the system into one closer to the traditional liberal model. At the same time, the conservative hopes of the Constitution makers have been no less frustrated: our political system does not maintain a constitutional equilibrium of economic classes, nor does it provide for the indirect election of an aristocracy who will be "proper guardians of the public weal." (The phrase is from *The Federalist* [No. 10].) The result has been neither liberal nor conservative in the traditional sense, but rather the politics of minorities rule which we have referred to earlier and will consider in detail subsequently.

At this point, we would emphasize what seems a reasonable conclusion from these historical developments: a constitution is not a political system; its principles do not necessarily prescribe political realities. Constitutional checks and balances may be radically altered in their meaning and effect by the growth of extra-constitutional political devices like the political party. But even this does not take us very far in understanding the nature of a society's politics. Like constitutional principles themselves other political institutions may serve the purposes of a liberal or a conservative or some other model of politics.

The character of a political system depends, in the final analysis, on more fundamental social and cultural considerations. Politics describes the ways in which men deal with conflict; governments are run by individuals; and constitutional principles are continually re-enacted and reformulated in the political activities of men. In consequence, it is the kind of answers that men give, explicitly or implicitly, to the questions of human nature, society, and truth that are important. For it is in the light of these answers that men define their political roles and expectations—as citizens, party politicians, administrators, and judges.

The resulting pattern of roles and expectations is expressed in the daily conduct of politics; in whether or not political parties are organized to conduct a public debate of public issues; in the role of interest groups and in their relationship to parties, legislatures, administrative officials and courts; in nominations, in campaigns, and in the behavior of voters when they go to the polls; in the attitudes of the man-in-the-street toward politics and in the attitudes of the politician toward the man-in-the-street; and in the media of communication through which political attitudes are simultaneously formed and reflected. Whether a political system approximates most nearly a conservative or a liberal or some other model will depend on the preceding variables, as well as on the underlying philosophical assumptions they express.

The principle of checks and balances expressed the conservative assumptions and hopes of those who formulated it; it was modified by amendment and usage in the light of the quite different assumptions and hopes of majoritarians. But, at any given time, the practical meaning and working of political and constitutional mechanisms will reflect the assumptions and hopes of the participants.

Federalism

Our very national designation—the United States of America—makes it clear that fifty states are united to form a nation, and that the result is a federal union. Federalism, as a principle, is a way of organizing the distribution of political power between a central or national government, on the one hand, and the governments of the areas into which the nation is divided (states, provinces, cantons, and so on) on the other. At the one extreme is the unitary state in which all political power is centralized in the national organs of government, and all subsidiary governments are the creatures of the national government. Great Britain is an example. At the other extreme is the confederation in which all political power is ultimately in the hands of the constituent states, and the national government is their creature with no independent powers of its own. American government under the Articles of Confederation (1781-1789) was an example.

THE BROAD OUTLINES OF AMERICAN FEDERALISM

Federalism stands between these two extremes, distributing power between a national government and the states in such a fashion that both have substantial powers, and both are bound by the terms of the arrangement. In the American system this is accomplished in the written Constitution, and the allocation of powers to nation and states therein provided may be formally altered only through a process of amendment in which both the national and state governments participate. The broad outline of this political relationship is stated in the Tenth Amendment: "The powers not delegated to the United States by the Constitution, nor prohibited by it to the States, are reserved to the States respectively, or to the people."

"The powers . . . delegated to the United States by the Constitution" are those which define the powers of the Congress (Article I, Section 8), the President (Article II, Section 2) and the national courts (Article III Section 2).

Article I

SECTION 8. The Congress shall have the power

1. To lay and collect taxes, duties, imposts, and excises, to pay the debts and provide for the common defense and general welfare of the United States; but all duties, imposts, and excises shall be uniform throughout the United States;

2. To borrow money on the credit of the United States;

3. To regulate commerce with foreign nations, and among the several States, and with the Indian tribes;

4. To establish a uniform rule of naturalization, and uniform laws on the subject of bankruptcies throughout the United States;

5. To coin money, regulate the value thereof, and of foreign coin, and fix the standard of weights and measures;

6. To provide for the punishment of counterfeiting the securities and current coin of the United States;

7. To establish post offices and post roads;

8. To promote the progress of science and useful arts, by securing for limited times to authors and inventors the exclusive right to their respective writings and discoveries;

9. To constitute tribunals inferior to the Supreme Court;

10. To define and punish piracies and felonies committed on the high seas, and offenses against the law of nations;

11. To declare war, grant letters of marque and reprisal, and make rules concerning captures on land and water;

12. To raise and support armies, but no appropriation of money to that use shall be for a longer term than two years;

13. To provide and maintain a navy;

14. To make rules for the government and regulation of the land and naval forces;

15. To provide for calling forth the militia to execute the laws of the Union, suppress insurrections and repel invasions;

16. To provide for organizing, arming, and disciplining the militia, and for governing such part of them as may be employed in the

service of the United States, reserving to the States respectively, the appointment of the officers, and the authority of training the militia according to the discipline prescribed by Congress;

17. To exercise exclusive legislation in all cases whatsoever, over such district (not exceeding ten miles square) as may, by cession of particular States, and the acceptance of Congress, become the seat of the government of the United States, and to exercise like authority over all places purchased by the consent of the legislature of the State in which the same shall be, for the erection of forts, magazines, arsenals, dockyards, and other needful buildings; and

18. To make all laws which shall be necessary and proper for carrying into execution the foregoing powers, and all other powers vested by this Constitution in the government of the United States, or in any department or officer thereof.

Article II

SECTION 2. 1. The President shall be commander in chief of the army and navy of the United States, and of the militia of the several States, when called into the actual service of the United States; he may require the opinion, in writing, of the principal officer in each of the executive departments, upon any subject relating to the duties of their respective offices, and he shall have power to grant reprieves and pardons for offenses against the United States, except in cases of impeachment.

2. He shall have power, by and with the advice and consent of the Senate, to make treaties, provided two thirds of the senators present concur; and he shall nominate, and by and with the advice and con-sent of the Senate, shall appoint ambassadors, other public ministers and consuls, judges of the Supreme Court, and all other officers of the United States, whose appointments are not herein otherwise provided for, and which shall be established by law: but the Congress may by law vest the appointment of such inferior officers, as they think proper, in the President alone, in the courts of law, or in the heads of departments.

3. The President shall have power to fill up all vacancies that may happen during the recess of the Senate, by granting commissions which shall expire at the end of their next session.

Article III

SECTION 2. 1. The judicial power shall extend to all cases, in law and equity, arising under this Constitution, the laws of the United States, and treaties made, or which shall be made, under their authority;—to all cases affecting ambassadors, other public ministers and consuls;—to all cases of admiralty and maritime jurisdiction;—to controversies to which the United States shall be a party;—to controversies between two or more States;—between a State and citizens of another State; —between citizens of different States;—between citizens of the same State claiming lands under grants of different States, and between a State, or the citizens thereof, and foreign States, citizens or subjects.

2. In all cases affecting ambassadors, other public ministers and consuls, and those in which a State shall be party, the Supreme Court shall have original jurisdiction. In all the other cases before mentioned, the Supreme Court shall have appellate jurisdiction, both as to law and fact, with such exceptions, and under such regulations as the Congress shall make.

3. The trial of all crimes except in cases of impeachment, shall be by jury; and such trial shall be held in the State where the said crimes shall have been committed; but when not committed within any State, the trial shall be at such place or places as the Congress may by law have directed.

The powers prohibited by the Constitution to the States are, for the most part, enumerated in Article I, Section 10:

Article I

SECTION 10. 1. No State shall enter into any treaty, alliance, or confederation; grant letters of marque and reprisal; coin money; emit bills of credit; make anything but gold and silver coin a tender in payment of debts; pass any bill of attainder, *ex post facto* law, or law impairing the obligation of contracts, or grant any title of nobility.

2. No State shall, without the consent of the Congress, lay any impost or duties on imports or exports, except what may be absolutely necessary for executing its inspection laws: and the net produce of all duties and imposts laid by any State on imports or exports, shall be for the use of the Treasury of the United States; and all such laws shall be subject to the revision and control of the Congress.

3. No State shall, without the consent of the Congress, lay any duty of tonnage, keep troops, or ships of war in time of peace, enter into any agreement or compact with another State, or with a foreign power, or engage in war, unless actually invaded, or in such imminent danger as will not admit of delay.

The relationship between national and state governments seems as explicit and clear as a written document could make it. The national Congress may legislate only where it can point to an express grant of power in the section quoted above. All other powers of government are reserved to the states. Yet, the whole problem of "states' rights" has led to endless controversy, and is an exceedingly complicated one. The relationship, seemingly so explicitly defined in the Constitution, has been modified continuously by interpretation, statutes, custom, and usage. It is a relationship which is constantly being contested in Congress and in state legislative halls throughout the land; in the courts, both state and national; in bureaucracies of various sorts; in election campaigns; and by ballots. The principle of federalism like that of checks and balances, has been a principle only in the sense of marking out an arena of controversy, of defining an issue around which the struggle to define democracy has continued to revolve.

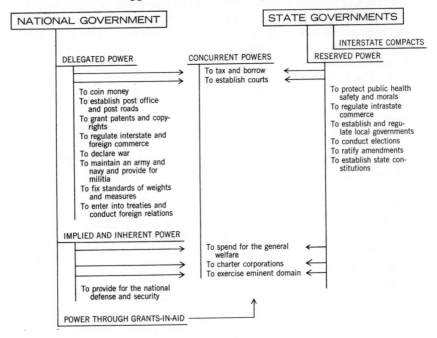

FIGURE 4. Federalism.

AMERICAN FEDERALISM: COMPROMISE OR PRINCIPLE?

In the Constitutional Convention federalism was a compromise, and a most necessary one; without it, it is unlikely any stable government at all could have been formed. The Connecticut Compromise (so-called because it was formulated by Doctor William Samuel Johnson of that State) sought a middle ground between those who would retain the full sovereignty of the individual states by not allowing the national government to act directly on individuals and those who wanted a strong national government capable of acting directly on individuals. In Doctor Johnson's words: "The two ideas embraced on different sides, instead of being opposed to each other ought to be combined; that in one branch the people ought to be represented; in the other the states." It was this compromise which laid the groundwork for the reconciliation of the interest of larger and smaller states, stifled most objections to a national government with real power, and paved the way for the elaboration of the federal system.

As Madison noted in *The Federalist* (No. 37), the result was that "the convention must have been compelled to sacrifice theoretical propriety to the force of extraneous considerations" because of "the interfering pretensions of the larger and smaller States."

A recent critic has warned us: "It is rather muddleheaded to romanticize a necessary bargain into a grand principle of democratic politics."[7] The warning, however trenchant, is a little tardy. The bargain described by Madison in *The Federalist* (No. 37) as an unavoidable compromise which could not be supported by "theoretical propriety" had already, in *The Federalist* (No. 51) become an example of the application of a principle. In that issue (written less than a month after No. 37) the federal principle had already become part of the conservative system of checks and balances and an "auxiliary precaution" against factious majorities:

> In the compound republic of America, the power surrendered by the people is first divided between two distinct governments, and then the portion allotted to each subdivided between distinct and separate departments. Hence a double security arises to the rights of the people. The different governments will control each other, at the same time that each will be controlled by itself.

Federalism had thus become an important part of the system whereby "ambition" could "be made to counteract ambition." From the conservative point of view, the most important aspect of federalism was that it removed political power from the states where democratic tendencies were most marked and where, sometimes, agrarian majorities ran wild (at least as conservatives were inclined to define "wildness"). Madison, in *The Federalist* (No. 51), summed up the conservative view of the danger of democracy in state governments and the advantages of a federal union:

> It can be little doubted that if the State of Rhode Island was separated from the Confederacy and left to itself, the insecurity of rights under the popular form of government within such narrow limits would be displayed by such reiterated oppressions of factious majorities that some power altogether independent of the people would soon be called for by the voice of the very factions whose misrule had proved the necessity of it.

The federal principle itself thus was counted upon to operate as an additional bulwark against majority tyranny and an additional safeguard of the rights of a propertied minority. At the same time, the preference of liberal democrats for decentralized government and retention of political power in the states reflected their own political and economic assumptions. They foresaw a strong national government supporting high duties on

---

[7]Robert A. Dahl, *A Preface to Democratic Theory* (Chicago: University of Chicago Press, 1956), p. 118.

imports and, in general, dedicating itself to the interests of the wealthy class and the large landholders.

Despite their general opposition to giving power to a national government, liberals gradually accepted the federal structure. Again, as in the case of checks and balances, their acceptance of federalism followed from their interpretation of its meaning and effect in the light of liberal principles. They saw the states as "laboratories of political science" in which their new ideas toward government could be experimented with, tested in practice, and copied in other states when they proved successful. They saw the union as necessary for the protection of newly won independence, but they did not intend that the new national government should do very much.

FEDERALISM: HISTORICAL DEVELOPMENT

The conflict between conservative and liberal interpretations of federalism centered on two issues: how powerful the national government was to be, and how conflicts between national and state governments were to be resolved. The first great conservative political party, led by Alexander Hamilton and John Adams, called itself the Federalists; the Jeffersonian liberals began their party career as the Anti-Federalists. The names concealed more than they revealed about the differences between them. The central question was not whether a federal system should prevail, but whether the federal division of power in the Constitution should be loosely or strictly interpreted. The Federalists, because they wanted to expand the national government, argued for a loose construction of the language enumerating its powers; the Anti-Federalists wanted to confine the powers of the national government to a strict and literal reading of the constitutional text.

The debate was first set off when, in 1790, Alexander Hamilton as Washington's Secretary of the Treasury, proposed the establishment of a national bank. There was no such grant of power in the Constitution; Hamilton argued that it was a power that, under the language of the final clause of Article I, Section 8, could be inferred to be "necessary and proper for carrying into execution" the powers that were expressly granted. The issue was decided by the Supreme Court in 1819 in favor of the Federalist position. In *McCulloch* v. *Maryland*,[8] the Court upheld the constitutionality of the second national bank (the charter of the first expired in 1811 without its ever having been tested in the courts) by accepting Hamilton's argument. In his decision, Chief Justice Marshall argued that the grants of power to Congress to lay and collect taxes, regulate commerce, coin and borrow money, and provide for the national de-

[8] 4 Wheaton 316 (1819).

fense are to be viewed as broad ends or goals of government activity; and that, therefore, they imply the existence of the power to do whatever may be "necessary and proper" for their accomplishment.

Thus he held that, whereas Congress was given no express power to charter a bank, its decision to do so was clearly a means to the accomplishment of the broad ends it is constitutionally empowered to promote. "Let the end be legitimate," Marshall summarized, "let it be within the scope of the Constitution, and all means which are appropriate, which are plainly adapted to that end, which are not prohibited, but consist with the letter and spirit of the Constitution, are constitutional."

The Court threw its authoritative weight behind the Hamiltonian argument for "loose construction," and the doctrine that the national government has "implied" and "resultant" powers to be inferred from those expressly enumerated became the basis for its tremendous growth in later years. The Hamiltonian argument came back, ironically, to haunt a new generation of conservatives when the instruments of the national government were controlled by liberals who undertook to use them to limit and regulate, rather than to promote, the interests of business. In changed circumstances, liberals and conservatives reversed sides on the question of states' rights and national power, which suggests again that the issue involved has never been a matter of fundamental political principle for any of the contestants.

The question has always been fundamentally that of marking out the legitimate boundaries of the power of popular majorities. Jeffersonians opposed national power when they saw it as a vehicle for protecting the property interests of a minority; they supported and used it when they saw it as an instrument of majority rule. Conversely, conservatives supported national power when they saw it as a check on the factious tendencies of local majorities; they opposed it and invoked the symbols of states' rights when majorities clamored for federal regulation of railroads and other reforms which invaded the property interests of minorities. When the high-sounding symbol of states' rights is invoked in political conflict, American history would seem to tell us, we would do well to take it only as window-dressing, as a clue that some important conflicts of interests and principles are involved, but never as a statement of what the conflict is really about.

The second major issue over which the Federalists and Anti-Federalists (or Jeffersonian Republicans) fought out the meaning of federalism involved the question of the nature of the Union itself. The Constitution is silent on whether the Union it established is indissoluble and on whether a state is obligated to comply with national legislation which it regards as unconstitutional. Did a state have the right voluntarily to secede? Did it have the right to nullify a national action as it applied to the citizens of the state? Did it have the right to interpose legislation of its own contrary to federal legislation, in order to prevent the latter from being enforced within the state?

These are all now, in a sense, "dead" issues; never resolved through political debate, they were for all practical purposes laid to rest on the bloody fields of the Civil War. Cries of "nullification" and "interposition" echoed across the land from some Southern states in the aftermath of the Supreme Court's desegregation decision, but they were cries from a buried past. They were, however, very live issues until they were settled by trial of arms. For the conservative, national power could operate within the confines of the constitutional equilibrium; there were no such safeguards on the power of the states. It was the very purpose of the federal union to limit and contain the factious majorities that might develop in the states. It was, therefore, unthinkable that a state could secede or that a temporary majority in a state could nullify national legislation. On the other hand, for the liberal the federal principle could only operate to safeguard liberty and popular government when the national government was not supreme. He saw the federal principle as another device for insuring that all government reflected the reasoned convictions of popular majorities.

John Taylor stated the liberal view most clearly in his argument: "The best restraint upon legislative acts tending to the destruction of a true republican government, consists of the mutual right of the general and state governments to examine and controvert before the publick each others' proceedings."[9] To modern ears this sounds more like a recipe for anarchy than for a "true republican government." Again, however, the argument becomes a more sensible one if we bear in mind that, historically, liberals expected that all government, national and state, would need do very little.

The initial battle in this struggle over the nature of the Union centered around the Alien and Sedition Acts. Federalists, alarmed about the influence of the Jacobin ideas of the French Revolution on the Jeffersonian societies, and seeking to cement their hold on the reins of government, passed these acts in 1798. Their effect was to make it a crime to criticize the government or its (then Federalist) officials. Jefferson and Madison, who had by this time become a staunch Jeffersonian and Jefferson's closest political compatriot, countered by drawing up the Virginia and Kentucky Resolutions and inducing the legislatures of those two states to adopt them. The resolutions rested squarely on Taylor's interpretation of federalism. They declared the acts to be unconstitutional, a clear usurpation of power by the national Congress, and thus, insofar as Virginia and Kentucky were concerned, null and void. The Virginia Resolution went further by proposing that states had the right to "inter-

[9] Taylor, *Inquiry*, p. 556.

pose" contrary statutes of their own to make even national enforcement of national law impossible within the state. Virginia and Kentucky called on the other states to adopt similar resolutions. The issue and the conflicting political philosophies underlying it were clarified in this contest, and the Alien and Sedition Acts were allowed to lapse.

At the Hartford Convention, the New England states' threat to secede because of the harm suffered by shipping interests in the War of 1812 illustrates how the federal principle became embroiled in the struggle of economic interests as well. So also does the extended debate between Senators Webster and Hayne in 1830. Here the threat of nullification arose over dissatisfaction in the South with the Tariff of Abominations of 1828. Senator Hayne, spokesman for the agricultural interests of the South, argued that tariff legislation passed in the interests of Northern manufacturers was intolerably oppressive to the Southern states and that, under the Constitution, nullification constituted a legitimate weapon with which a state could defend its vital interests. By this time, the issue of federalism had become so entangled in the struggle of economic interests and their moralistic rationalizations that it is difficult to discern what fundamental political principles, if any, were at issue. The debate was conducted over such matters as whether the Constitution had been created by the people as citizens of the United States or by the people as citizens of their respective states, and whether, therefore, the national government was the agent of the whole people or of the people acting through their states. But the arguments had become legalistic and states' rights seemed to be a mantle which could be, and was, donned by every interest which felt itself threatened by action in the national arena.

The issue of the nature of the federal union was settled when it became the battleground of forces that were moral as well as economic in the sectional rivalry that found its climax in the Civil War. Thereafter, the nature of the union was settled; the question of what the national government should do and what is better left to the initiative and discretion of the states continued, of course, to be a source of controversy in American politics. Much of that controversy has been characterized by legalistic pleadings about the intent of the Founding Fathers which serve to conceal or obscure the conflict of economic interests that lie at the heart of the matter. The invocation of states' rights in the controversy over tidelands oil in the years between 1947 and 1953 is a case in point. Partly, also, controversies have reflected efforts to deal with the very difficult problem for majoritarian theory of *which* majority should rule when there is a conflict between the majority views in local and larger political arenas. The control of alcoholic beverages and racial segregation illustrate this problem.

Finally, the controversy between national power and states' rights at times involves the traditional question of how the powers of government should be distributed so as to maximize freedom in society. To a considerable extent, the issue of federal aid to education would seem to turn on a fundamental controversy over this basic question. Perhaps the chief weaknesses of a federal system are that conflicts over the respective limits of national and state power promote a legalistic approach to issues ("Who has the constitutional prerogative?" rather than "What ought to be done?") and that, at the same time, the invocation of states' rights serves to conceal the interests and principles that are in conflict.

The Instruments of National Power. The history of American federalism is the record of the aggrandizement of power at the national level. The national government, restricted by the Constitution to those powers expressly delegated to it or implied therein, has come to exercise authority that would have astounded even the most ardent advocates of national supremacy at Philadelphia. Brought back to the America of the 1960's eighteenth-century Americans would find it hard to believe that the intervening changes could have been accomplished without extensive constitutional revision. Yet, only the Sixteenth Amendment, which authorized the federal income tax, directly expanded the powers of Congress and the President over economic life. Otherwise, the power emanating from Washington has grown slowly and informally, by constitutional interpretation and usage. This expansion comes in response to the fact that industrialization has raised new issues to the level of national debate, and that the pressures of majority opinion and of organized interests have undermined that portion of the doctrine of checks and balances embodied in the federal structure of government.

There are those who would say that what we have called constitutional interpretation is a euphemism used to conceal the fact that the Constitution has been stretched far beyond its clear and evident meaning. Senator Goldwater, in his widely read *The Conscience of a Conservative*, forcefully argues for this view: "The Constitution, I repeat, draws a sharp and clear line between federal jurisdiction and state jurisdiction. The federal government's failure to recognize that line has been a crushing blow to the principles of limited government."[10]

There seems to be a prima facie case for this assertion. How can the present scope of national activity be justified by the grants of power to Congress "to lay and collect taxes, duties, imposts, and excises, to pay the debts and provide for the common defense and general welfare of the United States," "to regulate commerce with foreign nations and among the several states, and with the Indian tribes," and to declare war and

---

[10]Barry Goldwater, *The Conscience of a Conservative* (Shepherdsville, Kentucky: Victor Publishing Company, 1960), p. 29.

provide for national defense? These are the constitutional provisions on which most of the growth of national power has rested. How far can the taxing power, the commerce power and the war power be stretched without making the federal limitations on the national government meaningless? Have they been stretched beyond all reasonable and meaningful limits?

The "War Power". Concerning the power of the national government to provide for the national defense and to declare and wage war successfully there seems to be little question. The national government has acquired tremendous power over the economy in discharging its war powers, not because of willful conspirators in Washington, but because of the changing requirements of national defense and the changed character of warfare. War has become total war; defense now means total economic and social mobilization, not because of the aspirations of power-hungry bureaucrats or advocates of socialist planning, but because of the technology of war itself. Who can doubt that national survival in the current contest with international communism involves the rate of growth of the economy, the capacity of the educational system to produce the skills and abilities necessary to a viable democratic order as well as an expanding economy, or the elimination of racial discrimination and segregation in all aspects of American life? Total war means total mobilization.

Some of these activities may be undesirable on other grounds. Indeed, the warfare state may even be incompatible with the maintenance of democracy in the long run. But, with respect to the question of the constitutional power of the national government, the nature of modern war means that the war power has become almost total power. The question is no longer whether the national government has the constitutional right to interfere in all aspects of economic and social life; modern war has virtually eliminated federalism as a system of constitutional restraints on the power of the national government. In one of its aspects this development is a healthy one. If there is no longer, in most matters, a *constitutional* question of what Congress has a legal right to do, there is still a *political* question of what and how much the national government should be asked to do. If we are forced to decide these questions as matters of public policy rather than as explications of a constitutional text, we shall have put the issues where, in a democratic society, they belong—squarely in the center of political controversy and debate.

The "Commerce Power" and the Power to Tax and Spend for the "General Welfare". Historically, the age of total war was clearly ushered in by World War II. Already, however, the power of the national government had been tremendously expanded in the development of the welfare state. The government had enacted legislation designed to regulate economic life; it had gone into business itself in some areas, most especially in the production and distribution of electrical energy, and in the provision of recreational facilities in the national park system; it had undertaken to plan the use and development of natural resources; it had erected a system of social security measures including old age and survivors' insurance, unemployment compensation, and minimum wage and child labor statutes.

Mainly, these measures were made under the grant of power to Congress to regulate interstate commerce and to tax and spend money for the general welfare. It should be noted here that there is no general grant to the national government of police power (that is, power to protect and advance the public "health, safety, welfare, and morals"). Thus, the national government may not enact legislation dealing with housing, wages, pornographic literature, or prostitution simply because the Congress and the President believe that such measures would contribute to the general welfare. It may, however, establish regulations on interstate commerce that have the effect of accomplishing these objectives. It may, for example, prohibit the movement in interstate commerce of goods produced in enterprises which pay less than an established minimum hourly wage. Or it may prohibit the use of the mails to defraud, even though there is no power to prevent fraud as contrary to the best interests of society.

The power to regulate interstate commerce turned out to be a formidable power, indeed. It has been used to justify national legislation designed not only to promote, control, and prohibit specific kinds of economic activity, but also to implement national policy on conditions of labor, the "white slave" traffic, racial discrimination, and so on. Moreover, interstate commerce has been defined so broadly by Congress and the courts that it includes virtually all economic activity. The power to regulate interstate commerce extends to the power to regulate the affairs of a small business engaged, for example, in selling rock and gravel products in a local market. Similarly, a farmer who grows only enough grain to feed his own livestock is nevertheless defined as being engaged in interstate commerce. Generally, the only persons who are excluded from national legislation regulating interstate commerce are those who, in the wording of the legislation, are deliberately excluded by Congress.

Is this an arbitrary and conscienceless abuse of the clear language of the Constitution? Not, it would seem, if we define commerce with relation not merely to a word in the Constitution, but with relation to the interdependent network of activity that makes up a modern industrialized economy. The rock and gravel delivered by our local businessman may be used by steel companies and other firms engaged in producing for an interstate market; it may be part of a roadbed that supports the vehicles engaged in the intricate system of transportation underlying the national economy. The farmer producing his own grain for his own livestock is affecting, nevertheless, the interstate market for grain and for livestock.

All business is interstate business because of the nature of the industrial and commercial system. The extent to which it ought to be subjected to promotion, regulation, or even abolition is a political rather than a narrowly constitutional or legal question in a modern, interdependent economy.

Similarly, the national government may tax or borrow and spend money, both directly and indirectly, for "welfare" purposes, even though it has no power in the Constitution directly to promote those purposes. Thus, during the Depression of the 1930's, the national government created and financed work programs designed to provide immediate relief for the unemployed, although there is no direct grant of such authority in the Constitution. Many of the "alphabet" agencies—the C.W.A. (Civil Works Administration), P.W.A. (Public Works Administration), W.P.A. (Works Progress Administration), C.C.C. (Civilian Conservation Corps), N.Y.A. (National Youth Authority)—represented national efforts to use the powers to tax, borrow, and spend to stimulate a flagging economy.

The national power to tax and spend may also be employed indirectly through the technique of grants-in-aid. Through this device, the national government makes funds available to the states for specific purposes, usually with a provision that requires the states to match federal contributions at some stated percentage thereof out of their own revenues.

The Social Security Act of 1935 was based on this principle which has since been extended beyond welfare to such programs as highway development, urban redevelopment, vocational education and rehabilitation programs, and others. Sometimes, as notably in the employment security program, federal funds are made available to the states on a tax rebate system, wherein state agencies collect unemployment security taxes for the federal government which in turn gives most of it back to the states to make unemployment insurance payments in amounts set by state legislatures.

Thus, the use of federal money in welfare and other programs may involve more or less of national government control, but in every instance grants-in-aid involve some measure of national initiative and control. In rare instances, national power has been used to stimulate state activity from which the national government hopes later to withdraw. Thus, Congress invested heavily in grants-in-aid to the states in venereal disease control and treatment programs, later cutting back its financial contributions in the hope that states would undertake to continue the programs on their own.

Whenever the national government undertakes to contribute financially to state programs—whether in highway construction, welfare, health, employment security, or resource development—state legislatures and local officials are left with less discretion than they would otherwise have. State agencies accepting federal welfare money must comply with all sorts of rules and regulations which they might otherwise prefer to do without. Specifically, in this program, all employees working for a welfare agency using federal funds must be under a merit system with an established, graduated wage scale which serves to frustrate traditional spoils operations in many states; all grants must be the same regardless of race, creed, or place of origin which is incompatible with traditional double living standards in some states; specific limitations are set on the various ways in which states may define residence in order to determine eligibility for aid; matching formulae must be met; and a plethora of reports must be submitted to Washington.

These restrictions, designed to insure compliance with minimum national standards, are bound to seem vexatious to state and local officials. Sometimes protests from the states are loud and insistent enough to induce Congress to yield to the views of the states. A good example was the Jenner Amendment to the welfare appropriation in 1954, which enabled states to print publicly the names of welfare recipients—a practice previously forbidden by the terms of federal legislation authorizing welfare grants to the states.

The Growth of National Power. How are we to account for the tremendous increase in the powers of the national government? Aside from the imperatives of national defense, how are we to explain the development of a range of national programs that affect almost all aspects of social life? It is important to distinguish between two general sources of demands for the expansion of national governmental power: the effort on the part of organized groups to secure governmental protection and promotion of their interests and the effort to use politics to resolve pressing public problems. This distinction is the same one we made earlier between policies undertaken to serve some conception of the public interest and governmental programs which reflect the push and haul of rival economic interest groups. The distinction is important, even though it is often difficult to apply it in practice.

A system of old-age pensions may reflect the philosophical conclusion that a free enterprise economic system in modern society destroys family responsibility for the care of the aged at the same time that it makes it impossible for most persons to provide for their own security. On the other hand, an increase in the amount of the pension may reflect the demands of politically potent "senior citizens" either organized as a pressure group or seen by politicians as constituting a voting bloc important in the next election. The approach to social security may take the form of issue-and principle-oriented debate, or it may be interest-motivated. The tremendous growth in the power of government in this century has reflected both motivations; underlying them both are some deep and far-reaching changes in American society and economic life.

The traditional order drew heavily on occurrences in the fateful year of 1776. A British economist, Adam Smith, published his *Inquiry into the Wealth of Nations,* a book which shook the foundations of traditional economic institutions as much as the American Revolution disturbed political ones. In it, Smith set forth a radical economic doctrine advocating a *laissez-faire* economy and proposing that free competition in the market place would provide an automatic regulator of economic activity. The functions of government were to be confined to keeping the domestic peace, enforcing private contracts, and securing the nation against attack. The key to Smith's theory was the claim that in a competitive market, price and output of all goods would be determined by the impersonal forces of supply and demand; economic activity would be regulated "as if by an unseen hand," rather than by the visible hands of men who had economic power.

The idea of an economy in which no man could have power over another man's sustenance or behavior fitted into the Jeffersonian agrarian ideal. The new American nation nurtured itself on Smith's doctrine, modifying it a bit with tariffs and other deviations from time to time. The theory was subsequently carried over, with modifications, to justify the industrial society that, after the Civil War, began rapidly to develop.

The results, however, were not quite what Smith had predicted. In addition to the rapidly growing industrial machine, there was the cycle of "boom and bust," the widening gulf between poor and rich, the economic whip that created a twelve-hour day in the new steel mills, the specter of child labor, the growth of new urban slums, and the wholesale corruption of politics by the new men of wealth.

By the end of the nineteenth century, many reformers, politicians, and economists began to realize that, although the use of governmental power (even operating through democratic institutions) might destroy the economic motivations of capitalism, it was equally possible that without governmental intervention capitalism might destroy democracy. The development of the trusts gave rise to the trust-busters; the muck produced muckrakers.

Underlying this ferment was the recognition that *laissez-faire* capitalism had not fulfilled on its central promise. The free market did not produce a society of small, independent entrepreneurs in which no man had economic power over his fellows. Unrestrained capitalism had produced a system of power. It had created corporations which were, in effect, "private governments" operating on autocratic principles. Once this fact was recognized, the conflict between democracy and unregulated capitalism could not fail to assert itself. Democracy, whether in its liberal or its conservative interpretations, insists that wherever power exists in society, it be made responsible to public purposes. Unregulated capitalism, the evidence was increasingly clear, meant irresponsible power.

However, existing privileges always die hard, and the beneficiaries of unchecked capitalism were supplied a handy body of doctrine that recognized and sought to justify the concentration of economic wealth and power. Toward the end of the century, a theory of "Social Darwinism" applied the ideas of evolution and natural selection—the "survival of the fittest"—to society. The rich and powerful, this thesis held, were entitled to their wealth and power because it evidenced their natural superiority. The poor were inferior and their condition was due to indolence, sloth, and indulgence of the passions and appetites. Some Protestant ministers helped the cause by asserting that "wealthiness is Godliness." To help the poor came to be viewed as not only sentimental but also socially dangerous, because it perpetuated the weak and demeaning elements in society.

Social Darwinism, however, was not a theory destined for popular acceptance by a nation that had more poor than rich and whose democratic commitment rested on the ideas of universal human dignity and equality of participation in formulating the goals of social life. When men of wealth conceded the fact of their economic power, it was virtually certain that it would be controlled and regulated to insure that it served the politically defined purposes of a society of equals.

The smug complacency with which economic power was embraced in high political circles was sharply shaken when William McKinley was assassinated and the colorful "cowboy," Theodore Roosevelt, became President. Promising the nation a "square deal," Roosevelt took after the "bad" trusts which he considered inimical to the public interest. Roosevelt did not break the trusts nor even seriously curtail their power. Neither did he secure popular acceptance of Presidents dedicated to governmental regulation of business, as the terms of Taft, Harding, Coolidge, and Hoover will attest. But he did drive home the point that economic power, like political power, in a democracy must always rest on consent; that it is a conditional grant, and the condition is that it be employed for politically approved public purposes. He also drove home the realization that government can regulate business without the whole nation collapsing.

Meanwhile, such critics as Thorstein Veblen took up the fight. The development of law and politics in industrial America, Veblen argued, had followed subserviently at the heels of business, so that "representative government means, chiefly, representation of business interests."[11] Veblen

[11]Thorstein Veblen, *The Theory of Business Enterprise* (New York: Scribner, 1904), p. 286.

himself was no reformer and he offered no advice, but the implication of his analysis was clear enough: the instruments of democratic politics needed to be employed to insure that private power was subordinated to public purposes. His argument was unpopular at the time and Veblen suffered for it personally.

Not until the Depression of the 1930's did these forces have their full impact. That decade saw an astounding increase in the powers of the national government. Prolonged mass unemployment was the triggering mechanism. But the responsibilities assumed by the government went beyond the obligation to provide work temporarily and insure full employment over the long run. It also undertook or expanded programs designed to protect investors and consumers against abuses of economic power; devised a social security program; conducted a program of integrated river valley development in the Tennessee Valley and embarked on other programs of electric power and resource development; established government agencies to make loans to farmers and undertook to insure that farm income maintained parity with nonfarm income; guaranteed the right of labor to organize and bargain collectively with employers; established minimum wage levels in industry; eliminated child labor; and provided limitations on working conditions of employed women. These activities were financed mainly from the proceeds of a federal income tax, the rates of which were made increasingly progressive. The result was governmental interference with the system of "natural" economic rewards and a deliberate political decision to redistribute the wealth, justified as necessary both to maintain full employment and to achieve justice.

These increases in the powers of the national government seem clearly to have been directed to the solution of problems occasioned by the concentration of economic wealth and power under unregulated capitalism. The response was at the national level because the problems were national in scope. The problems of an interdependent, industrial economy do not yield to local solutions.

FEDERALISM AND THE PUBLIC INTEREST

In some instances, the national government stepped in because state governments, for reasons rooted in their historical development, were unwilling to act. By and large, state governments in recent years appear to be more susceptible to the pressures of the most powerful interests and less responsive to popular demands for economic reform. Most often, the most powerful interests are property interests. The result is reflected, for example, in the structure of state and local, as contrasted with national, tax systems. The national income and corporation taxes are progressive; states and local communities rely mainly on sales, excise, and property taxes which are proportional or even regressive in their effects.

Partly, the susceptibility of state governments to the pressure of business and property interests is due to the structure of state governments, more specifically to the overrepresentation in state legislatures of rural areas which tend to be economically conservative. But partly, also, it is a function of the limitations inherent in local efforts to deal with an economic system that is national in organization and scope. Thus, states are in competition with one another to attract business and industry on which the level of income in the state will depend. To do this, local governments often appropriate public funds to chambers of commerce to be spent on advertising the community's attractions for industry. Most state governments have agencies of their own for this purpose. The success of these efforts generally depends on whether the state offers a "favorable climate" for business. In addition to such matters as the availability of power, cheap transportation, land, and a skilled labor force, a "favorable" tax structure with correspondingly low levels of welfare expenditures and the absence of a regulatory climate inimical to business freedom are also important.

Historically, after the Civil War, states competed with one another to see who could offer the most favorable conditions for business in their incorporation laws. More recently, the competition has extended to the whole range of tax, labor relations, regulation, and welfare activities. The states continue to find themselves in a situation in which there are very real pressures toward subordination of the public interest to the private interests of corporate business or labor. Perhaps it would be more accurate to say that there is tremendous pressure on the states to identify private business interests with the public interest, to accept what was for a long time the leading slogan of the business lobbies: "What helps business helps you."

The national government is under no such limitation. Because it is coextensive with the economy, it is uniquely able to avoid being divided and ruled by economic interests. It is uniquely capable of insuring that the economy is in the service of public goals. Although ordinarily these facts are not readily recognized, it seems likely that they underlie most of the debates about national power and states' rights. Those who identify the business interest with the public interest are likely to invoke the slogan of states' rights and eulogize the virtue of government that is close to the people. For those who take a different view, the national government seems in reality to be closer to the people than are the governments of the states.

We do not mean to imply that all the activities of the national government are undertaken in pursuit of a public interest that stands above the private claims of powerful groups or that, specifically, all federal programs that intervene in the economy are undertaken in order to insure that private economic power is made to serve public purposes. At the national level too, government often simply responds to private pressures, and national politicians often identify the balancing of private claims with the public interest. At the least, other interests than business—labor, for example—are likely to get a more even break in Congress than in state legislatures. At the most, national government in the present circumstances is capable of transcending all the private claims in order to deal with national problems created by industrialization and urbanization.

In practice, pressure politics and principled politics are both operative in national consideration of most issues, although one or the other may at different times be dominant. This matter is considered in greater detail in subsequent chapters. Our main concern now is to point to the greater difficulty at the state level of conducting government on any basis other than a response to private interests and to the pressures on state governments to favor the business interest over others. In any decision about whether a particular responsibility should be undertaken at the national or state level, these considerations should be an important element. They are not the only considerations involved, of course. Big government means big bureaucracy, "red tape," inflexibility of rules, the danger of officiousness in the attitudes of public officials, and the narrowing of diversity and variety in the national life. What this re-emphasizes, above all, is that the constitutional principle of federalism is not an oracle to which one can appeal for a solution to the problem of which levels of government should be relied on in particular cases. Decisions on these questions have become political rather than legal. We are now called upon to debate the kinds of questions that the Founding Fathers themselves debated. Here again, our heritage is not a constitutional catalogue of answers to political questions; it is, rather, one of controversy and of conditions which make continuing political debate possible.

4

THE CONSTITUTION:
DEMOCRATIC
BATTLEGROUND

[Limited Government & Judicial Supremacy]

LIMITED GOVERNMENT

THE THIRD MAJOR PRINCIPLE of American constitutionalism is that the powers of government are limited by the rights and the liberty of the governed. This principle is inherent in the very idea of *constitutional* government. As we have already seen, it is the purpose of a constitution to limit and restrain the exercise of political power; a constitution is a system of "effective, regularized restraints."[1]

The eighteenth century, with its faith in the process of establishing governments on a rational basis and its philosophy of natural rights, was an age of constitution-making. Americans, in particular, were experienced in the art of writing constitutions and impressed by the fruits of living under a fundamental body of law defining the scope and limits of govern-

[1]Carl J. Friedrich, *Constitutional Government and Democracy* (Boston: Ginn, 1946). As Friedrich maintains, a government is rendered constitutional by "establishing and maintaining effective restraints upon political and more especially upon governmental action" (p. 121).

98

mental power. One of the first groups of settlers had begun their adventure by agreeing to the Mayflower Compact. The political history of the Colonies had been, in some measure, a story of conflict over the terms of written Colonial charters and the rights of Colonists as subjects of the unwritten British constitution. In the process, the basic doctrine that citizens retain rights *against* the government as well as rights of *access to* the government came to be a widely shared article of the American political faith.

Governmental Power and Individual Liberty

The essence of constitutionalism, as we have suggested is that the powers of government shall be restrained to protect the liberty of citizens. In a democracy, the citizen plays a dual role: he is at the same time subject and ruler; he is bound by the laws that he participates in making.[2] The limitations that a democratic constitution places on a government relate to the dual roles of citizenship. They insure that the citizen as ruler is guaranteed those rights which are necessary, if he is to be able to influence and control the government. Also, they protect the citizen as subject from arbitrary treatment by those temporarily in control of the instruments of government.

The American Constitution, chiefly in the first ten Amendments, spells out the individual rights and liberties which are protected against governmental power. The most important of these are outlined below.

General Restraints on Government
No denial of life, liberty, or property without due process of law*
No *ex post facto* laws or bills of attainder*
No tax on exports*
No tax on imports***
Slavery may not be permitted*
Titles of nobility may not be granted*
No taking of private property for public use without just compensation*
Right to keep and bear arms**
No quartering of soldiers in private homes during time of peace**
Civil Liberties
Freedom of Religion*

[2]Joseph Tussman develops this distinction in an interesting and provocative way in his *Obligation and the Body Politic* (New York: Oxford University Press, 1960).

* Applies to both national and state governments
** Applies to national government only (but may apply to states through provisions of state constitutions)
*** Applies to states only

Freedom of speech*
Freedom of press*
Freedom of assembly and petition*
Political Rights
Right to vote without regard to sex, race, creed, or previous condition of servitude***
Civil Rights
Right to a writ of habeas corpus*
No unreasonable searches or seizures*
Indictment only by grand jury**
No double jeopardy* (but a person may be tried for the same offense under both federal and state law)
No compulsion to testify against oneself in criminal prosecutions** (but states may not coerce confessions)
Right to speedy, public trial by impartial jury* (jury trial not required of states but must be impartial where used)
Right to be tried in district where crime committed**
Right of accused to be informed of nature of accusation; no vague or ambiguous criminal statutes*
Right of accused to confront witnesses against him*
Right of accused to compulsory processes for obtaining favorable witnesses**
Right of accused to counsel in criminal cases*
Right to jury trial in common law suits**
No excessive bail**
No excessive fines or cruel and unusual punishments*

CIVIL LIBERTIES: THE RIGHTS OF CITIZENS AS RULERS

The role of the citizen as ruler in a democratic society quite obviously starts with certain political rights. The fundamental one is the right to vote in regularly scheduled elections in which the ballot is secret and the results are honestly counted and announced. The right to vote also implies the right to run as a candidate and to participate in the selection of candidates for public office.

These political rights are a necessary, but not a sufficient, basis for the democratic role of the citizen as ruler. They might all exist in a framework in which the citizen participates in politics but does not in any real sense control the government. Political rights themselves may even be the means by which citizens can be induced to troop to the polls to participate in a public ritual which permits them to be blamed for subsequent develop-

* Applies to both national and state governments
** Applies to national government only (but may apply to states through provisions of state constitutions)
*** Applies to states only

ments over which they exercised no real choice. This is the question, again, of the distinction between voting and political participation as a social act on the one hand, and participation which involves choice and responsibility on the other. The mere existence of political rights does not permit us to distinguish between free and unfree elections, or between free and engineered consent of the governed. It is scarcely possible to doubt, for example, that the Communist Party in the Soviet Union could afford the secret ballot, regular elections, and honestly counted returns. Whether or not they always do so is not the point: we stress here only that to do so would not seriously prejudice the controlling power of the Communist Party apparatus.

If political rights are not enough, what more is required? Again, we return to the crucial and fundamental matter of dissent. Democratic participation requires alternatives and the opportunity to choose. The existence of alternatives and choice, in their turn, depends upon the fundamental right to dissent and seek to persuade and join with others in an effort to make one's dissenting opinions prevail.

The class of rights which undergird and guarantee the possibility of dissent, and therefore of alternatives and genuine choice, are generally described by the term "civil liberties." They are the rights which are fundamental in the sense that they guarantee the openness and the competitive politics that are the basic conditions of democratic citizenship. In the United States, they are stated succinctly in the First Amendment to the Constitution and are often summed up as the "First Amendment Freedoms." They guarantee that the national government shall have no power to interfere with the intellectual freedom of citizens or with their freedom to associate with one another in common pursuit of their intellectual commitments and purposes. In the language of the Amendment itself:

> Congress shall make no law respecting an establishment of religion, or prohibiting the free exercise thereof; or abridging the freedom of speech, or of the press; or the right of the people peaceably to assemble, and to petition the government for a redress of grievances.

In addition to the fundamental guarantee therein provided, there are other sections of the Constitution whose purpose is to guarantee civil liberties. The Second Amendment, protecting the "right of the people to keep and bear arms," while no longer relevant, should probably be put in that category. Certainly the definition of treason in Article III, Section 3, was and continues to be an important limitation on one of the means by which political controversy and criticism might be curtailed. It provides the following:

Treason against the United States, shall consist only in levying war against them, or in adhering to their enemies, giving them aid and comfort. No person shall be convicted of treason unless on the testimony of two witnesses to the same overt act, or on confession in open court.

This section closes off what had been, in the history of government, an important means by which the state could rationalize its silencing of critics and its restraints on free thought and discussion. Treason has ever been the political counterpart of the charge of heresy in religious organizations. It is the means by which otherwise permissible criticism can be put beyond the pale of legitimate discussion and critics made to appear the enemies of society.

The gravity of the evil that the framers were seeking to guard against, and its fundamental incompatibility with democratic politics, were revealed in the period following World War II when aspirants for public office accused the members of the opposition party of "twenty years of treason"— a charge which, if made successfully, would have effectively ended competitive politics. This threat did not end with the demise of mccarthyism. The challenge of communism continues to lead groups on the radical right to the conclusion that socialists, leftists, New Dealers, and liberals all aid and abet the cause of communism and are, therefore, parties to treason. In defining treason as giving aid and comfort to the enemy and carefully defining the proof necessary for conviction, the Founding Fathers sought to remove this weapon from the struggle for power. These limitations on government assume that there are rights that inhere in individuals and have logical and moral priority over government, rights that no government is morally entitled to interfere with or curtail.

CIVIL RIGHTS: THE RIGHTS OF CITIZENS AS SUBJECTS

When we view the democratic citizen in his role as subject, we encounter a different class of rights which are derived from the ideal of a government of laws or equality before the law. Ordinarily designated *civil rights*, as distinct from civil liberties, these restraints on government protect the individual from abitrary, personal, or irresponsible use of governmental power. The basic principle that men who make and administer the laws are themselves subject to the laws was established early in the struggle for constitutional democratic government in England (England of course has no written constitution; this is a good example of an unwritten constitutional principle). The principle was established when it was decided that the King was not above the law—that is, that he could not rule by arbitrary decree or exact punishment except through the regularized procedures of established laws.

The limitations in the American Constitution that fall into this category may be thought of as seeking to achieve the protection of the individual as subject against arbitrary acts of government through the establishment of three principles:

1. *The ultimate power of government to coerce individuals—*to deprive them of property, or liberty, or in the final extremity, life—*may only be employed for violations of established, definite laws.* The following provisions of the Constitution contribute to the accomplishment of this purpose.

Article I, Section 9, prohibits Congress from inflicting punishment on individuals by legislative act and without judicial proceedings (bills of attainder); from passing legislation which retroactively makes an act a crime which was not a crime at the time it was committed, or from retroactively increasing the penalties for a crime or making conviction easier (ex post facto laws). These guarantees of civil rights, incidentally, reveal the close connection between civil rights and civil liberties. The arbitrariness involved in bills of attainder and ex post facto laws not only deprives individuals of "equal justice," such laws are also one potential means by which political dissenters might be punished for their dissent and political controversy be suppressed. Similarly, in modern totalitarian regimes, the substitution of decrees and the secret police for regularly established courts of law is a major instrument for enforcing conformity.

The Fifth Amendment prohibits the taking of private property for public use "without just compensation," and the question of whether compensation is just may be appealed from political officials into the courts. It makes an even more general provision: "No person shall be . . . deprived of life, liberty or property, without due process of law . . . ."

The Eighth Amendment prohibits excessive fines and "cruel and unusual punishments."

The purpose of these limitations is to provide for individuals a range of predictability within which individual responsibilty can operate. For even though, as everyone knows, "ignorance of the law is no excuse," unless it is possible for the individual to know clearly what the law is, and what the penalties for its violation are, there can be no range within which the individual can plan his own life and make his own choices. Making choices requires the possibility of anticipating consequences of alternative paths of action. If the government can change the rules retroactively or modify them so that they apply differently to different individuals, this condition no longer is present.

The basic principle was clearly formulated by Justice Jackson in his concurring opinion in the 1952 case in which the Supreme Court invalidated President Truman's seizure of the steel industry.[3] The authority of the government under the Constitution, Justice Jackson asserted,

---

[3]*Youngstown Sheet and Tube Co.* v. *Sawyer* 343 U. S. 579 (1952).

"reaches so far as there is law"; the due process provision of the Fifth Amendment guarantees "a private right that authority shall go no farther." These principles, Jackson continued, "signify about all there is of the principle that ours is a government of laws, not of men, and that we submit ourselves to rulers only if under rules." They are the minimum condition that must be met in order that "the public may know the extent and limitations of the powers that can be asserted, and persons affected may be informed from the statute of their rights and duties."

2. *In the use of its coercive power, government may not unnecessarily invade the privacy of individuals.* This principle is embodied in the following constitutional provisions.

Article I, Section 9, provides that the writ of habeas corpus may not be suspended except under conditions of "rebellion or invasion."

The Fourth Amendment guarantees "the right of the people to be secure in their persons, houses, papers, and effects, against unreasonable searches and seizures" and provides that warrants may be issued only "upon probable cause."

The Fifth Amendment protects individuals against "double jeopardy."

The Sixth guarantees defendants a "speedy" trial.

The Eighth prohibits "excessive bail."

These provisions protect the individual from harassment by the police; from search or arrest "on suspicion"; from the necessity of living in constant fear of the law-enforcing agencies of government.

3. *When accused of a crime, the individual is entitled to be judged fairly and impartially and to have available the means to his defense.* The guarantees of this principle, as they apply to federal criminal cases, are contained in the Fifth and Sixth Amendments. The Fifth Amendment requires indictment by a grand jury and protects the individual from being compelled "to be a witness against himself." The Sixth Amendment guarantees the accused the right to a public trial by an "impartial jury" in the state and district where the crime was committed, the right to be informed of the charges against him, the right to confront hostile witnesses and to subpoena friendly witnesses, and the right to a defense counsel.

It should be noted that not all these restrictions apply equally against the states. Most of the limitations on government in the Constitution are directed only to the national government. This is true of the entire Bill of Rights. The Supreme Court, in its interpretation of the due process clause of the Fourteenth Amendment that limits the state governments, has brought under the meaning of that phrase only those provisions of the first ten Amendments without which, in the words of Justice Cardozo, "neither liberty nor justice would exist." (For example, the following provisions have been held not to be necessary: protection against double jeopardy and self-incrimination, or the guarantees of indictment by grand jury and trial by jury. Nevertheless, the constitutions of most states do provide these guarantees, except for the requirement of indictment by grand jury.)

The importance of the civil rights that are guaranteed by the foregoing three principles would be difficult to exaggerate. If we need any reminding, the rise of modern totalitarian regimes emphasizes both their importance and the intimate relation between the guarantees of freedom of thought and speech and association on the one hand, and the limitations on arbitrary acts of government on the other. For the single most significant characteristic of modern totalitarianism is its use of terror as an instrument of governing. Terror is the means by which effective criticism of the regime is precluded. Terror rests, in Hannah Arendt's phrase, on the elimination of the "legal personality"[4] of citizens. It rests, that is to say, on systematic destruction of any legal order in which the rights and duties of individuals are clearly defined, and on the nonexistence of orderly procedures for establishing individual guilt or innocence. Terror, to be effective, must be anonymous, and it must destroy any important areas of predictability for the individual. Punishment by the state must be unrelated to any specific acts which an individual has committed or failed to commit. Punishment must be arbitrary from the point of view of individual moral responsibility.

It is not, of course, arbitrary from the point of view of "the movement": to be a Jew in Nazi Germany was, by definition, to be implicated in a conspiracy against the laws of race. But the point is that the legal order of a democratic society consists of regularized laws which make specific acts punishable, and it embodies procedures which require proof of individual responsibility. Such a legal order is the first line of defense against government by terror, and a necessary foundation for the freedoms of thought and expression which make responsible government possible.

Authority and Liberty: An American Consensus?

The tone of our discussion thus far might suggest that in the provision for limited government and individual rights and liberties we have at last located a bedrock principle on which our forefathers were agreed and from which our common political faith springs. It turns out, however, that this is true only in the same limited sense in which there has been agreement on the other principles of checks and balances and federalism. It is

[4]Hannah Arendt, *The Origins of Totalitarianism* (New York: Harcourt, Brace, 1951). See especially Chapt. 12, "Totalitarianism in Power."

no less true of limited government that we are closer to the truth if we see it as defining a problem rather than as posing a solution. Again there was agreement on the principle in spite of—or, perhaps more accurately, because of—disagreements over its meaning.

The conflict among the Founding Fathers should be immediately apparent from the circumstance that most of the rights we have been discussing are included in the first ten Amendments to the Constitution, rather than in the body of the document itself. For some, the system of balanced power set out in the document was as far as it was realistically possible to go in the direction of guaranteeing liberty; the Bill of Rights would do no harm, but neither would it do much good. In this view, liberty is to be discovered in the interstices of a balance of power, not in pronouncements which presume to declare fundamental truths. For others the Bill of Rights was the essence of constitutionalism, and freedom was to be achieved only by men who were consciously committed to it as a basic and enduring principle.

TOLERATION VERSUS LIBERTY

The conflict dividing the Founding Fathers on this issue was a fundamental one which reverts to the underlying philosophical issues that defined the conservative and the liberal positions. With respect to the problem of freedom, the two major positions are to be found in the conservative theory of toleration and the liberal theory of natural rights.

The approach of liberal democratic theory to this question we have already quite fully explored. The liberal faith in reason and the liberal commitment to natural rights led to the conclusion that liberty is something that men directly pursue and explicitly value. The free society is one in which the supreme value of freedom is the cardinal principle to which citizens are committed. In the last analysis, from the liberal point of view, it is only the dedication of free men to civil liberties that can effectively safeguard them. The rights of the individual will only be safe when other individuals accept Henry David Thoreau's principle that "under a government which imprisons any unjustly, the true place for a just man is also a prison."

From the conservative view of human nature and the conservative concern for social order and stability, the liberal faith in a commitment to abstract principle was a frail reed on which to rest men's liberties. A modern conservative has put their case aptly in the argument that freedom is essentially a by-product of toleration and comes to exist only in a "happily tolerant era," such as under those conditions in the Rome of the Antonine emperors as described by Gibbon: "The various modes of worship, which prevailed in the Roman world, were all considered by the people, as equally true; by the philosopher, as equally false; and by the magistrate, as equally useful." Gibbon concluded, "Thus toleration produced not only mutual indulgence, but even religious concord."[5] What Gibbon found to be the secret of religious toleration—a multiplicity of competing sects all of which accept the legitimacy of the others and none of which can hope to prevail—some of the Founding Fathers saw as the key to toleration generally. Madison expressed the argument clearly in *The Federalist* (No. 51):

> In a free government the security for civil rights must be the same as that for religious rights. It consists in the one case in the multiplicity of interests, and in the other in the multiplicity of sects. The degree of security in both cases will depend on the number of interests and sects. . . .

Civil rights and liberties, on this view, are not to be maintained by an appeal to abstract principle. If they are to prevail, it will be in spite of, not because of, what men seek in politics. If there is a wide enough variety of interests and desires in political competition, "ambition" may be "made to counteract ambition." Civil rights and liberties are only to be protected because no group has the power to curtail the liberties of others, not because any group is committed to a principle which protects others' liberties. The most that might be hoped for is that men who have lived for a long time in a carefully balanced pluralistic society may come even to see the policy of "live and let live" as a desirable one.

The distinction between the idea of toleration and the idea of freedom was developed by early liberals. "Toleration," Tom Paine argued, "is not the *opposite* of Intolerance, but is the *counterfeit* of it. Both are despotisms." Whereas intolerance "assumes to itself the right of withholding Liberty of Conscience,"[6] toleration no less despotically assumes the right of granting it. "Liberty of conscience," Paine argues, is not to be granted or denied by government to individuals; it is a natural right antecedent to government. And only if it is regarded as such will it be possible for individuals to control, and not be to controlled by, their government.

A political system which rests on the toleration of a broad plurality of groups, it might be pointed out, is one that is likely to be inhospitable to new ideas that propose far-reaching changes in society. Groups that have come to tolerate one another are likely to share an interest in maintaining the *status quo* in which each is likely to have a vested interest. Thus, it is just those groups and individuals whose liberties are most in need of protection who are most likely not fo find it.

In a regime of religious toleration, for example, it is the prevailing,

[5]Quoted in Daniel Boorstin, *The Genius of American Politics* (Chicago: University of Chicago Press, 1953), p. 135.
[6]Paine, *Rights of Man*, p. 64.

conventionalized modes of religious worship which are "mutually indulged." Precisely what is not indulged is the belief of those individuals who question the assumptions shared in what Gibbon called the "religious concord" of mutually tolerant religious beliefs. Similarly, where there is "mutual indulgence" between labor and management groups, there is likely to be little tolerance for those who would criticize the *status quo* in any fundamental way.

John Taylor, another Jeffersonian liberal, seems to have had these considerations in mind in his criticism of the phenomena of toleration. Government, Taylor argued, is likely to be made the "patron of the whole tribe of tenets" which at any time exist. The effect is to put the power of government behind the maintenance of the *status quo*, and to reverse the proper relation of ideas and power by making the former instruments for the power drives of politicians. Religious toleration, for example, violates "the faith of the political theory of the United States," a faith "which placed religion above the reach of the politician, that it might not by his arts be transformed from a consolation into a scourge." Toleration makes "religion a pander for avarice, ambition and tyranny." Taylor adds:

> If the people see [government] coining religion into power and money, under pretence of coining it into good morals; it will teach them also atheism and deceit. As a cunning government uses religion to cheat a nation, a cunning man will use it to cheat his neighbor; and in place of its being a bond of love, a preceptor of virtue, and the refuge of hope, religion would thus be made an engine of publick oppression and private fraud.[7]

Toleration, in short, is a conservative prescription for a condition of equilibrium among the several interests in a society. Where it is successfully achieved, the privacy and the liberty of individuals are protected from assaults by others. Liberty is to be insured and protected by diversity. A carefully devised constitution which will insure a balance among rival groups will protect men against themselves and their own innate tendencies to deprive others of their liberties. The liberal view, on the other hand, put its faith in the capacities of man's reason to discover and his good will to enforce the natural rights by which opinion, thought, speech, and writing are taken to be immune from governmental restriction. Men will have liberty when men take liberty to be the first principle of society and government. Otherwise, what will be tolerated is just those moderate and orthodox views which do not in any significant way challenge the *status quo* and which do not, therefore, stand in any real need of defense.

[7]Taylor, *Inquiry*, pp. 404-405.

THE PROTECTION OF FREEDOM FROM MAJORITIES

The second question on which the conflict between liberal and conservative theories of civil liberties was joined was the problem of how to protect these freedoms from the actions of majorities. This was the problem of majority tyranny, which we have already examined at some length. This conflict came to focus, as might have been expected, in two issues: the right of a majority to alter private property relationships; and the danger that a majority would eliminate or curtail the liberties of minorities to criticize and oppose or use their power to treat minorities arbitrarily or deny them equal treatment under the law. Using property rights as distinguished from human rights as a basis for limiting majority rule involves a fundamentally different view of the nature and scope of civil liberties. The question is whether majority rule is to be limited only by those intrinsic principles which justify it, or whether it is also to be limited by external principles which are opposed to it.

As we have seen, the title of any majority to have its way clearly depends on whether it is a majority which has been freely formed (that is, whether the conditions of free debate have prevailed) and on whether it has observed due process in the enactment and administration of its laws. These are qualities inherent in the majority process; they are the source of a majority's legitimate authority. The argument that a majority does not have a right to alter property relationships or the economic system through which they are derived, however, rests on the assertion that there are other principles, unrelated to majority rule, with which a majority has no right to tamper. Private property, in this view, reflects the natural inequalities of men; it is a transcendent principle which should restrict the exercise of majority rule and of those rights and liberties which are intrinsically necessary to majority rule.

This issue was implicit in the contrast between the protection accorded property and contracts in the body of the Constitution and the guarantees of civil rights and liberties in the first ten Amendments. After the Civil War it became crucial when majorities sought to regulate industry, set standards of wages and hours, enact a progressive income tax, and develop a wide range of other programs which had the effect of curtailing property rights and redistributing wealth and income.

LIBERTY TO DESTROY LIBERTY?

How far do civil liberties extend? Should freedom of conscience, of speech, and of writing extend to those whose objectives include the destruction of the regime of civil liberties itself? Are the prohibitions against governmental interference with thought and speech to be regarded as absolute? The wording of the First Amendment—"Congress shall make *no law* . . ."—suggests that this is what was intended, and no doubt it was by liberals like Jefferson, Paine, and Taylor. These men drew a rigid line between "the operations of the human mind," speech, and writing which are categorically immune from governmental interference, and behavior. Governments must have a legitimate power to regulate behavior so that they can preserve order and prevent violence. This position is clearly expressed in Jefferson's First Inaugural Address in which he extends the doctrine to cover even those who seek to change the fundamental bases of republican government: "If there be any among us who would wish to dissolve this Union or to change its republican form, let them stand undisturbed as monuments of the safety with which error of opinion may be tolerated where reason is left free to combat it."

Because conservatives did not share Jefferson's faith in the power of reason in the free market place of ideas, they could not share his unqualified endorsement of the sanctity and absoluteness of basic natural rights. In this view, as we have seen, it is not enough that men should control the government; government must exercise a reciprocal control over the irrational tendencies of men. In times of external threat and internal danger especially, as the Alien and Sedition Acts made clear, they believed that civil liberties must be balanced against the requirements of social order and stability.

The present century, with its two world wars, its revolutionary ferment, and American involvement in the Cold War, has intensified the struggle over the meaning of First Amendment freedoms. As we have already indicated, the Alien and Sedition Acts had raised the issue almost at the beginning of the nation's history. They evoked widespread and bitter debate, became an important issue in the campaign of 1800, and contributed to the downfall of the Federalists. The victory of the Jeffersonian Republicans insured that they would be allowed to expire.

It was not until World War I that any important cases involving the interpretation of these freedoms were decided by the Supreme Court. Partly this was because the Amendment applied to the federal government only. Until the enactment of the Fourteenth Amendment and its eventual expansion to require the states to guarantee the provisions of the First Amendment, state laws abridging these freedoms could not be challenged in the federal courts. Nor, of course, under the federal structure, could they be challenged by the Congress or the President. Consequently, it was not until 1931 that a state law abridging a First Amendment freedom was held completely invalid under the liberty clause of the Fourteenth Amendment.[8]

---

[8]*Near* v. *Minnesota*, 283 U. S. 1. Earlier, in 1925, the Court had held that the Fourteenth Amendment could be used to negate state legislation suppressing free speech (*Gitlow* v. *New York*, 268 U. S. 652).

During World War I, Congress enacted a Sedition Act under which approximately nineteen hundred people were prosecuted for alleged subversive activities or criticism of the federal government during and shortly after the war. Many radical publications were denied mailing privileges and groups advocating a variety of political innovations were cast under a cloud of suspicion. As one authority put it:

> The First Amendment had no hold on people's minds because no live facts or concrete images were then attached to it. Like an empty box with beautiful words on it, the Amendment collapsed under the impact of terror of Prussian battalions and terror of Bolshevick mobs. So the emotions generated by the two simultaneous cataclysms of war and revolution swept unchecked through American prosecutors, judges, jurymen and legislators.[9]

Since the end of World War I, a host of cases arising under the First Amendment have been before the Supreme Court. A vast literature on the meaning of civil liberties has also been developed. The range of judicial and scholarly opinion on the subject is now immense. The core of the problem—for judges, legislators, or citizens—is whether democracy is best served by balancing First Amendment freedoms against other values such as national security, or by taking an absolutist position for uninhibited freedoms in the areas covered by the First Amendment. One of the most influential advocates of the absolute sanctity of the First Amendment has argued that free speech must extend to everyone:

> There are no exceptions—Communists, Socialists, Fascists, Democrats, Republicans, the foolish, the wise, the dangerous, the safe, those who wish to overthrow the state, those who wish to keep it as it is. There is no reason to curb freedom of speech in time of danger or in war . . . . The time of danger is exactly the time to show people that you mean what you say.[10]

Such a pure view of freedom to speak has not, however, been very widely accepted in periods of crisis or danger, real and imaginary. During World War I, the general secretary of the Socialist Party was arrested and convicted under the Espionage Act of 1917 for mailing pamphlets to draftees urging them to oppose the draft. His appeal eventually went to the Supreme Court which unanimously upheld his conviction.[11] "In many places and ordinary times," said Justice Holmes for a unanimous Court, "the

[9]Zechariah Chafee, Jr., *Thirty-Five Years with Freedom of Speech* (New York: Roger N. Baldwin Civil Liberties Foundation, 1952), p. 4.
[10]Alexander Meiklejohn, *Free Speech and Its Relation to Self-Government* (New York: Harper, 1948), p. 50. On p. 27, he says, "To be afraid of ideas, any ideas, is to be unfit for self-government."
[11]*Schenck* v. *United States*, 249 U. S. 47 (1919).

defendants in saying all that was said in the circular would have been within their constitutional rights." But, he added:

> The question in every case is whether the words used are used in such circumstances and are of such a nature as to create a *clear and present danger* [italics ours] that they will bring about the substantive evils that Congress has a right to prevent. It is a question of proximity and degree.[12]

Holmes' relativism was a rigid relativism and his qualification of freedom would only apply in situations as serious as war or imminent violence. Words, then, had to be a proximate cause of serious consequence—"triggers of action" as Judge Learned Hand once called them. But even a rigid relativism in the law leaves open the door for further exceptions to the absolutist's position. Men were convicted and some went to jail for their words under the "clear and present danger" test.[13]

Later, however, Holmes and his colleague, Louis D. Brandeis, dissenting from the views of a majority of the court, attempted to demonstrate that the clear and present danger test did offer protection of the individual and limits on how far the provisions of the First Amendment could be stretched. In *Abrams et al. v. United States*,[14] the two dissented sharply from the conviction of another group of pamphleteers. Holmes' dissent, in which Brandeis concurred, attempted to clarify the limits of the clear and present danger test:

> I never had any reason to doubt that the questions of law that alone were before this court in the cases of Schenck . . . Frohwerk . . . and Debs . . . were rightly decided. I do not doubt for a moment that by the same reasoning that would justify punishing persuasion to murder, *the United States constitutionally may punish speech that produces or is intended to produce a clear and imminent danger that will bring about forthwith certain substantive evils* [italics ours] that the United States constitutionally may seek to prevent. The power . . . is greater in time of war. . . .[15]

Holmes added some persuasive arguments to his dissent and warned against making exceptions to the First Amendment unless the "emergency . . . makes it immediately dangerous to leave the correction of evil counsels to time." But the majority was not deterred from upholding this and other

[12]*Ibid.*
[31]*Frohwerk* v. *United States*, 249 U. S. 204 (1919) and *Debs* v. *United States*, 249 U. S. 211 (1919). The opinions of the Court in these cases were written by Holmes. Although the words "clear and present danger" were not used, the test of the Schenck case seems to have been applied. See Chapter 14 for an analysis of subsequent developments of this doctrine.
[14]250 U. S. 616 (1919).
[15]*Ibid.*

similar convictions.[16] In subsequent cases, as a majority of the Court further expanded the limits of permissible punishment of speech under the "bad tendency" test, Holmes dissented eloquently. "Every idea," he reminded his colleagues, "is an incitement."[17]

Out of the judicial use of the clear and present danger test and the extension of the Fourteenth Amendment to state legislation, grew the doctrine of the "preferred position." This doctrine, championed by Justices Murphy and Rutledge, held that the usual presumption of validity given to state legislation does not apply to laws restricting freedom of speech, press, or assembly. This approach, as developed by Justice Rutledge, still held that civil liberties must be balanced against domestic tranquility and national security, but it argued that the presumption must be in favor of liberty rather than its suppression. Rutledge put it this way:

> This case confronts us again with the duty our system places on this court to say where the individual's freedom ends and the State's power begins. Choice on that border, now as always delicate, is perhaps more so where the usual presumption supporting legislation is balanced by the preferred place given in our scheme to the great, the indispensable democratic freedoms secured by the First Amendment. That priority gives these liberties a sanctity and a sanction not permitting dubious intrusions.[18]

Rutledge then brought in the clear and present danger test when he stated, "Any attempt to restrict those liberties must be justified by clear public interest, threatened not doubtfully or remotely, but by clear and present danger."

This formula is not acceptable, of course, to those who argue the absolute inviolability of First Amendment liberties. Nor has it been accepted by all of the justices on the Court. Its most severe critic has been Justice Frankfurter, who called it a "deceptive formula" which unreasonably limits the power of legislatures; Justices Douglas and Black have argued for making the position of the First Amendment so "preferred" that virtually all intrusions are "dubious." In Justice Black's words, "The First Amendment provides the only kind of security system that can preserve a free government."[19]

Others have criticised the whole procedure of balancing the claims of individuals under the First Amendment against a public interest in order and security on grounds that, where the conflict is defined in this

[16]*Schaefer* v. *United States*, 251 U. S. 466 (1920), and *Pierce* v. *United States*, 252 U. S. 239 (1920)
[17]*Gitlow* v. *New York*, 268 U. S. 652 (1925)
[18]*Thomas* v. *Collins*, 323 U. S. 516 (1944)
[19]*Yates* v. *United States*, 354 U. S. 298 (1957)

way, the public interest will always overbalance the private claim. In their view, if a balance test is to be applied, it is not the *individual claim* to free speech but the *public interest* in maintaining freedom which should be weighed against other public goals. Quite clearly under this proposal the First Amendment side of the scales would be more heavily weighted.

The conflict over the meaning of civil liberties occasionally gets both intense and bitter. Individuals and groups who would restrict civil liberties to defend other values have sometimes been accused of bigotry or fascism by opponents. Those who argue for the primacy and inviolability of civil liberties have often been charged with abetting or sympathizing with the aims of the unpopular groups whose rights they defend. The American Civil Liberties Union has been for many years the leading organization dedicated to a defense of civil liberties against any intrusion or curtailment. Despite the fact that the ACLU numbers among its membership prominent Americans of different political persuasion, it was attacked by Senator McCarthy as an instrument of subversion and listed by a committee of the California State Legislature as a subversive organization. More recently several groups, including the California Department Convention of the American Legion, have urged that the ACLU be investigated by a congressional committee. In periods of national insecurity, apparently, the question is even raised of whether civil liberties should be extended to those who argue for the inviolability of civil liberties!

At this point, perhaps we do reach a bed-rock democratic principle. While the meaning and limits of civil liberties remain open questions, the principle of complete freedom to debate those questions is absolutely required. Within that framework there will be those who will say, with Judge Learned Hand, that the prohibitions of the First Amendment are "no more than admonitions of moderation." Others will reply, with Justice William O. Douglas, that "the idea that they are no more than that has done more to undermine liberty in this country than any other single force."[20]

CIVIL LIBERTIES VERSUS PUBLIC ORDER

Freedom of assembly is a corollary of freedom of speech. Free speech would be an empty liberty if one could not "peaceably assemble" an audience to hear the words spoken. But assemblies are not always peaceable, and when people assemble they may, in some circumstances, infringe on the liberties of others—the right not to listen, for example.

Every government must maintain the right and ability to use its police power to maintain public order. Legislatures and courts have real difficulty in finding a test for making exceptions to the right of

[20]William O. Douglas, *The Right of the People* (New York: Doubleday, 1958), p. 45.

assembly. "Incitement to riot" and "disturbing the peace" are vague criteria for limiting this right.

Does a city government have a right to prohibit any assemblies in streets and parks without a permit from a city director of public safety? The Supreme Court invalidated one such ordinance in Jersey City on the ground that it gave one man, the Director of Public Safety, the right to determine what assemblies could be held, which actually gave him the arbitrary power to restrict free speech.[21] The question of how far freedom of speech and assembly may be limited by ordinances designed to prevent breaches of the peace, however, has never been clearly resolved in public discussion or in the decisions of the courts.

A particularly difficult problem of free speech and assembly involves ordinances designed to curtail the use of sound trucks and other amplifying devices and the distribution of handbills which are subsequently tossed on the streets and become litter. One of the more interesting cases was *Saia* v. *New York*,[22] which involved the Jehovah's Witnesses—a group which often appears before the Supreme Court. Saia, a minister of this sect, lost his permit to use sound amplifiers because of complaints. Nevertheless, he continued his broadcasts and was soon arrested, tried, and convicted. His appeal eventually went to the Supreme Court.

Justice Douglas again took the purist position and held the law in violation of free speech, but Frankfurter dissented, pleading that uncontrolled noise was an "intrusion into cherished privacy" of people who might like to sit quietly in the park without benefit of Jehovah's Witness doctrine. The case is interesting because it put into clear focus the conflict between the rights of the speaker and the rights of people who do not wish to hear the message. Sound equipment extends free speech to areas in which it may not be welcome and makes the listener a "captive," as many citizens who complain about the loud and raucous noises coming from a nearby commercial area have discovered. A logical extension of Douglas' reasoning could, as Justice Jackson put it in his dissent, "render life unbearable."

In a case decided the following year the Court reversed its position and upheld a Trenton, New Jersey, ordinance preventing "loud and raucous" sound trucks from using the public streets.[23] Justice Reed supported the "loud and raucous" criterion as a valid exercise of the police power, although he would not go so far as his colleague, Justice Jackson, who would have upheld the right of a city to keep all sound trucks off the public streets. The Court has recognized here a conflict between the right of

---

[21]*Hague* v. *Committee for Industrial Organization*, 307 U. S. 496 (1939).
[22]334 U. S. 558 (1948).
[23]*Kovacs* v. *Cooper*, 336 U. S. 77 (1949).

speech and a counter claim of privacy. No clear solution has been devised by the courts or by public discussion.

CIVIL LIBERTIES AND PUBLIC MORALITY

Freedom of speech and freedom of the press may come into conflict also with the exercise of the police power to safeguard the public morality. Here again, the issue is whether the power of government should be applied to behavior or to ideas expressed in speech or writing. If censorship is admitted to be legitimate, the problem is how to construct criteria for determining when words are "pornographic" or "salacious," or when they "appeal to a prurient interest."

One approach developed by the courts, and adhered to until 1961, was the rule that "prior restraint" of what might appear in print was contrary to the meaning of a free press under the First Amendment.[24] Laws of libel and slander, the Court held, protect people who may have private cause for action after publication. To suppress publication of any material was held to be a basic interference with a free press. For a long time this principle was not seriously challenged. In 1961, however, the Court departed substantially from this principle when it upheld a city ordinance permitting censorship of movies before they could be displayed.[25] The case involved the moving picture "Don Juan," which the distributors had refused to submit to the censors. Justice Clark wrote the opinion for the five-man majority, and, in upholding the censorship ordinance, stated: "It has never been held that liberty of speech is absolute." Chief Justice Warren dissented sharply in a long opinion which went deeply into the history of censorship. He argued: "The decision presents a real danger of eventual censorship for every form of communication be it newspapers, journals, books, magazines, television, radio or public speeches."

Concluding his opinion, he made a strong plea for a more rigorous interpretation of the First Amendment: "No more potent force in defeat of [First Amendment] freedom could be designed than censorship. It is a weapon that no minority group, acting through government, should be allowed to wield over any of us."

It is not clear whether the majority of the Court intended the new doctrine to extend to preventing a publication from being issued. Nor is it certain that the case will have the effect of reopening the whole question of prior censorship in the future. Where censorship is admitted, the problem of insuring that the criteria employed are not arbitrary is a tremendously difficult one. There are those who argue that it is not

---

[24]*Near* v. *Minnesota*, 283 U. S. 697 (1931).
[25]*Times Film Corporation* v. *City of Chicago et al.*, 81 S. Ct. 391 (1961).

insuperable; others insist that no amount of logic and thought can eliminate the essential arbitrariness of the censor's role.

CHURCH AND STATE: A WALL OF SEPARATION?

The provision of the First Amendment which prevents the federal government from enacting any law respecting the establishment of religion was a "unique American experiment in the development of religious freedom and the separation of church and state."[26] Before its adoption, the Colonies had engaged in many discriminatory policies against members of certain religious orders, and some Colonies had established churches. Virginia officially recognized the Church of England, while Massachusetts, New Hampshire, and Connecticut were Congregationalist. In the matter of religious tests for holding office, only the constitutions of the states of New York and Virginia excluded religious affiliations from consideration, although New York as a colony had at one time excluded Catholics and Jews from suffrage. In Massachusetts and Maryland, only Christians could be governors, whereas in four other states the governor had to be a Protestant.

The enactment of the religious clause of the First Amendment settled some fundamental questions. It clearly ruled out a state-supported church and religious tests for public office or for the exercise of political rights. (Even on these points it was not until 1940 that the courts held that the Fourteenth Amendment extended these prohibitions to the states;[27] prior to that time they applied only to the federal Congress.) But the religious clause raised as many issues as it settled, and these have continued to provoke political debate and judicial contests.

Did the First Amendment merely declare that government may not "establish" a church? May government promote religion so long as it is neutral toward the claims of competing churches? Or did the Amendment establish, in Jefferson's phrase, "a wall of separation" between church and state which makes religion entirely a matter of private conscience and private association? "In God We Trust" is imprinted on our coins; we salute one nation "under God" in our pledge of allegiance to the flag; we use the Bible to take official oaths; adoption laws in several states are geared to religious beliefs; in California some of its laws include Christian Science practitioners as members of the healing arts; the three United States military academies require chapel attendance on Sundays; and chaplains are part of our armed forces.

The Christian religion and its ethical code permeate American life,

---

[26]Rocco J. Tresolini, *American Constitutional Law* (New York: Macmillan, 1959), p. 369
[27]*Cantwell* v. *Connecticut*, 310 U. S. 296.

but other religions are free to establish themselves without governmental interference. The Jewish, Buddhist, Mohammedan, and other churches will attest to this. Even agnostics and atheists can proclaim their beliefs, although, like members of non-Christian faiths, they are subject to nongovernmental pressures from less tolerant citizens who feel a nonbelief in God or a particular approach to His worship is cause for suspicion. When the government makes religious belief a matter of public faith, it adds to and supports these nongovernmental pressures. With the insertion of "under God" in the national flag salute, the atheist is faced with a dilemma since the secular oath cannot be given completely without including deference to a mystical force he disavows.

The same question arises in several other forms. May public funds be used to support nonprofit, parochial schools? In 1947, the Supreme Court held 5 to 4 that states may use public funds to transport students to nonprofit and parochial schools.[28] Justice Black's opinion ended with this statement about the "wall": "The First Amendment has erected a wall between church and state. That wall must be kept high and impregnable. We could not approve the slightest breach. New Jersey has not breached it here."

Four justices did think it had been breached, and there has been more adjudication on this matter by the Court. The next year, in *McCollum* v. *Board of Education*,[29] the Court held unconstitutional a released-time law permitting school buildings to be used for the teaching of various religious ideas while students not wishing to participate in the Catholic, Protestant, and Jewish instruction were not released from their secular instruction. There was some argument over the wall analogy and Justice Jackson, although concurring, felt that clearer legal principles must be provided than those given by Black or the wall might become as "winding as the serpentine wall designed by Mr. Jefferson for the University he founded." There was a good deal of bitterness in some church circles over this decision.

The released-time idea was not completely knocked down by the Court, however. It was upheld in *Zorach* v. *Clauson*,[30] wherein a New York plan called for released time religious instruction *away* from the school buildings upon written request of the parents. The Zorach decision may have reflected a judicial reaction to the storm of protest generated by the McCollum decision since 1952 was a time of growing religious influence. Where the issue of separation of church and state goes from here in the courts will be hard to anticipate, since there is considerable precedent on both sides of the question of how high the wall should be.

[28]*Everson* v. *Board of Education*, 330 U. S. 1.
[29]333 U. S. 203 (1948).
[30]343 U. S. 306 (1952).

A second major issue involving a continuous debate is the question of whether a majority has a right to write its religious convictions into law. In many states, for example, there are "blue laws" which are aimed at curtailing certain activities on Sunday. For example, the starting of athletic or other events before a certain time may be forbidden; or bars, liquor stores, and markets may be closed on Sundays. In some jurisdictions in which Catholics have been in a majority, dispensing of birth control information or contraceptive devices has been made illegal. Public authority may also be used in a positive way to enforce religious convictions. Should such Christian holidays as Christmas and Easter be celebrated in the public schools? In both the legal and the political arenas these questions continue to evoke controversy.

Thirdly, there is a range of issues that involve the question of whether, and under what conditions, government is entitled to regulate behavior that flows from religious conscience. Religious groups, the Supreme Court long ago asserted, may not engage in activities offensive to public morals.[31] But this doctrine is not as clear as it sounds. In 1944, the Court returned a case to lower courts because of its reluctance to interfere with religious freedom.[32] In this case, the issue was whether the defendant acted as leader of a religious sect or as a religious racketeer. The Court could not order him to cease his practices without undertaking to define a religion. To do so would make the government, via the judiciary, the arbiter of religious activity.

Conscientious objectors also raise the issue of freedom of religious belief. Every conscription law since World War I has granted exemption from military service to conscientious objectors as defined by statute. From time to time, the courts have had to decide just what a conscientious objector is, and some six thousand men, two thirds of them Jehovah's Witnesses, were held prisoner during World War II because they did not meet the legal definition of objectors.

These and many other questions are raised by the religious clause of the First Amendment. They suggest, above all, that even the most fundamental principles of democratic government cannot be authoritatively defined by a constitution or a corps of official interpreters.

Civil Rights and Liberties: Continuing Debate

We have examined very sketchily a few of the issues connected with the meaning and limits of the freedoms of speech, press, assembly, and religion. Changing conditions have given rise to new issues and new

[31]*Reynolds* v. *United States*, 98 U. S. 145 (1879).
[32]*United States* v. *Ballard*, 322 U. S. 78.

interpretations. The problem of defending civil liberties is also the problem of defining them. Since they are the liberties that make citizens also rulers, their defense must always be at the top of the agenda of a democratic society. What makes their defense difficult is that limitations on civil liberties are nearly always directed against unpopular and unorthodox ideas. In these circumstances what is likely to be lost sight of is the basic principle that liberty is always and exclusively for unpopular minorities. Freedom of thought is exclusively for those who think otherwise. There is never any problem of civil liberties for those who think and speak and write the thoughts that are orthodox at the time. *Every* society provides liberties for those who accept its prevailing ideas.

What this suggests is that civil liberties can be protected only when the majority is committed to the principles of liberty and their application to minorities. A similar range of issues arises in connection with the civil rights guaranteed by the other provisions of the Bill of Rights. These are dealt with subsequently.[33] In this area the problems generally arise as conflicts between the guarantees of due process described above and demands for more rigorous and efficient law enforcement. It is the person apprehended by the police, the person suspected of having committed a crime, who stands in need of the protections of due process. He is likely to get them only where the law-abiding majority is committed to due process for *all*.

In the American political system, the courts are the final arbiters of the meaning and limits of the Bill of Rights. But cases come to the courts because of the ordinances passed by city councils, laws passed by state legislatures and Congress, and the acts of public officials. Moreover, the courts respond, in the long run, to the political and intellectual climate of the country. No institutions, we may suspect, can long protect the civil liberties of a people who become indifferent to them or who come to value other goods more highly.

In 1947, the President's Committee on Civil Rights reported that it was essential to see that "all Americans are familiar with the fundamental rights to which they are entitled and which they owe one another." The report went on to say:

> This is not the case at present. In October, 1946, the National Opinion Research Center at the University of Denver, asked a cross-section of our adult population a series of questions about the Bill of Rights. Only one out of five Americans had a reasonably accurate knowledge of what is in the first 10 Amendments to the Constitution. Completely confused and inaccurate descriptions were offered by 12 per cent. More than a third had heard of the Bill of Rights but

[33]See Chapt. 14.

could not identify it in any way. Another third had not even heard of it. The NORC also reported that "Even among the best informed people, however—the more privileged, educationally, economically, and occupationally—less than a majority can satisfactorily identify the Bill of Rights." There is no excuse for this kind of ignorance.[34]

In the period since the Committee wrote we have seen the rise and fall of Senator McCarthy and the hunt for subversives, the social and political agonies of the school desegregation decision, congressional combat on civil rights legislation, "sit-ins," and a reassertion of a stronger attitude toward maintaining civil rights and liberties by the "Warren Court."

Nothing in this history suggests that the issues have been resolved or the threats to civil rights and liberties eliminated. Nor is it likely that they ever will be. Even the continuation of the controversy and the struggle, however, will depend on the existence of a public proud of its rights and liberties and alert to their abuse. To live in a democratic society is to share in responsibility for the continuing interpretation and enactment of its basic principles. In this sense, the Constitution was not written and adopted in 1789; it is being "written" and enacted by every generation of democratic citizens.

JUDICIAL SUPREMACY

THE FOURTH MAJOR PRINCIPLE of the American constitutional system defines the role of the courts in the process of government. The distinctive character of this role is that it includes the power to decide authoritatively and finally on the constitutionality of the acts of the Congress and the executive. Because the decision of the court is authoritative and binding on the other agencies, we have used the phrase "judicial supremacy" rather than the more common but less descriptive caption of "judicial review." Moreover, among the Founding Fathers it was only the question of the final and binding character of the decisions of the federal courts which was at issue.

There was general agreement that, in its absolutely necessary function of interpreting the statutes passed by Congress, the courts should have also the right to declare their findings with respect to whether statutes were compatible with the meaning of the Constitution. The issue was whether the courts' interpretation of the Constitution was to prevail over the views of other agencies which, under the doctrine of checks and balances, were equal and co-ordinate branches of government. The issue

[34]President's Committee on Civil Rights, *To Secure These Rights* (Washington: Government Printing Office, 1947), pp. 134-135.

was not whether the courts should have a right to *review* the constitutionality of acts of Congress, but whether, in this function, *supremacy* should mark their findings.

The Constitution itself, of course, is silent on this question. In Article III, Sections 1 and 2, it provides only the following:

> The judicial power of the United States shall be vested in one supreme Court, and in such inferior Courts as the Congress may from time to time ordain and establish....
>
> The judicial Power shall extend to all Cases, in Law and Equity, arising under this Constitution, the Laws of the United States and Treaties made, or which shall be made, under their Authority;—to all Cases affecting Ambassadors, other public Ministers and Consuls; —to all Cases of admiralty and maritime Jurisdiction;—to Controversies to which the United States shall be a Party;—to Controversies between two or more States....

The power of the Court to nullify an act of Congress as contrary to the Constitution was successfully asserted by the Court itself in the case of *Marbury* v. *Madison*,[35] but from the beginning some had argued that this power of the Court was inherently implied in the new system of government. On the surface, the arguments were those developed by Chief Justice Marshall in *Marbury* v. *Madison*. The Constitution, his decision held, expresses law which has a higher standing than ordinary legislation; hence, acts contrary to the Constitution must be void; hence, the Court must hold them to be invalid. In this view, a written constitution becomes meaningless unless the courts exercise the power authoritatively to maintain its provisions. Behind these legalistic arguments, however, stood the conservative political assumptions of the Federalists. The doctrine of judicial review was seen as a necessary barrier to the legislative supremacy of popular majorities which, despite the check and balance system, might come to control the other agencies of government. Against the onslaught of majority attack, the courts might be expected to protect the rights of minorities, as well as to enshrine national supremacy over states' rights.

The political, rather than legal, character of the argument for judicial supremacy was clear in the very circumstances in which it was asserted. The first legislation to reorganize the judiciary was passed in 1801, at the close of John Adams' administration, in order to carry out clearly partisan designs. It reduced the number of justices on the Supreme Court in order to maintain Federalist control, and it created new inferior federal courts to which Federalist justices could be appointed by the outgoing administration. It was the validity of one of these "midnight appointments" that

[35] 1 Cranch 137 (1803).

was at issue in *Marbury* v. *Madison*. Moreover, John Marshall, who delivered the opinion of the Court in the case, was a Federalist, appointed Chief Justice at a late hour to keep Jefferson from making the appointment.

For the liberal, constitution-making and constitutional interpretation were viewed as political, not legal, acts. Since a constitution is of fundamental importance, it is all the more necessary that those who make and interpret it be responsible to public opinion. Liberals granted, of course, that a written constitution must be respected if it is to be meaningful. But they denied that judges are peculiarly able to make such judgments. Liberals and conservatives alike were agreed on the necessity for the independence of the judiciary if equal justice was to be insured, but the very independence of the judiciary made it, for liberals, the worst possible place to locate final political authority. Judges must be counted on for even-handed administration of the laws. "But," John Taylor added, "the instant an individual is removed from the legislative or executive departments into the judicial, his nature is supposed to have been regenerated, his errours are sanctified, his intrigues are overlooked, and his responsibility commuted for the universal refuge of imposture, 'God and his own conscience.' "[36]

From the liberal assumptions, judicial supremacy would put popular majorities in the position of a Caspar Milquetoast and the court in the position of his wife: "I make all the major decisions and my wife makes all the minor ones; of course, she decides which questions are major ones." That is to say, the Court would be in the position of choosing what questions the popular agencies of government were competent to decide upon. But, if this was inadmissable, liberals were divided on the alternatives. Some looked to the separation of powers; with Andrew Jackson they would say to the Chief Justice (in connection with a later case), "John Marshall has made his decision, now let him enforce it." Others were more inclined to look to the federal principle and to the power of the legislatures in the several states as a counter to the political power of the courts.

In a subsequent chapter, the historical development of judicial review will be dealt with more fully. Here we wish only to emphasize that after the Civil War there developed in the United States what has been called a "Cult of the Constitution" in which the Supreme Court members acted as the "high priests." The Constitution then appeared to be precisely what we have been arguing it never was: a body of principles capable of settling political disputes, and the true meaning of which was to be discerned by a body of nine men who looked down on the political struggle from the Olympian heights of legal learning and objectivity.

[36]Taylor, *Inquiry*, pp. 198-99.

President Roosevelt's battle against the "nine old men" in the 1930's, and his eventual victory, seemed to reinforce John Taylor's earlier view that judges remain ordinary mortals who act politically from the perspectives of their own political philosophies. The Court itself, in its self-imposed limitations on its power to declare acts of Congress unconstitutional after 1937, seemed to recognize the political character of its function in interpreting the Constitution. Yet, in considerable measure it has continued to be "characteristic of the American system to confuse the legal and the moral and, in effect, to make the judges' view of public morality the law of the land." Morris R. Cohen, whose description this is, went on to argue that, during the early period of American history it was generally assumed, by liberals at least, that the individual conscience was the seat of judgment on the morality of the law. The development of judicial supremacy

> has changed this moral right of the people into a legal right of the judiciary. From the anarchy that would follow if every individual felt free to disobey what seemed to him an unjust law, we have been saved by a doctrine of judicial absolutism or infallibility. Presumably whatever a majority of the Supreme Court decides not only is the law but is also the original intention of the people, and conforms to the eternal principles of justice, or at any rate to the principles recognized by Anglo-Saxons since they roamed in the German forests.[37]

That the role of the courts in the American political system is still very much an open question is revealed by the fact that the most pressing of American political problems—the status of ethnic minorities—has been approached most importantly through judicial action. It was by judicial interpretation of the Constitution that equal access to education was declared to require the integration of schools. Generally, congressional and executive action have been used in this area to implement what the Court has declared to be fundamental public policy. The role of the courts since 1937 in serving as the bulwark of civil liberties and civil rights raises some interesting problems for political liberals, especially. Although they have been inclined to applaud the court's protection of cherished rights and liberties, they have been embarrassed, or should have been, by their reliance on a conservative device, removed from and superior to public opinion, for protection. One consequence, for example, has been the very unliberal identification of legality with morality to which we referred earlier. Should minorities have equal rights because it is the law of the land, or because they are entitled to rights which have fundamental and universal moral validity? Are the people "the only safe

[37]Morris R. Cohen, *American Thought: A Critical Sketch* (New York: The Free Press of Glencoe, 1954), pp. 143-144.

guardians of their own liberties," as Jefferson held, or do they require protection from themselves by a tribunal which is not responsible to them?

The resulting liberal dilemma has been underscored by conservatives who have pointed out that the recent role of the courts in protecting civil rights and liberties is a reaffirmation of traditional conservative doctrine. To paraphrase Peter Viereck, in the last analysis the question is whether we are to be ruled by men in black robes (the justices) or men in white sheets (the members of such bigoted organizations as the Ku Klux Klan). The old issues that divided liberal and conservative reassert themselves. Judicial supremacy, like the other articles of American constitutionalism, turns out to be unfinished business on the agenda of democratic discussion.

5

THE POLITICS OF
MASS SOCIETY

MANY YEARS AGO an acute observer of American democracy said:

> ... the species of oppression by which democratic nations are
> menaced is unlike anything which ever before existed in the world:
> our contemporaries will find no prototype of it in their memories. ..
> the old words despotism and tyranny are inappropriate; the thing
> itself is new; and since I cannot name it, I must attempt to define it.
> I seek to trace the novel features under which despotism may
> appear in the world. The first thing that strikes the observation is
> an innumerable multitude of men all equal and alike, incessantly
> endeavoring to procure the petty and paltry pleasures with which
> they glut their lives. Each of them, living apart, is as a stranger to
> the fate of all the rest—his children and his private friends constitute
> to him the whole of mankind; as for the rest of his fellow citizens, he
> is close to them, but he feels them not; he exists but in himself and
> for himself alone; and if his kindred still remain to him, he may be
> said at any rate to have lost his country. Above this race of men

stands an immense and tutelary power, which takes upon itself alone to secure their gratifications, and to watch over their fate. That power is absolute, minute, regular, provident, and mild. It would be like the authority of a parent, if, like that authority, its object was to prepare men for manhood; but it seeks, on the contrary, to keep them in perpetual childhood; it is well content that the people should rejoice, provided they think of nothing but rejoicing. For their happiness such a government willingly labors, but it chooses to be the sole agent and the only arbiter of that happiness: it provides for their security, foresees and supplies their necessities, facilitates their pleasures, manages their principal concerns, directs their industry, regulates the descent of property, and subdivides their inheritances—what remains, but to spare them all the care of thinking and all the trouble of living? Thus it every day renders the exercise of the free agency of man less useful and less frequent; it circumscribes the will within a narrower range, and gradually robs a man of all the uses of himself. The principle of equality has prepared men for these things: it has predisposed men to endure them, and oftentimes to look on them as benefits.[1]

These predictions are Alexis de Tocqueville's. Written in 1835 after a visit to the United States, his *Democracy in America* has in recent years been recognized as a classic, primarily because he put the problem of tyranny in a democracy in a new light. In his analysis of the dangers to freedom, he forecast the tendencies and problems of "mass society." In the excerpt quoted above, Tocqueville argues that, contrary to the views of the Founding Fathers, the real problem of faction is not that a majority will tyrannize a minority by forcing its will or opinion on them, but that all men will be gradually robbed "of all uses of" themselves. A "servitude of the regular, quiet, and gentle kind" may even appear as an outward form of freedom. "Sovereignty of the people" may still seem to exist even after the people have been spared "all the care of thinking" which is necessary to make their participation as citizens meaningful.

THE GROWTH OF MASS SOCIETY

ALTHOUGH HE MISSED MANY OF THE DEVELOPMENTS that contribute to this end, Tocqueville put his finger squarely on the phenomenon of mass society: the transition from a society of individuals or of identifiable social classes into the undifferentiated masses whose consent to be governed is engineered through the use of psychological techniques. We are

[1]Alexis de Tocqueville, *Democracy in America*, Phillips Bradley, ed. (New York: Knopf, 1948), p. 318.

still too close to the developments involved in this transition to be able adequately to assess their implications for the political system. Yet, most careful observers agree that Western society generally, and America in particular, stand at a watershed and that the underlying changes in the fabric of society are fundamental, even revolutionary. A neat summary of much of this concern might be taken from Herbert Muller's *Uses of The Past:*

> Let us spell out the worst about this notorious mass-man and his mass-culture. He has a meager idea of the abundant life, confusing quantity with quality, size with greatness, comfort with culture, gadgetry with genius. He has as little appreciation of pure science as of the fine arts, and as little capacity for the discipline that both require; although he may stand in awe of them his real veneration goes to the engineers and inventors, the manufacturers of True Romances and Tin Pan Alley airs. He is frequently illiberal, suspicious of "radical" ideas, scornful of "visionary" ideals, hostile to "aliens"; in America he has developed a remarkable vocabulary of contempt that manages to embrace most of mankind—the nigger, the mick, the chink, the wop, the kike, *et cetera.* He is the chief foe of the individualism he boasts of, a patron of standard brands in tastes and opinions as in material possessions, with a morbid fear of being thought queer or different from the Joneses; individuality to him is "personality," which may be acquired in six easy lessons or his money back, is then turned on to win friends and influence people, and is confirmed by the possession of "personalized" objects, which are distinguished only by having his initials on them. In short, he appears to be a spoiled child, fundamentally ungrateful to the scientists, political philosophers, social reformers, and religious idealists who have given him his unprecedented opportunities. He is therefore the natural prey of advertisers, politicians, millionaire publishers, and would-be dictators.[2]

We cannot pretend to make an exhaustive or authoritative account of the intellectual, cultural, and social changes that have played a part in the growth of mass society. The analysis that follows, however, may help to clarify some of the major tendencies that have implications for American politics.

Intellectual Changes: The Growth of Relativism

About two centuries ago, Oliver Goldsmith wrote,

> Logicians have but ill defined
> As rational, the human kind;
> Reason, they say, belongs to man,
> But let them prove it if they can.

[2] Herbert Muller, *The Uses of the Past* (New York: Oxford University Press, 1952), p. 232.

Since Goldsmith wrote, "logicians" themselves, in large numbers, have come around to his point of view. The result has been the development of an increasingly prevalent attitude toward morality and truth that is summed up in the phrase "moral" or "cultural" relativism, and in an attitude toward man that sees him as simply a network of conditioned responses. The crucial assumption underlying this attitude was expressed clearly by the British philosopher, Bertrand Russell: "Questions as to 'values' lie wholly outside the domain of knowledge. That is to say, when we assert that this or that has 'value,' we are giving expression to our own emotions . . . ."

The attitudes toward society and politics that follow from this assumption are fundamentally incompatible with the historic meaning of the democratic faith. In the first place, the concept of inherent rights of man, a doctrine that is absolutely necessary if we are to assert the universal validity of our own political system as against communism, simply makes no sense at all if it is true that all moral values are equally right, that "one idea is good as another."

For the same reason that relativism makes any claim to the universal moral validity of democratic principles impossible, it also makes democratic politics, in the traditional liberal sense, impossible. For if there is no way rationally to judge that one form of political society is better than another, then similarly there is no way to judge or to argue that any proposed change within a society is desirable or worthwhile. Conscious social change, proceeding from reasoned political debate, depends on the possibility of evaluating social conditions and institutions in the light of some conception of the public interest, of making judgments about good or bad, better or worse.

Cultural relativism undertakes to explain people's behavior, including their values, as evolving from the conditioning of plastic human nature into the responses desired in a particular cultural setting. It seems an adequate framework for explaining the behavior of most people in closed societies, in which all social institutions conspire to "interiorize" in the individual the stable and customary universals of the culture. But where does it leave the individual in an "open society"? Does the ideal of a community which offers its individuals alternatives and seeks to maximize their capacities for choice become meaningless? Most important of all for our purposes is the question of how, on the assumptions of relativism, the conflicts within a pluralist society are to be resolved.

One way out of the difficulty, and apparently an increasingly popular one, is to substitute statistical norms for ethical standards. "Keeping up with the Joneses" as a basis for behavior is a commonplace expression of this approach. At a more subtle level, norms based on statistical surveys of opinions and attitudes may be used as a basis for advertising and manipulation. In politics, this phenomenon is reflected in the tendency of candidates and parties to exploit public opinion polls in their favor.

These techniques, paralleling in politics the "everybody's doing it" approach to advertising, will be successful to the extent that people define what should be done on the basis of what most people want to do. It should be immediately clear that this tendency to use the average of what *is* being done as a definition of what *should* be done undermines the traditional meanings of democracy, both the liberal and conservative ones.

The standardization of values in an authoritarian society occurs through channels. An official party line sets the standards of orthodoxy. The individual is subjected to pressures—political, economic, social, and legal—to conform. In a mass democracy, on the other hand, conformity is a matter of social adjustment; the individual adjusts to the expectations of his peers, and he does it willingly. "If you want to get along, go along," a current slogan puts it.

Perhaps the heart of the matter lies in the fact that the conformity of mass society does not seem to the individual to be coerced. Where orthodoxy is a matter of conforming to rapidly changing fads and fashions of one's peers, there seems to be no visible source of authority. Where social acceptance becomes the major or exclusive goal of the individual, conformity does not require the sacrifice of other goals or values. This is likely to be the case for those who regard society as the source of all values anyway and who feel that, where values do conflict, they are simply relative. Individuals for whom social adjustment and approval are the ultimate goals are incapacitated even to recognize as tyranny those "regular, quiet and gentle" forms of manipulated but "voluntary" acquiescence in a standardized life.

As other critics have pointed out, the standardization of preferences and values in a democratic society is also likely to mean that the norms of conduct, precisely because they are not formulated or imposed by an elite, are likely to mean the reign of mediocrity. Norms which result from a desire to please everyone are likely to mean the repudiation of ideas of excellence in all areas of life. In such circumstances the pursuit of excellence, since it cannot by definition be achieved by a mass audience, will court resentment and lead to maladjustment for the individual.

The way in which relativism undermines the traditional models of democratic politics is seen most clearly in its consequences for the concept of a public interest. From the relativist point of view, the notion that there is a public interest which it is the purpose of reasoned debate to clarify and define is erroneous: "The question as to what is the common good can be answered only by subjective value judgments which may differ essentially from each other."[3] Where value judgments differ, no

[3] Hans Kelsen, "Foundations of Democracy," *Ethics*, October, 1955, p. 2.

appeal to reason or experience can be made: one opinion is as good as another. Translated into politics, this means that all interests must be accepted as equally legitimate. Appeals to the public interest appear as simply the gloss which all private interests use to conceal their special claims.

Similarly, if rational discussion of the public interest is not possible, then all appeals to the voter must appear as efforts to propagandize and manipulate. Propaganda comes to be defined as an ethically neutral term, because there no longer seems to be even the possibility of appealing to "opinion that is the result of reason and reflection," to use Paine's words. Democracy itself comes to be redefined as simply a matter of counting noses rather than heads, noises rather than arguments. Jefferson's injunction that "the will of the majority is in all cases to prevail" becomes the only admissible test of democracy; his condition that "that will to be rightful must be reasonable" is dismissed as essentially meaningless.

The public interest was the key to the traditional solution to the problem of faction. For liberal democrats, the reasoned opinions of a majority defined the standards against which the claims of special interests were judged. For conservative democrats, a balance of private claims permitted the public interest to be expressed by tradition and a responsible aristocracy. The relativist solves the problem of faction by denying that it poses a problem. From his perspective all political behavior is motivated by passion or interest. Politics is a struggle for power, and nothing but a struggle for power. The effort to subordinate the struggle for power to objectively valid public goals or purposes is a delusion.

The relativistic attitude toward values stems in part from what is perhaps the most prevalent interpretation of the meaning and character of scientific method. In this view, science is held to be purely descriptive, to permit only statements about the world as it is, never conclusions which express a preference about how it ought to be. It is impossible, according to this position, to get to an "ought" statement from any number of "is" statements. "Ought" statements express and refer to our internal feelings and desires, not to the external world; hence, they can never be verified or tested empirically. On these grounds, many philosophers have turned over the study of values to the psychologists. The conclusion is that values are purely subjective and simply relative to one another.

As a practical approach to life and politics, relativism probably owes most to a general understanding of *cultural* relativity. The inquiries of modern social science have systematically shown what increasing contact among cultures has revealed to common sense: human beings are in fact much more plastic than they formerly were assumed to be. The central tenet of the modern study of culture, the only hypothesis that makes human behavior intelligible, is the proposition that human behavior is learned; that, by and large, human beings behave the way they do and value the things they do because they have learned to act and think in these ways in the cultures in which they were reared. The tremendous diversity of cultural beliefs and practices seems to reinforce the view that there is nothing either right or wrong, but culture makes it so. The conclusion of cultural relativity is forced by the recognition that there is almost no kind of activity regarded by any society as good which is not also regarded by some other society as bad.

It is obviously tempting to go from the facts of cultural relativism to the conclusion of complete moral relativism, and from the inescapable conclusion that human behavior occurs within a cultural context to the position that therefore the individual can never transcend the values of his culture. Similarly, it is easy to see how the evidence that cultures in the past have sought to legitimatize the exercise of power through a wide variety of appeals to God, nature, history, and race leads to the conclusion that all such efforts are, and must be, equally fraudulent. The political philosophy of the past, including democracy in its historic form, seems only to reinforce the view. To paraphrase the late anthropologist, E. A. Hooton, man has insisted on playing the game of politics, not only with an ace up his sleeve, but with the smug conviction that God put it there.

It is undeniable that in the secular age in which we live, men in large numbers have abandoned belief in the absolute truths of religious faith. A recent study of the attitudes of American college students concludes that, while they "normally express a need for religion," their religious beliefs do "not carry over to guide and govern important decisions in the secular world. Students expect these to be socially determined ...."[4] The result appears to have been, notwithstanding the "religious revival" in America, that increasing numbers of men are no longer able to embrace "the intangible truths of the spirit" on which conservatives have sought to base governments. So also, and for the same reason, are many unable any longer to give loyalty to the liberal faith in human reason and individual choice on which democracy largely rested in the past.

For the individual, the result is a new type of "social character." The mass man who is the typical product of a relativistic culture has been described by David Riesman as "other-directed" in contrast to the "inner-directed" man of an earlier period.[5] The behavior of the inner-directed man was governed by internal norms or values. His course through life was directed by the values—largely imposed by parents and Church— which had come to form the content of his conscience. These values,

[4]Philip E. Jacob, *Changing Values in College* (New York: Harper, 1957), p. 2.
[5]David Riesman *et al., The Lonely Crowd* (Garden City, N. Y.: Doubleday, 1950).

"interiorized" in the process of growing up, functioned in a way analogous to the gyroscope, giving his behavior a self-contained direction and equilibrium.

The other-directed man, by contrast, has no fixed or definite standards of taste or judgment. He wants above all to "belong," to be liked, not to stand out from the crowd. He seeks to conform his behavior to the constantly changing expectations of others, rather than to any internalized standards of right and wrong. The analogy here is not the gyroscope, but radar. In search of cues from the groups to which he belongs, he sends out signals and guides his behavior by what he interprets to be the expectations of his fellows. Ray Ginger makes the same point in his study of Chicago when its leading public figures were such controversial men as the radical Governor Peter Altgeld and Clarence Darrow. However unlovely in many ways these men's personalities were, the question they put to themselves was, "Am I right?" This is to be contrasted with the question which appears to dominate the lives of current residents of suburbia: "Am I covered?"[6]

In this kind of society the threat is not so much the danger of the typically totalitarian mass movement of "true believers." The danger is not the susceptibility of people to totalitarian appeals, but their indifference to all ideological questions. It is not that the public interest will come to be identified with the final truths of some ideology interpreted by an infallible elite, but that the public interest will cease altogether to play a role in politics. The problem, as de Tocqueville pointed out, is the danger of tyranny "of the regular, quiet, and gentle kind." The problem comes to focus in the meaning of civil liberties, and in a form that the Founding Fathers never faced.

Madison, as we have seen, summed up an assumption shared by liberals and conservatives alike in *The Federalist* (No. 10). An enduring source of faction, he said, arises from the "zeal" of different individuals and groups "for different opinions concerning religion, concerning government, and many other points, as well of speculation as of practise." Man's opinions and his passions "will have a reciprocal influence on each other." Underlying Madison's whole argument is his assumption that "as long as the reason of man continues fallible, and he is at liberty to exercise it, different opinions will be formed." What he assumed, as a good child of the Enlightenment was bound to assume, was that when men are free to think, when they are not regimented by government, they will think. The only danger, then, would be the tendency for resulting opinions to be bigoted. What he did not foresee, the possibility that he did not allow, was a society of men free from the restraints of political authoritarianism and yet without "zeal for different opinions." He could

[6]Ray Ginger, *Altgeld's America* (New York: Funk and Wagnalls, 1958).

not imagine a society in which the legal right to think otherwise is guaranteed but not exercised, a society with freedom of political association, but with an apathy toward or an attitude of moderation on questions of public policy.

The growth and development of the tendencies of mass democracy suggest that Madison may have been wrong in concluding that the only way to eliminate faction based on "zeal for different opinions" is for political tyranny to destroy the liberty of opinion on which faction feeds, a remedy which along with his contemporaries he regarded as far "worse than the disease." We must now entertain the possibility that the legal existence of freedom of thought, speech, and association is no guarantee that thought will occur or that speech and association will furnish the means to rational choice in public policy. A society of men committed to the relativism of their own points of view may even lose the desire to have points of view. Bigoted political opinions may be swallowed up in the atmosphere of toleration, harmony and moderation, but the price will be the sacrifice of the commitment to reason on which the traditional liberal democratic theory rested.

Moreover, the person with convictions and commitment may find that the penalties of social ostracism and isolation under the conditions of mass society are even more onerous than political persecution. It seems to have been this possibility that Edmund Burke had in mind when he spoke of a dissenter in an equalitarian democracy:

> . . . individual sufferers are in a much more deplorable condition than in any other. Under a cruel prince they have the balmy compassion of mankind to assuage the smart of their wounds . . . but those who are subjected to wrong under multitudes, are deprived of all external consolation. They seem deserted by mankind, overpowered by a conspiracy of the whole species.[7]

Intellectual Changes: The Growth of Mechanism

Much the same sort of analysis might be made for the increasingly prevalent view that human nature is infinitely plastic and that men are essentially like machines and will react in determined ways to external stimuli. The distinguishing characteristic of a machine is that it does not make choices of goals or purposes which modify its own behavior. Consequently, if one understands the principles and mechanism of its operation, it becomes possible to cause it to operate in ways that the operator regards as desirable.

[7]Quoted in John C. Bennett, *Christians and the State* (New York: Scribner, 1958), p. 144.

The typical modern form of a deterministic, mechanistic view of man, like all things modern, tends to be secular rather than religious and to have its sources in psychology rather than theology. It sees man, not as an actor in some preordained Divine scheme of things, but rather as an organism which operates in accordance with certain internal psychological mechanisms which automatically translate external stimuli into determinate forms of responses. Just as access to the plot of the Divine drama would have enabled one to predict the behavior of the actors, so also it is assumed that knowledge of the internal psychological mechanisms will permit complete prediction of human behavior. To be sure, this is a different kind of machine, the only machine that has sensations of freedom and choice, but these are held to be illusions that stand really for the incompleteness of our knowledge of the determining mechanisms. Unlike the deficiencies in our knowledge of the Divine plan, these are potentially remediable. Moreover, also unlike the earlier theological interpretation, the expansion of our knowledge permits not only prediction but also control of behavior. Human nature is infinitely plastic; men can be conditioned and manipulated into almost any form of behavior, provided only that our knowledge of the determining mechanisms is accurate enough and our control of external conditions thorough enough.

The mechanistic view of man is rooted in pupular interpretations of the ideas of "all three of the great teachers of the 19th century—Darwin, Marx, Freud." The result is "a sort of secular Calvinism" which holds human behavior to be completely determined.[8] It seems likely that popular interpretations of the findings of psychoanalysis have provided the major reinforcement of the mechanist position. Freudian psychology introduced the concept of the unconscious, a concept that permitted explanation of many aspects of individual behavior not theretofore explicable. Essentially, this concept suggests that beneath the level of consciousness there are personality forces at work—drives, frustrations, conflicts, and so on—which are so threatening to the sense of self-importance and identity that they are repressed in consciousness. Yet they often operate to determine behavior in quite irrational or nonrational ways and completely without the awareness of the individual. Although Freud himself, and most other students of psychoanalysis, did not draw the conclusion that no individual ever knows the real motivations for his behavior and that therefore the intellect is simply an excuse-hunter for concealed drives and mechanisms, many versions of the popularization of psychoanalysis have arrived at this conclusion.

After Freud, "it was soon discovered not only that the gross symptoms

[8]Joseph Wood Krutch, *The Measure of Man* (New York: Grosset and Dunlap, 1953), p. 37.

136 / THE CONSENT OF THE GOVERNED

of insanity are the manifestations of irrational psychological processes but that in all human behavior intellect plays a role subordinate to that of the blind and irrational emotions."[9] From this point of view, reason appears to have been given to man not, as in traditional democratic theory, to direct his thought and action, but rather to conceal and camouflage the hidden forces of the unconscious that really do direct it. At best then, when men disagree, rationality is a cloak which may be useful "merely as a camouflage to conceal the real nature of the process of persuasion," which is inherently psychological rather than logical.[10]

This approach to human behavior led to the discovery that the democratic voter, like other men, can be most effectively reached not by rational argument but by appeals addressed to his subconscious desires, drives, and tensions. It led also to the development and refinement of the techniques of psychological manipulation, including subliminal projection. But even more important, the allegedly scientific character of the theory of mechanism served to offer a firm ground for the justification of the use of the techniques. For, if all appeals turn out to be emotional rather than rational, then psychological manipulation and conditioning appear as the only—and, therefore, the "democratic"—alternative to physical coercion. As one of the leading authorities in the field of public relations has put it, "The responsible leader ... must apply his energies to mastering the operational know-how of consent engineering and to outmaneuvering his opponents in the public interest."[11]

Two aspects of this statement are particularly remarkable. First, there is the obvious, but quite unintended, irony in the phrase, "consent engineering." Secondly, there is the appeal to a public interest which, in the premises, is completely spurious. For, where reason has been ruled out as the basis of political debate, the public interest can only serve as camouflage for the power aspirations or the rationally indefensible biases of the consent engineer. If propaganda and manipulation are viewed as the only possible approach to voters, there would not seem to be any room left for a public interest or for distinctions between good and bad propaganda; the only distinction is between effective and ineffective propaganda.

In the politics of the mass society, however, it is not simply that manipulation comes to characterize the politician's relationship to the electorate; the manipulative appeals themselves tend to focus around personalities and noncontroversial standards—"honesty," "sincerity," and similar catchwords—rather than around issues and principles of public policy.

[9]Franz Alexander, Our Age of Unreason (Philadelphia: Lippincott, 1942), p. 24.
[10]The phrase is from E. H. Carr, The New Society (Boston: Beacon, 1957), p. 72. Carr provides a very readable analysis of the effects of this assumption on traditional democratic theory.
[11]Edward L. Bernays, Public Relations (Norman: University of Oklahoma Press, 1952), p. 161.

This is, perhaps, due to the fact that politicians, as well as other elites in modern society, tend also to be other-directed men who themselves lack a set of guiding political principles. They may even be seeking to give the public what it wants—or, perhaps more accurately, to divine the lowest common denominator of its wants—in a psychological sense. The result is, as de Tocqueville foresaw, a government which still seems to rest on the consent of the governed, but in which that consent is no longer the product of conscious, reasoned choice of social goals and policies.

Social Changes: The Growth of Bigness

The broad intellectual tendencies we have been examining have been powerfully underwritten by a network of interrelated economic and social changes. Impressive among these is the sheer growth in the size of social undertakings. The growth in the size of national government is by now well known. The national budget for 1960 ($80 billion) was twenty times greater than it was in 1932 ($4 billion). The number of persons on the federal payroll has increased from approximately 600,000 to nearly 2.5 million in the same period. Similar development has occurred in industry. Five hundred corporations control two-thirds of the nonfarm economy; 150 corporations own one-half of all manufacturing facilities; the largest of the nonfinancial corporations, American Telephone and Telegraph, has a bigger annual budget than thirty-five of the states of the United States. In the same way, the size of labor unions, veterans' organizations, even organizations devoted to philanthropy, has grown.

In every case, size has led to bureaucracy, that is, to a rationalized organizational structure, which operates under settled rules of procedure. The growth of bureaucracies has been accompanied by several related changes. A new white-collar class of bureaucrats whose destinies lie within the organization has tended to replace the older middle class of independent businessmen and members of the professions. Whyte describes this new class as "organization men," chiefly characterized by the fact that they have abandoned the older "puritan ethic" of individualism for the "social ethic" of togetherness, harmony, and moderation.[12] Organization men, says Whyte, "tend to equate the lone individual with psychic disorder." Like Riesman's other-directed man, the organization man is a team player who has surrendered his own individuality to the organization as the necessary price for eligibility to climb in its ranks. He is a good committee member, an unassertive moderate, and an all-round "good fellow."

[12]William H. Whyte, *The Organization Man* (Garden City, N. Y.: Doubleday, 1956).

138 / THE CONSENT OF THE GOVERNED

Morover, he carries the qualities that stand him in good stead at the office to his home in suburbia where his easy congeniality leads him into the P.T.A., civic improvement clubs, and service organizations. But not into partisan politics. Partisan political activity means controversy and divisiveness. The man who is committed to the proposition that all truth lies somewhere in between competing claims to it, and that moderation is always the best policy, is not likely to be attracted to a partisan politics of issues. The political style of the mass man is characterized by withdrawal from conflict and controversy. Moderation between opposing points of view and the harmonious accommodation of rival interests seem to be the appropriate attitudes.

Large-scale organizations are characterized by an overriding concern with the morale of their members. In the human relationships of modern organizational life it may not be seriously misleading to see morale as a substitute for morality. The growth of the corporation has been accompanied, as Riesman argues, by a concern with human relations as the central organizational problem. Internally, this has meant the rapid expansion of personnel departments and harmony programs designed to secure the happiness and emotional well-being of employees.

Externally, the problem becomes one of public relations—to create and merchandise a favorable image of the organization. Virtually every large organization—including manufacturing corporations, government agencies, labor unions, and even universities—has a public relations department. The growth of specialized firms offering public relations skills and services has even acquired the collective name of "Madison Avenue." In both its internal and external expressions, this concern with people as the problem assumes that the problem of persuading and pleasing people is essentially a psychological process. Although none of the resulting activity is without some rational content, the underlying model of man on which it rests seems clearly to be a deterministic, mechanistic one. Thus, human relations in large-scale undertakings seem, in the interests of human harmony, to embody and to promote those modern conceptions of human nature which are clearly incompatible with the traditional democratic models, both liberal and conservative.

Individuals who increasingly confront these forces in their organizational lives are likely to carry over the same attitudes and expectations into the realm of politics. Enmeshed in organized bureaucracies which demand their uncritical loyalties, cogs in the wheels of intricate and highly interdependent organizations whose purposes and goals seem beyond their, or any men's, control or direction—men are not likely to see politics as a vehicle through which society and the future may be consciously subordinated to human purposes.

We might expect, in these circumstances, to find an electorate that is to an alarming degree apathetic or ignorant of issues, or both. Studies of voting behavior seem to argue that this is the case. We might expect also that among those interested in politics there is a marked concern with being "in the know," that for many of those who are not indifferent the focus of interest is in becoming what Riesman has called "inside-dopesters." The extent to which political discussion turns on the question of who will run for what office and who will be elected and not on the democratically critical questions of who *ought* to run and who *ought* to be elected is an obvious phenomenon.

Not only are these attitudes carried over into politics by voters, but also they seem increasingly to characterize the behavior of politicians and political parties. As we will see more in detail later, the rules of the game in American campaigns and elections in recent years have been rewritten under the impact of public-opinion polling, public relations and advertising technique, and the political styles appropriate to television and the other mass media.

Social Changes: The Growth of the Mass Media and Advertising

It is, perhaps, in the area of the mass media of communications that the impact of bigness comes most clearly into focus. The mass media, and television in particular, mean more than a technology which makes it possible to communicate with large numbers of physically dispersed people. They involve, potentially, the ability to control the information and ideas which are to be available to people. They constitute a framework in which the techniques of psychological manipulation can be effectively employed. They imply the existence of a mass-media market rather than a public. The appeals to this mass market are likely to be characterized by the standardization to taste, at the level of the lowest common denominator of tastes, say the severest critics; by a studied care in avoiding any idea or symbol that might be offensive to any group in the community; and by an avoidance of serious concern with controversial ideas and public issues. The result is essentially different from either the traditional liberal instruments of rival party presses and town-meeting-style party rhetoric and debate or the conservative instruments of tradition, reverence for constituted authority, and deference toward a responsible aristocracy that serves as the guardian of the underlying values and standards of taste for the society.

The crucial fact about the mass media—magazines, newspapers, radio, television—is that they are dominated by advertising; this for the simple reason that advertising pays the bills. With respect to radio and television, the only contribution of the consumer is the price of his receiver. In the case of magazines and newspapers, in many cases, "the real situation is that the advertiser buys the magazine for the 'purchaser,' and what the purchaser pays as the 'price' of the magazine is really only a kind of qualifying fee to prove that he is a bona fide potential consumer and not a mere deadhead on whom this handsome advertising spread would be wasted."[13]

It is the hold of advertising on the mass media that gives the latter their distinctive character, and advertising is perhaps the most distinctive institution of the mass society. We are talking here of advertising in its modern form as a device for stimulating consumption and the desire to consume, not as mere information-giving. It is in this sense that advertising is not only an institution, but one of those few crucial institutions that serves as "instruments of social control."[14]

Society controls individual behavior primarily through those central institutions which define the individual in a distinctive way and induce him to conceive of himself in the same way. Historically, the Church, the democratic political system, and *laissez-faire* capitalism, for example, offered models of man as a creature of God, as a rational participant in political life and as an independent producer. Advertising conceives man as consumer and encourages him to so conceive himself. The model of man as consumer demands that he have no set standards of taste and judgment. Participation in the consumption of standardized, mass-produced goods and services requires that individual tastes and values be fluid and manipulable. It is, therefore, the enemy of those older institutions that encouraged men to cling to traditional values or consciously to formulate their own standards. Advertising "has joined the charmed circle of institutions which fix the values and standards of society," but "it has done this without being linked to any of the socially defined objectives which usually guide such institutions in the use of their power."[15]

The effect of advertising in the mass society is strengthened by the fact that the media it largely controls are addressed to mass audiences. This means that the basic fact about the media is that "they are concerned not with finding an audience to hear their message but rather with finding a message to hold their audience." The result is an effort not to antagonize anyone (anything either controversial or unpleasant is to be avoided) or to leave anyone out (so, also, are subjects of special interest and treatment of any subject at higher levels of maturity or subtlety than can

---

[13]David M. Potter, *People of Plenty* (Chicago: University of Chicago Press, 1954), p. 180

[14]*Ibid.*, pp. 176 ff

[15]*Ibid.*, p. 177

be handled easily by the mass audience.) In view of the importance of the mass media as a vehicle of political debate, the political consequences of these developments are obvious.

By 1951, the total outlay for advertising in the United States had reached $6,548,000,000 ($199 per year per family) and exceeded the total spent on primary and secondary education ($152 per family, in 1949). In short, society spends more of its resources on the manipulation of its members as consumers than it does on their education as citizens.[16] Meanwhile, social adjustment and the consumer orientation to life have influenced the curriculum of the schools themselves. It should not be surprising if increasing numbers of people come to regard the purchase of a new automobile as a more important decision than the election of a President.

Social Changes: The Growth of Anomy

What makes it possible to speak of the mass society and the mass media is the evolution of the mass man. The mass man is the undifferentiated man who has lost those distinguishing characteristics that were provided by the liberal goal of the autonomous individual or, in the conservative view, by the formative influence and emotional ties of family, town, class, religious, occupational, professional, and social allegiances. The mass man is socially isolated and rootless; his is the face in the "lonely crowd." The term used by sociologists to describe this phenomenon of rootlessness—of the loss of deeply emotional social and ideological ties— is "anomy."

Anomy in modern society means that man is more mobile, both geographically and socially, than perhaps men have ever been before. But his very mobility, while it increases the frequency of his contacts with others, decreases their intensity and their meaning. The leveling process seems to result in a breakdown of distinctive class-oriented styles of life; men seem to slide, from one direction or another, into middle-class respectability.

The mass man is rootless in the sense of lacking membership in groups which give meaning to life by providing common purposes and values, shared emotional meanings, and relatively fixed patterns of status and role for the individual. These, the conservative reminds us, are a source of individual self-identity and self-esteem. At the same time, the mass man lacks roots in the sense of having lost the capacity to believe in the existence of an objective moral order that transcends both individual desires and cultural traditions. For the moral absolutes of the past, the mass man substitutes morale; for the quest for truth and justice, he substitutes the

[16]*Ibid.*, p. 178

quest for harmony. Having abandoned fixed standards of taste and preference, he is willing prey to constantly changing mass styles and fashions.

One critic provides a telling illustration of how these pressures affect traditional occasions and even the very young:

> The coming of Valentine's Day no longer means that the boy brings, shyly or boldly, to some girl he has mooned over all year a lacy heart and a declaration of love; but that every kid under pressure brings every other kid in his entire class some machine-produced greeting remembered the day before at the Five-and-Ten.[17]

Socially, intellectually and spiritually, the mass man is radically isolated. Yet his isolation—his freedom from the emotional and moral ties of genuine community—does not make him an autonomous individual. He does not fill the void created by the weakening of deep social ties with a sense of self-identity and purpose developed out of his own reflection. He does not substitute his own standards and values for those of tradition, habit, and social prejudice. Lacking a sense of purpose and moral standards of his own, he seeks to conform to constantly changing group expectations. He is manipulatable, and does not really mind being manipulated. Faced with the possibility of making his own choices, he avoids those situations in which choices must be made; he seeks to "escape from freedom" into the anonymity of the crowd. He is, in short, not the type of man that fits either the conservative or the liberal image of the free society.

The anomy that characterizes life in a mass society is related to changes in the basic institutions of character formation. There is wide agreement among anthropologists, sociologists, and social psychologists that the early years of childhood and the child-rearing practices of every society are crucial to the process of forming adult character traits. A review of the changes in childhood experience which are related to the growth of mass society is beyond our purpose here. Very generally, however, it is relevant to notice that the primary instruments of socialization in the past—the family, the Church, and the school—are generally believed to have declined in their influence over the development of the child. At the same time, the mass media (particularly television) and association with other children of the same age (peer groups) have come to play an enlarged role in the shaping of character. The effect is that those forms of direct adult control, and particularly parental control, by which traditional values were imparted to a new generation have been attenuated. At the same time, the newer influences of the mass media and

[17]Leslie A. Fielder, "Voting and Voting Studies," in Eugene Burdick and Arthur Brodbeck (eds.), *American Voting Behavior* (New York: The Free Press of Glencoe, 1959), p. 196.

the transitory and relatively superficial relations within peer groups operate to reinforce the characteristics of the other-directed, plastic, consumption-oriented, socially adaptive, and conforming mass man.

We need to recognize that the picture we have sketched of the mass man cannot be offered as an accurate or adequate portrait of American society. As Muller says, following his description which we quoted earlier:

> Yet he is much more than this, else he would never have got where he has. The "mass-man" is also a bogey—a monstrous abstraction that conceals the infinite varieties of common men, in interest, ability, character, and aspiration. It conceals all the degrees in culture, the frequent lustiness of the low-brow, the earnestness of the middle-brow. In particular it conceals the idealism that underlies the obvious materialism. This expresses itself in such commonplace sentiments as that every man ought to have a fair chance—a very novel commonplace, in the light of history. In times of crisis it has enabled such loyalty, fortitude, and unpretentious heroism as won the Battle for Britain. At all times it inspires an enthusiasm for vast cooperative enterprises, kindles the energy and imagination that have made the kingdom of common men the most adventurous in history. "An idealist working on matter" Santayana has called the American; and his fine enthusiasm might be touched to finer issues. Meanwhile it is again an inhuman spirituality that cannot see idealism in the effort to eliminate the poverty and wretchedness once accepted as the will of God, and to enable all men to enjoy the material well-being once enjoyed only by a privileged few—by aristocrats who could afford to exalt noneconomic interests and values because they took for granted their wealth and luxury, and seldom had to earn it.[18]

Professor Muller's assertion that mass man is a "monstrous abstraction" points out the fact that there may be more to actual common men than is contained in the philosophies of those who would manipulate him. The validity of the mechanistic view of man is open to question, and the effectiveness of the techniques of engineering consent is not yet clear. Politicians, however, have tended to assume their effectiveness. Consequently, much of the character of American politics is determined by their use which, in turn, reinforces belief in the validity of the mechanistic assumptions on which they are based.

We are interested in the impact of these tendencies on political techniques and processes and on our ideas about the meaning of democracy. In a broad sense, all the following chapters will be centrally concerned with the impact of mass society on American politics. In the remainder of

[18]Muller, *The Uses of the Past*, pp. 232-33.

the present chapter, we attempt a very broad and sketchy overview of the major political tendencies of what we may term a "mass democracy."

THE POLITICS OF MASS DEMOCRACY: A SUMMARY

IT SHOULD BE ALMOST IMMEDIATELY APPARENT that the tendencies toward mass society undermine both of the traditional American solutions to the problems of democracy. Insofar as these tendencies are in fact operative we would expect them to produce political consequenecs incompatible with either the liberal or the conservative models of democracy. These consequences may be seen more clearly by examining the actors in the American political drama—citizens, politicians, political parties, and pressure groups—and the changes in their roles which the forces of mass society might be expected to produce. We will then be in a position to sketch out the general characteristics of political campaigns and elections and the legislative, decision-making processes in a mass democracy.

The Mass Man as Citizen

Recent research into the political behavior of American citizens suggests that political apathy has been increasing along with the emergence of nonpartisan attitudes toward the political process. What this means is not simply that there has been a long range decline in voting, but also in such forms of participation in politics as the discussion of political issues, active participation in campaigns, and communication with elected officials. It also implies that, along with increased apathy and indifference, political participation has been less party- and issue-oriented, less concerned with controversial questions of public policy.

These phenomena are by-products of the tendencies we have been describing. Partisanship is not an effective device for "winning friends and influencing people." Most of us have heard the statement: "Two things I don't talk about are religion and politics." Steering clear of these two areas is a way of avoiding controversy in a situation in which controversy is likely to be offensive to one's more bland and conforming friends or to prejudice one's chances of being popular and getting ahead in the bureaucratic heirarchy. The easiest solution is not to have any convictions about public issues.

While apathy about controversial issues can be cloaked in the garb of nonpartisanship and independence, these are not a defense against pressures on people to vote, at least in the final elections. As real apathy has increased, the problem has been met by the typical mass technique of an organized public relations program to identify voting with the "American way of life." The effort to engineer a large voting turnout by mass advertising appeal is not likely, even if successful, to make voting more significant or to reduce the underlying causes of apathy. Large numbers of people trooping to the polls without any conception of the issues at stake are likely only to reinforce the harmony, "just-folksiness" and middle-of-the-roadness of mass democracy. These are likely to be the voters who will be influenced by the endorsement of a movie star or baseball hero and most susceptible to the smiling charm of a politics of personality.

The mass-man's retreat from politics is not likely, however, to be complete. He may, as we indicated earlier, be attracted to the role of "inside-dopester," and the personality aspects of rival politicians may arouse his interest. But his retreat from the public world of politics is likely at the same time to be a retreat into the private world of consumption. Therefore, he may see politics as a vehicle for the satisfaction of his private desires. And probably he will see politicians as messenger boys to be evaluated by their success in securing and advancing his private claims. Public goals will diminish in importance, and the taxation necessary to finance them is likely to appear as an onerous burden.

The Mass Man as Politician

The politician in a mass democracy is likely to be convinced that incumbency is all. The role most likely to win him office is that of representing the interests of his constituency rather than positions on the issues in the broader community. Where his constituents' interests are in conflict, he will play the role of neutral broker, seeking to work out compromise arrangements satisfactory to all. In the legislative arena, he will be an astute horse trader in behalf of his constituents' interests.

His public face will be cast in the image constructed for him by the professional public relations firm he has retained to guide his campaigns. If he has any strong convictions on public issues, he will publicly play them down. The cardinal rule will be inoffensiveness: never say anything that might alienate any significant group of voters. His stance will be in the middle of the road; his byword, "moderation"; all in all, he is the "ideological missing man."

Parties and Pressure Groups in Mass Democracy

We have seen how, in both liberal and conservative theory, the political party was viewed as a central institution in achieving responsible government. In the liberal democratic model that underlay American political practice it was the function of the parties to organize political debate and policy making around alternative views of the public interest. This was viewed as necessary if government was to be held responsible to the citizen at election time. It assumed that the parties stood above the interest groups, screening their demands through party principles.

In the politics of mass society, interest groups become stronger than political parties. Parties become, in effect, loose coalitions of interest groups. Since both parties seek, above all, to win elections each seeks to put together a package that will appeal to all organized groups. The differences between the parties are thereby minimized, reflecting only differences in judgment about what combination will be a winning one. The resulting bargains will shape the platforms of the parties and result in support of particular candidates. Parties, in short, seldom operate to organize the debate of public policy alternatives. They no longer stand above group interests; they serve, rather, as clearinghouses and brokers for the interests.

The Electoral Process in Mass Democracy

In a fully developed mass democracy, candidates and parties would go to the public on the basis of bargains struck among interest groups. Campaign appeals would not be based on rival principles or policies; elections would tend, therefore, to be personality contests with candidates packaged and merchandised by professional experts in public relations. The campaign and the electoral process would be exercises in mass manipulation of the electorate, planned by consent engineers.

What makes the impact of mass society on elections alarming is the new light in which electoral processes have been put by the rise of modern totalitarian regimes. It used to be commonly assumed that the act of voting was a primary, perhaps even the most important, test of whether a government is democratic. The rise of modern totalitarianism shattered this easy assumption. Beginning in the 1930's, in fascist, nazi, and communist regimes, voters began to troop to the polls in large numbers (often over 90 per cent). Nor is it enough to argue that they do so under compulsion. Apparently, they vote often with enthusiasm and feeling. The question we have now to face is, what is the significance of the voting act? What criteria must be met before the act of voting can be held to have genuinely democratic significance?

One solution commonly offered for this question is the simple distinction between a totalitarian vote cast for or against a single candidate or slate and the democratic provision of options or choices between two or more candidates or parties. But does this distinction carry us far enough? What is the significance of the vote in a totalitarian society? What does it mean to the millions of voters who cast their ballots for the single slate of candidates? The best answer seems to be that voting in a totalitarian society is primarily a social and psychological, rather than a political, act. It seems primarily to be a way of securing the psychological comfort of conformity, of expressing one's solidarity with the nation, one's integration into the basic values of the society, one's emotional oneness and belongingness in the total community.

A *political* act, as that term is used here, is distinguished by the fact that it is part of a procedure for settling differences and for allocating power, prestige, and influence. In this sense, only the ruling elite in a totalitarian society performs political acts; the remainder of society performs the social acts which sanctify, legitimatize, and bind the political decisions of the elite. It would seem to be crucial to the idea of democracy, at least in its historical meaning, that the civic roles of citizens should have political, as distinct from social, meaning and that the act of voting should be a political act. The existence of two or more candidates or parties in no way insures that the citizen is a participant in political decisions, as we have defined that word. Voting, even in a nominally two party politics, may be an act that has primarily social rather than political significance.

Whether the vote is a political act will clearly depend on the extent to which the options, provided for the citizen at the polls, offer the possibility of genuine choice between alternative principles, programs, and policies. Unless they do—if, for example, political competition for the vote is personality-oriented rather than issue-oriented—then the voter's choice will at best reflect his preferences for such personal qualities as sincerity, friendliness, amiability, leadership, grooming, and charm. It will not reflect his judgment about what policies are in the public interest or how the competing claims to increased wealth, status, prestige, and power in society are to be weighed and accommodated. A nominally and formally competitive political system, under the conditions of mass society, may serve to conceal the fact that citizens are participating socially in the legitimatizing of decisions rather than politically in the making of them.

The Decision-Making Process in Mass Democracy

After the election, the same process that shaped the party platforms and the positions of the candidates would operate to shape policy in the legislature, the administrative agencies, and the courts. The basic process is, of course, the bargaining and compromise of rival interests. The basic rule of the game is that no important interest may be adversely affected without its consent.

Under these conditions, the majority that puts candidates and parties into office determines only *who* the official policy makers will be; it does not determine *what* policies will be implemented. These will be the result of group bargaining and compromise. As A. Lawrence Lowell, a political scientist and president of Harvard University, foresaw in 1913, a mass democracy means an "age of brokers" and an "age of advertisement."[19] "Brokerage" describes the process of resolving the conflict of interests in mass democracy; "advertisement" describes the techniques of organizing and engineering consent in the electoral process.

There is disagreement about how closely this description of the politics of mass democracy fits the facts or describes the tendencies of the actual workings of the American political system. Certainly as a factual description, this picture is greatly overdrawn—how greatly may be judged better in the light of subsequent chapters. But as a model which clarifies the direction in which recent tendencies are leading us, it may provide us with a perspective necessary both to understand and to evaluate the present condition of our political system.

Just as there is disagreement over how far along the road to the politics of mass democracy we have traveled, so also is there disagreement on whether we should relax and enjoy the journey and anticipate the destination. The tendencies of mass democracy are attacked by traditional liberals and conservatives alike, although for different reasons. But they are defended equally sincerely by the proponents of a relatively new theory of democracy. This new model, as might be expected, gives less place to enlightened and rational citizens or to tradition; it gives none at all to a public interest. It finds in group interests the basic data of politics. And it makes the compromising and balancing of group claims the uniquely democratic solution to the problem of politics. Both the fact that it is already widely held, and the fact that it claims to justify some of the major tendencies of modern political life, entitle it to serious and systematic consideration. It is to this model of democracy as minorities rule that we now turn.

[19]Lowell, *Public Opinion and Popular Government*, pp. 58-61.

6

DEMOCRACY
AS MINORITIES RULE

MANY OF THE CHARACTERISTICS of mass democracy described in the last chapter have always existed in the United States. Politics in American democracy has always involved a considerable amount of "brokerage": parties have always tended, among other things, to accommodate the interests and claims of rival social and economic interests; the party platforms have reflected the political horsepower of organized groups; some politicians have tended to define their role as political brokers. The practices we have been describing are not new. What is new is the tendency for American politics to become nothing but the brokerage of minority interests. This could only happen when the process of minorities rule had been developed into a theory of democracy, for otherwise the accommodating of competing interests was bound to occur within a framework in which the pursuit of a public interest was regarded as the norm of the democratic process. The unfettered conflict of minority interests can only occur where democracy is itself defined as the process of compromise.

149

Only after World War I did such a theory come to be advanced by political theorists, and only in the period since World War II has it come to be widely accepted.

CALHOUN AND THE CONCURRENT MAJORITY

To UNDERSTAND why this came to be so, we need to examine briefly the political philosophy of John C. Calhoun, for he was the first to develop a systematic justification of the theory of brokerage politics which, in the twentieth century, has become the model which actual American politics most nearly approximates. Long-time Senator and for one term Vice-President of the United States, Calhoun was another in the long line of politician-philosophers so prominent and distinctive in the American tradition (and, perhaps, destined to be one of the casualties in the growth of mass democracy). Calhoun was writing to defend the institution of slavery in the South from the growing abolitionist sentiment in the North. As T. V. Smith says, it was his peculiar lot "while losing his cause to win his case," for although slavery was doomed, the political theory he devised to protect it has become the orthodox defense of current American political institutions.

Calhoun focused his attack on the constitutional system of checks and balances. The members of the Convention of 1787 were right, he agreed, about the necessity for constitutional checks on majorities, but the system they had erected failed to work because they did not take into account the dynamic nature of interest groups in society and the development of political conflict along sectional lines. He saw, moreover, that the rise of party machinery made the constitutional equilibrium ineffective. A political party, organized for example on the principle of equality and therefore opposed to slavery, if it could become a national majority, would be able to control the Congress, the Presidency, and finally the Court. It would, then, be able to force its views on the recalcitrant minority. The numerical strength that could be mustered by northern industrial and commercial interests would lead to control over the various branches of government and would mean public policy on tariffs, internal improvements, and fugitive slave laws inimical to the agrarian and slave-holding interests of the South.

Why would the rule of a northern majority in these circumstances be wrong? Calhoun's answer was that majority rule is always, in its very nature, tyranny over the minority. We need to see what assumptions were necessary to support this conclusion, for it is a basic postulate of brokerage rule.

Men, Calhoun asserted, are basically social animals in the sense that they require to live in society for the fulfillment of their natural needs and desires. At the same time, man is basically antisocial in the sense that he "is so constituted, that his direct or individual affections are stronger than his sympathetic or social feelings."[1] The essential egoism of human nature leads necessarily to "the tendency to a universal state of conflict, between individual and individual; accompanied by the connected passions of suspicion, jealousy, anger and revenge. . . ."[2] Government, in these circumstances, is the only agency which can avert the "state of universal discord and confusion" which would otherwise result. But government must be administered by men who are equally self-interested and hence can always be used by some men to enforce their wills on others.

Society, accordingly, comes to be composed of groups of men organized to promote their own basically economic interests as against the selfish interests of other men; politics is to be inclusively defined as a struggle for power. Moreover, the interests of the groups involved in this struggle are rationally and morally incommensurable—that is, there is no way for men to judge objectively or impartially between their respective claims on society; they cannot be weighed or evaluated against each other. For, if any man or group of men is allowed to judge, he must simply prefer his own interest against others. He will, to be sure, dress up his decision in the language of moral justification, but this must be recognized for the rationalization it is bound to be.

In Calhoun's view, there are no abstract standards of the public interest or justice which men, whether a majority or a minority, can be relied on to discover or apply. For when men's desires and interests are at stake, one man's opinions are as good as another's, one man's interests as legitimate as any other's. Human values, in short, are rationalizations of interests and desires. They are, from any rational point of view, simply incommensurable. All interests, and accordingly all competing social groups, must be taken to have been born equal.

On these assumptions, it necessarily follows that majority rule—and, of course, minority rule as well—is sheer coercion. The noncoercive use of the powers of government requires the equal treatment of all organized groups. Equality of treatment cannot be guaranteed through a static equilibrium established in a constitution, nor through reliance on Madison's "representatives whose enlightened views and virtuous sentiments render them superior to local prejudices and to schemes of injustice." No static balance is possible because there is no way of determining objectively

---

[1] John C. Calhoun, "A Disquisition on Government," in *The Works of John C. Calhoun*, Richard K. Cralle, ed. (New York: Appleton-Century-Crofts, 1954), Vol. I, p. 3.

[2] *Ibid.*, p. 4.

when the conflicting forces are in equilibrium; this is a judgment that would have to be made by men, and like all human judgments it will inevitably express self-interest. The only alternative to force in government, Calhoun concluded, is the process of securing the universal assent of all rival interests to every proposed public policy—that is, the process of compromise. A genuinely constitutional government, one that would control the human propensity to use others for one's own purposes, must insure that compromise is the only basis for resolving disputes.

It should be obvious that Calhoun was making a direct frontal assault on both the liberal and the conservative positions. The nature of this attack is clarified if we put the issue in the familiar language of faction. Calhoun attacked the idea that factions are undesirable but, given the nature of man, inevitable—an assumption shared by liberals and conservatives alike. For Calhoun they were simply inevitable, and they exhausted the stuff of politics. In his view, it is meaningless to conceive a government which regulates interest groups in some conception of a public interest. The only real alternative to tyranny, he concluded, was so to structure a government that all public policies would reflect compromises voluntarily agreed to by the factions themselves.

Applying this theory to the sectional conflict of his own day, Calhoun worked out the principle of the "concurrent majority." What he proposed was a constitutional revision which would provide dual instruments of government in the North and the South, including a President in each, and which would insure that no national policy could be adopted without the assent of each. The way to accomplish this was obviously to give each of the rival interests an absolute veto on any proposal made by the other. The result would be to force the conflicting sections to compromises in which there would be mutual sacrifice. The rival parties, he argued somewhat lamely, would be motivated to compromise because the alternative—stalemate or war—means anarchy, which all men recognize as the worst of all possible evils.

Calhoun's argument for the application of this theory to the settlement of the issue of slavery never got a very serious hearing. But his argument is much broader than that issue. What he presented was a radically different model of democratic politics, one in which the pursuit of truth and public morality no longer was regarded even as a possible goal of political life. It made factional strife the exclusive reality of politics and argued that the only problem was to keep any interest from winning. Its basic operational principle was that every organized group should have a constitutionally protected absolute right of veto over any proposed legislation.

Calhoun's argument follows logically from his premises. If it is true that (1) men are universally dominated by self interest, and in particular by their economic interests; (2) politics may be inclusively described as a struggle for power among competing interest groups; and (3) all social values are subjective and simply relative to one another, then it follows necessarily that neither the traditional conservative nor the liberal solutions to the problem of controlling political power is valid. The conservative faith in a static constitutional equilibrium or in the stewardship of a responsible elite will break down, as men who represent the majority point of view come into control of the several branches of government. The liberal ideal of the electorate as a body of reasonable men to whom reasoned appeals are made was from the beginning a visionary, unrealistic dream, the consequences of which are pure coercion in the form of majority tyranny. On his assumptions, the conclusion he drew is logically inescapable; the only possible alternatives in government are coercion or compromise. In Calhoun's words, "Force is the conservative principle of absolute and compromise of constitutional governments. . . ."[3] The necessary conclusion is that democratic government means government by compromise as a basic political principle.

CONCURRENT MAJORITY
IN THE AMERICAN TRADITION

THE IRONY of Calhoun's role in American history is that, even in its larger meaning, his theory of democracy as compromise had few takers and remained largely outside the framework of American political theory for at least another seventy or eighty years. His reputation as a political theorist and his theory itself have been revived only in the last thirty years or so, when the discovery was made that a theory devised to support the position of the South before the Civil War provided the theoretical justification for the actual system of politics that had gradually come to prevail in American life! Of course, the origin of the theory, or Calhoun's intentions when he developed it, is completely irrelevant to its validity and adequacy. But we are faced with the interesting question of how the principle of concurrent majorities (more accurately, in multigroup society, a system of rule of concurrent minorities) and government by compromise (the modern term is "broker rule"), rejected or ignored when first proposed, came to be the dominating feature of our political system.

What makes Calhoun's role doubly ironic is that the very institutions of checks and balances which he condemned as inadequate to guard against majority rule came to work largely in the way he thought desirable. Without the constitutional guarantee of the right of interest-group veto,

[3] *Ibid.*, p. 39.

154 / THE CONSENT OF THE GOVERNED

which he regarded as necessary, how did these groups come to have something like the very veto power that he urged? One thing seems clear: the constitutional system of checks and balances was never really incompatible with the rule of compromise, as he imagined it was. The Constitution had arranged the instruments of government so as to delay the translation of majority opinion into law and make majority rule difficult. But it did not make it impossible, as the Jeffersonians and Jacksonians demonstrated. At the same time, and for the same reasons, the constitutional provisions made a system of minorities rule equally possible where conditions, like those of mass society, inclined men in that direction. As many close observers have pointed out, the system of separation of powers and checks and balances tends to make it easier to block governmental action than to advance it. "The result, of course, is that not only have interest groups flourished in such constitutional soil, but they have developed chiefly along the lines of thwarting governmental action."[4] Thus interest groups have tended to become, in Riesman's phrase, "veto groups" very much like those required in Calhoun's theory.

The major obstacle to the success of the theory of democracy as a compromise of interests was the then still-dominant liberal faith that the end of government is justice and the public good. Men were held to be capable of enough rationality and selflessness to pursue these objectives through reasoned argument and discussion. And private interests were to be evaluated in the light of the majority's reasoned view of a public interest. Calhoun's theory was unimpressive and unpersuasive in the America of his day because it involved the view that "morality was absent from politics or that it might come about automatically" through the mutual accommodation of conflicting interests.[5] The philosophical premises of the America of abolitionism, the Transcendentalist movement, the Chautauqua circuit, and the Lincoln-Douglas debates were fundamentally opposed to the egoism, power, and moral relativism of the theory of compromise.

By 1913, the assumptions of American political life had changed so much that, as we have seen, Lowell could describe the underlying political

[4]Robert E. Lane, "Political Character and Political Analysis," in Heinz Eulau, Samuel J. Eldersveld, and Morris Janowitz (eds.), *Political Behavior* (New York: Free Press of Glencoe, 1956), p. 120.
[5]Alfred De Grazia, *Public and Republic* (New York: Knopf, 1951), p. 248. De Grazia concludes his comment with, "even though everyday politics affirmed the idea as a working principle." But it is not clear whether "everyday politics" affirmed that "morality was absent from politics" or that morality "came about automatically" from the clash of private interests. It makes a difference, and the second possibility sounds more like a kind of magic than something that "everyday politics" could "affirm."

climate as the "Age of Advertisement" and the "Age of Brokers." Lowell saw in "the same conditions that have caused the great development of advertising, where the mass of the public must be reached," the factors that produced the political broker "in the class of transactions which affect a smaller class of persons."[6]

Lowell recognized the inevitability of a considerable amount of brokerage in a pluralistic society: ". . . the mincing of political power into very small morsels," he argued, following Sir Henry Maine, "naturally makes the wire puller the leader."[7] The function of the broker is "as needful for political as for commercial life, as proper and as honorable." But there are grave dangers:

> The really serious evil comes when the brokerage is not confined to formulating public opinion, but degenerates into a traffic in public measures without regard to any public opinion on the measures themselves, or into a traffic in private legislation and in appointments to public office. It is these last things that have brought politics in America into discredit.[8]

Lowell was among the first analysts of American politics to see clearly its modern characteristics of mass manipulative appeal and the brokerage of interests. He also saw these developments as threats to the organized politics of issues and the leadership of public opinion on issues which he thought to be necessary to democracy. This reveals clearly the extent to which the development of a system of minorities rule occurred gradually and without conscious intent; the theory was developed to justify it after the fact.

THE MODERN THEORY OF MINORITIES RULE

THE THEORY of broker rule in its modern form dates from Arthur Bentley's *The Process of Government*, published first in 1908.[9] Bentley's work, even though it brings Calhoun up to date by couching the argument in the language of scientific method and value relativism, actually had little impact when it was published. In more recent years, both Calhoun and Bentley have been rediscovered, and a host of writers have clarified and developed the argument that identifies the brokerage of interests with the process of democratic decision-making. The major assumptions

---

[6]Lowell, *Public Opinion and Popular Government*, p. 60.
[7]*Ibid.*, p. 62.
[8]*Ibid.*, p. 64.
[9]A later edition is: Arthur F. Bentley, *The Process of Government* (Bloomington, Ind.: Principia Press, 1949).

and arguments in this theory include the following: (1) Politics is a struggle for power. (2) The elements in this struggle in a democracy are organized interest groups. (3) The stability of democratic politics requires overlapping membership in groups and the selection of legislators, administrators, and judges who will define their roles as mediators of group compromise. (4) Democracy cannot operate under other than brokerage techniques. These elements of the brokerage model are examined briefly below.

Politics as Power

To the theorist of compromise, the scientific study of politics must confine itself to the study of power relationships. Underlying this assertion is the positivistic assumption that values are psychological data, the primary purpose of which is to cloak interests, needs, and desires which are rationally incommensurable. From this point of view, it is a mistake to believe that political values or principles play any real causal role in politics. As Bentley put it, "It is the power of the underlying interests which pump all the logic into theory that theory ever obtains." The devastating effect of this proposition on the traditional liberal model is obvious. The trouble with the liberal view of democracy was that, in it, "the political community had some of the characteristics of an Oxford debating society, policy emerging from endless argument, with reason presiding in the speaker's chair."[10]

According to the theory we are considering, this is a hopelessly utopian dream, even as an ideal, because it rests on a mistaken view of the nature of politics. It makes any understanding of the actual political processes of democracy impossible. A legislature, for example, can never be understood as long as it "is taken for what it purports to be—a body of men who deliberate upon and adopt laws." In order to discover where "the real law-creating work is done" it is necessary to trace any policy from "its efficient demand [by an interest group or groups] to its actual application." When this is done it will always turn out that the legislature was not "Moses the law-giver" but "merely Moses the registration clerk."[11] If the legislature fails accurately to reflect the balance of power in the political arena, the function will be taken over by the President or the courts; hence, the fluctuation over time in their respective influence.

For the same reasons, the traditional liberal concern for the pursuit of the public interest becomes meaningless where the struggle for power is

[10]Earl Latham, *The Group Basis of Politics* (Ithaca: Cornell University Press, 1952), p. 6.
[11]Bentley, *The Process of Government*, p. 163.

held to be the only political reality. If empirical realities are the only realities, "the existence of an interest of the nation as a whole" could only be proved by showing that it describes a condition of political fact—that is, a condition in which there is unanimity among all the special interests. It cannot "describe any actual or possible political situation within a complex nation." Accordingly, the "public interest" can never be more than "a tremendously useful promotional device."[12]

Similarly, the assumption that politics can be described only as a power struggle rules out the conservative's contention that "higher law," tradition, a settled social system of status and role, or a responsible elite can safeguard the civilized values which alone can make power responsible. Just as was the case with Calhoun, if values and ideals are assumed merely to reflect power aspirations, the problem of democracy appears in a new light: majority rule is tyranny; so also is the influence of a governing class, however responsible.

The Group Basis of Politics

Brokerage theory assumes that interest groups are the basic elements in the political system. An interest group has been defined by one exponent of the theory as "any group that, on the basis of one or more shared attitudes, makes certain claims upon other groups in the society for the establishment, maintenance, or enhancement of forms of behavior that are implied by the shared attitudes."[13] It is true, of course, that organized interests—groups characterized by interaction and organized to exert pressure on centers of decision-making—tend to proliferate in a pluralistic, free society. No one denies this. It is what Paul Appleby meant when he said that "noses count in politics but noises do too. Big noises count extra." But what group theory asserts is that politics is nothing but the struggle of interest groups: "The only opinion, the only will, which exists is the opinion, the will, of special groups."[14] From this perspective, political society is seen only as a process of group competition for power.

As we have noted, American politics in the twentieth century seems to fit the model of group rivalry and compromise rather well. To understand the significance of this fact we need to get a clearer view of what group theory implies and what other approaches to politics it excludes. It denies, in the first place, that the ballot box can be the primary means by which sovereign, choice-making individuals hold the exercise of

[12]Latham, *The Group Basis of Politics*, pp. 50-51.
[13]David Truman, *The Governmental Process* (New York: Knopf, 1951), p. 33.
[14]John Dickinson, "Democratic Realities and Democratic Dogmas," *American Political Science Review*, May, 1930, p. 291.

governmental power responsible. The proponents of group theory assert that it "does not lose sight of the individual," since groups may be seen as existing to fulfill the desires, wants, and values of the individual.[15] But it does see the group as both the source of individual attitudes and the channel through which they are given political effect. It sees government as *responding* to the desires of individuals by reflecting the competing demands of interest groups, rather than as *responsible* to the individual's convictions about public issues.

Secondly, group theory denies that the political process can be meaningfully conceived in terms of majority and minority opinion on public issues. It holds that "we cannot correctly describe the actual operations of democratic societies in terms of the contrasts between majorities and minorities. We can only distinguish groups of various types and sizes, all seeking in various ways to advance their goals, usually at the expense, at least in part, of others."[16] In the light of this analysis of democratic politics as group struggle, the concept of majority rule is a myth, a part of the folklore, which can never in fact be reflected in political reality. Public policies must be seen as the resultant of the competition and compromise of private interests. As a leading spokesman for the theory puts it:

> The legislative vote on any issue tends to represent the composition of strength, *i.e.*, the balance of power, among the contending groups at the moment of voting. What may be called public policy is the equilibrium reached in this struggle at any given moment, and it represents a balance which the contending factions or groups constantly try to weight in their favor.[17]

The legislature serves as "referee" in the group struggle, "ratifies the victories of the successful coalitions, and records the terms of the surrenders, compromises, and conquests in the form of statutes."[18] Insofar as the legislature does more than umpire the game and serve as a cash register, it is not because the parties organize a debate of the public interest which the majority translates into policy. It is rather that legislatures are groups themselves and "show a sense of identity and consciousness of kind that unofficial groups must regard if they are to represent their members effectively."[19]

In the third place, not only is group theory incompatible with the

---

[15]Latham, *The Group Basis of Politics*, p. 54.

[16]Robert A. Dahl, *A Preface to Democratic Theory* (Chicago: University of Chicago Press, 1956), p. 131.

[17]Latham, *The Group Basis of Politics*, p. 36.

[18]*Ibid.*, p. 35.

[19]*Ibid.*, p. 37.

traditional liberal faith in the autonomous individual and public debate of the public interest. It is similarly opposed to the conservative assumption that the struggle for power is to be controlled and moderated by a responsible aristocracy or by social norms and values internalized in individuals through the process of socialization and hallowed by tradition. Particularly, in its emphasis on the utilitarian, economic character of the interests of dominant groups, the theory denies that the consensus in society on intangible but fundamental values is a significant political variable, as the conservative insists it must be. For group theory, the most significant political attribute of human beings is a conscious or unconscious need to "belong." It is this need which leads individuals to adjust to changing group norms and to surrender their political destinies to the process of compromising group interests. Here, as elsewhere, the model of minorities rule is a rationalization of the politics of mass society.

Group Conflict and Stable Equilibrium

Where interest groups have free access to centers of decision-making, where interests tend to be economic rather than ideological and doctrinaire, and where all interests respect the rules of the game, the result is presumed to be a condition of equilibrium. This condition among competing interests is held, in the group theory of politics, to constitute justice in democratic societies. The whole system of group equilibrium will be a stable one only if all the important groups in society accept the basic rule of compromise and refrain from doing serious violence to the interests of other groups.

What makes a stable equilibrium possible is the fact that "no single group affiliation accounts for all of the attitudes or interests of any individual except a fanatic or a compulsive neurotic."[20] Individuals belong to many groups with the result that group membership is overlapping. The fact of overlapping membership guarantees that no group can command the total loyalty of its members and that, therefore, its demands on other groups will be less drastic and its leaders more amenable to compromise. If the leadership of any group seeks to go too far, its members who may also belong to other groups that would be hurt thereby will balk and curb its ambitions. An individual may even belong to directly opposed groups, "as when a man who belongs to a local improvement association that is demanding the repaving of a neighborhood street is also a member of a taxpayer's group that is opposing an appropriation for this purpose."[21] It is this condition of overlapping and contradictory memberships which insures that the rules of the game are respected, that each group will be neither:

[20]Truman, *The Governmental Process,* p. 508.
[21]*Ibid.,* p. 157.

... intransigent or doctrinaire. It must make every conceivable effort to compromise, relying on its veto only as a last resort. For if any player wields this weapon recklessly, the game will break up— or all the other players will turn on him in anger, suspend the rules for the time being, and maul those very interests he is trying so desperately to protect.[22]

In some cases, group theorists admit, "overlapping membership" may not always be extensive enough to "obviate the possibility of irreconcilable conflict"—in the case of labor unions and the National Association of Manufacturers, for example.[23] Where eighteenth-century theorists might have embarked on a search for what Madison called "auxiliary precautions," modern behavioral science claims to discover them in empirical reality. Where overlapping membership is inadequate, the "relative stability" of the American political system is to be explained by "the second crucial element . . ., the concept of the unorganized interest or potential interest group."[24] An "unorganized interest" refers to people with shared attitudes and expectations who are not yet organized to make demands on other groups. The claim is that organized interests, recognizing the possible serious disturbances to the system which might result "if these submerged, potential interests should organize," provide "some recognition of the existence of these interests" and give "them at least a minimum of influence." For similar reasons, such groups as churches, which are not organized to exert political pressure, will still wield political influence because the politically powerful groups recognize and respond to their potential political mobilization.

Potential groups are also held to be a balance wheel which operates to protect and enforce that unorganized interest which a majority has in maintaining the basic values of the society. Thus, majority attitudes are reflected in politics, in spite of the fact that they are not organized through political parties. Attacks by any group on these widely held but largely unorganized interests will be checked by existing organized groups or by new ones born as a result of the attacks.

Proponents of brokerage democracy often cite the Civil War, the political parties of France, and communist and fascist movements as examples of the instability of political situations in which the competing units (parties, in this case) command the total loyalty of their members. We might note, parenthetically, that another way of putting this condition is that groups required by group theory are not aggregations of individuals;

[22]John Fischer, "Unwritten Rules of American Politics," *Harper's*, November, 1948, p. 30.
[23]Truman, *The Governmental Process*, p. 510.
[24]*Ibid.*, p. 511.

they are, rather, collections of the partial interests of individuals. Thus, if groups are the actors in the political drama, individuals, as individuals, have been read out of politics. Furthermore, the system will be more stable the more schizophrenic are its citizens—the more, that is, they hold to conflicting interests which they make no effort to rank or reconcile. It is tempting to note that while there is an old axiom which holds that two heads are better than one, this is not such an obvious advantage when they are on the same person, as they seem to be here.

Not all theorists of compromise make their case rest on the moderation and self-restraint of interest groups. Some, like T. V. Smith, see the burden of compromise as resting on the shoulders of politicians precisely because groups are too committed to their own interests to be up to it themselves. As he claims:

> Each side has a material stake, but one which has been heavily moralized; and each cause alike is now drenched in patriotism. Equally honest men, with causes equally sincere, meet in such manner that neither side can permit the other to have its way without both loss of face and impairment of self-respect. That's politics.[25]

In Smith's analysis, every side would like to have its own complete way. For democracy to exist, however, a "new way" must be devised which "is the way of neither, in which each gets enough of what it wants to observe a truce in the spirit of sportsmanship . . ."[26] It is the democratic politician's task to enforce compromise by devising these new ways. Politicians are society's "generalized specialists in conciliation"; it is their role to invest "the legislative process with the accolade of moral midwifery."[27] If he is to perform his function effectively the legislator must make the following assumptions: (1) "All major interests in a given society are equally legitimate"; (2) "representatives of the great legitimate interests are equally honest"; and (3) "ideals (justice, for example) cannot be invoked to settle issues that involve quarrels as to what the ideals are."[28] These are the assumptions that make it possible for the legislator—or the administrator or the judge—to maintain the neutrality that an effective conciliator must possess. They define the role of the politician in the brokerage model. How this role diverges fundamentally from that envisioned by liberals and conservatives should be clear.

---

[25]T. V. Smith, "Compromise: Its Context and Limits," *Ethics*, October, 1942, p. 3.
[26]T. V. Smith, *Discipline for Democracy* (Chapel Hill: University of North Carolina Press, 1942), p. 105.
[27]T. V. Smith, "Compromise: Its Context and Limits," *op. cit.*, p. 2.
[28]T. V. Smith, *The Legislative Way of Life* (Chicago: University of Chicago Press, 1940), p. 26.

Brokerage Politics as the Politics of Democracy

The alternative to brokerage politics, in Calhoun's theory, is held to be coercion. The alternative to the politician who can "rise above principle" in order to serve the higher "principle of toleration and compromise" is "authoritarian systems [which] push upon the people bodies of fixed principles without counting the desires of the people."[29] Basically, the argument is that any effort to found democratic politics on processes other than compromise (majority rule, for example) must result in dividing society into armed camps organized around radically opposed ideological principles. Political parties would come to represent warring principles divided by a "no-man's land" and, as a consequence, defeat would appear intolerable to the loser. The toleration on which democracy depends would not be possible under these conditions. What makes submission to the victor tolerable for the vanquished is the substantial similarity of the parties, and this can be achieved only when both parties operate as brokers of the major interests in society. If, in the political struggle, "the desire to accomplish one's purpose turns into a desire to annihilate one's opponent, the outcome is civil war." And this will be the case if it is ideas rather than interests that are at stake: "Material interests can be compromised, principles cannot. A man who sensibly will not fight his neighbor over depredations in his garden will fight him over being called a liar."[30]

The balance the parties strike may differ slightly—the Republicans being inclined toward a heavier weighting of the business interest and the Democrats of labor, for example—but their chances of success depend on each of them finding a place for all the major interests in its "package."

THE CHALLENGE OF MINORITIES RULE TO
TRADITIONAL DEMOCRATIC THEORY

THE WAYS IN WHICH THIS MODEL of minorities rule differs from traditional democratic theory are fundamental. Its basic assumptions are different and, as a consequence, it envisions radically different roles and functions for citizens, legislators, administrators, judges, political parties, and interest groups.

[29]Latham, *The Group Basis of Politics*, p. 224.
[30]Jacques Barzun, *The House of Intellect* (New York: Harper, 1959), p. 146. Barzun's is an interesting position. He seems to want to protect the purity of the "House of Intellect" against the corrupting influence of politics. One may doubt, however, whether the life of reason will long be honored in a society that has given up hope of making its politics rational.

Out of the challenge of the theory of broker rule to traditional models of democracy, many interesting and significant questions emerge. We have, somewhat arbitrarily, selected four of them for special attention: (1) Does the role envisioned for the citizen in the theory rest on a more realistic and adequate assessment of human nature? (2) Is a politics of minorities rule the only way to insure social peace and toleration? Do other alternatives invite internecine warfare and chaos? (3) What role does compromise play in the several models of democratic politics? (4) Is the principle of compromise as it operates in the system of broker rule an adequate method of making political decisions?

The Role of Citizens in Democratic Politics

Despite the claims of its proponents (referred to earlier), the theory of broker rule does lose sight of the individual, at least in the Jeffersonian sense. It does so explicitly because it rests on a theory of human nature which sees the individual as a collection of interests, desires, and preferences as these are reflected in his group memberships rather than as a conscious, reasoning animal making judgments on public issues. Similarly, it loses sight of the individual in the traditional conservative sense. The concept of group membership required by the theory fragments and makes trivial the social relationships of the individual, robbing him of that sense of established status in a well-ordered society which earlier conservative theories of balance had sought to protect.

The model of broker rule is willing to take human nature as it finds it in mass society—egoistic, consumption-oriented, group-adaptive. It is willing to accept the tendency of the mass man to conceive himself as a consumer and a conformist to group fashions. It denies the conservative demand that government ought to control man's passions and his egoism by denying that self-gratification is evil. It promises, as did the classical economic theory of *laissez-faire*, that public virtue will emerge from the compromise of private vices. It repudiates the liberal conviction that politics ought both to permit and to encourage man to see himself as a rational participant in shaping his collective destiny.

With respect to the question of human nature, the issue has been forcibly put by Robert Dahl:

> In a rough sense, the essence of all competitive politics is bribery of the electorate by politicians. How then shall we distinguish the vote of the Soviet peasant or the bribed stumble-bum from the farmer who supports a candidate committed to high support prices, the business man who supports an advocate of low corporation taxes, or the consumer who votes for candidates opposed to a sales tax? I assume that we wish to exclude expressions of preference of the first kind

but to include the second. For if we do not exclude the first, then any distinction between totalitarian and democratic systems is fatuous; but if we exclude the second, then surely no examples of even the most proximate democracies can be found to exist anywhere. We can hardly afford to read the human race out of democratic politics.[31]

The question involved here is not simply, as Professor Dahl puts it, whether the interest-motivated vote of the farmer, the businessman, or the consumer is to be "excluded from the category of the democratic"; the further question is whether it is to be *identified* with the democratic. If self-interest is taken as a basic datum of democratic politics, to the exclusion of issue and principle-oriented behavior, then it becomes difficult, indeed, to exclude the "bribed stumble-bum." It would appear to us that the only real distinction is that the stumble-bum has what the economists call a high "liquidity preference"; perhaps, also, he could even be accounted more rational, since he knows more precisely how much it takes to bribe him. Or, perhaps, the important distinction is that stumble-bums are not organized and hence are at a disadvantage by having to play the game as individuals. On the assumptions of relativism, what the stumble-bum sees as his interest would seem to be as legitimate as the farmer's desire for price supports.

The really crucial point, as Professor Dahl subsequently makes clear, is that we cannot in any event simply define democracy as the way most people behave. What we must look for, in his words, are "the conditions that may be used as limits against which real world achievement can actually be measured."[32] Democracy, that is to say, is a set of ideals to be approximated as nearly as possible. If the ideals of democracy must be, in some sense, unreal, it has been the historic office of liberalism to insist that they be genuinely heroic as well. If, as liberalism has insisted, the noblest human capacity is for examining one's preferences and narrowly defined interests in the light of the widest possible range of evidence and alternatives, then any theory of politics which does not embody the development of this capacity in its ideals has fundamentally "read the human race out of democratic politics." More accurately, the theory of broker rule offers no resistance to those pressures of mass society which encourage men to repudiate their own humanity in their roles as citizens.

The consequences of the theory of broker rule for citizenship are most sharply revealed in the electoral process. Clearly, where significant

---

[31]Dahl, *A Preface to Democratic Theory*, pp. 68-69.
[32]Professor Dahl defines such Utopian limits (*ibid.*, pp. 70 ff.), but none of them requires men to behave other than materialistically or egoistically.

policies emerge from the continuous interplay of group interests, elections cease to have the significance they were assumed to have in earlier models. Specifically, they would no longer be characterized by opposing political principles or by rival programs for the solution of what are taken to be public problems; elections would no longer be *political* contests, as we defined that word in the last chapter. In a system of broker rule, campaigns are likely to be characterized by a politics of personality, by a scrupulous avoidance of any appeal which might alienate any group of voters, and by the pervasive use of the psychological techniques of consent engineering. Shared interests (for example, in a new dam or a defense plant) in a constituency may be cultivated. So, also, may those particular group interests (for example, in a tariff, or price supports) which do not adversely affect other groups in the constituency. "Something positive for everybody (at least everybody who is organized); nothing negative for anybody" is likely to be the rule.

The point is this: nonrational manipulation and organized bribery will operate in the competitive politics of every democracy. But they will only be the *essence* of the political process in a mass democracy which accepts them as legitimate and inevitable. Men have lived in the past in a political system whose normative demands required that they see themselves as responsible participants in formulating the rules of their common life. To some extent (and that was all anyone could ever hope for), they have lived up to that ideal. If it ceases to live as an ideal, if it is replaced by a new ideal which encourages and legitimatizes private claims and manipulative appeals, we may expect that organized bribery will indeed become the *essence* of democratic politics. The pressures of mass society seem to lead in that direction. The extent to which they will have their way will depend, in some measure, on whether men picture the normative order of democracy in the way it is conceived in the model of minorities rule.

The Requirements of Toleration

In the theory we have been considering, it is commonly argued that a system of majority rule, organized in a party system that divides the electorate along ideological lines, is inherently unstable. In such circumstances, it is said, political positions tend to become highly moralized, with the result that the winning side feels justified in making life intolerable for the losers, and the losers lose also the stake in the system that makes defeat tolerable.

It seems impossible to refute this argument. If political rivalries become polarized into warring ideologies, no reconciliation will be possible. The result is warfare, not politics. For example, insofar as this situation is still reflected in the relations of North and South on the racial question, the liberal solution of public discussion and majority rule is clearly unworkable, as a basis for resolving political conflict. The issue, from the point of view of the participants, will not be debatable, nor will the minority be willing to accept the rule of the majority on the question. The point is that, although in these circumstances the system of majority rule breaks down, so does every other political system except dictatorship (which may break down too, if the dictator lacks the force necessary to impose his will.)

The problem of racial segregation illustrates this fact. Discrimination has been attacked in decisions of the Supreme Court, in Executive Orders of Presidents, and in statutory enactments of Congress. It seems not to matter whether the decision is taken through the conservative device of judicial interpretation of the "fundamental law" of the Constitution or through the liberal political device of majority decision. Whatever the method, the decisions are unacceptable to important elements in the South.

If any people value other substantive principles more than they do the liberal principles of reason, discussion, and majority rule or the conservative principles of tradition, "higher law," or the stewardship of a responsible elite, then neither the liberal nor the conservative solutions to the problem of resolving political disputes will work. For the same reason, neither will the principle of compromise work. As some of the leaders of southern opinion have made clear, they are no more willing to accept the compromise of gradual integration than the principle of immediate integration. It is integration they are opposed to, because the highest value in their social philosophies is the value of segregation. It is much less plausible in these circumstances to expect the conflicting parties to accept the higher validity of compromise as a principle than it would be to expect them to abide by the decisions of a national majority or a decree of the Supreme Court.

No democratic system will work unless the principles which underlie it have broad acceptance in the community. Where there is no fundamental cultural and moral consensus, where a significant minority prefers insurrection to the acceptance of political decisions, no method of making these decisions will work, and no constitutional government is possible.

The real question, then, is whether a system of majority rule tends to produce those conditions which destroy the prospects for domestic peace. It is certainly not self-evident that it should have this effect. On what grounds could it be argued that encouraging men to take philosophical positions on such questions as the meaning of justice will turn them into ideological zealots and bigots? Are democratic socialists, welfare-staters, and economic liberals just a short step, or series of steps, away from the fanatic Communist? A small and articulate segment of society would say yes, but most informed persons would disagree. Neither are economic conservatives and believers in *laissez-faire* or the elimination of the income tax a step away from fascism. The evidence shows clearly that the zealot and the bigot—the "true believers"—who pose the threat to democratic processes represent personality patterns which are reactions to certain threatening or frustrating life experiences (including, perhaps, the anomy and loneliness of mass society).[33] They are not produced by, and perhaps are even less likely to be found in, a political system that operates through the organized debate of real and principled policy alternatives.

The Role of Compromise in Democratic Theories

The problem of the role played by compromise in democratic politics is not nearly so simple as our discussion up to now has suggested. The complicating consideration is that whereas brokerage theory elevates compromise into the cardinal principle of the system, it is also true that every form of democratic politics—including the majoritarian model—involves compromise. The important problem is to define the kind of compromises that are required, and the roles they play, in different theories of democratic politics.

There are two major alternative views of the place and function of compromise in democratic politics. (1) The first—illustrated by, and embodied in, the brokerage model of democracy—is that compromise is the *principle* that ought to be used for the settlement of disputes—that is, that public policies ought to reflect the compromises of rival interest groups. (2) The second—contained in the traditional liberal democratic theory—is that, not compromise, but the reasoned debate of public goals and issues ought to be the basis of public policies. What role does compromise play in the latter alternative?

The crucial fact of political life in an open society is that there is not only a plurality of organized interest groups; there is also a plurality of views about what the issues are, what goals should be pursued, what policies should be adopted. Even when politics is issue-oriented, there are never simply two clear-cut philosophies of political action. It is never a simple question of capitalism versus socialism, liberalism versus conservatism, idealism versus realism, or any other duality. In an open society, we must start with the fact that there are not simply two alternatives. There are many. Ideological dissent is a crucial fact of democratic politics,

---

[33]Provocative analyses of the authoritarian personality may be found in Erich Fromm, *Escape From Freedom* (New York: Farrar Straus, & Cudahy, 1941); T. W. Adorno et al., *The Authoritarian Personality* (New York: Harper, 1950); Zevedei Barbu, *Democracy and Dictatorship* (New York: Grove Press, 1956); and Eric Hoffer, *The True Believer* (New York: New American Library, 1958).

the fact from which the necessity of compromise inevitably follows.

Consider the political implications of this fact. One possibility is that those people who agree completely on matters of public policy might act together politically in a political party. This alternative would have the advantage of enabling them to vote and to seek to influence policy without the necessity of compromising their views. It is the only alternative that would. For even though there are other persons with whom we might agree, for example, on the proper principle of taxation or the basis of the government's response to corporate monopoly, we find that these people are both unenlightened and intransigent with respect to public policy on education, or the problems of the cold war. With them, we cannot engage in common political action without compromising some of our own political philosophy. Nor they with us.

We do not really have any alternative but to compromise. If we insist on our own political party to avoid it, and others do also, we are confronted by a second basic fact of democratic politics: In order for political questions to be decided by majority vote, it is necessary that, *at the point where the vote is decisive*, the options be narrowed down. If every political philosophy that exists were represented by a political party, the process of compromise would simply be shifted from the political party to the legislature. In order for the legislature to reach agreement on any public policy, it would be necessary to form, through compromises among groups of parties, proposals on which to vote. Voting requires that a proposal be made to which finally one says Aye or Nay.

It is obvious that something like this happens in the multiparty systems of some of the parliamentary governments of Western Europe. The voter in those systems can avoid much of the compromise that we must accept in a two-party system, for he can find a party much closer to his own position than he could where there are only two parties. But, at that point where effective decisions are made, further compromises are necessary. Those politicians who are party leaders then make decisions as to which further compromises of the voters' conscience are to be made. The resulting compromises, and the policies and programs of the government, are not subjected to popular vote or to the test of public debate. The effort in a democratic political system to avoid altogether the necessity of compromise succeeds only in making the process of compromise irresponsible, by removing it from public view and its results from public debate and judgment.

From the perspective of the majoritarian model of democratic politics, the role and limits of compromise can be defined: *Compromise is legitimate and desirable when it is necessary in order to permit or facilitate the formulation of alternatives for public debate and majority decision.* Compromise is a necessary technique of common political action. Moral choice in politics can seldom be a choice between absolute good and incarnate evil from anyone's standpoint. It is necessary, in order for politicians and parties to provide the electorate with reasonably clear alternatives and to clarify these alternatives in public debate, that politicians compromise some of their own principles in the development of party principles. This partial sacrifice, done in order to participate effectively in politics, does not imply the abandonment of the political quest for principles of public morality. Rather, it is a necessary means of that quest. We must compromise our moral principles in order that principles of morality, and not the principle of compromise, may be employed to resolve the conflict of private interests.

When the compromise of private interests is viewed as the principle on which public policies are to be based, it means that the quest for principles of the public interest has been abandoned. The basic difference between the traditional liberal theory of democracy and more recently popular views is that, in the former, compromise is viewed as a necessary *tactic* in an organization of politics which permits majority decision on public issues. In broker or minorities rule theories, compromise plays the role of a fundamental *principle* which is a substitute for majority rule and for the public interest.

Compromise and Democratic Politics

The case for compromise as the basic democratic principle is an attractive one. Everyone gets part of what he wants except for the unorganized. Here is the first apparent gap in the theory. The solution it offers the unorganized, who never get dealt in to the "fair deal," is a simple one: organize. This is no solution at all for the individual whose expectations in politics can only be satisfied by an organized partisan debate of policy alternatives. Beyond this, it is not even clear that it is very helpful advice for those who are at an economic disadvantage by their lack of organization.

There is some evidence which suggests that organization is often not so much the means to influence as a result of it. In American politics, the important interest groups have most often been able to organize effectively only *after* their claims had been given public recognition as in harmony with a public interest. For example, business interests were able to organize for effective political action after they had grown strong in a climate that held private enterprise to be necessary to promote maximum economic welfare for all. Effective farm organization occurred after the independent farmer had become a symbol of American ideals and, indeed, largely after the government had undertaken to facilitate recruitment of membership for what became the largest farm organization. The period of effective labor organization followed the passage of the Wagner Act in 1936, which gave labor, as a matter of justice, the necessary legal and political help. None of this would have been possible under a brokerage system, and, where such a system is in operation, advising the unorganized to organize is something like prescribing that a drowning man should learn to swim. What he clearly requires is some fairly active concern for his welfare on the part of the bystanders who are swimmers.

The unorganized constitute a special and difficult problem for the theory. The celebrated political cartoonist, Herbert Block, has pointed to one aspect of the problem:

> We don't need to be concerned about pressure groups, according to one pleasant theory, because they tend to balance each other off. That would be comforting if it were true. But too often the only balance that's achieved is the lightening of John Public's pockets on both sides at the same time.[34]

Even from the point of view of the organized, the method of compromise is open to attack. The basic issue here is underscored in two recent studies of the national legislative process made by prominent political scientists. Earl Latham, in *The Group Basis of Politics*, studied the steel industry's effort to legalize the basing-point pricing system, after the Supreme Court held it to be in violation of the antitrust statutes. Stephen K. Bailey analyzed the passage of the Employment Act of 1946.[35] Their analyses agree that the processes of policy-making, as they observed them, fit closely the brokerage model, and their studies are fascinating accounts of the interplay of group interests and group pressures. They both find the Congress and its committee system, the parties, and administrative agencies to be structured so as to facilitate the process of group bargaining and compromise.

Latham sees the process as a vindication of the efficiency and the "democratic" character of American political machinery. Bailey, on the other hand, sees the process as illustrating "the difficulty of formulating meaningful ethical norms in the hurly-burly political world of appetites, pressures, rationalizations, and compromises."[36] "Put in its baldest form," he writes:

> The story of S. 380 adds up to the fact that majority sentiment expressed in popular elections for a particular economic policy can

---

[34]Quoted in Robert A. Horn, *Groups and the Constitution* (Stanford: Stanford University Press, 1956), p. 165.
[35]Stephen K. Bailey, *Congress Makes a Law* (New York: Columbia University Press, 1950).
[36]*Ibid.*, p. xi.

be, and frequently is, almost hopelessly splintered by the power struggles of competing political, administrative, and private interests, and is finally pieced together, if at all, only by the most laborious, complicated, and frequently covert coalition strategies.[37]

Bailey goes on to observe that majority rule and political responsibility are closely correlated. What is missing from American politics, and what is needed, is "a responsible political system which will reflect the will of the majority and which will enable the citizens to hold identifiable rulers accountable for policy decisions."[38] Responsibility, in Bailey's sense, is at the heart of the liberal doctrine of progress, of faith in man's ability to control his own social destiny and to shape the future to fit human values. The principle of compromise is incompatible with this faith in progress as a consciously controlled change, because a policy which is the result of compromise does not constitute a consciously defined direction into the future. From the liberal point of view, compromise is aimless, or power-directed, drift.[39]

From the conservative point of view, a regime of compromise undermines the capacity of leaders for statesmanship and the capacity of followers to believe in the ultimate truths of what Walter Lippmann has called the "public philosophy." Compromise itself, from the conservative assumptions, can only operate where it is underwritten by a basic social consensus on ultimate values enshrined in tradition and a stable social system.[40] The rule of compromise as a basic principle, by its encouraging men to follow their interests and their impulses and by its dissolving all the traditional restraints on power-motivated man, must ultimately destroy the constitutional order itself.

Clearly the issues we are considering go to the root of what the meaning of democracy is. It is the basic character of American political processes that are now being called into question. We cannot approach the problem without seeking to understand the basic theoretical positions that are in conflict. Finally, we cannot discharge our obligations as democratic citizens without committing ourselves to some model of how democratic politics ought to operate, and then seeking to mold political reality to our ideals.

[37]*Ibid.*, p. 237.
[38]*Ibid.*, p. 239.
[39]For a comprehensive critique of the theory of compromise from a liberal perspective, see Francis M. Myers, *The Warfare of Democratic Ideals* (Yellow Springs, Ohio: Antioch Press, 1956).
[40]For a similarly comprehensive critique of compromise from a conservative position, see John H. Hallowell, *The Moral Foundation of Democracy* (Chicago: University of Chicago Press, 1954).

7

PARTIES, PRESSURE GROUPS, AND PUBLIC RELATIONS

PARTIES AND PRESSURE GROUPS: INSTRUMENTS OF DEMOCRATIC POLITICS

Both POLITICAL PARTIES AND PRESSURE GROUPS are unofficial instruments of government—that is, they are not provided for in the Constitution and they are not among those governmental institutions whose actions are binding on the society. Yet their unofficial actions have a most important bearing on how public decisions are made. It may even be, as our earlier discussion should have made clear, that they are the most crucial of all the institutions of a democratic society. They are the devices through which political competition is organized, and the *competitive* nature of democratic politics is perhaps its most distinctive characteristic. The nature of its political parties, the conditions of party rivalry, and the relationship of parties to pressure groups go a long way toward defining the character of a society's politics. Specifically, these arrangements will largely reveal which of the democratic models under consideration most nearly infuses and inspires a nation's political life.

Political parties and pressure groups are the agencies through which political demands are formulated and expressed. Most pressure groups in American politics clamor for recognition of the material claims of their members. This is an inevitable part of the politics of a pluralistic society, and anyone who would understand American politics must look at the power structure of the society and assess the political muscle of a host of competing groups seeking to get "what, when, and how" they can. But such information is not adequate to present a comprehensive picture of the nature of American politics. Much depends on the extent to which the parties operate as clearinghouses of interest groups, and the extent to which they also operate to regulate and restrain the interests in the light of party principles. The character of pressure groups and of political parties and the nature of their interrelationships determine both how political demands are formulated and how conflicting demands are reconciled.

Both parties and pressure groups make use of all the devices of political influence—including the techniques of heat and light—to achieve their goals. In both cases, these groups measure their success not only in terms of what positive objectives they achieve but also in what they prevent from happening. For example, tax depletion allowances for the oil industry were achieved after vigorous efforts by the petroleum lobby, whereas the prevention of a system of national health insurance has been a major objective of the American Medical Association lobby. So also with political parties. The Democrats may seek to enact new welfare programs and to prevent the downward modification of progressive tax rates; Republicans may wish to make the regulation of labor unions more stringent and to prevent the expansion of public power facilities.

Differences Between Parties and Pressure Groups

Yet, with all their similarities there are important differences between parties and pressure groups. The first such difference is that parties organize the electorate in elections. They are instruments for organizing majorities. No matter how much or how little parties are organized along ideological lines, it is in the nature of party organization to select nominees and to seek to elect them to public offices. In a two-party system, for reasons we will shortly examine, the parties are likely to be broad-based groups able to appeal to a fairly wide range of interests and philosophies. Within this framework the party operates to select its candidates and help them successfully through the campaigns and elections.

Pressure groups are neither so broad nor so open. Membership is generally limited to those who share a common affiliation and interest (for example: labor unions, barbers, bankers, school teachers) or to those who subscribe to a specific position on a particular issue (for example: tax

reform, capital punishment, civil liberties, separation of church and state).
Pressure groups do not run candidates—officially, at any rate—although
they give strong support to those they believe will be favorably disposed
to their aims. They cannot pretend to the breadth of appeal or the com-
prehensiveness of program that would qualify them to enter the lists to
carry a slate of candidates into office. They concentrate, rather, on influencing the position of the parties and the decisions of official agencies of
government.

The other major distinction of concern to us here is that although
pressure groups seek to *influence* the government, the political parties
seek to *organize* and *control* it. We noted earlier that political parties
have undermined the system of separation of powers by cutting across
it in their efforts to control all of the governmental agencies. Because they
organize political power, the parties are the central institution of a democratic society. Responsible government is possible only where parties
compete for the right to organize and control the government by offering
alternative candidates and programs to the electorate.

This distinction is illustrated by the occasional efforts of pressure
groups to behave like political parties. Sometimes, a group which lacks
either a broad set of principles for dealing with issues or a broad-gauged
appeal to a wide range of other groups has tried to achieve its aims by
organizing as a party. Prohibitionists, successful with the Eighteenth
Amendment as a pressure group in the Anti-Saloon League, organized
themselves as a party since its repeal. Vegetarians are another example.
In the nature of the case, neither group has those characteristics necessary
for appealing to the electorate as a party or organizing the government
if successful.

The Nature and Purpose of Political Parties

The political party systems of democratic societies are not all alike.
The differences among them depend upon the extent to which political
practices more nearly reflect one or another of the models we have
described. The continuum along which they range has ideal types at its
poles. At one extreme is the party system of the brokerage model. Here
the parties are not characterized by philosophical or ideological differences,
and the chief difference between them at any given time is that one of
them is in power and wants to stay there while the other is out and wants
to get in. As one expert has put it, "The first consideration of the party
is to get elected, and the second to get re-elected."[1] The path to election

[1]Henry B. Mayo, *An Introduction to Democratic Theory* (New York: Oxford University Press, 1960), pp. 90-91.

and power in a multigroup society is a winning coalition of groups, and it is this coalition that defines the position of the parties. Since both parties share the same exclusive objective of getting elected, the character of the coalitions they engineer is likely to differ only very marginally.

At the other pole of our continuum is the party system of traditional democratic models. Here the parties grow out of a desire on the part of those who feel similarly about how the government should be operated to organize and present candidates who reflect their common principles. The basis of organization centers around a body of ideas and aims at capturing adherents in the course of public debate. In a two-party system, the ideological centers of gravity of the parties will be compromises, in the sense and for the reasons described earlier. Similarly, there is likely always to be substantial overlap in the positions of the parties. The parties undertake to judge the conflicting claims of rival interests against party principle; conversely, interests are attracted to support one or the other of the parties, but on the party's terms.

These two polar conceptions of the nature and function of political parties and the role of pressure groups in each are illustrated graphically in Figure 5.

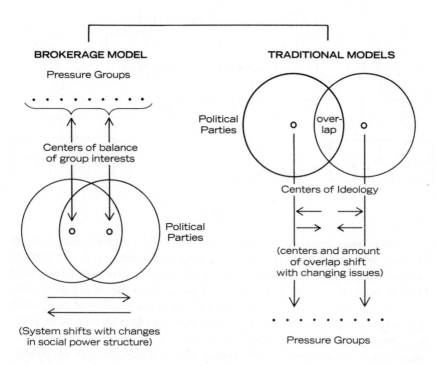

FIGURE 5.

We offer here a word of caution. We are dealing with ideal types which are useful in understanding and evaluating situations and tendencies in the "real world." The polar types we have identified are limits approximated by actual party systems rather than categories into which party systems can be classified. We turn now to the question of how they apply to American parties.

The Formal Structure of American Parties

Political parties in the United States are structured in such a way that they reach down from a national organization to the grass-roots level of local precincts. They roughly follow the federal organization of the nation. Below the national committees are state central committees followed, generally, by county central committees, below which are precinct organizations presided over by precinct chairmen. In chart form, they look something like Figure 6 below.

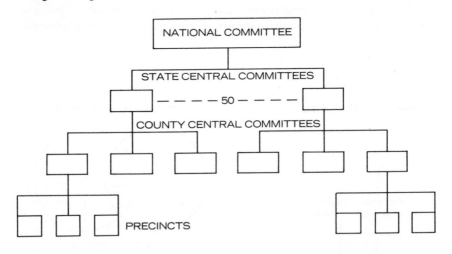

FIGURE 6.

Some states have additional organizations by congressional districts or state legislative districts, and some large cities use wards or districts (usually city council districts) as an organizational structure (Tammany Hall, in New York City is a good example of this type of organization).

There is wide variation from state to state in the location of real power in this hierarchy. Formal power always rises from bottom to top. In practice, however, real power may be retained at the local levels of party organization. Party policy will reflect the real distribution of power. If it is retained at the local levels and fairly evenly distributed, for example, the state organization is likely to have "a policy of no policy."

The bottom level of party organization, the precinct or ward, is concerned with the continuous details of seeing that voters register, know where to go to vote, and get to the voting place. They also take care that the opposition does not raid their ranks and keep a jealous watch to insure that their own party is distributing a fair share of political rewards to deserving and/or influential constituents. Precinct captains or committeemen are usually either elected at primary elections or in precinct caucuses open to all registered members of the party, but there are many variations in method.

There is no common pattern of party organization above the precinct level. The next higher party organs may be the county central committees, or there may be district committees between the precinct and county levels. Whatever the intermediate structure, it comes to focus in a state central committee which is the official governing agency of the party in all of the states. The most common pattern for constituting the membership of central committees within the states is a pyramid of successive elections from lower committees to the next higher units. There is also variation in the basis of representation and, therefore, in the size of central committees.[2]

County central committees are generally responsible for local campaigns for all offices within their jurisdiction (city, county, judicial, legislative, and congressional, if they are big enough to contain a whole congressional district). They also are the basic unit of representation to the state central committees. The activities of county committees vary from state to state, but patronage matters are a universal concern. This is particularly important in such spoils-system states as New Mexico, in which state jobs are often portioned out on a loose percentage ratio to the counties which contributed most to getting their candidates elected.

State central committees are usually composed of members selected by county central committees. Sometimes they are augmented by candidates or incumbents in office, as in California, and become very large organizations. Alabama elects its state central committees at the primary election, and other states use the chairman and vice-chairman of the county committees as a state central committee. State central committees co-ordinate county activities, raise funds, devise strategy to conduct the campaigns, and call in speakers from outside the state to support local candidates (a prize is to get the President personally to lend his prestige

[2]California is a good example of the variety of ways central committees are formed. Los Angeles County has seven members for each of its thirty Assembly districts, whereas San Francisco has five members for each of its six districts. Most of the rural or "cow" counties select their members from supervisorial districts. The number of central committee members varies from about twenty to over two hundred.

and influence to gubernatorial, congressional, and lesser candidates). State committees also do a lot of work on national campaigns by trying to deliver their state to the victorious party which, in turn, means more federal loaves and fishes for their state.

The national committees of the parties are basically clearinghouses and co-ordinating bodies for the state organizations. But they are increasingly making use of professional staffs to conduct research and put out party propaganda. Both the Republican and Democratic national committees have a committeeman and committeewoman from each state and territory. However, the Republican Party has included the state chairman from each state which has a Republican governor or a Republican majority in its congressional delegation, or which voted for the Republican Presidential candidate in the preceding election. This puts Republicans in the Democratic South at a disadvantage in the national party councils.

State laws govern most party activity, including the method of selecting national committee members. The extent to which party activity and organization are regulated by law varies widely from state to state. Campaigns against boss-type politics and attempts to neutralize partisanship have resulted in such measures as California's late cross-filing law (allowing members of each party to run on the primary ballots of the other) and state laws requiring open primaries.

On the surface, the formal party structure seems to provide for a considerable degree of centralized authority. In fact, though, the central organs of the party are relatively powerless, and the parties tend to be loose coalitions of sectional, economic, ethnic, religious, and local political groupings. The primary responsibility of the national committees is to plan and conduct the party presidential nominating conventions each four years. They are not, in any important sense, policy bodies. The conventions themselves are the scene of a complex interplay of the parties' office holders, leaders of city and state machines, leaders of important interest groups and, increasingly, the leading candidates who have successfully built up an imposing public image and public support in the pre-convention campaigns. In all this elaborate and complex jockeying for power, there are no mechanisms out of which a clear picture of party policy might emerge. It may almost be said there is no national party organization, at least in the sense of an authoritative and powerful national organ of the party which defines party policy, exerts a significant influence on the selection of candidates for national office, or influences the behavior of its members who hold national office.

On the other side of the picture, three recent developments are worthy of note. First is the fact that the chairmen of the national committees seem, in recent years, to have acquired somewhat more standing as national party spokesmen. In both parties, the national chairman is formally chosen by the national committees, but in actuality he is the choice of the party's presidential candidate. He has no formal mandate to speak for the party, nor any political machinery for making his views effective. Yet, recently strong chairmen have sometimes emerged as semiofficial spokesmen for the party position. This is especially possible for the chairman whose party is out of power in the White House.

The second development has been the sporadic creation in both parties of advisory policy committees, created by the national committees to develop and publicize party positions on issues. The most successful of these has been the Democratic Advisory Council, established by the Executive Committee of the Democratic National Committee in 1956. The Council defined its own purpose, in a statement approved by the Executive Committee, as that of providing "a collective voice for the Democratic Party, representing on a year-round basis the millions of Democrats who may or may not be represented in either House of the Congress."[3]

Many of the party's leading national figures (including Harry Truman, Eleanor Roosevelt, Adlai Stevenson, Senator Hubert Humphrey, and Governor G. Mennen Williams) have served on the Advisory Council. The Council has, in turn, created advisory committees on important policy areas (foreign policy, labor policy, urban problems, economic policy, and so forth) and has distributed its policy statements widely. The creation and strengthening of such organs in both parties might go a little distance toward remedying the lack of effective party machinery.

A third development is that of the mass media. The effect is to create a national audience and to centralize in the national party organization the technical experts in the exploitation of the media. These changes, explored more fully subsequently, provide the national party leaders with an independent source of popular strength and weaken their reliance on local interests and machines. Even though they tend to produce stronger national parties, they do not necessarily make for national party debate of issues. This will depend on how national party power is used and, specifically, on the extent to which its use is dominated by the techniques of advertising.

Party Structure and Incumbent Politicians

The history of the Democratic Advisory Council reveals another obstacle to the strengthening of party machinery. The official Democratic leadership in Congress (from 1956 to 1960, House Speaker Sam Rayburn

[3]Stephen K. Bailey, *The Condition of Our National Political Parties* (Santa Barbara: The Fund for the Republic, 1959), p. 10.

and Senate Majority Leader Lyndon Johnson) refused membership on the Council. What this suggests is that, in the absence of effective formal party organization, actual control of party affairs may gravitate largely into the hands of party office holders and the groups from which they derive support. At the state and local level, this control is in some states formally recognized in party organization which gives incumbents and their appointees a dominant position on the central committees. At the national level, insofar as there is a national party leader, it is the President when his party is in power. The party out of power tends to be identified with its representatives in the House and Senate. The control of the national party by "out-party" congressmen is largely a matter of their filling what would otherwise be a vacuum. Understandably, they resent and oppose the development of any formal party organization which would provide the machinery for developing national party policy and for disciplining those party office holders who do not support it.

One effect of the control of the national parties by their incumbent congressmen seems to be moving the party system in the direction of the brokerage model. There are two major reasons for this. First, and most important, is that incumbent politicians, of all people, are most likely to regard the winning of elections as both the proximate and the ultimate end of politics. Where they control a party, the purpose of the party is likely to be defined exclusively as the winning of elections. In a society of strong and well-organized private interest groups this is likely to mean, in Professor Bailey's phrase, "a politics of 'boodle' and accommodation."[4] In the second place, as we will see more fully in a later chapter, legislators become members of a "club" in which they share certain outlooks and attitudes as well as procedures for moderating differences and reconciling disagreements. The rules of the "club" are no doubt necessary to maintain the mutual respect and indulgence required by the legislative task. But, at the same time, if carried over into control of party affairs, they can hardly fail to have the effect of making the parties more noncommittal on matters of policy, and less inclined to the kind of proposing and opposing that makes responsible (as against responsive) government possible.

These tendencies are reflected in the operations of the campaign committees maintained by the party members in both houses of Congress. These committees are "mutual-aid" devices for their members. They show little concern for the positions that congressional candidates take on policy questions; they seem interested exclusively in electing, and largely in re-electing, incumbent Democrats or Republicans. One careful observer has concluded, "In a large measure, the continued existence and importance of the senatorial and congressional campaign committees symbolize the

[4] *Ibid.*

desire of congressional leaders to protect their interests when they believe these interests to be counter to the ambitions of the national party organization."[5]

We may summarize by saying that the parties are weak and decentralized. The formal structure does not provide for effective national organization; real power gravitates into the hands of state and local organizations and of the parties' office holders. The result is to make it less possible for the parties to give direction to government policy or to maintain an independence from interest groups. Organized minorities have an open arena in Congress largely because of the lack of party leadership and discipline. The over-all consequence is a party system approaching the brokerage model.

Informal Aspects of Party Organization

The formal party organization is only part of the picture of partisan political activity in the United States. Formal party organizational efforts to select and elect candidates are augmented and influenced by informal organizations affiliated with the party, and by closely allied nonparty groups.

Since the legal basis of party organization is state rather than federal, there is a wide range of variation in the practices of the several states. Often there are informal party organizations or nonparty organizations that work to influence the nomination of particular candidates or to impress a given set of policies on the party. Sometimes, informal party organizations develop in order to circumvent the legal restrictions on the activities of parties themselves. Thus, in California the Democratic Clubs and the Republican Assembly arose in order to bypass state law which forbade formal party organs from endorsing candidates in the primaries. Many candidates not very well liked by party "big-wigs" have been successful by relying on these organizations for support—in money as well as enthusiastic leg-work—in their constituencies. Sometimes, as notably with the California Democratic Clubs, these organizations exert a significant influence in pushing the party to accept a particular set of policies. Insofar as they are successful, the result is to produce more principled party competition in the traditional mold.

Another type of informal organization operates as a "front" for the formal party apparatus and is ordinarily created by the party leadership itself. These organizations are ordinarily temporary and designed to further the campaigns of the party's candidates. Examples include the "Citizens for Joe Doakes," "Lawyers for Smith," "Independents for Jones," and

[5]Guy B. Hathorn, quoted in *ibid.*, p. 11.

"Taxpayers for Brown" groups that proliferate in election years. Also, each party arranges "front" committees of the other party to endorse its candidates: "Democrats for Eisenhower," "Republicans for Kennedy." Most often the "independent" committees are organized, staffed, and managed by the party's campaign headquarters. Their purpose is to make a "nonpartisan" appeal to the voters of the other party and to the members of interest groups. Their effect is to undermine the partisan debate of issues. The increase in this kind of activity in recent years may be another indication that the party system is moving farther away from the traditional model.

AMERICAN PARTIES: TWEEDLEDEE AND TWEEDLEDUM?

AMERICAN PARTIES have always, at least periodically, been accused of being Tweedledee and Tweedledum. The argument that there are no real, significant ideological differences between them which would offer the voter a meaningful choice is not a new cry in American political life. Historically, a good case can be made that the cry has been unjustified, that the parties (with some significant exceptions and despite surface similarities) have taken substantially different positions on public issues.

The Historical Situation

In the past, the conflict between the two American parties appears to have had both social class and ideological dimensions. We have had a "conservative" and a "liberal" party, not in the sense in which we have until now used those words, but in the different sense of attitudes toward social and particularly economic reform. There have been periods, such as the "Era of Good Feelings" during the administrations of Presidents John Quincy Adams and Monroe, when the distinction between the parties became so blurred they eliminated party lines almost entirely. But after 1828, the old party lines were re-established. They had had their origins in the first conservative party, the Federalists, which drew its strength from "well-to-do farmers, urban merchants, persons of English extraction, and members of such high-status churches as the Congregationalists and the Episcopalians." The Federalists were opposed by the Jeffersonian Republicans, whose support was based on the "urban workers, poorer farmers, persons of non-English background such as the Scotch-Irish, and members of the (then) poorer churches like the Presbyterians and the Catholics."[6]

[6]Seymour Martin Lipset, *Political Man* (Garden City, N. Y.: Doubleday, 1960), p. 292.

These basic, class-oriented distinctions have continued to furnish the centers of gravity of the two parties. The Whigs, who took over the mantle of the conservative party from 1836 to the eve of the Civil War drew their strength from the old Federalist sources. The Democrats continued to be the party of the poorer classes and the waves of immigrants. After 1865, the Republicans inherited both the support and leadership of the northern Whigs. A writer in the 1860's said of the politics of New York, from 1828 onwards: "The mass of large and little merchants have, like a flock of sheep, gathered either in the Federalist, Whig, Clay, or Republican folds. The Democratic merchants could have easily been stored in a large Eighth Avenue railroad car."[7]

In the latter part of the nineteenth century, the social cleavage of the parties was blurred somewhat by the tension between small farmers and urban workers and by the Negro issue, but the basic distinction remained. Recent studies of the class basis of historical party loyalties confirm Charles Beard's comment in 1917 that "the center of gravity of wealth is on the Republican side while the center of gravity of poverty is on the Democratic side."[8]

The most recent research shows that this continues largely to be the case. Outside the South, the major sources of Republican strength continue to be professional, executive, and white-collar groups; upper-income groups; the college-educated segment; higher-status religious groups; and the small-town rural areas. Democratic strength still centers around labor, lower-income groups, and minority ethnic groups. At the extremes, these party loyalties continue to be strongest. If the population is grouped into four income brackets, 70 per cent of the poorest group were Democrats in 1950, whereas only 31 per cent of the most prosperous group were Democratic. In 1955, a study revealed that in corporations employing more than 10,000 workers, only 6 per cent of the executives were Democrats; in firms employing more than 1,000, 8 per cent were Democrats; in firms employing more than 100, 12 per cent of the executives were Democrats.[9] The social factors related to party affiliation are illustrated in Figure 7.

These differences in social class composition of the parties have been accompanied by ideological differences. In a meaningful sense, there have tended to be, particularly in periods of crisis, real differences in the positions of the parties. The Democrats have been the "liberal" party in the sense that they have generally pursued policies which would provide

[7]Quoted in *ibid.*, p. 293.
[8]Quoted in V. O. Key, *Politics, Parties and Pressure Groups*, 4th ed. (New York: Crowell, 1958), p. 235.
[9]Lipset, *Political Man*, pp. 286-87.

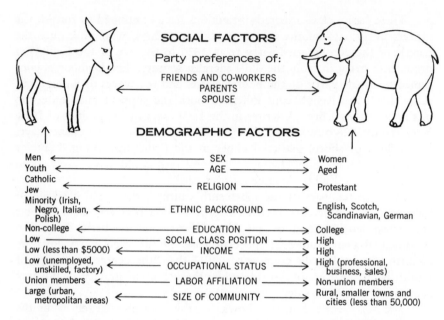

SOCIAL FACTORS

Party preferences of:

FRIENDS AND CO-WORKERS
PARENTS
SPOUSE

DEMOGRAPHIC FACTORS

Men ⟵	—— SEX —— ⟶	Women
Youth ⟵	—— AGE —— ⟶	Aged
Catholic Jew ⟵	—— RELIGION —— ⟶	Protestant

Minority (Irish,
  Negro, Italian, ⟵
  Polish)
	—— ETHNIC BACKGROUND —— ⟶	English, Scotch,
		  Scandinavian, German

Non-college ⟵	—— EDUCATION —— ⟶	College
Low ——	SOCIAL CLASS POSITION —— ⟶	High
Low (less than $5000) ⟵	—— INCOME —— ⟶	High

Low (unemployed,
  unskilled, factory) ⟵
	—— OCCUPATIONAL STATUS —— ⟶	High (professional,
		  business, sales)

Union members ⟵	—— LABOR AFFILIATION —— ⟶	Non-union members

Large (urban,
  metropolitan areas) ⟵
	—— SIZE OF COMMUNITY —— ⟶	Rural, smaller towns and
		  cities (less than 50,000)

FIGURE 7. Social and demographic factors in party strength.

the disenfranchised with access to political power and the disadvantaged with access to economic opportunity. De Tocqueville described the conflict between the parties, in the 1830's, in this way: "The deeper we penetrate into the inmost thoughts of the parties, the more we perceive that the object of one is to limit and that of the other to extend the authority of the people."[10] The authority of the people was extended by the progressive elimination of restrictions on the franchise, by the elimination of such restrictions on popular control as the indirect election of senators, and by the creation of such devices for bringing government closer to the people as the initiative, referendum, and recall. The alleviation of the plight of the economically disadvantaged took shape in programs directed toward labor reform, progressive income taxes, aid to the farmer, minimum-wage legislation, unemployment compensation, social security—the whole network of social legislation covered by the term, the "welfare state." The central objective that runs through the history of American political liberalism has been, as Emerson said a century ago, to facilitate "in every manner the access of the young and the poor to the sources of wealth and power."[11]

The role of American political conservatism has been to challenge

[10] De Tocqueville, *Democracy in America*, Vol. I, p. 168.
[11] Quoted in Lipset, *Political Man*, p. 309.

these liberal reforms and to speak for the necessity of restraints on popular rule—in President Hoover's phrase, "more business in government and less government in business." Applied to the issue of public policy in the recent past this has meant that the Democrats have favored the "welfare state," the Republicans a "welfare society"; the Democrats have been the "pro-government" party, the Republicans "anti-government"; the Democrats have had a pro-labor bias, the Republicans pro-business.

Factors Obscuring Party Differences

If there have been real and significant differences between the parties, how are we to explain the frequent popular charges that they are Tweedledee and Tweedledum? There seem to be several features of two-party democratic politics which insure that the parties will not become radically opposed ideological camps engaged in internecine warfare and which conceal or gloss over such underlying differences as may exist.

In the first place, party controversy has been sporadic, the significant cleavages occurring during periods of crisis. In periods of economic prosperity, like the prolonged prosperity since World War II, the differences between the parties have a tendency to narrow. This is particularly true of the current political scene, because the other major areas of potential controversy—civil liberties, civil rights, and foreign policy, for example—have not been areas of partisan debate. The issue of civil rights and liberties cuts across party lines. In the area of foreign policy, often a partisan issue prior to World War II, bipartisanship has confined debate to accusations (by the party out of power) of running behind in the missile race or to promises of providing "more bang for a buck." This situation is shown in Figure 8.

A second, and perhaps more fundamental, reason for a narrowing of party differences is rooted in the nature of the two-party system itself. A two-party system only works effectively when both of the parties have the normal support of something approaching 50 per cent of the electorate. But under the economic conditions of the past, the liberal party has had a built-in advantage: its programs carried an economic appeal to the lower classes, which have always been a majority. The conservative party must win working-class support to bolster its chances of winning elections. To do so, it has had to accept the reforms of the liberal party. Republicans in the 1950's, for example, did not urge the repeal of New Deal and Fair Deal reforms. Candidate Eisenhower, in 1952, promised the farmers 100 per cent of parity, and President Eisenhower pushed through Congress with Democratic support significant extensions of the social security program.

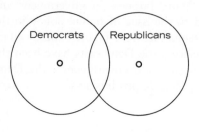
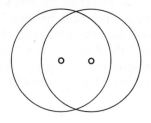

1936   *1960*

(Depression; four years of experience with the New Deal; domestic, economic issues predominate)

(Eight years of prosperity; foreign policy predominates with bipartisan approach; chief domestic issue to continue prosperity with no basic philosophical or institutional change)

FIGURE 8.

The fact that both parties in their campaigns must seek the support of the marginal and uncommitted voters in the middle means that the Republican presidential candidate must ordinarily be to the left of the Republican representatives in the Congress if the party is to appeal to enough independent or ordinarily Democratic voters to win. Inevitably, in the past, if the conservative party was to have a chance of winning elections, there was bound to be a considerable amount of "me-tooism" in our politics.

Thirdly, these characteristics of a two-party system are exaggerated in the United States by the loosely confederative nature of the national parties described above. Because the party in opposition almost ceases to exist as a national organization with national leadership it is not very likely that it will play the role of loyal opposition in criticizing, formulating issues, and framing alternatives.

A fourth factor is an increasing deference of American parties to the nonpartisan bias which has characterized a large segment of the electorate. No doubt, this bias is caused by a typically American deep-rooted aversion to power. It has sometimes—as in the case of the "Citizens for . . ." and the "Independents for . . ." organizations—led the parties to present a more noncommittal face to the voters than their real differences would justify. Occasionally, this bias leads a party to offer itself to a popular hero, rather than to select one of the tried and true party leaders as a candidate. The most recent example was the wooing of General Eisenhower by both parties on the assumption that his prestige, popularity, and nonpartisanship would provide a strong "coattail" whereby the party and its other candidates could be pulled into office. For the Republicans, who finally did convince him to run, this proved to be a sound prediction. Two years later, however, when Eisenhower was not a candidate, the Democrats regained control of Congress.

The Role of Third Parties

No adequate analysis of the American party system is possible without a consideration of the role of minor parties, particularly of those which have arisen from time to time to challenge the two major parties from a broad ideological position. Historically, third parties have often furnished the lever by which one of the major parties has been moved to a change of position, with a consequent intensification of major party competition. Thus, in the 1890's, much of the program of the People's Party (the "Populists") was taken over by the Democrats under the leadership of William Jennings Bryan, only to have Teddy Roosevelt "steal all of Bryan's thunder" for the Republicans in 1904. Subsequently, Roosevelt himself led a third-party movement to further his reforms. The Progressives made a creditable showing at the polls in 1912, syphoning off enough Republican votes to insure the election, by a plurality, of Woodrow Wilson.

The most recent third-party effort occurred in 1948. The Progressive Party, led by Henry Wallace, attempted to attract liberals on the plea that the two major parties offered no real choice, particularly in the area of foreign policy. In this case, the effort was a signal failure. It had no visible impact on the positions of the major parties, partly because Wallace, for reasons that have never been clear, permitted Communists to take control of, and wreck much of, the organization.

Third parties have served in the past as a lever on the two-party system in another way. By furnishing opportunity for voters to cast a protest vote, reflecting their dissatisfaction with the "me-tooism" of the major parties, they have probably caused the latter to respond by increasing somewhat the difference between their respective centers of gravity. This is particularly true of the Socialist Party, which polled nearly a million votes in 1920. Many a registered Democrat and Republican found in Eugene V. Debs, and later in Norman Thomas, an opportunity to protest. Not all the Socialist vote was mere protest, by any means. The planks in the Socialist platform, almost without exception, found their way into the platforms of one of the two major parties. In 1932, "the Socialist Party came much nearer to anticipating the depression measures than did the major party platforms for that year."[12]

[12]Charles Edward Merriam and Harold Foote Gosnell, *The American Party System*, 4th ed. (New York: Macmillan, 1950), p. 60.

Future Prospects for Competitive Party Politics

Few informed people would contend that there are not now some significant differences between the major parties. The more debatable questions are whether there is as much difference as there should be, and whether the trend is toward a narrowing of the differences. No doubt, it is partly true that the recent apparent similarity between the parties reflects those continuing factors discussed above. But only partly. Perhaps it is also true that the moderation of current American politics is a consequence of deeper changes in the style of life attendant on the growth of an "affluent society," the breakdown of social class distinctions and, perhaps, the "end of ideology" in a relativistic, tolerant mass society.

In these circumstances, social stratification and status and income differentials continue to exist, but it is hardly realistic to conceive of them as social class distinctions in the old sense. Certainly, they are not generally seen that way by Americans, the vast majority of whom think of themselves as being middle class. The lower income groups may persist in voting Democratic, but not so firmly and not for class or ideological reasons. It can certainly be overbalanced in national campaigns by charismatic, "above-the-parties" appeals of particular personalities and by attempts to lure traditional opponents to vote for a "good man" rather than class interest. Thus in 1956, 43 per cent of trade-union members voted Republican for Eisenhower, as against 27 per cent in the congressional elections of 1954. The trade unionist-become-suburbanite very likely tends to vote Republican just as the suburban vote generally tends to be heavily Republican. This does not mean that the trade unionist, for example, has become a conservative in the traditional social-class sense; it may be that more than anything he is becoming a moderate, and the Republican Party probably has appeared in the public image in recent years as the party of moderation.

Many observers have noted that the economic differences which continue to exist no longer mean different styles of life for those at different economic levels. Such distinctions as continue to exist involve the difference between colored and black and white television, between a new car every year and one every several years, between a hand-tailored suit and a machine-made product that is virtually indistinguishable. These differences are not likely to lead to political controversy centering around the question of economic justice. It is true, of course, that this affluence is not universally shared. About 15 per cent of America's family units have incomes of less than $2,000 per year. But the point is that politics, when it is dominated by the balancing of the claims of the organized "haves," ceases to concern itself with providing justice for the remnants of "have-nots" who lack both status and organization.

The crucial consideration might well turn out to be that moderation is the political way of life of man in mass democracy, capable of being disturbed only in the improbable event of a severe economic crisis. If so, political parties, the potential instruments for organizing a system of political debate and rule by popular majorities, will continue to be ineffective for the purpose. In the past, they have been weak and decentralized except where a popular and strong President or presidential candidate could align them behind his political program. Given the basic climate of moderation which seems to have roots deep in the social and intellectual changes we have examined, the recent similarity of the parties may be unlike the temporary lulls in party controversy that have occurred in the past.

The likelihood of a restoration of more vital partisan debate is further reduced by the habit of voters and candidates alike to regard legislators increasingly as primarily representatives of the constituency's interests rather than as representatives of identifiable positions on national issues. For a time, it seemed that the campaign for the Presidency, addressed to a national electorate, was destined to emerge as the only forum for the debate of national issues. Certainly, this accounts for much of the increase in the power and prestige of the Presidency in this century.

However, mass democracy exerts pressure on presidential candidates to act as brokers of private interests on a larger scene. Even if the pressures are resisted, presidential candidates alone, in a system of separation of powers with decentralized parties, cannot provide responsible government. The Southern Democrat-Republican coalition in Congress, and the supremacy of interests over parties there, will continue to obscure party differences and frustrate party competition. Still, the role of the presidential contest is an important factor in keeping alive issue-oriented controversy in party politics. The Kennedy-Nixon debates over national network television, in 1960, suggested some of the possibilities. Whether they will be developed or whether presidential campaigning will yield to pressures of winning elections and mollifying all the major interests or succumb to the allure of professional public relations techniques is an open question.

THE NATURE OF THE PRESSURE SYSTEM

At the same time that the kind of political parties required by majoritarian democracy have been undermined by the party's brokerage role, interest groups—the instruments of minorities—have become increasingly bureaucratic, strong, and effective.

The development of industrialization and urbanization in a mass society created the kind of group life which is the ideal milieu for the brokerage process. The consequent development of highly integrated interest groups, organized nationally, caused a breakdown of the old sectional basis of politics. The closing of the doors to immigration helped to eliminate the role of ethnic groups in the political process. The effective use of political power by business interests after the Civil War provided a lesson in practical politics for agriculture and labor. Public policies more and more reflected simply a compromise of the power positions of vocal, interested minorities. From a politics resting on the Jeffersonian ideal of "special privilege for none," American politics seemed increasingly to reflect the unspoken assumption of "equality of special privilege for all organized groups." The process was speeded up by the economic affluence of World War II and its aftermath in the United States. A 50 per cent rise in the standard of living in the decade following the war seemed, for the first time in history, to provide enough "privilege" to go around.

Types of Pressure Groups

In addition to the increase in their size and organizational structure, interest groups have undergone other significant changes that contribute to the dominance of the brokerage process. In order to see what these changes are, we need to distinguish between two general types of pressure groups. The distinction is between the organization devoted to securing differential economic or status advantages for its members and the one devoted to promoting some particular public principle in which its members have no stake other than their intellectual commitment. We may label these two types as "private interest groups" and "public interest groups" to distinguish their central concerns. Examples of the first type are the private power lobby (the Association of American Light and Power Companies), the real estate lobby (National Association of Real Estate Boards), the A.F.L.-C.I.O., and the Farm Bureau Federation. Examples of public interest groups are the American Civil Liberties Union, the American League to Abolish Capital Punishment, the Planned Parenthood Association, the American Association for the United Nations, and the John Birch Society. The test, as a leading political scientist has recently put it, is a dual one: whether the benefits sought by the organization are exclusive or nonexclusive; whether membership is open or confined to those with a common, exclusive interest. His illustration of the distinction deserves further consideration:

> Is it possible to distinguish between the "interests" of the members of the National Association of Manufacturers and the members of the American League to Abolish Capital Punishment? The facts in the two cases are not identical. First, *the members of the A.L.A.C.P. obviously do not expect to be hanged.* The membership of the A.L.A.C.P. is not restricted to persons under indictment for murder

or in jeopardy of the extreme penalty. *Anybody* can join A.L.A.C.P. Its members oppose capital punishment although they are not personally likely to benefit by the policy they advocate. The inference is therefore that the interest of the A.L.A.C.P. is not adverse, exclusive or special. It is not like the interest of the Petroleum Institute in depletion allowances.[13]

This distinction is admittedly difficult to draw in practice. Some pressure groups are a combination of both material interest and general interest. For example, veterans' groups like the American Legion work strenuously for such clientele benefits as pensions, home loans, and educational benefits while, at the same time, they lobby for anticommunist legislation, loyalty programs, and other measures of a general application.

In addition, most private interest groups clothe their claims in an appeal to principle. Sometimes the claim is too disingenuous or naïve to be credible: "What's good for General Motors is good for the country." Often, however, such claims deserve a hearing: "The depletion allowance is necessary to create the incentive for oil exploration on which America's defense capability and economic future rest." Sometimes, too, what appears to be a public interest group is a front for a private interest. A "Facts Forum" may be subsidized by Texas oil millions, or a committee to promote "constitutional government" may derive its sustenance from large corporations.

Recent Changes in the Pressure System

Despite these difficulties in application, the distinction is crucial to an understanding of recent changes in the composition and pattern of pressure groups. These changes, in turn, have had important consequences for the role of pressure groups in the political system.

There appears to have been, in the first place, an increase in the number and importance of private as against public interest organizations. Historically, public interest groups have played an important role in influencing political parties and legislatures to adopt their principles. The abolition societies, the Women's Christian Temperance Union, the Daughters of the American Revolution, the Suffragettes, and the Anti-Saloon League are obvious examples. The Izaak Walton League played an instrumental role in securing conservation policies at the turn of this century. There are still such groups in existence, and they continue to be politically active. But their relative number and influence has declined, and they now operate on the fringes of the political arena with little chance

---

[13]E. E. Schattschneider, *The Semisovereign People* (New York: Holt, Rinehart & Winston, 1960) p. 26.

of being considered by politicians or parties as spokesmen for a principle. Instead, they are seen as "featherweight" organizations to be weighed into the balance of interest with the "heavyweight" economic interest groups. The effect of this development is exaggerated by the tendency of legislators to define their role as neutral brokers. When they do so, the influence of pressure groups is almost entirely dependent on the amount of "heat" they can generate. For the broker-legislator, heat is heat no matter who applies it. The American Civil Liberties Union and the American Friends Service Committee enter the arena armed with matches, the private interest groups with blowtorches.

Secondly, what we are here calling "private" interest groups decreasingly define and justify their private interests in terms of public principles. Business groups—chambers of commerce, trade associations, and the National Association of Manufacturers, for example—formerly defended their interests as entitled to legitimate expression because the entire community had a stake in the creation of an economic system of the "survival of the fittest" or of private enterprise, competition, and *laissez-faire*. In recent years, chambers of commerce seem more concerned with local prosperity even where this means coming to the defense of local examples of "creeping socialism"—government dams, arsenals, power facilities, and other projects which bring payrolls and prosperity to the local scene. The steel industry seeks legal authorization of basing-point pricing, not on the grounds of a competitive system with which it is obviously incompatible, but on the obligation of representatives of steel-producing states to safeguard the economic prosperity of their constituencies. The effectiveness of this appeal can be judged by the following: when this issue came to a vote in the House, all but two members of Pennsylvania's fifteen-man Democratic delegation voted to legalize the system, even though it very obviously conflicts with traditional party position on monopoly and economic concentration.[14]

It would appear that private interest groups generally see themselves as rivals in a contest for advantage, entitled to be given a "fair" weighting rather than to have their claims to a public interest considered.

Thirdly, interest groups less and less represent identifiable, conscious interests of *individuals* and more and more are becoming compromises engineered by the professional bureaucracy of the organization. Labor unions, for example, tend to be *responsive* to the conflicting desires of their membership as these are interpreted by the leadership, rather than *responsible* for consciously determined goals. Thus, skilled craftsmen have a stake in promoting wage differentials based on skill; women workers want maternity benefits and equal pay for equal work; night workers want

[14]Latham, *The Group Basis of Politics*. See especially chapters 4 and 5.

greater shift differentials; elderly members want better pension provisions. Union leaders, like politicians, attempt to reconcile the pressures so as to contribute to the stability and growth of the organization.

The same process characterizes the shaping of the demands of trade associations, associations of government employees, and other organizations. In short, making private interests bureaucratic has come to mean that they too are brokerage houses, rather than instruments for defining and pursuing conscious goals of public policy or for reflecting the opinions of their members. Collectively, they constitute a mart in which parties and politicians tend to play the neutral role of referee.

Activities of Pressure Groups

The inclusive objective of pressure groups is to influence public policy in some desired direction. The techniques which will promote that objective are varied: gaining access to and influence in the centers where governmental decisions are made, developing favorable attitudes among the public at large and in other groups, or influencing the nomination and election of favorably disposed candidates.

In their efforts to influence directly the making of governmental policies, pressure groups operate within and before legislative bodies at the federal, state, and local levels. In their efforts to affect policy administration and interpretation, they appear before regulatory commissions and other administrative agencies.

The agent of the pressure group is the lobbyist. We will describe and analyze his activities in a later chapter on the legislative process. Here we only note that the lobbyist may be a member of the organization he represents or he may be a skilled public relations expert, ex-legislator, or career lobbyist retained by the organization to achieve certain objectives for a fee—sometimes a flat fee and sometimes a contingency fee based upon his success.

The lobbyist, however, is only a small part of pressure group operation. Personal contact with those who can make political decisions is important, but a report from the House of Representatives Select Committee on Lobbying Activities had this to say:

> Our investigation has convinced us that the business of influencing legislation is dominated by group effort, and that individual activities by persons known as "lobbyists" are subordinate. Much of the money expended to influence legislation is spent in pamphleteering or advertising to obtain legislative aims. We do not wish to discredit the activities of individual lobbyists, or indicate that they are altogether without importance. We do believe that the printed word is much more extensively used by organizations as a means of pursuing legislative aims than personal contacts with legislators by individual

lobbyists. The record on one of the most active lobbying groups investigated (the Committee on Constitutional Government) supplies clear proof of this proposition. Its principal function is the distribution of pamphlets and books, and releases under Congressional frank, as a part of campaigns to influence legislation. It also utilizes other and more direct lobbying techniques, but places more reliance on pamphleteering than any other method of influencing legislation. Lobbying activities of this kind increasingly overshadow the traditional techniques of contact and persuasion.[15]

It should be noted that printed materials are distributed not only to those people who make the final decisions but also to influential individuals and groups. Businessmen, teachers, medical practitioners, and members of labor unions and other organizations are constantly receiving pamphlets from various pressure groups for their information. Often they bear the open invitation to write one's congressman, legislator, or executive official to express one's agreement with the cause. Recipients of this barrage of material might wonder about its effectiveness as they toss large quantities of it into the wastebasket, but the amount of mail received by legislators attests to its influence in activating many of those who receive it.

Pressure groups work to influence elections of sympathetic candidates as well as to influence legislaton after election. An example of their effectiveness is described in R. Cragin Lewis' account of the intensive efforts of the medical profession to support candidates of its choice.[16]

A case in point was the Florida Democratic primary contest between Claude Pepper and George Smathers in 1950. Senator Pepper was an advocate of national health insurance which was tainted with the label "socialized medicine." He told the Florida physicians flatly that he was "sticking by the administration's health plan. I just don't care about your 2,000 votes."

The reaction of the physicians was quick and effective. Doctors from all parts of the state contributed a hundred dollars apiece, and their wives staged a series of fund-raising parties to sweeten the treasury. Mr. Lewis describes the results:

> Professional reserve melted away. Doctors got out their patient lists, dashed off hundreds of personal letters. From Tallahassee to Ponce de Leon, people began to tell each other, 'My doctor thinks it's a good idea to vote for Smathers.' Some patients wrote answering notes that gave M. D.'s a rare glimpse of their own influence: 'Didn't know you were interested. I assure you I'll vote for him . . .' 'Re-

[15]*House Report No. 3239* (Washington: Government Printing Office, 1951), p. 3.
[16]"New Power at the Polls: The Doctors," *Medical Economics*, January, 1951, pp. 73-79.

ceived your card and am going to please you. Hadn't even planned to register.'

On election day, medical workers phoned every professional man in the state before noon. More than 70 percent, they found, had already voted. In some small towns every phone number in the book was called. By the time the primary balloting was over, George Smathers was a shoo-in.[17]

Money and Influence

Activities of pressure and interest groups cannot be conducted without considerable amounts of money. How much they spend depends upon several factors: (1) the availability of revenue—that is, some have steady and abundant sources of funds while others rely upon hand-to-mouth collections of contributions; (2) how anxious they are to achieve results—for example, a particular bill before a legislative body might present a fundamental threat or opportunity and generate an all-out effort; (3) how much good-will advantage might be expected to accrue from supporting causes peripheral to the group's major interest—for example, support given to education or higher teachers' salaries; and (4) how much chance of success is predictable.

It is difficult to get a reliable estimate of total expenditures of pressure groups because their activities take so many different forms. Attempts have been made by Congress and many states to require financial reporting by lobbying groups but the laws are so written that reporting requirements are easily evaded and the figures reported never tell the full story. For example, many organizations assign employees to supply "information" which can be interpreted not to be "influence." In any event, lobbying is just a part of the over-all activity, it by no means tells the story of the total expenditures.

Lobbying expenditures are interesting, however, as a very rough and grossly understated index of who spends what. The *Congressional Quarterly* has compiled the figures which compare the top spenders for 1959 and 1960. It is interesting to note that in 1960 the Veterans of World War One of the U.S.A., Inc., known as the "Wonnies" in Washington, led the list by spending almost twice as much as the next group (AFL-CIO). The reason was that the "Wonnies" put on a vigorous campaign for pensions during 1960 which cost a reported amount of $200,623, although they spent nothing in 1959. The table follows:

Top Spenders

Ten organizations reported spending more than $75,000 on

[17]*Ibid.*, pp. 76-77.

lobbying during 1960. Each is listed below, with spending figures for both 1960 and 1959.

Organization	1960	1959
Veterans of World War One of the U.S.A. Inc.	$200,623	"None"
AFL-CIO (National headquarters)	129,157	$132,053
American Farm Bureau Federation	101,412	105,038
American Legion	99,220	102,132
National Education Assn.	96,914	106,399
International Brotherhood of Teamsters	95,765*	242,951
American Petroleum Institute	91,420	35,549
National Federation of Post Office Clerks (AFL-CIO)	85,260	74,406
National Farmers Union	78,841	82,156
National Housing Conference	76,367	78,571

Fifteen other groups reported spending in excess of $50,000 during 1960:

International Assn. of Machinists, Washington, D.C. Lodge (AFL-CIO)—$72,734; American Medical Assn.—$72,634; National Assn. of Home Builders—$69,497; American Trucking Assns.—$69,373; Brotherhood of Locomotive Firemen and Enginemen (AFL-CIO)—$67,792; National Assn. of Letter Carriers (AFL-CIO)—$66,692; National Committee for Insurance Taxation—$64,590; Nation-Wide Committee of Industry, Agriculture and Labor on Import-Export Policy—$61,613; U. S. Savings and Loan League—$58,752; Railway Labor Executives Assn. (AFL-CIO)—$56,000; AFL-CIO Industrial Union Department—$55,731; National Federation of Independent Businesses—$55,011; American Hospital Assn.—$54,052; National Conference for Repeal of Taxes on Transportation—$53,059*; National Retail Merchants Assn.—$51,161.

*Spending reports filed through first three quarters of 1960 only.[18]

Other lobbies registered before Congress range from the Associated Third Class Mail Users ($13,200.03 reported) to the West Coast Inland Navigation District ($2,507.10 reported) and include all types of organizations and activities.[19]

Pressure groups are no less active at the state level. In fact, there were 515 organizations registered to lobby before the California state legislature in 1961, a substantially larger number than the 284 which were registered in Washington, D.C.

The scope and strength of the pressure system, and the dominance within it of private interests, serve to underscore some of the forces that

[18]*Congressional Quarterly*, May 5, 1961, p. 771.
[19]*Ibid.*, pp. 772 ff.

promote the processes of minorities rule. The underlying problem, first clearly set out by Madison, remains: how to devise the means for subordinating the conflicting claims of private groups to a public interest without destroying the pluralism out of which the pressure system inevitably grows. The supremacy of the party system, it would seem, offers the major alternative to the supremacy of the pressure system.

THE DECLINE OF THE POLITICAL BOSS

THE GROWTH OF BUREAUCRACY, the rise of a new group of masterminds of politics skilled in the arts of manipulation and the employment of the mass media, and the homogenizing of American society have all contributed to toll the death knell for the political boss and his machine. Machine politics, presided over by a boss and organized through district leaders and ward heelers, based its strength on unassimilated ethnic and immigrant groups and economically underprivileged people. The machine distributed jobs, groceries, buckets of coal, and other favors and arranged for funerals and marriages for the faithful and the poor, the Irish, the Catholic, the Poles, and the Jews.

In the past, the machine and its boss have often been powerful enough to control and "deliver" the politics of a city or a state. Curley of Boston, "Big Bill" Thompson of Chicago, Hague of Jersey City, and Crump of Memphis were some of the colorful figures who were powerful enough to demand and receive consideration in the selection of candidates and the development of the platforms of the national party.

An analysis of New York City politics—the historic home of Tammany Hall, the strongest and most enduring of the machines—reveals the forces at work to undermine their traditional sources of strength and change their character. A recent study[20] finds that the district leader, the key to the machine's traditional organization and power, has become a mere functionary of a system in which real power has gravitated into the hands of the top party leaders, municipal bureaucrats, public relations firms, and leading businesses which contract with the city. The result, according to these observers, is a shift from a system that with all its faults was responsive to the people (particularly to the poorest and most disadvantaged part of the population) to a system which is almost completely removed from their desires and grievances.

The authors of this study point out that, in 1959, New York had more than 600,000 people on its municipal payroll and argue that, unlike

[20]Fred J. Cook and Gene Gleason, "The Shame of New York," *The Nation*, October 31, 1959, pp. 261-321.

the traditional boss, this powerful bureaucracy was increasingly dedicated to serving its superiors rather than the people of the city. The poorest citizens seeking relief for their poverty or their grievances now deal with a vast and impersonal bureaucracy rather than with a sympathetic (for whatever reasons) and personal "boss." With respect to the new system that has replaced the old machine, the authors hold that "power speaks only to power." They go on to state that:

> The power is of many kinds and degrees, but its varying forms have one thing in common. It is derived from the top, not from the bottom. The men who control the $2 billion-a-year city government deal only with their counterparts—with the men who wield millions in private finance, with the men whose fortunes control all the large media of public opinion, with the new emperors of Madison Avenue who, through the cultivation of the technique of making a rancid herring smell sweet, have become the go-between in every big deal.

This, say the authors, has left the district leader

> . . . shorn of his functions as the Lord Bountiful and guardian of his people; and as he has lost this elemental reason for existence, he has been deprived of the influence his following used to give him with the men upstairs. No longer is he the source of food to the starving, jobs for the needy. Welfare is administered by one of those great, impersonal city agencies directed from the top at City Hall. The finding of jobs is the function of the employment bureau. The services that cater to the most fundamental needs of the people now filter down from the top. One cannot understand what is happening in today's New York unless one understands the significance of this change.[21]

This is not the place to argue the relative merits of ward heelers and bureaucrats, but these authors have indicated that New York City politics, like politics in many other places, has been turned upside down—that is, the local party leaders tend to become functionaries in a system in which power and influence flow downward. The result has been to make a bureaucracy of the political system which increasingly ignores the sentiment, however self-seeking or illogical, of the people. Rather than being responsive to public sentiment, the new powers in politics ignore it, or, if they cannot ignore it, they manipulate or engineer it with professional skill to serve their ends.

The old political boss, more often corrupt than not and usually completely indifferent to a public interest defined in any way but expediency,

[21] *Ibid.*, p. 262.

at least heard the voice of the oppressed—and responded somehow. Not many people weep as the corpses of machines are laid to rest, but the homogenized brokerage politics that is taking its place also seems to concentrate power, albeit in different places, and operates with as much cynicism as the machine. Whereas the machine, for reasons of its own power, responded to the needs of unorganized individuals with problems, brokerage politics offers to see that the demands of organized groups—the National Association of Manufacturers, the AFL-CIO, the Farm Bureau Federation, and the others—are all responded to in rough proportion to their political power.

THE RISE OF PUBLIC RELATIONS

IN AN EARLIER CHAPTER, we sketched briefly the political impact of the growth of the mass media, and we have made frequent references to the parallel growth of the techniques of public relations. In the present section, we examine, more specifically but still very broadly, the growing influence of the techniques of advertising on politics.

In describing preparations for the 1950 congressional campaigns, the New York *World Telegram* ran a story under the headline: "The Hucksters Take Over GOP Campaign."[22] The story had symbolic significance: the decade of the 1950's seems to mark the large-scale introduction into politics of the uses of the mass media and of the techniques employed to merchandise mass-produced articles in a culture of mass consumption. The story itself described the advertising paraphernalia which the National Committee and Congressional Campaign Committees were making available to Republican candidates: dramatized radio spot announcements, newsletters, street interview techniques, and visual aids of various sorts.

In 1952, both television and Madison Avenue made their first large-scale entrance into presidential politics. Both party conventions became carefully staged television spectaculars. Television coverage was concentrated in metropolitan areas and available to more than 50 per cent of the voters of the nation.[23]

During the campaign, the Republican Party was represented by the prominent New York advertising agency of Batten, Barton, Durstine and Osborn, whose professional influence was evident in the use of media, the treatment of issues, budgeting, strategy, and timing in the campaign. The Democratic standard bearer, Adlai Stevenson, dissented vigorously

[22]Vance Packard, *The Hidden Persuaders* (New York: McKay, 1957), p. 155.
[23]Charles Thomson, *Television and Presidential Politics* (Washington: The Brookings Institution, 1956), p. 1.

from the public relations trend with the observation that "the idea that you can merchandise candidates for high office like breakfast cereal is the ultimate indignity to the democratic process."[24] In 1952, the Democrats made little use of professional persuaders, and those they used had less voice in policy decisions. By 1956, however, the Democrats had been converted. They retained an advertising agency of their own and organized the campaign in close consultation with the professional public relations men. The age of the advertising men in politics had apparently arrived. By the beginning of the 1960's, candidates for even the humblest of offices were no more likely to enter the fray without hired professional help than an old-style politician would have been to forget the birthdays of his leading constituents.

The Role of Public Relations in Politics

Very early in this process, one of the first and most successful of the experts in campaign management, Clem Whitaker of California's Whitaker and Baxter, noted that "managing campaigns founded on sound public relations principles and using every technique of modern day advertising is no longer a hit or miss business directed by broken down politicians."[25] Whitaker's statement points to the pervasive influence of the professional expert in a campaign, but it does not very precisely define his role. Is he an essentially neutral expert who gives technical advice on the relative effectiveness of alternative techniques and approaches, prepares publicity releases that dramatize and maximize the audience for the candidate's position, and provides access to—besides serving as a contact with—the mass media? Or is he also cast in a policy-making role, creating the image of the candidate to be projected to a mass audience and helping to select the issues to be emphasized?

Perhaps this distinction between technical advice and policy-making is too pat. There are some fairly obvious ways in which technical advice operates to shape policy in a campaign. The expert, for example, may advise a politician that he cannot hold a television audience for a fifteen-minute speech, and that ten- to thirty-second "spot" announcements provide the most efficient use of limited campaign funds. Obviously nothing very meaningful can be said about complex social issues in twenty seconds, even if the time is devoted to a brief statement by the candidate himself. Still less can be said if it is used for professionally produced animated cartoons.

The intent of this technical advice is to saturate the audience through

---

[24]Quoted in Packard, *The Hidden Persuaders*, p. 172.
[25]Quoted in William Lee Miller, "Can Government Be Merchandized?" *Reporter*, October 27, 1953, p. 12.

repetition of the candidate's name or through identifying him with some simple and homely virtue. Insofar as issues are dealt with at all, they are given in capsule form, set forth in slogans, and relieved of intellectual content. The 1952 presidential campaign offers some instructive examples. The campaign plan called for candidate Eisenhower to deal with issues through a series of very brief, taped, and uncomplicated inter-views. A voice would present the candidate with an issue; he responded in "short, simple and hopeful" terms. For example:

> VOICE: Mr. Eisenhower, can you bring taxes down?
> EISENHOWER: Yes. We will work to cut billions in Washington spend-
> ing and bring your taxes down.

Or:

> VOICE: Mr. Eisenhower, what about the high cost of living?
> EISENHOWER: My wife Mamie worries about the same thing. I tell her
> it's our job to change that on November 4th.[26]

The Republicans reportedly spent about $1,500,000 on about forty-nine of these station-break spots in selective parts of the nation in the final three weeks of the campaign.[27] The Democrats, although they spent only a small fraction of that amount, countered with spots of their own. One of these went as follows: "Sh-h-h-h-h. Don't mention it to a soul, don't spread it around . . . but the Republican Party was in power back in 1932 . . . 13,000,000 people were unemployed . . . bank doors shut in your face . . . ."[28] Not even the most enthusiastic huckster could claim this to be a meaningful debate of issues.

It may almost be said that the over-all purpose of public relations in politics is to set the issues of the campaign in such a way that they are no longer issues in the traditional sense. Here again, the 1952 campaign is instructive. The Republicans were "successful in establishing with the voter their definition of the issues at stake . . .," which were "the govern-ment's handling of the Korean War, subversives in government agencies, and corruption." Polls demonstrated their success in making these im-portant to voters.[29]

But are these really *issues*? The war and corruption themes were essentially charismatic appeals ("I will go to Korea"; the "moral crusade") on universally desired goals. In neither case was there any hint of policy or program for dealing with the issue, or even efforts at defining the

[26]Stanley Kelley, Jr., *Professional Public Relations and Political Power* (Baltimore: Johns Hopkins Press, 1956), p. 189.
[27]*Ibid.*, p. 190.
[28]*Ibid.*, pp. 190-91.
[29]*Ibid.*, p. 200.

character and causes of the evils under attack. In the case of the subversion issue in government, the party traded on the climate created by Senator McCarthy and sought to read the opposition out of the democratic political arena ("Twenty Years of Treason" was one campaign theme).

This is a presentation of issues that are no longer issues. The appeal is addressed to stimulating emotional reactions, so that no one will be alienated, and so that opposition is difficult or impossible. Much the same might be said of some of the issues created by the Democrats in the 1960 campaign. "Getting this country on the move again" is hardly a controversial position on a real issue. The issues, so framed, bear more than a superficial similarity to the "issue" of eating a "breakfast of champions" or preventing cavities. We do not mean to imply that this was all there was to either the Democratic or the Republican campaigns. We are here examining only the impact of advertising techniques on politics. Politicans have by no means surrendered all control to professional persuaders. What we are arguing is that when public relations techniques have determined the character of campaigns, there has been a tendency to define real issues out of existence.

Occasionally, the professionals have even identified one of their problems as a tendency of the candidate to upset his "image," which has been carefully built up, or to take positions on issues which have a negative effect on the campaign. Thus Whitaker observed that "an automobile is an inanimate object; it can't object to your sales talk—and if you step on the starter, it usually runs. A candidate on the other hand can and does talk back."[30] Another public relations consultant commented about "the generality of candidates": They "only know they're ambitious and not much else. We take them from there."[31]

Not all of those engaged in professional campaign management take a cynical view of the candidates or of their own roles. Most of them sincerely believe that they are producing a wider familiarity with the candidates and with political questions than would otherwise be possible. In any event, our concern is not with their motivations but with the impact of the new techniques on political processes. One result seems to be a contribution to producing candidates who fit the description the late Governor Long of Louisiana gave to one of his opponents: "He won't say nothing, he won't promise nothing, and if he gets in he won't do nothing."[32] At the same time, it is an open question, of course, whether this is an improvement over the type of old-style boss which Long himself epitomized.

[30]*Ibid.*, p. 222.
[31]*Ibid.*, p. 234.
[32]Quoted in A. J. Liebling, "A Reporter at Large: The Great State," *New Yorker*, June 4, 1960, p. 74.

The Politician and the Professional Expert

Public relations techniques are the techniques of reaching and moving mass audiences. As such, they are in considerable measure the by-products of a consumption-oriented mass society generally, and of the domination of mass media by advertising in particular. Politicans are forced to compete for the attention of the voter with the entertainment provided in the mass media by other advertisers. In the circumstances, it would be surprising if they did not turn for help to those who have been successful in these media.

With the growth of new kinds of audiences and new techniques of reaching them, the old rules no longer apply and the old techniques become irrelevant. The politician is uncertain about what approaches will be most effective, and he operates always within a very limited budget. The costs of campaigning are increased by the new media through which he must communicate, and the decisions on how to use very limited funds become more difficult.

The politician may not be certain that the experts know very clearly about the relative effectiveness of various techniques (it is very possible that no one as yet knows very much about it), but his own uncertainty is apt to lead him to trust those who have at least mastered the maze of technical detail involved in a candidate's getting access to mass audiences. Another factor which sometimes operates to increase the candidate's willingness to put his campaign in the hands of a professional is pressure exerted on him by large contributors to his campaign who have themselves relied on public relations in their own enterprises.[33] Sometimes campaign contributions are made in the form of direct payments for professional consultation or management.

The Impact of Public Relations on American Politics

It seems obvious that the intrusion of professional public relations techniques into all stages of campaigns has far-reaching consequences. But the precise nature of these consequences is not so obvious. There are differences of opinion, for example, on how these changes are affecting the voter, how they are influencing the type of candidate likely to enter politics and likely to be elected, and more broadly what they do to traditional models of democratic politics.

As a result of the use of public relations techniques in the mass media, it has been contended, the average American citizen is becoming less apathetic, better informed, and more rational. One authority, for example, has recently claimed that television has:

[33]Kelley, *Professional Public Relations and Political Power*, p. 205.

brought about an infinite broadening of public participation in our democratic processes. It has given all Americans a clearer understanding of trends and issues. It has given them a personal acquaintance with their leaders and with those who aspire to leadership. It has increased the degree of independent thinking . . . . It has resulted in balloting based more on reason than on emotion.[34]

It is a fact that 1952 and 1956 saw the largest turnout of eligible voters in a presidential contest in recent decades. But it is not necessarily true that this fact reflects a decline in *political* apathy. As we will see in the next chapter, it is difficult to discover what the act of voting means. Insofar as it is a response to spot announcements, candidate images, or a noncommittal issue in capsule form, an increase in voting must be accounted an increase in *social* as distinct from *political* participation. We are entitled to wonder whether public relations techniques in politics do not overcome apathy in much the same way that the diversions of television programming overcome boredom.

Even though some people credit professional public relations with reducing apathy, its low level of intellectual content and its emotive appeal have been justified by others as techniques necessary to capture the attention of an apathetic, gullible, and ill-informed citizenry. As one professional remarked of the use of faulty and misleading statistics, "Jello isn't very solid either, but they sell a hell of a lot of it."[35] The difficulty with this rationalization is that these qualities of the citizen are not simply the stimuli to public relations techniques; they are also a consequence of their use. The mass media, as we have seen, constitute instruments of social control and character formation. When they are the vehicles for modern consent engineering, they induce people to see themselves as consumers of candidates and issues rather than as political participants shaping public policies.

Under the necessity of mass audience appeal, it is inevitable that the choice of candidates should come to be made on different grounds. "Availability" is the term used to describe the qualities that give a presidential candidate a good chance of being elected. Traditional availability meant that the candidate should be white, Protestant, from a large and pivotal state, and not identified too closely with particular interests or with either wing of the party. President Kennedy laid the religious criterion to rest in 1960. Still, it was these traditional criteria which were being applied when, during the campaign the story went around that the ideal Democratic vice-presidential candidate would be "a dirt-farmer from Kansas named Martin Luther" (Kennedy, of course, was a wealthy Catholic from industrial New England).

[34]Sig Mickelson, "TV and the Candidate," *Saturday Review*, April 16, 1960, p. 14.
[35]Quoted in Kelley, *Professional Public Relations and Political Power*, p. 234.

These traditional criteria seem to be yielding to new ones: a well-known name, a good television personality, personal ability to finance and organize the "pre-sales" campaign and the build-up. Stanley Kelley, on whose study we have relied heavily in this section, even suggests that the political public relations man may become a "talent scout."[36]

These changes are not necessarily bad. The old-style politician was often a product of machine politics and boss rule. It has been contended that the "new breed of politician . . . created by television . . . is an improvement over the past. He cannot hide behind showmanship and oratory. He is facing his audience on an infinitely more searching, more intimate basis than ever before."[37]

If the problems of public life are more complex than they have ever been, it is also true that the mass media present opportunities for political education never before even approximated. The mass media have created a national public which makes it possible to confront national issues. As the Kennedy-Nixon debates in 1960 made clear, television can be a tremendously flexible and useful vehicle for the organization of competitive politics. It can, indeed, put candidates on their mettle in ways not heretofore possible.

The all-important question is what the politicians, the audience, and the parties imagine their roles in the new media to be. Whether they contribute to genuine political debate and to a more responsible political system will depend on what models of democracy inform the behavior of the participants. We see no reason to abandon the conclusion that, where the media are dominated by public relations techniques, the tendency will be to cheapen and make trivial political debate and to contribute to what has been termed a politics of "organized irresponsibility."[38]

POLITICIANS, PEOPLE, AND POLITICAL POWER

DEMOCRACY DEMANDS that political power and public policy be made responsible ultimately to the people: "The people shall judge." But judge what? Who are the people? And through what political instruments is their voice to be registered and made effective?

By now, it should be clear that democrats are by no means agreed on what the legitimate and proper role of the people is. "The people," meaning "the many," may participate as one of the counters in a system of constitutional checks and balances, as found in the conservative model;

---

[36]*Ibid.*, p. 225.
[37]Mickelson, "TV and the Candidate," p. 51.
[38]Charles Frankel, *The Case for Modern Man* (New York: Harper, 1956).

"the people," meaning the electorate, may dictate the broad outlines of public policy through party debate and majority rule, as found in the liberal model; "the people," organized into pressure groups, may rule through the principles of compromise and the mutual accommodation of their conflicting interests, as found in the brokerage model; "the people," as a mass audience, may choose among competing merchandising appeals in much the same way they choose a toothpaste or a breakfast cereal.

It is clear that political power has shifted from the people in the first or conservative sense to the people in one of, or a combination of, the latter three senses. Whether or not he ever did, the American "common man" has long since ceased to regard the House of Representatives as "his" branch of government, speaking for his interests and opinions in a delicately balanced constitutional order. From Jacksonianism to the present, Americans have regarded all the agencies of political power, including and perhaps especially the Presidency, as vehicles of their will. Probably this process is, for all practical purposes, irreversible. If so, the real question is the extent to which "the people" organized as a public, "the people" organized as interest groups, or "the people" organized as a media market have inherited power.

The sense in which the people rule will be determined by the character of pressure groups, political parties, and the mass media, and by the pattern of their relationships. Political parties are the potential instruments through which a "public" may be organized to assert the primacy of public goals over private claims. In a pluralist society, "group man" can always be counted on to be articulate; "mass man," a product of recent social change, reacts to the calculated slogans and issue-less techniques of political merchandising. "Public man," the ideal of traditional theory, is almost completely inarticulate unless his voice is organized politically through political parties with principles which stand above the interests and dominate the political uses of the mass media.

When the realities of political life are viewed in this way, much of the frustration and cynicism which so often leads to an "escape from freedom" can be avoided. In a pluralist society, pressure groups are a desirable and inevitable means through which persons petition their government. Nor is there any way compatible with freedom to eliminate fraudulent or manipulative political advertising. The problem—if one exists —is political, and its solution must be found in devising or modifying political instruments for organizing the competition for power along different lines.

From the radical right and the radical left alike come proposals to solve the problems of democracy by eliminating the pluralism and openness which produce pressure groups or professional persuaders. Typically, their appeal is to transcend competitive politics, to find something better than politicians, to go above the strife of party controversy. It may be possible—in our view, it is both possible and desirable—to transcend the clash of private groups and to find alternatives to the competition of political hucksters. But the only approach consistent with democracy must look to the reorganization of political competition through politicians and parties. Appeals to rise above partisan politics turn out, on analysis, to reflect a loss of faith in democracy itself.

Still less can the politican be made the villain in the piece (assuming that one finds present practices less than satisfactory). If he too often succumbs to the temptation to dodge his way through the conflicting interests, if he listens too earnestly to the siren songs of the political advertising men, it may be for the sake of his political survival. In other words, he may be trying to give constituents what he believes they want. And his successes may reaffirm this judgment.

Few politicians have adopted completely these conceptions of their role. American political history is full of examples of courage of a political sort.[39] But political courage will be more common when it is politically rewarded. The roles of politican and citizen are interdependently related. Again, the character of the party system plays a crucial role in defining both.

[39]President Kennedy popularized some of these in *Profiles in Courage* (New York: Harper, 1956).

8

CITIZENSHIP
AND
VOTING BEHAVIOR

In the traditional theory of democracy, democratic citizenship involved an underlying tension between conflicting roles. On the one hand, the individual was seen as a private person, engaged in a competitive struggle with others for income, power, prestige; on the other, he was seen as a public person, a moral agent participating with others in defining the public principles by which private claims were to be judged.

More recently, in theory and practice, the public side of the citizen's dual role has come under attack. The fundamental crisis in democratic politics has come to focus, in one of its dimensions, on the behavior of citizens as voters.

THE MASS ELECTORATE:
DEMOCRATIC THEORY AND REALITY

Bluntly, the issue is this: traditional democratic theory makes certain assumptions about and places certain demands on the democratic

208

voter. Specifically, the average citizen is required to be (1) interested, (2) informed, and (3) capable of making reasoned choices.

We are already familiar to some extent with the model from which these requirements stemmed. In it, a competitive politics made responsible government possible because the appeal of politicians was presumed to be to the "liberal public"—in C. Wright Mills description, a body of reasoning men to whom reasoned appeals could be made. This public, in its turn, was presumed to consist of individuals who were vitally concerned about public affairs; who voted on the basis of their opinions about public problems rather than on their special interests or vague and irrelevant emotional appeals; and who had a knowledge of the issues and arguments necessary to an independent, individual, informed judgment. In short, the voter was presumed to perform an act of independent, interested, and informed choice among alternative principles of the public good. Not habit, nor the determinism of social status, religion, sex, age, income, or other environmental factors, nor yet emotional response to personalities or glittering but meaningless generalities were to determine his vote. Independent, reasoned, principled choice was held to be necessary if government was to be truly responsible to the electorate.

In the last two decades, sociologists, social psychologists, and political scientists have turned their attentions to the problem of describing and explaining the behavior of voters. As a result of the growing body of research in this area, it is now possible for us to make some generalizations about such questions as why people vote or abstain from voting and why they vote in the ways that they do. The most general observation we can make is that the evidence suggests a wide gulf between the traditional model of the democratic voter and his actual behavior.

The Voter: Interested or Apathetic?

More voters turn out on election day in totalitarian than in democratic countries, and in no other major democratic nation is participation at the polls so limited as in the United States. This is the more surprising because the United States was the first nation to achieve universal adult suffrage. Yet 60 per cent of the eligible electorate is considered a good turnout in Presidential elections (only in 1952 and 1956 did the figures go this high), and in local elections it often goes as low as 10 per cent. Moreover, many of those who do vote are herded to the polls by interested parties or pressure groups. They are not highly motivated and often vote more out of a sense of civic obligation (a feeling that is stimulated by popular pressures ranging from a nationwide campaign organized by the Advertising Council of America to the active efforts by the Boy Scouts to shame their elders into voting) than out of a sustained interest in public affairs.

Voting is only one avenue of political participation. But if the other possible means by which the average citizen can influence politics are considered—reading and listening to campaign materials, talking politics with friends and associates, contributing financially to parties and candidates, and working actively in political campaigns—it is still apparent that "a decline in political participation has been occurring in the United States concomitant with the emergence of a 'nonpartisan' set of attitudes toward the political process."[1]

Both apathy and nonpartisanship operate to reduce the popular basis of democratic consent for governmental policy: apathy for obvious reasons, and nonpartisanship because party leadership and the competition of the parties provide the means to responsible government. Nonpartisanship very likely is promoted by some of the same causes that underlie the growth of political apathy, and in many cases it may even be simply a more respectable way of expressing one's apathy. Thus, for example, that apparently growing body of voters who regard themselves with pride as "independents" contains a large proportion who turn out not really to care very much one way or another. The independent is usually the least interested and motivated voter, and he is in fact very likely not to vote at all. Recent research discloses that "the more strongly the voter favors or opposes parties and candidates, the more interested he is in the election."[2] When partisan commitment is weakened, interest is decreased.

There is much about the causes and character of political apathy that we do not know. However, recent research gives us clues as to some of the factors involved. It also suggests that political apathy in some of its dimensions is not simply a response to politics but reflects those more deep-seated social and cultural developments which we have earlier described as mass society and popular culture. The three sources of apathy with which we will be particularly concerned are: (1) withdrawal from politics because of the threats that it may pose to the individual, (2) "disengagement," which is the result of feelings of alienation from politics, and (3) apathy that reflects a sense of futility.[3]

POLITICS AS A THREAT TO THE INDIVIDUAL

For whatever truth there is in Riesman's analysis of the mass man as "other-directed," it is obvious that it should operate in the direction of increasing political apathy and disinterest. For political choice is inherently

[1]Samuel J. Eldersveld et al., "Research in Political Behavior," in Eulau, Eldersveld and Janowitz, Political Behavior, p. 72.
[2]Bernard R. Berelson, Paul F. Lazarsfeld, and William N. McPhee, Voting (Chicago: University of Chicago Press, 1954), p. 25.
[3]Our analysis is based extensively on Morris Rosenberg, "Some Determinants of Political Apathy," Public Opinion Quarterly, Winter, 1954, pp. 349-66.

a divisive process, basically at odds with the longing for harmony. Participation in partisan and controversial political activity may be seen as a potential source of disapproval in the groups with which one associates. Typical of this attitude is the following response of an interviewee in a recent study: "We don't discuss politics much. I think it's sort of like religion. It's personal, and I don't like to get into arguments. When politics comes up in conversation I always say—'Let's talk about something else.' "[4]

The potential controversy in politics may be seen as a threat to harmony in the home, the neighborhood, local civic groups, and in the occupational field. In all but the last area, it is likely to be a source of apathy primarily for those who have an overdeveloped dependence on group approval for justification of their own actions. In the occupational field, especially in large-scale organizations, political apathy may be more an expression of realistic expediency than a direct desire for congenial togetherness. Such an expression seems to underlie this reaction: "Well, it's a personal subject. . . . You see, in my field there is no harm in avoiding unnecessary conflicts, and politics are subject to strong sentiments. . . . I have to maintain relations among employees and management, and I try to avoid trouble points."[5]

It is true, on the other hand, that occupational and other groupings may be a strong source of support for political participation. A labor union, as well as a trade association or a professional organization, may exert pressures on the individual to participate actively in politics for certain causes or candidates. More loosely, where there is political agreement among occupational associates this tends to support political interest and involvement in the members. In this connection, one of the most significant results to come out of recent research into voting behavior relates to the important effects of cross-pressures on the individual. A voter is subjected to social cross-pressures when his environment is not politically homogeneous. He may find himself in political conflict with his wife or his family, with his close associates or his neighbors, or with the members of religious and social groups to which he belongs. There is a strong tendency for most people to associate in face-to-face groups mainly with persons who share the same political dispositions, but when conflict does occur one possible response is to avoid making a choice by withdrawing from political participation. This is apt to be especially true of those persons who can find a sense of their own worth only in the approval of others, an attitude which in the opinion of many observers is characteristic of mass society.

In addition to the threatening social and occupational consequences

[4]*Ibid.*, p. 352.
[5]*Ibid.*

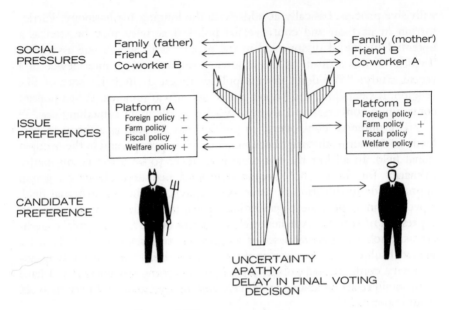

SOCIAL
PRESSURES

Family (father)
Friend A
Co-worker B

Family (mother)
Friend B
Co-worker A

ISSUE
PREFERENCES

Platform A
Foreign policy +
Farm policy   −
Fiscal policy +
Welfare policy +

Platform B
Foreign policy −
Farm policy   +
Fiscal policy +
Welfare policy −

CANDIDATE
PREFERENCE

UNCERTAINTY
APATHY
DELAY IN FINAL VOTING
DECISION

FIGURE 9. The cross-pressured voter.

which may stimulate a retreat from politics, there is another possible source of threat to the individual. Interest in politics, as we have suggested, seems to go along with the commitment of individuals to partisan and controversial positions and a willingness to defend them. This may take the form of commitment to a particular party or of deep feelings about issues or of strong identification with candidates, but, whatever form it takes, interest in politics ordinarily involves the individual in situations in which he risks being shown up as wrong or as uninformed in one way or another. It involves exposing oneself to the risk of ego deflation.[6] Just as some persons enter politics to enjoy the ego inflation that goes with being "in the know" and the chance to rub an occasional elbow with celebrities and to engage in the game of "name-dropping," so others stay out because of the hazards to personality. This type of person, when asked whether he discussed political questions, commented: "No, since I don't understand too much about politics, I just keep my mouth closed. . . . I don't think I am capable enough to take an active part. I just feel I lack the ability. . . . I don't know what would be required of me."[7]

Although we lack reliable data on the relative importance of the threatening consequences of politics for some types of personalities, there

[6]Ibid., p. 353.
[7]Ibid., pp. 353-54.

seems little doubt that they are clearly a factor in promoting apathy in others. Probably, the number of people who see the controversy of politics as undesirable and threatening has been increasing in recent years. As one political scientist has put it:

> By withdrawal the citizen may avoid a painful choice. He does not have to choose between two reference groups with different policies; he does not have to bring together in his own mind mutually incompatible ideals which are all dear to him; he does not have to risk alienating friends, customers, superiors, or in-laws; he does not have to expose himself to incompetence. All around him are people who are also apathetic who give him reassurance that he is not too derelict in his duties in this behavior.[8]

Perhaps it is significant that the word "apathy" is derived from a Greek word meaning to "not suffer."

THE ALIENATED VOTER

Political interest and activity imply the existence of effective incentives for the individual citizen. Political questions and issues, that is to say, must be felt to have some significance for the individual. He must be able to see that these questions, or for that matter politics itself, relate to his life and to his important concerns in one way or another. There is evidence that this condition is lacking for many people in contemporary politics.

In the traditional democratic model, we should recall, politics was viewed as the arena in which men could collectively control their collective destinies. Politics was a means by which society could be continuously adapted to men's moral purposes and public goals. A paradox of recent society is that while politics increasingly affects men's lives as the boundaries of governmental activity are expanded, the individual's feeling of control and competence and his sense of mastery over the future seem to have diminished: ". . . people no longer feel confident that they can affect their destiny, in anything that matters, by political action, individual or collective."[9] When people are asked about issues in campaigns there is always a sizeable "don't know" response; this often means really "don't care."[10] And not caring stems from an inability to see direct and important consequences affecting oneself or society from the victory of one side or the other.

These attitudes may even characterize persons who are politically

---

[8]Robert E. Lane, *Political Life* (New York: The Free Press of Glencoe, 1959), p. 47.
[9]David Riesman and Nathan Glazer, *Faces in the Crowd* (New Haven: Yale University Press, 1952), p. 33.
[10]Berelson, Lazarsfeld, and McPhee, *Voting*, p. 309.

active in campaigns. One study found that even active party workers are "not typically motivated by ideological concerns or plain civic duty"[11] but by the sources of ego inflation noted above. This suggests that even among those who are politically active, for a great many the psychological incentives are social rather than political. Political issues themselves often seem to many persons abstract, distant, and impersonal. As contrasted with family, job, and friends, the subject matter of politics seems not to relate to their personal lives. This is especially true in a culture in which material goods and private living standards are perhaps the basic criteria by which progress is defined and evaluated.[12] Insofar as politics is concerned with the problems of the total society (that is, with a public interest), it is not likely to be psychologically compelling for those persons who are engrossed in the day-to-day satisfaction of immediately personal needs. Where no clear ideal of citizenship as a *public* role infuses people's attitudes toward politics, the *private* test of "what's in it for me" becomes the only one. In an increasingly complex society, and especially one whose major problems are involved in foreign policy which is formulated in a bipartisan framework, the relevance of public issues to private concerns seems increasingly remote.

As the authors of one study have put it, "Citizens who vote only when they percieve some special direct benefit can be derived therefrom are not likely to vote when the vision of that benefit is lacking."[13] Their study showed that persons whose lives were dominated by their businesses or jobs were quite frequently indifferent about elections, and that this tends to be particularly true of those whose businesses have no direct connection with government. The attitudes are particularly apparent in the following response:

> I don't think politics or election results will or do affect my own life very much. Regardless of who is in power, I'll keep my job and my home. . . .I realize that politics does affect me, but it still doesn't seem to really touch me. . . .I think the fundamental thing is that we don't feel directly related or affected. . . . It doesn't affect us inwardly.[14]

In a system of competitive politics, parties and candidates must seek to overcome a sense of alienation of large numbers of voters and to engage them in the campaign. This effort sometimes takes the form of seeking to make politics an attractive form of diversion or entertainment in com-

---

[11]*Ibid.*, p. 307.

[12]See John Kenneth Galbraith, *The Affluent Society* (Boston: Houghton Mifflin, 1958).

[13]Berelson, Lazarsfeld, and McPhee, *Voting*, p. 167.

[14]Rosenberg, "Some Determinants of Political Apathy," p. 363.

petition particularly with the entertainment furnished by the mass media. The persons to whom this appeal is addressed are typified by this respondent in an interview study:

> People like to be entertained. . . .and get away from the troubles of the day. . . .They've got enough troubles of their own without carrying the weight of the world. . . I would say politics are dull in comparison to other news. . . .I see much more excitement in this story about the plane crashes than in this story about Eisenhower and the story on farm price supports.[15]

To compete for this man's attention, politics must be given the same warmth and personal and emotional appeal as a plane crash or a television western, and with no greater demands for rigorous and difficult analysis. It is doubtful that politics lends itself to effective competition in this kind of market. And it is certainly clear that, even if it did, the result would not be the development of a system of competitive politics designed to achieve responsible government and the organization of democratic consent. Yet, there seem to be forces operating in a democratic political system to force politics in the direction of increased personalization and subjective and emotional flavor in the competition for the entertainment of the electorate. There is, as one astute observer has put it, a sort of Gresham's Law of politics by virtue of which the beatitude tends to drive the epigram out of circulation.

The immediate cause of this phenomenon is that political campaigns must be pitched to those whose votes are likely to be influenced. Especially is this true of the minority party (that is, the party which has a minority of registered adherents). Both parties must, of course, seek to activate their partisans and insure that they get to the polls. But the majority party must also seek to hold its potential waverers, and the minority party must make these marginal supporters of the opposition its major target. As we have seen, there is an especially high proportion of apathetic persons among this very group of "undecideds." The result is that campaigns tend to be keyed to those sorts of appeals likely to activate voters who have a heightened sense of alienation. The marginal voter tends to exert even more than his due share of influence on campaign techniques and strategy. And this influence is exerted in directions other than rigorous analysis of public issues or sustained debate of a public interest.

APATHY AND FUTILITY

In addition to the threatening personal consequences of politics and the alienation of the individual, a third major source of political apathy

[15]*Ibid.,* p. 362.

is his sense of futility that he is powerless to affect the course of political decisions, the belief that the individual vote really makes no difference anyway, and the conviction that political power is effectively maintained by an elite who are not genuinely susceptible to the influence of the average citizen and voter.

These feelings of futility may arise from several sources. They may be rooted in the feeling of being dwarfed by the size of the electorate as when the individual feels that his is only an insignificant single vote destined to be overwhelmed by the huge number of the votes and voices of other participants. Or they may reflect the individual's feeling that he is weak in relation to powerful and usually anonymous forces—a vague "they" who make up the City Hall crowd or the political machine or simply the "government"—who will continue to run things as they wish and for their own benefit, despite anything that citizens might do at the polls. Or, they may stem from a conviction that the parties do not offer the voters real alternatives, that pressure groups are the real, effective agencies of politics, and that the role left for the individual as voter is accordingly negligible. Finally, they may flow from a resentment at being made the objects of manipulation by high-powered opinion engineers.

The attitude that a single vote cannot be important when there are large numbers of voters going to the polls is a common one. The size of modern electorates does tend to make the influence of the individual voter appear *deceptively* small. We say "deceptively" because it is not the total vote that the individual must compete against in order to be effective, but rather the number constituting the margin between the candidates. Where over seventy million people vote in a presidential election, the influence of a single vote looks small indeed. But where elections are won by as little as one vote per precinct in the country, the picture appears quite different. Yet sizable numbers of people continue to believe, with this respondent, that "voting doesn't make that much difference. What can an individual do about it? He can't really do much. My vote will always count, yet one vote one way or the other doesn't make much difference."[16]

In phases of political activity other than voting, the problem is more difficult. Can the individual exercise any really effective influence over the activities and decisions of the parties? If he is a loyal and faithful party worker because he is committed to the principles for which he believes the party stands and because he believes in the necessity for party responsibility, what does he do when he is asked by the leaders of the party to help organize a group of "Independents for Smith"? Can he exert any real influence over his party's local central committee, to say nothing of its state and national committees? Can he influence the choice of

[16]*Ibid.*, p. 355.

nominees for public office? One person expressed the cynical view of the possibilities of individual influence in these areas in this way: "I don't know how party politics go or anything, and maybe I am wrong, but it seems that you end up doing little things like telephoning or licking stamps. You don't have any control over things."[17]

This person's picture of "how party politics go," although it does not rest on first-hand experience, is accurate for much partisan activity on the American scene. There are significant exceptions, perhaps the most notable of which is the growth of the Democratic Clubs in California, and in most places the opportunities for individuals to play a more active and influential role are present where the motivation and the will exist. Yet there are real problems in these areas. They seem to be not so much a matter of the geographical distance between the individual and the centers of political decision-making as of organizational distance. The presence of several echelons of party organization between the individual and the levels at which significant decisions are made, along with the absence of effective organizational means for the participation of rank-and-file party members in the making of important decisions on policy and candidates, contribute to the feeling that the individual is used by the party for purposes that he has not helped to formulate.

In a political system like ours, in which the primary, if not the exclusive purpose of party organization is assumed by politicians and voters alike to be the winning of public office, it is almost inevitable that all those who are involved except those who will occupy the seats of power or those who will personally benefit through patronage or favor will in fact be used by the party machines as "power fodder." Where this is a source of apathy it cannot so easily be dismissed by argument or an appeal to the facts; at the most, it can be pointed out that the opportunities for more significant participation are there for those who have the desire and the will to use them. If that desire is absent, there is point to the futility expressed in such comments as this one: "I think that the higher levels of party organization are closed to ordinary citizens. . . . A couple of guys get together in some room . . . and when they come out, the party nomination has been made. You never know."[18]

There are, of course, other factors operating to promote a sense of futility about politics. Even the casual reader of the newspapers is aware that politicans frequently develop a special election-year psychology which makes it exceedingly difficult to pass legislation which might prove to be unpopular among significant groups of voters. Necessary but unpopular legislaton—tax bills, for example—may be put over to the following session

[17]*Ibid.*, p. 362.
[18]*Ibid.*, p. 358.

of the legislature when, it is hoped, the citizens who oppose it will have had time between elections to forget, or at least to forgive, their representatives for their votes. Awareness of this situation may lead the individual to feel that his influence is both intermittent and indirect.

Occasionally, too, individuals come to be disillusioned by the knowledge that some measures on which they are asked to judge are deliberately misrepresented and misleading. It sometimes happens that a measure presented as in the public interest is a front for private interests. Thus, a measure which has been presented as justified in the interest of conserving oil resources may turn out to be supported by large oil companies because it also increases their control of the market. Or a bill may be introduced to limit interest rates that can be charged by small-loan companies, but it may also contain provisions lifting the maximum limits on the loans that such companies can make and removing all limits on interest rates charged for large loans. Thus, a bill which appears on its surface to restrict small-loan companies may in fact be secretly supported by the loan companies themselves. Whereas such instances are by no means the rule in politics, when they become known the result may be to lead some people to conclude that all politics is a masquerade behind which powerful interests pull the strings.

Those who, for whatever reasons, develop a sense of futility about the role of the average citizen in politics are likely to have their views reinforced by the financial aspects of political campaigns. Especially as the costs of campaigning continue to rise those who see themselves as powerless are likely to regard all campaign contributions as purchases of special favors. Witness the comment of one person on a Boston campaign for mayor: "He spent too much money campaigning. I thought of where all those funds came from."[19]

Feelings of futility about politics are related to demographic characteristics in the population. Thus, the person who believes that he can exert a significant influence on politics is likely to be college educated, from upper-income and higher-status occupational groups, male, white, and residing outside the South in a metropolitan area. A heightened sense of futility is associated with the following characteristics: grade school education, female, Negro, low income, unskilled workers and farmers, Southern residents, and residents of rural areas.[20]

In part, these results reflect the objective access of different groups to political power and influence. People of higher socio-economic status are more likely to know, or to know persons who know, successful politi-

[19]Murray B. Levin, *The Alienated Voter* (New York: Holt, Rinehart & Winston, 1960), p. 60.
[20]Angus Campbell, Gerald Gurin, and Warren E. Miller, *The Voter Decides* (Evanston, Ill.: Row, Peterson, 1954), pp. 187-215.

cians; they are more likely to have experienced situations in which efforts at political influence have been successful. Persons of lower socio-economic status, on the other hand, are much less likely to have come close enough to the seats of the mighty to feel any sense of control or participation. Similarly, women and Negroes are only recently enfranchised groups and in many respects are still second-class citizens.

We must be careful, however, about drawing conclusions from statistical correlations like those above. It is true that education and higher socio-economic status tend to promote a sense of involvement and obligations of civic participation, and that lack of education and lower socio-economic status tend to promote feelings that a vague and powerful "they" are really running things. Partly, at least, this futility is a product of ignorance of the political process and governmental institutions: people tend to fear what they do not understand. But it would be a mistake to assume that education and increased status, for example, are cures for a sense of futility.

The uneducated are more likely to believe that "most major policy decisions are the work of 'wire-pullers' and pressure groups and the product of 'backroom deals.' "[21] But, paradoxically, this is close to one modern sophisticated analysis of the realities of the democratic process. It is, indeed, a reasonably accurate, though somewhat crudely put, restatement of the brokerage model of democratic politics. If the term "wire-pullers" is replaced by "lobbyists," and "committee sessions" and "bargaining situations" substituted for "backroom deals," the resulting description is not too wide of the mark.

Although education is likely to refine one's descriptive language, it does not necessarily any longer alter the picture of political reality from which the futility of the uneducated is derived. As the descriptions in the high school civics books catch up with the realism of present-day political science, it is even less likely to do so. Whether or not one feels a sense of futility about the resulting picture will depend on whether one continues to cling to a normative model of democratic politics which is inconsistent with this picture. This kind of futility stems from a feeling that (under the conditions of politics-as-it-is) the individual cannot play the significant role that he *ought* to play. Increased knowledge of the brokerage character of modern politics may have the result of producing futility and apathy if the individual clings to something like the traditional model of democracy in which the individual vote rather than the group interest is held to be the basic datum of politics.

It is likely that some such considerations as these are responsible for the growth of a new-style futility in recent years and an apathy that finds its expression among the most highly educated. So long as one clings to

[21]*Ibid.*, p. 188.

something like the traditional majoritarian or conservative models of democracy, the picture of Congress as a body whose "main business" is "the hammering out of a series of compromises between many special interest groups," and of parties whose "one purpose is to unite the largest possible number of divergent interest groups in the pursuit of power"[22] will be a frustrating one. In these circumstances one is likely to conclude, with Bernard Rosenberg, "I could care less about who won in November, but with some effort."[23]

In addition to this essentially intellectual rejection of the politics of compromise, there is a psychological sense in which increased knowledge of political realities may produce a heightened sense of futility. We have already noted that political interest and motivation may be party-centered, issue-centered, or candidate-centered. And we have noted also that people subjected to cross-pressures are less likely to be politically active. Where cross-pressures involve conflicts for an individual in these motivational factors (that is, where his party, issue, and candidate preferences cannot be reconciled), the extent of political participation tends to be reduced.[24] The looseness of party lines in a system of broker rule seems likely to increase the incidence of these cross-pressures. At the same time, increased education and political knowledge are apt to increase the individual's awareness of these cross-pressures where they exist. Here again, education under present conditions may promote, rather than retard, tendencies toward the retreat from politics.

The Vote: Reasoned Choice or Conditioned Response?

In the traditional rhetoric of democracy not only was the voter assumed to be interested, he was also described as performing an act of reasoned choice which was at once informed, independent, and principled. Recent research sheds light on the extent to which these requirements are typically met by the American electorate. The results reveal a striking contrast between democratic theory and democratic reality. It turns out that a large percentage of voters cast their ballots without much information about the issues, the candidates, and the parties; and they vote on the basis of the influence of family and close associates, economic interests, socio-economic status, or unconscious, psychological factors. We turn now to a brief review of some of the research findings as they relate to the requirements that the vote be informed, independent, and principled.

THE VOTE: INFORMED JUDGMENT OR "VISCERAL RESPONSE"?

Everyone is familiar with examples of experiments which show how

[22]Fischer, "Unwritten Rules of American Politics," *Harper's*, November, 1948, p. 31.
[23]"Comments," *Dissent*, Winter, 1959, p. 11.
[24]Campbell, Gurin, and Miller, *The Voter Decides*, pp. 157-59.

few voters are able to name or recognize the names of their representatives in Congress, state legislature, or city council. According to the authors of one study of voting behavior, most voters do not consider their vote as carefully or act as knowledgeably as when, for example, they are considering the purchase of a new home or car.[25] Some voters do not see the issues as important or relevant enough to their own immediate concerns to justify the time and effort necessary to inform themselves properly for an intelligent voting decision. Some others vote almost habitually out of party commitment and use their allegiance to a party label as a substitute for seeking information and listening to argument.

In addition to the voters who are uninformed, there is apparently a large amount of misinformation among voters. In a nationwide study of the 1952 campaign, one-third of the persons in the sample believed that the parties had the same position on the two major issues of the campaign; another one-fourth admitted that they did not know the parties' positions.[26] A study of the 1948 Presidential election revealed that on two of the crucial issues in the campaign (the Taft-Hartley Act and price controls) to which the candidates paid extensive attention in the mass media, only about one-third of the voters were highly accurate in their definitions of the positions of the candidates. Another one-third had highly or completely inaccurate perceptions of the candidates' stands.[27]

The general tendency working here seems to be for voters to see the candidates they support as agreeing with *them* on issues and the opposing candidates as disagreeing with them, irrespective of the positions the candidates have publicly taken. For example, 70 per cent of the Republicans who favored price control saw the Republican candidate, Thomas E. Dewey, as also favoring price control even though his public speeches and statements clearly indicated his opposition. Voters, in other words, perceive political reality in a highly selective way so that what Walter Lippman has called "the pictures inside people's heads" often are falsifications of the political reality outside. The more partisan the voter, the more likely he is to make this kind of misperception. The result is that partisanship leads to misperception which reinforces the original partisanship which leads to further misperception. These tendencies are aggravated where the actual, objective situation is ambiguous, as it often is in political campaigns. It is not true, however, that the attitudes of voters are evidence-proof stereotypes in their perception of the candidates.

The more an individual is exposed to the campaign (through newspapers and other mass media and campaign speeches and materials), the more likely he is to perceive the positions of the candidates accurately.

---

[25]Berelson, Lazarsfeld, and McPhee, *Voting*, p. 310.
[26]Campbell, Gurin, and Miller, *The Voter Decides*, p. 125.
[27]Berelson, Lazarsfeld, and McPhee, *Voting*, pp. 215-33.

Accuracy of perception also increases with educational level, interest, and membership in organizations, but exposure to the channels of political communication is the most influential variable. This suggests that much of the misinformation which voters take to the polls is a result of not caring sufficiently to expose themselves to the campaign.

With respect to another group of voters who are not so much misinformed as uninformed, the voting decision seems to be made on grounds to which information about the issues is simply irrelevant. These are the voters whose behavior is based on "visceral responses," to use the refined expression—"gut reactions," in Levin's less elegant but more descriptive phrase. Here are some reasons voters offered for their choices of a candidate in a Boston mayorality campaign: "Don't like his looks"; "smug—looks crooked"; "something about his eyes"; "looked icky, talked funny—the sound of his voice"; "a good man to his family"; "a real gentleman"; "just the way he spoke, I feel he is honest."[28] Considerations equally remote from the issues operate in presidential campaigns; the hair styles and taste in apparel of the candidates' wives, for example, have been matters of political comment and influence.

THE VOTE: AN INDIVIDUAL OR A SOCIAL ACT?

The requirement that the voter be informed was supplemented by the expectation that in casting his ballot he would behave independently as an individual. His decision would then reflect his own thinking about public issues and not his ties to socio-economic status, the pressures of the members of groups to which he belonged, or other types of social compulsion. The evidence available about how people actually behave conflicts with the requirements of the democratic model. The voting decisions of individuals tend in the first place to be group and not individual acts. Voting behavior turns out to be correlated statistically with a wide range of social characteristics. The most significant correlations tie voting behavior to (1) socio-economic status, (2) group loyalty and allegiances, and (3) geographical and regional characteristics. These relationships are illustrated in Figure 7 on page 184.

We need, however, to remember that statistical correlations do not, in themselves, establish any causal connections. Nor do they tell us anything at all about the reasons for any particular individual's vote. "Still," as professor Clinton Rossiter has put it,

> if we mind our step and are alert to the pitfalls, we can make excellent use of the broad generalizations that the Democrats are a party of the South, the city, the poor, the unions, the hard-luck farmers, the immigrants and their children, Negroes, white suprem-

[28]Levin, *The Aliented Voter*, pp. 44, 63.

acists, the young, the least educated, and the most educated; the Republicans a party of the North, the country, suburbia, the rich, the middle class, the business community, the good-luck farmers, the old stock, the middle-aged, and the college graduates. In making these generalizations, we must note that we are speaking of tendencies more than of imperatives. Both parties can still claim to be all things to all men.

Above all, we must be careful to pay homage to American individualism. As we travel over the political landscape we may come across the perfect demographic Democrat—a poor, young, unionized, Roman Catholic, second-generation, un-skilled laborer named Grabowski with an eighth-grade education and a lumpy bed in Buffalo—and find that he votes the straight Republican ticket, or the perfect demographic Republican—a well-to-do, middle-aged, salaried, Protestant, seventh-generation, top-management executive named Hoover with a college degree and a lovely home in Scarsdale—and find that he votes Democratic and, in addition, throws in $500 a year. The Republicans will be happy to have Grabowski's vote, the Democrats will invite Hoover to sit at the head table at the Jefferson-Jackson day dinner, and political demographers will be reminded once again of the hazards of their trade.[29]

The most common and well-documented conclusion of all the studies of the behavior of American voters is that persons in lower-income groups tend to vote Democratic while those in upper-income groups tend to vote Republican. Income appears to be, then, an independent variable in determining voting behavior. Most other variables associated with socio-economic status—for example, occupation, education, age—turn out to be dependent variables which cancel out when differences in income are controlled. Thus, except for the very highly educated, the greater the amount of education a citizen has the more likely it is that he will vote Republican. This does not mean, as Democrats are quick to point out, that there is any connection between being educated and seeing the Republican light, for the correlation between education and political preference turns out really to be an expression of the basic relation between income and political preference. Higher education is associated with higher income, and, where income is controlled, educational differences in voting decisions disappear.[30]

The same thing is true of age differences. Younger persons tend to be more liberal and are more likely to vote Democratic, but again this correlation disappears where socio-economic status is controlled. Religion,

[29]Clinton Rossiter, *Parties and Politics in America* (Ithaca: Cornell University Press, 1960), pp. 105-106.
[30]Berelson, Lazarsfeld, and McPhee, *Voting*, p. 334.

however, probably plays an independent role in some limited ways. While it is true that political differences among Protestant denominations (a higher percentage of Episcopalians vote Republican than do Baptists) disappear where income and occupation are controlled, the same does not seem to be true for Catholics and Jews. Even at the same income and occupational levels, Catholics seem to be more Democratic than Protestants, Jews more Democratic than Catholics.

Generally, however, it seems true that in considerable measure persons tend to vote with their pocketbooks. This does not mean that the motivation is purely economic. It may be above all a matter of status in the community. In American society, income is without much doubt the chief avenue to status. The motivation, however, to a conservative point of view among the well-to-do may be fundamentally a matter of accommodating oneself to the prevailing views and attitudes appropriate to the status in which one finds oneself or perhaps, even more importantly, the status to which one immediately aspires. In any event, the close relationship between voting behavior and socio-economic status suggests quite clearly that the decision of large numbers of voters cannot in any meaningful sense be regarded as an independent choice exercised by a consciously choosing individual.

There is one point that needs clarification. If the vote is so largely correlated with socio-economic status, how do the Republicans ever manage to win elections in the light of the fact that there are many more members of the lower economic classes than of the upper classes? The first factor is that, as we have seen in the earlier section, there is a higher percentage of voters among high-status persons than among wage earners. For example, one study found that 75 per cent of all executives and 74 per cent of all professional workers voted in 1948 and 1952, as compared with only 47 per cent of wage workers.[31]

The second reason is that the correlation between voting preference and socio-economic ties is by no means unity; that is, there are persons at all levels of socio-economic status who vote for the candidates of both parties. At the same time, the vote is more cohesive in the higher socio-economic range than in the lower. In most surveys, fully 75 per cent of those persons engaged in business, professions, and white collar employment vote Republican; a considerably smaller majority of wage workers vote Democratic. If it were not so, the Democrats would always constitute a majority party.

For the same reasons, the commitment of the lower-income groups to the Democratic party is more easily overcome than is the case with high-

[31]Angus Campbell and R. L. Kahn, *The People Elect a President* (Ann Arbor: University of Michigan, Survey Research Center, 1952), p. 109.

status groups. For example, when President Eisenhower was first elected in 1952, members of labor unions shifted to the Republican side in large numbers even though the Democrats still maintained a small majority of the labor-union vote. Interestingly enough, the only major group in American society, other than Negroes, which did not shift its vote in the Republican direction was the professional and managerial class. Among higher-status groups, in this election at least, the Republican majority and the Democratic minority both tended to be much less susceptible to change than was the case with lower-status voters.[32]

Apart from considerations of socio-economic status, there is another major category of influences which suggests that most voters do not vote independently. These influences flow from the effect on the individual of group membership and the pressures toward group loyalty and conformity. Included here are the influences of the family and of religious, ethnic, occupational, and other primary or "reference" groups.

Most people live within a homogeneous environment. It is perhaps inherent in the nature of group life that the more personal forms of social relationship involve common values and common ways of defining situations and resolving conflict for individual members. Especially those groups which sociologists term "primary groups"—those that involve immediate, continuing, intimate, face-to-face relationships—have available to them the capacity to reward their members for conformity and to punish them for deviation from group norms. These are the groups in which individuals, by and large, define themselves, and in which they satisfy the fundamental human needs for acceptance, affection, and approval. The ultimate threat of ostracism from those groups to whose approval one looks for a sense of his own importance is perhaps the ultimate punishment. The mechanisms by which groups structure the political perceptions of their members are complex and subtle, and the process is often an unconscious one in which the individual is not aware of having been influenced. This process operates in subtle ways even on individual evaluations of political events that are of little concern to the group. At the other extreme are cases where political attitudes are very closely linked with basic values of the group, and in which the individual is more likely to be consciously aware of deviation from group norms and to experience guilt feelings when he deviates.[33]

It is for these reasons that the family appears to be the primary unit in fashioning political preferences. Voting studies disclose that, in fully 90 per cent of all family situations, husband and wife agree in their voting decision. In upwards of 70 per cent of the cases, voters adopt the political

---

[32]Campbell, Gurin, and Miller, *The Voter Decides*, p. 153.
[33]*Ibid.*, p. 204

preferences of their parents and grandparents. These data are even more impressive when we take into account the testimony of psychiatrists that, in a large although undetermined number of cases where individuals depart from the voting preferences of their parents, the reasons are still to be found in primary group relationships. The deviant voter is often expressing his "resentment against his own group, rebellion against authority figures, or the wish to defend himself against an unbearable amount of submissiveness and to show his independence by his deviant vote."[34] Many psychiatrists have testified to the frequency of situations in which a divergence in political opinion and belief between the individual and his parent appears to reflect an unconscious and infantile need to usurp or overthrow the dominance of a parent figure.

The political experience of most people occurs within the framework of like-minded group association. Most political discussions carried on by citizens occur in homogeneous primary groups, and the exchange consists of mutually reinforcing observations on the campaign, candidates, and issues, rather than through debates. In most situations in which voters start out with views different from those that prevail among their primary associates, they modify them in the direction of conformity. People who are subjected to cross-pressures and conflict in their primary allegiances tend to vacillate and withdraw, or they reinforce one alternative over the other by looking to "wider associations in the surrounding communities."[35]

The available data lead us to the conclusion that voting is primarily a social rather than an individual act, and that most persons in casting their ballots register the preferences and attitudes dominant in the groups to which they belong. The average voter votes the way trusted people around him are doing, even though he may be firmly convinced that his decision is uniquely his own, undetermined or uninfluenced by social pressure.

We have already indicated that certain religious affiliations, specifically among Roman Catholics and Jews, appear to have an independent influence on voting behavior, the latter in a more marked way than the former. The same thing is also true of ethnic group membership. For example, voting behavior reflects a tendency on the part of those who have Scandinavian, German, or English-Scotch background to vote Republican, much more than do those of Irish, Italian, and Polish descent. Some partial data suggest that these results are probably attributable to the length of time that the various groups have lived in this country, more recent immigrant groups tending to be Democratic and all groups tending to become more

[34]Franz Alexander, "Emotional Factors in Voting Behavior," in Burdick and Brodbeck (eds.), *American Voting Behavior*, p. 302.
[35]Berelson, Lazarsfeld, and McPhee, *Voting*, p. 100.

Republican as they are integrated into American society and as opportunities for status advancement come to be available to them.[36]

In addition to group influences on voting, there are broader geographic and regional voting patterns in American political life. The most familiar of these is the sectional Democratic vote of the South. With the exception of 1928, when some of the southern states bolted the Democratic ticket because of the Catholicism of its candidate, Alfred E. Smith, the South was solidly in the Democratic camp at least until 1952, when Stevenson lost Florida, Texas, and Virginia to Eisenhower. Arkansas, Mississippi, Alabama, Georgia, and South Carolina have never gone to the Republicans since the Civil War. The states that border the solid South exhibit a clear tendency toward the Democratic party, although most of them were carried by Eisenhower in the 1952 and 1956 elections.

Until very recently, New England seemed to constitute a Republican hinterland, matching the solid South in its loyalty to the Republican cause. In recent years, however, Massachusetts, Rhode Island, and Connecticut have turned up on occasion in the Democratic camp; Maine and Vermont have, since 1958, elected Democratic candidates in state-wide contests. The Rocky Mountain states, especially Wyoming and Colorado, have been leaning toward the Republicans. The same is true for Oregon. Most of the states, however, have been genuinely two-party states, in which the contest is close as Figure 10 reveals.

Within the states themselves, there are varied patterns of community political preference. The large urban centers have been Democratic bastions which, in election returns, smother the Republican majorities returned by rural areas. Largely since World War II, the phenomenon of the growth of suburbia promises to introduce a new element into the traditional urban-rural split. In the same period, there have been other homogenizing influences—for example, the growth of mass media, the spread of industrialization into previously rural areas, the importance of defense industry in the economies of most states, the external and internal threats of communism, the dominance of foreign policy issues, and (with the exception of the Puerto Rican migration to New York) the end of significant new ethnic immigration. The effect of these developments will probably be the progressive elimination of ethnic and regional voting patterns.

THE VOTE: PUBLIC INTEREST OR PRIVATE BENEFITS?

In the middle of the nineteenth century, John Stuart Mill stated clearly an important premise of traditional democratic thought. The voter, he said, "is bound to give it [his vote] according to his best and most

[36]Campbell, Gurin, and Miller, *The Voter Decides*, p. 78.

States in which Republicans won all six times.
Total electoral votes in 1964 – 40.

States in which Democrats won all six times.
Total electoral votes in 1964 – 56. (disregards
Third Party victories in Louisiana, Alabama, Mississippi and South Carolina in 1948 and in Mississippi in 1960)

States in which Republicans won four or five times.
Total electoral votes in 1964 – 75.

States in which Democrats won four or five times.
Total electoral votes in 1964 – 91.

States in which each party won three times. Total
electoral votes in 1964 – 265.

FIGURE 10. Geographic distribution of party strength for six
presidential elections, 1940-1960.

conscientious opinion of the public good."[37] Research suggests that most
voters may lack this essentially altruistic motivation, and that most votes
are cast for candidates or parties from which the voter expects definite
and tangible benefits to accrue to himself. In considerable measure, the

[37]Quoted in Henry B. Mayo, *An Introduction to Democratic Theory* (New York:
Oxford University Press, 1960), p. 75.

arguments of candidates are rationalizations of the interests of the audiences to which they are addressed. Personal advantage, rather than a standard of the public interest, seems to be the major basis of appeal in American politics.

There are two sorts of appeals to private interest which characterize political campaigns. There is first the appeal to the interests of organized groups: the promise to farmers to vote for high support prices; promises to labor to vote for increased minimum wage requirements or liberalized industrial accident or unemployment insurance laws; promises to specific industry groups to safeguard local products from foreign competition through tariffs; promises to elderly citizens to increase social security benefits; and so forth.

The second appeal is reflected in the situation in which candidates promise to secure differential advantages for all their constituents against others. Examples would be the location of a new state college or university in the district, a new county fair ground supported by state funds, reclamation projects, parks and recreational facilities, and government defense installations. This process is revealed in attitudes of California Congressmen in the period since World War II. California has twice as much in defense contracts as the next leading state. This means that the protection of this economic advantage has become a major staple in the campaign of incumbent congressmen who claim to be responsible for this pleasant state of affairs and to stand jealous guard over the efforts of less favored states to reverse the situation.

Whichever of these two forms the appeal to private interest takes, one of its consequences is to minimize the role of a public interest in political debate and electoral contests. If politics is a matter of interests, the incumbent can lay claim to effectively representing all interests in his constituency. His opponent is reduced to the difficult task of seeking to maintain that he can do the same thing better. Thus, the tendency on the part of voters to cast their ballots on the basis of their economic interests is reinforced by campaigns in which private interests are the ground of appeal.

In this area of the motivation behind the decisions of voters, we have focused on the appeal to private interests in campaigns because there is very little data on voting behavior that sheds direct light on the question. To what extent do veterans vote for increased veterans' benefits, farmers for higher support prices, workers for liberalized labor benefits, wealthy people for reduced income taxes, bankers for higher interest rates, or the voter in the Fourth Congressional District for a local flood control project? We do not know directly. Analysis of campaign techniques suggests that politicians assume that appeals to private interest are the most effective. But this evidence only reflects the judgment of politicians on the matter. They are, presumably, the "experts" here. Still, they might be wrong.

There are enough successful politicians who have operated on contrary assumptions (Senators Morse of Oregon, Douglas of Illinois and Goldwater of Arizona are some) to suggest that there is at least a reservoir of public concern for political principles.

There are other data that support this interpretation. For example, the Democratic party, over the last several decades at least, has shown much the greater inclination to support governmental programs of immediate concern and interest to the aged: housing, old-age assistance, medical care. Those who are approaching or have reached retirement age, if their votes reflect their interest, ought to be voting Democratic. In all recent elections, however, those who are 55 and over constitute the most heavily Republican age group in the country, and in every case a majority of those voting have voted Republican. This suggests that factors other than private interest are involved in their vote. At the same time, it may be that some of this elderly group are the custodians, so to speak, of earlier attitudes toward politics and that they have been much more resistant to the growth of interest politics than other groups. In this connection, it may be of importance to have found that the students in our classes overwhelmingly expect and predict that the vote of elderly persons will be determined by their stake in old-age benefits. Perhaps this dichotomy between the voting behavior of the elderly and the expectations young people make about the way the elderly will vote reveals the extent of the shift in the American scene to a politics of private interests.

The Vote: The Impact of Suburbia

During the first quarter of this century, American politics was revolutionized by the migration from farm to city. In the period since 1940 particularly, the major population movement has been from the central city into the suburban community. The following estimated population figures tell the story: in the suburbs of the large metropolitan areas there were 15 million people in 1920; by 1940, there were 23 million; 35 million by 1950; and 53 million by 1960. By that date, slightly more than one-fourth of all Americans lived in suburban communities. In the decade from 1950 to 1960, while the major cities increased in population by about 10.7 per cent, the suburbs of the largest cities increased by 48.6 per cent.[38] Most analyses of the political behavior of suburbanites suggest that there is a suburban conservatism. In the elections from 1952 through 1956, Republican majorities in the suburbs overwhelmed the traditional Democratic majorities in the cities proper.

[38]Wilbur C. Hallenbeck, *American Urban Communities* (New York: Harper, 1951), p. 202; *U.S. News and World Report*, November 25, 1955, p. 35; and *Statistical Bulletin*, Metropolitan Life Insurance Co., July, 1961, p. 1.

Practical politicians, as well as scholars, have noted this trend. On election night in 1952, Jake Arvey, Democratic potentate in Illinois, is reported to have said. "The suburbs beat us."[39]

As scholars have pointed out, in 1952 the commuter country around such large cities as New York, Chicago, Cleveland, Detroit, and Milwaukee rolled up heavier Republican majorities than these cities proper gave the Democrats.[40] In the 1954 congressional elections, New York City voted 65.9 per cent Democratic, while the suburban areas in Suffolk County gave only 30.9 per cent of their votes to the Democrats. Similar results came in from such areas as Chicago, Philadelphia, and most other large metropolitan sections. Although some political studies have contested this generalization, most of the voting data supports the assertion of a predominantly Republican suburbia. The reasons for this phenomenon are by no means clear, although some aspects of it seem to be clearly worked out. We know, for example, that suburban life has certain characteristics. It tends to be marked by ethnic, religious, racial, and socio-economic homogeneity at a middle-class level which suggests a generally conservative political orientation.

There are two major, and conflicting, explanations for the Republican voting pattern of suburbia. The first of these is that Republican preferences are produced by exposure of new residents to a conservative and Republican environment, one in which new friends and neighbors share conservative values and in which the political attitudes acquired in large urban Democratic districts are regarded as lower-class habits. This explanation in terms of group association has been challenged by others who argue that socio-economic status considerations are more important. In this view, the new suburbanite is seen as a person who is already upwardly mobile before he joins the suburban community. It is a well-established thesis that the impact of social mobility on groups that are climbing their way up the status ladder is to make them more sensitive to the political norms of the groups into which they are climbing. As one observer has said:

> Anyone who aspires to move upward on the social scale will almost certainly sense the fact that the political coloration of the level toward which he is moving is more Republican than the one which he is leaving. This does not mean of course that he will necessarily change his politics as his social status improves, but he will become increasingly aware that Republican values are the accepted standards of the people whose approval he seeks.[41]

[39]Louis Harris, *Is There a Republican Majority?* (New York: Harper, 1954), p. 124.
[40]Samuel Lubell, *Revolt of the Moderates* (New York: Harper, 1956), p. 112.
[41]Angus Campbell, "The Case of the Missing Democrats," *New Republic,* July 2, 1956, p. 13.

Another possible explanation sees suburbia as the habitat of the "other-directed" man and the center of popular culture. Its style of life is epitomized in the quest for diversion and for "belongingness." If so, it is not correct to characterize the political attitudes appropriate to it as conservative in the traditional, middle-class sense (involving a commitment to *laissez-faire* and business interests, and opposition to progressive taxation and government programs of economic amelioration). The conservative attitudes reflected, after all, certain ideological commitments. And ideology, this argument runs, is contrary to the political style of the typical suburbanite. The attitudes of suburbia, some observers have held, spell "the end of ideology," conservative or otherwise.[42]

In this view, the political style appropriate to the dominant tendencies of suburban life is characterized by moderation and a commitment to the middle-of-the-road. The suburban Republican majorities in the 1950's reflect the fact that, under Eisenhower's leadership, the Republican party had become the party of moderation. Not conservatism, but "conservative liberalism" and "moderate progressivism" were the slogans of the Eisenhower years. If so, the Republicans cannot take for granted a suburban majority. This was indicated in 1960 when the Democrats picked up substantial strength in the suburbs. In Cook County, Illinois, for example, the Republican vote dropped from 56.8 per cent of the total in 1956 to 43.5 per cent in 1960. This 13.3 per cent loss more than doubled the nationwide figure.

Whatever the character of voting behavior in the suburbs, and whatever the explanations for it, one thing is clear: these developments lend no support to the hope that there are tendencies operating to reinforce a picture of the voter as an independent, deliberating member of a public organized to make reasoned choices of public policy. The picture of the voter as threatened by apathy, incapacitated by ignorance, manipulated by group pressures, and motivated by private interests emerges clearly enough from the data to pose a dramatic challenge to our traditional ideas of what a citizen as voter ought to be.

THE VOTER AND THE CRISIS
IN DEMOCRATIC THEORY

So WE HAVE COME TO AN IMPASSE, many believe, in the theory of democracy: we are forced to admit that citizens do not cast their votes in the way that traditional theory required for the system to work. Are we,

[42]Daniel Bell, *The End of Ideology* (New York: Free Press of Glencoe, 1960).

then, to say that the system has not worked, and should we try changing the behavior of voters to fit the model so that it will work? Or are we to say that it has worked, and, therefore, we need to find out how and why it has worked and to revise our theory of democracy accordingly?

In recent years, a significant school of thought has pursued the second of these alternatives. Many theorists argue that there is nothing wrong with the American voter; the problem lies with the traditional theory which imposed impossible—and unnecessary—demands on him in his role as citizen. In the following section, we present such a case—not the only one, but a representative and leading one.[43]

The Case for the Irrational Voter

According to this argument, a major difficulty in traditional democratic theory has been that it took as its point of departure the individual citizen rather than the political system. If we can transcend our inherited tendency to think in individualistic terms and think first about what we want a democratic political *system* to do, we will be able to discover why our own has worked as well as it has and why it has even worked better, perhaps, than it would have if voters had behaved as they "should." We will even discover that irrational individuals are necessary in order to make the system behave rationally.

What is it then that a democratic *system* ought to do? Although there are many ways of answering this question, there seem to be at least three qualities that have inhered in our own politics and that help to account for the fact that we live under the oldest existing constitutional republic. These qualities are (1) the ability to reconcile stability with flexibility and change; (2) the provision of a balance between consensus and cleavage; and (3) the creation of a framework within which the conciliation of the rival claims of conflicting groups in society can be peacefully achieved. We shall consider briefly how the actual characteristics of American voting behavior contribute to the meeting of these three tests.

STABILITY AND FLEXIBILITY

Any workable democratic system must provide for both stability and change. It must be capable of adapting itself to new conditions, but, at the same time, it must avoid the instabilities and fluctuations of power that characterize some of the Latin American "democracies," for example. It may be argued that the American system provides a strikingly successful solution to this problem and that it does so because of, rather than in

---

[43]The argument follows fairly closely, but not entirely, the analysis presented in the final chapter of Berelson, Lazarsfeld, and McPhee, *Voting*.

spite of, the fact that its citizens behave irrationally. Our survey of voting behavior research revealed that only a minority of citizens vote independently after carefully weighing the arguments and alternatives, but that most voters are influenced in their decisions by the way trusted people around them are voting, by their perceived economic interests, or by an almost biological attachment to the party label of their parents or of their geographical areas. If all citizens voted independently, the result would be government by fits and starts without the necessary stability and continuity of policy. In the American system, stability is provided by the role of habit in the voting decisions of a majority of citizens. These ties of habit tend to be self-perpetuating, precisely because they are not rational or reflective or principled. Voters do, to be sure, modify their political preferences, but this is a very gradual and, from the point of view of the individual voter, an almost unconscious process.

On the other hand, the element of flexibility in the system is provided by the independent voter who is likely to change his mind during the course of the campaign. As we have seen, the so-called independent is even further from the ideal of what a citizen ought to be than the biological, "my-party-right-or-wrong," partisan. He is likely to be inconsistent in his beliefs, caught in cross-pressures, but unlike the donkey between two bales of hay, not likely to care very much anyway. Thus, two groups of citizens, neither of whom embodies the traditional virtues of citizenship, may provide the political system with the desirable qualities that ideal citizens could not furnish.

CONSENSUS AND CLEAVAGE

Democracy means freedom of association and of ideas and a resulting pluralism of interests and values. At the same time, democratic government requires a consensus on the underlying procedures and values of its political processes. If democratic pluralism is to be reflected in politics, there must be some correlation between political party membership and socio-economic, ethnic, and other affiliations. The correlation, however, must not be too close, else there will be "total political war between segments of the society."[44] If, for example, all labor union members or all Catholics or all lower-income families were Democrats, and all business and professional groups or all Protestants or all high-income families were Republicans, the political system would break down. Under such conditions, the losing side in an election would be unwilling to accept a defeat that seemed to mean oppression by the victorious side.

We have seen in our survey of voting behavior that some voters do cast their ballots on the basis of their own considered principles, but most

"*Ibid.*, p. 320.

voters seem to be either patently and systematically bribed by organized appeals to private interests made by the politician and the party, or to be influenced by habit, emotion, or other nonrational considerations. It has been argued that the system works well because most voters do not meet the requirement of voting on the basis of principle. The argument may be summed up in the proposition that, however repugnant it may be to our individualistic tradition, in politics as elsewhere in modern industrial mass society, the division of labor is a necessary condition. Just as not everyone can be expected to be his own baker and shoemaker, so not all citizens can be expected to play the role assigned to them by the individualistic tradition. They play their different, largely irrational, roles; in the interconnection of these roles is to be found the rationality of "mass politics."[45]

THE PEACEFUL CONCILIATION OF GROUP INTERESTS

In the view we are considering, perhaps the major problem of politics is seen as the peaceful and willing conciliation of the rival claims made on public policy by competing individuals and groups. The social, cultural, and political conditions which make possible an environment in which a politics of conciliation and compromise can prevail is a central problem for any democratic system. On this assumption, it can be argued that the highly motivated and interested citizen of the traditional model can only increase the temperature of politics to the point where the climate is too heated for an effective politics of accommodation.

We have noted that only a minority of American voters seem highly motivated and interested, still more are mildly involved, and a large and apparently growing group is apathetic. From one point of view, this is a fortunate circumstance, for otherwise we should not expect that an electoral decision would be accepted on all sides and that the wounds of a heated campaign would heal rapidly when the election is over. A society in which the voting turnout approaches 100 per cent, in the absence of compulsory voting, is on the verge of revolution. Highly involved voters who see politics as a crusade for their conceptions of social justice are not the ingredients of a situation in which the compromise necessary to democracy can prevail. Indifferent or very lukewarm involvement on the part of large numbers of citizens reflects a general satisfaction with the *status quo* and provides the foundation for the process of conciliation and compromise of interests on which the success of a democratic system rests.

[45]*Ibid.*, p. 321. It should be noted that although these arguments are taken largely from Berelson, Lazarsfeld, and McPhee, these men do not offer them as an unqualified basis for the rejection of "the classical theory of liberal political democracy." They argue, rather, for the need for a "revision" of traditional theory.

The arguments on each of these three points all emphasize "the collective properties that reside in the electorate as a whole and in the political and social system in which it functions."[46] Citizens are not required to be members of or to aspire to membership in a homogeneous electorate characterized by interest, independence, and rationality. What makes the system work, it is held, is that the citizens are a heterogeneous group with a mixture of different and contradictory properties; in the balance of these properties lies the clue to a successfully operating democratic system.

The Case for Traditional Democratic Theory

Must we accept the position that what we know of the behavior of voters forces us to abandon or drastically to modify the traditional theory of liberal democracy? We think not, and for the following reasons:

1. It must be admitted that the traditional requirement of the citizen, "if pushed at all, becomes an impossible demand on the democratic electorate," at least in the sense that under modern conditions we are not likely to find anything like a majority of ideal citizens. But the theory of democracy has never claimed to be a description of actual political societies. Its description of the democratic voter was never offered as a picture of the average voter. It is, rather, an ethical norm of behavior. The democratic political system is, among other things, one in which this norm lives as a criterion against which citizens are continually urged to measure their behavior as citizens. The men who formulated this theory were never under the impression that group loyalties, habit, passion, and self-interest could be eliminated from politics. But they understood that they could be contained and superceded only so long as there were public norms of behavior that made contrary demands on citizens.

It would make as much sense to argue that the religious norm of love as a basis for human relations ought to be abandoned because the empirical evidence on prejudice, war, rivalry, and other forms of aggression proves that most men hate. Judged on this basis, not even the most proximate example of a religious society could be found in the world. But the crucial fact is this: insofar as there are differences in the behavior and relations of men in the world, certainly the ideals that men hold help directly to explain them. Every ideal, if it is to be meaningful, makes impossible demands on people; that's what makes it an ideal.

There is, in this sense, always a gulf between the ways in which people do behave and the ways in which their values require them to behave. This gulf produces feelings of guilt and frustration in individuals.

[46] *Ibid.*, p. 312.

It is a sign of our times that another reason sometimes offered for abandoning the traditional norms of citizenship is that these resulting guilt feelings are undesirable. It is true that guilt and frustration, carried too far, become the sources of the raw materials for mass movements and totalitarianism. It is also true that they serve as the stimuli to conscious change and control of human destiny. And the normless man is a ripe target for the kind of manipulation Orwell has described in *1984*.

2. The argument that the political system works in spite of—or because of—the apathy and irrationality of large numbers of voters rests basically on the claim that it maintains domestic peace and order without the imposition of uniformity or irresponsible political power. This reconciling of unity and diversity, this balance between consensus and cleavage, between stability and change, is no mean accomplishment and not lightly to be challenged. We would ask whether the unity, the consensus, and the stability may not in some important respects be more apparent than real. It is true that the large numbers of Americans who stay home on election day may be regarded as indicative of confidence in the basic governmental process, of a unity that is reflected in the feeling that, whichever way the election goes, things will not turn out badly.[47]

Before we accept this as a wholesome condition we should want to know what kind of satisfaction with the system is involved. More specifically, it is important to discover the extent to which political apathy reflects the attitudes of what C. Wright Mills has called "cheerful robots"— that is, persons who no longer view themselves as moral agents and who have largely lost their capacity to be concerned with the effort to control their own destinies. Insofar as this is true (and as we have seen, we have little evidence here), the consensus may not be either a very meaningful or a very democratic one. Studies of voting behavior seem to show that nonvoters are much less committed to civil liberties and have a greater susceptibility to appeals to authority and conformity and to the charms of the charismatic personality.[48]

From this standpoint the abandonment of the burden and opportunity to participate in defining the common concerns and in directing the collective destiny of society may be regarded as one of the basic symptoms of that drift toward a totalitarianism of spirit which, as de Tocqueville warned, can grow even inside a technically open society. The problem extends also to the question of the meaning of the vote itself under the

---

[47]See, for example, John P. Roche and Murray S. Stedman Jr., *The Dynamics of Democratic Government* (New York: McGraw-Hill, 1954), p. 128; also Lipset, *Political Man*, p. 32.

[48]Samuel A. Stouffer, *Communism, Conformity and Civil Liberties* (Garden City, N. Y.: Doubleday, 1955), pp. 83-86.

conditions of mass society and attitude engineering. The fundamental question is "in what sense and to what degree" voting itself has become "a symbolic gesture of the surrender of personality."[49]

Neither apathy nor participation for the sake of participation indicates the existence of consensus in any meaningful sense. For the apathetic, politics is hopeless; for those who participate without intellectual or moral commitment, it is meaningless. Consensus must be something more than "a mere bracket to enclose diversity" in Professor MacIver's phrase, and diversity itself is politically creative only when pluralist forms of association are related in some fashion to consciously chosen public goals. Moreover, the alienated man, whether he votes or stays home, no longer believes that the open, normal, and traditional channels of political choice and political responsibility are operative. If he is not apathetic, his interest is likely to be that of the "inside-dopester" described by Riesman. And if he has hopes of influencing political decisions, he is likely to conclude that the only real channel is behind-the-scenes personal influence. He is, accordingly, more likely to resort to it, and as it becomes generally accepted, "the stigma attached to it tends to disappear," and the standards of political morality become progressively blurred until "the political community becomes normless."[50]

3. Consensus, unity, and stability are alleged to be combined and balanced by this heterogeneous electorate with cleavage, diversity, and openness to change. But we would question the meaning and the character of the diversity and flexibility of such a system. The magic formula of a balance between stability and flexibility is an attractive one in a world rent by political strikes, revolutionary violence, civil war, and civil disturbances. In all such periods, men have been willing to pay a high price, and understandably so, for peace and order. Yet, in modern conditions, one may question whether democracy can survive if men are widely afflicted with that failure of nerve which leads them to sacrifice all other political values at the altar of stability and balance. Most importantly, a heterogeneous electorate in which habit, the desire to conform, private interest, emotion, or even reason plays its appropriate role in the total balance of forces may produce a very stable and nonrevolutionary system. But, it does so at the sacrifice of traditional values of liberty and individuality. For those values got their political meaning in men's ability to control their own collective destiny through the conscious choice of alternative

---

[49]Fiedler, "Voting and Voting Studies," in Burdick and Brodbeck (eds.), *American Voting Behavior*, p. 195. See also the Appendix in Levin, *The Alienated Voter*, and Lane, *Political Life*.
[50]Levin, *The Alienated Voter*, p. 64.

public policies. In this sense, the citizen was presumed to be the source of political power, his voice at the polls determining the fate of politicians and the course of public policy.

The significant fact about new "realistic" models of democratic politics is the contention that the *system* is rational only because citizens in large numbers behave irrationally. The flexibility of the system depends especially upon that group of citizens which is least influenced by issues and principles. One may inquire, then, about *how* the system adapts itself to change; what gives direction to the changes that are effected? There would seem to be two possible answers. First, it might be a political elite skilled in the ability to manipulate the anxieties, the emotions, and the desires of the marginal voters—the cross-pressured, uncertain, mildly concerned independent whom we have examined. The second possibility is that campaigns and elections are a largely meaningless facade behind which the real forces of local and special interests operate freely in their incessant struggle for differential advantage. This is, of course, the picture of a system of minorities rule, which we have already examined. In this case, political change is simply a response to the constantly shifting and changing balance of economic and social forces in a pluralist society. It is aimless, not consciously determined by anyone.

Both of these alternatives involve the surrender of the liberal possibility of man's consciously and purposefully steering his course into the future. They invite man to enjoy the fruits of tranquillity in the present at the necessary price of surrendering his responsibility for the future. They encourage men to cease struggling against their own irrationality which turns out to be, happily, the very prerequisite of a rational political system. As was the case with the traditional theory of *laissez-faire*, private vices are transmuted into public virtues, as if by an unseen hand.

This is not to deny that the system does produce tranquillity in a balancing of stability and flexibility, nor to minimize the value of that tranquillity. It is rather to argue that it is not the only political virtue. We would want to insist that any political system is to be judged also, and primarily, on its consequences for individuals, including their capacity to participate as citizens in the conscious, reflective choice of public goals and policies. And we would argue that a theory of democracy is inadequate which involves no greater demands on its citizens than to be their own sweet, apathetic, uninformed, self-interested and manipulated—but indispensable—selves.

Those who argue for replacing the hopelessly "idealistic" and optimistic eighteenth-century view of the role of the citizen with a "realistic" model more in keeping with the actual behavior of voters base their case on the desirability of recognizing man-as-he-is. This position neglects, we believe, the basic truth expressed by Goethe: "When we take man as he is, we make him worse; but when we take man as if he were already what he should be, we promote him to what he can be."[51]

[51]Quoted in Viktor E. Frankl, *From Death Camp to Existentialism* (Boston: Beacon, 1959), p. 110.

9

LEGISLATORS
AND
THEIR ENVIRONMENT

L EGISLATURES ARE THE KEY INSTITUTIONS OF REPRESENTATIVE DEMOCRACIES. This chapter analyzes the role of legislators, their characteristics, the environment in which they operate, and the effects of these considerations upon public policy. The following chapter will be concerned with the methods, procedures, and structures through which legislation is made.

THE ROLE OF THE LEGISLATOR

DURING THE 1959 SESSION of the lower house of the California legislature, the Assembly chaplain offered the following prayer:

Ever-present God, We seek immediate attention to our prayer for we think we can afford only a few moments, and, please, God, answer our prayer instantly. If you have any word of guidance for us, speak promptly, but, please, God, do not expect promptness from us. Carelessly some of us waste the time of others who must wait in committee and on Assembly floor while we get ourselves organized. You know our excuses: the telephone, an office visitor, we just couldn't make it on time. We mean we could have, but did not. Forgive our self-deception and our lack of courtesy to others. Help us, O God, to be present and ready for every duty, and thank you, God, for your prompt attention.—AMEN.[1]

The chaplain's candor was refreshing and his implicit plea that the legislative sessions should have first call on the time of a legislator is understandable. It minimizes, however, the great burden of work facing legislators, particularly United States congressmen who represent large constituencies. Much of the work has to do with matters not directly concerned with enacting laws—errands for constituents, correspondence, political party matters, speeches, and other time-consuming duties. All these things distract the legislator from his primary responsibility of acting upon proposals before his legislative house.

In Congress itself, his responsibility is enormous. The matters he must consider and vote upon are staggering in both variety and quantity. He must pass upon legislation in almost every area of human affairs. Within constitutional limitations, the congressman confronts a variety of measures, including appropriations for innumerable governmental activities both domestic and foreign; taxation measures to raise the money for appropriations; proposals to guarantee civil rights and liberties to minority groups; public housing bills; welfare proposals; demands for policy declarations covering the political activities of civil servants and military personnel; agricultural programs; social security measures; veterans' benefits; debt ceilings; tax depletion allowances; inquiries into foreign policies; federal-state-local governmental relationships; lobbying activities; aid to education; criminal procedures and penalties; immigration matters; bankruptcy regulations; new federal judicial districts and new courts to handle special kinds of cases; atomic energy; defense weapons; wages and hours legislation; and bills for the regulation of interstate commerce, communications, securities, aircraft, and other areas of the national economy.

Some sessions of Congress will be more concerned with some of these areas than others. Some Congresses will be known for their action on particular monumental measures such as social security, foreign aid, or land grants for state institutions of higher learning. Others may become known, perhaps unfairly, for their inactivity. For example, President Truman's 1948 campaign included many attacks upon "that no good, do-nothing Eightieth Congress."

[1] *Assembly Daily Journal*, May 6, 1959, p. 3281.

The broad outlines of congressional authority are found in the First Article of the Constitution. States also outline legislative authority in their constitutions. The powers of and restrictions upon legislative authority vary among the several states, but, in all of them, as in the federal government, the legislature is the main source of our body of law. There is still "judge-made" law, to be discussed in the chapters on the judiciary, but it composes much less of the total body of law than it once did.

LAWS AND MEN

A TIME-HONORED APHORISM of American politics holds that "we have a government of laws, not of men." This implies that law is a moral cut or two above the decisions of mere mortals. Many devotees of the law have carried such assumptions to the point where they look to constitutions, statute books, and judicial decisions for answers to moral questions on the premise that within these legal documents lies the key to moral direction. According to this reasoning, one could find in the written law the answer to such moral dilemmas as the proper treatment for homosexuals, the method of dealing with civil liberties, the desirability of fair-trade laws, or the discretion of an administrative official in dealing with agricultural problems.

We must ask ourselves, however, who makes the law and by what standards it is made. The answer to the first question in a democracy is obvious. Law is made by men, capricious creatures that they are, and law reflects the characteristics of men, including their greatness and their pettiness.

It is for this reason that legislative bodies are the most distinctive structural characteristic of democratic government. When one speaks of the British Parliament, the Congress of the United States, the North Dakota State Legislature or the Sacramento County Board of Supervisors, he is referring to that body of persons chosen by constituents in a given area to represent them in enacting measures for the public benefit. Democracy assumes that people will participate in shaping their own destiny and will prescribe the rules by which they will proceed to fulfill it. Legislative bodies are the basic means to this end. Laws and ordinances passed by these bodies determine the rules which executives administer and enforce and which courts will judge. Constitutions, executive vetoes, and judicial review may sometimes thwart the legislative will, but the long-run course of public policy is usually set by legislatures.

The proper function of legislative bodies and the standards to be employed in law making raise more difficult questions. If one conceives

that their theoretical mandate is to represent the public interest, many of
the activities observed in these chambers can lead to the conclusion that
the public interest takes strange forms at times.

THE DIFFICULTY OF EVALUATING LEGISLATURES

LEGISLATURES ARE THE LOCUS OF MOST OF THE SOCIAL FORCES of the
society they represent. It is here that these forces become pressures for
recognition or demands for solutions to social problems. Politics in its
most elaborate forms is involved in a bewilderingly complicated way to
reach solutions to these problems. Many standards and measurements of
legislative activities are applied to attempt an understanding of the process,
but these often leave even the most sophisticated observer doubtful of the
accuracy of his appraisal. Even at the purely descriptive level it is difficult
to discover, for example, how a particular law was passed or why another
failed of enactment.

The effort to explain the activities of a legislature involves an assessment of complex pressures, motivations, rules, and procedures not
completely intelligible to the participants themselves and likely to leave
the citizen who has not been behind the scenes of the legislative pageant
hopelessly lost. Did the Civil Rights Bill pass because of any real congressional attitude that such a bill was "good," or did it get through
Congress because one political party knew it could roast the opposition
by presenting it an issue that would tear it to shreds? Or did it pass
because politicians of both parties in the North and West were seeking
to cultivate significant organized groups of voters? Do we have a tax
depletion allowance for the oil industry because it is in the public interest
or because it was horse-traded by congressmen partial to the oil lobby
for a favorable vote on another issue, such as civil rights?

The answers to these questions are not simple and are sometimes
impossible. No one person, even a congressman himself, can have available
all the cloakroom conversations, cocktail party chatter, and luncheon
talk around the capitol. The personal motivations, ambitions, or fears of
a legislator all have an effect on what he does. So does the influence of
important bureaucrats, lobbyists, constituents, wives, secretaries, and his
political party. The best that can be hoped for is a plausible explanation
not too far removed from what happened in particular cases and a broad
view of the general characteristics of the decision-making process.

We do know, however, a good deal about some of the methods of
persuasion and influence as well as legislative convictions that lead to
laws. We also know a good deal about certain congressmen. Senator Doe
always votes for the public utilities, and Representative Roe is the man

who always supports and often sponsors antitrust legislation. Such information is useful in predicting the outcome of certain bills. It is particularly useful to the lobbyist who accumulates such information so that labor can predict how many solid votes it has on particular issues or the oil lobby can judge its chances for desired legislation. For the lobbyist, this is important information since he must avoid writing checks on his accumulated good-will account with legislators for what are likely to be lost causes. It also permits him to concentrate his attention on "fence-sitters." These legislators are given even more thorough attention because it is the "fence-sitters" who often decide important issues and who are most subject to persuasion.

Briefly, we can gather a good deal of empirical evidence about legislators and the means they use to achieve their ends. We also can draw some general conclusions about the most significant characteristics of the process through which public policies are adopted. But our picture will surely remain incomplete.

WHAT IS A LEGISLATOR?

AFTER THE VOTES ARE CAST, the political posters swept up, and the autumn air cleansed of the political smog of the preceding months, the victors in the contests for legislative seats emerge triumphant and anxiously await the day they will begin or continue to make laws for the rest of us to obey. But who is this victorious peer and what will he do when he makes our laws? Legislators are typical representatives of the society which chooses them.[2] The appeals and promises of the campaign were many and varied. Yet, in one way or another, each managed to appeal to a majority of the voters in his constituency.

There are sharp differences, though, in the way that a legislator may perceive his role; that is, in the self-image from which he defines his relationship to constituents, interest groups, party, and his own conscience. We can identify three broad models which may define the politician's role, generally, and his conception of the public interest, in particular.

Models of the Legislator's Role

1. A legislator may conceive himself as a political errand boy or cash register, whose obligation it is to mirror faithfully his constituency and

[2]An interesting appraisal of what legislators are and do may be found in Richard L. Neuberger's "I Go to the Legislature," *Survey Graphic*, July, 1941, pp. 373-376; or Jerry Voorhis' *Confessions of a Congressman* (Garden City, N. Y.: Doubleday, 1947).

246 / THE CONSENT OF THE GOVERNED

skillfully to negotiate in the legislature for their attitudes or interests, whatever they may be. Such a legislator is inclined to keep his "ear to the ground and his nose to the wind," seeking to gauge shifting public sentiment and attitudes as these are reflected in public opinion polls, letters from home, and the importunities of delegations of citizens. He is likely to regard what he learns as a mandate which deprives him of the right of independent judgment. When his constituents do not speak with a clear, near-unanimous voice—either in their attitudes on such a question as capital punishment or in their interests in such a question as taxation or minimum wage legislation—the appropriate posture for the political errand boy is the role of broker. In this circumstance, he may seek that solution which is tolerable, if not desirable, from the points of view of persons and groups with conflicting attitudes or interests. If this is impossible he can, in the last resort, avoid a position and find occasion to be in a conflicting committee meeting or the men's room when a vote is taken.

Lacking a political philosophy of his own, or at least unwilling to allow it to interfere with his political career, the broker politician who is a political mirror must rely in his campaigns upon organizational support and his personality. Ideally, a 100 per cent American with an attractive wife, war record, broad grin, glad hand extended, three lovely children; of the middle class but from humbler origins; who is hard-working, honest, able, and sincere—such a man offers himself as a charming personality who will do well because he is so typical of what all of us see ourselves to be. He must be able to play the role of "egghead" before audiences of intellectuals, and to shift to a wholesome folksiness before other groups. He must have a facility at role-playing to fit the flexible public image created by professional public relations advisers, if he is able to afford them.

2. Another general type of legislator is the "hack" who usually sets the low horizon of remaining in office as the highest virtue. The hack spends his time toiling the vineyards of his party, the political machine, the dominant interest group, or the press which operates in his constituency with enough strength to determine elections. He is often content to front for the political boss, party wheelhorse, or newspaper editor who flashes him signals and pulls his strings on all issues of importance. Sometimes the bosses will permit their hacks to join a harmless and popular movement. Thus, a tool of a boss may become famous for his righteous stand against narcotic peddlers, or famous as a crusader against pornographic comic books. Still, he knows that his political office and his political future depend upon other backstage forces which can make him or break him at will, and would not hesitate to do so on appropriate occasions.

Hacks are seldom bothered by any great pangs of doubt about the public interest or the rationality of constituent demands. As a result, they are very often noted for their personal services to their supporting constituents. This can take such forms as arranging appointments with bureaucrats for someone seeking a government contract, unsnarling a serviceman's war bride from the Bureau of Immigration's red tape, or getting a job for the boss' nephew just out of college. The hack gladly performs these services so long as they do not arouse the forces for which he fronts.

3. The third general type of legislator is the idealist. Idealists rarely exist in pure form, since the rigors of politics are often fatal to this delicate species unless they make some adaptation to their environment. Idealists are of two general types: the generalist and the specialist.

The generalist refers all political issues to his own conception of the public interest. Sometimes, the idealist is prone to see all issues as black-or-white moral matters and to deliver pious lectures to his colleagues on almost any subject, reminding them that the public interest will be thwarted if his moral guidance is not followed.

The specialist generally embraces a single cause and becomes famous for his dedication to it. He may be dedicated to the repeal of the income tax, the public ownership of basic industries, vegetarianism, the Townsend Plan, prohibition, or other causes. This type is fading in importance in current politics. Champions of single causes usually possess immoderate, if not eccentric, qualities which current society seems to frown upon and, as a result, penalizes them politically.

Idealists usually try to campaign on issues, but their efforts often fail disastrously if their opponents are distracting the electorate with circus tactics. Many idealists suffer greatly because they know they must often play the advertising game to get elected, and the brokerage game to get bills passed in the legislatures. To an idealist, these compromises of conscience do not come easily. He often finds the brokerage way of legislation to be a cynical, if not appalling, threat to his conception of democracy.

The above types of legislators are by no means definitive descriptions of actual individuals. There is a reciprocal relationship between every legislator and his constituency, and the realities and requirements of political life create dilemmas for every legislator. No matter what his self-image, a legislator whose constituency is made up predominantly of labor votes would hesitate to introduce legislation designed to thwart labor unions. Similarly, any legislator is likely to do whatever is necessary to retain a large government installation in his district or to secure an important public works project for his constituents. Still, the way in which a legislator meets these problems and makes his decisions will tend to hinge on his ideal image of his relationship to the electorate. In general, the dominant emerging type in American politics appears to have, for reasons discussed earlier, the cash-register orientation.

THE LEGISLATIVE ENVIRONMENT

THE BUSINESS of a legislature is conducted in an environment which shapes the pressures and sets limits of action in legislative conduct. Part of this environment is formal, derived from structural and constitutional factors and formalized rules of procedure. This formal background is considered in the next chapter. Now we are concerned with those informal arrangements which involve the role of lobbyists and political parties in the legislature, and with those informal arrangements which define the relationships of legislators to one another.

Legislators and Lobbyists

The lobbyist, as well as the journalist and the academician, is interested in the characteristics and the motivations of legislators. Clues to their power drives, vanity, integrity, and other factors may be significant for the lobbyists' tactics. Legislators' constituencies carefully are studied and analyzed by lobbyists to discover the composition of forces they contain. The lobbyist then plans his strategy on the assumption that the legislator will be influenced by the relative strength in his district of labor, real estate interests, newspaper editors, educational interests, Catholics, professional men, Protestants, small business interests, Jews, civil servants, ethnic groups, motel operators, liquor interests, the oil industry, manufacturers of various commodities, corn growers, dairy farmers, or local governmental units. Some lobbyists gather and catalogue information about the personal habits of lawmakers. Representative Doe likes two martinis before a roast beef dinner; one of his colleagues does not drink; another likes night clubs with lots of brass in the band and girls in the line; another likes a quiet dinner with good conversation; another, the theatre. Some legislators can be flattered; others like to argue; a dirty joke goes over well with some, but angers others; some want information in turgid reports full of facts and figures; others think statistics are lies. Overt requests to some legislators by a lobbyist mean a No vote, whereas other legislators seek out the stand of all affected interest groups on an issue.

How is this information used by those attempting to influence legislation? It depends on the legislator; the approach will be tailored to his individual characteristics. Assume a lobbyist is retained by the teachers' organizations in his political jurisdiction to work for higher salaries for the profession. He may drop off a mimeographed report with the secretaries of several legislators, knowing that the legislators are favorably interested and will read the report in order to shore up their arguments. He may arrange a luncheon with a few legislators to talk over the proposal and to point out why he thinks they should vote for it. He may take a few more out on the town that evening and do nothing more than let his guests know whom he represents. For others, he may be able to arrange a block of seats for a good play in town, or he might dig up some information desired by a legislator on a problem totally unrelated to his interest. His task is complicated by the necessity of tailoring his approach to the individual characteristics of legislators. The application of pressure is always delicate: too little may cost him his bill; too much may cost him his job. If he builds up widespread resentment, he becomes ineffectual, and no organization can afford lobbyists who are not well considered by the people they are attempting to influence.

The stereotype of the lobbyist has generally been a portly character dressed in cigar butt and elk tooth, his pockets stuffed with cash for the ready purchase of favor, and followed by a brace of shapely ladies of easy virtue who are readily available to those in influence. There have been such characters and may be a few left, but they have rapidly given way to the new type of lobbyist. He is usually a sincere, professionally trained man, skilled in human relations and the manipulative arts, who really likes people and enjoys the "good life." If he is also intellectually committed to the goals of the organization he represents and if, figuratively, his eyes grow moist when his organization's name is mentioned, he is even more effective. A true believer who is competent and intelligent makes the most effective lobbyist. He puts the legislator in a very difficult position. When the legislator dealt with the stereoype lobbyist he knew he was being used if he gave him aid. When he deals with the new model, he has difficulty sorting out truth from fancy, no doubt because the lobbyist himself is often confused on this point. In a society which increasingly submits to the engineering of desires by public relations experts, it is difficult for the citizen, the legislator, or even the lobbyist to extricate himself from the quagmire of contrived stratagems.

The influence of the modern lobbyist is increased by the complexity of the legislative task. The legislator is confronted with a range of activity which is virtually impossible for a human mind to comprehend. Generally, he cannot and admits it. He may base many decisions upon party platform, advice from a highly respected colleague, information from public officials, or articulated demands from constituents. But many things remain in doubt, and it is here that the lobbyist can often be of help as well as influence. In many instances, lobbyists will supply information, often of a high quality, on matters in which they have no interest. This serves to help the legislator as well as to ingratiate the lobbyist with the legislator. It can also muddy the waters of influence to the point where it is increasingly difficult to sort out biased from unbiased information.

In some situations, effective lobbying requires no great skill. There are many constituencies in which a single interest wields, or is thought to wield, a determinate amount of political influence. In these cases, the representative himself may be counted on by the lobbyist to "work the floor"—that is, to line up support from his colleagues. All that is needed to activate him is a word from the lobbyist indicating what his organization seriously wants. The legislator himself then becomes lobbyist, armed with the potent weapon regular lobbyists do not have—his vote on other issues. In every state legislature, for example, the representatives from the districts where the large state offices are located are likely to regard the support of the large number of state government employees in their districts as absolutely essential to their political careers. No matter what their own political philosophies, they are likely to lobby for the legislative program of the state employee's association and against legislation which might reduce the number of state employees or adversely affect their salaries, rights, or privileges. Yet again, the dominant interest might be an economic organization or a newspaper. If a single interest is politically powerful enough, the initiative may even come from the representative himself, as in the case of the state legislator who told one of the authors: "I finally got a good editorial in my home town newspaper, but it took me six bad votes to do it."

The techniques of influence, it would seem, have been polished, refined, and made more subtle in recent years. At the same time, the effort to raise the question of the morality of manipulative techniques or the question of the relation between group pressures and the search for the public interest seems to have slipped into the limbo of being old-fashioned, quaintly moralistic, or fault-finding. These questions, however, are made more rather than less significant and pressing by a recognition of the pervasive influence of lobbies.

Political Parties and the Legislator

Political parties are basic instruments of responsible government. If they are to play this role, however, more is necessary than that they provide voters with significantly different alternatives. They must also be strong enough to organize the debate and the vote in the legislature.

Every legislature must provide organized means for formulating the proposals on which the legislators will finally be called on to say Aye or Nay. If the parties are not the instruments through which proposals are formulated and alternatives drawn, that function will be performed by other groups. In a pluralist society, it seems that the alternative to party government is pressure-group government.

In 1913, California provided a dramatic and instructive example.

During the "progressive" era of Hiram Johnson, Californians were dis-illusioned with the corruption of political parties and the control exercised over them by dominant interest groups. In revolt, they passed a series of reform measures, including crossfiling, with the objective of minimizing the power of the parties. The reforms succeeded—in virtually eliminating effective political parties. But they succeeded also in *increasing* corruption and the power of dominant interest groups. They failed to accomplish their underlying purpose because they rested on a typically American fallacy we have often alluded to—the myth that the problem of controlling political power can be solved by eliminating it. Over a period of time, the reforms created a vacuum in the legislature which was filled by the pressure groups. Where formerly the legislature was organized by the dominant party it came to be organized on the basis of deals worked out by the lobbyists for the powerful interests. Lobbyists actually negotiated among themselves the appointment of speaker and committee chairmen. Instead of pressure groups seeking a party, candidates sought pressure groups. Within the framework of the pressure system itself, a structure of power developed. A master lobbyist, in the employ of several of the major interests, emerged as the invisible king of the legislature. Holding court in the Senator Hotel, across the street from the Capitol, Artie Samish summoned his minions in the legislature to appear and receive orders.[3] At one point, Earl Warren, then the Governor, pleaded that Artie had more power in the legislature than the Governor (which was very likely the case), and Samish himself on one occasion proclaimed, "The hell with the Governor; I run this state."

The lesson which it took Californians until 1959 to learn is that nonpartisan politics means an almost complete surrender of political power to the most powerful interests. Effective power is shifted out of the legis-lature and into the "lobby."

From the point of view of the legislator, he is left with little effective partisan organizational protection and no support. No longer able to look to his party for campaign funds or campaign workers, he looks elsewhere and takes help where he can find it. At the same time, the lack of effective party organization in the legislature means that proposals are usually formulated by pressure groups themselves and the legislator receives neither party pressure on his vote nor party protection. This is not likely to mean that he becomes "independent" or rises above politics. It only means he is forced to rely heavily on pressure groups for political support.

The principle seems clear: parties and pressure groups are *alternative* devices for organizing the legislative process; the strength and influence

[3]Lester Velie, "The Secret Boss of California," *Colliers*, August 13 (pp. 12-13; 71-73) and August 20 (pp. 12-13; 60-64), 1949.

of the one is at the expense of the other. The party with its program based upon its platform and principles is the only instrument yet devised for exerting any responsible control over the power aspirations of groups. It is not, however, a mere matter of the *strength* of party organization. Parties must be able to exert influence over their members in the legislature, but their power must be exerted in the service of party principle and not the mere balancing of interests.

In Congress, the power and effectiveness of party organization is something of an open question. There is agreement on the effectiveness of party discipline in organizing Congress (that is, on such matters as party control over the election of the presiding officers and committee chairmen). There is disagreement, however, on the effectiveness of the parties in formulating a legislative program which reflects party principles and in inducing party members to vote the party position.

One authority has concluded that the pressure of the party is the most important influence on a majority of Congressmen. He claims, too, that legislators who are independent of their parties are not treated kindly by the electorate.[4]

In the view of others, the party system breaks down in Congress, party lines being crossed so often in the vote that party responsibility becomes impossible. The endemic rash of what one critic has called "coalition fever" means, in this interpretation, that interest coalitions largely displace party policies in congressional voting.[5]

The major coalition in Congress is, of course, the northern Republican-southern Democrat vote. Its significance in cutting across party lines is revealed by the following tabulation for the Eighty-sixth Congress (1959-60) and the first year of the Eighty-seventh Congress (1961):[6]

	TOTAL ROLL CALLS	COALITION VICTORIES	
		No.	% OF TOTAL ROLL CALLS
1961			
Both Chambers	320	47	15
Senate	204	31	15
House	116	16	14
86th Congress			
Both Chambers	602	74	12
Senate	422	57	14
House	180	17	9

[4]Julius Turner, *Party and Constituency* (Baltimore: Johns Hopkins Press, 1951), pp. 70-71 and 174-179.
[5]James Burns, *Congress on Trial* (New York: Harper, 1949), p. 43.
[6]Adapted from *Congressional Quarterly*, November 3, 1961, p. 1796.

The weakness of party control in the Congress can be gauged by several other measures as well. One clue is simply the number of bills introduced during a session. In Congress, the figure is never less than several thousand. By contrast, in the British Parliament where there is strict party control and discipline, there are likely to be perhaps ninety bills (comprising the majority party's legislative program) considered.

The lack of party discipline in Congress is largely a result of the looseness of the party organization described earlier. The legislator does not owe his election as much to party affiliation, organization, and finances as he does to his own resourcefulness in securing local support. He is apt, therefore, to be much more sensitive and responsive to local interests and needs than to the party's position on national issues. He "tends to vote in the legislature as the local pressures upon him seem likely to influence his fate at the next election."[7] If his party had a greater influence on that fate, he would be more inclined to reflect that influence in his votes.

These pressures acquire special urgency in the House where the two-year term never permits the legislator to stop running for office. He is made especially anxious to cater to the interests of his constituency and the wishes of the dominant interests in it and is less likely to see issues in terms of the party's conception of a national interest.

THE DILEMMAS OF A LEGISLATOR

No MATTER IN WHAT MODEL a legislator defines his role he confronts inevitable dilemmas. Conflicting pressures on him create problems for which there is no simple solution—perhaps no solution at all. Is he entitled completely to neglect his constituents' interests in pursuit of his view of the national interest? To what extent should he serve the powerful interests in his constituency (on which his chances of re-election will largely depend) at the expense of the interests of the unorganized? What compromises of his principles are justifiable in order to secure a part of a political loaf? When does compromise become surrender or give way to expediency?

The Legislator and His Constituents

American politics, we have often noted, is strongly oriented toward local and private interests. Voters ordinarily expect that the legislator will promote the interests of his constituency. The strongest interests,

[7]Mayo, *An Introduction to Democratic Theory*, p. 90.

which are likely to have backed the legislator's campaign, expect to be served and, if they are not, their retribution in the next campaign is almost certain.

The problem of constituents for the individual legislator is complicated and difficult. This is true whether he comes from a constituency which is dominated by a single interest or from one in which there is a variety of sometimes conflicting interests. In the former case—if, for example, he represents a working class district in Detroit or an important natural gas-producing state—he is likely to feel that on crucial issues he has no alternative but to vote against a labor reform bill which the Auto Workers dislike, or for a bill to exempt natural gas wells from price regulation. (In 1956, all fifty-eight of the representatives in Congress from the leading gas-producing states of Arkansas, Kansas, Louisiana, Oklahoma, and Texas—liberals and conservatives alike—voted for removing controls on the price of natural gas at the well!) On issues which affect the dominant interest, he is likely to lose his freedom of action and even the opportunity to consider the question of the public interest. On issues unrelated to the dominant constituency interest, however, he may play his hand more freely.

His situation may be more confining if he represents a constituency with a diversity of economic interests. For in this case, it is likely that the lobbyists themselves will not be so prone to identify their interests with the "American way"; they are more likely to take a "reasonable" position which expresses a willingness to compromise with other interests in order to produce a "fair" solution to conflicts. The legislator in these circumstances may play a freer hand, but he is under considerable pressure to perform the neutral function of mediator between conflicting interests. He will often tend to seek solutions that will find a balance agreeable to the several interests. The point is that no matter what the interest group composition of his constituency, the role of interest groups makes it difficult for a legislator to approach his task as the application of a philosophical position to public issues.

The legislator can serve his constituents' interests, as a close observer of and participant in the Washington scene has put it, "only by frequent and perhaps distasteful compromises, and the line between compromise and corruption is often shadowy."[8] The price the legislator pays for being able to serve his constituents' interests successfully may be the ability effectively to promote his principles. His constituents' interests may directly conflict with his view of the public interest (as, for example, when he is committed to a low-tariff policy but seeks protection for

<hr>

[8]Telford Taylor, "The Ethics of Public Office," *Saturday Evening Post,* April 16, 1960, p. 94.

dominant local industries). More broadly, if he works hard and actively to promote his principles, he is likely to violate the unwritten rules that make it easier for other legislators to satisfy their constituents' interests. If he insists on doing so, he will forfeit his own effectiveness.

This situation was dramatically illustrated in a recent session of the California State Senate. A freshman Senator sought, on the floor, to remove committee amendments emasculating a bill which would have required the marking of gasoline octane ratings on pumps. By long-standing Senate tradition, committee action is seldom challenged on the floor and never by freshman Senators. Vigorous pressure for the amendments had come from the powerful oil lobby; no discernible organized pressures sought to protect the bill. The Senator had lined up enough votes to remove the amendments on the floor, but just before the vote was taken several of his colleagues asked to be excused from their vote pledge. The Senator found the powerful lobby opposing him and the traditions of the Senate itself too formidable a combination. His explanation to the press was frank:

> Some of the men said the heat they were getting from their home districts was too much [the "heat," of course, was applied by the petroleum industry, not consumers]. A couple of them won recent elections by close margins and indicated that if they voted with me they would not be returning to the senate.
>
> There's no sense in making an issue of it. Somewhere along the line there would be a rollcall and I'd just be putting people on the spot for a losing cause. Maybe in a couple of years things will be different and we can try again.[9]

It is hard to see what might happen so that "things will be different"— except a strengthening of political party organization and principles so that legislators are less susceptible to the power of the oil lobby. In the absence of that, it seems more likely that freshman senators will learn to behave according to the rules of a game that gives constituent and private interests priority over the legislator's conception of the public interest. It does not follow that all or even most legislators want it this way.

A democratic legislature can never be Utopia, and complete consistency and unblemished conscience can never be expected of democratic legislators. The idea that they can be is a dangerous illusion in a democracy for it leads to those efforts to "rise above politics" and those demands for perfection in which "the good becomes the enemy of the better." If we demand more principle in politics, we need to remember that this will result from an *increase* in principled controversy. To demand

[9]*The Sacramento Bee,* May 5, 1959.

uncompromised principle and purity of motive would make the "good" an impossible goal and the "better" an unworthy one.

The Legislator: Conscience or Compromise

Under what conditions is the legislator justified in sacrificing his own principles to the prevailing sentiment in his constituency or to the compromises worked out in the legislative arena? These are not easy questions. William Benton, former United States Senator from Connecticut, put them to his one-time colleagues in the Senate with interesting results. Ralph Flanders, Republican of Vermont who retired after a long and distinguished career in the Senate, replied:

> There is a saying to the effect that "a Senator's first duty is to get re-elected." This sounds a bit cynical, but there is a real vein of truth in it.
> If I were a Southern Senator and were facing the Little Rock situation, I would be strongly moved to avoid the extreme segregationist position, but would also avoid crusading for anti-segregation. I would join the moderates so far as seemed safe and hope for re-election, knowing that if I were defeated in the primaries my place would be taken by a rabid segregationist.[10]

Another distinguished Republican, Representative John Vorys of Ohio, took an opposite view:

> I am extremely cautious about calling political decisions moral issues. On the other hand, I think that Congressmen and Senators are expendable rather than indispensable, and no Congressman or Senator should cast a vote he knows is wrong in order to be re-elected. It makes no difference whether the wrongness is on a moral, legal, economic or other issue. . . .Taking the example you mention, I think that if a Southern Senator is opposed morally to segregation he should vote his convictions and take his medicine. For one thing, he might be surprised to find how many people admire that kind of courage.[11]

The same position was upheld vigorously by Democratic Senator Wayne Morse of Oregon who replied:

> Too often and too readily politicians—when they vote against something they know is in the public interest—fall back upon the excuse that "I know it is right but people don't understand it."

[10]William Benton, "The Big Dilemma: Conscience or Votes," *New York Times Magazine*, April 26, 1959, p. 12. Copyright by The New York Times. Reprinted by permission.
[11]*Ibid.*

What these politicians don't understand themselves is that it is part of their function in representative government to get the facts across to the people so they *will* understand. Instead, they become panhandlers for votes. We have many in public life who are afraid or unwilling to be defeated. Winning is their only goal, not true public service.[12]

The question at issue is whether the legislator is justified in doing what is necessary to win elections. If he does so, he may justify his actions with the argument that he is giving the voters what they want. This argument must be rejected on grounds that voters cannot know what they want, in a democratic sense, unless politicians formulate alternatives. Yet, the problem is not so simple. The legislator knows, for example, that his vote on many important issues is overlooked or even unknown to his constituents. He also knows his vote on a single issue, dramatized in his constituency, may cost him an election. He has not one, but many, principles. Should he take defeat for voting to repeal a loyalty oath when he might be re-elected on his votes on other issues if only he could make the voters aware of them? There are no simple answers here.

Another major problem of conscience for the legislator arises from the nature of democratic processes. The issues with which a legislature deals are complex, and there are many approaches to their solution. Yet, when a bill finally reaches the floor, the legislature must vote on a single measure which reflects both the complexity of the problem and compromises among rival viewpoints. The individual can vote Aye or Nay; there is no opportunity to follow up with qualifying conditions. Unable to vote his convictions in the record, the legislator faces the tremendously difficult problem, as President (then Senator) Kennedy put it, of "wondering when a compromise is one of accommodation or one of principle," and he must do it in "a glare of publicity," in "an irretrievable manner, on a permanent record, and with only the answer of an 'aye' or 'nay' to choose between."[13]

Legislators draw the line at different places. Senator Morse, for example has been a life-long battler for civil rights. In 1957, he was the only senator outside the South who voted against the Civil Rights Bill. He did so because he saw it as an inadmissable series of compromises with "the civil rights guarantee of the Fourteenth Amendment. I do not accept the view that such a compromise is ever justified."[14] Others, like Vice-President (then Senator) Johnson incline to the position that politics

[12]*Ibid.*, pp. 12 and 83.
[13]*Ibid.*, p. 84.
[14]*Ibid.*, p. 83.

requires the acceptance of considerably less that a whole loaf. "It is essential," he commented, for a political leader to yield or withdraw on some issues so that he will be "able to pick the terrain upon which he will give battle."[15] Still others are so concerned with accommodation that their principles are difficult to discern.

"Politics," an old saying goes, "is the art of the possible." This will always express an important truth about democratic politics. But it is not necessarily the whole truth. It may be that what makes "what is possible" also a movement in the direction of what is desirable is the presence of those politicians in the system who stand firm for the presently impossible. It is a presumptuous and misguided citizen, however, who will judge too quickly, too harshly, or too certainly every vote which appears to be a sacrifice of principle by a legislator.

WHO ARE THE LEGISLATORS?

IN ADDITION TO the general question of the relationship of politician to constituents and to his conscience, every legislator confronts other problems that involve his relationship to his party, to the executive branch, to other legislators, and to particular issues with which he is especially concerned. He also has the problem of adapting his own strengths and weaknesses in interpersonal relations, public speaking, and the devising of strategy for the legislative situation in order to maximize his effectiveness. As a result, it is possible to categorize legislators into a wide variety of types depending on how they react to this variety of demands. This categorization may be the result of the substance of legislation identified with the legislator, such as civil liberties, foreign affairs, or highway construction; or by the method he uses to achieve his objective, such as a reputation as a compromiser, a strategist, or an orator. Usually, it is a combination of both, but most legislators get themselves typed during their careers to the point where their political futures are often determined by their deserved or undeserved reputations. And, like actors, the type may not be deserved nor indicate the real or potential qualities of the individual legislator. Without attempting to be definitive, some of the legislative types are presented below to suggest how legislators either by their conceptions of their role or by the evaluations of others find themselves known to the public.[16]

A legislator may be one of the following:

[15]*Ibid.*, p. 84.
[16]Journalistic and academic observers of American politics very often discuss politicians as types. Our list is a general assessment of some of these observations, as well as some of our own.

1. An agent for the executive branch of government. He may represent the whole program of the administration or a segment of it, such as defense, agriculture, housing, or some other phase of the administration's legislative desires. This role often falls to the leadership of the executive's party in the legislature.

2. An agent for the program of an administrative agency, even though it is in opposition to the executive's desires for the program. A congressman who is known as a spokesman for the program of the Air Force or the Corps of Engineers would illustrate this type of activity.

3. A spokesman and champion of a pressure group and sponsor of legislation desired by such pressure groups. Many congressmen have had a difficult time explaining their close associations with the power lobby, the natural gas lobby, or labor unions. Too close an identity with pressure group interests often has detrimental effects on aspirations for national office.

4. A champion of a cause, such as civil liberties, antitrust legislation, or lower taxes. Wyoming's Senator O'Mahoney is noted for his championing of antitrust legislation, and Senator Eastland of Mississippi is identified with his desire to preserve the "southern way of life" in the face of legislation and judicial opinion extending civil rights to minority groups.

5. A strategist and champion of the political position of a party. The late Senator Taft's efforts in behalf of the Republican party which earned him the title "Mr. Republican" is an example.

6. A self-styled "statesman" in the grand design who rises above the petty aims of party and pressure groups and sees himself as the personification of the Truth. These people often have difficulty finding a haven for their ideas, if not their egos, within any political organization.

7. A "bad boy" (the late Senators Bilbo and McCarthy are examples) whose career is built upon a roughshod treatment of the ethical rules of our society. Such a role is risky, since one may ride high on an emotional binge, but when sanity returns the comedown is usually abrupt and often complete.

8. A political maverick. An example is Senator Langer of North Dakota or Senator Lausche of Ohio, who tend to run astray of party discipline and are at times quite unpredictable.

9. An elder statesman. Senator Hayden of Arizona, for example, does not seek the limelight but is consulted and admired by his colleagues for his wise counsel and great knowledge of legislative affairs.

10. A parliamentarian and strategist able to operate the creaking machinery of the legislative mill and get things done without breaking the machine down. Senator Russell of Georgia is known for his abilities in this direction.

11. A errand boy for constituents. He will guide them through the

bureaucratic labyrinth, see that appointments are granted to people from home, and arrange for tours of visitors.

12. A "hatchet man" for the party, a role which often falls to a personality type who delights in bursting the pompous poses of the opposition, and whose attack flirts with charges that the opposition is dishonest, subversive, or dupes of sinister forces. This can also be a risky business relative to one's political future. Such tactics can have a serious boomerang effect.

13. The bright young man with intellectual aspirations. He writes books and articles, sometimes very able ones, about his conception of the theoretical and practical aspects of his job.

14. A compromiser who is famous for his ability to get people together and get bills through Congress, even if it requires virtually emasculating the bill to do it. Several senators are noted for their abilities to reconcile the many opposing forces in Congress.

15. A flowery orator whose purple and bulbous rhetoric appeals to the sentimental and the pious in man. There are still many political figures noted for their uses of embellished oratorical utterances which cause embarrassment, rapture, or amusement, depending upon his listeners' orientation. Sadly, however, this type seems to be on the wane.

16. A political extremist, either to the right or left of the existing middle, who speaks seriously of a political philosophy of the distant past or dim future. Extremists also find difficulty retaining their position, particularly when moderation is popular. Congress did, however, contain members of the John Birch Society, an extremist right-wing group, in 1961.

17. A nonentity who is colorless, votes right to satisfy enough constituents, and laboriously tends his political fences to prevent a breakthrough of any sort. Legislative bodies, particularly at the state and local level, ordinarily contain a good number of nonentities, but their chances of reaching the United States Senate are very limited.

A list like this could be extended at great length, but it should illustrate the great variety of personality traits which are found in every legislative body. These traits are spread over the whole range of human characteristics—a fact that makes a study of legislative bodies extremely difficult. The study of legislatures involves the study of legislators. Examining legislators is examining human behavior, a task to which the whole area of the social sciences is dedicated. The tools of the social scientist are as yet inexact and imperfect, and so are many of his conclusions. When we turn our attention to the study of legislatures, we must accept these same limitations.

Again, none of the above illustrative types is intended as an inclusive description of individual legislators. Most legislators are a combination of types who display these varied characteristics on various occasions. Such a variety is both frustrating and fascinating to those politicians, lobbyists, academicians, and others who are constantly attempting to analyze and predict political behavior.

Professional, Social, and Personal Characteristics of Legislators

There are other characteristics of the legislator which must be considered. He will almost without exception be a member of some church. In the Eighty-sixth Congress, 85 of the 100 senate members were Protestants, 12 were Roman Catholic, two were Jewish, and only one did not give a religious preference. In the House of Representatives, out of the 432 members (there were five vacancies in a total of 437 seats), 328 were Protestants, 90 were Roman Catholics, ten were Jewish, one was a Sikh, and four did not state their affiliations.[17] Significantly, no member of either house was a declared atheist or agnostic. Even though America may not be a really religious society in any profound sense—clergymen are very rarely elected to public office, for example—Americans do seem to insist that their politicians adopt a nominally religious posture.

The legislator also will have professional or other occupational connections that are important in his role as a legislator. The dominant profession is law. Lawyers are more able to adjust their professional life to political activity, and campaigning for political office can serve as a form of advertising compatible with professional ethics. Lawyers also help to shape the methods of operation of legislative bodies, since the ethics of the profession demand that a lawyer argue his case regardless of what he personally thinks about it. Corporation lawyers and those practicing predominantly in the field of civil law often act as brokers among various interest groups within and without the courtroom, and many of them transfer this technique into legislative bodies when they are elected to them.

For the Eighty-sixth Congress, the *Congressional Quarterly* summarized the backgrounds of the members as follows:

> Attorneys again predominate in the 86th Congress, accounting for more than one-half the membership. Nearly one-third of the members have backgrounds in either business or banking.
>
> Almost 98 per cent of the Senators and 86.5 per cent of the representatives have had prior experience in politics or civil service. Sixty-two per cent of the Senate and 59 per cent of the House are veterans of the armed forces.

[17]*Congressional Quarterly*, January 8, 1960, p. 61.

Some members have engaged in more than one profession which explains why percentages in the following breakdown total more than 100. A few, such as housewives, fit into no professional category. Two Representatives are ministers.

	85TH CONGRESS		86TH CONGRESS	
	Senate	House	Senate	House
Agriculture	21%	11%	17%	10%
Business or Banking	29	30	29	29
Journalism	9	7	12	8
Law	61	54	62	52
Medicine, Engineering	4	2	3	1
Teaching	18	11	16	9

The average age of Representatives was 51.7 years and Senators 57.1 years in the 86th Congress. In the same Congress the youngest representative was 30 years old and the oldest was 91.[18]

The social class background of legislators may also be considered important to the legislative process. Most legislators are representative of some range of middle-classness, upper or lower. This may have some effect on the position legislators will take on specific issues, but attempting to explain political positions from financial and social background leads one into so many qualifications that valid generalizations from such studies become almost impossible to make. This gets particularly difficult in second-generation class backgrounds, as the political attitudes of Nelson Rockefeller, John Kennedy, and Averill Harriman attest. Also, the different political positions of former President Truman and Vice-President Nixon, who both claim lower middle-class backgrounds, illustrate the difficulty in attempting generalizations.

THE "CLUB"

Most students of organization realize that the power used to make institutional policies often lies somewhere in the organization other than in the top boxes on the organizational chart. A secretary to an executive may have a good deal of influence on corporate policy; an assistant professor may force issues upon equivocating administrators of his college; or a low-ranking budget analyst may throw a large and cumbersome bureaucracy into all sorts of agonizing justifications of its activities. So it is with legislatures. If one posed the question of the locus of power in the United States Congress, he would get a plethora of answers from a host of "informed" sources. Republicans would have one answer, Demo-

[18]Congressional Quarterly: Student Guide, Spring, 1959, p. 12.

crats another; labor leaders would offer their views, manufacturers theirs; leaders of minority groups theirs; and Capitol newspaper correspondents would have still others. But all would probably agree upon several key figures in both houses who had a great deal of influence upon congressional decisions.

The shifting sands of political fortune can change the power structure in Congress quite drastically. This is most noticeable when the political climate changes or the hue and cry goes up, and is successful, to "throw the rascals out." Generally, however, the shift in power alignments is more gradual and has an almost infinite number of factors working continuously to change it. To describe the power structure adequately in any particular Congress is difficult, especially for "outsiders," and even the memoirs of "insiders" are not always completely reliable. Power in legislative bodies rests on such factors as personal charm, seniority, voting strength in the constituency, the ability to compromise and get people together, social prestige, favor with the President, erudition, honesty, cunning, bluntness, dependability, wit, humor, eloquence, or even, as Senator Joseph McCarthy proved, the ability to cow one's colleagues into submission. As we pointed out earlier, there are many types of legislators. Leadership and positions of power in legislative bodies are often derivative from either the self-image or public image of the legislator as a person.

Legislatures are more than a haphazard collection of elected representatives who are thrown together to make laws. They are exclusive "clubs" to which the admission is open only to those who have survived the rigorous test of campaigning successfully for office. This is a hard test. Those who survive it and gain admission soon develop a strong sense of *esprit de corps* which transcends the verbal discord and power struggles that take place in legislative chambers. The United States Senate is often referred to as the most exclusive "club" in the United States, open only to one hundred of more than 175 million people. Although there are all kinds of members with a variety of professional backgrounds, upon election to the Senate all of them share an important common attribute—membership in the "club."

The "club" has rules and etiquette. New members are to be seen and not heard. Before they are admitted to high councils of the "club," they must serve their apprenticeship and prove their worthiness. The new member must be a "workhorse," not a "showhorse," tilling the vineyard and leaving the headlines and the glamour to the older hands. The new member gets what office space is left over after his colleagues with previous service have made their choices. He sits at the foot of the table at official dinners. He does not speak on the floor often, for this is a breach of tradition; in fact, he is not even supposed to deliver eulogies and flattery, a practice common among legislators, unless he has been around long enough to have earned the right to praise his colleagues. A veteran senator has illustrated the tradition in this story of a freshman who did not know his place:

> When I came to the Senate, I sat next to Senator Borah. A few months later, he had a birthday. A number of the older men got up and made brief, laudatory speeches about it. Borah was pleased. Then a freshman Senator—one who had only been in the Chamber three or four months—got to his feet and started on a similar eulogy. He was an excellent speaker, but between each of his laudatory references to Borah, Borah loudly whispered "That son-of-a-bitch, that son-of-a-bitch." He didn't dislike the speaker personally. He just didn't feel that he should speak so soon.[19]

The Senate folkways are elaborate, and admission to the inner circles of command depends upon one's observance of them before he can expect his elders to bestow on him the longed-for nod of acceptance.

The "club" not only has serious effects upon behavior but tends to encourage brokerage politics on the part of its members. Whereas integrity is recognized as desirable, brashness and flaunting of erudition is not. One accommodates his fellow "club" members and is expected to do some careful horse trading, often at a disadvantage since the inner circle has most of the best horses, to get his bills passed. Some members have gained admission to the "club" eventually by flouting the rules and "kicking the door down," but this takes a rare and dramatic personality as well as the ability, over a period of time, to gain personal respect. If the member attempting this tactic does not kick hard enough, he is in trouble when his bills begin their way through the legislative labyrinth. If a member served well on unimportant committees, and behaved properly in other ways, his bills will meet with some success. If he has flouted or defied the rules, his legislative objectives are likely to suffer and his constituents may be put on a slim diet of "pork." The same is true of committee assignments. The good spots go to the most acceptable applicants if seniority does not dictate otherwise. Pressure groups are much aware of the advantages the "club" provides them, and they carefully cultivate the friendship of its informal directors.

Lower houses of legislative bodies have some of the "club" atmosphere, but their larger size and frequent elections with consequently higher turnover of members make them less charmed circles than are upper houses. What is true of the United States Senate is also true of the upper houses

[19]From Donald R. Matthews, "The Folkways of the United States Senate: Conformity to Group Norms and Legislative Effectiveness," *American Political Science Review*, December, 1959, p. 1066.

in most states. State senates are quite exclusive, as many an eager freshman has discovered. In fact, members of most upper houses hardly acknowledge the existence of the lower house; when they do, they often refer to it as "that group across the Capitol," "those other fellows," or, as one state senator put it, "that mob over there."

Some legislative leadership is formally established. By definition of their offices and the manner of selection, the Speaker of the House, majority leader in the Senate, minority leaders in both houses, and party whips will have a good deal of power. Their partisan colleagues usually have selected them because of some characteristics of leadership. There are, however, some members of Congress who avoid assuming formal positions of leadership, since they feel more effective operating from the sidelines. Many legislators, for example, are very adept at calming troubled waters or at in-fighting in the privacy of offices but are very poor at publicly leading their colleagues.

Positions of prominence, such as majority or minority leader in the Senate, generally go to Senators whose abilities are recognized by both the public and their colleagues. The personal characteristics of the legislative leaders may differ greatly, but they almost without exception have considerable ability in organizing their party colleagues for legislative battle.

Such personal differences were illustrated in the change in Republican Senate leadership in the Eighty-sixth Congress. Former Majority, and later Minority, Leader Senator Knowland of California was a doggedly determined, almost humorless man who pushed forward for what he thought was right, even when the President and other members of his party periodically chafed at some of his public expressions. He was often quite successful, as one may note in his influence on the United States' relationships with Nationalist China.

When Senator Knowland quit the Senate and ran unsuccessfully for Governor of California, he was succeeded as majority leader by Senator Dirksen of Illinois. Whereas Senator Knowland's public utterances were coldly serious and unembellished, Senator Dirksen is famous for his oratory, unctuous to the point where one observer dubbed him the "Wizard of Ooze."[20] Senator Knowland was not a man to compromise his principles, but Senator Dirksen was selected because his voting record and political career clearly indicated he could be flexible on many issues. Also, he was often able to get opposing points of view reconciled into a compromise. Knowland appeared somewhat indifferent to personal animosity, but Dirksen is highly sensitive to it. For example, at the 1952 Republican convention,

[20]William B. Furlong, "The Senate's Wizard of Ooze: Dirksen of Illinois," *Harper's*, December, 1959, p. 44.

Dirksen almost caused a rebellion when he pointed a finger at Thomas E. Dewey and intoned accusingly, "You took us down the road to defeat." When boos and shouts came from the floor, Dirksen ". . . sipped a glass of water daintly—pinky neatly curved—and said with prim precision: 'I did not mean to precipitate a controversy.' "[21]

Both Dirksen and Knowland have been effective leaders of their party, although they are very different types. Where the party puts a premium on appeals to moderation and harmony, it is likely that leaders of strong partisan views and personal commitments like Knowland will give way to more pliable leaders like Dirksen.

Prevailing political attitudes also have an effect on the selection of legislative leadership. If the nation is sharply divided on issues, such as the economic crises of the 1930's, forceful leaders able clearly and emphatically to state their party's views are more in favor. But if the mood is one of harmony and if political success is gained from being moderate, as in the late 1950's, leadership tends to adopt this role. Senator Lyndon Johnson's selection as Democratic Majority Leader, in 1954, reflected the desire of his party to be "less controversial" then it would be under a more doctrinaire leader.[22] Senator Johnson's greatest praise stemmed from his ability to compromise factions and to get along reasonably well with a President of the opposite political faith. Many members of Senator Johnson's own party grumbled about his propensity to compromise, but since the Democrats have appeared anxious to avoid the charge of being extremists in a time of moderation he did his job effectively. Without strong party identity on public issues, an increasing number of moderates will probably find a position of leadership. But a revolt of the moderates does not imply a breakdown in party organization and discipline for power purposes. Moderates need power to be moderate just as extremists need power to be extreme. Legislative leaders are likely to continue to be men who can organize their party's quest for power.

Internal fights occasionally develop which reflect the parties' dissatisfaction with the organizational effectiveness of its leadership. An example was the struggle for the House Minority Leader position between Republican representatives Joseph W. Martin and Charles A. Halleck in the Eighty-sixth Congress. Martin had been Minority Floor Leader since 1939, with the exception of the Eightieth and Eighty-third Republican Congresses in which he was Speaker. Halleck was Majority Leader when Martin was Speaker, and Martin's unofficial assistant in the Eighty-fourth and Eighty-fifth Congresses. Halleck was a more vigorous fifty-eight years

[21]*Ibid.*, p. 45.
[22]See William S. White, "Who is Lyndon Johnson?" *Harper's*, March, 1958, for an interesting appraisal of Senator and, later, Vice-President Johnson by a well-respected reporter on national politics.

of age, while Martin was seventy-four and not in the most robust health. Each had support from both the liberal and conservative segments of his party, but Martin intimated that Vice-President Nixon had intervened on his opponent's behalf. As he put it, "All I know is that all his [Nixon's] people were against me—actively against me." After it was decided to use a secret ballot, which permitted some reluctant members to vote against Martin without having to do so openly, Halleck emerged triumphant. Martin, after twenty years of leadership, was turned out to pasture.

Cruel treatment, one might say, and reasons for it ranged from Martin's age to the failure of Republicans to win enough congressional seats in the preceding three elections. As Martin said, election reverses "had the boys confused. They wanted a fall guy." As politicians are prone to do, they tried to soften the blow for Martin by offering him a variety of honorary offices, but these were rejected with Martin's succinct statement, "After twenty years as leader, what the hell do I want those for?" Honorary office could not remove the sting of defeat.[23]

Power shifts fascinate students of legislatures, and the attempt to identify them or predict what will happen fills much space in newspapers and magazines when a new Congress or legislature is about to convene. Indeed, there seems to be a tendency for this concern with power and personalties to take precedence over the discussion of issues in contemporary political conversation.

The game goes on and on. Reporters report, professors analyze, lobbyists manipulate, editors editorialize, and novelists fictionalize while the legislator swims in his goldfish bowl under the bright light of scrutiny, neither completely understood nor misunderstood. Yet citizens must judge legislators, and, if their judgments are to be meaningful, they must be undertaken in the light of what one considers to be the legislator's proper function. Errand boy, broker. or principled party politician? Or a combination in what proportions? The decision is a difficult but vitally important one. And after the citizen has defined the role of the ideal legislator, he must face the difficult task of applying it to men with human motivations operating in the almost bewildering complexity of pressures and forces which an open and pluralistic society produces. This is the public role of the citizen. Dictators have lost their heads for failure to solve simpler problems! The costs of indifference or failure in a democracy are more widely shared but, in the long run, no less severe.

[23]*Congressional Quarterly*, January 9, 1959, pp. 43-44.

10

LEGISLATIVE
ORGANIZATION
AND PROCEDURE

As WE HAVE SEEN, complexity is perhaps the best descriptive term that can be applied to the legislative process—in fact, human beings seldom have devised a more elaborate contrivance of rule, ceremony, regulation, and detail than is found in democratic legislative bodies. Some of the ceremonies seem bizarre to the casual observer from a gallery. The peculiar spectacle of an extended debate and speech-making while members of the audience read newspapers, gossip, and caucus; the general confusion of members coming and going while business is being conducted; the droning of the voices of clerks reading bills to an inattentive audience; the shuttling of pieces of legislation around to various committees; the befuddling method of taking test votes; and the ceremonial forms of address are a few of the more obvious and superficial spectacles which may seem to the uninitiated to be useless, time consuming, or silly.

Many visitors to legislative halls are annoyed when they see their representative reading his local newspaper while earnest speeches are being made or at hearing him refer to a political enemy as his "distinguished colleague." Such observations lead to many cynical statements about congressmen, state legislators, and local politicians. The "Senator Snort" of the cartoons, the "Claghorn" of the radio, and "Senator Phogbound" of the comics all attest to this derision. Good humored it may be, but it is a stereotype which contains very little truth and is generally unfair.

In every case, there are good, if not always sufficient, reasons for practices which seem quaint or ridiculous to the uninitiated. Ceremonial forms of address illustrate this. Senator Stephen M. Young of Ohio, attributing the quotation to the late Senator and Vice-President Barkley of Kentucky, described the practice in this way:

> If some colleague refers to you as the "distinguished senator from Ohio" consider yourself lucky. If this same colleague refers to you as "the able and distinguished senator from Ohio" be on your guard, for the knife is getting sharper. If, however, your colleague refers to you as "the able and distinguished senator from Ohio and my friend" then duck fast for he is trying to see if the jugular vein is exposed. And in case your colleague refers to you as "my very good friend, the able, distinguished and outstanding senator from Ohio" then run for your life.[1]

When a congressman uses the elaborately formal modes of address customary in the Congress, there are good and sufficient reasons. Personal animosities must be muted and restrained in a group of men working so closely together and trying to achieve conflicting goals. Formal modes of address—"the honorable gentleman from . . ."—help to concentrate the debate on issues and to avoid personalities. The senator who, more than anyone in recent years, violated the dignity of the Senate and disrupted its orderly procedures—the late Senator Joseph McCarthy—was also most prone to putting his colleagues on a first-name basis. In most democratic legislatures, formality and titles of address may be desirable to facilitate the processes of orderly debate of issues.

Similarly, if a legislator reads a newspaper while a colleague is speaking, it is probably because this is the only time he has to read it. If he makes ambiguous statements on current issues, it may be that he has been so bombarded by shrill demands for a position that he wants to investigate the matter more deeply before making a declaration of his views. Legislators are often attacked because they do not take a consistent stand on every issue. By necessity, some of them may "go along" with something they do not like in order to conserve their strength for issues they consider vital.

[1]*Sacramento Bee,* February 10, 1960.

Some legislative practices are understandable but more difficult to justify. Legislators are exposed to all sorts of external pressures and demands. Some of the rules of legislative bodies seem designed to provide mutual protection against outside forces. Where political parties are too weak to protect an individual against pressure groups or his constituency for an unpopular vote, the organization and procedural methods of the legislature may provide some shelter. This helps explain some procedures and rules, such as voice votes, committee control of bills, closed committee hearings,[2] control of its membership by each house of the legislature, and methods of censuring colleagues who bring disgrace to the legislative institution. In addition to such formal rules and procedures, the informal ethics of the club, as we have seen, also often operate to protect legislators against outside pressures.

BICAMERALISM

IN THE UNITED STATES, the federal government and all the states except Nebraska have bicameral, or two-house, legislatures. Nebraska's experiment with a unicameral, or single-house, legislature has not caused other jurisdictions to follow in this direction.

It is often argued that two-house legislatures are inefficient. By management analysis standards they are. There is duplication of function, a pet peeve of efficiency experts. Everything is done twice. Hearings on

[2]Closed hearings exclude the public from attendance while testimony is being taken and decisions are made. Many closed hearings are held on matters where government security is involved and classified information is discussed. Other closed hearings may not involve security but are held because the committee members feel it would be better to conduct them privately. There is considerable debate over the extensive use of closed hearings. Criticism usually centers around the question of whether the public is entitled to observe committee action unless there are vital reasons why it should be excluded. The importance of the issue is reflected in the following figures compiled by *Congressional Quarterly* (April 21, 1961, p. 669):

Year	Total Meetings	No. Closed	Per Cent Closed
1953	2640	892	35
1954	3002	1243	41
1955	2940	1055	36
1956	3120	1130	36
1957	2517	854	34
1958	3472	1167	34
1959	3152	940	30
1960	2424	840	35
1961 (Jan. 3–March 31)	687	229	33

bills are generally held separately. Votes are taken separately in each house. Rules apply only to the house that makes them. Each house has its own committees to deal with the same subject matter, and each has is own officers and attaches.

Bicameralism has virtues, however. It gives two full-dress considerations to all important, and even unimportant, measures. The different bases of representation provide different perspectives on these measures. Longer terms in upper or smaller houses, such as the United States Senate, prevent rash or hasty action on emotionally charged bills. Two houses, in short, give a greater range of attention to public policy. The popular representation found in numerically larger lower houses assures a responsive vote to public sentiments. The territorial representation generally found in upper houses allows for the expression of other perspectives. In Congress, each of the houses occasionally prevents the passage of a bill rushed through the other on a surge of expediency or emotion.

Bicameralism also presents problems. It leads to delays and bickering. Over forty years ago, one authority described the Senate and House of Representatives as being "strangers to each other."

> Save for conference committees, they might as well sit at opposite extremes of the continent or at different times of the year. The leaders confer once in a while, no doubt, but for the rank and file there is neither acquaintance nor interest. Rarely does a Senator deign to enter the House. Rarely does a Representative go to the other end of the Capitol from motives other than those of curiosity, unless he has occasion to consult a Senator from his own State in some personal or political matter.[3]

This estrangement partly reflects the weakness of national political parties, and it makes it difficult to fix political responsibility for ignoring or overriding a majority opinion. It also tends to facilitate the occasional irresponsible passage of a bill by one house, in the confidence that the other will let it die in committee.

The absence of effective co-ordination between the two houses is particularly evident when they pass widely different versions of the same bill. In this circumstance, conference committees are used to resolve differences between the two houses. Very often this results in bargains at half-way points between the bills of each house. If one house knows the other will force a bill to conference by amendments, it very often loads the bill with excessive demands to insure itself a good bargaining position. When both houses do this, a bill gets so far out of shape when it goes to a conference committee that the eventual resolution of differences may be nothing like the intentions of either house.

[3]Robert Luce, *Legislative Procedure* (Boston: Houghton Mifflin, 1922), p. 141.

The idea that popularly representative lower houses are the best vehicles for the expression of a public interest or of majority opinion is questionable. One often finds that civil rights and liberties, for example, receive treatment more in keeping with the basic ideals of democracy in upper than in lower houses of legislatures. It is even difficult to support the position that a more numerous lower house, based on population rather than area, is ordinarily more responsible to majority opinion. In Congress, for example, the Senate in recent years has been more responsive to the problems of urban majorities than has the House. Partly, this is because House members tend more to represent local interests than positions on national or even state-wide issues and because even the smallest states have been urbanized in recent years. Partly, it is due to distortions in representation caused by methods of legislative districting discussed in the following section.

LEGISLATIVE DISTRICTS

REPRESENTATION IN THE LOWER HOUSES is presumably based on population. So far as the distribution of representatives among the states is concerned the requirement is now automatically met by procedures which reallocate seats in the House to correspond with population changes in the states as revealed by the decennial censuses (except that each state is guaranteed at least one representative). But within the states, the basis for electing their respective quotas of congressmen is decided by the states themselves. Occasionally, when a state's congressional delegation is increased, the additional representatives may be elected at large; when states have lost seats they have even on occasion elected the entire delegation at large. But ordinarily, congressmen are elected from districts which are created by the state legislatures.

Congressional district lines are drawn in a political atmosphere; the party which controls the legislature at the time of the redistricting will use its power to maximize its control. The most common device is to establish districts which concentrate the opposition party's strength in as few districts as possible while securing a narrow but safe margin for themselves in as many districts as possible. For example, when the Republicans redistricted California in 1950, the Twenty-sixth Congressional District in Los Angeles County was drawn to contain nearly a 90 per cent Democratic majority. In 1960, the Democrats had their turn, and some Republican districts were nearly as lopsided. In both cases, the party in control of the state legislature insured itself more of the congressional seats than the size of its majority would have justified.

When districts are drawn in this way, they sometimes have odd boundaries. In 1811, a Massachusetts political cartographer, named Elbridge

Gerry, drafted a congressional district designed to keep his Federalist opponents out of power. Because the "boundary" lines resembled a salamander, one of his Federalist opponents preferred to call it a "gerrymander," after its creator. The term has become part of our political vocabulary as descriptive of the imaginative partisan geography used in most states.

Another effective device available to state legislatures is the "silent" gerrymander. This is the refusal to redraw district lines to reflect population shifts within the states. The major population shift in recent decades in all of the states, of course, has been from rural to urban areas. State legislatures, controlled by rural interests, have partially disenfranchised big city residents by declining to redistrict. The effect of gerrymandering, explicit and silent, is partially seen in the differences in the size of the constituencies represented in the House. The 1960 census indicates that the average Representative served 410,481 persons. In 1961, the largest number of constituents was served by Rep. James B. Utt (R) in California's Twenty-eighth district. It contained 1,014,460 persons. The smallest district, the Sixth Kansas, represented by Robert Dole (R) had 244,706 constituents. The 1960 election returns showed the average number of voters for the 262 seats held by Democrats was 359,459, whereas the 174 Republican seats averaged 430,380 voters.[4]

The plight of the urban voter has been steadily growing more serious. Underrepresented in the House of Representatives, his only recourse is to his state legislature where he is even more underrepresented. In those states which lack machinery for securing legislation by initiative measure, the courts seem to be his only hope. But the courts have declined in the past to interfere. In 1962, however, the Supreme Court handed down a decision which leaves a tremendous number of questions unanswered but which clearly makes the Constitution and the federal courts accessible to voters who have been rendered politically impotent by minority rural control of state legislatures.[5]

A group of voters in Tennessee entered a civil action in a federal district court, claiming the legislative districting in the state denied them "equal protection of the laws accorded them by the Fourteenth Amendment to the Constitution of the United States by virtue of the debasement of their votes." The district court dismissed the case on the grounds that it lacked jurisdiction. The decision was appealed to the Supreme Court, which held that the dismissal was in error and remanded the case to the district court for hearing. The case led to a rather bitter division among the Supreme Court justices on the question of whether the federal courts

[4]*Congressional Quarterly,* February 17, 1961, pp. 275 ff. What this suggests is that Democrats had controlled more state legislatures when states were redistricted.
[5]*Baker et. al.* v. *Carr et. al.* 30 L. W. 4203.

should be empowered to order state legislatures to district themselves in accordance with judicial interpretation of the "due process" clause of the Fourteenth Amendment. In a concurring opinion, Justice Clark cited evidence and statistics in support of the view that equal protection had clearly been denied urban voters. Moore County, for example, had a total population of 2,340 whereas Rutherford County had 25,316, but both had the same representation in a Tennessee Legislature which had not been redistricted since 1901.

Justice Frankfurter dissented in a lengthy opinion which Justice Clark referred to as "bursting with words that go through so much and conclude with so little." The majority's decision, Frankfurter had argued, would "charge courts with the task of accommodating the incommensurable factors of policy which underlie those mathematical puzzles." In Frankfurter's view, the courts were being plunged into a "quagmire" of political considerations to which judicial processes are inadequate and inappropriate. Judicial review in this area does present important and difficult problems, and it is still not clear whether, how, and in what circumstances the courts will be able to redress the grievances of gerrymandered voters.

THE NECESSITY FOR LEGISLATIVE
ORGANIZATION AND PROCEDURE

ANY DELIBERATIVE BODY WHICH MAKES POLICY requires some procedural framework, be it "Roberts' Rules of Order" in a student council or the elaborate rules of each house of the United States Congress. Size alone necessitates this, and as size increases, rules and procedures often increasingly limit the freedom of the individual member. In the United States, lower houses of the legislature are almost always larger than upper houses. For example, the 435-member House of Representatives is over four times as large as the Senate, and the entire membership must face election every two years. To organize such a large institution which has as its purpose the deliberation and creation of public policy requires some necessary restrictions on the activities of its members. Debate must be limited, and a tight control over the measures coming before the House must be exercised. Committees, in such a large body, become important and powerful since they control the flow of legislation.

In the Senate, only one-third of the Senators face election every two years so there is a greater guaranteed continuity of membership. This, along with its smaller size, insures organization and procedures different from those of the House. Its rules and procedures give the individual Senator more opportunity to make his views known.

There are many other factors that make organization and procedure essential. The variety of areas and interests represented in a legislature requires some procedural mechanism which guarantees them a fair hearing. The competition of rival political parties must be regulated. Methods must be found to prevent obstructionists from thwarting the flow of legislation; minorities must have protection from tyranny of the majority; members must be protected from legal action for their statements in the legislature; and many other safeguards are necessary.

Rules and regulations are means devised by a legislature to achieve its objectives rather than ends in themselves. The objectives of individual legislators may be diametrically opposed—that is, one legislator may look to procedure as a means of getting a law enacted while one of his colleagues may look to the same procedure as a device to prevent such enactment. Rules and procedure attempt to provide the battlefield and code of conduct on which legislative jousting takes place.

Some legislators are masters of the intricacies of the procedural labyrinth. They can find their way in its endless passageways until their desired goals are obtained. Others flout procedural formalities as much as possible. They emphasize the virtue of their goals and often point out that they are being frustrated by antagonists with procedural roadblocks.

Efficiency of Legislative Organization and Procedure

The economic growth of the United States and the complexity of the problems created by rapid social change have led to dramatic changes in the structure and organization of the executive branch of government. Congress, on the other hand, in spite of these changes, goes along in just about the same way it has for generations. One author summed up the situation, in 1953, as follows:

> Congress meanwhile had changed little in the intervening decades. For the most part it was still operating with the same machinery and methods, the same facilities and services, that it had inherited from the era of Thomas Bracket Reed [1880's]. Overworked and underpaid, often lampooned by the press and unfairly critized by the thoughtless, our national legislature had fallen from its once high estate. Few any longer regarded it as the keystone of the federal arch. With Congress overwhelmed by its great responsibilities, operating under its ancient ritual, the streamlined age of the Giant Clipper, radar, and the atomic bomb seem to have passed it by.[6]

[6]George G. Galloway, *The Legislative Process in Congress* (New York: Crowell, 1953), p. 8. Even the academic study of government has largely ignored legislative activities. Most government curricula in most colleges deal heavily with the executive and courts but have few courses on legislation.

Granted the truth of this statement, the question of how one would gear Congress to the twentieh century remains difficult. To make it bigger would only aggravate the problems. To streamline its procedures might result in more laws being made, but it might also be less democratic in making them.

Making laws does not lend itself to the generally accepted standards of efficiency. For example, a law that has been filibustered, amended countless times, heard by many committees, and sent to several conference committees before it at long last was passed might still be a very efficient action of Congress in that the public interest is well served. It may well be that efficiency is the advantage of tyranny; the strength of democracy lies in the very "inefficiency" of its methods for determining the goals and purposes of political society.

This is not to say that the structure and procedures of Congress now serve this democratic process well. The question we must ask of congressional organization is whether it facilitates the process of democratic decision-making. And, of course, our conclusions will depend on which model of the democratic process we apply. With this in mind we turn to the organization of Congress.

Debate and Its Limitations

The responsibility for enacting laws makes legislative bodies a forum for the debate of public issues. Few, if any, of the nation's important laws have been unanimously agreed upon by all members of Congress. Debate reflects the range of political perspectives held or articulated by congressmen. Debate, however, cannot go on forever, or many of the pressing political issues would never be solved.

In Congress, the size of the House of Representatives works against the free and unlimited debate still used in the Senate. The House Rules Committee is charged with allotting time to debate bills. It does this by a special order specifying the time for debate allotted to the most important bills (except appropriations). The time is then divided equally between the parties. The chairman of the committee in charge of the bill rations out the time to majority members wishing to speak while the ranking minority member does the same for the opposition. Sometimes, many members who would like to discuss the bill are eliminated by the time factor, and often those who do enter the debate have only a few minutes to make their views known. Also, debate can be closed by a motion for the "previous question," and a majority vote on this motion stops debate (technically called "cloture") to bring the issue up for final vote. If the "previous question" passes before any debate on the measure has been held, a brief time, usually forty minutes equally divided between the parties, is allowed. Floor leaders of the political parties are influential in the managing of debate and in calling for cloture.

In the Senate debate is not easily limited. There is a strong tradition of free discussion which occasionally blossoms into a filibuster—an extended marathon of words and procedural delays which can frustrate the business of the Senate almost indefinitely. From 1949 to 1959, cloture could not be obtained without a two-thirds vote of the entire Senate membership. In 1959, a struggle over this issue ended with the adoption of Rule 22, which made cloture somewhat easier by only requiring a two-thirds vote of members present and voting, rather than of the whole body. But extended debate and delay can still occur, and it is difficult to muster enough votes to stop a real or threatened filibuster.

The history of the filibuster is a colorful story. Filibusters can be extended talks on any subject, since the discussion does not have to be germane to the issue. The individual record was made by Senator Strom Thurmond, who talked for twenty-four hours and 18 minutes against the Civil Rights Act of 1957. Other individual endurance performances were Senator Morse's twenty-two-hour and twenty-six-minute talk against the Tidelands Oil Bill and Huey Long's fifteen-hour and thirty-minute talk on an amendment to the National Recovery Act in 1935. Subjects range from Long's elaborate recipes for home-made liquor, turnip greens, and corn pone to the best technique of swinging a golf club, the evils of Wall Street, motherhood, and raising children.

Extended speeches are only one way to conduct filibusters. Other techniques include delaying parliamentary tactics; quorum calls, roll call votes, points-of-order and appeals from them, and extended questions and answers. Difficult as it is, cloture is usually the only effective weapon against a filibuster, but a strict enforcement of Senate rules can help. Senators have to stand and cannot walk around when speaking, they cannot use nonparliamentary language and can be taken "off their feet" if they do, and they cannot have clerks read their material. A less effective but more sensational technique to combat the filibuster is to keep the Senate in long sessions so that the talkers will become too tired to continue. This tactic has limitations, however, since physical fitness is a prime requisite for verbal endurance tests.

Much legislation filibustered to death is often needed or desirable but is killed because it is unpopular with powerful private or sectional interests. Southern Senators, for example, have used the filibuster many times to kill civil rights legislation. Between 1865 and 1946, thirty-seven measures exclusive of appropriations were killed by filibustering. It is estimated that about four times this many appropriation bills have met their deaths by this same device. On a heated issue it may take a long time to "talk a bill to death." In 1890, the southern filibuster against a bill calling for federal supervision of elections lasted twenty-nine days.[7]

Filibusters are particularly effective toward the end of a congressional session, since the pressure of time works in favor of dropping the bill being talked to death.

Often bills are dropped or passed over when cloture of debate is not obtained and a filibuster threatens. This happened in 1962 on a civil rights bill directed against the discriminatory use of literacy tests in the South. The bill would have made a sixth-grade education automatic evidence of literacy for voting. Neither Democratic Majority Leader Mansfield nor Republican Minority Leader Dirksen could muster enough votes in their parties to support the cloture petition, so the bill died. An almost identical proposal was part of the 1960 Republican platform. The northern Democrats thought this would secure enough Republican votes for cloture to overcome the opposition of southern members of their own party. Their hopes, however, proved futile.

Free debate is susceptible to such obstructionist abuse that there have been many attempts to change the rules to make cloture easier. Its chief advantage, however, is that it can assure a full-scale debate as well as a depth of criticism and analysis of measures before the Senate. Even a filibuster can be used to awaken the public to an important issue. These broad considerations have done as much to retain free and full debate in the Senate as have the powerful minority blocs who see it as a device to gain their ends. The abuse of free debate is more possible when political parties lack the strength to discipline members who wish to use their right to unlimited discussion as a power device to enhance a narrow interest. Stronger parties with stronger platforms might do much to make free debate more responsible.

PARTY CONTROL OF THE LEGISLATURE

THE POLITICAL SETTING OF LEGISLATIVE BODIES finds two parties, one a majority and the other a minority, contesting for power. This political contest sets the tone of much procedure. Both major political parties fight earnestly, sometimes even viciously, for political control of Congress and other legislative bodies. The power conflicts between the two parties come to focus in their efforts to control the organization of legislatures. Organizational control means the power to designate the presiding officers and committee chairmen, to hold a majority of seats on the committees, and to control the order of business. On these questions, party discipline and

[7]Bertram M. Gross, *The Legislative Struggle* (New York: McGraw-Hill, 1953), pp. 374-375.

cohesion are rigid, and deviation rarely occurs although it is sometimes threatened.

This unity on organizational issues is in sharp contrast to the divisions in Congress on legislative issues which rarely follow strict party lines. The alignment of southern Democrats with northern Republicans on many issues is a case in point. On organizational questions, the southern Democrats stay with their party; but on other legislative issues, they incline to vote with the Republicans.

At the national level, neither party has any wild dreams of ever completely driving out the opposition. Procedure is devised to give the majority party strength but also to assure the voice of the minority party will be heard. Both parties are aware that democratic government demands opposition. They are also conscious that they will themselves almost certainly be a minority at some future time and are therefore sensitive to the rights of the minority party. Moreover, whereas each party unites itself to control the legislature, they do not want such overwhelming control as one might imagine.

Having too large a majority, as President Franklin Roosevelt discovered, aggravates the already serious problem of party discipline and cohesiveness on legislation. If one party has an overwhelming majority, its individual members may feel less personal obligation to support the party's position, and the party tends to break up into internal factions which quarrel with one another rather than with the opposition. The minority party gains considerable strength, if it is united, from such an occurrence. What most party leaders seek is a comfortable majority which is not so big it becomes indifferent to the opposition but big enough to insure the passage of the party's legislative program. It is convenient for a party to have a comfortable enough majority so that party members who have some political reason related to their constituency, a major interest group, or their consciences may be allowed to vote against the party on particular issues. But the party's position may be weakened if its majority is so big that the party members ride off in all directions at once.

Briefly, when a political party captures Congress it sets out to organize the institution so that it will be able to get its program under way. If it is fortunate enough to be of the same party as the chief executive, it has both an opportunity and a responsibility to see that it is set up so the executive program will have a good chance of success. If the chief executive is from the other party, it may organize itself so it can saddle the executive and his party with blame for failures and unpopular policies and secure for itself the credit for the successes.

The organization of the legislative body and its committees is only the first stage of conflict. Party allegiances are generally adhered to on these questions, but they fly apart on others. A governor facing an emotionally charged issue, such as capital punishment, may find his faithful supporters in bitter combat over the issue. So will a President when he takes a controversial stand on a volatile issue, such as national defense or federal aid to education. Political attacks on governmental institutions, such as Franklin Roosevelt's attempt in 1937 to "pack" the Supreme Court by lowering the retirement age and increasing the membership from nine to fifteen, can also cause dissension in the ranks. Such problems of partisan desertion also can occur on less dramatic issues. Party discipline is not enough to guarantee victory on a public issue, particularly when powerful and vocal interest groups are involved and when individual legislators feel that they owe little to their national party organizations and platforms.

The combination of partisan cohesion on organizational issues, and the abandonment of partisan loyalties on others, causes an endless shifting of alliances among the membership. A majority and minority leader may engage in a bitter parliamentary battle on an organizational question but find themselves close allies on a bill dealing with natural gas regulation. They may break apart again on a tax measure. Constituents, personal convictions, or sympathy toward articulate interest groups are likely to contribute to this.

LEGISLATIVE LEADERSHIP AND ORGANIZATION

THE LEADERSHIP OF A LEGISLATIVE BODY is selected from the membership of its majority party. Occasionally, in bicameral legislatures different parties control the two houses. Majority leadership in upper houses may be further complicated when the official presiding officer, the Vice-President in the United States Senate and the Lieutenant-Governor in most state senates, is not from the majority party. Official presiding officers are usually unable to vote except in case of a tie, but their ability to use their position to party advantage has many possibilities. Vice-President Nixon, for example, was a Republican presiding over a Senate controlled by the Democrats for six of the eight years (1954 - 1960) he held the office. On a few important issues, his vote to break a tie was a distinct advantage to his party. He also used his position as presiding officer to assist his party in many ways, particularly in bringing public attention to political maneuvers by Democratic Senators.

An important official in upper houses is the President *pro tempore* who presides in the absence of the official leader. In the United States Senate, he assumes the presiding office in the event of the Vice-President's death, resignation, or succession to the presidency. The majority party's nominee for the office is virtually assured election, although the minority party puts up a candidate as a gesture.

The House of Representatives selects its own presiding officer, who is called the Speaker. Each party places a candidate for Speaker before the House, but party discipline is such that the majority party is victorious.

The real struggle for leadership occurs in the party caucus or conference. Each house of Congress has its party conferences to select its leaders. In addition to securing agreement on nominees for President *pro tempore* and Speaker, as well as Secretary to the Senate, Clerk of the House and other administrative aides, party conferences are used in both houses to select the majority and minority floor leaders, assistant floor leaders, often referred to as whips, and the membership of each party's committee on committees.

The internal struggles in party conferences sometimes involve a challenge to the existing leadership of the party. Sometimes the challenge is serious but unless it reflects deep-seated grievances, as it did in the case of Minority Leader Martin's difficulty discussed previously, the threat to party unity ordinarily keeps it in bounds and renders it ineffectual.[8]

The selection of committee membership by the committee on committees of each party is a crucial step in the organization of party power. Until 1910, when the House of Representatives rebelled against the iron-fisted rule of Speaker Joseph G. Cannon, the Speaker virtually handpicked members of committees. Since Cannon's dethroning, the House has adopted a method of selecting committees which involves a much broader participation by party members. The party leaderships informally agree upon the total membership and party ratios of each House committee. The Democratic caucus elects their members of the Ways and Means Committee who also serve as the party's committee on committees. This committee then draws up the committee assignments and submits them to a party caucus for approval. When the caucus agrees upon the list, a resolution containing it is submitted to the House.

The Republican committee on committees in the House is made up of one member from each state having at least one Republican in its delegation. It prepares a list which is submitted for approval to the party's policy committee, which in turn reviews the list and incorporates it in a House resolution. The Democrats have developed a list of committee priorities based upon considerations other than strict seniority but the Republicans, according to Minority Leader Charles A. Halleck did not, as of 1960, follow any firm rule but seniority.[9]

In the Senate, the Democratic Steering Committee and the Republican Committee on Committees each works up a list of committee members. In the case of the Democrats the list must be submitted to the party caucus

---

[8]In 1959, there developed some rumblings of dissatisfaction within the Democratic party both in the House and the Senate. The "two Texans," the late Speaker Rayburn of the House and Senate Majority Leader Lyndon Johnson, were criticized by their own party for being both too authoritarian with party members and too much committed to compromise with the opposition.

[9]*Congressional Quarterly: 1961-62 Guide to Current American Government*, p. 18.

for approval. The Republicans do not require submission to a caucus. The lists then go to the Senate in the form of resolutions for acceptance. Senate tradition and knowledge of the rituals of seniority make approval almost automatic so that rarely does any adjustment occur on the floor.

The Seniority System

Both houses of Congress select committee members on the basis of the personal preferences of the congressmen if the rule of seniority does not interfere. If the number of Senators or Representatives requesting membership on the same committee is so large that all of them will not be able to be placed on it, seniority then applies and those with the longest tenure get the seats. Seniority also applies to the committee itself. That is, the members with the longest service on the committee get the positions of leadership. Thus, a relatively new member of Congress may have committee seniority over one of his elders who joined the committee at a later time. The member of the majority party with the greatest committee seniority becomes chairman; his counterpart in the opposition party will probably be chairman in the future if the political climate changes.

Probably no aspect of congressional procedure has been subjected to such prolonged and fundamental attack as the seniority rule. Its tenacity is partly explained by the two main advantages it provides the legislators. One is that it keeps partisan members of Congress from feuding bitterly among themselves over committee posts, since seniority is a deciding factor to which all give recognition. No doubt it is largely for this reason that most congressmen find that the longer they are in Congress the better the seniority rule looks and the easier it is to accept. The second advantage is that seniority provides a buffer against pressure groups and the executive branch turning on the heat for the location of particular legislators on committees they are anxious to "stack."

The chief disadvantage of seniority is that it tends to favor one-party regions, such as the South, who return the same congressmen year after year and thus gain a disproportionate control over Congress. Elections in these one-party areas generally turn on a stand on local interests. There is less conflict over national issues than in areas with competitive politics with the result that, except for those regional or sectional issues like race relations in the South, committee chairmen are freer to act as political brokers on issues of national or international scope. Seniority also protects mediocrities who continue to be elected. It gives them a means to float to the top positions of power and prestige unless drastic action prevents it. Sometimes seniority produces chairmen of key committees who are out of sympathy with the objectives of their party and its presidential leadership. Thus, a President devoted to foreign aid might find an old-style isolationist as chairman of the Senate Foreign Relations Committee. Seniority, in short, makes party responsibility and discipline difficult.

The Struggle for Committee Assignment

The formal procedures of committee selection are devices which serve as both conveniences and inconveniences to those members interested in getting on particular committees. Such procedures are also of concern to groups other than Congress itself. Political parties, private interest groups, the President, government agencies, and geographic areas are all anxious to place elected representatives partial to their interests on appropriate committees. Within the limitations of seniority and other procedural formalities, they often work to influence the choice of members for particular committees.

Aspirations of individuals in Congress to be placed on certain committees run the gamut of human motivations and drives. Some want to be on a committee in order to promote their own views by furthering or frustrating specific legislation; some want an assignment that can be dramatized to their constituents; some want to be on "pork-barrel" committees which deal with projects of importance to their districts; others feel they can serve various interest groups important to them by being placed on appropriate committees. Still others, particularly aspirants for a national reputation, may feel they can get a lot of publicity and political mileage out of certain strategic committee assignments. In the case of television and the other mass media, this is likely to mean committees investigating sensational matters and well enough financed to hold public hearings. World-wide travel can also be a lure for membership on some congressional committees. The motivations are almost without limit and in the case of individual legislators are no doubt mixed.

Committee appointments are a matter of considerable importance to the political parties as well as to individual legislators. Within the limits of seniority and other criteria, they work over membership lists with the most extreme care. Key committees must be stocked with enough talent so that if seniority dictates a mediocrity or a maverick as chairman, the party can still have a committee member who is an articulate spokesman for the official party position. There are always some "duty" committees concerned with mundane matters. These committees usually have a membership composed of a large number of freshmen with an occasional oldster or two. Such "pork-barrel" committees as post offices, civil service, public works, veterans affairs, and others are carefully staffed and controlled by the majority party to handle what spoils are available within the limits of civil service. "Pork" committees are also used to get some politically advantageous distribution of government construction and other spending projects located in strategic spots throughout the country. Decisions on the location of defense plants and military installations, and the efforts of congressmen and governors to get their "fair share" of such installations, have become a serious political concern. The composition of the armed services committees, for example, is likely to be reflected in the distribution of military payrolls among the states.

Special interest groups are ever on the alert when committee members are being selected. They apply a good deal of pressure on political parties or wherever else it might be effective to see that committees are staffed so that their particular interests will be given a favorable and sympathetic audience. Agricultural groups have been quite effective in loading agriculture committees of both houses of Congress (and most state legislatures) with sympathetic members. Other interest groups, such as business, labor, medicine, law, education, and oil, exert pressure to get members on or keep members off committees in which they are interested.

THE COMMITTEE SYSTEM AND LEGISLATION

COMMITTEES OF LEGISLATURES are a basic feature of their organization. They serve as subgroups of the legislature and they are responsible to the entire body. In this way, work can be divided and the multitude of legislative proposals can be given more attention, albeit by a smaller group, than if the whole house had to deal with them. Committees also control the flow of legislation. They are very important politically since a program of a political party can often be thwarted by a hostile committee. The party that controls a legislature usually controls its committees. But this control extends only to party affiliation, and if a member of the majority party not in tune with the official position of his party becomes chairman of a key committee, he can cause his party a good deal of difficulty.[10]

Committee chairmen, by virtue of the power of the chair and by tradition, generally have a great deal of control over their committees. If they are unable to control their committees, on key issues at least, they usually try to rearrange the membership so that they can. Even the threat by a committee chairman to resign if his committee does not support his position may be effective, since such resignations would undermine, in effect, the seniority system.

[10]President Kennedy, for example, unsuccessfully employed all his power and influence in an effort to force his legislative program through the Democratically controlled House Rules Committee in the Eighty-seventh Congress. Its chairman, Howard W. Smith of Virginia, was not sympathetic to many of the Kennedy measures. Even though the Rules Committee was enlarged (some said "packed") with a few more liberally oriented members, Representative Smith, with the power of the chairmanship and the help of votes cast by sympathetic members, was still able to block several Kennedy measures.

The power of congressional committees, in combination with the seniority system and the lack of party cohesiveness, contributes to the difficulties in achieving party responsibility for legislative performance. Democrats, particularly, find it difficult to manage a legislative program and steer it through Congress when a large number of their party members, some holding key chairmanships, are in sympathy with the opposition. The Eighty-seventh Congress, for example, had a good deal of the Democratic platform of the 1960 election before it in the form of legislation. This legislation had strong support from President Kennedy, who was popular, articulate, and powerful. He used a variety of techniques and a large corps of aides to solicit support. His efforts, however, ran headlong into the committee power of Democrats whose political philosophies were more in keeping with the conservative wing of the Republican party than with the Democratic program. As a result, the President's legislative accomplishments were limited and the "New Frontier" still remained on the horizon. Liberal Democrats are often frustrated by the legislative impotence which follows electoral triumphs and organizational control. Effective remedies, however, would require national party and congressional reform.

Types of Committees

There are several types of committees used by legislatures to conduct their business. Every political jurisdiction has its own variations in its committee structure and in the power of committees over legislative matters. In fact, in some jurisdictions there is marked difference in committee structure and power in the two houses of their bicameral legislatures.

The following are the main types of committees used by legislatures (the list by no means encompasses all the variations found throughout the United States):

1. *Standing committees.* These committees are organized around legislative subject matter. They are permanent—that is they exist continuously until the house they serve decides to abolish them. Standing committees handle such subjects as foreign affairs, agriculture, appropriations, armed services, un-American activities, and rules.

In 1946, Congress reorganized its committee structure and, among other things, reduced the number of standing committees in both houses of Congress. The number of standing committees varies, but the House of Representatives usually has about twenty and the Senate about fifteen.

2. *Special committees.* Special committees, or "select committees" as they are sometimes called, are created to look into specific subjects. They are usually temporary. They hold hearings and conduct investigations but generally cannot report bills for action. The 1946 congressional

committee reorganization bill passed the Senate with a provision that special committees be abolished. The House struck out this provision, and both houses still use select committees.

3. *Joint committees.* These are committees with a combined membership from both houses of a bicameral legislature. Joint committees can efficiently eliminate duplicate hearings and can present a single bill for action in both houses. They are not very popular, however, because members of each house are likely to feel their independence is jeopardized. Also, the tendency of senators or upper house members to dominate joint committees is not taken kindly by the membership of the lower house.

Some state joint legislative committees are very important. California's Joint Legislative Budget Committee has a great influence on the state's fiscal affairs. With a permanent staff of about thirty professionals, it supervises an independent budget analysis for the state and makes recommendations to both houses of the legislature.

4. *Subcommittees.* All the above-mentioned committees can use subcommittees. The power of the full committee chairman to create them and to appoint the membership and chairmen is an important source of his influence. The main purpose of subcommittees is to divide the work of the larger committee into categories where more thorough inquiry can be made. For example, a committee on agriculture could break down its work so that one subcommittee could look into parity prices, another into soil conservation, another into crop research, and still others into the various problems coming before the full committee. Subcommittees can become very important—sometimes to the point where they overshadow the full committee. They cannot report bills out to the floor for action since they are responsible to the full committee and report to it. By tradition, however, their reports are ordinarily accepted by the parent committee. The number of subcommittees varies with each Congress, but there are generally more than one hundred in the House and more than fifty in the Senate.

5. *Conference committees.* These are temporary committees appointed for the purpose of resolving differences between the versions of a bill as passed by the two houses of the legislature. Members are appointed by the presiding officer of each house. In Congress, they usually consist of the interested senior members of the committees which were in charge of the bill in the respective houses. Conference committees report back to their respective chambers on the compromise or agreement reached in conference. Sessions are secret and unrecorded, and the report must be signed by a majority of the conferees from each house. Conference committees theoretically decide only those issues disagreed upon by the two houses—that is, they are not free to change the features of a bill on which both houses were in accord. If the conference report is accepted

by both houses, the bill, with modifications contained in the conference report, is passed. If either house votes down the report, a new conference committee may be appointed or the bill may be allowed to die.

Committees of the Congress

Congress modifies its committee structure as new problems develop and old ones are resolved. The following list of committees in the Eighty-sixth Congress illustrates that most of the subjects are of continuous concern but some, like Atomic Energy and Aeronautical and Space Science, are products of a modern age:

House	*Senate*
Agriculture	Agriculture and Forestry
Appropriations	Appropriations
Armed Services	Armed Services
Banking and Currency	Banking and Currency
District of Columbia	District of Columbia
Education and Labor	Finance
Foreign Affairs	Foreign Relations
Government Operations	Government Operations
House Administration	Interior and Insular Affairs
Interior and Insular Affairs	Interstate and Foreign Commerce
Interstate and Foreign Commerce	Judiciary
Judiciary	Labor and Public Welfare
Merchant Marine and Fisheries	Post Office and Civil Service
Post Office and Civil Service	Public Works
Public Works	Rules and Administration
Rules	Select Small Business
Un-American Activities	Select Committee on Improper Activities in the Labor Management Field
Veterans Affairs	Aeronautical and Space Science
Ways and Means	
Select Small Business	
Science and Astronautics	

Joint

Atomic Energy
Defense Production
Economic
Internal Revenue and Taxation[11]

[11]*Congressional Quarterly: Student Guide*, Spring, 1959, p. 20.

Staff Assistance to Committees

The staff assistance available to committees depends upon the amount of funds allotted them, the importance of the issues under consideration, and the desire of the legislature to have information. Many legislative committees are able to employ their own staff or "consultants," as they are often called. Others must rely upon what help they can get from the executive departments. Since committee chairmen have discretion over whom the committee will employ, there is always a problem of appointing staff members as a repayment for a political debt. Some staff members are zealous partisans of a political cause, others show a particular fondness for certain pressure groups, and others may be embarassments to the whole legislature, either because of their ineptitude or their independence.[12]

On the other hand, many legislative committees avail themselves of the best talent they can find. Some committee staffs have done a monumental job of gathering and analyzing information vital to efficient legislation.

There are, however, problems contingent upon the staffing of committees in relation to minority membership. For example, in the Eighty-seventh Congress there was complaint from the Republican party, a minority in both houses, that they did not have proper staff assistance to present them information to support a position contrary to that of the majority party. Contributing to this discontent was the fact that the Democrats not only controlled the staff of congressional committees, but also they had access to information from the executive branch which their party controlled, too.

The problem raised by the Republicans is a serious one which many states have confronted. Some states—Wisconsin is a good example—have helped solve it by establishing a centralized research agency which gathers information requested by legislators from either party. The quality of this research is often excellent and provides, if not a partisan argument, a body of data from which a political position can be derived. Congress has not yet developed such an agency but with the growing complexity of issues it must resolve, it is quite possible it may do so in the future.

---

[12]The House Special Committee on Legislative Oversight in 1958, which looked into the activities of regulatory commissions, employed a staff member so zealous in his duties that he caused a great deal of discomfort to his committee. He was fired, but out of his zeal several regulatory agencies had trouble. See William S. Fairfield, "Dr. Schwartz Goes to Washington," *Reporter,* March 20, 1958, pp. 24-28.

The Investigating Power

Gathering information necessary for legislation is an important function of committees. Hearings are one source of information necessary to an enlightened vote on specific bills before a legislature. There are many problems, however, which legislatures wish to explore in order to determine whether laws are necessary or desirable. Such exploration of legislative problems is an important function of committees and one which has aroused a good deal of political and legal controversy.

There have been many very important investigations in the past which have led to some of our more fundamental laws. In the preceding several decades, congressional committees have investigated such important and pressing national problems as organized crime, business monopolies, fraudulent stock and bond sales, farm problems, atomic energy, space exploration, education, un-American activities, and political corruption. Laws regulating business and labor relationships, antitrust acts, farm legislation, and the Securities and Exchange Act have resulted from such investigations.

Investigations are sometimes conducted by full committees (standing, special, or joint), but generally they are undertaken by subcommittees. The Eighty-sixth Congress, for example, had a total in both houses of forty-one investigating committees, most of them subcommittees, which were authorized to spend $15,565,695 for investigations.[13]

The control of the legislative power to investigate is basically a problem for the legislature itself. The informal rules of the "club" and the ethical purview of legislative bodies have an effect on those who tend to abuse the power. Senator Joseph McCarthy was halted in his free-swinging investigations because he violated the dignity of the Senate. Others have also been limited by Congress and state legislatures when they have gone too far. Sometimes, however, they have not been halted before extensive and serious damage has been done to the lives and reputations of individuals often innocent of any crime and guilty only of thinking or acting in a way not approved by the investigators.

Proposals to curtail investigating power must be carefully and cautiously considered. The power to legislate requires the power to investigate. Formalized restraints to prevent abuses may seriously curtail access to important information. A decent respect for private rights in the legislature and a public opinion alert to their invasion must be the ultimate safeguards.

---

[13]*Congressional Quarterly*, April 22, 1960, p. 673. This is in addition to the other committee expenditures not connected with investigations. All this money may not be used; the Eighty-fifth Congress authorized $12,118,280 but spent only $9,717,796.

Introduction of Bills and Committee Hearings

Every measure introduced into a legislature is called a bill. It may be a potential statute or one of various types of resolutions.[14] The sponsor of a bill may state a preference for referral to a particular committee and struggle to achieve his preference. In the Senate, bills are assigned to committee by the President and in the House by the parliamentarian on order of the Speaker. Sometimes, however, the decision on referral is vital to the bill's chances, and the real struggle may be to decide whether a favorably or unfavorably disposed committee shall have jurisdiction.

Figure 11 illustrates the several stages from introduction to final enactment through which a bill must go in order to become a law.

Rarely is a piece of legislation the sole creation of the individual legislator who introduces it; usually, even the idea is not originated by him. A bill may have been drafted by some governmental agency as part of the executive's legislative program; it may be introduced at the request of, perhaps even be written by, a particular interest group; a group of legislators may draw up a bill in which they have a common interest; the legislator may introduce private bills[15] for constituents in need of special relief; or he may introduce bills at the suggestion of constituents.

Several legislative bodies adopt the practice of allowing the author of a bill to have the words "by request" placed under its title. This is a note either to the Speaker to send the bill to the graveyard or to the first committee chairman to administer the *coup de grace* to the bill. This courtesy between legislators allows them to introduce the whims and fantasies of their constituents and then dispose of them for one another by killing them when the phrase "by request" appears. Cynical perhaps, but effective. In Congress "by request" on bills generally means that the author's responsibility has ended with the bill's introduction, and he is not interested in pushing the bill actively through committee. Committee action, it scarcely needs adding, is often negative.

After a bill is referred to a congressional committee, it is placed on the committee calendar. Most proposed legislation dies on the calendar. If

---

[14]Regular bills introduced into the house of Representatives are entitled "H.R. 500" or whatever the number happens to be, and in the Senate, "S. 500." Joint Resolutions, which can become law also, are entitled "H.J. Res. 500" in the House and "S.J. Res. 500" in the Senate. Concurrent Resolutions, which do not become law but declare a sentiment or desire of Congress, are entitled "H. Con. Res. 500" in the House and "S. Con. Res. 500" in the Senate. Single House resolutions which do not become law but declare an attitude of one house (sometimes aimed at the other) are entitled "H. Res. 500" or "S. Res. 500" in the respective houses. All these bills go to committees.

[15]Private bills are for the benefit of a particular individual. They are used, for example, to appropriate money for the relief of an individual who is unable to sue the government because of its sovereign immunity.

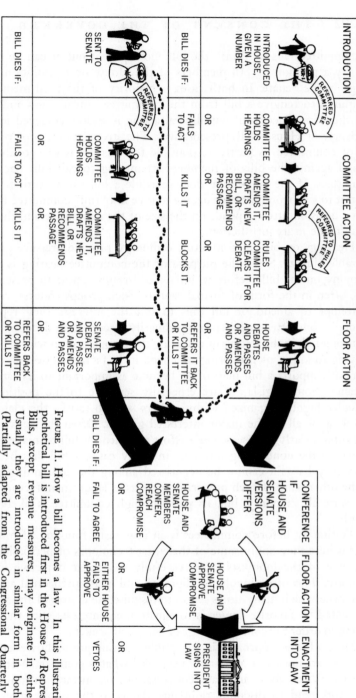

Figure 11. How a bill becomes a law. In this illustration a hypothetical bill is introduced first in the House of Representatives. Bills, except revenue measures, may originate in either House. Usually they are introduced in similar form in both Houses. (Partially adapted from the Congressional Quarterly and the Journal of the National Education Association.)

the committee fails to "hear" the bill and report it out, it can be rescued only by a petition of 218 members of the House or a resolution of discharge in the Senate. In both cases, a majority of the total membership is required to remove a bill from the committee's jurisdiction and return it to the floor. Successful withdrawal action is seldom achieved in either the Senate or House of Representatives. The strong tradition of the sanctity of committees is partly responsible for this. So is the possibility or reprisal against the bills of members attempting to call bills back from committees. If the committee does schedule a bill for a hearing, it may assign it to a subcommittee or decide to give it a "full" committee hearing. Such a decision often depends on the size of the committee and the range of substance in its jurisdiction.

Hearings on bills in committee ordinarily provide pressure groups a favorable climate. Since the purpose of the committee hearing is to take testimony on the bills before it, interested groups appear to present their cases, often in the form of formal reports. Such groups endorse, support, or attempt to amend or kill bills to suit the interests they represent. Although committee members are ordinarily interested in deciding on the merits of a bill, in the setting of a hearing the emphasis is on who is pushing it, trying to kill it, or proposing to amend it. In fact, the question of who favors or supports a bill may often become as important to its fate as its substance. Some legislators are especially sensitive to the position of a particular highly organized lobby; others seek to satisfy the claims and objections of all of the major interested groups. Often the activity of a committee clearly focuses on the effort to amend a bill to make it satisfactory to the contending interests. In many cases, a bill dies because a satisfactory bargain cannot be negotiated among the contending parties. On the other hand, if such powerful interests as labor, manufacturers, and real estate all support a bill, its path through committee is likely to be smooth.

Testimony before committees is an important function of lobbyists, and it is here they apply some of their best techniques of persuasion. The most able of the lobbyists work carefully to appear objective in their testimony. This often involves a dignified and quasi-intellectual approach to the issue which many times serves to disguise the desires of the interests represented. A favorite device is to equate their interests with the public interest, in order to avoid the charge of being self-seekers.

Most of this approach is for public consumption, however, since legislators are not naïve and know very well what is going on. Very often there have been more intimate conversations on interest group desires. Legislators tend to discount righteous claims to the public interest by lobbyists as "window dressing" or "violin music." Whether committee members or their staff scratch the surface to reveal the true nature of the testimony depends, as much as anything else, on their desire to probe deeply. If a legislator is sympathetic to the lobbyist, he will probably let the testimony stand. In fact, he may bulwark the testimony and make it more plausible by asking leading questions to draw out the lobbyist. On the other hand, an unsympathetic legislator often asks probing and, for the lobbyist, embarassing questions. He may, if he feels strongly about the measure, expose the testimony as being misleading and publicly censure the lobbyist.

Lobbyists can provide legislators excuses, grounds for action, or even convince them of the worthiness of their case. The best lobbyist is one who persuades his audience of the validity of his claims. But in his attempts to convince he must avoid, if at all possible, getting himself into a position of vulnerability where he is "one-upped" by his equally skilled opponents.

The testimony of lobbyists often appeals to such symbols as the "American way of life," "creeping socialism," "selfish exploitation," and other clichés full of emotion and empty of precision. But in spite of the perfection of the science of persuasion, many arguments by interest groups are paradoxical and almost humorously inconsistent. For example, the steel industry has consistently dressed up its case with the slogans of *laissez-faire* competition, yet devoted all its energies to legislation legalizing basing-point marketing systems which artificially raise and protect the price of steel. In the same way, labor unions support featherbedding in the form of "full-crew" laws while at the same time paying deference, when it suits their convenience, to the notions of pride in workmanship.

Appearances before committees by persons other than those employed to do so is uncommon. The testimony of Mr. Harry Golden before a Senate Committee in 1945 put it this way: "Anytime a bill is presented to the Congress, I can close my eyes and visualize who will appear. They will be about the same people who usually testify for or against a bill. You never have any new blood."[16]

The function of committees in hearing bills is to acquire information about the bill, as well as to cull out from the plethora of measures introduced into legislatures those they think are deserving of consideration. This function is often used for other than its original purposes. Many times, important bills favored by a majority of the legislature will never reach the floor because they have been bottled up in a powerful committee. On the other hand, committees sometimes duck their responsibilities and report out bills which are not deserving of passage but are so highly pressured the committee passes the buck to the total legislature.

When a bill survives committee hearings, the committee has several

[16]Quoted in Gross, *The Legislative Struggle*, p. 290.

possible courses of action in reporting it back to the whole house. It can recommend that the bill be passed as introduced, that it be passed with amendments made by the committee, or that it be defeated. This last alternative of reporting a bill unfavorably is very infrequently used because committees themselves have a most effective means of killing bills, either by not considering them or by tabling them. Few bills dealing with important matters survive committee deliberations without amendment. One congressman put it succinctly when he said that Congress would amend the Bible if it were before them for action. One might add that the variety of interest group pressures would doubtless make the original intent hard to discover in the committee report.

When there are a large number of amendments suggested by a committee, very often they are put into a "clean" bill, which is assigned a new number and reported to the floor for action. On the floor, all committee amendments must be acted upon (approved, altered, or rejected) before a vote is taken on the measure itself. Committees do not always return unanimous agreements on the course of action to be taken on bills in their report back to the whole house. Minority or dissenting opinions by a member or members of the committee are often submitted to the house along with the majority opinion. Dissenting opinions can recommend completely different action or modified action in the form of additional amendments. A bill generally has a better chance for favorable action if the committee is unanimous in its recommendations.

BROKERAGE POLITICS AND COMMITTEES

THE PROCESS of creating and staffing committees reflects the complex interplay of political forces. To recount accurately or definitively all the factors entering into the final accommodation would be impossible. The result, however, is an intricate balance of prestige, power, ambition, statesmanship, self-interest, and political stratagems of all kinds. Indeed, the test of political leadership in a legislature is often largely measured by how well the committees were put together. If it is a good job, political programs will move. If it is a poor job, programs bog down. If it is a very bad job, there will probably be some changes made in the leadership.

The carefully constructed committees can be predicted to act in various ways. Some of them will block certain types of legislation deliberately; others will move legislation through rapidly; others will conduct elaborate hearings; others will spend a lot of time amending bills; and still others will serve as brokerage houses for a host of interest groups wanting something.

Committee hearings and deliberations are suited perfectly to the free play of pressure groups and the compromise of their differences. Except for executive sessions, committee meetings are open to the public; yet, they are for the most part private and unpublicized. The spotlight of publicity which attends floor debate serves to encourage legislators to frame their arguments in a broad public context. Floor debate and its publicity can also shine the light of public attention on the private interests and their stakes in the outcome. Neither of these conditions ordinarily obtains in the committee room. It is thus especially significant that the role of floor debate in legislative bodies has continuously declined while the power of committees has increased. Even in the Senate, traditionally the central forum of American public life, the role of floor debate has been progressively usurped by committees. The sheer weight of legislative business exerts pressures in this direction.

The process is complicated by the power of committee chairmen. Committees can bottle up a bill which the majority wants by simply refusing to take it up or report it out, by referring it to a subcommittee, or by reporting it out too late in the session for action. In most legislative bodies, including Congress, committee chairmen are often powerful enough to frustrate the wishes of a majority of the committee members. A chairman through his control of the agenda and of subcommittees, and with a swift and strong hand on the gavel, can often have his own way. In many committees, there are traditions, part of the rules of the "club," which dictate against a frustrated majority demanding a roll call vote of the committee or appealing from a ruling of the chair.

Committee control over the fate of legislation may increase with the growing complexity of the issues themselves. If this happens, as it appears to have with the military-industrial situation, group pressures can be more intensely applied and bargains more easily made.

FLOOR ACTION AND DEBATE

WHEN BILLS ARE RETURNED to the house in which they originated, they are placed upon the appropriate calendar.[17] In Congress, bringing

---

[17]The House of Representatives has several different calendars which are used for various types of bills. These are the *Union Calendar*, which contains all appropriation and revenue bills; the *House Calendar*, which lists public bills other than those dealing with financial matters; the *Private Calendar*, which contains all private bills; the *Consent Calendar*, to which noncontroversial bills from the *Union* and *House Calendars* can be removed and considered in order of their listing on the first and third Mondays of each month and passed only if they receive unanimous approval; and the *Discharge Calendar*, where bills with a favorable petition to discharge them from a committee (the petition requires 218 signatures) are placed and

bills up for floor debate is a complicated process. In the House, even those bills reported favorably by committees usually have to clear the powerful Rules Committee. A bill goes to the floor only after it has been scheduled by the Rules Committee as a special order of business. If the committee declines to schedule it, a petition of discharge is necessary to bring it before the House for debate and action. For the reasons already discussed, this is exceedingly difficult to achieve. In the House, appropriation and other important bills are debated before the Committee of the Whole House. This is a procedure by which the House converts itself into a committee and thus avoids having to follow the intricate formal procedure with which it has encumbered itself for regular business. The Senate does not use the Committee of the Whole except for treaties.

Debate on legislation displays wide ranges of ability, wit, erudition, and style. There are congressmen who speak with calm and reasoned dispatch and those whose rhetoric virtually lifts the dome off the Capitol in a mist of homilies, biblical references, and sentimental maxims. Great spellbinders seem to be diminishing in the ranks of congressmen, and their loss takes something of the drama out of political debate. Much of the debate, in any event, is for public consumption since committee action and informal commitments give a degree of predictability to the outcome of most legislation.

Floor Amendments and Riders

Congress, unlike many state legislatures, makes extensive use of floor amendments to bills. Very often, these are intended to cut the very heart out of the bill or alter its basic intent.

Another type of amendment, often coming from the floor, is the rider. Riders are designed to achieve a purpose not originally intended by the bill. On the 1918 agriculture appropriations bill, for example, the "drys" attached a rider calling for the wartime prohibition of intoxicating

---

considered on the second and fourth Mondays. A sixth calendar contains bills which the President has vetoed.

The Senate uses only one legislative calendar but has an *Executive Calendar* reserved for the confirmation of treaties and presidential nominations of officials.

Placing bills on various calendars is virtually automatic, but occasionally some deft maneuvering goes on in efforts to secure unanimous consent through the Consent Calendar. If any objections are raised to a member's bill on the Consent Calendar, it goes back to either the House or Private Calendar from which it came and cannot be put on the Consent Calendar again during the session. Many bills are noncontroversial, and the Consent Calendar speeds up action on these bills, but members at times attempt to move something to the Consent Calendar, often after a good deal of cloakroom conversation, even at the risk of losing it. Timing is important for such moves, since there is a twilight zone between the controversial and noncontroversial.

liquor. Riders can embrace subject matter which is totally unrelated to the provisions of a bill. Senator Morse, for example, attempted to attach an anti-poll tax rider onto the Tidelands Oil Bill before the Senate in 1946. Fortunately for the tidelands interests, the rider was killed along the way, although it was not ruled out of order. A threatened filibuster by southern Senators against the anti-poll tax rider was thus avoided. Riders seem to attach themselves like barnacles to legislation which seems likely to pass without difficulty. Such a situation provides an opportunity for many congressmen to get a "free ride" for some favorite cause, if they can hook it onto something going by with a lot of momentum.

Often legislative horse trading comes into play at this point, and the sponsor must agree to riders as the price of enough votes to get his bill passed. The effectiveness of the use of the rider also reflects the separation of powers and the fact that the President does not have an item veto power. The item veto, which many states provide their governors, allows the executive to veto, and often to reduce, specific items in appropriation bills. The President's lack of this power precludes him from taking out riders by vetoing them out of a bill. In short, he must either approve or veto the whole bill. Congress very often attaches riders which the President wants to a bill that is otherwise distasteful to him. A reverse situation also applies—that is, an obnoxious rider can be attached to a highly desired piece of administrative legislation.[18]

If the amending process from the floor of a legislative chamber gets too far out of hand, it can result in a practice, occuring in some state legislatures, known as bill hijacking. This is a device by which one legislator takes little more than the number and title of a bill and rewrites it completely by amendment. For example, a bill increasing welfare benefits to the aged by ten dollars a month may be amended to reduce the benefits ten dollars a month and to place restrictions on the receipt of such benefits. The bill has then been hijacked so that its effect is the opposite of what was intended. In many legislatures, including Congress, hijacking is discouraged by informal tradition. Even where it is permissible, it is discouraged by fear of reprisal. Carried very far, it introduces a degree of viciousness and irresponsibility into the legislative process which thwarts the whole system.

Amendments and riders are effective techniques in the brokerage process of politics. Many amendments are designed to satisfy special interest groups or to make bills politically palatable to constituents. The

[18]In 1961, President Kennedy was presented with a bill revising the immigration laws in several respects desirable to him. It also contained a provision changing the appellate jurisdiction on rulings by the Immigration Service from federal district courts to circuit courts, which he reportedly did not want. The bill was signed, however.

end of much of the maneuvering which flowers into amendments is legislation that often misses the point it originally tried to make. The strong
and straightforward principles of the Truman Administration in its original
request to Congress for the Full Employment Act (1946) were reduced to
legislation qualified to meet the demands of the major industrial, labor,
and agricultural interests. Such legislation might be hailed as a victory by
those who acclaim the validity of "hammering out laws on the anvil of
compromise" but to those who believe the principle of full employment to
be vital, the thunderous declaration of an aggressive governmental
responsibility for the economic security of its citizens emerged as a mild
squeak.

Test Votes

During the course of consideration of bills in Congress and other
legislative bodies, a vote on an amendment may be a test vote designed
to permit the leadership to discover the prospects for favorable final action
without risking the bill itself. Which amendments will be used as tests of
the final vote depends upon the stratagems employed by the floor mana-
gers. When an amendment, for example, would tend to destroy a bill, the
vote is usually a test. If the amendment passes, the bill can be dead for all
practical purposes, and usually those who support a destructive amendment will vote against final passage of the bill. There are both offensive
amendments, designed to cripple bills, and defensive amendments, designed
to thwart the offense and preserve the original purpose of the bill. The
vote on riders is also very often a test of a bill's strength. If the backers
can keep the barnacles off their bills, it is an indication of its strength. If
they are unable to do this, the bill may become so encumbered that it
could never pass or survive a presidential veto.

Other stratagems used to test legislation under debate are votes on
procedural questions, such as the validity of a point of order, a motion
to table a bill (which in effect kills it), and a vote on a motion to recommit
a bill to committee for further study.

These procedures for dealing with bills under debate do not begin
to exhaust the intricacies of procedure. Many a newly elected representative
of the people has discovered the complexity of the process as he has
watched his legislation disappear into the mysterious caverns of procedure.
It is both a frustrating and fascinating experience, and most freshmen legislators have taken the sage advice of their more battle-scarred elder brethren
to sit quietly on the sidelines and keep their mouths shut and their eyes
open.

The Vote

After a bill has been fully debated, and if it survives the laborious
process from introduction to final vote, the question put to the House of

Representatives is "Shall the bill be engrossed and read the third time?" The vote is on final passage and if it is affirmative, the bill is engrossed; that is, it is reprinted with all of its amendments put in their appropriate places and sent on to the Senate. Senate procedure is similar although simpler than in the House. If the bill passes the second house without amendment, it goes on to the President for his action. If the two versions are not the same, the bill will go to conference, and action is taken on the report before it goes to the President.

The President may approve the bill or veto it and return it to Congress with a message stating his reasons. Or, if Congress has adjourned and he cannot send it back, he can effect a pocket veto by not acting upon the bill. If Congress is in session and the President does not either approve or veto the bill, it automatically becomes law ten days after he has received it.

In the votes on the floor, Congressmen may pair votes, which means they enter into an agreement with a colleague on the opposite side of an issue to withhold their votes if one or both of them are absent when the vote is taken. In such cases, one is paired for and the other paired against an issue. Pairs are recorded in the *Congressional Record* but are not counted in vote totals.

If members do not want to vote they do not have to, even though they are present; both precedent and procedure guarantees the right to abstain. Voting may be by voice vote, with the Speaker deciding which side has it. If the vote is close or a member demands it, the vote may be by division, which requires members to stand and be counted. Or, the vote may be by roll call when a member demands it.

Article I, Section 5, of the Constitution provides for the recording in the *Journal* of "yeas and nays of the members of either House on any question . . . at the desire of one-fifth of the members." Any member may arise and ask for the yeas and nays. This request forces his often reluctant colleagues to declare themselves. Because of the necessary declaration of a stand on the bill before the house, the roll call is seldom used. If a roll call is obtained, it is still difficult to get one-fifth of the members to demand a recording of the vote in the *Journal*. An alert observer, however, can get the vote on a roll call, and some of the more adept are able to get it on a division by remembering which members stood on each side of the vote.

THE LEGISLATIVE PROCESS AND
RESPONSIBLE GOVERNMENT

THE SCOPE OF LEGISLATIVE ACTIVITIES in the United States is indeed broad. The authority of Congress and state legislatures is not without limits however, since the system of constitutional government in the United States not only grants power to legislative bodies but restricts them as well. The phrase "Congress shall make no law. . . ." which begins the First Amendment and the limitations upon Congress found in Article I, Section 9, of the Constitution are important restrictions on congressional action. These are principles which symbolize the limitations on the national legislature in acting in areas considered inappropriate to the proper functioning of a federal government composed of citizens with certain guaranteed freedoms. States also place restrictions upon their legislatures through their constitutions. The Constitution of the United States also restricts the states. It does this by express limitations, such as those in Article I, Section 10, and the Fourteenth Amendment, and by implication in granting certain exclusive powers to the federal government.

Within the purview of these limitations, however, the legislative power is basic to creating the broad policies of government. Legislatures cannot be evaluated by any one criterion alone. The people who are legislators, the environment they work in, various concepts of the purpose of the legislature, the individual and collective concepts of a public interest within and without legislatures, and the rules and rituals by which legislative activity is conducted are all relevant to the study of the legislative process.

Legislation passed in the United States by the national Congress has ramifications all over the world. Big armies, more and better bombs, tariffs and foreign aid are but a few legislative products which affect the whole world. Domestic actions also have widespread ramifications. If sectional interests kill civil rights legislation through the manipulation of the legislative machinery, not only do the second-class citizens denied their first-class rights suffer, but also the nation has a difficult time explaining this "democratic" action to its enemies and its allies.

As for the average citizen, the action of Congress or his state or local legislature is very important. If lobbies or interest groups he is associated with gain him special favor, he can enjoy these fruits. But they may be bitter fruit to others—maybe even to that heterogeneous mass called "the public." What we seek to find from legislative activity in the final examination is a key to understanding the values and moral tone of the society the legislature serves. If the principle of representative government is valid, there is no better place to look.

The problem is one of organizing political power in order that it may be made responsible. In practical terms, as we have argued earlier, this comes down to a question of the relationship between political parties and pressure groups. If the central purposes of the parties is seen as providing an organizational framework within which the accommodation of group interests can be achieved, the congressional parties and the

Congress itself are reasonably well organized for the task. The looseness of party discipline on all except organizational matters, the committee system, seniority rules, and much of the formal and informal procedure and rules contribute to an organization of power through shifting coalitions of groups.

If Congress is organized quite efficiently to conduct the brokerage process, the same cannot be said of its efficiency in providing a debate of public issues and in reaching decisions for which political parties may be held accountable. The public issue of the nation's health is different from a battle between the organized medical profession and other groups. Conservation of resources is not the same thing as satisfying the demands of timber, oil and mining interests, labor unions, recreation interests, and organized commercial and sport fishermen.

The essential difficulty confronting the legislator who seeks to apply his principles to the solution of *public* issues is his frustration at being unable to put issues beyond the special demands of organized groups. For the individual legislator, the problem is practically insurmountable. Only as a member of a political party organized in the legislature to promote party principles which stand above the interests does he have much of a chance. Once the inevitability and ubiquity of power is recognized, the problem of its organization emerges as the crucial one. If it is to be organized to pursue a public interest, political parties must be the instruments of its organization. The concern of the eighteenth century with the problem of faction is as important to democratic politics today as it was then. Factions have been honed and polished by the development of highly sophisticated techniques of human relations and persuasion. They have also become respectable. Through the practice of persuasion, they have convinced many Americans that not only are they respectable, they are also the basic instruments of democratic policy-making. "Nationally advertised brands are best; those that are not advertised must be inferior." This logic applied to political issues would require those who wish to accomplish something to organize and advertise.

As we have seen, academicians have not been oblivious to this development in American politics, and some have proffered optimistic theories which identify the brokerage model with democracy. Others, both liberal and conservative, view the same developments with alarm. The issue is an important one. In fact, it is so important that any discussion of the legislative process becomes meaningful only when it is examined in the light of these rival views of democracy.

II

THE PRESIDENT
AND
HIS ADMINISTRATION

THE PRESIDENCY: THE OFFICE AND THE MAN

THE PRESIDENT OF THE UNITED STATES wears many hats in playing his many roles. He is the chief Republican or Democrat, depending upon current political fortunes. He is in charge of strategy, the distribution of political awards, and fence-mending for his party. He is chief legislative leader and has a program which he pushes by methods ranging from persuasion to heavy and stinging lashes from the political bull whip. He is the main spokesman and leader of the nation in foreign affairs. He is commander-in-chief of the armed forces, who must serve as referee and final authority in the pulling and hauling of the rival services. He is the ceremonial head of state, who greets distinguished visitors and adds his presence to national ceremonies that range from throwing out the first baseball of each new season to buying the first box of girl scout cookies and talking by telephone to the returned astronaut. And he is commander-in-chief of the bureaucracy, which makes him chief administrator of the nation.

The expansion in the powers of the executive branch in recent years has intensified constitutional conflicts among the three branches of the federal government, conflicts which have existed in varying degrees since the Constitution was adopted. Theodore Roosevelt had trouble getting appropriations from Congress. There was a power collision when he sent the Navy halfway around the world, exhausting his available funds, and then said it was up to Congress to,bring it back. Woodrow Wilson lost his health and his dream of United States leadership in a strong League of Nations when the United States Senate, led in this fight by Senator Henry Cabot Lodge, refused to approve American participation. Both Franklin Roosevelt and Harry Truman came into conflict with the courts and with Congress over the extent of executive power. President Kennedy ran into difficulty in asking Congress for grants of executive power to regulate tariffs and to control recessions. In early 1962, when his bill to create a new cabinet post on Urban Affairs was bottled up in committee, he forced the House to a roll call vote, which he lost, by exercising his power to effect reorganizations of the executive branch, subject to congressional veto. (Under the existing Reorganization Act, presidential reorganization proposals become effective in the absence of a veto by either house within sixty days.)

In these conflicts the President is armed with the constitutionally prescribed powers of the office. Beyond these, he can bring to bear the inestimable influence of his position as the only public official with a mandate from the national electorate. Over a hundred years ago, de Tocqueville said that "the laws allow him to be strong but circumstances make him weak."[1] Changing circumstances since that time have made him strong. The importance of foreign policy in recent years and the role of the President as party and legislative leader may even point to the need for more executive power and indicate, contrary to de Tocqueville's comment, that the law does not provide sufficient strength.

Presidential Styles in Leadership

Americans look to their President for guidance and leadership. Periodically, Presidents speak to the nation on important issues and during crises. From these occasions much of the character and personality of the President emerges.

Historian Eric F. Goldman has pointed out that the public statements of Presidents, albeit largely "ghost-written," are directly related to the quality of their Presidencies. As he puts it, "what Presidents have done with words has expressed a lot about them, bad and good." He continues with an illustration:

[1] *Democracy in America*, Vol. 1, p. 126.

Go in any place on the long roll of American Chief Executives and the White House words call up the memory of the administrations. Take George Washington, an aging general playing father to a squalling infant nation, and the words are firm, paternal, magisterial. Or Thomas Jefferson, a remarkable combination of the gentleman scholar and the hardheaded politician, using a prose that is a striking amalgam of the elegant and the wily. Or piddling, indecisive James Buchanan, mincing along from flaccidity to inanity. Or Abraham Lincoln, that great President and great human being, incapable of writing even a hasty letter that is not touched with wisdom and compassion. Or the nothing Rutherford B. Hayes, talking and writing a nothing prose. Or the rambunctious Teddy Roosevelt, lecturing the corporations or any other deviator from The Good and The True in sentences that shrill like a runaway calliope.[2]

Goldman observes that Woodrow Wilson, in his prose,

drove ahead in his God-lashed way, rarely failing to intimate that his program had a decided connection with divine revelation. (The cynical old French Prime Minister Georges Clemenceau put it: "God gave us only Ten Commandments. Wilson brings us Fourteen Points.") The Wilson prose, most of which he hammered out himself on a battered typewriter brought from his Princeton days, had a constant summons to redemption. On the occasion of his famous first inaugural in 1913 the crowd hushed, as if in church, when the new President reached his climax, speaking of lifting "our life as a Nation to the light that shines from the hearthfire of every man's conscience. . . .The feelings with which we face this new age of right and opportunity sweep across our heartstrings like some air out of God's own presence, where justice and mercy are reconciled and the judge and the brother are one."[3]

By contrast, according to Goldman, Truman used a "shoot from-the-hip decisiveness, a brash confidence in the face of anything"; Coolidge's prose was "as crabbed as the Coolidge policies"; Eisenhower was adept at "expressing in a friendly muddle of words his faith in a sunny muddling through"; and Kennedy's prose is "carefully burnished, tautly disciplined, astute and hard-driving, humorous in its wary way, and cool, so very cool."[4]

There is much more to a President than his public speeches, but since the President is the focal point of the political attention of the whole nation, his prose will be listened to very carefully. From his words the people derive hope, despair, frustration, anger, and, above all, a sense of

[2]Eric F. Goldman, "Presidential Prose," *Holiday*, April, 1962, p. 11.
[3]*Ibid.*, pp. 11 and 14.
[4]*Ibid.*, pp. 14, 16, 18, and 19.

national purpose. "The business of the country is business"; "We have nothing to fear but fear itself"; "Grass will grow in the streets"; and "We must move ahead." Words, but how they are said and who says them at what time have been important to the whole nation.

Presidential Styles in Administration

Personality characteristics also show up in a chief executive's administration. A contrast between the types of administration the nation had under Franklin Roosevelt and under Eisenhower suggests several personality differences between the two men. Roosevelt ran a loose-jointed administration which was the bane of the efficiency expert who looked to organization charts, clear lines of communication, and standard operating procedures as the right and proper way to do things. Roosevelt's cabinet was a quarrelsome collection of able individualists—some of them have been called "prima donnas"—who went directly to "the boss" with complaints and who directly sought the favor of their chief.[5]

Roosevelt's cabinet leaked like a sieve to the press, although some of the leaks were opened by the President. Roosevelt let his cabinet go along in this fashion, but at times he would deal directly with subordinates to the cabinet members in the various departments, and, it is alleged, bypassed his cabinet members on several occasions by taking charge of things personally. The administrative pattern was also complicated by advisers like Harry Hopkins,[6] who had a great deal of power but no definite place in any structural apparatus. Hopkins served as sort of a personal trouble shooter for the President. Roosevelt also piled organization upon organization and had fantastic overlaps of jurisdictions of various governmental agencies. He got things done in spite of this organization inefficiency and his administration was creative even though it was a structural mess.[7]

President Eisenhower's concept of administration was quite different from that of Roosevelt. Eisenhower's military background, and the fact that he was not as intrigued with the political aspects of his job as was Roosevelt, no doubt contributed much to the difference. Where Roosevelt seldom, if ever, avoided the politics of administrative situations, Eisenhower

[5]For an interesting account of some of the doings of the cabinet, see Harold Ickes, *The Secret Diary of Harold Ickes: The First Thousand Days* (New York: Simon and Schuster, 1954).
[6]See Robert E. Sherwood, *Roosevelt and Hopkins*, 2 volumes (New York: Bantam, 1950).
[7]For an account of Roosevelt's organizational creations and his built-in "espionage" system of acquiring information, see Arthur M. Schlesinger, Jr., *The Coming of the New Deal: The Age of Roosevelt*, Volume 2 (Boston: Houghton Mifflin, 1959).

attempted, at least early in his administration, to divorce politics as much as possible from administering the government. Instead of the free-wheeling informality of Roosevelt's cabinet meetings, Eisenhower's cabinet always had a carefully planned agenda which was distributed in advance. Discussion was not allowed to roam hither and yon but focused on the issues at hand. Eisenhower also introduced the military staff concept to his cabinet and, in his own words, he gave "way on a number of personal opinions to this gang [the cabinet]."[8] He regarded his cabinet as advisers who were to be respected and whose collective judgment should be a guide to action, rather than a collection of people with interesting ideas which he might or might not follow. Eisenhower also delegated a great deal of authority to his cabinet officers and other administrators. His knowledge of what was going on in the inner workings of bureaucracy was often severely limited—so much so, that many members of the press accused his administration of drift and lack of direction. He relied mainly upon the techniques of persuasion rather than orders to his subordinates and, unlike Roosevelt, would not circumvent his administrators or short-circuit the lines of authority to get his wishes into action.

Briefly, Roosevelt dominated his administration and got his way whereas Eisenhower was influenced by his cabinet and often followed its lead. The contrast in power between Roosevelt's various secretaries of state and Eisenhower's Mr. Dulles is a case in point. Roosevelt was, in effect, his own Secretary of State, but Eisenhower relied heavily upon Mr. Dulles for foreign policy decisions. In short, the chief executive's role as chief administrator depends upon his conception of the office and the importance he attaches to administrative matters in comparison with his other duties.

THE PRESIDENT AS SPOKESMAN FOR A PUBLIC INTEREST

AMERICANS ARE AMBIVALENT about the extent and use of presidential power. In the political dialogue centering around the desirability of the welfare state, the President is generally the person and the Presidency the institution which bear the brunt of the thrust and parry of the argument. As party chief and as leader of public opinion, the President is the source of most social legislation. Furthermore, to curtail the welfare state is to curtail the activities of the executive branch of government. This continuing argument over the scope and range of presidential

[8]Robert J. Donovan, *Eisenhower: The Inside Story* (New York: Harper, 1956), p. 64. This author deals extensively with the Eisenhower concept of administration.

power is often made in general terms. There are, however, specific instances where the power collisions between the President and a private interest give the debate a sharp focus.

Two Presidents have experienced difficulty in a clash with the same private group and the results of their behavior in these situations have left a clear mark on American political history. President Truman had difficulty with the steel industry in 1952. Ten years later, in 1962, President Kennedy collided with the same industry. The circumstances, actions, and results in the two cases were different; taken together they illustrate the range of methods available to a President in exploiting the full power and influence of the office.

Steel represents a large industrial establishment which enters into contractual agreements with its well-organized employees. Labor-management negotiations take the form of industry wide bargaining and revolve basically around wages and fringe benefits. The historical pattern is for wage increases to be followed immediately by industry-wide price increases. Steel has been referred to often as the barometer of the economy —that is, when steel goes up in price everything else tends to do so also. Thus, the wage-price spiral in steel exerts inflationary pressure throughout the economy.

For a long time, the price of steel was considered a matter for the industry to determine, but recently there has been a growing body of opinion which holds that steel pricing policies should be consistent with the public interest in economic growth and monetary stability. In 1952, during the Korean War, (or "police action"), union and management officials deadlocked in negotiations. Part of the machinery of wartime emergency wage and price controls empowered the Wage Stabilization Board to make findings in labor disputes. In this case, the W. S. B. proposed a package of hourly and fringe benefit increases totalling $.225 as a basis for settlement. Charles E. Wilson, Director of the Office of Defense Mobilization (parent organization of the Wage Stabilization Board), considered the package a "serious threat in our effort to stabilize the economy."[9] President Truman disagreed, and Mr. Wilson resigned. The recommended package was accepted by the union but vigorously opposed by management. If it were enforced, industry officials argued, a twelve-dollar per ton price increase was necessary (although they may have taken less); President Truman responded with the promise that if a price rise is necessary "in the interest of national defense, it will be granted," but he refused to commit himself to any specific amount. Later, steel management presented the union an offer less than the "package," and Philip Murray

[9]Alan F. Westin, *The Anatomy of a Constitutional Law Case* (New York: Macmillan, 1958), p. 4.

of the union turned it down and served notice of a strike. Industry began banking its furnaces.

President Truman's problem was to avert a strike. He could invoke the politically distasteful cooling-off provisions of the Taft-Hartley Law; he could grant the industry's price request; or, although legal opinion was divided as to his power to do so, he could seize the mills and put them under government operation. He chose to seize the mills.

President Truman's action precipitated a national debate. He defended his position as being in the public interest and within the emergency powers implied in his constitutional position as chief executive and commander-in-chief of the armed forces. He told his "fellow Americans," on April 8, 1952:

> You may think this steel dispute doesn't affect you—you may think it's just a matter between the Government and a few greedy companies. But it isn't. If we granted the outrageous prices the steel industry wants, we would scuttle our whole price control program. And that comes pretty close to home to everybody. . . .[10]

On April 9, Clarence Randall, President of Inland Steel, responded for the entire steel industry (he was angry, as his remarks reveal):

> I am here to make answer on behalf of the steel industry to charges flung over these microphones last night by the man who stood where I stand now. I am a plain citizen. He was President of the United States. . .but actually it is not the President of the United States to whom I make answer. It is Harry S. Truman, the man, who last night so transgressed his oath of office, so far abused the power which is temporarily his, that he must now stand and take it.[11]

Mr. Randall emphasized the rights of private property and its ownership by "one million people" and asked parents whether their boys were "making $1.70 an hour in Korea." His response was bitter, stimulated no doubt by the bitterness in the President's attack.

The press took up the battle, but it was not decided there. The steel industry entered suit and, after hasty processing through the lower courts, the Supreme Court upheld its claim.[12] The decision stated that there is no implied grant of emergency power to the President in the Constitution sufficient to justify his abrogation of the separation of powers in this case. The power claimed by the President, the Court ruled, constitutionally resides in the Congress, and the Congress had not expressly delegated it to the President. Truman had lost his battle in the courts.

[10]*Ibid.*, p. 16
[11]*Ibid.*, p. 18.
[12]*Youngstown Sheet and Tube Company et. al. v. Sawyer*, 343 U. S. 579 (1952).

Ten years later the President and the steel industry faced each other again.[13] This time it was President Kennedy who invoked the public interest against a steel price increase. Secretary of Labor Goldberg had persuaded labor to make moderate demands; the matter had been discussed with steel executives, and the President was under the impression that no price increase would be made. But shortly after the contract was signed, on April 10, 1962, United States Steel announced a six-dollar per ton increase in price, an action quickly followed by the Republic, Bethlehem, Jones and Loughlin, Pittsburg, National, and Youngstown companies. On April 11, President Kennedy scheduled a nationally televised press conference and icily levelled charges that the decision to raise steel prices was a threat to the "public interest":

> Simultaneous and identical actions of United States Steel and other leading steel corporations increasing steel prices by some $6 a ton constitute a wholly unjustifiable and irresponsible defiance of the public interest.
>
> In this serious hour in our Nation's history, when we are confronted with grave crises in Berlin and Southeast Asia, when we are devoting our energies to economic recovery and stability, when we are asking reservists to leave their homes and families for months on end and servicemen to risk their lives—and four were killed in the last two days in Vietnam—and asking union members to hold down their wage increases, at a time when restraint and sacrifice are being asked of every citizen, the American people will find it hard, as I do, to accept a situation in which a tiny handful of steel executives whose pursuit of private power and profit exceeds their sense of public responsibility can show such utter contempt for the interests of 185 million Americans.
>
> If this rise in the cost of steel is imitated by the rest of the industry, instead of rescinded, it would increase the cost of homes, autos, appliances, and most other items for every American family. It would increase the cost of machinery and tools to every American businessman and farmer. It would seriously handicap our efforts to prevent an inflationary spiral from eating up the pensions of our older citizens, and our new gains in purchasing power.

The President then pointed to the favorable earnings position of the companies and added some clear threats of executive retribution:

> The facts of the matter are that there is no justification for an increase in the steel prices. The recent settlement between the industry and the union, which does not even take place until July 1st, was widely acknowledged to be non-inflationary, and the whole

[13]During the Eisenhower Administration, in 1960, Vice-President Nixon had persuaded the steel industry not to raise prices immediately after a wage increase.

purpose and effect of the Administration's role, which both parties understood, was to achieve an agreement which would make unnecessary any increase in prices. Steel output per man is rising so fast that labor costs per ton of steel can actually be expected to decline in the next 12 months. And in fact, the Acting Commissioner of the Bureau of Labor Statistics informed me this morning that, and I quote: "Employment costs per unit of steel output in 1961 were essentially the same as they were in 1958."

The cost of the major raw materials, steel scrap and coal, has also been declining, and for an industry which has been generally operating at less than two-thirds of capacity, its profit rate has been normal and can be expected to rise sharply this year in view of the reduction in idle capacity.

Their lot has been easier than that of 100,000 steel workers thrown out of work in the last three years. The industry's cash dividends have exceeded $600 million in each of the last five years, and earnings in the first quarter of this year were estimated in the February 28th Wall Street Journal to be among the highest in history.

In short, at a time when they could be exploring how more efficient and better prices could be obtained, reducing prices in this industry in recognition of lower costs, their unusually good labor contract, their foreign competition and their increase in production and profits which are coming this year, a few gigantic corporations have decided to increase prices in ruthless disregard of their public responsibilities.

The Steel Workers Union can be proud that it abided by its responsibilities in this agreement. And this government also has responsibilities which we intend to meet. The Department of Justice and the Federal Trade Commission are examining the significance of this action in a free, competitive economy. The Department of Defense and other agencies are reviewing its impact on their policies of procurement and I am informed that steps are underway by those members of the Congress who plan appropriate inquiries into how these price decisions are so quickly made and reached, and what legislative safeguards may be needed to protect the public interest.

His concluding statement raised the whole issue of the public responsibility of powerful private groups:

Price and wage decisions in this country, except for very limited restrictions in the case of monopolies and national emergency strikes, are and ought to be freely and privately made, but the American people have a right to expect in return for that freedom, a higher sense of business responsibility for the welfare of their country than has been shown in the last two days.

Some time ago I asked each American to consider what he would do for his country. And I asked the steel companies. In the last 24 hours we had their answer.[14]

Mr. Roger Blough, Board Chairman of United States Steel, responded for a part of the steel industry. In contrast to the historical pattern, the industry had not solidly followed United States Steel's price leadership; Inland and Kaiser steel companies announced they would not raise prices. Other steel companies followed suit, particularly when they found the Attorney General and Congress acting to explore violations of antitrust statutes and to investigate price collusions. Also, government contracts were awarded to companies not raising their prices. In the face of all these pressures, the industry reconsidered and rescinded the increase. President Kennedy won his battle and graciously stated in his press conference that his administration "harbors no ill will against any individual, any industry, corporation, or any segment of the American economy."

There are many reasons why President Truman lost his case while President Kennedy won his. Both Presidents stood on the public interest as justification for their actions. Both took their cases to the people. But, whereas President Kennedy chose to make this informal arena the decisive battleground, President Truman chose to risk his formal constitutional powers in the courts. Contrary to de Tocqueville's observation, circumstances prompted him to seek greater strengh than the law allowed him. But where formal powers had failed, President Kennedy made informal power succeed. It is true that the informal pressures of public opinion which Kennedy exploited were backed by the use of, and by threats to use, such formal executive power as control over the allocation of defense contracts and antitrust prosecutions. His formal power to recommend to Congress and his informal power as party leader were also available to threaten, for example, changes in the tax laws unfavorable to the steel industry. The over-all lesson seems clear: the Presidency is an office of tremendous potential power, the effective utilization of which requires the skillful blending of formal and informal—constitutional and political— sources of strength. When the office is so employed, its power may seem, as it did to many of President Kennedy's opponents, virtually unrestrained and even dictatorial.

THE PRESIDENT AS CHIEF EXECUTIVE

THE EXECUTIVE POWERS of the President are exercised through a multitude of administrative agencies. The growth of government, over which Americans have been so deeply concerned, occurs primarily in

[14]*Sacramento Bee*, April 12, 1962.

these agencies—both by the creation of new ones and the expansion of old ones. Congress and legislatures generally are more fixed in size and function than is the executive branch of government. The judicial system expands enough to quicken the pace of its business, but its duties and responsibilities also remain more fixed than those of the executive.

Executive functions are by far the most elastic of the three branches of government. The executive has even taken over many legislative and judicial functions. Quasi-legislative powers have been delegated to many executive agencies. This allows these agencies to make rules and regulations which not only concern the workings of the agency but also large segments of the public.

The rule-making powers of the federal Departments of Agriculture and of Health, Education and Welfare or of a state highway commission are examples of this. The executive can also enforce these administrative rules through the use of quasi-judicial powers. This power allows executive agencies to conduct investigations, hold hearings, and decide cases within authorized jurisdictions. The hearings and decisions of the Civil Service Commission can be a matter of job or no job to a federal employee. The decision of a state welfare board can mean pension or no pension to the mother of a needy child or an aged person. Court review of these matters is generally confined to the question of whether the agency operated in good faith within the authority delegated to it by the legislature. Facts are seldom tried again in the courts.

The Problem of Executive Control

The almost explosive expansion of the executive branch has created tremendous problems of over-all co-ordination, control, and responsibility. In the American constitutional system, the final authority and responsibility for administration cannot be alienated; they rest squarely on the shoulders of the lonely man in the White House.

The complexities of the federal service and that of many of the states are such that many students of administration feel something must be done to relieve the chief executive of his burdens.[15] Suggestions include giving the Vice-President some administrative duties and creating various "assistant President" offices which would be more than advisory in nature. Presidents themselves have chafed at the numerous demands upon their time. Many of them would like to be freed of routine so they could devote more time to the awesome responsibilities of making basic policy

---

[15]The Hoover Commission of 1949, which recommended many changes in the structure of the federal executive agencies, led to several "little Hoover Commissions" in the states.

decisions. As a result, much delegation has been made by some Presidents to cabinet members, to "administrative assistants," such as Sherman Adams under President Eisenhower, or to ministers without or with various portfolios, such as Harry Hopkins under President Roosevelt.

The American public and Congress, however, have not been enthusiastic about having others act in the name of the President. There seems to be a popular view that Presidents should know all the answers to press conference questions regarding the workings of bureaucracy. Even the substitution of Vice-President Nixon, early in the Eisenhower administration, to throw out the first baseball while the President engaged in his preferred recreation of golf caused such bitter comments among those who regard this ceremony as a part of the "American way of life" that it did not happen again. We demand a lot from our chief executives. We not only expect them to cut ribbons for highways, pay tribute to national heroes, and entertain visiting dignitaries, we also expect them to know what an atomic reactor is, how it works, how much it costs, and how the votes will go in upstate New York. Woodrow Wilson once said: "Men of ordinary physique and discretion cannot be Presidents and live. If the strain be not somehow relieved, we shall be obliged to be picking our chief magistrates from among wise and prudent athletes—a small class.[16]

Even though the White House office staff numbers about four hundred people, many of whom work to organize and funnel information for the President, no one man could possibly expect to acquire or be adequately briefed on all of the information these people collect. When he is not briefed, the press has a field day at the presidential press conference.

Executive Administrative Aides

Since we have yet to develop a group of supermen from which we could select our Presidents and governors, it has been necessary to equip our chief executives with subordinates who can aid in carrying out the administrative burdens of such offices. The most important staff aid in the federal system is the Executive Office of the President. It took a long time to get the President more than two or three secretaries for help, but in 1937 the President's Committee on Administrative Management, a group of academically and practically trained experts in administration, decided that the President needed more than clerical help and recommended he be given six administrative aides who should have, in the now legendary words, a "passion for anonymity." Two years later, as part of the Reorganization Act, Congress authorized these positions but

[16]Quoted in F. M. Carney and H. F. Way, *Politics 1960* (San Francisco: Wadsworth, 1960), p. 65.

not without some spirited and eloquent debate regarding the sacred principle of separation of power. Congress also viewed with alarm the growing power of the President. Some of the fears expressed misgivings about the fact that Congress has through the years given the executive branch more and more personnel and more and more power. At the same time, Congress has denied itself much of the same kind of assistance and has delegated away much of its authority to administrative agencies.

The Executive Office of the President now consists of over one thousand permanent staff, including the approximately four hundred members of the White House staff mentioned earlier. It also contains all sorts of special consultants and temporary help.

In addition to the White House staff, the following are the chief agencies of the Executive Office of the President:

1. *The Bureau of the Budget.* This office is composed of economists and administrative analysts who study the national economy and federal governmental agencies and put the executive budget together for presentation to Congress. The staff of the bureau attempts to make use of the best techniques of administrative and budget analysis in preparing the budget. The net result of such efforts is a mass of complex data to support appropriation requests. The federal budget, like that of most states, is a bewildering compilation of such "line items" as telephone charges, travel funds, and other bits and pieces of information. The 1949 Hoover Commission Report recommended a performance budget, which attempts to relate what agencies spend with what they do, rather than exhaustively to list the minutiae of their expenditures. In 1950, Congress requested a performance budget in its Budget and Accounting Procedure Act, and the Bureau began working in this direction. If the performance budget is further developed, it should help in providing Congress with the devices for speedier decisions. As yet, however, the line-item approach is still popular with Congress.

2. *Office of Civil and Defense Mobilization.* Through its Director, this agency advises the President on the development and co-ordination of the nation's civilian, military, and industrial resources. It advises on defense materials, stockpiles commodities considered necessary for defense and war, and advises on the use of governmental contracts to maintain a strong industrial potential and productive capacity for emergency use should the occasion arise.

3. *National Security Council.* This agency is a creature of Congress (1947) designed to provide top-level advice on how the nation's foreign, military, and domestic policies can be integrated to protect the nation's security. The law provides that its membership shall include the President, the Vice-President, the Secretary of State, the Secretary of Defense,

and the Director of the Office of Civil and Defense Mobilization. Ordinarily, the President invites other key officials to sit in the Council's meetings. They may include the Director of the Central Intelligence Agency, the Chairman of the Joint Chiefs of Staff, the Secretary of the Treasury, the Director of the Bureau of the Budget, the United States Ambassador to the United Nations, and the Under Secretary of State.

4. *Council of Economic Advisers.* This group, created by the Employment Act of 1946, consists of three members appointed by the President with Senate confirmation. The Council has a small but highly professionalized staff. The chief duties of the Council are to make general analyses of the national economy and inform the President on these matters. The President uses the Council's reports as a basis for his recommendations to Congress in his required annual Economic Report to that body. The Council has been subject to criticism for being "soft-headed" as well as "eggheaded" in its recommendations, particularly when it suggests that increased welfare and public works programs might be desirable. The business community and labor have both chafed under its recommendations upon occasion. Nevertheless, Presidents since 1946 have relied heavily on the Council's advice in formulating programs for avoiding the "boom-bust" cycles of the past. The President's proposals must run the course of congressional procedure, including consideration by the Joint Economic Committee, which was also created by the Employment Act.

PRESIDENTIAL POLICY AND THE MEN
WHO MAKE IT

IN THE PERFORMANCE of his role as chief policy-maker for the nation, the President can make use of his politically appointed cabinet as well as the advisors in the Executive Office. The cabinet consists of the heads of the ten major departments of the federal government: the Secretaries of State, Treasury, Defense, Interior, Agriculture, Commerce, Labor, and Health, Education and Welfare, and the Postmaster General and Attorney General.

There has been a marked tendency in recent years for Presidents to rely more heavily on the members of the Executive Office than on the heads of the regular government departments. There are many reasons for this. Partly it is a matter of the increasing complexity of the presidential task and his increased responsibility for over-all policy leadership and co-ordination. Particularly in the area of foreign policy in an age in which almost all aspects of society are involved, it is obvious why the President would come to rely on those agencies of co-ordination and policy planning whose responsibility and vision is not limited to traditional departmental boundaries. The same considerations apply to domestic policy. The Council of Economic Advisers, for example, is in a position to make recommendations on problems of economic stability and growth which cut across the jurisdictions, and the limited perspectives, of the Departments of Labor, Commerce, Agriculture, Interior, Treasury, and Health, Education, and Welfare, as well as of independent agencies like the Securities and Exchange Commission, the Federal Trade Commission, and the Federal Reserve Board.

Partly, also, the President's reliance on the men in the Executive Office is due to the fact that they are, in a unique sense, "his men." With few exceptions, his hand is free in making appointments, since the requirement of Senate confirmation applicable to the heads of regular departments does not apply. Without the requirement of Senate confirmation, the President need not worry about "senatorial courtesy," and he need not consider the damage which might be done his position by the harassment of a single senator on even those nominations which eventually will be confirmed. The appointees to positions in the Executive Office are not likely, therefore, to have their allegiance to the President fragmented by conflicting loyalties.

These same considerations help to explain why the Vice-President has not emerged as an assistant President. Although the traditions of the presidential nominating conventions of both parties virtually assure the presidential nominee of the power to name his running mate, his actual choice is likely to be circumscribed. The nomination of the party's standard bearer will most often have involved conflicts among the interest group and ideological factions of the party. The imperative necessity in filling the second place on the slate is to heal the wounds. The vice-presidential nomination is likely to furnish the salve of reconciliation. Therefore, he will probably represent a different orientation from the President.

There are exceptions, of course. Candidate Eisenhower, because of his ability to appeal to all segments of the party, had a relatively free choice of running mates. Early in his administration, he made clear that his relationship to Vice-President Richard Nixon was an almost unique one in our recent political history. Nixon, the President repeatedly affirmed, was "the most valuable man on my team." This relationship led, during the Eisenhower Administration, to the Vice-Presidency becoming a much more important and influential office than it has been in any other recent period.

Even so, if there was an assistant president to Eisenhower, it was not Vice-President Nixon but Sherman Adams, a member of the White House Staff whose official title was Assistant to the President. It was

Adams who—until his resignation under pressure in the Goldfine "influence" scandal—played the role of understudy to the President and who was, during several serious illnesses of the President, the voice of the Presidency. The pattern of presidential reliance on the staff of the Executive Office continued in the Kennedy Administration.

PRESIDENTIAL LEADERSHIP AND THE SEPARATION OF POWERS

IN THE AMERICAN CONSTITUTIONAL SYSTEM the problem of effective and responsible policy leadership is posed directly by the separation of powers. In parliamentary systems, like that of Great Britain where the executive and his cabinet are chosen from the majority party in the legislature, they have almost automatic legislative support for their programs. If they do not, the executive and his cabinet can be removed. This is not the case where the executive is a separate branch of government elected for a fixed term. He may or may not have political support, and his ability to provide legislative leadership and to organize an effective and dynamic administration can suffer severely if he does not. President Hoover in his last two years in office, President Truman during the Eightieth Congress and, to a lesser extent, President Eisenhower in his second term were all handicapped administratively as well as politically by Congresses dominated by the opposite party.

Complications result from congressional control of appropriations and of the President's legislative program. By overriding a presidential veto, Congress can force the President to administer a law to which he is opposed. The device of administering a law to death has been tried at times but is not a very effective method of dealing with a hostile Congress. This is a device where the executive takes a law he does not like and enforces it to the letter and very last comma. President Truman threatened to do this with an immigration bill he opposed. Perhaps a better example was Oklahoma Governor Edmondson's treatment of the state's dry laws, which prohibited the sale of alcoholic beverages. He won reluctant support by enforcing the dry laws as they had never been enforced before which caused a great outrage among those accustomed to the illegal consumption of spirits. Will Rogers is reported at one time to have said, "Oklahoma will be dry as long as the voters can stagger to the polls." Events proved him right: when the governor enforced the law so well the voters had to walk soberly to the polls, they voted to make Oklahoma wet.[17]

Even where the Presidency and Congress are controlled by the same

[17]"Parching Oklahoma into Repeal," *Business Week,* March 21, 1959, p. 32.

party, the weakness of American parties and the concomitant influence of interest groups in Congress force the policy leadership role on the President. At the same time, they put formidable barriers in the way of his ability to generate the necessary congressional support. Presidential-congressional hostility is virtually built into the system.

In this context, the President's increasing reliance on a loyal and able White House staff, however necessary to carry out the responsibilities of his office, may very well have its disadvantages in other ways to a Congress already jealous of and frustrated by the gradual aggrandizement of executive power. A vigorous and powerful staff of presidential aides and consultants is likely to appear as insult heaped on past injuries. Men who have weathered the arduous trial of popular election could not be expected to take kindly to the fact that, often very young and sometimes academic "Johnnys-come-lately" over whom they have almost no control have more power than they.

Even the Vice-President, who has weathered the election trial and who presides over the Senate, is never very fully trusted or admitted to membership in the legislative "club." Not even a Vice-President who formerly sat in the "club's" inner circles can escape being a part of the "enemy" executive's apparatus. Vice-President Lyndon Johnson, formerly majority leader and the most powerful member of the Senate, apparently has not been able to retain enough of his influence in Congress to save major portions of President Kennedy's legislative program. The hopes of many that the combined congressional experience of President Kennedy and Vice-President Johnson would provide adequate sail and rudder for a legislative program floundered on the reef surrounding the "club."

An important part of the duties of the White House staff is to act as liaison with Congress and to generate support for the executive program. It is not an easy nor an enviable duty. In effect, it asks a group of men wholly identified by the manner of their appointment and their undivided loyalty with the President to overcome the rivalry, animosities, and jealousies inherent in the separation of powers and reinforced in our political history. And it asks them to do the job without the one tool that might be effective—the power of party discipline and common loyalty to party principles. Without any heavy artillery for political persuasion, the legislative liaison men increasingly rely upon cajoling, wheedling, endearment, and manipulation. They tend to become lobbyists for the President, and his program takes on the characteristics of another pressure group demand in Congress. Little wonder that they fail so often, and that the problem of coherent, responsible policy-making remains the central problem of the system.

In state governments, most governors have similar problems, although in some, the governor as leader of a strong state party organization and as dispenser of patronage, is in a stronger position. In many states, however, the governor is confronted with a formidable obstacle to his ability both to exercise executive control and to provide policy leadership. His problems result from the long ballot, in effect in a large number of states, by which many additional executive officials are elected directly by the people.

Most governors have executive secretaries in varying numbers who handle such matters as appointments, legislative liaison, press relations, departmental co-ordination, executive clemency for criminals, and others. But a governor, like the President, still has personal responsibility for these matters. In long-ballot states, the governor usually tends to surround himself with officials over whom he has political control. For example, sometimes a governor has an attorney general from the opposite political party, which can result in the governor having his worst political enemy for his legal counsel. When this happens, governors often "borrow" lawyers from departments they control or sometimes, if they are fortunate, get enough funds to hire their own legal counsel to help make certain that the attorney general gives "proper" opinions and prosecutes cases in court adequately. If he does not, the governor is in a position to do battle in the legislature or in the press.

THE PRESIDENT AND FOREIGN POLICY

OF ALL THE ROLES PLAYED by the most powerful elective official in the world, none matches in its importance and in the power that attends it the President's position as chief formulator and executor of the nation's foreign policy. The force of circumstance has seen to its importance, while the ineffectiveness of checks and balances in this area has increased the power of the Presidency almost by default.

Foreign Policy in the Nuclear Era

The circumstances which have led to a preoccupation with foreign policy in the executive establishment have revolutionized the relations between nation—states. The international system of the nineteenth century was characterized by domination of Asia and Africa by European powers who occasionally engaged in fraternal wars. War could be held to be "the continuation of diplomacy by other means," and when it broke out it was fought with limited means and for limited ends. Most often it was restrained by shifting coalitions of states in a system of balance of power. America, for her part, withdrew in "splendid isolation" to carry out the conquest of the frontier and the "grand experiment" in democracy, except of course for the mantle of protection thrown over Latin America by the Monroe Doctrine. In the twentieth century, the world of international politics changed in all its important aspects and so, of necessity, did the American posture toward it.

In the aftermath of World War II, fundamental changes, long brewing beneath the surface of international tradition, erupted violently. The war left only two superpowers—Russia and the United States—and it soon became painfully evident how tenuous their wartime alliance had been. The Cold War which rapidly developed between them was marked by some enormously important features which distinguished it from earlier international conflicts.

First, the superpowers sought a division of the world into opposing armed camps—the Soviet satellite system facing the system of Western alliances. Second, the communist challenge to the West was ideological, and therefore total. More than economic interests or political prestige were at issue. Mutually exclusive ways of life, each claiming universal validity, were in contention, and whereas the democratic ideology contemplated a triumph over the minds of men through experience and persuasion, the communist techniques rested on the necessity of violence in the revolutionary struggles which would win the world for socialism. Third, the awakened masses of Asia, Africa, the Middle East, and Latin America were undergoing "the revolution of rising expectations." Their increasing demands for an end to foreign political domination, reflected in a tremendous wave of nationalist movements, destroyed the old European empires. And their determination to alleviate poverty and to secure the fruits of industrialization and modernization provided fertile ground for communist penetration. It became increasingly evident that a major arena of the Cold War was the struggle for the support of the "uncommitted," underdeveloped nations. Finally, the technology of war, already become total in the mass bombings of World War II, had developed into the Frankensteinian dimensions of nuclear weapons that threatened total destruction and made war "unthinkable." Yet, the Soviet Union and the United States were engaged in a spiralling sruggle to achieve and maintain superiority in new weapons.

The effect of all these changes was to make the Cold War, as well as preparations for a hot one, a matter of total competition. Every facet of society has a relationship to the struggle. Older distinctions between foreign and domestic policies seem misleading in this new context. An effective foreign policy for carrying on the struggle must be almost a complete and integrated social policy. At the domestic level, it clearly involves the health and the growth rate of the economy, the effectiveness of the educational system, the vitality of the political system, and the elimination of the racial discrimination and segregation which handicap us so seriously in our approach to the underdeveloped areas. At the level of the explicit formulation of foreign policies, total competition requires that these domestic concerns be related to the sources of international tension and conflict described above. Ideally at least, the resulting policies should reflect a clear and realizable national purpose.

In the application of foreign policy, the problem of co-ordination and control is staggering. Intelligence information on the capabilities and intentions of other countries, strategic military planning, programs of ideological warfare, the conduct of diplomatic relations and of our role in international organizations, the development of economic aid pro-grams—these are but a few of the many considerations which must be meshed into policies applicable to a constantly shifting set of circum-stances and opportunities. This is the tremendous burden which, in the main, comes to rest on the President.

Foreign Policy and Federalism

The national government, under the Constitution, has exclusive power to make treaties and to carry on relations with other governments. The power to engage in international relations, the Supreme Court has held, is inherent in a nation-state and was acquired by the United States in 1776 when sovereignty was wrested from the British Crown.[18] This power, moreover, has been used as the basis for federal action in areas which would otherwise be beyond the constitutional competence of the national government.

In 1914, for example, Congress passed a law regulating the hunting and killing of birds which migrate between Canada and the United States. The federal district courts ruled that the law was an unconstitutional assertion of congressional power in an area reserved to the states under the Tenth Amendment. Subsequently, the United States entered into a treaty with Canada on this subject and, after the treaty was duly ratified by a two-thirds vote of the Senate, Congress enacted a law providing for even more rigorous protection of the migratory birds. This time, the Supreme Court upheld the power of Congress to act in this area as necessary to comply with a treaty.[19] The Court ruled that, whereas ordi-nary acts of Congress became "the supreme law of the land" only when made "in pursuance of the Constitution," treaties become "supreme law" when "made under the authority of the United States" in the exercise of a power which must "somewhere reside in every civilized government." The Court added that the treaty-making power is subject to constitutional

[18]*United States* v. *Curtiss-Wright Export Corporation*, 299 U. S. 304 (1936).
[19]*Missouri* v. *Holland*, 252 U. S. 416 (1920).

limitations, but implied that states' rights are not among these. More recent decisions have reinforced this view.

The power acquired by the national government in carrying out foreign policy which would otherwise remain in the domain of the states has prompted considerable concern in recent years. During most of the decade of the 1950's, the so-called "Bricker Amendment" was the focus of this controversy. This proposed constitutional amendment, named after its chief sponsor Senator John W. Bricker of Ohio, would have restricted the power of Congress under the treaty-making power to "legislation which would be valid in the absence of a treaty." Another provision would have operated to limit the power of the President which is presently derived from his ability to make "executive agreements" with other countries which have the force of treaties but do not require ratification by the Senate. The amendment would have permitted Congress to control the negotiation of all international agreements.

The Power of Executive Agreements

The presidential power to commit the nation through executive agreements without the consent of Congress is a formidable one, and it has been used to consummate most of the international agreements to which the United States has been a party. Such important commitments as the Atlantic Charter, the Yalta agreements, and Roosevelt's trade of American destroyers for British bases on the eve of World War II were all consummated by the President as executive agreements. They make it easy to understand why the Congress would resent an evasion of the constitutional role of the Senate in treaty-making.

The President as Chief Diplomat

But, even without the executive agreement, there are factors operating to make the President the chief foreign policy-maker. Partly, his power stems directly from the Constitution. With the consent of the Senate, he appoints ambassadors and all other official representatives in foreign countries, and he has the exclusive power to "receive ambassadors and other public ministers." From this power, the President directly derives the exclusive authority to recognize or refuse to recognize other governments since recognition is formalized by an exchange of ambassadors. The importance of recognition as an instrument of foreign policy was illustrated by Theodore Roosevelt's recognition of Panama within a few hours of an American-backed "revolt," Franklin Roosevelt's recognition of the Soviet Union in 1933, and the controversy over the refusal of American Presidents to recognize Communist China in recent years.

The President as Commander-in-Chief

The Constitution also makes the President "Commander-in-Chief of the Army and Navy." Although the power to raise armies and to declare war are expressly delegated to Congress by the Constitution, in practice the President's power as commander-in-chief permits him to create a state of war which Congress may well find impossible to reverse. Presidential power has often been used in this way, the most recent example being President Truman's commitment of troops to resist North Korean aggression in 1950. In 1958, President Eisenhower sent American forces into Lebanon, though armed conflict was averted. Eisenhower went to Congress for a resolution supporting the move after it was made, not because it is constitutionally necessary, but in order to impress the outside world with the firmness and solidity of American purpose.

The Cuban invasion of 1961 involved the use of American military forces, but more importantly the Central Intelligence Agency (in the Executive Office), which apparently planned, co-ordinated, and supervised the operation. When the landings at the Bay of Pigs faltered, the President alone decided not to commit American air power to insure their success. There were two striking characteristics of the ill-starred Cuban invasion attempt. The first is that the plans which had been in preparation for months by the Eisenhower Administration were applied by the Kennedy Administration, without Congress even being informed of what was going on. And in the second place, the venture was not intended as a prelude to war, but rather as a para-military operation disguised as a revolution.

In this new area of undeclared, guerrilla-type conflict, the President's power is virtually unrestrained since he not only can commit American personnel and materiel, he can do so under the cloak of secrecy. Congress is thereby barred from expressing its disapproval through its power over appointments and appropriations, and, at the same time, presidential decisions in this area are removed from public scrutiny and criticism.

THE PRESIDENT AS CHIEF FOREIGN POLICY-MAKER

APART FROM THE SPECIFIC POWERS of the Presidency in the field of foreign relations, his position as a chief of state makes him the only authoritative representative of, and spokesman for, the nation. No other figure in the country could conceivably represent us at a summit meeting with other heads of state. The Supreme Court recognized this fact in the Curtiss-Wright case when it referred to the President as "the sole organ of the Federal Government in the field of international relations."

The President's real power, however, probably stems as much from the complexity of formulating a foreign policy in an age of ideological conflict and total war as it does from his constitutional position. The basic fact is simple, and perhaps also disturbing: if the President did not make foreign policy, no one else could. No other individual or agency is in a position to weigh the bewildering variety of relevant considerations and to integrate them into coherent and purposeful policy. The President's access to information as well as to expert advice is not available to Congress, which finds itself at a serious disadvantage in not having the background information which would make possible intelligent appraisal of presidential foreign policy. The system of checks and balances was not designed to insure responsibility in such circumstances; the effort to apply it would make any coherent foreign policy impossible. The emergence of the pre-eminent position of the President in foreign policy is basically a response to the need for policy. We have yet to devise ways to make the exercise of his power responsible.

The Machinery of Foreign Policy-Making

The institutional machinery available to the President in the making and conduct of foreign policy is impressive and, unavoidably, impressively complicated. The Secretary of State is ordinarily the most important cabinet member. The department over which he presides is a prolific source for the gathering and analysis of information on all of the countries of the world; it has responsibility for the conduct of our diplomatic relations and negotiations; it carries on intelligence and research programs; and it has responsibility for the execution of technical and economic assistance programs. It is charged with co-ordinating the activities of all its own and other governmental agencies engaged in planning and executing foreign policy. And it has a responsibility to advise the President on over-all policy and on specific policy problems.

The problem of co-ordinating the activities of the State Department has led to frequent reorganizations of its many bureaus and offices—without, say its critics, any very satisfactory results.

The complexity of the problem is seen in the fact that there are many other agencies outside the State Department involved in foreign policy activities. A partial list would include the following:

The Defense Department develops military policy, administers the programs of military aid to other governments, and collects and evaluates intelligence information.

The Department of the Treasury recommends policy on and administers financial and monetary relations with other governments and with international agencies.

The Departments of Commerce, Labor, and Agriculture all contain branches which help formulate and administer phases of our economic relations with other countries.

The United States Tariff Commission's role has been accentuated in recent efforts to work out new relationships with the European Common Market countries.

The Central Intelligence Agency collects and analyzes intelligence data which, in the modern world, means much more than espionage. The great bulk of the information collected is from "open" sources and includes data on geography, cultural customs, public opinion, industrial development, political conditions, and transportation systems, as well as on military forces and plans. In an age of total conflict, intelligence also becomes total, and the agency which collects and evaluates it is cast in a more important policy role. The actual power of the C.I.A. and the range of its activities, however, cannot be described because no "outsiders," including the Congress, know. Its operations are highly secret, and its budget is concealed from Congress by distributing it in smaller amounts throughout the budgets for other agencies.

The United States Information Agency carries on propaganda programs through the Voice of America, maintains field offices and libraries in foreign countries, and encourages and helps foreign students to come to the United States for study.

The National Security Council is the chief instrument for co-ordinating the mass of information, plans, and programs and for fitting them together in policy. The Council meets weekly and wields an influence that led John Fischer to describe it as "Mr. Truman's Politburo." The President himself presides over the discussions which seek to integrate foreign political, military, and economic programs with domestic policies in the quest for national security.

The Operations Co-ordinating Board is directly under the National Security Council and reports directly to it. The Board's task is to see that Council policies are carried out by the operating agencies in an integrated manner. There are, in addition, many interdepartmental committees established to co-ordinate related programs in separate agencies.

All this elaborate machinery operates to provide the President with advice; the basic policy decisions are his alone. The co-ordinating mechanisms assist him in the integrated application of policies; the responsibility, however, remains his.

The Politics of Foreign Policy

Although the President alone has potential access to the resources and the information necessary for decision, Congress has the power to grant or withhold appropriations for foreign policy programs. And Congress is often inclined to look at the President's requests with a suspicious eye. In addition to its constant desire to protect congressional prerogative against executive encroachment, the concern of Congressmen to protect and advance their constituents' interests and the influence of pressure groups in Congress are likely to lead to congressional-presidential conflict.

When a conflict occurs, the President is at the same disadvantage on foreign policy issues as he is on other matters. On the whole, the President cannot rely on interest group support for his policies. Even where executive agencies have the built-in support of private groups—the armed services can count on their own private associations and on the major veterans' groups, for example—it is likely to be exerted against the President through congressional committees.

Nor can the President count on active and knowledgeable public support. All the polls show that not more than one out of four voters has even a basic knowledge or undersanding of foreign affairs. Many of those who know something about it show a tendency to oversimplify, to see issues in black and white, and to demand an inflexibility of policy positions incompatible with rapidly changing events.

General public indifference combines with the weakness of pressure group support for broad national policies to increase the influence of pressure groups who oppose specific aspects of policy. As a result, the alternative to congressional rubber-stamping usually takes the form of nit-picking and tampering rather than of sustained review, criticism, and debate of broad policies. Congressional frustration of the President's policies may take other forms. At the behest of national-origin pressure groups, for example, Congress during the 1950's passed several resolutions calling for the liberation of the satellite nations of Eastern Europe and even of nationality groups within the Soviet Union which had never been independent nations—"Cossackia," for example. The resolutions had no legal force but they did appear to the Soviet Union as provocative threats in situations in which presidential policies might have dictated an opposite approach. Neither a meaningful consensus nor responsible criticism and debate is possible in this environment.

In the absence of effective political parties, the machinery of checks and balances creaks cumbersomely along where domestic policies are concerned; in the area of foreign policy, it has broken down almost completely. Presidential power over foreign policy is awesome. We have yet to develop the means to make it responsible. We return to this problem in the final chapter.

12

BUREAUCRACY
AND THE
PUBLIC INTEREST

THE BUREAUCRATIC WILDERNESS

To WANDER THROUGH THE LABYRINTH of bureaucracy and explain all
of the agencies and their activities would require a work of bewildering
detail. Both the 1949 and 1955 Hoover Commissions inquiring into
government organization found that the federal government was a fantastic
collection of all sorts of agencies which had mushroomed during our
history and solidified into permanent concerns. "Great confusion," said
the 1949 Hoover Commission,[1] but the situation had improved by 1955
when about 70 per cent of its 1949 recommendations were carried out.
Bureaucracy, however, kept growing. In 1949, there were 2,100,000 persons, exclusive of the military, working for the federal government. As of
December, 1961, there were 2,672,946.[2]

[1]*Report on the General Management of the Executive Branch* (Washington: Government Printing Office, 1949), pp. 3-4.
[2]U.S. Civil Service Commission, *Monthly Report of Federal Employment*, December,
1961.

In addition to the Executive Office of the President and the ten departments of cabinet rank, the range of other federal administrative agencies is indicated in Figure 12. (The chart shows only the "more important" agencies.)

Some of these agencies report to the President, although their directors or administrators are not members of the cabinet. Examples are the Veterans Administration, the United States Information Agency, and the Housing and Home Finance Agency. Other agencies are "independent" establishments over which Congress and the President exercise only budgetary and appointing power.

While the agencies which report to the President ordinarily have at their heads a single responsible director, many of the independent agencies are multiheaded. The size of their governing bodies ranges from the three Commissioners of the Tennessee Valley Authority to the twenty-five member Board of the National Science Foundation.

In addition to these program agencies, there are housekeeping agencies which do not deal directly with the public. These agencies service the bureaucracy with people (the United States Civil Service Commission, headed by three commissioners) or supply it with the bureaucratic fuel of paper, mimeograph ink, desks, charts, pencils, and other supplies and services (the General Services Administration, headed by an administrator).

The General Accounting Office (G.A.O.), headed by the comptroller-general, has been a controversial agency ever since it was established in 1921. Focal point of the difficulties was the power given to the comptroller-general by Congress which liberated him from executive control by giving him a fifteen-year term and prescribing the conditions for which he could be removed. John R. McCarl, the first incumbent, made full use of his power to settle claims for or against the government, prescribe accounting procedures, investigate fiscal transactions of all sorts, and to report all violations of the law to Congress. The G.A.O. conducted continuous warfare with the executive and reported all violations of the law (and, some say, of the comptroller's prejudices) to Congress to the point where the 1937 Committee on Administrative Management complained that the comptroller was hampering the management of almost all federal agencies. The controversy abated, however, as a result of relapsed zeal on the part of later comptrollers-general, and after the passage of the Corporation Control Act of 1945 required business-type audits for those federal agencies classified as government corporations.

GOVERNMENT CORPORATIONS

THE GOVERNMENT CORPORATIONS which had occasioned much of this conflict are multiheaded, semiautonomous agencies. The Tennessee Valley

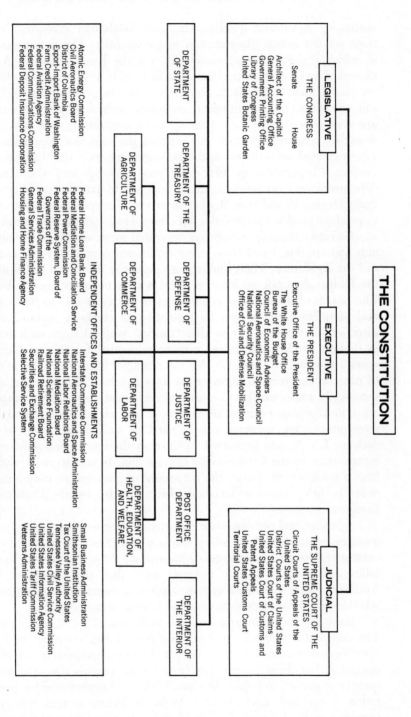

Figure 12. The Government of the United States. This chart, of course, shows only the more important agencies of the Government.

Authority is without question the most celebrated example. Corporations are not a new phenomenon in government. The first corporation in which the government took part was the Bank of North America chartered by the Continental Congress in 1781. In 1791, Congress chartered the First United States Bank. Since that time, the government has been in and out of several governmental corporate activities. Such organizations are very effective in times of emergencies, and during wars and depressions they tend to proliferate. For example, the economic depression of the 1930's created several new agencies, beginning with the Reconstruction Finance Corporation in 1932 and mushrooming into the Roosevelt Administration's numerous agencies designed to get the economy rolling again. During World War II, over twenty new corporations were created to produce needed commodities in certain areas, such as rubber and metal.

Government corporations are organized something like a private business and are thus freed from many traditional controls by the executive and the legislature. Their budgets are generally brief, and the Bureau of the Budget does not go into details as it does on other agency budgets. The boards of directors or commissioners often are able to make a good deal of policy without specific legislative or executive authorization or direction, even to the extent that "profits" realized from such activities as the sale of electrical power may be reinvested for the production of other commodities. The T.V.A., for example, has invested in a variety of projects designed to improve the area in which they operate but not specifically authorized by Congress. Government corporations, since they are akin to private business, do not enjoy sovereign immunity and, unlike most government agencies, can be sued, as well as sue. Some of them, such as T.V.A., are permitted to develop their own personnel systems independent of the Civil Service Commission. In recent years, there has been a tendency to restrict the autonomy of government corporations in order to bring them under more direct control by the President and Congress.

A second, and perhaps more important, factor working against government corporations is the hostility aimed at them from defenders of private enterprise. No government agency has aroused the opposition of the power lobby and other economic interests more than the Tennessee Valley Authority. Such activities sometimes appear as creeping socialism to those who identify democracy with capitalist economic institutions.

State and local governments also make use of the corporate device. The compact between New York and New Jersey creating the Port of New York Authority is a good example. This is an administratively efficient operation, but there are protests from several sources that it is not adequately responsive to public demands. Cities use corporations for transportation, water, and other services. As in the federal system, this type of operation makes for more flexible administration, but it raises serious questions about public control. Its flexibility actually results from a lack of public control through elected representatives and frees the administrator from having to answer for all his actions.

INDEPENDENT REGULATORY COMMISSIONS

IN THE ADMINISTRATIVE STRUCTURE of American government, there is a unique type of administrative agency known as the independent regulatory commission. These organizations, sometimes called the "headless fourth branch of government," are figuratively adrift from the traditional administrative structure of government. Created by Congress, they are not clearly tied down to either the executive, legislative, or judicial branches of government, although they exercise all three types of power. Commissions serve as their policy-making bodies. The size of the commissions varies—the Interstate Commerce Commission has eleven members and the Federal Power Commission has five—but all commissions are engaged in regulating specific activities of the economy within very broad policy lines established by Congress. They act in a legislative capacity by making rules which have the force of law, in an executive capacity by administering and enforcing the law, and in a judicial capacity by conducting hearings and issuing orders. Commissioners are appointed for overlapping terms by the President, who can remove them only for specific reasons.

The leading or "big six" regulatory commissions are as follows:

1. *The Interstate Commerce Commission.* Originally created in 1887 to regulate railroads, its powers have been expanded to include the regulation of routes, rates and safety of, and conflicts between, all means of interstate transportation except air.

2. *The Federal Trade Commission.* Created in 1914 to regulate economic competition so it will be "free and fair," it has two basic functions: to issue cease and desist orders when it finds unfair trade practices existing; to study and investigate questionable business practices and make reports of its findings.

3. *The Securities and Exchange Commission.* Founded in 1934 after the stock market collapse, it supervises the entire securities market and administers statutes providing for securities regulation.

4. *The Civil Aeronautics Board.* Established in 1938, it makes civil airline rules and regulations (enforced by the Civil Aeronautics Administration), determines rates, allocates routes, adjusts disputes over routes, investigates accidents, and conducts other functions related to air transportation.

5. *The Federal Communications Commission.* Created in 1934 to

regulate radio and telephone, telegraph, and submarine cable communications in interstate and foreign commerce, its functions have been expanded to include television. It has general supervision over these activities, and it can require the extension of service, award franchises, regulate rates, and conduct investigations.

6. *The Federal Power Commission.* Established in 1920, its original responsibility was for the licensing of hydroelectric projects on navigable waters of the United States. Since then, its functions have been continuously expanded by the Natural Gas Act (1938), which gave it authority over the transportation and sale of natural gas in interstate commerce; the Flood Control Acts of 1938 and 1944, which authorized the Commission to recommend hydroelectric projects at dams held by the Department of the Army and to regulate the price of power so produced; and Executive Order 10485 (1953), which authorized it to issue permits for power projects on the borders of the United States.

The Problem of Political Responsibility

When this type of independent organization drifts too far away from the regular branches of government, the question of who will pull it back into proper constitutional orbit causes much confusion. Franklin Roosevelt found that Presidents cannot remove commissioners on these bodies at will without trouble from the courts and objection from Congress, which provides the conditions for which the President may remove commissioners.[4] Such conditions do not include a political or economic philosophy contrary to that of the President. Congress may, of course, redefine the functions of the commissions, change the size or conditions of their governing bodies, or eliminate them altogether. And the courts may declare that a commission has no statutory authority to perform certain functions, or is required by its organic statute to perform others.

But why are such circuitous measures necessary to change a governmental agency's policy? Part of the answer lies in the structure of the commissions. The structural difficulties stem from the facts that these agencies are governed by commissioners who generally serve longer terms than the President; that commissioners cannot be replaced by the President except for generally few and specific causes set out by Congress; that effective political control is difficult, particularly if there are holdovers from a previous administration or if the law demands bipartisan membership as it nearly always does; and that there is no congressional or executive veto of commission actions. These structural characteristics tend to remove the commissions from responsibility to the elected branches of govern-

[4]*Humphrey's Executor* v. *United States*, 295 U. S. 602 (1935).

ment. This very independence from political controls operates to make the commissions more susceptible to other, and often less desirable, influences.

Independent Commissions and Brokerage Politics

During the Eisenhower administration, the Special Subcommittee on Legislative Oversight of the House Committee on Interstate and Foreign Commerce conducted a broad investigation of regulatory agencies. The purpose was to deal with an underlying problem which had been evident to close observers for a long time. The commissions, largely freed from responsibility to the regular branches of government and subjected to the pressures of the interests they were designed to regulate, often were improperly influenced or controlled by those interests.[5]

The whole concept of public regulation is based on the assumption that private economic groups are not always governed by a self-discipline which subordinates their interests to broader interests. Business and other private interest groups, the regulatory concept assumes, will tend to regard whatever they can legally get as legitimate. The purpose of regulation is to subordinate these interests to the public interest. When the legal agency regulating them is independent of other controls, however, the techniques of lobbying can be sharply focused on a small group of men. The pressure can become most intense, particularly if the general attitude of politicians is that the claims of all groups must be, by good brokerage practice, treated "fairly." In the power vacuum created by non-partisan commissions, the public interest is undefined, and effective power passes into the hands of the well-organized and powerful private interests. Political columnist Doris Fleeson has described the process in an analysis of the role of an effective lawyer-lobbyist before the Federal Power Commission.

> LIGHT—The chief value of Thomas G. Corcoran's appearance before the Harris subcommittee is its brilliant illumination of the way in which federal regulatory agencies are determining the prices consumers must pay for essential goods and services.
>
> To save himself, Corcoran, a brilliant technician with a rare background in government, is having to explain and justify the system under which he and his natural gas clients have become rich. While the consumer plays no discernible role in it beyond that of final bill payer he can at least be grateful that his nullity rarely has been more clearly exposed.

---

[5]The Committee had conducted over three years of investigation. The result was legislation aimed at more stringent regulation of improper or corrupt influence on the commissions (H.R. 4800 and H.R. 6774, Eighty-sixth Congress). These measures, however, failed of passage.

What Corcoran is describing in essence is a kind of gray area between what is allowed by law and what is encouraged by present custom.

Corcoran argued that his many off the record contacts with the federal power commissioners were made in broad daylight and constituted only a lawyer's duty to "take care of his client up to the limits of the law on the books at the time." What he expects of the commissioners was revealed in his description of a talk with William R. Connole, the commissioner whom President Dwight D. Eisenhower refused to reappoint.

According to Corcoran, Connole said: "I don't want to talk to you about the merits of the case." To this Corcoran said he replied: "I don't have much time to talk to you anyway."

POLICY—Such arrogance has been possible because administration policy has been that regulatory commissioners must be in harmony with the interests they regulate. The case of Connole, only commissioner to oppose several gas price raises, indicates they will get fired if they are not.

In such case, all that remains for the industry is to take care of the other side of the street. In Corcoran they have one of Franklin D. Roosevelt's brain trusters who helped write the laws establishing the regulatory agencies. He has maintained his New Deal contacts with Speaker Sam Rayburn and Senate Majority Leader Lyndon B. Johnson who, as Texans, sympathize with the general aims of the oil and gas industry. Sources friendly to Johnson have pointed to Corcoran as a major architect of Johnson's bid for the presidency.

The expensive fact is that natural gas prices have risen 40 per cent since 1951, three times as fast as the general cost of living. It has become also a $50,000,000,000 industry.

TREATIES—This, according to Counsel Robert W. Lishman of the Harris subcommittee is the result of negotiation, not regulation. In short, what has happened is that the government has ceased try to regulate but only to negotiate treaties beween the government and the gas interests.

Such lawyer-lobbyists as Corcoran are private ambassadors for the industry and the Eisenhower appointed commissioners are ambassadors from the White House. What they agree is in the realm of the possible then is done.

One hurdle remains—the Supreme Court, which continues to direct FPC to regulate natural gas prices. The federal courts also have had something to say about ex parte contacts by lawyers with agency heads, a privilege which Corcoran contends is upheld by a statute called the Administrative Procedures Act.

In a case involving such contacts by a television station operator with federal communications commissioners, the District of Columbia court of appeals last year held that private approaches to FPC members had vitiated its action and the entire proceedings must be reopened.

Thus it appears that what results Corcoran may have achieved through FPC contacts still may have to run the gauntlet of the federal courts and may not stand.[6]

There are several approaches to the problem of how to prevent regulatory agencies from becoming the tools of the private interests they are supposed to regulate. Legislative measures have aimed at publicizing and reforming the techniques of influence on the commissions. H.R. 4800 of the Eighty-sixth Congress would have used criminal procedures with maximum penalties of one year in jail and/or a $10,000 fine to stop such practices as failing to place all communications of the agency (including summaries of telephone calls) in a public file, attempts privately to influence commissioners and employees of regulatory agencies, and the failure to file notice in advance of appearances before any commission proceeding. Such proposals would not change the existing structure of the commissions.

Another school of thought holds that there is little use in attempting reforms in the procedures of the commissions since the basic structure is such that there is no way effectively to prevent abuses inherent in the whole concept of a special, autonomous, small, and nonpartisan group regulating vast industries. Former C.A.B Commissioner Lewis J. Hector, an advocate of a basic change in the whole structure of these commissions, submitted a seventy-page report to the President upon his resignation in 1960. Among his criticisms of the present structure was the argument that the Civil Aeronautics Board "is so divided in opinion that it is impossible to tell on any specific point just what Board policy might be." Concepts of a public interest are splintered and fragmented; the private interest is clearly defined and cohesively represented. This is an almost unavoidable situation which is intensified when members of different political parties and economic philosophy are on the same board. He also stated: "The inability of Congress to control the policies of the agencies it has created and the inability of the executive to coordinate their policies . . . may well be the most urgent reason for a substantial change in the machinery for government control of business.[7]

But Mr. Hector also underscored a situation which is perhaps even more important than control by Congress and the President. Pointing to the ethical problem and the difficulties it causes, he stated:

---

[6]*Sacramento Bee*, May 23, 1960. (Used by permission of the United Feature Syndicate). The column is included in its entirety since it gives an able reporter's insight into many problems concerned with the workings of these commissions.
[7]*Congressional Quarterly*, March 11, 1960, p. 429.

No man can possibly work all day every day with the same people in the same industry and discuss all aspects of it informally as a policy maker and then from time to time wipe every bit of that out of his mind in order to become a judge and decide a case solely on the record. . . .The system is actually so inviting to improper influence that it will inevitably occur from time to time.[8]

Both columnist Fleeson and ex-Commissioner Hector show that structure poses grave problems. They also share the conviction that basic theoretical notions of economic regulation need some re-examination.

The problem focuses upon the very nature of regulation. To regulate something, you have to say a frequent and emphatic No to private claims. But in a climate of positive thinking and harmonious personal relationships, it is hard for a small group of men to accept the role of consistently being the "bad guys." As a result, it is much easier to negotiate than to regulate, and the brokerage method of balancing claims (even though the people of the United States may be one of the claimants) can operate so the regulator sees himself as a reasonable man doing his job. Inject into this the smooth and fast-talking lobbyist who has only a handful of people to convince rather than a large mass of men, as he does when he works on a legislature, and it is easy to see why it would be simpler and more comfortable to negotiate than to regulate. But effective regulation does not always, if ever, result from treaties negotiated between producer and consumer. The producer is articulate and organized while the consumer is a faceless mass, often unrepresented by a spokesman, and generally without political force since consumers are by definition nonpartisan (Democrats and Republicans, Northerners and Southerners, farmers and factory workers all use gas.)

The problem of regulation also exists in state and local government. Sometimes "boards" and "commissions" are appointed to regulate certain interests. Some states even go so far as to construct these boards and commissions so that negotiation rather than regulation is built into the structure. A classic example is the seven-man California State Board of Forestry. The law reads in part:

There shall be a State Board of Forestry of seven members appointed by the Governor with advice and consent of the Senate. . . .
    One member shall represent the pine producing industry.
    One member shall represent the redwood producing industry.
    One member shall represent forest land ownership.
    One member shall represent the range livestock industry.
    One member shall represent agriculture.
    One member shall represent the beneficial use of water.

[8]Ibid.

The aforementioned six members shall be persons of practical knowledge and experience in the field they are to represent. One member shall be appointed from the general public at large.[9]

Brokerage politics could not be better expressed in the law. The public interest has one-seventh of the total voice, it would appear that it would have to be loud and clear to be heard above the din of the special interests given a legal voice. It seems much more likely that the lone and lonely public member will be forced to define his role as broker to the other six. And it is highly probable that the protection of the best interests of the people of the state will be identified with the settlements reached by the ambassadors from the affected private interests.

Another popular and growing form of regulation used in state and local government is the licensing board for professions and trades. Such boards are typified by licensing and examination boards for medical practitioners, plumbers, lawyers, funeral directors and embalmers, optometrists, furniture and bedding inspectors, accountants, dry cleaners, barbers, electricians, psychologists, contractors and pest exterminators.

Theoretically, licensing is an exercise of the police power designed to protect the public health, safety, or welfare. All too often, however, the licensing function turns out to be a protection of the profession or trade being regulated. Indeed, licensing boards are usually initiated at the behest of the industry itself. Licensing is justified to protect the public against inadequately trained practitioners of a particular calling. Most often, however, its real purpose or effect is to use the power of government to give existing practitioners monopoly power to limit competition. Sometimes, it is even the competition of the public itself, as when the law provides that the home owner cannot do his own plumbing or electrical work because only licensed practitioners are allowed to do so. Generally, the home owner can do his work if it will pass inspection, but inspection is also often controlled by the trade. In most jurisdictions, the licensing of professions and trades is done by members of the group themselves—plumbers license plumbers, accountants examine accountants —which makes public control difficult. As a result, the members of these boards tend to become publicly supported and official spokesmen for the activities they are supposed to regulate.[10] If one takes a close look at legislation sponsored by such groups, it is often evident that the purpose of regulation is to provide protection and a more favorable climate for the group's activities.

[9]California *Public Resources Code*, Sec. 505.
[10]At one time, the state of New Mexico transferred money from a licensing board's revolving fund to the general fund. The board objected strenuously, contending that licensing fees paid by the group licensed belonged to them. It was difficult, if not impossible, to convince the board that license fees are public revenue.

The problem of regulating industries and professions so that the public is properly represented continues to be an important one in American government. In one of its aspects, the problem depends on the extent such activities need to be and ought to be regulated. The argument rages between classic concepts of *laissez-faire* and increased public control of the economy. But when public regulatory agencies become pressure groups or brokers for the interests they regulate, the public stands little chance to benefit. If the public's interests are to prevail, they must be politically organized. Responsible and competitive political parties, experience teaches us, are the only effective democratic device for accomplishing this purpose. The effort to accomplish regulation through nonpartisan agencies makes impossible the organization, definition, and protection of a public interest. The resulting vacuum will be filled, as it has been, by those private groups whose organization is strong and whose interests are clearly defined.

THE PROBLEM OF BUREAUCRACY

AMONG THE MORE FASHIONABLE PARLOR GAMES of a large number of Americans is that of damning the governmental bureaucrats. Somehow, in the public mind, employees of governmental bureaucracies are bureaucrats; those who staff corporate and other private bureaucracies are not. The corporate executive's briefcase is full of "know-how"; the bureau chief's contains only a rulebook. Status goes to the hard-headed businessman who has "met a payroll," whereas the public employee, be he federal, state, or local, must often accept the stigma of being stereotyped as a bumbling plodder with two left hands who enjoys nothing more than packaging the most simple problem in bales of mimeographed minutia bound with endless yards of red tape.

Such generalities are highly questionable. Very likely public employees are of about the same quality as their business counterparts. Bureaucracy, public or private, leaves much the same marks on those who are the cogs in its wheels. It is often true that there is a high degree of idealism and dedication on the part of the public employee which focuses upon service to people rather than personal gain. This is an important factor, and one which should give many of our public servants a more deserving reputation than they now enjoy. Elevating the bureaucrat to first-class status with his private enterprise counterpart, however, does not mean that bureaucracy does not present some real problems related to the conduct of public business.

Perhaps it is more realistic to conceive of bureaucracy and the bureaucratic way of life as a phenomenon of size rather than of the public or private nature of the organization. Governments are big—the federal government is huge—but so are the private corporate organizations in which the vast majority of Americans make their livings, the unions by which they are represented, the educational systems in which they get their schooling, and the churches in which they worship. Bureaucratic procedure is usually the result of the necessity of large organizations to prescribe rules, regulations, and formal procedures for carrying out the organization's activities. Paul Appleby has related the bizzare problems he encountered in trying to order an ironing board from a large department store chain with a mail-order service.[11]

Some veterans, on the other hand, have been driven almost to distraction trying to figure out how the forms supplied them by the Veterans Administration should be filled out, and they stand in awe of the elaborate machinery necessary to secure veterans' benefits. Appleby's ironing-board incident indicates what happens occasionally when necessarily formalized procedures are mechanically applied to individual cases. The veteran painfully answering what he considers a host of irrelevant questions does not often consider that such questions may be important factors for deciding cases other than his own. When masses of people must be dealt with by large organizations, settled rules and procedures are necessary, and they inevitably will be arbitrary or redundant in individual cases.

Even the strange cant of the bureaucrat—as someone once said, "I love you" becomes "complete assurance of maximum affection is hereby implied"—has a purpose. It is an attempt to get the most widespread understanding possible by deadening prose until it loses any emotional impact. "I love you" causes emotional reactions in the reader of the phrase. "Assurance of maximum affection" transmits the idea without unnecessarily stirring feelings of romance. An absurd basis for a marriage or a friendship, and perhaps a dehumanizing basis for any social relationships, nevertheless, it is a necessary price of large-scale, formal organization.

Bertrand Russell, in his Nobel Prize acceptance speech, stated that most officials prefer to say No rather than Yes, since they derive greater feelings of satisfaction and power from turning someone down than by giving him what he wants. Perhaps Lord Russell is correct, but it should be pointed out that governmental and private organizational procedures are designed to insure that the public official or store clerk does not say No rather than Yes. If each public official could arbitrarily decide how persons coming before him should be treated, the basic democratic doctrine of equality before the law would be destroyed. Many individuals feel that their situation is unique and therefore should be treated differently from John Doe's. When the public official applies the rules and decides

[11]Paul H. Appleby, *Big Democracy* (New York: Knopf, 1949), pp. 59 ff.

accordingly, a person who is disappointed often grumbles that the bureaucrat is intellectually and morally bankrupt since he cannot recognize the uniqueness of the case and use his discretion. But discretion is just what rules, regulations, and procedures are designed to prevent. While the denial of discretion prevents the official from considering unusual circumstances, it also stops him from capriciously turning away deserving people. We are all, in short, treated with maddening uniformity, a situation quite difficult for people tending toward individualism to understand. It has been argued that the development of mass society and mass man has led to a greater toleration if not acceptance of bureaucratic treatment. It can also be argued that large bureaucracies acting impartially toward the society they serve may have contributed to the creation of the mass man, since individualism becomes buried under the increasing and necessarily impartial treatment by big government, big business, big labor, and big education.

To protest the size of government and to look longingly at the past era of *laissez-faire* as a condition which should be resurrected is about as futile as wishing an industrial society would go away so that we could return to a pastoral and simple life of small farms and small businesses. Myths die hard, and one of the hardest to dispose of is that a complex government can operate without a large number of employees. Government grows because people demand that it grow by supplying them services and protecting them to an extent not previously done. Even the most stalwart defenders of *laissez-faire* put their demands upon government. The national farm program administered by the gigantic United States Department of Agriculture or the Reconstruction Finance Corporation, which makes loans to deserving business enterprises, will attest to this. It is obvious that big military establishments require large numbers of men, but not so obvious is the fact that big budgets require a large number of budget analysts and accountants; that a federal home loan program causes the employment of people of a variety of talents to administer it; or that the enactment of antitrust legislation requires an investigative and legal staff to enforce the law. In short, every time governments create new programs, expand old ones, or enact new regulatory laws, people are needed to administer them. The process of such enactments goes on continuously as demands multiply, but the reverse situation of doing away with old programs seldom occurs. Government just seems to keep growing, and despite the political oratory of election campaigns, no political party seems to succeed in making it significantly smaller or in reducing expenditures. Vice-President Alben Barkley facetiously explained the derisive nature of the word "bureaucrat" when he asked the rhetorical question "What is a bureaucrat?" He supplied the answer by saying "a bureaucrat is a Democrat who has a job some Republican would like to have."

Civil Servant or Spoilsman?

In the United States, as in many other countries, there is a strong feeling that civil service based on some degree of merit selection is the best method of picking government employees. This notion rejects the thesis often attributed to Jackson and still practiced in many state and local governments that "to the victor belongs the spoils"—that is, the victorious political party should have the jobs to pass out to the politically faithful. Civil service denies this thesis so completely that many civil service laws virtually deprive the civil servant of all the political rights guaranteed to the rest of the population. Civil servants are not denied the vote to be sure, but they are often denied the right to campaign actively for political candidates, endorse legislation or ballot propositions, or to run for partisan political office. Civil servants are, however, permitted to organize and push for legislation and administrative rules and regulations that will make their tenure in office and their privileges and fringe benefits more secure and attractive.[12] Thus, while they are often deprived of their public vote as democratic citizens, they are never denied their private roles as interest group members. Perhaps it is significant that the latter would seem to many a more serious deprivation of democratic liberties.

CIVIL SERVANTS

"Civil service" is the term generally applied to the use of merit selection of employees. This selection involves the use of competitive instruments, such as written examinations. These are designed to measure either general intelligence or a substantive knowledge, such as engineering or accounting. "Unassembled" examinations are also used in the federal and other civil service jurisdictions. These examinations consist of applications stating the candidate's education, experience, or other relevant information. Selection is then made on the basis of the "best qualified" candidate as determined by the appointive authority. Merit appointment attempts to select the "best person for the job" regardless of his political orientation.

---

[12] A good example of such an organization is the California State Employees Association which supports favorable legislation such as retirement benefits and higher appropriations for salaries, and more rigid rituals governing dismissal of civil servants. This organization will also supply an attorney for its members facing dismissal hearings by the State Personnel Board. It is a very powerful lobby at both the legislative and administrative levels.

"Best person" is interpreted to mean the ability to perform the tasks for which he is to be employed or, in some instances, general aptitude or intelligence. There are often preferences given to veterans in civil service jurisdictions. This means that a veteran may have points added to his score just because he is a veteran. If he is a disabled veteran, he often gets more points. Such preferences dilute a pure merit selection because extra points are not the result of performance or qualification to do the job.

Since the Pendleton Act of 1883, the federal civil service has been increasingly professionalized with an increasing number of jobs placed under merit selection. There has also been a tendency to increase civil service coverage of policy jobs so that in event of a partisan change in administration the policies or philosophy of the previous administration will have a better chance to continue. One might ask how such a practice could be established if merit is the criterion for selection. Through the use of unassembled examinations, interviews, and the nature of the work itself, it is often quite simple to recruit people who are sympathetic to the administrative position.

Another motive for increasing the merit system coverage is that it takes patronage out of the hands of future administrations. An example of the problem of extending merit system coverage occurred during the New Deal period when jobs multiplied rapidly and the merit system was extended to cover not only many of the new positions but old ones as well. When the Republican party, after twenty years in waiting, finally got back "in" with the Eisenhower administration, it found itself saddled with a large bureaucracy well covered by the protective cloak of civil service and oriented to Democratic policy. The Republicans found it essential to do some declassifying—that is, taking certain policy-making positions out of the merit system—in order to have a bureaucracy that would respond more rapidly to their demands. Often, some of these positions are reclassified after the political party in power has made its appointments.

Most merit-protected public employees are career people who can shift their ideas and methods to a new set of political principles without too much of an intellectual trauma. Sometimes, however, the more dedicated may find it necessary to leave the public service if the policy changes are too severe. The motivation into public service is often the result of a sense of dedication and idealism. If policies change so that these motivations cannot be satisfied, life in bureaucracy can be miserable.

Even though the ideal bureaucrat might be a bright but intellectually plastic individual, it is too much to expect a whole governmental structure, especially in the United States, to be staffed with such types. In some European countries where bureaucracies are recruited from higher social strata, the personal problem is not so great, and a shift in political fortunes does not cause as much concern. In the United States, however, there is a good deal of mobility between private enterprise and government. Indeed, many people seem to feel that the solution to governmental problems is to import business executives to run the government with their business acumen. Some of these business executives have been distinguished public officials; others have failed miserably because they could not adjust to the "goldfish bowl" of public scrutiny. Still others have not understood organizations dedicated to service rather than profit. Much of the impetus in establishing schools of public administration stems from the idea that public service is unique enough to warrant a special type of education and that the transference of business administrative techniques to government will not adequately serve a meaningful conception of the public interest.

SPOILSMEN

The spoils system operates on a theory entirely different from a civil service or merit system. Public employees in the spoils system, unlike the politically restrained merit-system employee, are by definition active participants in the political process. In a firmly entrenched spoils system one often finds key posts in the bureaucracy going to county chairmen of the victorious political party. The state of New Mexico has, at times, been a good example of such a situation.[13]

New Mexico politicians have often used the bureaucracy to build political power and fill the party coffers by requiring percentage payments of state employees' salaries to be "contributed" to a party worker each month. Although this practice is increasingly frowned upon and periodically suspended by New Mexico officials, it has been an important source of party funds. The promise of lucrative jobs is also a means of getting "doorbell-pushers" out in their districts to see that the vote goes properly. Since the dominant party controls all the jobs, it is able to get prospects for even the more lowly positions of stenographers and file clerks out for party work. Spoils systems sometimes have odd salary schedules since the "payoff" often goes to people with limited experience. A good vote-getter who cannot type or file may be paid a high salary for extremely mundane tasks. It is also not uncommon to find elected officials rewarding personal cronies, occasionally even their mistresses, with good jobs, although their duties may be unrelated to serving the public interest.

In short, the chances for incompetence and corruption are generally more favorable in a spoils system than in a merit system. An enlightened spoils system, however, can work well if officials accept the notion that

[13] The observations that follow are based on the experiences of one of the authors as a New Mexico bureaucrat.

good administration is good politics and appoint competent members of their party rather than political hangers-on to governmental positions. Neither party has complete claim to competent people within its ranks, and it is possible to find accountants, lawyers, administrators, psychiatrists and clerks within both parties.

The most serious drawback to the spoils system is the tendency for plans to extend only until the next election. There are two basic reasons for this. The first is that the party in power cannot expect to commit the rival party, or even rival factions within its own party, to programs over which it may have no control. The second reason is that since spoilsmen are dedicated party workers whose future employment depends upon victory at the polls, they will often plan their programs to build the political power of their administration. In states where governors are prevented from succeeding themselves, future plans often must be dropped of necessity, and many of the spoilsmen have difficulty in keeping themselves in grace with the lame-duck governor while trying to court favor with his likely successor. In such an event, the public service may suffer while political fences are being erected or mended.

Spoils systems have long been under attack by organizations dedicated to improving the public service, such as professional personnel administrators' organizations, civic leagues, the League of Women Voters, and organizations of civil servants. The federal government has also contributed to the attack by demanding that certain federal matching programs, such as public welfare, employment security, and public health, be administered by people with merit protection working under a graduated and approved pay schedule. In some states, such agencies are the only ones which have a merit system and they are periodically reviewed by the federal government to see that the spoilsmen keep their distances.

Bureaucracy and the Role of the Expert

Public service on most any level contains almost all the professions and skills society develops. Government agencies employ engineers, physicists, educators of all sorts, doctors, lawyers, professional administrators, typists, clerks, accountants, sanitation experts, social workers, efficiency experts, biologists, chemists, librarians, cooks, loggers, bulldozer operators, carpenters, painters, plumbers, steam fitters, public relations men, mechanics, policemen, mailmen, key-punch operators, janitors and gardeners. A few jobs, such as salesmen, are not found in government, and a few such as mailmen, are not found in business, but generally governmental jurisdictions employ just about every occupational type one can imagine. As government assumes new functions such as control of atomic energy or space exploration, the diversity of its employees increases. Also, as government grows in both size and complexity, the role of the expert in government becomes increasingly important and problematical.

The chief problem connected with experts practicing their expertise, a fancy word meaning "expertness," is to keep them in tune with the public interest. To do this, many schemes have been proposed which would keep the expert "on tap, not on top." Some of the proposals include continuous surveillance by legislative committees to see that the legislative intent establishing the agency and setting out its powers and duties is carried out. Another is to see that political appointees always dominate the administrative structure so that the chief executive can insist that his political desires be reflected in the organization. Thus the President's cabinet is composed of politically appointed heads of the major agencies of government. A third type of control, not used in the federal system but popular in many state and local governments, is to use the long ballot. This means that many of the major department heads are elected directly by the people. For example, California popularly elects its attorney-general, state treasurer, secretary of state, state controller, superintendent of Public instruction, four members (by district) of the State Board of Equalization (primarily a tax collecting agency), and its lieutenant-governor. These officials may or may not be of the same political party as the governor. A long ballot system of election can raise havoc with the chief executive's political control of his party. For example, in 1952 the governor of New Mexico was the only elected Republican official. He had a good deal of trouble operating the administrative machinery of the state with a Democratic attorney-general, treasurer, auditor, superintendent of public instruction, lieutenant-governor, and others. The legislature was strongly Democratic, particularly in the state senate. His program, which included a job classification system and uniform salary scales, kept getting slammed against the rocks of partisanship, since there were direct dealings between elected Democratic officials and the legislature of which the governor had no knowledge.

Even with political control, however, the problem of a responsible bureaucracy composed of experts remains. Many writers in the field of public administration concern themselves with this problem, and quite common among them is the notion that the generalist should dominate the specialist.[14]

[14]In his address before the American Sociological Society on December 28, 1936, Arthur E. Morgan succinctly stated the issue: "One plausible explanation for the breakdown of great climaxes of human culture is that there came to be so many specialists and so few generalists that the co-ordinating and integrating forces of society became too weak to make effective synthesis of the riot of specialization." From J. M. Pfiffner, *Public Administration* (New York: The Ronald Press, 1946), p. 21.

What is a generalist? It is often suggested that he is a "specialist in generalization" trained to have a broad view of things. Unfortunately, however, as an examination of college catalogs in public administration reveals, the specialist in generalization usually comes out of college a specialist in public administration just as the engineer, physicist, business administration major, or statistician is a specialist in his field. As in most academic areas, there has been a tendency, with some present signs of reversal, continuously to narrow the base of the discipline of public administration by adding more courses in that area at the expense of electives in other fields. Instead of the student learning to make a decision on the basis of a broad knowledge of the culture, literature, and philosophy of his civilization, he is taught how to do this in a course in decision-making. So, even the training of generalists, if such is the goal, tends to become a specialty replete with its own jargon and esoteric literature.

Perhaps the desired generalist should be defined not by formal training but by a state of mind. Thinking big or broadly is not easy in an era of specialization necessitated by complexity. The lure to know more and more about less and less is a built-in temptation of modern life. A political scientist becomes a "specialist" in public law but further specializes in administrative law and then may narrow this to state administrative law, perhaps the administrative law of Michigan, or maybe even administrative law in Michigan's workman's compensation cases. And so it goes. The amount of data is so great in so many narrow areas that one may be drawn into it so completely that after a while he loses touch with the broader areas of a field.

To maintain a generalist position is most difficult, particularly for the public official whose daily tasks tend to focus on special areas. He has to know his business, but he also has to equate this with the elusive public interest. How he does this depends upon his state of mind and the kind of persons he is. This may or may not be a result of his education. People who think small may think just as small had they pursued liberal arts rather than cost accounting.

Experts, however, are necessary. People broadly familiar with literature and the arts could not build atomic submarines without an additional knowledge of physics and engineering, just as the atomic physicist would be unable to prosecute an antitrust suit through the courts without legal training. Government needs experts who know what they are doing. Without expert advice on the consequences of policies, government programs may be doomed in advance to failure (the ill-fated Cuban "invasion" of 1961 was a dramatic example). Similarly, even the best grounded intentions of the public, Congress, or the President will be frustrated where the expertness necessary for implementation is lacking. Such circumstances produce that heightened sense of frustration and futility which undermines popular government.

When the often necessary tent of secrecy has been dropped over the bureaucrat's operation, the frustration becomes even greater. The question of the public interest then becomes more difficult to explore as some congressmen and citizens discovered when they wanted to find out more about the role of the highly secret Central Intelligence Agency in the Cuban invasion. "We must trust our sincere public officials" is often the medicinal dose offered an excited public waiting to "do something" but not knowing what to do. In a democratic society, such a dosage goes down hard, even if it is necessary, because none of us likes to feel we cannot be informed of what is happening to our destiny. At the same time, we want to be loyal to our government. To equate disloyalty with incisive probing into political and administrative blunders or questionable policies is a device which has been used with disappointing frequency and equally disappointing results. This applies also to the technique of substituting slick public relations for honest policy statements.[15]

To solve the problem of political control of experts is not easy, and will continue to be a key issue in both the study and practice of politics. The problem is insoluble wherever secrecy is deemed necessary. We may have to accept secrecy in some areas; we ought not, however, fool ourselves that it is compatible with democracy. Generally, perhaps the key to the solution is that the expert must retain a humility and acceptance of the fact that he is a public servant who in the last analysis must submit to the public's orders as expressed by their representatives. This may be a lot to ask of generals, physicists, accountants, and others who are appalled at public and even legislative misinformation about their fields of specialization. But purpose must dominate technique if a democratic public is to be adequately served.

PUBLIC RELATIONS AS AN ADMINISTRATIVE TOOL

EARLIER, we discussed the use of public relations and advertising techniques in electing candidates, influencing them after they are elected, and manipulating public attitudes on specific issues. These same techniques are used increasingly in public administration to sell the public on a governmental or departmental program. The techniques can focus around top political personalities, such as the President or a governor of a state. But they can be directly focused on an agency program, such as the Veterans Administration, a great user of spot announcements on radio and

---

[15]The multiplicity of conflicting statements regarding the capture of the American U-2 pilot by the Russians in 1960 not only confused the public but also angered many people because the news releases were not always the truth.

television designed to inform the agency's clientele what the agency can do for it.

"Information officers," as they are called in most jurisdictions, are used to inform the public of agency programs. For example, fish and game departments in many states have made use of information officers to print bulletins and issue press releases on such matters as bag limits for fish, the merits of shooting limited numbers of doe during deer season, the problem of producing adequate pheasants for hunters, and the virtues of fish and game conservation. A real question arises as to whether this type of activity is informing or propagandizing the public.

Federal agencies also use direct promotional devices to win support for their programs. The radio commercials of the Veterans Administration are paralleled by activities of the Department of Agriculture, the Treasury Department, all branches of the Department of Defense, and the Department of Labor; in fact, all government agencies, including independent regulatory commissions, engage in this activity in varying degree.

The basic questions involve the purpose and content of public relations. Is it a matter of informing the public or is it an effort to promote public acceptance of a program? Can this distinction be made? One of the country's leading authorities defines public relations as ". . . the attempt, by information, by persuasion, and adjustment, to engineer public support for an activity, cause, movement, or institution."[16]

Such words as "information, persuasion, and adjustment" are vague enough to cover the whole catalogue of political sins and virtues but it is the engineering of public support that is bothersome. The Civil Service Assembly, an organization devoted to understanding and improving the public service, has recognized the delicacy of governmental use of public relations techniques and insists that publicly employed public relations men must use "legitimate" means to "educate" and to "inform" the public. They also add: "Public relations have to do with the development and maintenance by any legitimate means of *favorable* [italics added] attitudes on the part of the people with whom the agency comes in contact."[17]

It is a peculiar comment on democracy, if we accept Mr. Bernays' definition of public relations, to find the public employing people to persuade them that the public's agencies are doing well by them. It is no answer to say that the agencies are acting on the orders and in behalf of the policies of elected officials. Even where this is true, it means that one of the parties is using the machinery and finances of government, not to

[16]Edward L. Bernays, *The Engineering of Consent* (Norman: University of Oklahoma Press, 1955), pp. 3-4.
[17]*Public Relations of Public Personnel Agencies* (Chicago: Civil Service Assembly, 1941), pp. 5-7.

administer its programs but to manipulate public opinion in its favor. Presidents as politicians, and their parties, have a right and an obligation to carry their views to the public. But as chief administrator of the governmental apparatus he can have no such democratic right nor can any of his subordinates. The basic principle involved is simple but important: If the opinions of the public are to control the government, these opinions must not be controlled by the government.

The problem is aggravated in those situations in which an administrative agency's program is closely linked with the interest of a private group. In these cases, government machinery and personnel of persuasion may be directly used for the betterment of a private interest. One observer has provided a striking example in the development of security programs for defense contractors:

> In the case of the industrial security program, which is in operation for classified defense contract work, we find a leading organization of industrialists calling attention to the sweet, nonsecurity uses of security. Says the foreword of the National Industrial Conference Board Study on Industrial Security (published in 1952): "Even if you don't have a trained saboteur in hire, industrial security can pay off in peacetime. It can help you rid your plant of agitators who create labor unrest, who promote excessive grievances, slowdowns and strikes, and encourage worker antipathy toward management. These actions cost your company money."
>
> Believe it or not, this advice to businessmen on the anti-labor applications of security was reprinted in 1955 in a pamphlet, "Disaster Planning for the Oil and Gas Industries," * published by the National Petroleum Council, an organization which also functions as the Petroleum Advisory Council to the Department of Interior of the U. S. Government.
>
> * This pamphlet...bears the notation that it is "published in response to request of Office of Oil and Gas, Department of Interior."[18]

Perhaps the most difficult problem of government public relations is how to reconcile persuasion with the democratic ideal of rationality. Rational men are appealed to on the basis of their intellects, not their glands. It seems to be an axiom of public relations that the test of the legitimacy of any campaign to "put something over" is its success. Glands rather than intellect are often the target.

The same techniques may, of course, be employed *against* an administration. According to a recent report, one public relations firm persuaded

[18]Benjamin Ginsburg, *Rededication to Freedom* (New York: Simon and Schuster, 1959), p. 33.

a governor to veto a bill without ever contacting the governor. It merely arranged to have "objective" sounding propaganda opposing the bill cross the governor's desk in such a barrage that he changed his mind.[19]

Persuasive techniques employed by private interests on administrative agencies may often strain at ethical limitations. Ordinarily, however, conflicting interests will operate partially to cancel out one another's extravagances. In any event, it is difficult in a free society to regulate the private use of manipulative techniques. But this is not a justification for allowing public, administrative agencies to become the province of the professional experts in attitude engineering.

Public information services can be a very useful activity of governmental agencies. If an agency confines itself only to dispensing information requested—favorable and unfavorable from the agency's point of view—it can contribute to public enlightenment. But with agencies whose continuity and growth depend upon public support of their programs, and with personnel generally committed to the programs as well as to keeping their jobs, it is difficult to insist that they forego those efforts to create good public relations which have become so basic to the conduct of all nongovernmental organizations. This, however, is a legitimate demand of democratic citizens. Few people would argue that a "ministry of propaganda" in a government is consistent with the consent of the governed. For the same reason, neither can there be a whole series of smaller propaganda offices and officers attached to specific governmental agencies. The public relations approach *to* government by private groups poses a constant and unavoidable threat to responsible administration and popular consent; when it is used *by* government to engineer the attitudes of the electorate, the stream of popular, responsible consent is polluted at its source.

BUREAUCRACY AND THE PUBLIC INTEREST

BIG GOVERNMENT AND THE PROBLEMS OF PUBLIC CONTROL have concerned many scholars of administration, as well as the many polemicists who argue the virtues and vices of governmental assumption of functions traditionally left to private initiative in a simpler and less interdependent world. Bigness is a fact. Whether it is inevitable and whether it is, on the whole, desirable, are still moot questions. So also is the problem of how to keep government responsible to public control. This is the recurring

[19]R. L. Heilbroner, "Public Relations: The Invisible Sell," *Harper's*, June, 1957, pp. 28-29.

problem of how to keep the vague concept of the public interest paramount in the minds of bureaucrats who serve the public and legislators who create public agencies, and in the programs of clientele who benefit from the activities of bureaucracy.

The problem is also posed by the recurring conflicts among rival bureaucratic interests and activities. The armed services argue over who has the best weapons and delivery systems and who is best qualified to employ them. When President Truman stated that he thought the Marine Corps should be abolished, a great furor ensued, the Corps alerted its past and present members, appealed to their *esprit de corps,* and had its top brass appear before Congress to plead successfully for its retention.

President Eisenhower's suggestion that all services should be under one command and wear the same uniform aroused admirals, army and air force generals, and civilian partisans of the services to action, and the services remain separate.

Farmers will not hear of curtailing the multitudinous activities of the Department of Agriculture which, through its extension service, teaches them how to raise more crops and then, through its bureau's dealing with crop surpluses, buys the surplus for storage.

Antitrust advocates and civil libertarians try to get the Department of Justice to follow their ideas; the business community works hard to keep the Post Office Department from getting authorization for increased rates on bulk mail deliveries; labor leaders try to head the Labor Department in their direction; businessmen try to make the Department of Commerce into a super chamber of commerce; the American Medical Association fights any notions of public health insurance that might exist in the Department of Health, Education, and Welfare while pension advocates work on the same agency to support legislation for larger benefits; and the Secretary of State is subjected to periodic public and congressional censure for leading or not leading the nation to the brink of war.

Agencies without cabinet rank have the same difficulties, even the highly secret Central Intelligence Agency when its activities get publicized. And independent regulatory commissions are periodically embarrassed by findings that their officials are enjoying very cozy relationships with the industries they regulate.

The problem involves not only outright corruption but the more subtle forms of thwarting the public interest. Often these emerge from officials' sincere convictions that the public interest is identical to the private interests with which the agency finds itself associated. In democratic politics the public interest, we have argued before, is at any given time the product of political debate and the competition of the political parties. Where parties do not play this role, the public official is deprived of guidance and support. Individually isolated, he has the same difficulty in pursuing such an abstract concept as does the legislator, judge, or citizen. As a result, bureaucracies very often rely upon brokerage processes to solve problems facing them. The Defense Department is inclined to see that all the services get their share of things; small and large farmers are each given their due by the Department of Agriculture (large farmers are more politically potent; thus, have more "due"); the Post Office sees that its clientele (mailers are organized and potent; householders are not) is treated fairly; and the Justice Department spreads itself among the many demands put upon it. Sometimes such brokerage is dictated by the chief executive through his politically controlled cabinet members, but many delegated areas of decision deep down in the organization charts also tend to operate on the brokerage model.

Administrative agencies vie with one another for appropriations from legislatures. In the making of a budget the brokerage process also operates. At both the national and state levels, the method of arriving at a budget is predicated on taking the departmental requests, carving them to the bone through analysis, and coming up with a final figure somewhere between the agency's request and the budget analyst's recommendation. The figure is usually agreed upon at a hearing before the head of the budgeting agency. The claims of the agencies and of the budget analysts are both considered equally legitimate. As a result, budgeting tends to become a game in which the agencies often pump their budgets full of air while the budget analysts cut it to the quick, with both sides hoping for a result somewhere near what each really felt was correct.

If one side is able to generate more influence than the other, the agency may end up with a bloated budget or an inadequate one, depending on which side is victorious in the struggle. At times, these differences are taken to the legislature, but this is risky for both sides since the compromises of the legislature are often made on politically different criteria than those of administrative agencies under the executive. Also, since both the budgeting agency and the program agency are ordinarily controlled by the executive, it looks bad to see them quarrel before the legislature, which might very well say "a plague on both your houses."

Legislatures, pressure groups, clientele, and many other forces work on bureaucracies to achieve their ends. But how does the public interest get served? The difficulty this question poses is reflected in the recent comment of one student of the problem:

> American writers in the field of public administration have evolved neither a unified or consistent theory to describe how the public interest *is* defined in administrative decision-making. Neither have they constructed theoretical models with the degree of preci-

sion and specificity which is necessary if such models are to be used as a description of, or as a guide to, the actual behavior of real people.[20]

Although this plea for precision may be difficult if not impossible to achieve, it indicates that ferreting out the public interest and discovering how it is pursued have proven frustrating tasks to students of administration.

The solution of the basic problem of a responsible bureaucracy will largely depend upon whether party organization can overcome the discontinuities and rivalries between Congress and President which are inherent in the separation of powers. Legislative bodies must themselves be organized to make responsible party government possible, and to exercise enough control and ask enough questions so that the public will know what goes on. But it is difficult to hope for much more than brokerage if legislatures create a host of agencies dedicated to special interests. This seems to be the tendency in many governmental jurisdictions, particularly in the creation of regulatory commissions and, on the state and local level, licensing boards, which all too often become tax-supported lobbies for pressure groups.

The President, on his part, can exercise responsible control over the bureaucracy only if, as party and legislative leader, he can protect the principles and programs of his Administration from the pressures of private groups operating directly on and through Congress. In the absence of sustained and strong presidential leadership, the major restraint on the brokerage process in the parties and in the Congress is removed. If parties and Congress are dominated by private interests, it is unrealistic to expect a President to be able to harness the bureaucracy in the service of the national principles and policies on which he was elected. He will be able to do so only insofar as he can apply effective strategies of personal persuasion, influence, and pressure on Congress and on powerful private groups. He is not without weapons in this struggle, but the odds against him are high. And he must constantly bear the burden of knowing that whenever he is outmaneuvered, and segments of the bureaucracy succumb to pressures from outside, the public will not blame the constitutional principle of separation of powers, the weakness and the brokerage character of the political parties, or the dominance of interests in the Congress. The President alone will be held responsible. It is an unfair game, and the President deserves better of enlightened public criticism.

[20]Glendon A. Shubert, Jr., " 'The Public Interest' in Administrative Decision-Making," *American Political Science Review*, June, 1957, p. 366.

13

COURTS
AND
THE RULE OF LAW

LAW AND SOCIETY

"WHAT IS THE LAW?" Socrates used to ask his fellow Athenians. The question is a simple one only at first glance, as many an Athenian found out. Over the centuries, it has been approached from a variety of vantage points and remains worth asking. We might begin with the proposition that law is the power of a government to control the behavior of its subjects by commanding or forbidding certain actions and by attaching a penalty to a violation of these commands. The content of the law is derived from that body of precepts by which a society lives. The source of these precepts may be an absolute ruler of some sort, an aristocracy selected on such a standard as heredity or wealth, the people of the society themselves either through representatives or on their own initiative, judges selected either by appointment or election, or a society's traditions with their sources shrouded in the mist of antiquity.

Social control can be exercised by means other than law. Custom, habit, folkways, and mores all influence people to act in certain ways.

Law is more formalized, and its command to action is backed with the power of the state. Law continues to perform, however, the major social function performed by tradition in earlier societies. Social life requires some range of predictability; individuals and groups must be able to anticipate the consequences of their actions in the reactions of others. Where the "cake of custom" has been crumbled, law as the command of the state steps in to insure predictability in social relations. Law is like custom in another respect: its commands and proscriptions have behind them a moral force. Custom may be obeyed in a traditional society because the individual is really unaware of the possibility of alternative actions. The "good" and the customary are interwoven in the fabric of social life and inculcated in the processes by which children are "socialized." Law most often develops in society as a codification of group values. Indeed, law is often formalized custom. The effectiveness of law, like the effectiveness of custom, continues to depend upon the acceptance of its moral content by those over whom it would be effective. A legal system is a substitute for physical might. It may be that in matters of the law, as Thomas Hobbes long ago said, "When nothing else is turned up clubs are trumps." But the vitality of a legal system will depend on its ability to make this situation the exception.

The existence of law presupposes a community—that is, a set of values by which a society resolves the issues on which its existence depends. At some stage of its development, the community establishes a basic legal order which determines the methods of creating laws. It also decides how laws are to be interpreted and enforced. Since specific laws always eventuate from conflicts and controversies, the machinery for making and interpreting laws tends to be used by the most powerful and influential segments of society in order to implement their interests or values. Law, then, is never a system of abstract, perfect justice. It must, however, rest on a claim to widely applicable and valid principles of justice from which a moral obligation to obey may be derived.[1]

FREEDOM AND THE LAW

THE ROLE OF LAW, its meaning, and the method by which it is enacted and interpreted are basic expressions of the political philosophy of every society. The distinction between a free and a totalitarian society is directly related both to the sources and the meaning of the law. When we talk of majority rule, we mean the right of the majority to declare the legal rules for society. We are accustomed to thinking of dictatorship as including

[1]Left out of account here are those laws which are purely expedient devices to regulate areas of human relations in which values are not involved. Laws which regulate automobile traffic are examples.

a system of unjust laws enacted and enforced without the consent of those subject to them. In modern totalitarian regimes, the development and refinement of the techniques of "random terror" exemplify the importance of even unjust laws. The random use of these techniques—the punishment of people for no apparent reason or without legal justification— means the elimination of law and predictability. The individual is deprived of any "legal personality." In this respect, Hannah Arendt argues, the modern totalitarian regime not only destroys the old legal order but also deliberately prevents the erection of a new one. Arbitrary decrees to carry out the demands of a "movement" and the use of the techniques of random terror deprive the citizen of any legal status.[2]

The citizen of the fully developed totalitarian state is in the same position as those unfortunates in the period following World War I who found themselves stateless, unwanted, and unaccepted in the legal system of any nation state. Wandering from state to state in Europe without legal personality in any nation, they were dealt with at the whim or caprice of police agencies. They dramatically illustrated the final plight of men who do not live under a law: the only way they could improve their condition was to come under the law by breaking it. For only then did they become "legal persons" and acquire such minimum legal rights as the right to be saved from starvation in prison. The fullest achievement of human rights requires a particular kind of legal order. The one condition in which there are no human rights whatever is the absence of a legal order altogether.

LAW IN DEMOCRACY

IN A FREE SOCIETY AND A DEMOCRATIC POLITICAL SYSTEM the legal personality of citizens is guaranteed by all those requirements of due process described earlier. Due process refers to those procedures designed to guarantee rights to the citizen as a subject of the law. The democratic citizen is creator of the law as well as its subject, thus law and morality bear a distinctive relationship to each other in democratic societies.

In closed societies and authoritarian political systems, law is regarded as the authoritative expression of the values of society. The moral personality of the citizen is identified with his legal personality: not only obedience to the law, but also allegiance to the values it expresses are the obligations of citizenship.

In a democratic society, legality and morality are never identical. In Arendt's words, "The genius of law in a free society is that it only tells

[2]Hannah Arendt, *Origins of Totalitarianism*. See especially Chapter 12, "Totalitarianism in Power."

citizens what they must not do; never what they ought to do." This characteristic of democratic laws derives from the fact that they are instruments which express the values of a majority in a climate in which minorities retain the basic right to continue to criticize, oppose, and seek to amend or repeal majority decisions. The empirical question of "What is legal?" is relevant only to the citizen's role as subject of the laws; as maker of the law, it is the value question of "What is right?" which is relevant.

A law-abiding citizenry is necessary to any organized society, but obedience to existing laws in democratic societies cannot require a commitment to the worth of the law in question. Indeed, earlier generations of democratic thinkers went further. In the Revolutionary period, M. R. Cohen says, "Not only Democrats like Jefferson but Federalists like James Wilson, living at a time when the Revolutionary tradition was vivid, found it easy to think that the people had a right to disregard the law when it seemed to them unjust or contrary to conscience."[3] Not many would go so far under the interdependent conditions of modern society.

Traditionally, Americans have been ambivalent on this question. The right and the supremacy of private conscience are continuously reasserted in one form or another (for example, by the individual's substitution of his judgment for the stop sign). Private conscience is protected by the law itself. For example, the law makes provisions for conscientious objectors and people whose conscience will not permit them to salute the flag. At the same time, Cohen went on to add, the development of American constitutionalism has tended to change "this moral right of the people into a legal right of the judiciary." The acquisition by the courts of the right to determine the conditions under which a law need not be obeyed reflects the complexity of modern society and is not a fatal blow to democratic values. But the democratic citizen cannot take the further step of believing that his duty to obey the law is also a duty to substitute the law for his own conscientious judgment of what is right. The distinction is important because the conditions of mass society appear to have reinforced the tendency to identify what is moral with what is legal. The tendency is incompatible with the citizen's political role as maker of law.

THE NATURE OF THE JUDICIAL PROCESS

"A JUDICIAL DECISION IS A SOCIAL EVENT," wrote Felix S. Cohen. "Like the enactment of a federal statute or the equipping of police cars with

[3]Morris R. Cohen, *American Thought, A Critical Sketch* (New York: The Free Press of Glencoe, 1954), p. 143.

radios, a judicial decision is an interaction of social forces."[4] Such social events do not occur arbitrarily, however, for the legal process is an elaborate and rigorous one which has developed intricate procedures designed specifically to rule out arbitrary action whenever possible. Most Americans are familiar, perhaps superficially, with the elaborate ceremonials connected with the operation of the legal process. The strange cant of the lawyers liberally sprinkled with Latin phrases; the awesome atmosphere of many courtrooms which exude dignity and justice; the robed judge sitting remotely upon his raised bench while lawyers, clerks, and other court attaches speak to him in required subservience; the oath taken on the Bible; and the jury box with stern-faced peers attentively listening to the proceedings—all bring to the courtroom a dramatic tenseness. The social events and their drama have not escaped the attention of writers, and the American novel, theatre, movie house, radio, and television have fed us almost as much courtroom drama as they have "horse" opera.

The judge is a public servant charged with judging controversies and dispensing justice. As a public servant, his area of operation is disciplined, steeped in tradition, and circumscribed by highly formalized precedents, rules, and procedures. The precedents, rules and procedures have not been established or developed merely to make the judge's task difficult. They attempt to reduce any tendencies toward arbitrary or capricious action by some human being wearing the judicial ermine. Even the judicial apparatus of a hierachy of courts with an increasing number of judges is designed to insure an adequate review of judicial action by the collective review of others skilled in the same discipline. The entire judicial structure, in fact, is based upon the assumption that human beings, even judges, can err. There are procedures, to insure against judges' mistakes, by means of which a litigant may challenge in a higher court the validity of the proceedings in a lower one. These characteristics of judicial proceedings are probably responsible for the tendency of Americans to hold judges in such high esteem that, at times, they seem to overlook the fact that the judge is a human being.

The Nature of Judicial Decisions

Legal rules and ritual and the structure of the court system are important factors in determining the quality of justice, but equally important are the human beings who wear the judicial robes. How does the judge operate? Do his decisions reflect his own values and philosophy? Or does

[4] F. S. Cohen, "Transcendental Nonsense and the Functional Approach," in F. S. Cohen and M. R. Cohen, *Readings in Jurisprudence and Legal Philosophy* (Englewood Cliffs, N. J.: Prentice-Hall, 1951), p. 479.

he deduce them mechanically from precedent? Or, does he follow the procedure of the irreverent Rabelais' Judge Bridlegoose:

> ... having well and exactly seen, surveyed, overlooked, reviewed, recognized, read, and read over again, turned and tossed over, seriously perused and examined the bills of complaint, accusations, impeachments, indictments, warnings, citations, summaries ...
> I posit on the end of a table in my closet all pokes and bags of the defendant and then allow unto him the first hazard of the dice according to the usual manner of your other worships.... That being done, I thereafter lay down upon the other end of the same table in my closet the bags and satchels of the plaintiff ... and forthwith [give] him his chance....[5]

Bridlegoose has two kinds of dice, however: large and small. When there are few bags on each end of the table, which means the issue is clear, he would use his "other large, great dice, fair and goodly ones," but when there are many bags on the table (that is, there are many small issues), he would use his "little, small dice."

Most judges would, of course, reject Bridlegoose's theory that judicial decisions have no more foundation than a hazard of the dice, but the theory of the hunch or intuitive process has been well defended by members of the judiciary. Federal Judge Joseph Hutcheson, playing on Rabelais' description of Bridlegoose, once said:

> I, after canvassing all the available material at my command, and duly cogitating upon it, give my imagination play, and brooding over the cause, wait for the feeling, the hunch—that intuitive flash of understanding which makes the jump-spark connection between question and decision, and at the point where the path is darkest for the judicial feet, sheds its light along the way.[6]

This description at least has the merit of emphasizing the inadequacy of the theory that the making of judicial decisions is an essentially mechanical process of applying the law to particular cases. In this mechanical view, judges are seen as simply matching the proper tint card of law and precedent to the color of the case, thus producing an automatic decision. In some aspects of judicial decision, however, it is immediately clear that discretion is involved. Thus decisions rendered by different judges for violations of the same law show a wide variation in penalties. For example, the statistician of the City Magistrates' Court of New York reported in 1916 that 17,075 persons were charged before the magistrates with intoxication. Of these cases, 92 per cent were convicted, but the record

---

[5]*Gargantua*, Book III, in Cohen and Cohen, *Readings*, p. 441.
[6]Joseph C. Hutcheson, "The Judgment Intuitive: The Function of the 'Hunch' in Judicial Decision," 14 *Cornell Law Review* 277-278 (1929).

indicated that one judge dismissed 79 per cent of this class of cases. The same agency also reported that in cases of disorderly conduct one judge heard 566 cases and discharged one person, whereas another judge discharged 18 per cent, and another 54 per cent of the cases.[7] Such "unscientific" and inconsistent application of the law has led Felix S. Cohen to observe:

> Concretely and specifically we know that Judge So-and-So, a former attorney for a non-union shop, has very definite ideas about labor injunctions, that another judge. who has an unfortunate sex life, is parsimonious in the fixing of alimony; that another judge can be "fixed" by a certain political "boss"; that a series of notorious kidnapings will bring about a wave of maximum sentences in kidnaping cases.[8]

The tendency in this age of objectivity and science is to recoil from such subjectivity, particularly in the administration of justice. It is impossible, however, to avoid the conclusion that judges *interpret* the law and, in the process, apply their own values and are influenced by the political, economic, and social environment in which they act.

Judicial Decisions: Pickax or Case Knife

The discretionary element in judicial decisions and the influence of social and economic forces are often concealed by the ritual and tradition of the judicial process. Confronted with a need to change the law or precedent in response to changed conditions or social forces, courts sometimes resort to "legal fictions," which make it possible to pretend that fundamentally nothing has been changed.

This process has been likened to the approach of Tom Sawyer and Huck Finn to digging Jim out of jail.[9] Tom, who was an authority on all matters of the right and proper and traditional ways for prisoners to dig themselves out, explained to Huck that "case knives" (table knives) were the only appropriate tool: ". . . it's the *right* way—and it's the regular way. And there ain't no *other* way, that ever *I* heard of, and I've read all the books that gives any information about these things. They always dig out with a case knife. . . ." Huck, not knowing any better and not caring "shucks for the morality of it, nohow," was all for getting on with the

[7]Charles G. Haines, "General Observations on the Effects of Personal, Political and Economic Influences in the Decisions of Judges," 17 *Illinois Law Review* 96 (1922).
[8]F. S. Cohen, "Transcendental Nonsense and the Functional Approach," in Cohen and Cohen, *Readings*, p. 481.
[9]Roscoe Pound, "Law in Books and Law in Action," in Cohen and Cohen, *Readings*, p. 419.

job with picks, but Tom would not "stand by and see the rules broke—because right is right, and wrong is wrong, and a body ain't got no business doing wrong when he ain't ignorant and knows better." After digging until midnight with case knives but with little visible result except blisters, even Tom began to see the advantages of "letting on," and said to Huck, "Gimme a case knife." Huck tells the rest of the story:

> He had his own by him, but I handed him mine. He flung it down, and says, "Gimme a *case knife.*"
> I didn't know just what to do—but then I thought. I scratched around amongst the old tools, and got a pickax and give it to him, and he took it and went to work, and never said a word.
> He was always just that particular. Full of principle.

And so they dug Jim out with case knives that were really pickaxes, but form, precedent, and rules were followed as in many judicial decisions where it is necessary to relabel the pickax a case knife.[10]

Legal fictions conceal the subjective elements involved in decisions which modify the law or apply it to new conditions. They also serve to dramatize the broader truth that judicial discretion is not only unavoidable but necessary to the flexibility of the legal system and to the search for justice. Like the concept of the public interest in a democracy, justice is never perfectly or finally achieved but remains an abstraction pursued by men of good intentions within an ordered framework of procedure and precedent.

SOURCES OF AMERICAN LEGAL PRINCIPLES

IF THE ESSENCE OF LEGAL ORDER IS SUMMED UP IN THE ATTRIBUTES OF JUSTICE AND PREDICTABILITY, this is also the source of the major problem of law. Particular standards of justice tend to develop into rules or principles of law. In Justice Cardozo's definition, a rule of law is "a principle or rule of conduct so established as to justify a prediction with reasonable certainly that it will be enforced by the courts if its authority is challenged. . . ." Thus, law is not simply a series of particular commands.

---

[10]A good example of the case knife, pickax routine would be the situation in California (similar to that in other states), which restricts the legislature from enacting certain statutes relating to a specific county. The courts have allowed the legislature to classify counties, however, and enact legislation for particular classes of counties. California has fifty-eight counties and oddly enough, there are fifty-eight classifications of counties. When the California legislature enacts a law applicable to "all counties of the fourteenth class," it is, of course, enacting a law for only one county. But since the pickax is a case knife, all is well with proper precedent.

Every legal system is a body of principles, applicable to a range of discrete social situations, and slowly evolved by the decision of concrete cases. Since the variety of specific human acts and human relationships is almost limitless, only a body of legal principles applicable to a wide range of situations can insure justice and predictability. Yet, in the nature of the case the general principle cannot contain and include all possible specific cases. Particularly, it cannot encompass new acts and relations that develop from changes in one part of society or another. The problem, for every legal system, is how to reconcile the need for stability of legal principles which predictability requires with the need for change and flexibility which the quest for justice requires in a changing society.

In the United States, there are generally four sources of legal principles: constitutional law, statutory law, common law, and equity. The first two stem from deliberative bodies which announce new legal principles; the latter two represent judge-made law. Of course, both constitutional principles and legislative enactments have to be interpreted when they are applied to particular cases. Thus, the development of legal principles derived from the Constitution or statutes still allows considerable leeway for the making of law by the courts.

Moreover, even in the areas of common law and equity, where principles of law are developed by judges rather than by legislatures, the principles themselves are hardened into precedent which not only limits the discretion of judges but also the flexibility of the legal system itself. Thus, judges make law in any legal system, but in none do they make it out of whole cloth. For this reason, every legal system, by virtue of its commitment to predictability, has built in tendencies to *rigor mortis* that the urge to justice must find ways of overcoming. This problem is illustrated in the common law itself.

Common Law and Equity

The common law developed in England after the Norman Conquest. A system of Royal Commissioners, empowered by the King to decide cases throughout the realm, was under the obligation to develop rules of law. Originally, all regular matters were handled in the traditional system of local courts that predated the Norman Conquest. Where the local courts proved inadequate—for example, when a controversy arose between litigants from different areas—a petition could be made to the King for intervention. In such extraordinary matters the King might, in the exercise of royal prerogative, hear the case personally or through a Royal Deputy. The decisions of the Royal Commissioners evolved into the common law. This was a reaction to the necessity of providing relief against the rigors of an established legal system under changed circumstances. In societies where the art of legislation had not matured, this became the function of the ultimate interpreter of law—the King—in the exercise of his "prerogative of grace." The King's grace was gradually evolved into a body of law presided over by judges. Common law, because of its ability to accommodate to social changes, moved far beyond the adjustment of legal relations in feudal society and became the basis of modern Anglo-American law.

This process can best be illustrated by an example. Let us imagine that Smith has a dispute with Jones which is novel in that nothing exactly like it has happened before. The common law judge would search past cases similar to this one and attempt to find a principle applied to cases where the facts were substantially the same (the rule of *stare decisis*). If *stare decisis* failed him because there were no precedents, he would decide on the basis of "right reason" what should be done. By so deciding, he would be establishing precedent himself.

By the fourteenth century, the common law had begun to be crystallized into fairly settled rules and principles. On the basis of these principles, the courts issued writs, entitling a petitioner to have his case heard. For a time, new writs were issued for new types of cases—for example, contracts, wills, titles, torts (injuries sustained by one individual as a consequence of the actions or negligence of others), and crimes. The list of permissible writs tended to become inflexible as the precedents of common law had hardened into principles. New kinds of writs allowing the courts to hear new types of litigation were not available. The common law had grown to satisfy the requirement of predictability, but its very development made it a cumbersome way of satisfying the demands of justice in new conditions.

The response to the rigors of common law precedent paralleled the development of common law itself. The solution was revived appeals to the King's grace. By the reign of Edward III (1327-1377), the King began to formalize the new procedures by referring the numerous petitions addressed to him to his Chancellor. From this developed the High Court of Chancery whose decisions came to be known as "equity."

Cases in equity were not subject to ordinary common law or statutory provisions. In its broadest sense, equity implies a natural form of justice based upon right reason. It developed out of appeals to the King's own person to do justice in cases where neither common law nor statutory remedies were available. The type of concern to which equity extended is perhaps illustrated by the injunction. The injunction is the "strong arm" of equity. It is a court order which generally prohibits a person or persons from doing something the court deems unjust or inequitable to some other person or party. Injunctions can be temporary, permanent, or for a specified period of time. They can prevent things from happening that are planned for the future. Cases at law, on the other hand, must wait until the event has occurred before there is a case.[11]

But again, the quest for new principles of justice hardened into precedents that provided predictability. By the latter half of the sixteenth century, the principles upon which cases were decided in the Chancery had tended to become settled and, hence, precedents for the guidance of subsequent Chancellors. Equity continued to be characterized by greater opportunity for judicial experimentation and innovation than common law. With the development of democracy, however, legislation became the major source and method in the quest for principles of justice.

The role of judge-made law in interpreting statutes is important in the United States because of the common law tradition in the American courts. The formal distinction between the common law and continental or Roman law, such as that of France or Louisiana, is that the common law is based upon past precedents whereas the Roman law is based upon applying statutes enacted by some governmental body. As we have seen, the common law tradition imposes the responsibility on judges to distill rules of law from precedents.

The jurist operating under continental law would have a different task, however. He would search all the codes of law used in his political jurisdiction and find the statute that most nearly squared with the case. One might liken the process to a housewife matching tint cards to the color of paint she wants. When she came as close as possible, she would select that color. If there were no paint near the color she desired, she would be out of luck. So would our continental jurist without his statute.

Although this distinction is oversimplified, it does illustrate the different approaches to law in the common law and the continental traditions. With the development of statutory law, the courts necessarily became involved in the interpretation of statutes. But, in his approach to this problem, the judge who operates in the common law tradition will bring to his task the greater judicial freedom and flexibility of that tradition. Thus we get a remarkably different interpretation of laws passed by legislative bodies given by different judges. For example, we find many judges making interpretations of legislative intent which are difficult for other judges, lawyers, and legislators themselves to accept.

---

[11]Other remedies in equity include nuisance abatement, alimony awards, divorce decrees, mortgage foreclosures, wage garnishment, and bankruptcy receiverships. A few states still have courts of equity, and others provide for equity procedures in their regular courts. In most states, however, the distinction between the common law and equity is disappearing. Also, much of both common law and equity is being put into statutory law.

Statutory Law

The importance of common law in the United States is increasingly overshadowed by statutory law. Federal law is all statutory law, although federal cases involving citizens of different states are tried under the common law of the state wherein the trial is held. Within the states, much if not most of the common law has been codified into or superceded by statute law.

Statutory law goes beyond the common law and supercedes it if conflict arises. It takes much of the discretion out of the judges' hands by prescribing definitions of crimes or civil situations and the penalties or rights of contestants under the statutory provisions. Statutes can prescribe the grounds for divorce and classify crimes, define the types of crimes that constitute the classes, and name the penalties for these crimes. Also, they can define what constitutes certain tort actions, the conditions under which the State will waive its sovereign immunity from suit, and declare the kind of conditions which may be placed upon contracts in certain instances.

Criminal and Civil Law

In all the codified or written law jurisdictions in the United States (federal, state, local), law is divided into the two broad classifications of criminal and civil. Criminal law defines offenses against the public; civil law governs the relations between individuals. Since common law was never taken over by the national government, all federal crimes are statutory crimes. Most state crimes have been crimes at common law (for example, assault, battery, kidnaping, rape, homicide, burglary, arson, larceny, forgery), but for the most part they have been embodied in and defined by statute. Except for exclusively federal matters, civil law belongs almost entirely to the states. Although now embodied in statutes for the most part, some of the civil law of the states had common law origins (for example, real property, personal property, contracts, sales, torts, domestic relations, inheritances, wills). Other areas of civil law owe their origins directly to statutes (for example, corporations, bankruptcy, mining, irrigation, taxation, administrative law).

Criminal law is concerned with wrongs against society, and prosecution is by the political jurisdiction against the individual; the United States versus John Doe, California versus Mary Roe, or the City of Syracuse versus John Doe, Jr. Crimes are classified according to their seriousness, the two most common classifications being felonies and misdemeanors. Felonies are major crimes, such as murder, armed robbery, and rape. Felonies are in turn often classified in degrees depending on the intent, premeditation, or some other standard the legislature may prescribe.

Misdemeanors are minor crimes which have limited penalties, seldom involving fines above one thousand dollars or more than six months to a year in jail. Traffic tickets, building code violations, petit theft, vagrancy, and other minor infractions of the law are usually misdemeanors. Local government ordinances define misdemeanors only.

The common law holds there is no crime without both an act and an intent to do wrong or to act in a criminal manner. Statutes may make acts crimes without intent, such as statutory rape which applies to girls under a certain age although no criminal intent was evident; or they may make intent punishable without an act, such as a conspiracy to advocate the overthrow of the government by force or violence although no act of force or violence occurred.

Criminal trials are exacting in their demands for proof of guilt. The individual on trial must be appropriately brought before the bar. This is done either by grand jury indictment in federal cases or by a grand jury or substitute that satisfies the due process of law requirements of the Fourteenth Amendment in state cases. He is presumed innocent until proven guilty beyond any reasonable doubt, and if he elects to have a jury, their decision must be unanimous. If convicted, the criminal faces a variety of penalties ranging from death to a lecture by the judge.

One problem with justice in a federal system is that penalties for crimes vary so greatly from state to state. Some states allow the death penalty for the more serious crimes while others do not. At the same time, statutory limits on the penalties for specific crimes vary widely from state to state. In some instances, such as kidnaping and interstate traffic in women for purposes of prostitution, the crime has been made a federal offense in order to insure adequate punishment and to indicate national disapproval of such crimes.

Civil law governs relations between individuals and between individuals and the public not involving public offenses. Civil law generally revolves around contracts, torts, civil rights, and other such matters. Civil law has been defined as that law which is not criminal and, while this may be similar to saying chemistry is what is not physics, it reflects the difficulty of precise definition.

In civil actions, proof is by a preponderance of evidence rather than beyond any reasonable doubt as in criminal law. Juries may or may not be used, depending upon the wishes of the contestants and the constitutional provisions of the states. If juries are used, they can often be less than twelve members, and their decision may require only a majority of the jurymen rather than unanimity.

There are instances in which some acts are subject to both civil and criminal action. Many criminal acts are subject to recovery by tort action. For example, under the Sherman Anti-Trust Act, a firm may be convicted of the crime of conspiring to "restrain trade"; at the same time, an injured competitor may recover in a civil suit as much as treble the damage it has suffered.

THE ROLE OF THE COURTS IN
AMERICAN GOVERNMENT

THE SEPARATION OF POWERS IN THE UNITED STATES gives the judiciary a place of unusual importance and influence. Its unique power stems from its role as final arbiter of the federal and state constitutions. Since Chief Justice Marshall's opinion established the precedent of judicial review of legislation, American constitutionalism has endowed the courts with the power to serve as guardians of the principles of the Constitution and its Amendments.

Statutory and Constitutional Interpretation

The institution of judicial review has been termed judicial supremacy since the decisions of the court on constitutional matters are binding on the other branches of government. This doctrine is a unique American contribution to political institutions. To understand its significance, it is necessary to distinguish clearly between statutory interpretation and constitutional interpretation. In a legal system which has an independent judiciary, the courts interpret the statutes they are called upon to apply in the cases that come before them. Did Congress in enacting the Taft-Hartley Act mean to exclude states from legislating in the same area? The courts have said Yes, and have invalidated more restrictive state legislation on that ground. But when the court is interpreting a statute, the way is completely open for the legislative body to overrule the court's interpretation through amending the statute to make its intention clear. Thus, in the case of labor legislation, bills were introduced into Congress to amend the Taft-Hartley Act to permit state right-to-work laws to supercede federal law. A partial victory for this point of view was achieved in the Landrum-Griffin labor bill, in the 1959 session, which permitted state labor relations agencies to apply state law to cases which the National Labor Relations Board had declined to hear. But the point is that there is nothing in the court's decision interpreting the statute to prohibit the Congress from going further.

Similarly, a court may decide that a particular law requires a governmental agency to do something that the agency has failed to do. Thus, the Supreme Court held that the Natural Gas Act *requires* the Federal Power Commission to regulate the interstate rates of natural gas. One result of the Court's decision was a political attempt to amend the Act to exempt the rates from federal regulation. In this case, the effort was successful in Congress, although the bill was vetoed by President Eisenhower on grounds that the natural gas lobby had used undue pressure in its efforts to get the bill passed.

In these cases, the Supreme Court's decision was based on statutory interpretation. The Court had decided only what Congress had intended when it wrote the statute in question. After such cases are decided, Congress has complete authority to redefine its intent if it disagrees with the Court's interpretation. But when the Court considers the constitutionality of congressional acts its decision is binding on the Congress. The recourse is not amending the law but amending the Constitution or, perhaps, waiting long enough for the judges to change their minds.

The Courts as Political Institutions

There is no question that in the United States the courts, either through interpreting constitutions and statutes or acting under the common law, have a tremendous influence on our destiny. They may order, in eloquent ambiguity, our reluctant Southland to integrate its schools "with all deliberate speed"; demand that an economic empire break up its holdings because it has competed so well it is becoming a monopoly; tell a religious group its children will have to salute the flag but, upon pondering the matter later, decide they do not have to after all; send people to their deaths; tell children with which parent they must live; keep us from reading books which might corrupt our morals; and tell the President of the United States that he and his cabinet are without power to take over the steel industry.

It is obvious that many of these decisions are *political* in the sense that they lay down or modify the course of public policy and arbitrate between conflicting groups and values in society. The political character of the courts' role is further revealed in the history of judicial review of legislation.

The Constitution (Article I, Section 10), for example, is explicit in stating that "no state shall . . . pass any . . . law impairing the obligation of contracts." This is not vague language, and for a long time the Court interpreted it almost literally. In a series of four decisions,[12] Chief Justice Marshall and the Court made the contract clause a powerful instrument for the protection of property rights.

[12]*Fletcher v. Peck*, 6 Cranch 87 (1810); *New Jersey v. Wilson*, 7 Cranch 164 (1812); *Dartmouth College* v. *Woodward*, 4 Wheaton 518 (1819); and *Sturges v. Crowninshield*, 4 Wheaton 122 (1819).

After the War Between the States, justices unfavorably disposed to social legislation relied upon the contract clause to protect the right of employers to hire labor as cheaply and for as many hours as possible. At the same time, efforts to organize labor were frustrated by court-supported "yellow-dog" contracts forbidding employees to join unions, and by court decisions that unions were monopolies which violated the liberties protected by the Fifth and Fourteenth Amendments. Such judgments by his colleagues on the Supreme Court led to one of Justice Holmes' sharpest dissents. In *Lochner* v. *New York*, a case invalidating a New York statute limiting to sixty hours the work week of bakers and confectioners, Holmes stated:

> This case is decided upon an economic theory which a large part of the country does not entertain. If it were a question whether I agreed with that theory, I should desire to study it further and long before making up my mind. But I do not conceive that to be my duty, because I strongly believe that my agreement or disagreement has nothing to do with the right of the majority to embody their opinions in law .... The Fourteenth Amendment does not enact Mr. Herbert Spencer's Social Statics. ... Some of these laws [limiting hours of work, etc.] embody convictions or prejudices which judges are likely to share. Some may not. But a constitution is not intended to embody a particular economic theory, whether of paternalism and the organic relation of the citizen to the state or of *laissez-faire*.[13]

As the United States grew and as efforts to deal with the problems of industrialism began to collide with private property rights, the contract clause lost most of its power. In 1934, the contract clause became almost an historical anachronism when, in *Home Building and Loan Assn.* v. *Blaisdell*,[14] Chief Justice Hughes' opinion in a five-four decision upheld a Minnesota statute preventing foreclosures on property during the Depression. After this decision, the contract clause as a protection of property rights against legislation was seldom used, demonstrating, as Pritchett puts it, "the present-day superfluity of the clause."[15]

The contract clause is still in the Constitution, but circumstances have changed. So have the viewpoints of the justices on the Court, particularly on the relationship of private contracts to the public interest. The Court changes its mind, at times reversing itself, not particularly because the language of the Constitution is vague, but because circumstances

[13]198 U. S. 45 (1905).
[14]290 U. S. 398 (1934).
[15]C. Herman Pritchett, *The American Constitution* (New York: McGraw-Hill, 1959), p. 658.

and the political demands of society change. Perhaps even more important, justices with different systems of values and perspectives become members of the Court.

Sometimes, the Court's actions have been in accord with popularly held values, but at other times its judgments have aroused heated political controversy. When the latter occurs, the Court is catapulted into political conflict over its role in a democratic society. Sometimes, these attacks involve the Court as an institution; at other times, attacks are aimed at particular justices; and sometimes, both the Court and the justices are criticized.

In recent years, the courts have voluntarily withdrawn from part of the political arena. Since 1937, court decisions have reflected a self-imposed restraint on declaring legislation outside the field of civil liberties and civil rights unconstitutional. Within those areas, however, and in their exercise of the function of statutory interpretation, the courts remain near the center of the political stage.

THE COURT STRUCTURE IN THE UNITED STATES

IT IS THROUGH THE AMERICAN JUDICIAL SYSTEM that law gains its meaning and interpretation. The court system is structured to provide for extensive hearings and for appeal and review of legal decisions. Indeed, the very structure of our parallel system of courts in the federal and state governments is probably one of the most extensive areas for judicial interpretation ever devised.

The structure of courts in the federal judiciary as well as in individual states is a fairly neat hierarchical arrangement. It proceeds from trial courts or courts of original jurisdiction on up to appellate courts and culminates in a Supreme Court which is the capstone of justice. The three-layer system is the most popular although some more sparsely populated states, such as New Mexico, only have two layers of courts with appeals going from the trial court directly to the Supreme Court. States also have a variety of minor courts, or courts of limited jurisdiction, such as justices of the peace, juvenile courts, small claims courts, traffic courts, and family courts.

In the three-level court structure used in the federal system, the trial court or court of original jurisdiction is the federal district court of which there are over one hundred, some with more than one judge or court, scattered throughout the country and its territories. Above the federal district court are the circuit courts of appeals. There are eleven circuits with the states being grouped into ten of these. The District of Columbia, where federal business is centered, is an eleventh circuit. On top of the pyramid is the United States Supreme Court.

Federal district courts usually operate with only one judge presiding, although some types of cases require three judges. The circuit courts have three judges, and the Supreme Court has nine, so as one proceeds up the ladder of justice he finds that more heads will ponder his fate. In addition to the three-level hierarchy of courts in the federal system, there are the following special courts created to hear special cases:

1. *The United States Court of Military Appeals.* This court reviews the findings of courts-martial. It reviews the record of all cases affecting generals or flag officers or cases in which the sentence is death. It will also hear cases by order of the Judge Advocate-General or by granting a review to a petition by the accused.

2. *The United States Court of Claims.* This is a special court established to review claims against the United States arising usually from contracts and sometimes torts. The United States has waived its sovereign immunity from suit in certain instances, and this court hears many of these cases.

3. *The United States Court of Customs.* A special court established to review the appraisal of imported goods and other decisions of customs collectors.

4. *The Court of Customs and Patent Appeals.* This court hears appeals from the Court of Customs as well as cases arising from the Patent Office on decisions regarding applications for patents or interference with patents and trademarks.

All the federal courts, except the Supreme Court, are creatures of Congress, since Article III, Section 1, of the Constitution states: "The judicial power of the United States shall be vested in a Supreme Court, and in such inferior courts as Congress shall from time to time ordain and establish."

The authors of the Constitution anticipated such an establishment of courts, and they put in some safeguards on the selection, retention, and compensation of the judges of future inferior courts: "The judges, both of the supreme and inferior courts, shall hold their offices during good behavior and shall, at stated times, receive for their services, a compensation, which shall not be diminished during their continuance in office."

The Selection of Judges

Judges for all federal courts are appointed by the President with the consent of the Senate. The practice of "senatorial courtesy"[16] is often extended to the senator from the state in which district court appointments are to be made.

The quality of justice in any legal system is very largely dependent

---

[16]A practice wherein senators will not vote for nominees who are unacceptable to the senator of a nominee's home state.

upon the quality of appointees to the bench. The appointing power of the President, the tradition of senatorial courtesy, and the selection of judges are all political processes. Judges are appointed basically on the premise that there will be some political mileage gained from their selection. About the best the people can hope for is that their President will be sold on the idea that good justice is good politics. Presidents are usually able to find acceptable appointees from the ranks of their own party, for it would be an indication of political weakness to rely upon the opposite political party for judicial talent.

Like all political appointments, judges must generally satisfy political considerations first and be qualified candidates second. As a result, many eminent jurists have never received the highest reward of their profession, a Supreme Court appointment. If an appointment is made from the ranks of the opposition, it is generally quite evident that this is to take care of some political consideration of pressing importance, such as satisfying the growing by-product of the national quest for harmony known as "bipartisanship" (sometimes erroneously referred to as "nonpartisanship"). Or the consideration could be a reward to a good friend from past associations such as President Truman's appointment of his former Republican colleague in the Senate, Harold Burton.

Appointments to federal district court judgeships are usually made on the advice of some sort of party organization and after consultation with the senator from the state involved, particularly the ones from the President's own political party if there are such. Over 90 per cent of such vacancies have been filled from the ranks of the President's party during the past seventy years.[17] The Department of Justice, the F.B.I., and the American Bar Association's Committee on the Federal Judiciary all scrutinize the candidate to see that he is loyal and qualified after the party has determined his political worth. Circuit court appointments follow the same process although political party organizations play a lesser role. Many circuit court appointments are filled by promotion from district courts.

The appointees to the Supreme Court are the most important to the President and his party. Presidents have all sorts of suggestions offered but generally attempt to place people on the Supreme Court who will bring to the bench a philosophy of government and a value system similar to their own. Very often, Supreme Court justices are selected on the basis of careers outside the judiciary, such as Chief Justice Earl Warren, who distinguished himself as Attorney General and Governor of California. Many former United States Attorney Generals—Tom Clark, James C. McReynolds, and Harlan F. Stone are examples—have been elevated to a Supreme Court seat. Several former senators and representatives have found

[17]Pritchett, *The American Constitution*, p. 114.

places on the bench; so have cabinet members and others who have brought attention to themselves and their beliefs.

Some Presidents have also appointed personal friends to the court, a charge often leveled at former President Truman regarding his appointments of Harold Burton, Sherman Minton, Tom Clark, and Fred M. Vinson. Other justices come from lower federal courts and some from state tribunals such as Oliver Wendell Holmes, who had served a distinguished career as both Associate and Chief Justice of the Supreme Court of Massachusetts. In short, Supreme Court justices come from all sorts of backgrounds with a wide range of talents and a variety of legal philosophies.

There have been instances when Supreme Court justices have failed to fulfill the expectations of those appointing them. When President Theodore Roosevelt appointed Holmes to the Supreme Court, he expected Holmes to help him "bust" some trusts. There was a good deal of social intercourse and a mutual affection between the two men, based on Roosevelt's fascination with Holmes' erudition and wit and Holmes' admiration of Roosevelt's energy, courage, and candor. But after the Northern Securities case,[18] in which Holmes dissented from the Court's decision upholding the enforcement of the Sherman Anti-Trust Act and attacked the whole idea of trust-busting, Roosevelt was furious with his appointee, and the friendship between the two men virtually ended.

A similar instance was the appointment of Justice McReynolds by President Wilson in 1914. McReynolds, as Assistant Attorney General in charge of antitrust prosecutions under Theodore Roosevelt, and later as Attorney General under Wilson, had shown himself to be an energetic and able lawyer who successfully won many cases and gained a reputation as a fearless trust-buster. On the Supreme Court, however, he became a cantankerous and ardent champion of *laissez-faire* and rugged individualism. He grumbled at his colleagues to the point where Chief Justice Taft described him as "a continual grouch" who "seemed to delight in making others uncomfortable."[19]

In spite of the caution exercised by Presidents in their appointments to the judiciary, candidates may behave differently than expected or hoped for. But the probability that the nominee will act in a predictable fashion sometimes causes the Senate to delay or deny confirmation. This happened in the case of John J. Parker in 1930, who was held to be anti-labor and anti-Negro. The Senate thoroughly aired the political, social, economic, and other views of the candidate before they denied his appointment. Justice Brandeis was only able to gain confirmation by a strict party vote, and Charles E. Hughes was opposed as being overly friendly to the business

[18]193 U. S. 197 (1904).
[19]Tresolini, *American Constitutional Law*, p. 649.

community when he was nominated and eventually appointed to the Court for the second time in 1931. Even Earl Warren did not escape some scrutiny before confirmation, and, oddly enough, most of it came from his own party.

Many bar associations are continuously suggesting that prior judicial experience would be advantageous, and bills have been introduced into Congress requiring such experience. This argument, however, rests mainly on a theory of constitutional jurisprudence that gives experience and knowledge of procedure a high value. It loses its force if the judges' role is regarded as more broadly political than narrowly legal and mechanical. Moreover, some of our greatest Supreme Court justices attest to the fact that their backgrounds, which did not include judicial experience, have brought much to American justice. As Herman Pritchett points out,[20] if previous judicial experience had been required in the past, the nation would have been denied Marshall, Storey, Taney, Miller, Bradley, Hughes (first appointment), Brandeis, Stone, Frankfurter, Jackson, and Warren.

Methods of selecting judges for state courts vary widely. Many states retain the electoral process, although some have made judicial elections nonpartisan. Others use appointment by the governor for some or all of the courts. Still others, like California, use a combination of election and appointment for the appellate courts wherein the governor nominates from a "screened" list, and the people confirm his choice by election. If they do not confirm the governor's appointment, he then appoints some other candidate from the screened list.

The question of how to select a judge is a difficult one. If we rely on appointment, a political hack may get on the bench. But if we rely on election, we may get fooled by eloquent oratorical spellbinders who are incompetent. How does an elector judge a judge? By what standards does he measure the abilities of candidates to weigh precedent against justice? There is no panacea. It is a difficult problem which many states are considering carefully. Various plans have emerged and some of them, like California's, are designed to satisfy the demands for the popular selection of judges while, at the same time, admitting that a governor may be able to select better candidates than would result from elections.

Jurisdiction of the Courts

In the federal system of government in the United States, there are two court systems to which each citizen is subject. Whether the federal or

---

[20]Pritchett, *The American Constitution*, p. 115.

state courts have jurisdiction depends upon the nature of the case. The federal courts are used for cases arising under the jurisdiction stated in Article III, Section 2, of the Constitution as limited by the Eleventh Amendment. This jurisdiction extends to cases arising out of the nature of the controversy and the nature of the parties. Examples of cases arising from the controversy would be those coming under the Constitution, statutes and treaties of the United States, and all cases dealing with admiralty and maritime law. Treason, for example, is a crime defined in the Constitution with the power of setting the penalties delegated to Congress except that "no attainder of treason shall work corruption of blood, or forfeiture except during the life of the person attainted."

Cases arising out of the nature of the parties would include cases affecting ambassadors and other diplomats, contests between states which go directly to the Supreme Court, and controversies to which the United States is a party. Contests between states may be long, drawn-out affairs, as in the case between Arizona and California, in continual litigation since the mid-1930's, over water from the Colorado River. Several other states have come into the case since their water may be affected by any eventual decision, and the whole thing becomes more involved as it proceeds. No solution seems to be on the immediate horizon.

State courts have jurisdiction over all cases which are not federal, although state judges are bound to uphold the United States Constitution. The types of cases are somewhat different, since the federal courts do not use the common law except when controversies arise between citizens of different states or to which the United States is a party. In that instance, the common law of the state where the trial is held is used. Courts of unlimited jurisdiction in the states hear cases arising from the common law, suits in equity, criminal prosecutions, civil contests, and probate matters. Minor state courts hear only those cases falling within their limited jurisdiction, such as juvenile cases, misdemeanors, family matters, or traffic violations.

The use of the appellate courts is similar in both federal and state systems. Cases which are appealed to higher courts usually go up on what is called a writ of *certiorari*, which is an order of a higher court to review the decision of a lower court. In such instances, the case is reviewed on matters of law rather than fact, although the question of what is law and what is fact is one that often causes a good deal of legal bickering. The appellate court upon review has a good deal of discretion over the disposition of the case. It can uphold or reverse the lower court's decision, modify the sentence, or order a new trial. Generally, review by a higher court is at the discretion of the higher court, although in several states there is an automatic review by higher courts over some cases. The Supreme

Court of California, for example, is required to review all cases where the death penalty has been given. The effect of a refusal by a higher court to grant a review of a lower court decision is to sustain the judgment below. This is often done, and it serves the purpose of upholding the lower court while avoiding the necessity of saying why.

The hierarchy of courts is a guarantee of thorough review to insure the criminally accused or contestants in a civil matter not only their "day in court" but their "days in court." They can travel up either the federal or state pyramid, depending on the jurisdiction over their case, and can move from the state supreme court to the federal Supreme Court, if the latter thinks there is a federal issue warranting a grant of *certiorari*. They can appeal the questions whether the procedures in their trials conformed to the requirements of due process and whether the law under which they were convicted is constitutional.

Within this structure and procedure, the courts define and play their political role in society. In this realm, the courts have several options and, to a considerable extent, they themselves define what their political role will be. In the next chapter, some of these options are described and their political consequences analyzed.

14

THE COURTS
IN AMERICAN POLITICS

T HE PRECEDING CHAPTER should have made it clear that while the courts in the American governmental system are, inescapably, political as well as legal agencies, the character of their political role is open to various interpretations. At any given time, it is shaped by the attitudes of judges themselves and by the expectations of citizens and the reactions of citizens and political agencies to the decisions of the courts. Historically, the interaction of these forces has led the courts, at one time or another, to wield their political power and influence by playing the role of guardian of the moral code of society, by guaranteeing due process against the pressures of other agencies of government, by offering themselves as oracles of basic principles of public policy, or by serving as umpires of conflicting principles and brokers of conflicting interests in society.

The question of which of these various political roles courts ought to emphasize and how they ought to play them will depend on what one sees their legitimate place in democratic politics to be. The role of the courts, like the roles of other agencies of democratic government, is to be defined with relation to the competing models of democratic politics examined in previous chapters. With this in mind, we turn to an analysis of some of the ways in which the American courts have played the roles of moral guardian, guarantor of due process, oracle, umpire, or broker.

THE COURT AS MORAL GUARDIAN

THE TRADITION of American law makes the judiciary the trustee of the moral code of society in two important ways. First, the courts are responsible for applying and interpreting laws designed to safeguard the public morals. Secondly, the courts are the guardians of a legal heritage which itself embodies and reflects certain moral postulates. Both of these circumstances have posed significant and unresolved dilemmas for the courts in defining their role.

The Court as Guardian of the Public Morals

Historically, there seems to have been a distinctive American tendency to write into the law anything and everything that a majority thought to be moral. Many foreign observers of American society, ranging from Alexis de Tocqueville to Gunnar Myrdal, have been interested in our concern with law and our "worship of the Constitution." Myrdal had this to say:

> Americans are accustomed to inscribe their ideals in laws, ranging from their national Constitution to their local traffic rules. American laws thus often contain, in addition to the actually enforced rules (that is "laws" in the ordinary technical meaning of the term), other rules which are not valid or operative but merely express the legislators' hopes, desires, advice or dreams.[1]

An examination of the laws, both statutory and judge-made, of the United States and of many individual states would bear out Myrdal's thesis. In a society which describes itself with the oft-repeated phrase that its is "a government of laws," there has been an almost literal translation of this to mean that there ought to be a law on every possible subject. We find, for example, that for a while Americans sought to prevent the consumption of alcoholic beverages by an amendment to the United States Constitution, that the Constitution of California limits boxing matches to ten rounds, that in Kansas it is against the law to swallow snakes and other reptiles in public, and that a successful suicide is a crime in many places.

[1]Gunnar Myrdal, *An American Dilemma* (New York: Harper, 1944), p. 14.

Such enactments ordinarily express the moral indignation or the code of ethics of enough lawmakers or a highly vocal pressure group to get the law "on the books." They seek to regulate behavior in areas regarded by others as essentially matters of private judgment and concern. When such moral postulates are enacted into law, they are often inadequately enforced and violations are common and sometimes flagrant. The hip-flask, speakeasy, and organized bootleg crime during the Prohibition Era attested to the fact that many Americans did not regard even the Constitution as a legitimate source of authority over this aspect of their private lives.

The enacting of a code of personal morality into law often produces some interesting moral hairsplitting, both by legislatures and by the courts. Gambling, in all states but Nevada, is prohibited in many of its forms. But often we find that betting on horses is legal although the slot machine, crap table, and roulette wheel are outlawed and smashed with zeal if discovered. It cannot be gambling that is bad, then, but specific forms of it. There has been much interesting legislative debate attempting to distinguish between the moral implications of the dog race and the horse race; the former is against the law and the latter is legal in many states.

The major burden of moral exigesis, however, falls on the courts. When a legislature passes a law against pornography, the court must decide whether *Lady Chatterley's Lover* is a pornographic book. Courts will be called on to decide what portions of the bare anatomy will "appeal to a prurient interest," and the same courts may decide that the latest "sex kitten's" sweater, while covering the flesh but enticingly accentuating what is underneath, is permissible. The courts' dilemma, however, is an expression of the confusions and inconsistences in the moral attitude of society, and of the difficulties of seeking to apply the law to areas of private taste and judgment.

The Court as Trustee of the Legal Heritage

At the heart of the Anglo-American legal system are certain assumptions about the nature of man. These assumptions hold that man is a rational creature, capable of making rational choices between right and wrong, and that when wrong choices are made he can expect to pay penalties which he deserves. The view of legal punishment as retribution and atonement for bad or wrong actions follows from these assumptions. Justice Holmes put it this way: "My aim and purpose have been to show that the various forms of liability known to modern law spring from the common ground of revenge. . . . In the criminal law and the law of torts it is of the first importance."[2]

[2]Oliver Wendell Holmes, *The Common Law* (Boston: Little, Brown, 1881), p. 37.

The assumptions about human nature and behavior, from which the legal principles of personal responsibility, punishment, and atonement were derived, came to be part of our legal system before the development of modern, scientific analysis of human behavior. The knowledge and the theories of modern sociology and psychology are, on some fundamental points, at odds with the traditional assumptions of the law. Much modern behavioral science selects as its operational assumption a theory of determinism which holds that the behavior of men, like that of other animals, is to be explained entirely as conditioned responses to stimuli. A person's response to a given situation at a given time is entirely the result of his earlier conditioning. Thus, if enough knowledge of the ante-cedents were obtainable, it would be possible to predict his actions. In this view free will is meaningless. Responsible choices between the alter-natives of right and wrong are never the real basis of behavior. If the wrong choice (from society's point of view) is made, the man making it must be conditioned into the right (or socially acceptable) way of doing things. Further, he cannot legitimately be punished by society or held responsible for wrong behavior when he could not in any relevant sense have behaved differently.

The logical end of social determinism would hold that society rather than the criminal must assume responsibility for criminal acts, for it was environmental conditions which caused the criminal to act as he did. The slum theory of juvenile delinquency, the emotional stress theory of alcoholism, and the disturbed mother-father relationship theory of homo-sexuality are all indications of the effort to find causal factors or determi-nants of certain types of crimes and misbehaviors.

The search for causal factors is important to justice in its broad sense, and has long been a factor in criminal law. To the common law standards of defining a crime—that is, both an act and an intent—it adds a reason for committing the act or having the intent. This has sometimes resulted in acquittals in cases in which the accused had committed an illegal act with premeditated intent. A good and not uncommon example of this type of case would be the irate husband who, upon discovering that he is the cuckold in a love triangle, seeks out either his wife or her paramour and shoots one or both of them dead. If the drama occurs in middle-class suburbia rather than the slums, the husband's chances of acquittal are fairly good because, whereas the intent was there as well as the act, his reason for doing his intended act may be considered adequate explanation by many of his peers occupying the jury box.

The courts of most states have increasingly relied upon psychiatric and other expert help in searching out the reasons for many acts. Very often, the question revolves about the issue of the sanity of the individual. The classic standard of legal insanity throughout the English-speaking world is the McNaughten Rule. This rule holds that in a plea of insanity it must be proven that the person making the plea was laboring under such a defect of reason that he was unable to know the nature or quality of his act or was unable to know that his act was wrong.

The McNaughten Rule, however, has been challenged as inconsistent with modern scientific evidence. A recent decision,[3] partially recognizing these objections, caused a stir in both the professions of law and psychiatry. The Durham Rule, resulting from the decision, holds that an accused is not criminally responsible if his unlawful act was the *product* of mental disease or mental defect. The implications of this rule would change the test of legal responsibility in a significant way. The product of a mental illness is a different test from whether, at the time the act was committed, the accused was able to determine right from wrong. It would make a wide range of psychological reasons for an act relevant and admissable.

The current controversy over punishment of criminals attacks the very foundations of Anglo-American law. A recent report of the committee on psychiatry and law of the Group for the Advancement of Phychiatry, entitled "Criminal Responsibility and Psychiatric Expert Testimony,"[4] points up the issue quite clearly:

> Attacks upon the law by psychiatrists and the defense of the legal position by lawyers have engaged a disproportionate share of our attention and exertions at the expense of significant psychological insights which can no longer be ignored. A re-examination of not only the basic premises of the criminal law but also of its actual operations is needed if lawyers and psychiatrists are to attain a better inter-communication and understanding.
>
> As expressed in contemporary law, responsibility is regarded as a function of the intellect, of conscious volition with definite boundaries and degree. Modern psychiatry recognizes the role of the intellect, but would give to the emotions and unconscious a greater weight in the balance of forces in mental life, and would assert that their boundaries and degree are not readily ascertainable.

The role of punishment by society still has its strong advocates, however. The focus is often put upon organized crime and the necessity of holding out a social whip against those who wish to practice such illegal professions as burglary or embezzlement. Retribution, both severe and certain, is deterrence and if determinism becomes the basic assumption of criminal acts, say its critics, anyone could do almost anything and explain it by trauma in childhood. "Benevolent social reformers," says M. R. Cohen:

[3]*Durham* v. *The United States*, 214 F2d 862 (1954).
[4]Report No. 26, 1954.

are apt to ignore the amount of cold calculating business shrewdness among criminals. . . .Men will risk their lives if they think that there is some chance of winning something. And while many take long chances, as in lotteries, it is a fact that professional crime, like any other business, ceases to grow in extent where the chances of failure rise. That is why bandits do not try to rob the United States Treasury or the mint.[5]

It is one thing to insist that psychological and sociological explanations of human behavior be given judicial notice in criminal law. But before the concept of rational man capable of choice is thrown out the window, we might consider the implications in civil law. It would be an interesting situation if John Doe, a party to a contract with used-car dealer "Honest" Roe, could appear in court for release from an otherwise legitimate contract on the basis that he was not responsible for entering into the agreement because his mother denied him love. It would be equally ridiculous to find the party responsible for a tort pleading that he should not be held liable for recovery by his victim because his wife had been unfaithful. The prospects of shifting the burden of responsibility for one's actions from the individual to society are awesome, and it is questionable whether a society could or should ever assume the burden.

Both lawyers and behavioral scientists are deeply concerned with the proper treatment of criminals. The scientific approach to human behavior has not demonstrated the desirability of abandoning the assumption of personal responsibility for one's acts. Much carefully tested behavioral evidence shows very clearly, however, that retribution and atonement for a social act is not usually the most effective solution for either society or the individual. On the other hand, lawyers are not anxious to give up traditional approaches to punishment and chart new courses until these new methods of treatment and rehabilitation can be proven a better solution. The dilemma centers around establishing the most meaningful appraisal and understanding of man. This is a problem as old as human history and it is far from resolved.

The burden of dealing with it falls inescapably on the courts. What, no doubt, they will continue to search for will be solutions which reconcile responsibility with justice. Sometimes this may be based upon scientific evidence offered by an expert, but at other times it will probably be a subjective selection of the right treatment made by the judge. The basic assumption of individual responsibility over which the courts stand guard is also a basic premise of political democracy. The courts in a democratic system cannot avoid seeking solutions to the dilemmas which this assumption occasions.

[5]"Moral Aspects of the Criminal Law," 49 *Yale Law Journal* 987 (1940).

THE COURT AS GUARANTOR OF DUE PROCESS

THE QUALITY OF LAW in any society depends to a considerable extent on the character of the agencies through which laws are enforced. Police agencies stand between the citizen and the courts. In a democracy the citizen, as we have seen, has rights *against* the government. These rights are established by the procedural guarantees in the Bill of Rights against the possible caprice, arbitrariness, overzealousness, or brutality of the law enforcement agencies. These rights are secured and enforced largely by the role of the courts in marking out the boundaries of private rights and official uses of power.

Law Enforcement and Due Process

Enforcement of federal laws and their prosecution are the responsibilities of the Department of Justice under the direction of the Attorney General, who is a cabinet member. The chief law enforcement arm of the Department is its Federal Bureau of Investigation. This agency, known to every citizen as the F.B.I., has achieved near autonomy under the leadership of its energetic chief, J. Edgar Hoover. The F.B.I. is a national police force which employs about fourteen thousand people, of whom over six thousand are agents. Mr. Hoover and his agents enjoy an enviable position of prestige achieved by the almost unadulterated adulation of the mass media of radio, newspapers, magazines, television, and movies. These media tend to create the impression that the national interest will be well served only if the F.B.I. is left alone and not subjected to criticism. The danger in adulation of a law enforcement agency in a democracy was dramatically illustrated by reaction to recent cases in which the Supreme Court called the F.B.I. to account for careless observance of civil rights. The decisions of the Court aroused shrill horror in some superpatriots who felt the Court was turning the Bill of Rights into a "suicide pact" and who demanded that Chief Justice Warren be impeached.

What the Court has done is to limit the F.B.I. to a quite rigid interpretation of constitutional methods of obtaining and using evidence in its investigations of crime and subversion. In *Kremen* v. *United States*,[6] the court held that the F.B.I. could not search and seize the contents of a cabin without a warrant and use the evidence in court. The use of information supplied by informers to the F.B.I. was seriously curtailed in *Jencks* v. *United States*,[7] when the court held that the source of such information must be disclosed to the defendant. Justice Brennan had this to say:

[6]353 U. S. 346 (1957).
[7]353 U. S. 657 (1957).

We hold that the criminal action must be dismissed when the government, on the ground of privilege, elects not to comply with an order to produce, for the accused's inspection and, for admission in evidence, relevant statements or reports in its possession. . . .

The burden is the government's . . . to decide whether the public prejudice of allowing the crime to go unpunished is greater than that attendant upon the possible disclosures of state secrets and other confidential information in the government's possession.

These decisions insist that in a democracy a police force must comply with established standards of justice based upon individual liberties. Enforcing the law in a democracy is not as easy as in a totalitarian state, where the inconveniences of civil liberties do not clutter up the process. The court has told the F.B.I. that it will have to endure these annoyances even though a criminal may now and then elude its talented agents. The carefully recruited, highly trained, and competent staff of the F.B.I. has permitted it to avoid many of the potential dangers of a secret police force. But here, as elsewhere, "eternal vigilance" remains "the price of liberty," and vigilance must seek to insure the political and legal responsibility of police agencies.

Local police forces, usually staffed with personnel much less qualified than the F.B.I. agents, also pose problems for the maintenance of civil liberties and general democratic standards in law enforcement. State courts have the same responsibility within their jurisdiction to see that these standards are maintained and that even "bums" and criminals are protected against brutality, arrest on vague suspicions, or invasion of privacy. Our standards of justice at the local level depend heavily upon the quality of law enforcement officials and judges available to the community.

The protection of the procedural guarantees of the Bill of Rights is always difficult because these guarantees do, in fact, raise problems for law enforcement agencies. The civil rights in question are those generally found in Amendments Four through Eight. They include the protections against unreasonable searches and seizures, double jeopardy, self-incrimination, and excessive bail, as well as such guarantees as trial by jury, access to counsel, and the right to confront witnesses in criminal trials.

These rights are an important part of the tradition of justice in the United States. Under the terms of the Constitution, however, like the rest of the first ten Amendments, they apply only to the national government. The court has shown itself quite aware of their importance but has sometimes been reluctant to impose them upon the states. The question for the courts is whether they are to be extended to the states under the clause of the Fourteenth Amendment which guarantees due process of law. For example, in 1937, in *Palko* v. *Connecticut*,[8] a condemned murderer

[8]302 U. S. 319 (1937).

who had been tried twice by the state of Connecticut entered a plea that he had twice been put in jeopardy of his life. He asked that the Fourteenth Amendment be extended to protect him from double jeopardy by applying the restriction to states. His plea was denied by the Supreme Court on the grounds that this guarantee was not essential to "ordered liberty." In this case, Justice Cardozo attempted to explain the Court's position in sorting out those liberties it would protect with the Fourteenth Amendment and those it would not. After explaining that such liberties as freedom of speech, press, religion, assembly, and right of an accused to counsel were protected by the Amendment while others were not, he said:

> The line of division may seem to be wavering and broken if there is a hasty catalogue of the cases on the one side and the other. Reflection and analysis will induce a different view. There emerges the preception of a rationalizing principle which gives discrete instances a proper order and coherence. The right to trial by jury and the immunity from prosecution except as the result of an indictment may have value and importance. Even so, they are not of the very essence of a scheme of ordered liberty. To abolish them is not to violate a "principle of justice so rooted in the traditions and conscience of our people as to be ranked fundamental. ..." What is true of jury trials and indictments is true also, as the cases show, of the immunity from compulsory self-incrimination.

The more zealous civil libertarian might chafe at such reasoning and argue with Justice Douglas, concurring in *Joint Anti-Fascist Refugee Committee* v. *McGrath*,[9] that "it is procedure that spells much of the difference between rule by law and rule by whim or caprice."[10]

Many "hard cases" come to the Supreme Court on procedural issues. One of the most bizarre was *Louisiana* ex. rel. *Francis* v. *Resweber*,[11] one of the few cases which have come before the Court on cruel and unusual punishment. Francis, a young Negro sentenced to death for murder, had been placed in the electric chair but when the switch was thrown some mechanical difficulty prevented his being killed. He tried to prevent a second attempt on the grounds of double jeopardy and cruel and unusual punishment but the court, in a five-four decision turned him down. Justice Reed had this interesting comment for the Court:

> Even the fact that petitioner has already been subjected to a current of electricity does not make his subsequent execution any more cruel in the constitutional sense than any other execution. The cruelty against which the Constitution protects a convicted man is

[9] 341 U. S. 123 (1951).
[10] Justice Frankfurter has said: "The history of American freedom is, in no small measure, the history of procedure," in *Malinski* v. *New York*, 324 U. S. 401 (1945).
[11] 329 U. S. 459 (1947).

cruelty inherent in the method of punishment, not the necessary suffering involved in any method employed to extinguish life humanely. The fact that an unforeseeable accident prevented the prompt consummation of the sentence cannot, it seems to us, add an element of cruelty to a subsequent execution.

After this decision, Francis was again strapped in the electric chair. This time it worked and he was properly killed.

Many of the procedural due process cases cause the courts a great deal of difficulty in maintaining Justice Cardozo's line of division between fundamental freedom and freedoms not fundamental. True, many of the cases involve sordid situations and characters who do not command public sympathy or admiration. A case in point was *United States* v. *Rabinowitz*,[12] which involved a stamp forger (Rabinowitz) who sold his altered and artificial goods to collectors. Federal officers acting under a proper warrant arrested him but also ransacked his office for evidence, although they had no warrant to search his premises. The illegal search yielded 573 forged postage stamps which were later used as evidence to convict him. Rabinowitz appealed, but by a four-three decision the Court upheld the conviction. Commenting in his dissent, Justice Frankfurter entered a plea for the Fourth Amendment as a fundamental liberty and scolded his colleagues for subordinating this Amendment to the unpleasant case before them. He said:

> The old saw that hard cases make bad law has its basis in experience. But petty cases are even more calculated to make bad law. The impact of a sordid little case is apt to obscure the implications of the generalization to which the case gives rise. Only thus can I account for disregard of the history embedded in the Fourth Amendment and the great place which belongs to that Amendment in the body of our liberties as recognized and applied by unanimous decisions over a long stretch of the Court's history.
>
> It is a fair summary of history to say that the safeguards of liberty have frequently been forged in controversies involving not very nice people. And so while we are concerned here with a shabby defrauder, we must deal with his case in the great theme expressd by the Fourth Amendment. A disregard of the historic materials underlying the Amendment does not answer them.

What Justice Frankfurter said of his colleagues is even more true of society generally. In many current controversies concerning such things as police brutality, the apprehension of narcotics offenders, or coerced confessions, the attitude is often expressed that the "known criminals" and those "probably" guilty of heinous crimes deserve rough treatment

[12]339 U. S. 56 (1950).

anyway. So what if there was a violation of accepted standards of justice? It is difficult to arouse the "respectable majority" over the maltreatment of the "undesirable element" of society, except in a case of extreme cruelty[13] or after it is too late—when an innocent person has been victimized.

Police departments often appear hysterical over any attempts to create a body of lay citizens to investigate charges of brutality or corruption. In Los Angeles, the American Civil Liberties Union has been charged with all sorts of misguided efforts if not outright subversion in its attempts to establish a police review board to safeguard civil rights.[14] The same thing has happened in numerous other cities. The big question seems to be whether we wish to allow some criminals to go free rather than compromise the civil liberties all Americans expect to enjoy or whether we are willing to forego some of these liberties in order to give law enforcement officials more efficient means to do their jobs. It is not an easy question for we demand a peaceful and tranquil society, and law enforcement is often difficult in a democracy. We are annoyed when some of our major criminals seem to evade the law, or are put behind bars for the evasion of income tax or some other charge which has to be used because conviction for the real crimes cannot be made—albeit, sometimes because of corruption or payoff to appropriate sources of influence. Yet, as Frankfurter so well put it, we cannot allow a "sordid little case" to tear down the structure of American justice.

The extension of the Fourteenth Amendment to include procedural rights of citizens of all states has recently been greatly extended. In *Elkins* v. *United States*,[15] a sharply divided five-four Court held that the Fourteenth Amendment extended part of the Fourth Amendment to the states and, in this instance, stopped the so-called "silver-platter" doctrine. This rule allowed evidence illegally obtained by *state* officers to be introduced as evidence in a federal criminal trial, although similar evidence obtained by *federal* officers was barred by the Fourth Amendment. Until this decision, such evidence could be used and the courts would not exclude it because of its source. The dissenting opinion of Justice Frankfurter was strongly opposed to extending the Fourth Amendment to the

[13]A case in which brutality of disgusting proportions was used on a prisoner is *Apodaca* v. *United States*, 188 Fed. 2nd 932 (1951). This type of treatment eventually works to the detriment of good law enforcement, as most leaders of police work will attest.

[14]See Norman B. Moore (Sergeant, Los Angeles Police Department) "Police Review Boards," *California Peace Officer*, November-December, 1960. The editorial caption reads, "A Page Out of the Communist Manual," and a boxed editorial comment opens with the sentence: "No matter what names are used by sponsors of so-called 'Police Review Boards' they exude the obnoxious odor of Communism."

[15]80 S. Ct. 1437 (1960).

states by means of the Fourteenth. Justice Frankfurter was to have an opportunity to dissent again, with three of his colleagues, when in 1961 the Court extended the Fourth Amendment through the Fourteenth to all citizens of all states.

In the case of *Dollree Mapp* v. *Ohio*,[16] Justice Clark, for the Court, held that all states must comply with the prohibition against illegal searches and seizures. The Mapp case involved a flagrant violation of the defendant's rights which ended the Court's limited application of the Fourth Amendment to the states. Justice Clark summed up the argument with this:

> Having once recognized that the right to privacy embodied in the Fourth Amendment is enforceable against the States, and that the right to be secure against rude invasions by state officers is, therefore, constitutional in origin, we can no longer permit that right to remain an empty promise. Because it is enforceable in the same manner and to like effect as other basic rights secured by the Due Process Clause, we can no longer permit it to be revocable at the whim of any police officer who, in the name of law enforcement itself, chooses to suspend its enjoyment. Our decision, founded on reason and truth, gives to the individual no more than that which the Constitution guarantees him, to the police officer, no less than that to which honest law enforcement is entitled, and, to the courts, that judicial integrity so necessary in the true administration of justice.

The future will no doubt see further changes in the application of the rights enumerated in Constitutional Amendments Four through Eight to the states. There seems to be a growing awareness that many of the procedural guarantees of the Bill of Rights are essential to ordered liberty. The distinction between substantive and procedural rights breaks down in application. Liberty in a democratic society requires that citizens be free from arbitrary governmental action. This demands a guarantee of both substantive and procedural rights, for the substance of due process cannot exist without procedural safeguards. The courts would seem to be uniquely qualified to play the role of protecting the rights of individuals against overzealousness or abuse of power by law enforcing agencies.

Legislative Investigations and Due Process

The role of the courts as protector of individual rights and guarantor of due process occasionally comes into conflict with its position as one of three presumably equal and independent branches of government. The position of the courts as final arbiters of the Constitution, however, makes

[16]81 S. Ct. 1684 (1961).

them in effect the judges of the constituional limits of their own power, as well as of the legislative and executive powers. As a result, when the courts' power to accord individuals the guarantees of due process collides with the exercise of legislative and executive powers, it is the courts which decide which must give way. The other agencies may be restrained by the courts; the restraints *on* the courts are largely self-imposed. The constitutional system of separation of powers, however, often operates as a significant source of judicial self-restraint.

One important arena in which the courts have faced this problem in recent years surrounds actions of Congress and state legislatures in pursuit of their powers of investigation. Legislative bodies have the power to compel witnesses to appear before them and to punish them for contempt if they refuse to co-operate in the inquiries of investigating committees. These inquiries, described in an earlier chapter, often involve a personal examination and cross-examination of witnesses in a legislative setting which lacks the procedural rigors of the courtroom. Sometimes the questions asked a witness may be held to infringe upon constitutional rights and rules of due process. If he declines to answer, his recourse is often an appeal to the courts from contempt proceedings of Congress. The courts are then forced to define their role as guarantor of due process in its relation to the legislative power of investigation. The result is that these are "hard cases," which often narrowly divide the court.

The rights and powers of congressional investigating committees became a judicial problem after Congress gave itself the power to punish for contempt. In 1789, Congress empowered its committees to administer oaths and take testimony, and made false statements by witnesses subject to the "pains, penalties, and liabilities of perjury."[17] The Supreme Court upheld this exercise of congressional authority in *Anderson* v. *Dunn*[18] but held that a person imprisoned under this statute could not be confined beyond the session of Congress in which the contempt occurred. Congress remedied this in 1857 by enacting a law which made contempt a misdemeanor—an indictable offense with appropriate punishment attached.

An early court decision held that Congress is limited in its investigations by the separation of powers. It also held that the subject matter of investigations must be relevant to contemplated legislation, and that the resolution establishing the committee must indicate an interest in legislation on the subject being investigated.[19]

---

[17]Pritchett, *The American Constitution*, p. 192. The chapter on the investigatory power of Congress is an excellent account of its history and use.
[18]6 Wheaton 204 (1821).
[19]*Kilbourn* v. *Thompson*, 103 U. S. 168 (1881), in which the court held Congress did not have "a general power of making inquiry into the private affairs of a citizen."

The Court later abandoned the last requirement in a decision which held that it was not necessary for a Senate investigating committee to declare by resolution what it contemplated doing with the information it gathered—in this case, information on the corruption of senators.[20] In 1927, the Supreme Court received a case arising out of the Teapot Dome scandal. The Senate wanted to talk to Attorney General Harry Daugherty's brother, Mally. Lower courts held that the Senate was exceeding its powers in conducting an investigation which seemed to be more in the nature of a trial. The Supreme Court reversed the lower courts and held that it was an appropriate investigation and that the "power of inquiry—with processes to enforce it—is an essential and appropriate auxiliary to the legislative function."[21]

More recent developments have found the court again confronted with the constitutional relationship of individual rights to legislative power. During the span of McCarthy hearings, the Supreme Court had generally exercised self-restraint, refusing to invoke constitutional rights as limits on the investigating activities of the Wisconsin Senator's subcommittee and other investigatory bodies. Later, when the "Warren Court" adopted a firmly defensive position on civil rights generally, the courts did begin to take cases involving legislative investigations, thus abandoning a strict interpretation of the principle of the separation of powers.

In 1957, the court, in one day, temporarily placed two explosive charges on the doorsteps of Congress and state legislatures. One of these was the Watkins case,[22] which went to Congress; the other was the Sweezy case,[23] which was delivered to state legislatures.

The Watkins case concerned an official of the Farm Equipment Workers Union who had appeared before a subcommittee of the Committee on un-American Activities in 1954 and had answered all questions about his past activity freely and fully. He denied he had ever been an official member of the Communist Party but admitted that he was very cooperative with the Party and its members at certain times in his past. Watkins refused, however, to tell the committee if he knew whether people whose names were read to him had been members of the Communist Party. He did not invoke the "self-incrimination" clause of the Fifth Amendment, which Congress itself had not challenged as a legitimate *constitutional* ground for refusal to answer (some Congressmen had challenged it, however, as a legitimate *moral* ground by helping

[20]*In re Chapman*, 166 U. S. 661 (1897).
[21]*McGrain* v. *Daugherty*, 273 U. S. 135 (1927).
[22]*Watkins* v. *United States*, 354 U. S. 178.
[23]*Sweezy* v. *New Hampshire*, 354 U. S. 234.

to popularize the ingenuously vicious phrase, "Fifth Amendment Communist.)'" Watkins had, instead, based his refusal to answer on his constitutional right to silence where, in his judgment, his answers might lead to unjust harm being visited on others.

The Court's decision, while finding in favor of Watkins, did not turn on the constitutional issue. The case was actually decided on the point that the committee's instructions from Congress did not "spell out that group's jurisdiction and purpose with sufficient particularity." The Court thus left the door open to Congress to remedy the situation. But in spite of the narrowness of the decision, Chief Justice Warren, speaking for the Court, made clear that the investigating power itself was subject to constitutional limitations:

> Clearly, an investigation is subject to the command that the Congress shall make no law abridging freedom of speech or press or assembly. While it is true that there is no statute to be reviewed, and that an investigation is not a law, nevertheless an investigation is part of law-making. It is justified solely as an adjunct to the legislative process. The First Amendment may be invoked against infringement of the protected freedoms by law or by lawmaking.

The Court went even further in taking explicit notice of the fact that infringements on civil liberties and due process by legislative investigators must be judged by the social consequences of the investigative process, as well as on narrowly legal considerations:

> Abuses of the investigative process may imperceptibly lead to an abridgment of protected freedom. The mere summoning of a witness and compelling him to testify, against his will, about his beliefs, expressions or associations is a measure of governmental interference. And when those forced revelations concern matters that are unorthodox, unpopular, or even hateful to the general public, the reaction in the life of the witness may be disastrous.

The Court here expressed concern over the tendencies of legislative committees to act like courts of law without extending to witnesses the customary legal procedural guaranties.

The Sweezy case involved a situation in New Hampshire in which the legislature delegated its investigating power to the state's attorney general, who in turn made sweeping inquiries into "un-American" activities in New Hampshire. Among those called before the attorney general, acting as a one-man investigating committee, was Professor Sweezy, who lectured at the University of New Hampshire. The attorney general questioned Mr. Sweezy at length on many subjects, including the content of his classroom lectures. Sweezy refused to answer certain questions on the grounds that his constitutional liberties were being invaded. He was convicted for contempt by the New Hampshire courts, and his case went to the United States Supreme Court.

Chief Justice Warren, speaking for the Court, held that the questions asked Sweezy were an invasion of academic freedom. Warren had reservations about the delegation of power to the attorney general because, in his view, it separated the power to investigate from the power to direct its use. Warren also argued that constitutional protection does extend to legislative investigation:

> There is no doubt that legislative investigations whether on a federal or state level, are capable of encroaching upon the constitutional liberties of individuals. It is particularly important that the exercises of the power of compulsory process be carefully circumscribed when the investigative process tends to impinge upon such highly sensitive areas as freedom of speech or press, freedom of political association, and freedom of communication of ideas, particularly in the academic community.

The concurring opinions of Justices Frankfurter and Harlan denied that the internal affairs of New Hampshire were of concern to the Court and joined the majority only on the grounds of an invasion of Sweezy's rights under the First Amendment.

The trend established in the Watkins and Sweezy cases did not continue, however, for in a series of five-four decisions involving legislative investigations the court upheld contempt convictions and would not allow the First Amendment as sufficient grounds for refusing to answer committee questions.

Two years after the Watkins and Sweezy decisions, the Court had a similar pair of cases before them. One of these was *Uphaus* v. *Wyman*,[24] which again involved the one-man legislative investigating committee of New Hampshire—Attorney General Wyman.

Uphaus ran a summer family camp for a group called "World Fellowship," which had as one of its purposes the discussion of world peace. Uphaus is a lay clergyman who has been a life long pacifist. New Hampshire law requires the preparation by all public facilities of guest registration lists and requires that these lists be available to appropriate officials. Even though the attorney general had access to them, he demanded a guest list from Uphaus, who refused to give it to him. Uphaus was subsequently convicted of civil contempt. In civil contempt cases, the sentence is indefinite. The convicted person has the "key to his release in his pocket," since all he has to do to gain his freedom is comply with the court order:

24360 U. S. 72 (1959).

in this case, to deliver the guest list. The appeal from the conviction went to the Supreme Court and was denied. Justice Clark wrote the opinion of the Court upholding the conviction. He put the interests of government, in this case New Hampshire, above the constitutional provisions of the First Amendment. He said: ". . . the governmental interest in self-preservation is sufficiently compelling to subordinate the interest in associational privacy of persons who, at least to the extent of the guest registration statute, made public at the inception the association they now wish to keep private."

The dissenters would have reversed the conviction. Justice Brennan did not feel that New Hampshire had sufficient grounds to invade the privacy of Mr. Uphaus, particulary since the guest list was already available to the attorney general. Brennan also dealt with the social pressures individuals suffer when brought before investigating committees, simply because they hold views contrary to conventional opinions:

> For in an era of mass communication and mass opinion, and of international tensions and domestic anxiety, exposure and group identification by the state of those holding unpopular and dissident views are frought with such serious consequences for the individual as inevitably to inhibit seriously the expression of views the Constitution intended to make free.

In another 1959 decision, which involved a university professor who had been convicted for refusal to answer, the Court upheld the contempt conviction and backed away from its suggestion in the Sweezy case that academic freedom should be accorded special protection.[25]

In a dissenting opinion, Justice Black again dealt with the social consequences of legislative abuse of witness. His views were similar to those expressed by Warren in his opinion for the Court in the Watkins case, and Brennan in his dissent in the Uphaus case. Justice Black said:

> Finally, I think Barenblatt's conviction violates the Constitution because the chief aim and purpose of the House Un-American Activities Committee, as disclosed by its many reports, is to try witnesses and punish them because they are or have been communists or because they refuse to admit or deny communist affiliations. The punishment imposed is generally punishment by humiliation and public shame. There is nothing strange or novel about this kind of punishment. It is in fact one of the oldest forms of governmental punishment known to mankind; branding, the pillory, ostracism, and subjection to public hatred being but a few examples of it.

On the same day in 1961, the court decided two more cases in which

[25]*Barenblatt* v. *United States*, 360 U. S. 109.

they refused to extend the protection of the First Amendment to witnesses appearing before the House un-American Activities Committee.[26] Both cases resulted from a foray of the Committee into Atlanta, Georgia, in search of "un-Americans." Oddly enough, the committee evidently did not consider the perpetrations of violence by white citizen councils and expedient politicans during racial integration struggles as within its purview, and the two cases which finally reached the Supreme Court both involved integrationists and opponents of the committee itself. Wilkinson, a member of an Emergency Committee on Civil Liberties, had a long record of opposition to the committee. He came to Atlanta to speak against and to organize opposition to the committee and was subpoenaed to appear as a witness. The committee put a series of questions to Wilkinson, all of which he refused to answer on the ground of the First Amendment. He was subsequently tried and convicted for contempt.

The Braden case was similar in that Braden, white integrationist, had sent several letters asking people of both races in the South to write their congressmen protesting the attacks on the Supreme Court which had followed the school desegregation decision and urging that Congress discourage the un-American Activities Committee from harassing integrationists. Braden was called before the committee and refused to answer questions on the grounds of the First Amendment. He, like Wilkinson, was eventually convicted of contempt and his case appealed to the Supreme Court. In both cases, a five-man majority again asserted the Barenblatt decision as ruling and declined to invoke the First Amendment as a defense for refusing to answer the committee's questions. The four dissenters were vigorous in their opposition. Justice Douglas argued that opposition to the committee (quite widespread at the time) was an important factor in the calling up of the witnesses and that such opposition was beyond reach of the committee's legitimate jurisdiction. Justice Black again expressed his fear that the committee's tactics were promoting those conditions in which "government by consent will disappear to be replaced by government by intimidation."

On May 21, 1962, the Supreme Court decided six cases in this area in a single opinion.[27] Four of the cases grew out of investigations of the Internal Security Subcommittee of the Senate Judiciary Committee; the other two involved the House un-American Activities Committee. All the petitioners had been convicted of contempt for refusing to answer questions put by the committees. The Supreme Court held that the

[26]*Wilkinson* v. *United States*, 81 S. Ct. 567; and *Braden* v. *United States*, 81 S. Ct. 584.
[27]*Russell* v. *United States*; *Shelton* v. *United States*; *Whitman* v. *United States*; *Liveright* v. *United States*; *Price* v. *United States*; and *Gojack* v. *United States*, 30 L. W. 4352.

indictments were faulty because they did not state the subject under inquiry by the investigating committee. The constitutional issue of the First Amendment was avoided, but in a concurring opinion Justice Douglas stated "no indictment, however drawn, could in my view be sustained under the requirements of the First Amendment." The dissenters, however, regarded the majority opinion as a serious break with the precedent set in Braden, Wilkinson, and Barenblatt Cases. Justice Clark held that the decision "abruptly breaks with the past."

This decision was not happily received by several congressmen. Democratic Senator John B. McClellan, chairman of a Senate subcommittee which has inquired into many things, including the activities of Teamster Union official James Hoffa and the financial affairs of Billie Sol Estes, was particulary unhappy with the majority opinion of the Court. In a statement to the press, he said:

> The action of the Supreme Court. . . seems to make it crystal clear that Congress cannot rely upon the Courts to punish contumacious witnesses who appear before its committees.
>
> Thus, it appears that in these circumstances the only recourse left to Congress, if it is to have any protection at all, is for it to exercise the inherent power of each House to uphold its own prerogatives and to punish directly contempt or contumacy of witnesses appearing before it.[28]

The court's decision and Senator McClellan's reaction to it may presage a new struggle over the separation of powers.

The present position of the Court involves a basic political conflict. A reluctance to restrict the range of inquiry of investigating committees collides with an obligation to protect individual liberty and due process. The dilemma was well pointed out by Justice Brennan:

> I fully appreciate the delicacy of the judicial task of questioning the workings of a legislative investigation. . . . However, our frame of government also imposes another inescapable duty upon the judiciary, that of protecting the constitutional rights of freedom of speech and assembly from improper invasion, whether by national or state legislatures. [29]

Justice Brennan's statement focuses upon the difficulty of the court's role as the guardian of due process working in a context of separated political power. The Court's inability to translate its concern for due process into rules restraining the investigative power is understandable. Regular standards of law and evidence would provide a straight-jacket, seriously

[28]Los Angeles *Times*, May 23, 1962, p. 26.
[29]*Uphaus* v. *Wyman*, 360 U. S. 72 (1959).

crippling the legitimate ends of legislative investigations. Self-restraint by the legislature, in the circumstances, seems the most effective restraint.

It is doubtful whether more vigorous and strict judicial application of the First Amendment and the rules of due process to individual cases would very effectively deal with the problem which has concerned Warren, Black, or Douglas. The most serious invasions of liberty and due process which have ensued from investigations involve, in Justice Black's words, the "disastrous" consequences "in the life of the witness." The courts cannot devise and enforce constitutional rules which could protect individuals against a suspicious and intolerant public. In such a political climate, the power to subpoena and compel testimony can result in social "punishment" even if formal constitutional restraints are enforced. The courts, however, might still play the political role of reminding or persuading legislators and the public of the importance of individual liberties and due process of law in a democratic society.

THE SUPREME COURT AS ORACLE: EQUAL PROTECTION OF THE LAW

THE CAPSTONE OF JUSTICE in the United States is the Supreme Court. Other courts must concern themselves with constitutional issues, but it is the Supreme Court which has the final and authoritative power to interpret the Constitution. This function requires that the Justices of the Court make interpretations and pronouncements on the meaning of the Constitution. They must not only declare what it legally requires but what it morally implies.

The function of extracting moral implications places the justices in the role of oracles. As we pointed out earlier, the Constitution has been approached differently by various justices. Some shy away from their oracular function and prefer to concentrate on legalities or, at least, to shroud their moral judgments in legalistic technicalities. Others look to the Constitution as much more than a legal document and emphasize the view that it is a set of basic principles by which men conduct their political lives.

We have noted earlier that the Supreme Court has exercised its oracular function differently during various historical periods. During its early period, the Court used its power to establish the operating framework of separated power and a federal system of government. During much of the nineteenth and early twentieth centuries, it protected private property from the onslaught of social reform. The New Deal of Franklin Roosevelt saw it briefly hold the line against the bloodless revolution in traditional relationships of the government to private sectors of the society. But even after its self-restraint in the mid-1930's—the "switch in time that saved nine"—when the court was threatened with enlargement, it did not give up its oracular function.

Its new focus in the middle of the twentieth century has been upon the civil rights and liberties of citizens. About the middle of the 1950's, the Court made a pronouncement that has rocked the nation when it decided that racial segregation in public schools must end. Segregation had been ended by the Court in many areas, but the final blow came in 1954 with the decision that segregated schools are incompatible with the Fourteenth Amendment. The decision illustrates how the Court can overturn long-established precedents and cut across the grain of accepted social customs. Attacks on the court were many and varied, but they tended to divide themselves into two categories. One type of attack held that in playing oracle, the justices had usurped a power that properly belongs in the legislature. The other group held that the justices were bad oracles.

In the following section, we pause to review the position of the judiciary in the history of racial segregation as an illustration of the Court's oracular role.

The Constitutional and Political Background of Segregation

The emancipation of the slaves and the passage of the Thirteenth, Fourteenth, and Fifteenth Amendments, which, respectively, outlawed slavery, extended "equal protection of the laws" to citizens of all states, and guaranteed the right to vote to all citizens of the United States regardless of "race, color or previous condition of servitude" did not liberate the Negro from discrimination. In 1866, Congress passed a civil rights act shortly before it passed the Fourteenth Amendment. The law was designed to give Negroes equality in the courts and in commercial activities. In part it read:

> Citizens of every race and color [shall have] the same right in every State and Territory . . . to make and enforce contracts, to sue, be parties, and give evidence, to inherit, purchase, lease, sell, hold, and convey real and personal property, and to full and equal benefit of all laws and proceedings for the security of person and property, as is enjoyed by white citizens, and shall be subject to like punishment, pains, and penalties and to none other . . . .

Between 1866 and 1875, a total of five civil rights and reconstruction acts were passed by the "radical Congress" which were aimed at giving the Negro immediate equality and at thwarting the efforts of state legislatures to curtail the Negroes' rights. The stormy period of reconstruction following the Civil War was one of rising racial tension, particularly in the old Confederacy, and a long contest between Congress and the states developed over the rights of former slaves.

In 1875, Congress passed a civil rights act designed to prevent any public form of discrimination against Negroes. The law provided that all persons regardless of race or color were entitled to the "full and equal enjoyment of accommodations, advantages, facilities, and privileges of inns, public conveyances on land or water, theatres, and other places of public amusements." This law was based upon the assumption that Congress had the power to enact legislation that would enforce the Fourteenth Amendment, not only by negating state action but also by affirmatively forbidding private individuals from exercising discrimination.

The Supreme Court disagreed, however, and in 1883 it declared the Civil Rights Act of 1875 unconstitutional.[30] Justice Bradley wrote the court's opinion, which held that the Fourteenth Amendment meant that Congress could only enact corrective legislation where states had violated the Amendment's provisions. The opinion held also that Congress had no power to enact "primary and direct" legislation—that is, to pre-empt power to legislate on the subject of equal accommodations. Following this line of narrow construction, the opinion stated that the Civil Rights Act "superceded and displaced" state legislation rather than just corrected it:

> It [the Civil Rights Act] ignores such legislation, and assumes that the matter is one that belongs to the domain of national regulation. . . . What we have to decide is, whether such plenary power has been conferred upon Congress by the Fourteenth Amendment, and, in our judgment, it has not.

In a lone and lengthy dissent, Justice John M. Harlan stated that the Court's opinion was "too narrow and artificial" and that "the substance and spirit of recent amendments of the Constitution have been sacrificed by a subtle and ingenious verbal criticism." Harlan made a well-documented argument that the Court had inadequately interpreted the intent of the constitutional amendments. His interpretation of the Thirteenth and Fourteenth Amendments included the following:

> If the constitutional amendments be enforced, according to the intent with which, as I conceive, they were adopted, there cannot be, in this republic, any class of human beings in practical subjection to another class, with power in the latter to dole out to the former just such privileges as they may choose to grant. The supreme law of the land has decreed that no authority shall be exercised in this country upon the basis of discrimination, in respect to civil

[30]*Civil Rights Cases,* 109 U. S. 3 (1883).

rights .... To that decree—for the due enforcement of which, by appropriate legislation, Congress has been invested with express power—everyone must bow....[31]

The majority of the court in the Civil Rights Cases ignored these fine words, however, and only Harlan would have followed them.

To modern men, Justice Harlan's views probably sound more logical and correct. But they have been a long time gaining acceptance. With the blessings of the majority opinion of the court, restrictions of all sorts in the areas prohibited by the 1875 Act befell the Negro. In fact, recent bus boycotts, the 1960 demonstrations or "sit-ins" by Negroes protesting discrimination in restaurants and stores, and the 1962 "freedom rides" indicate how long this discrimination has lasted.

After the Civil Rights Cases and the resurgence of southern political power in Congress following the Reconstruction Era, civil rights legislation lapsed. Post-Civil War legislation dealing with civil rights was almost eliminated by 1910, through judicial construction as well as legislative modification. It was not until late in the 1950's that Congress made serious legislative attempts to restore some degree of equality to the Negro and other minority groups. In 1956, the House of Representatives passed a civil rights bill (H.R. 627), but it did not reach the Senate. In 1957, a civil rights bill was passed. In 1960, after much manuevering and some filibustering, a stronger civil rights bill was enacted. Both of these laws were passed under the authority of Congress to enforce the Thirteenth, Fourteenth, and Fifteenth Amendments "by appropriate legislation" and will no doubt call for broader judicial interpretation than the Civil Rights Cases gave to it.[32]

[31]Harlan's protest against narrow construction of the Fourteenth Amendment was against a trend the Court had established in the Slaughter House Cases, 16 Wall 36 (1873), in which the court decided that state legislation (Louisiana) granting a monopoly to one firm to slaughter all animals in the New Orleans area did not abuse the privilege and immunities of some one thousand butchers who were thus denied work. In the majority opinion, Justice Miller offered: "In the light of the history of these amendments . . . it is not difficult to give a meaning to this clause [equal protection of the laws]. The existence of laws in the States where the newly emancipated Negroes resided, which discriminated with gross injustice and hardship against them as a class, was the evil to be remedied by this clause, and by it such laws were forbidden."
[32]One analysis of the Civil Rights Cases states that the opinion "served notice that the federal government could not lawfully protect the Negro against the discrimination which private individuals might choose to exercise against him. This was another way of saying that the system of white supremacy was mainly beyond federal control." Alfred H. Kelly and Winfred A. Harbison, *The American Constitution, Its Origins and Development* (New York: Norton, 1948), p. 491. Present civil rights laws are aimed at state laws and practices, but such things as fair employment legislation would affect private individuals and groups.

During the long period of congressional inactivity in the area of civil rights, the status of these provisions depended primarily upon judicial construction. The narrow interpretation of both the Slaughter House Cases and the Civil Rights Cases gave the southern states a basis for enacting a number of laws restricting the freedom of the Negro. Such things as the grandfather clause,[33] poll taxes, the all-white primary, elaborate tests to qualify for voting, and other laws and ordinances authorizing segregation of the races were passed. Segregation of the races was given judicial sanction in *Plessy* v. *Ferguson*,[34] which upheld a Louisiana statute requiring railroads to provide separate cars for the two races. The Court held that separate but equal facilities were not incompatible with the Fourteenth Amendment. In fact, Justice Brown in the majority opinion held that segregation had nothing to do with superiority or inferiority. The opinion stated:

> We consider the underlying fallacy of the plaintiff's argument to consist in the assumption that enforced separation of the two races stamps the colored race with a badge of inferiority. If this be so, it is not by reason of anything found in the act, but solely because the colored race chooses to put that construction upon it.
>
> If one race be inferior to another socially the Constitution of the United States cannot put them upon the same plane.

Only Justice Harlan, as in the Civil Rights Cases, dissented. He attacked the reasoning of the Court and argued that segregation recognized classes based upon race, and that "our Constitution is color blind": "The law regards man as man, and takes no account of his surroundings or of his color when his civil rights as guaranteed by the supreme law of the land are involved."

Plessy v. *Ferguson* helped racial segregation become a southern tradition. For a long time, the doctrine of separate but equal lay unmolested although there was growing awareness that while "separate" was well enforced, "equal" was not. Negro facilities were remarkably inferior, and Negroes were often denied an equitable share of tax-supported services and facilities.[35]

By the late 1930's, the court began to take a close look at "equal"

---

[33]There were several versions of the grandfather clause, but generally they required descendants of persons who were not qualified to vote before or during the Civil War to pass a maze of literacy and other tests which the rest of the population did not have to take. The court ruled the grandfather clause illegal in both *Guinn* v. *United States*, 238 U. S. 347 (1915) and again in *Lane* v. *Wilson*, 307 U. S. 268 (1939). Both cases applied to Oklahoma's attempts to use this "sophisticated" means of discrimination, as Justice Frankfurter called it.

[34]163 U. S. 537 (1896).

[35]President's Committee on Civil Rights, *To Secure These Rights*, pp. 81-82.

facilities. In *Missouri* ex. rel. *Gaines* v. *Canada*,[36] the Court decided that since Missouri had no law school for Negroes it must admit them to its white law school. Like many southern states, Missouri paid the tuition of Negro law students at law schools in other states which accepted them. The court held that this practice did not provide equal treatment to residents of the same state. Equality was denied solely on the basis of color. White students had a law school in Missouri. Negro residents of Missouri were obliged to be educated in the law in another state. Thus there was not equal treatment.

This same doctrine was asserted in *Sipuel* v. *University of Oklahoma*,[37] and in 1950 the court went a step farther and held that Negroes could not be segregated after being admitted to a graduate school.[38] Separate but equal suffered another blow in *Henderson* v. *United States*,[39] where the court ruled that segregation of Negroes in railroad dining cars under rules of the Interstate Commerce Commission denied equal treatment of the races.

The Plessy doctrine was, in short, increasingly and steadily being weakened by judicial decisions. In *Sweatt* v. *Painter*,[40] the court laid the foundation for the final reversal of the separate but equal doctrine. In this case, Sweatt, a Negro, was denied admission to the University of Texas Law School, and when he sued to be admitted he was turned down by the lower court on the grounds that Texas was building a law school for Negroes. The Texas courts all refused to grant Sweatt's request on the grounds that separate but equal facilities would soon be available. When the case reached the United States Supreme Court, Chief Justice Vinson's opinion for the Court carefully compared the facilities of the existing law school with those being prepared for Negroes. He found that the latter would be in no way "equal" to the established law school and reversed the Texas courts. Vinson, however, carefully avoided a re-examination of the rule of *Plessy* v. *Ferguson*, and the case turned narrowly on the point that the Negro law school would not be equal to the white law school.

Judicial Enforcement of Equality

In 1954, the final reversal of *Plessy* v. *Ferguson* was carried out by the Supreme Court in *Brown et. al.* v. *Board of Education*.[41] In effect, the decision foreshadowed an end to the pattern of segregation of the South.

[36]305 U. S. 337 (1938)
[37]332 U. S. 631 (1948).
[38]*McLaurin* v. *Oklahoma State Regents*, 339 U. S. 637 (1950).
[39]339 U. S. 816 (1950).
[40]339 U. S. 629 (1950).
[41] 347 U. S. 483.

Since this decision, the whole structure of racial segregation, which reposed on the separate but equal doctrine, has been weakened. "Sit-ins," boycotts, and other protests by the Negro press the issue of equality, and when cases come to the federal courts, "separate but equal" no longer provides a convenient way out of the difficulty.

The resulting struggle, aside from its sporadic violence, involves an intense debate over the judicial process. It raises questions, for example, about the role of precedent in the decisions of judges. The pattern of precedent, or *stare decisis*, regarding school facilities for different races had been at one time on the side of separate facilities for the races. "Separate but equal" was the clear precedent for many years, with the courts permitting a strict enforcement of "separate" on a loose interpretation of "equal." In the *Brown* case, equality of facilities was challenged directly; and the court, finding some precedent in the law but more justification in psychological and sociological theory, decided that separate but equal was incompatible with the "equal protection of the laws" of the Fourteenth Amendment to the Constitution.

Since the Brown decision, the whole structure of American political life has begun to deal more specifically with the rights and liberties of minority groups. Congress and many state legislatures are passing laws aimed at the various remaining areas of discrimination, though almost never without heated struggles. The executive branch of government in several states as well as in the federal government has tightened up the enforcement of antidiscrimination statutes. Both political partites deal with the issue of discrimination in their platforms.

The Supreme Court, in short, has helped make the subject of equal rights and race relations an unavoidable part of political discourse through its decisions on the subject. The exercise of its oracular role has made the Court, in this area, more than the final appellate jurisdiction in the judicial hierarchy. In often eloquent opinions, it declares the moral postulates at issue in the cases which come before it. Sometimes, the values expressed reveal sentiments held by individual justices which they try to impose upon the rest of society. Sometimes the moral position asserted by the Court leaves doubt and confusion among many segments of society. The Court can hold back surges of social reform, but it can also force social changes more rapidly than some would prefer. But whether or not one agrees with Supreme Court interpretations of moral issues, most citizens have a high respect for the Court as an oracular institution. Indeed, when other political agencies default, it often falls to the Court to introduce moral questions into political dialogue. Both majority opinions and sharp dissents are high quality fuel for the democratic machinery through which public issues are debated.

THE SUPREME COURT AS UMPIRE:
FREEDOM VERSUS NATIONAL SECURITY

THE SUPREME COURT does not always find clear meaning in the Constitution from which it can make oracular pronouncements. The Constitution means different things to different justices, which often causes them vigorously to contest one another's views and to divide themselves into two or more groups of oracles.

This division often results from the ambiguity of the Constitution itself. Constitutional provisions are subject to such a variety of interpretations that very often the principles derived by different justices collide. For example, the essence of the Constitution—that is, all its provisions—are held by some justices to put national security and preservation of the government above any specific constitutional provision, such as the First Amendment. Other justices, however, consider the freedoms of the First Amendment, particularly freedom of speech, to be so basic to democratic government that only the most extreme abuse of this liberty would justify curtailing it.

If national security comes into conflict with free speech, it must be assumed that free speech can threaten this security. Speech advocating extreme positions, such as the overthrow of the government by force and violence, must then be curtailed. It is here the justices face the great difficulty of finding proper grounds for making exceptions to the rule of free speech.

Earlier we discussed the development by Justice Holmes of a "clear and present danger" test as one which would permit exceptions to free speech. This test would require a showing that the words in question would pose an immediate threat of substantive evils which Congress is empowered to prevent—falsely shouting fire in a crowded theatre was his example. In subsequent cases, however, the Court substantially diluted this doctrine as it confronted particularly difficult decisions regarding the relative merits of free speech and national security.

The cases which follow illustrate some of the approaches which Supreme Court justices have taken to this problem. To umpire these constitutional conflicts the court is unable to ignore the potential violence of mob action and the inflamed passions and fears which can result from an unlimited freedom of speech. The record of such happenings cannot help but make anyone wonder when the appropriate time to gag a speaker arrives. The temptation is, at times, almost irresistible, and the problem has caused much soul searching by our Supreme Court justices.

A good example of a responsible concern over the possible civil chaos to which uninhibited free speech could lead was contained in Justice Jackson's dissent in *Terminiello* v. *Chicago*.[42] Terminiello was a defrocked Catholic priest who specialized in anti-Semitic tirades and splenetic blasts at both the Roosevelt Administration and the Roosevelt family. He was a disciple of hate-monger Gerald L. K. Smith. At the time of his arrest, he was speaking to a large audience of believers while a mob of non-believers picketed the building outside, charged the doors, and threw rocks at the windows of the auditorium.

Terminiello was subsequently arrested under a city ordinance for causing a riot. He was later convicted and his conviction was upheld by the Illinois appellate courts. The Supreme Court reversed the Illinois courts on the ground that the ordinance was faulty. Justice Jackson, recently returned from his duties as allied prosecutor at the Nuremberg war crime trials of high-ranking Nazis, dissented sharply. He held the incident "was a local manifestation of a world-wide and standing conflict between two organized groups of revolutionary fanatics, each of which has imported to this country the strong-arm technique developed in the struggle by which their kind has devastated Europe." In answer to the majority of the Court, Jackson had this to say:

> This court has gone far toward accepting the doctrine that civil liberty means the removal of all restraints from these crowds and that all local attempts to maintain order are impairments of the liberty of the citizen. The choice is not between order and liberty. It is between liberty with order and anarchy without either. There is danger that, if the court does not temper its doctrinaire logic with a little practical wisdom, it will convert the constitutional Bill of Rights into a suicide pact.

The concern Justice Jackson expressed was reflected in a series of decisions, made by the Supreme Court during the 1950's, dealing with the relationship of free speech to subversion. One of these cases involved a test of a provision in the Taft-Hartley Act requiring all union officials to sign a noncommunist affidavit.[43]

The Court, speaking through Chief Justice Vinson, upheld the loyalty oath provision on the ground that it was a reasonable protection of the security of the nation. Vinson said that if constitutional government ". . . is to survive it must have the power to protect itself against unlawful conduct and, under some circumstances, incitements to commit unlawful acts. Freedom of speech thus does not comprehend the right to speak on any subject at any time."

Justice Jackson in a concurring opinion made a distinction between

---

[42] 337 U. S. 1 (1949).
[43] *American Communications Association* v. *Douds*, 339 U. S. 382 (1950).

the Communist Party and other political parties and concluded that the requirement of an affidavit was reasonable for the Communist Party, because it advocates the overthrow of the government. Justice Black, who holds a different view of the First Amendment, dissented on the ground that "not the least of the virtues of the First Amendment is its protection of each member of the smallest and most unorthodox minority."

Another case in which the court was faced with the problem of subversion was *Dennis* v. *United States*.[44] Dennis and ten other Communists had been convicted under the Smith Act of 1940, which made advocacy of the overthrow of the government by force or violence a crime. Chief Justice Vinson spoke for the Court and again argued that national security is essential to any kind of freedom. He said:

> Overthrow of the government by force and violence is certainly a substantial enough interest for the government to limi. speech. Indeed this is the ultimate value for any society, for if a society cannot protect its very structure from armed internal attack, it must follow that no subordinate value can be protected.

Vinson's decision again brought a sharp dissent from Justice Black, who challenged the whole concept of "reasonableness" which was emerging as a justifiable judicial test to limit free speech:

> So long as this court exercises the power of judicial review of legislation, I cannot agree that the First Amendment permits us to sustain laws suppressing freedom of speech on the basis of Congress' or our own notions of mere "reasonableness." Such a doctrine waters down the First Amendment so that it amounts to little more than an admonition to Congress. The Amendment as so construed is not likely to protect any but those "safe" or orthodox views which rarely need its protection. . . .

The issue of curtailing free speech came up again in *Feiner* vs. *New York*,[45] when a zealous graduate student from Syracuse University was arrested for haranguing a comparatively small crowd on the streets of Syracuse. Chief Justice Vinson, speaking for the majority and using the test of reasonableness, said he agreed with the trial court's findings that a "clear danger of disorder" existed and that Feiner had defied the police officers who told him to stop speaking after a member of the audience threatened to do it himself. But what price do we pay for order? The consequences of casting freedom to speak, however violently, against the desire for order and tranquility, and having the former give way to the latter, are disturbing to many believers in democratic theories of

[44]341 U. S. 494 (1951).
[45]340 U. S. 315 (1951).

government. If this were to be the test, all one would have to do to stop a speech would be to mill around the speaker in a disorderly fashion.

The Vinson Court was sharply divided on the issue of civil liberties. The fear of cynical use of liberty to cover up plans to curtail democracy and the assertion that it is the unpopular and noxious opinions which must be protected if freedom of speech is to mean anything are fundamental differences in political philosophy. Under Chief Justice Warren, the Court has been more favorably disposed to First Amendment freedoms. The trend established in the Douds, Dennis, and Feiner cases was temporarily halted in *Yates* v. *United States.*[46] In this case, the Court held that the Smith Act, under which Dennis had been convicted, did not outlaw the abstract theory of overthrow of the government. Justice Harlan said that to be punishable under the Smith Act advocacy must go beyond a mere belief in "violent revolution" and must urge others "to do something, now or in the future, rather than merely to believe something." Justice Black, with the concurrence of Justice Douglas, went further to state: "The First Amendment provides the only kind of security system that can preserve a free government—one that leaves the way open for people to favor, discuss, advocate or incite to causes and doctrines however obnoxious and antagonistic such views may be to the rest of us."

Justice Black's view of the meaning of the First Amendment differs sharply from the position taken by Chief Justice Vinson and others who feel that the ultimate necessity for national security requires a reasonable interpretation of specific constitutional provisions. To Justice Black, the First Amendment is a first principle of democratic government which means just what it says. This he oraculary proclaims in a clear and often eloquent voice.

Chief Justice Vinson's view of a reasonable interpretation of First Amendment liberties holds that they are by no means absolute but relative to his oracular view that a secure nation comes first.

The relativism inherent in the test of reasonableness was subsequently further developed into the judicial doctrine of balance. In the Barenblatt case, Justice Harlan, speaking for the court, made both national security and free speech relative and put the Court in the role of umpire. Upholding Barenblatt's conviction, he commented: "We conclude that the balance between the individual and the governmental interests here at stake must be struck in favor of the latter, and that therefore the provisions of the First Amendment have not been offended."

Justice Black responded with this:

To apply the court's balancing test under such circumstances is to read the First Amendment to say "Congress shall pass no law

[46]354 U. S. 298 (1957).

abridging freedom of speech, press, assembly, and petition, unless Congress and the Supreme Court reach the joint conclusion that on balance the interest of the Government in stifling these freedoms is greater than the interests of the people in having them exercised." This is closely akin to the notion that neither the First Amendment nor any other provision of the Bill of Rights should be enforced unless the court believes it is *reasonable* to do so.

The controversy over umpiring civil liberties cases, which often narrowly divides the Court, is just one area where the Court balances the legal claims before it. The Court must adjust conflicts between various private sectors of society, as well as between government and individuals or groups.

THE JUDICIAL PROCESS AS BROKERAGE

OFTEN THE DOCTRINE of reasonableness or balance puts the court in the role of compromiser or broker of conflicting claims over what the law means. In fact, this doctrine has been expanded into a theory of jurisprudence which sees the law and the courts as simply "one more level of official compromise in the never-ending march and counter-march, thrust and parry, among economic groups, enforcement agencies, legislators, and executive functionaries."[47] This position defines the function of the courts in the minorities rule model of democracy. Thus Bentley, the father of the modern theory of broker rule, saw law as the outcome of the political process of adaptation of group interests in which the process of pressure exerted "by group against group" has worked itself out into a provisional balance.[48]

According to this theory, the balancing of interests is the central task of the judge, just as it is of the politician. In this process, the judge, like the politician, must posit the equal legitimacy of all competing claims. On this assumption, the judge then "should aim at all times, and in all the compromises and adjustments and reconcilings involved in the legal order, to give effect to as much of the whole body of social interests as possible."[49]

This balancing theory of the law gets credence from the fact that the traditional balancing goddess of the law is blind. But this need not imply,

[47]Latham, *The Group Basis of Politics*, p. 53.

[48]Bentley, *The Process of Government*, p. 272.

[49]Roscoe Pound, in Felix S. Cohen, *Ethical Systems and Legal Ideals: An Essay on the Foundations of Legal Criticism* (Ithaca: Great Seal, 1959), p. 5, note 6. Cohen develops an able criticism of Pound's views.

as the theory of balance assumes, that justice, any more than the public interest, is simply the automatic product of group accommodation. The courts may seek to conserve traditional concepts of justice, or they may seek to elaborate new ones. In either case, they are seeking standards which transcend and regulate group conflict. This is clearly the case in the Court's desegregation decision or its restrictions on searches and seizures. The court was not serving, in the latter case, as "one more level of official compromise" between the interests of law enforcement agencies, lawyers, the American Civil Liberties Union, and criminals; it was asserting a principle of justice. Both conservatives and majoritarians would regard this as the central function of the courts, although the majoritarian would argue that legal principles should be responsible to the political process.

THE JUDICIAL PROCESS AND MAJORITY RULE

Chief Justice Hughes once suggested that the "law is what the Court says it is." If so, even a government of laws is rule by men. Within the discipline of the law, it is they who will ultimately decide which balance scales to use. As Justice Frankfurter declared:

Judges are men, not disembodied spirits. Of course a judge is not free from preferences or, if you will, biases. But he may deprive a bias of its meretricious authority by stripping it of the uncritical assumption that it is founded on compelling reason or the conceived power of a syllogism. He will be alert to detect that though a conclusion has a logical form it in fact represents a choice of competing considerations of policy, one of which for the time has won the day.[50]

Choosing among competing considerations of policy involves an assessment by the judge of his place in the structure of American government. To many judges, the right of a majority to enact laws through legislatures must be regarded as a principle to be preserved even though the laws might be foolish. To others, the role of oracle requires the judge to overrule legislative and executive action where it collides with a judicial interpretation of the Constitution.

The judicial process is not a simple one, and the judge often finds he is without the necessary rules and procedures which would make it easier. Former Supreme Court Justice Cardozo summed it up well:

[50]Felix Frankfurter, "Some Observations on the Nature of the Judicial Process of Supreme Court Litigation," in Alan F. Westin (ed.), *The Supreme Court: Views from the Inside* (New York: Norton, 1961), p. 41.

"They do things better with logarithms." The wail escapes me now and again after putting forth the best that is in me, I look upon the finished product, and cannot say that it is good.

I have given my years to the task, and behind me are untold generations, the judges and lawgivers of old, who strove with a passion as burning. Code and commentary, manor roll and year book, treatise and law-report, reveal the processes of trial and error by which they struggled to attain the truth, enshrine their blunders and their triumphs for warning and example.[51]

Cardozo's sigh for a logarithm is a wistful plea for the certainty of exactness which comes from the iron laws of mathematics applied to problems. It would be much easier and more comfortable to do it this way, but a judge true to his calling, as Cardozo recognized, must be denied such comfort. He has to follow "right reason," sometimes to the point of being unreasonable.

The power of the courts and the discretion of judges raises fundamental questions about the relationships of the judiciary to majority rule. The courts can thwart social reform, or they can overturn established customs. They can defy majority demands for changes in the *status quo*, or they can press the sensitive nerve of a national guilt complex about the second-class treatment of a racial minority. Is such power, exercised by "nine old men" who are removed from public control, compatible with the principles of popular sovereignty and majority rule?

The key to this question, we believe, lies in the realization that the actual political power of the courts will be determined by how citizens, politicians, and political parties view the role of the courts. If the justices are seen as oracles, whose decisions are authoritative pronouncements of the true meaning of the Constitution and of public morality, their decisions will replace public debate and responsible political processes.

On the other hand, if the commitment to democratic processes is deeply rooted and widely shared, the role of the judiciary will be seen as that of clarifying social values and public issues. In these circumstances, judicial decisions may put the focus on an issue which will require the majority not only to think about it but let its views be known. The courts can act as both a brake and accelerator upon popular demands and force a value judgment on issues which otherwise might be expediently avoided. The Supreme Court is an elite; but an elite of oracles can serve a majority, either as a goad to action or as a conscience to stop hysterical overaction. Responsible government may be threatened where the judges' views of public morality are made the law of the land. Responsible government is destroyed where judge-made law becomes an authoritative and

---

[51]Benjamin N. Cardozo, *The Paradoxes of Legal Science* (New York: Columbia University Press, 1928), pp. 1-2.

closed definition of the public interest no longer subject to public debate and modification by statute or constitutional amendment. The law may be "what the court says it is." Behind the law and the judges, however, there stands a higher court of appeal—the sovereign tribunal of public opinion.

15

THE NEW AGENDA
OF
DEMOCRATIC POLITICS

W̲ᴇ ᴀʀᴇ ᴇɴɢᴀɢᴇᴅ, ᴀʟʟ ᴏᴠᴇʀ ᴛʜᴇ ᴡᴏʀʟᴅ, in a defense of the Western conception of freedom and democracy. Our problem is that we are not at all clear whether in defending democracy we are defending hot dogs, baseball, and Mom's apple pie or the rights of man. And if the latter, what are these rights specifically, and how are they to be realized in a political system?

At the root of our problem is the fact that the actual political system, as we are able to observe it in operation today, is at fundamental odds with the traditional ideas and assumptions on which democratic government was founded. This crisis in the traditional order of democratic politics raises a whole new range of questions.

UNFINISHED BUSINESS OF THE OLD ORDER

Rᴏᴜɢʜʟʏ, ꜰʀᴏᴍ ᴛʜᴇ ᴇɴᴅ ᴏꜰ ᴛʜᴇ ᴄɪᴠɪʟ ᴡᴀʀ ᴛᴏ ᴡᴏʀʟᴅ ᴡᴀʀ ɪɪ, the political system itself was unquestioned. The problems of politics involved, for the most part, the use of existing political arrangements to extend

411

political and economic opportunities to a wider range of citizens. There remains some unfinished business on the agenda of this traditional order: the extension of full political and civil rights to minority racial groups, particularly the Negro, and the use of governmental power to improve the conditions and opportunities of the unorganized who have not shared in the growing affluence of American society. At the same time, the brokerage character of political processes makes the solution of these problems difficult. Indeed, they remain as problems because, in the nature of the case, they do not respond to brokerage solutions.

The plight of the Negro, for example, can only be intensified, not resolved, by seeing Negroes as an interest group entitled to have their private claims weighed fairly against the claims of other organized groups. The National Association for the Advancement of Colored People was not begun as a Negro organization, but as a nonracial organization for the promotion of an ideal held to be valid for all. The principle of equal rights can never be achieved by a Negro lobby, or represented in politics by the response of politicians to the Negro vote in the large industrial areas outside the South. If the problem is approached within the framework of "countervailing power" and the compromise of group interests, the "American dilemma" and the international embarrassment which results from it can only be endlessly prolonged.

A similar problem exists with those groups which have not shared very fully in the affluence of the economy. These are the groups of people who are not organized, for whom organization is difficult, and who, even if they were organized, would be dwarfed by the political bargaining power of rival groups. They include migrant farm workers, technologically displaced unskilled workers, and the elderly. They are, in a sense, the "left-overs" from a system of minorities rule. Such groups are unable to acquire the recognized status of minorities and, even if they were, they would not be dealt fully into the game. Since their present situation is largely the result of the operation of broker rule, it is unlikely to be relieved by continued application of the same rules.

If effective political organization as pressure groups is impossible or unlikely for some, the other side of the coin is the situation in which the power of effectively organized groups is not matched by the countervailing power of other groups, and is not likely to be. The farm bloc, for example, is well organized and politically effective. The farm program, on the other hand, is generally admitted to be a colossal and irrational failure. If the interests of farmers are well attended to, the same cannot be said for the public interest in the rational management of farm surpluses and effective land use and conservation. These are public problems which are not susceptible of solution through political processes that respond only to group and constituency interests.

THE NEW PROBLEMS OF POLITICS

IT MAY STILL BE ARGUED THAT THE BROKERAGE PROCESS HAS, on the whole, successfully allocated political power and economic advantage to produce a sharing of the economic pie compatible with a rapid increase in its size. The left-overs aside, American politics has been a successful instrument for the solution of economic problems. But democracy cannot afford to minimize the importance of finding ways of dealing with the remaining pockets of privation and poverty. Solutions will depend on the working of political instruments through which these are seen as public problems rather than simply as private grievances.

The major problems of politics in the years ahead, however, will no longer be primarily economic. The growth of delinquency, crime, alcoholism, and drug addiction rates makes clear that poverty is not the root of all evil. Universal education has not produced a cure-all for ignorance and indifference; some say it has not even been a solution to illiteracy. The growth of the metropolis has been scarred by urban blight and the frustrations of suburban commuters. The wealthiest people in the history of the world live in communities that are seldom graced by beauty and charm and are often blighted by neglect and the absence of civic pride.

American economic affluence is no mean achievement, and is not to be underestimated. We mean rather to emphasize that our very achievements have created a new range of problems, and that these problems will not respond to the political processes of group accommodation which have been so effective in producing our affluence. If this is true of such problems as migrant labor, civil liberties, crime and delinquency, alcoholism, and urban renewal, it is even more true of a whole range of problems associated with America's involvement in international politics.

The Challenge of Foreign Policy

Since the end of World War I, the United States has found itself increasingly involved in world affairs. This involvement was neither sought nor welcomed by many strong forces within the nation. Isolationism to which the country succumbed when President Wilson tried to lead it into the League of Nations, operated to put off the day when the United States would assume the international responsibilities that her power, wealth, and influence required. The rise of dictators between the wars and the appalling degradation of human dignity which accompanied their crude nationalism proved that a powerful democratic society cannot retreat from foreign entanglements if it is to survive. World War II not only pitted two powerful military alliances against each other, but it also tested the vitality of political institutions constructed around the notion that free men can govern themselves. One brand of dictatorship was defeated. But the "brave new world" which we faced in 1945 has developed a new division of power and a political cleavage which has left both sides angrily contesting for influence, alliances, and military establishments capable of wreaking almost unimaginable destruction on each other.

The problems created by international tension and the challenge of communism have become the major concerns of domestic politics. In addition, all other internal problems must now be seen in the light of their international implications. It has long been traditional to distinguish between domestic problems and foreign problems. Indeed, the constitutional structure of the federal government provides different processes for the consideration of these two categories. Now, however, defense production and its relation to the national economy, diplomatic relationships, foreign aid, racial problems, the exploration of outer space—all have implications for the Cold War. Senator Hubert H. Humphrey emphasized the meshing of foreign and domestic policy when, in discussing the role of the Senate in foreign policy, he said:

> Foreign policy was an occasional and tangential function of the Senate in the eighteenth and nineteenth centuries. Today the mind and will of the Senate are never free from the burdens of the United States in the vast realm beyond the borders of its legal jurisdiction. The old distinction between *domestic* policies and *foreign* policies has given way to a new concept of *national* policies, each of which bears upon the course of events at home and abroad. The understanding of our national character and purposes abroad is deeply affected by laws dealing with immigration, civil rights, tariffs, subsidies, and other "domestic" matters. Our capacity to lend substance to our stated goals is determined to no little extent by tax and budget laws.[1]

The entanglement of domestic and foreign issues is well illustrated by the relationship of defense production to the health of the national economy. Out of the Cold War and balance of terror have come a series of decisions to accelerate defense production in all phases. In the early stages of the Cold War, Harvard economist Sumner Slichter, commented: It "... increases the demand for goods, helps sustain a high level of employment, accelerates technological progress and thus helps the country to raise its standard of living. . . .So we can thank the Russians for helping make capitalism in the United States work better than ever."[2]

In the period that followed, the crash program for the development

---

[1]H. H. Humphrey, "The Senate in Foreign Policy," *Foreign Affairs,* July, 1959, p. 526.
[2]From an address to a bankers' convention in 1949. Quoted in Fred J. Cook, "Juggernaut: The Warfare State," *The Nation,* October 28, 1961, p. 300.

of a hydrogen bomb, the development of delivery systems, the race into space, and foreign military and nonmilitary aid programs have all operated to underwrite economic prosperity.

On the other side, it has become gradually apparent that the struggle against communism is not exclusively, nor even primarily, a military struggle. Its crucial dimensions are political, ideological, and economic. This means that a just, healthy, and expanding economy is itself an instrument of American influence, as well as a necessary base for foreign economic and technological aid programs. Continued racial discrimination is perhaps our major national liability in the underdeveloped countries of Asia, Africa, and Latin America. Economic recession, unemployment, and unused industrial capacity would also make more plausible the communist claim to provide superior methods of social organization.

Democracy and the Warfare State

The prosperity which has been stimulated by the defense economy raises new and serious political problems. President Eisenhower, in his last major presidential address, issued a solemn warning of the dangers associated with the development of a military-industrial complex which permeates almost every facet of American life. The United States, he noted, had been compelled to "create a permanent armaments industry of vast proportions" and to maintain a defense establishment of three and one-half million persons. He continued with further warning:

> This conjunction of an immense military establishment and a large arms industry is new in American experience. The total influence—economic, political, even spiritual—is felt in every city, every statehouse, every office of the federal government. We recognize the imperative need for this development. Yet we must not fail to comprehend its grave implications. Our toil, resources, and livelihood are all involved; so is the very structure of our society.
>
> In the councils of government, we must guard against the acquisition of unwarranted influence, whether sought or unsought by the military-industrial complex. The potential for the disastrous use of misplaced power exists and will persist. We must never let the weight of this combination endanger our liberties or democratic processes. We should take nothing for granted. Only an alert and knowledgeable citizenry can compel the proper meshing of the huge industrial and military machinery of defense with our peaceful methods and goals so that security and liberty may prosper together.[3]

[3]*Congressional Quarterly*, March 24, 1961, p. 464. This issue contains a careful analysis of the impact of the military lobby (pp. 463-478). See also Cook, "Juggernaut: The Warfare State."

The extent and the influence of the military-industrial complex are difficult accurately to gauge. Partly, the reason is that the interests of the military lobby mesh into the pressure system generally. Thus, for example, the State of Georgia, whose Representative Vinson and Senator Russell are chairmen of the respective Armed Services Committees, ranked fourth among the states in 1961 in the estimated federal payroll for active duty military personnel stationed in the states. Similarly, an issue of the magazine, *Army*, of February 1, 1961, carried four articles by active duty army officers supporting expansion of the Nike-Zeus antimissile program, advertisements by the prime contractor and major subcontractors, and a map showing the distribution of the $410 million in contracts for the project among 37 states.[4]

In 1959, a House Armed Services subcommittee, headed by Representative F. Edward Hebert, conducted a probe into political influence in defense contracting. Its report showed that 1,400 retired military officers in the rank of major or above (including 261 generals) were employed by the top one hundred defense contractors. Several instances of entertainment of the military by defense contractors were also reported and, although the committee found no evidence of real misconduct, the hearings did point out a disturbing network of interrelations of the armed forces with defense contractors.

Cast in the brokerage system, the military-industrial complex has even wider ramifications. Perhaps, it might more adequately be called the military-industrial-labor-state-local complex, since all are involved. Governors descend upon Washington to support their state's congressional representatives' claims for a "fair share" of defense contracts; local chambers of commerce and other groups vie with one another in making attractive offers to defense plants; economically depressed areas are given defense priorities; and all defense appropriations in the Congress have strong political overtones as bargaining takes place among congressmen eager to better the economic conditions of their constituents.

When, occasionally, the Secretary of Defense announces that all defense contracts will be made exclusively on defense requirements and efficiency, it is not at all clear that his voice carries from the Pentagon to Capitol Hill. The problem is complicated because here, as elsewhere, the distinction between public and private interests is clearer in principle than it is in practice. California's king-sized share of defense contracts (in 1961 it had nearly one-fourth of the value of all defense contracts—more than twice as much as its nearest competitor, New York—and one-third of its work force engaged in manufacturing was employed directly by defense related industries) has become a political staple in the public

[4]*Congressional Quarterly*, March 24, 1961, p. 469.

speeches of its incumbent congressmen regardless of party. The promise to maintain the state's favored position is, of course, couched in the language of the public interest: California's "fair share" is at least as much as it already has because the state contains the necessary facilities and skilled work force necessary for efficiency in the defense effort. The argument, of course, is transparently circular, but it seems good enough to put a frosting of national interest on the cake of California's vested interest in prosperity.

What the military-industrial complex illustrates is the difficulty of getting a national interest recognized as a basis for judgment in a political setting dominated by organized interest groups and the promotion of constituency interests. National defense requirements, like the other aspects of foreign policy, do not respond to the politics of group accommodation in a climate of countervailing power.

Democracy and Foreign Policy

The problem of devising responsible instruments for the expression and implementation of public goals in the area of foreign policy is further complicated by the absence of organized political debate. In the period since World War II, we have developed a desire for unity of purpose under the generally agreed upon assumption that foreign policy should be bipartisan. The late and distinguished Senator Vandenberg, who was one of its major architects, preferred to call it "nonpartisan," thus suggesting that the absence of partisan debate was due to the presence of a clearly discernible national interest about which there was no real room for disagreement. On other occasions, however, he justified the policy as necessary in order that we might "unite our official voice at water's edge so that America speaks with maximum authority."[5] For Senator Vandenberg, as for the rest of us, there has always been some confusion about whether a consensus *exists*, or whether it is necessary that we act *as if* if did.

Whether regarded as bipartisanism or nonpartisanism, what this policy implies is not that politics stops at the water's edge, but rather that it is excluded from the processes of our own political system with respect to policies that involve our relations with the outside world. The difficulty is that the elimination of politics is also the elimination of most of the devices for insuring political responsibility. So far as the citizen is concerned, his vote, where it involves foreign policy, becomes merely an exercise in patriotism and social solidarity. In the absence of the regular mechanisms of choice and accountability, he endorses a blank check made out to the "successful candidates."

[5]From Humphrey, "The Senate in Foreign Policy," p. 533.

Moreover, where bipartisanism has ruled out public debate of basic policy questions, there is a tendency for technical considerations to dominate policy decisions. In the absence of public debate on the political desirability of atomic testing, for example, the decision is likely to turn on whether it is militarily and technically advantageous. Congress is the first casualty in the triumph of the experts and the technicians. Senator Humphrey, for example, suggests that the Senate is handicapped in discharging its constitutional role of participation in foreign policy-making, because it lacks any real "countervailing expertise" which would permit it to evaluate the "impressive case by the Administration."[6]

Nor does it necessarily follow that effective control over foreign policy passes from Congress into the hands of the President. Deprived of congressional and public support for any clear, broad policy, even he may on occasion lack the countervailing expertise that would provide options to the recommendations of the technical experts in his own administration. One suspects that the 1961 Cuban "invasion" and the 1960 U-2 incident are cases in point.

Bipartisanism also makes it difficult to take new directions in foreign policy. A President who wishes to make a change in a policy of containment, massive retaliation, absolutely "cheat-proof" inspection systems, or of any other basic strategy of the Cold War will have difficulty marshalling consent for his proposals. Any basic change will disrupt a unity which has very likely been reflected in a delicately contrived balance of interests. The absence of congressional debate makes it more likely that constituency interests will be controlling in congressional behavior. If the President goes to his constituency—the voters—they are not likely to have any basis for evaluating the new proposals, since foreign policies are not part of the national political dialogue. Moreover, since the public has been conditioned to accept the necessity of consensus on past policies to protect the nation's vital interests, the President's task may involve a very difficult process of reconditioning the public mind. Bipartisanism, in short, seems to build an inflexibility into the area of foreign policy where flexibility is most vitally necessary.

The crux of the matter is that our new foreign policy problems (with all this now implies) cannot even be approached, much less resolved, through the brokerage process which has come so largely to shape our approach to traditional problems. At the same time, the traditional processes of partisan competition and debate have been ruled out. Where foreign policy questions have come to be the most important political questions, the problem of devising instruments of responsible government becomes a pressing and fundamental concern.

[6] *Ibid.*, p. 534.

DEMOCRACY AND THE CONSENT OF
THE GOVERNED

THE MID-TWENTIETH CENTURY, with its nuclear explosives, men in orbit, jet propulsion, and casual conversation about exploring the moon, finds the American citizen in a peculiarly paradoxical political situation. Government, as we have seen, permeates American life to an extent almost unforeseeable even a generation ago, and political decisions have ramifications through the whole structure of the social and economic systems of the country. But instead of an increase of political involvement by the citizen, there is a tendency for him to regard the government as an external intrusion on his important affairs or as a vague, and generally benevolent, source of economic benefits and national well-being. Where government decisions determine how one's life will be conducted or ended, it is ironic that the citizen's political role should so often finish a poor last to the many other claims on his time—business, family, social, fraternal or recreational. What attention the average citizen does devote to politics is hopelessly inadequate to cope with the issues at stake.

The continuous crises in Berlin since World War II, for example, do not overly excite many citizens who seem to feel, as a student so well put it, that the Berlin situation is a "crazy complicated mess I could never figure out." Foreign policy issues introduced tremendous complexity into a political structure which already made great demands on the citizen. Agricultural problems, public welfare programs, and educational and economic policies have already overburdened even the conscientious citizen's spare time. For the unconscientious, the situation is hopeless.

We must face the hard fact that American democracy proceeds without even the minimum involvement of voting for about 40 per cent of the electorate in presidential elections and many more than that in local elections. Even those who do involve themselves by voting are often uninformed or vague about the issues at stake.

The nonparticipation of large numbers of voters leads the student of democratic politics to a serious examination of the relationship of theory to practice. If American politics contains large numbers of citizens who do not participate or only casually participate out of a vague sense of duty, we must ask ourselves whether we should revise our theory to square with our practice or change our practice so it is more compatible with our theory.

There are many indications that the character of politics has changed with the emergence of mass society. In fact, it appears that political groups which are issue-oriented are often relegated to the limbo of extremists. The peace marcher, the civil libertarian, the antisegregationist, and the income tax repealer are all dismissed as extremists, while those who relegate him to this position seek the middle way. To be a middle-of-the-roader is a political virtue proudly proclaimed in campaign material. But Americans must ask themselves who built this road and where it leads as we proceed down its middle. Obviously, a middle stand delimits controversy and the consideration of ideas which, while they may be extreme, might also offer some vigor to our political dialogue. Moreover, there is at least a possibility that an extreme position might be extremely right.

Public reaction to the emergence in recent years of movements of the radical right illustrates our dilemma. The anticommunist crusades, the John Birch Society, and the anti income tax, anti-United Nations "committees for constitutional government" have been attacked in most of the mass media and by all but a very few politicians because they are radical. So, at one time, were the ideas of democracy, freedom, and civil liberties. Whether a position, seen from the middle-of-the-road, appears radical is irrelevant to its right to enter the arena of political debate.

Similarly, whether a position is radical is no basis for the individual citizen either to accept or reject it. Some of the groups and movements in what has come to be labelled the "radical right" ought to be criticized and rejected by citizens, but not for their radicalism. The more relevant questions would ask whether the positions taken by a group are supported by evidence and by sound argument and whether its tactics are compatible with continuing political dialogue and the individual freedoms which make it possible. The real problem with many modern radical groups is that they substitute emotional appeals for argument, suspicion for evidence, and innuendo for proof. Thus, they eventually see everyone who does not agree with them as both misguided and dangerous. The existence of such peripheral groups is not necessarily evidence of a breakdown in the processes of democracy. When men are free to form their own opinions, James Madison reminded his fellow citizens, some opinions will be passionate, intolerant, and fanatic. It is, rather, the character of our overwhelming reaction to these groups which should be disturbing. For, by and large, our leading public figures and the mass media have had nothing to offer more fundamental than the charge of extremism and the alternative of moderation and harmony.

What we are suggesting is that involvement in politics, an understanding of issues, and a commitment to principles are vital to Americans if they wish to control their own destinies. If they do not choose to do this, or if the almost infinite complexity of modern politics overwhelms them to the point where they are willing to abandon this responsibility, then they must be prepared to accept the consequences and follow the government where it takes them. The question of whether the leaders will lead the citizen well is not so much the point as whether they will lead in accordance with the consent of the governed. Consent does not mean falling in line behind a leader of good intentions who will try his best. Rather, it means that those who follow have rationally concluded which direction their leaders should take.

This kind of consent requires much of the citizen. He must give some of his best efforts rather than his left-over time to examine political issues. Long ago in ancient Athens, Pericles, leader of its Golden Age, argued that involvement in public affairs was the vital element in Athenian democracy: "We are a free democracy. We do not allow absorption in our own affairs to interfere with participation in the city's; we yield to none in independence of spirit and complete self-reliance, but we regard him who holds aloof from public affairs as useless."

The collapse of Athenian democracy is a tragic and complex history. But important to its decline were demagogues whipping up emotional mob passions while respectable Athenians avoided the vulgarity of the mob, lamented the extremism of its leaders, and pursued their private lives—unmindful of Pericles' eloquent wisdom.

The Crisis in Citizenship

Even if it were not for the overarching importance of foreign policy problems, Americans in mid-century still should return to fundamentals and consider again the question of the meaning of democratic government and the institutions and attitudes appropriate to it. As we might expect in a democratic society, the crisis in the political order has its roots in the attitudes of individual citizens toward politics.

Americans have always prided themselves on their receptivity to change, their flexibility and inventiveness, and their hospitality to new ideas. This quality of openness was transmitted into a sense of the unfinished business of building a democratic society. The pressures of mass society, in the view of one penetrating critic, have not eliminated the average American's eagerness to "try new things and new methods." But they have confined it to those activities which do not "make him look 'different' or 'peculiar.' "[7] Political involvement which reflects one's principles and commitments is one of the earliest casualties of this limitation. Citizens tend to retreat into the private world of consumption where trying the new is the only way to avoid being peculiar. This preoccupation with personal economic affairs, de Tocqueville pointed out, "saps the virtues of public life."

Under these conditions, the consent of the governed ceases to mean

[7]Gabriel A. Almond, *The American People and Foreign Policy* (New York: Harcourt, Brace, 1956), p. 59.

that citizens have exercised conscious, reasoned choice. There may still be competitive elections, and the efforts of competing consent engineers may even be said to give the public what it wants. The question, however, is whether consent in a democratic society is simply a matter of giving people what they want. People are not born with "wants"; they develop them in a social setting. The character of a society's educational system, its system of mass communications, its group life, and its political system—all contribute to defining the conditions in which human wants are developed. If people are to participate politically in defining the goals of their public life, it is necessary that these institutions be in good democratic repair to open up alternatives, sharpen the skills of critical choice, draw men into a public discourse, and provide information and reasoned argument. Only then can the contest for political power be genuinely competitive. This suggests that education and the mass media should be high on the agenda of a democracy concerned not to give people what they want but what they "think best."[8]

The Responsibilities of Citizenship

Criticism of the existing order of American politics need not involve either an underestimation of its achievements and virtues or a plea for Utopian perfectionism. The politics of group conciliation maintains social peace and order, eliminates bigotry and fanaticism, and has resulted in a wider sharing of economic plenty than any other society has ever achieved. Moreover, despite its lack of provision for direct responsibility to majority opinion, the system no doubt responds, cumbersomely but surely, in the direction of widespread and sustained popular desires.

Similarly, if much of the appeal by politicians to citizens is manipulative, there are still advantages in the existence of a plurality of manipulators. Certainly, this condition is preferable to an exclusive monopoly of the instruments of manipulation in the hands of party or state. To borrow a figure from democratic philosopher Boyd Bode, it is much worse to be bawled out by a policeman than by one's wife. But dictatorship and totalitarianism are not the only alternatives to the politics of compromise and manipulation. It is true that they are likely to be the result if, out of frustration and despair and righteous indignation, men seek to elevate politics by transcending it. Perfectionism, as modern conservatives have ably and persistently warned, has a habit of defeating its own purposes. The demand for total victories and total solutions to problems, the cry for leaders who will rise above politics and parties, the tendency to see those who disagree as traitors—these are the characteristics of the modern

[8]See Tussman, *Obligation and the Body Politic,* pp. 110-112.

mass movements which lead to totalitarianism. Democratic alternatives must stay within the bounds of competitive politics, which encompasses pluralism, conflict, disagreement, compromise, and manipulation. The problem is not to *eliminate* self-interest and emotion or the play of pressure groups and public relations. Rather, it is to make the legislative process something more than the result of group pressures, and politicians something more than moral midwives—in short, to make the electoral process something more than a patriotic holiday.

The fundamental problem is to decide what model of democracy is to serve us as a basis for evaluating the existing order. Only then can we make judgments about the adequacy of current organization and function of campaigns and elections, political parties, pressure groups, Congress, the Presidency, and the courts. In any event, there is no simple panacea. The processes of democratic government will reflect the expectations of its citizens and the demands they make on themselves. If citizens generally make the care of their private interests paramount, effective political power will be increasingly transferred to the agents of pressure groups and to those skilled in the uses of the mass media; the effective political process will increasingly reflect the compromise of private claims.

On the other hand, one may find these tendencies to be incompatible with the development of the highest promises of popular government. Insofar as this occurs, the changed demands that citizens will make on themselves and on their politicians and political parties will themselves be the primary instruments of political reform.

Constitution of the United States

[In Convention, September 17, 1787]

PREAMBLE

We the people of the United States, in order to form a more perfect union, establish justice, insure domestic tranquillity, provide for the common defense, promote the general welfare, and secure the blessings of liberty to ourselves and our posterity, do ordain and establish this Constitution for the United States of America.

ARTICLE 1.   LEGISLATIVE DEPARTMENT*

Section 1. Congress*

*Powers Are Vested in Senate and House**

1.* All legislative powers herein granted shall be vested in a Congress of the United States, which shall consist of a Senate and House of Representatives.

Section 2. House of Representatives

Election of Representatives

1. The House of Representatives shall be composed of members chosen every second year by the people of the several States, and the electors in each State shall have the qualifications requisite for electors of the most numerous branch of the State Legislature.

*Headings and paragraph numbers have been inserted to assist the reader, and are not part of the Constitution. The original Constitution contains only article and section numbers. These headings and paragraph numbers were prepared under the direction of the Chief Clerk of the California Assembly.

Qualifications of Representatives

2. No person shall be a Representative who shall not have attained to the age of twenty-five years, and been seven years a citizen of the United States, and who shall not, when elected, be an inhabitant of that State in which he shall be chosen.

Apportionment of Representatives

3. Representatives and direct taxes shall be apportioned among the several States which may be included within this Union, according to their respective numbers, which shall be determined by adding to the whole number of free persons, including those bound to service for a term of years, and excluding Indians not taxed, three-fifths of all other persons. The actual enumeration shall be made within three years after the first meeting of the Congress of the United States, and within every subsequent term of ten years, in such manner as they shall by law direct. The number of Representatives shall not exceed one for every thirty thousand, but each State shall have at least one Representative; and until such enumeration shall be made, the State of New Hampshire shall be entitled to choose three, Massachusetts eight, Rhode Island and Providence Plantations one, Connecticut five, New York six, New Jersey four, Pennsylvania eight, Delaware one, Maryland six, Virginia ten, North Carolina five, South Carolina five, and Georgia three.

(This clause has been superseded, so far as it relates to representation, by Section 2 of the Fourteenth Amendment to the Constitution.)

Vacancies

4. When vacancies happen in the representation from any State, the executive authority thereof shall issue writs of election to fill such vacancies.

Officers of the House—Impeachment

5. The House of Representatives shall choose their Speaker and other officers; and shall have the sole power of impeachment.

Section 3. *The Senate*

Number of Senators

1. The Senate of the United States shall be composed of two Senators from each State, chosen by the Legislature thereof, for six years; and each Senator shall have one vote.

(Superseded by Amendment XVII.)

Classification of Senators

2. Immediately after they shall be assembled in consequence of the

first election, they shall be divided as equally as may be into three classes. The seats of the Senators of the first class shall be vacated at the expiration of the second year, of the second class at the expiration of the fourth year, and of the third class at the expiration of the sixth year, so that one third may be chosen every second year; and if vacancies happen by resignation, or otherwise, during the recess of the Legislature of any State, the executive thereof may make temporary appointments until the next meeting of the Legislature, which shall then fill such vacancies.

(Modified by Amendment XVII.)

Qualifications of Senators

3. No person shall be a Senator who shall not have attained to the age of thirty years, and been nine years a citizen of the United States, and who shall not, when elected, be an inhabitant of that State for which he shall be chosen.

President of Senate

4. The Vice President of the United States shall be President of the Senate, but shall have no vote, unless they be equally divided.

Officers of Senate

5. The Senate shall choose their other officers, and also a President pro Tempore, in the absence of the Vice President, or when he shall exercise the office of President of the United States.

Trial of Impeachment

6. The Senate shall have the sole power to try all impeachments. When sitting for that purpose, they shall be on oath or affirmation. When the President of the United States is tried the Chief Justice shall preside: And no person shall be convicted without the concurrence of two-thirds of the members present.

Judgment on Conviction of Impeachment.

7. Judgment in cases of impeachment shall not extend further than to removal from office, and disqualification to hold and enjoy any office of honor, trust or profit under the United States: but the party convicted shall nevertheless be liable and subject to indictment, trial, judgment and punishment, according to law.

Section 4. Election of Senators and Representatives— Meetings of Congress

Election of Members of Congress

1. The times, places and manner of holding elections for Senators and Representatives, shall be prescribed in each State by the Legislature

thereof; but the Congress may at any time by law make or alter such regulations, except as to the places of choosing Senators.

(See Amendment XX.)

Congress to Meet Annually

2. The Congress shall assemble at least once in every year, and such meeting shall be on the first Monday in December, unless they shall by law appoint a different day.

(Changed to January 3d by Amendment XX.)

Section 5. Powers and Duties of Each House of Congress

Sole Judge of Qualifications of Members

1. Each House shall be the judge of the elections, returns and qualifications of its own members, and a majority of each shall constitute a quorum to do business; but a smaller number may adjourn from day to day, and may be authorized to compel the attendance of absent members, in such manner, and under such penalties as each House may provide.

Rules of Proceedings—Punishment of Members

2. Each House may determine the rules of its proceedings, punish its members for disorderly behavior, and, with the concurrence of two-thirds, expel a member.

Journals

3. Each House shall keep a Journal of its proceedings, and from time to time publish the same, excepting such parts as may in their judgment require secrecy; and the yeas and nays of the members of either House on any question shall, at the desire of one-fifth of those present, be entered on the Journal.

Adjournment

4. Neither House, during the session of Congress, shall, without the consent of the other, adjourn for more than three days, nor to any other place than that in which the two Houses shall be sitting.

Section 6. Compensation, Privileges and Disabilities, of Senators and Representatives

Compensation—Privileges

1. The Senators and Representatives shall receive a compensation for their services, to be ascertained by law, and paid out of the Treasury of the United States. They shall in all cases, except treason, felony and breach of the peace, be privileged from arrest during their attendance at the session of their respective Houses, and in going to and returning

from the same; and for any speech or debate in either House, they shall not be questioned in any other place.

Disability to Hold Other Offices

2. No Senator or Representative shall, during the time for which he was elected, be appointed to any civil office under the authority of the United States, which shall have been created, or the emoluments whereof shall have been increased during such time; and no person holding any office under the United States, shall be a member of either House during his continuance in office.

(See also Section 3 of the Fourteenth Amendment.)

Section 7. Mode of Passing Laws

Special Provision as to Revenue Laws

1. All bills for raising revenue shall originate in the House of Representatives; but the Senate may propose or concur with amendments as on other bills.

Laws, How Enacted

2. Every bill which shall have passed the House of Representatives and the Senate, shall, before it become a law, be presented to the President of the United States; if he approve he shall sign it, but if not he shall return it, with his objections to that House in which it shall have originated who shall enter the objections at large on their Journal, and proceed to reconsider it. If after such reconsideration two-thirds of that House shall agree to pass the bill, it shall be sent, together with the objections, to the other House, by which it shall likewise be reconsidered, and if approved by two-thirds of that House, it shall become a law. But in all such cases the votes of both Houses shall be determined by yeas and nays, and the names of the persons voting for and against the bill shall be entered on the Journal of each House respectively. If any bill shall not be returned by the President within ten days (Sundays excepted) after it shall have been presented to him, the same shall be a law, in like manner as if he had signed it, unless the Congress by their adjournment prevent its return, in which case it shall not be a law.

Resolutions, Etc.

3. Every order, resolution, or vote to which the concurrence of the Senate and House of Representatives may be necessary (except on a question of adjournment) shall be presented to the President of the United States; and before the same shall take effect, shall be approved by him, or being disapproved by him, shall be repassed by two-thirds of the Senate and House of Representatives, according to the rules and limitations prescribed in the case of a bill.

Section 8. Powers Granted to Congress

Taxation

1. The Congress shall have power to lay and collect taxes, duties, imposts and excises, to pay the debts and provide for the common defense and general welfare of the United States; but all duties, imposts and excises shall be uniform throughout the United States;

Loans

2. To borrow money on the credit of the United States;

Commerce

3. To regulate commerce with foreign nations, and among the several States, and with the Indian tribes;

Naturalization and Bankruptcies

4. To establish an uniform rule of naturalization, and uniform laws on the subject of bankruptcies throughout the United States;

Coin

5. To coin money, regulate the value thereof, and of foreign coin, and fix the standard of weights and measures;

Counterfeiting

6. To provide for the punishment of counterfeiting the securities and current coin of the United States;

Post Office

7. To establish post offices and post roads;

Patents and Copyrights

8. To promote the progress of science and useful arts, by securing for limited times to authors and inventors the exclusive right to their respective writings and discoveries;

Courts

9. To constitute tribunals inferior to the Supreme Court;

Piracies

10. To define and punish piracies and felonies committed on the high seas, and offenses against the law of nations;

War

11. To declare war, grant letters of marque and reprisal, and make rules concerning captures on land and water;

Army

12. To raise and support armies, but no appropriation of money to that use shall be for a longer term than two years;

Navy

13. To provide and maintain a navy;

Military and Naval Rules

14. To make rules for the government and regulation of the land and naval forces;

Militia, Calling Forth

15. To provide for calling forth the militia to execute the laws of the Union, suppress insurrections and repel invasions;

Militia, Organizing and Arming

16. To provide for organizing, arming, and disciplining, the militia, and for governing such part of them as may be employed in the service of the United States, reserving to the States respectively, the appointment of the officers, and the authority of training the militia according to the discipline prescribed by Congress;

Federal District and Other Places

17. To exercise exclusive legislation in all cases whatsoever, over such district (not exceeding ten miles square) as may, by cession of particular States, and the acceptance of Congress, become the seat of the government of the United States, and to exercise like authority over all places purchased by the consent of the Legislature of the State in which the same shall be, for the erection of forts, magazines, arsenals, dockyards, and other needful buildings;—And

Make Laws to Carry Out Foregoing Powers

18. To make all laws which shall be necessary and proper for carrying into execution the foregoing powers, and all other powers vested by this Constitution in the Government of the United States, or in any department or officer thereof.

(For other powers, see Article II, Section 1; Article III, Sections 2 and 3; Article IV, Sections 1-3; Article V; and Amendments XIII-XVI and XIX-XXI.)

Section 9. Limitation on Powers Granted to the United States

Slave Trade

1. The migration or importation of such persons as any of the States now existing shall think proper to admit, shall not be prohibited by the Congress prior to the year one thousand eight hundred and eight, but a tax or duty may be imposed on such importation, not exceeding ten dollars for each person.

Habeas Corpus

2. The privilege of the writ of habeas corpus shall not be suspended,

unless when in cases of rebellion or invasion the public safety may require it.

Ex Post Facto Law

3. No bill of attainder or ex post facto law shall be passed.

Direct Taxes

4. No capitation, or other direct, tax shall be laid, unless in proportion to the census or enumeration hereinbefore directed to be taken.
(Modified by Amendment XVI.)

Duties on Exports

5. No tax or duty shall be laid on articles exported from any State.

No Commercial Discrimination to Be Made Between States

6. No preference shall be given by any regulation of commerce or revenue to the ports of one State over those of another; nor shall vessels bound to, or from, one State, be obliged to enter, clear or pay duties in another.

Money, How Drawn From Treasury . .

7. No money shall be drawn from the Treasury, but in consequence of appropriations made by law; and a regular statement and account of the receipts and expenditures of all public money shall be published from time to time.

Titles of Nobility

8. No title of nobility shall be granted by the United States: And no person holding any office of profit or trust under them, shall, without the consent of the Congress, accept of any present, emolument, office, or title, of any kind whatever, from any King, Prince, or foreign State.
(For other limitations see Amendments I-X.)

Section 10. Powers Prohibited to the States

Powers Prohibited, Absolutely

1. No State shall enter into any treaty, alliance, or confederation; grant letters of marque and reprisal; coin money; emit bills of credit; make anything but gold and silver coin a tender in payment of debts; pass any bill of attainder, ex post facto law, or law impairing the obligation of contracts, or grant any title of nobility.

Powers Concerning Duties on Imports of Exports . .

2. No State shall, without the consent of the Congress, lay any imposts or duties on imports or exports, except what may be absolutely necessary for executing its inspection laws: and the net produce of all duties and

imposts, laid by any State on imports or exports, shall be for the use of the Treasury of the United States; and all such laws shall be subject to the revision and control of the Congress.

Powers Permitted With Consent of Congress

3. No State shall, without the consent of Congress, lay any duty of tonnage, keep troops, or ships of war in time of peace, enter into any agreement or compact with another State, or with a foreign power, or engage in war, unless actually invaded, or in such imminent danger as will not admit of delay.

ARTICLE II. EXECUTIVE DEPARTMENT

Section 1. The President

Executive Power Vested in President—Term of Office

1. The executive power shall be vested in a President of the United States of America. He shall hold his office during the term of four years, and, together with the Vice President, chosen for the same term, be elected, as follows

Appointment and Number of Presidential Electors

2. Each State shall appoint, in such manner as the Legislature thereof may direct, a number of electors, equal to the whole number of Senators and Representatives to which the State may be entitled in the Congress: but no Senator or Representative, or person holding an office of trust or profit under the United States, shall be appointed an elector.

Mode of Electing President and Vice President

3. The electors shall meet in their respective States, and vote by ballot for two persons, of whom one at least shall not be an inhabitant of the same State with themselves. And they shall make a list of all the persons voted for, and of the number of votes for each; which list they shall sign and certify, and transmit sealed to the seat of the Government of the United States, directed to the President of the Senate. The President of the Senate shall, in the presence of the Senate and House of Representatives, open all the certificates, and the votes shall then be counted. The person having the greatest number of votes shall be the President, if such number be a majority of the whole number of electors appointed; and if there be more than one who have such majority, and have an equal number of votes, then the House of Representatives shall immediately choose by a ballot one of them for President; and if no person have a majority, then from the five highest on the list the said House shall in like manner choose the President. But in choosing the President, the votes shall be taken by States, the representation

from each State having one vote; a quorum for this purpose shall consist of a member or members from two-thirds of the States, and a majority of all the States shall be necessary to a choice. In every case, after the choice of the President, the person having the greatest number of votes of the electors shall be the Vice President. But if there should remain two or more who have equal votes, the Senate shall choose from them by ballot the Vice President.

(This paragraph has been superseded by the Twelfth Amendment to the Constitution. See Amendment XX.)

Time of Choosing Electors and Casting Electoral Vote..

4. The Congress may determine the time of choosing the electors, and the day on which they shall give their votes; which day shall be the same throughout the United States.

Qualifications of President

5. No person except a natural-born citizen, or a citizen of the United States, at the time of the adoption of this Constitution, shall be eligible to the office of President; neither shall any person be eligible to that office who shall not have attained to the age of thirty-five years, and been fourteen years a resident within the United States.

(See also Article II, Section 1, and Fourteenth Amendment.)

Presidential Succession

6. In case of the removal of the President from office, or of his death, resignation, or inability to discharge the powers and duties of the said office, the same shall devolve on the Vice President, and the Congress may by law provide for the case of removal, death, resignation or inability, both of the President and Vice President declaring what officer shall then act as President, and such officer shall act accordingly, until the disability be removed, or a President shall be elected.

Salary of President

7. The President shall, at stated times, receive for his services, a compensation, which shall neither be increased nor diminished during the period for which he shall have been elected, and he shall not receive within that period any other emolument from the United States, or any of them.

Oath of Office of President

8. Before he enter on the execution of his office, he shall take the following oath or affirmation:—"I do solemnly swear (or affirm) that I will faithfully execute the office of President of the United States, and will to the best of my ability, preserve, protect and defend the Constitution of the United States."

Section 2. Powers of the President

Commander in Chief

1. The President shall be Commander in Chief of the Army and Navy of the United States, and of the militia of the several States, when called into the actual service of the United States; he may require the opinion, in writing, of the principal officer in each of the executive departments, upon any subject relating to the duties of their respective offices, and he shall have power to grant reprieves and pardons for offenses against the United States, except in cases of impeachment.

Treaties and Appointments

2. He shall have power, by and with the advice and consent of the Senate, to make treaties, provided two-thirds of the Senators present concur; and he shall nominate, and by and with the advice and consent of the Senate, shall appoint ambassadors, other public ministers and consuls, Judges of the Supreme Court, and all other officers of the United States, whose appointments are not herein otherwise provided for, and which shall be established by law: but the Congress may by law vest the appointment of such inferior officers, as they think proper, in the President alone, in the courts of law, or in the heads of departments.

Filling Vacancies

3. The President shall have power to fill up all vacancies that may happen during the recess of the Senate, by granting commissions which shall expire at the end of their next session.

Section 3. Duties of the President

Message to Congress—Adjourn and Call Special Session....

He shall from time to time give to the Congress information of the state of the Union, and recommend to their consideration such measures as he shall judge necessary and expedient; he may, on extraordinary occasions, convene both Houses, or either of them, and in case of disagreement between them, with respect to the time of adjournment, he may adjourn them to such time as he shall think proper; he shall receive ambassadors and other public ministers; he shall take care that the laws be faithfully executed, and shall commission all the officers of the United States.

(See also Article I, Section 5.)

Section 4. Removal of Executive and Civil Officers

Impeachment of President and Other Officers

The President, Vice President and all civil officers of the United States, shall be removed from office on impeachment for, and conviction of, treason, bribery, or other high crimes and misdemeanors.

(See also Article I, Sections 2 and 3.)

ARTICLE III. JUDICIAL DEPARTMENT

Section 1. Judicial Powers Vested in Federal Courts

Courts—Terms of Office and Salary of Judges

The judicial power of the United States, shall be vested in one Supreme Court, and in such inferior courts as the Congress may from time to time ordain and establish. The judges, both of the Supreme and inferior courts, shall hold their offices during good behavior, and shall, at stated times, receive for their services, a compensation, which shall not be diminished during their continuance in office.

Section 2. Jurisdiction of United States Courts

Cases That May Come Before United States Courts

1. The judicial power shall extend to all cases, in law and equity, arising under this Constitution, the laws of the United States, and treaties made, or which shall be made, under their authority;—to all cases affecting ambassadors, other public ministers and consuls;—to all cases of admiralty and maritime jurisdiction;—to controversies to which the United States shall be a party;—to controversies between two or more States;—between a State and citizens of another State;—between citizens of different States;—between citizens of the same State claiming lands under grants of different States, and between a State, or the citizens thereof, and foreign States, citizens or subjects.

(See also Eleventh Amendment.)

Jurisdiction of Supreme and Appellate Courts

2. In all cases affecting ambassadors, other public ministers and consuls, and those in which a State shall be party, the Supreme Court shall have original jurisdiction. In all the other cases before mentioned, the Supreme Court shall have appellate jurisdiction, both as to law and fact, with such exceptions, and under such regulations as the Congress shall make.

Trial of Crimes

3. The trial of all crimes, except in cases of impeachment, shall be by jury; and such trial shall be held in the State where the said crimes shall have been committed; but when not committed within any State, the trial shall be at such place or places as the Congress may by law have directed.

(See also Fifth, Sixth, Seventh, and Eighth Amendments.)

Section 3. Treason

Treason Defined

1. Treason against the United States, shall consist only in levying war against them, or in adhering to their enemies, giving them aid and comfort.

Conviction

2. No person shall be convicted of treason unless on the testimony of two witnesses to the same overt act, or on confession in open court.

Punishment

3. The Congress shall have power to declare the punishment of treason, but no attainder of treason shall work corruption of blood, or forfeiture except during the life of the person attainted.

ARTICLE IV. THE STATES AND THE FEDERAL GOVERNMENT

Section 1. Official Acts of the States

Full Faith and Credit

Full faith and credit shall be given in each State to the public acts records, and judicial proceedings of every other State. And the Congress may by general laws prescribe the manner in which such acts, records and proceedings shall be proved, and the effect thereof.

(See also Fourteenth Amendment.)

Section 2. Citizens of the States

Interstate Privileges of Citizens

1. The citizens of each State shall be entitled to all privileges and immunities of citizens in the several States.

Fugitives From Justice

2. A person charged in any State with treason, felony, or other crime, who shall flee from justice, and be found in another State, shall on demand of the executive authority of the State from which he fled, be delivered up, to be removed to the State having jurisdiction of the crime.

Fugitives From Service

3. No person held to service or labor in one State, under the laws thereof, escaping into another, shall, in consequence of any law or regulation therein, be discharged from such service or labor, but shall be delivered up on claim of the party to whom such service or labor may be due.

("Person" here includes slave. This was the basis of the Fugitive Slave Laws of 1793 and 1850. It is now superseded by the Thirteenth Amendment, by which slavery is prohibited.)

Section 3. New States

Admission or Division of States

1. New States may be admitted by the Congress into this Union; but no new State shall be formed or erected within the jurisdiction of any other State; nor any State be formed by the junction of two or more States, or parts of States, without the consent of the Legislatures of the States concerned as well as of the Congress.

Control of the Property and Territory of the Union

2. The Congress shall have power to dispose of and make all needful rules and regulations respecting the territory or other property belonging to the United States; and nothing in this Constitution shall be so construed as to prejudice any claims of the United States, or of any particular State.

Section 4. Protection of States Guaranteed

Republican Form of Government

The United States shall guarantee to every State in this Union a republican form of government, and shall protect each of them against invasion; and on application of the Legislature, or of the executive (when the Legislature cannot be convened) against domestic violence.

ARTICLE V. AMENDMENTS

Amendments, How Proposed and Adopted

The Congress, whenever two-thirds of both Houses shall deem it necessary, shall propose amendments to this Constitution, or, on the application of the Legislatures of two-thirds of the several States, shall call a convention for proposing amendments, which, in either case, shall be valid to all intents and purposes, as part of this Constitution, when ratified by the Legislatures of three-fourths of the several States, or by conventions in three-fourths thereof, as the one or the other mode of ratification may be proposed by the Congress; provided that no amendment which may be made prior to the year one thousand eight hundred and eight shall in any manner affect the first and fourth clauses in the ninth section of the first article; and that no State, without its consent, shall be deprived of its equal suffrage in the Senate.

ARTICLE VI. GENERAL PROVISIONS

The Public Debt

1. All debts contracted and engagements entered into, before the

adoption of this Constitution, shall be as valid against the United States under this Constitution, as under the Confederation.

(See also Fourteenth Amendment, Section 4.)

Supreme Law of the Land

2. This Constitution, and the laws of the United States which shall be made in pursuance thereof; and all treaties made, or which shall be made, under the authority of the United States, shall be the supreme law of the land; and the judges in every State shall be bound thereby, anything in the Constitution or laws of any State to the contrary notwithstanding.

Oath of Office—No Religious Test Required

3. The Senators and Representatives before mentioned, and the members of the several State Legislatures, and all executive and judicial officers, both of the United States and of the several States, shall be bound by oath or affirmation, to support this Constitution; but no religious test shall ever be required as a qualification to any office or public trust under the United States.

ARTICLE VII. RATIFICATION OF THE CONSTITUTION*

Ratification of Nine States Required.

The ratification of the conventions of nine States, shall be sufficient for the establishment of this Constitution between the States so ratifying the same.

DONE in convention by the unanimous consent of the States present the seventeenth day of September in the year of our Lord one thousand seven hundred and eighty-seven and of the Independence of the United States of America the twelfth. In witness whereof we have hereunto subscribed our names,†

* The Constitution was ratified by the States in the following order:
    1. Delaware—December 7, 1787.
    2. Pennsylvania—December 12, 1787.
    3. New Jersey—December 19, 1787.
    4. Georgia—January 2, 1788.
    5. Connecticut—January 9, 1788.
    6. Massachusetts—February 6, 1788.
    7. Maryland—April 28, 1788.
    8. South Carolina—May 23, 1788.
    9. New Hampshire—June 21, 1788.
    10. Virginia—June 25, 1788.
    11. New York—July 26, 1788.
    12. North Carolina—November 21, 1789.
    13. Rhode Island—May 29, 1790.
† There were sixty-five delegates chosen to the convention; ten did not attend; sixteen declined or failed to sign; thirty-nine signed. Rhode Island sent no delegates.

G? Washington—Presid^t
and deputy from Virginia

New Hampshire
{ John Langdon
Nicholas Gilman

Massachusetts
{ Nathaniel Gorham
Rufus King

Connecticut
{ Wm Sam^L Johnson
Roger Sherman

New York . . . . . Alexander Hamilton

New Jersey
{ Wil: Livingston
David Brearley.
W^M Paterson.
Jona: Dayton

Pensylvania
{ B Franklin
Thomas Mifflin
Rob^T· Morris
Geo. Clymer
Tho^S FitzSimons
Jared Ingersoll
James Wilson
Gouv Morris

Delaware
{ Geo: Read
Gunning Bedford jun
John Dickinson
Richard Bassett
Jaco: Broom

Maryland
{ James McHenry
Dan of St Tho^S Jenifer
Dan^L Carroll

Virginia
{ John Blair—
James Madison Jr.

North Carolina
{ W^M Blount
Rich^D Dobbs Spaight.
Hu Williamson

South Carolina
$\begin{cases} \text{J. RUTLEDGE} \\ \text{CHARLES COTESWORTH PINCKNEY} \\ \text{CHARLES PINCKNEY} \\ \text{PIERCE BUTLER} \end{cases}$

Georgia
$\begin{cases} \text{WILLIAM FEW} \\ \text{ABR BALDWIN} \end{cases}$

The word, "the," being interlined between the seventh and eighth lines of the first page, the word "thirty" being partly written on an erasure in the fifteenth line of the first page, the words "is tried" being interlined between the thirty-second and thirty-third lines of the first page and the word "the" being interlined between the forty-third and forty-fourth lines of the second page.
Attest WILLIAM JACKSON Secretary

Amendments

AMENDMENT I

Restrictions on Powers of Congress

(SECTION 1.) Congress shall make no law respecting an establishment of religion, or prohibiting the free exercise thereof; or abridging the freedom of speech, or of the press; or the right of the people peaceably to assemble, and to petition the Government for a redress of grievances.

(Proposed September 25, 1789; ratified December 15, 1791.)

AMENDMENT II

Right to Bear Arms

(SECTION 1.) A well-regulated militia, being necessary to the security of a free State, the right of the people to keep and bear arms, shall not be infringed.

(Proposed September 25, 1789; ratified December 15, 1791.)

AMENDMENT III

Billeting of Soldiers

(SECTION 1.) No soldier shall, in time of peace be quartered in any house, without the consent of the owner, nor in time of war, but in a manner to be prescribed by law.

(Proposed September 25, 1789; ratified December 15, 1791.)

AMENDMENT IV

Seizures, Searches and Warrants

(SECTION 1.) The right of the people to be secure in their persons, houses, papers, and effects, against unreasonable searches and seizures, shall not be violated, and no warrants shall issue, but upon probable cause, supported by oath or affirmation, and particularly describing the place to be searched, and the persons or things to be seized.

(Proposed September 25, 1789; ratified December 15, 1791.)

AMENDMENT V

Criminal Proceedings and Condemnation of Property

(SECTION 1.) No person shall be held to answer for a capital, or otherwise infamous crime, unless on a presentment or indictment of a grand jury, except in cases arising in the land or naval forces, or in the militia, when in actual service in time of war or public danger; nor shall any person be subject for the same offense to be twice put in jeopardy of life or limb; nor shall be compelled in any criminal case to be a witness against himself, nor be deprived of life, liberty, or property, without due process of law; nor shall private property be taken for public use, without just compensation.

(Proposed September 25, 1789; ratified December 15, 1791.)

AMENDMENT VI

Mode of Trial in Criminal Proceedings

(SECTION 1.) In all criminal prosecutions, the accused shall enjoy the right to a speedy and public trial, by an impartial jury of the State and district wherein the crime shall have been committed, which district shall have been previously ascertained by law, and to be informed of the nature and cause of the accusation; to be confronted with the witnesses against him; to have compulsory process for obtaining witnesses in his favor, and to have the assistance of counsel for his defense.

(Proposed September 25, 1789; ratified December 15, 1791.)

AMENDMENT VII

Trial by Jury

(SECTION 1.) In suits at common law, where the value in controversy shall exceed twenty dollars, the right of trial by jury shall be preserved, and no fact tried by a jury, shall be otherwise re-examined in any court of the United States, than according to the rules of the common law.

(Proposed September 25, 1789; ratified December 15, 1791.)

AMENDMENT VIII

Bails—Fines—Punishments

(SECTION 1.) Excessive bail shall not be required, nor excessive fines imposed, nor cruel and unusual punishments inflicted.

(Proposed September 25, 1789; ratified December 15, 1791.)

AMENDMENT IX

Certain Rights Not Denied to the People

(SECTION 1.) The enumeration in the Constitution, of certain rights, shall not be construed to deny or disparage others retained by the people.

(Proposed September 25, 1789; ratified December 15, 1791.)

AMENDMENT X

State Rights

(SECTION 1.) The powers not delegated to the United States by the Constitution, nor prohibited by it to the States, are reserved to the States respectively, or to the people.

(Proposed September 25, 1789; ratified December 15, 1791.)

AMENDMENT XI

Judicial Powers

(SECTION 1.) The judicial power of the United States shall not be construed to extend to any suit in law or equity, commenced or prosecuted against one of the United States by citizens of another State, or by citizens subjects of any foreign State.

(Proposed March 4, 1794; ratified February 7, 1795; declared ratified January 8, 1798.)

AMENDMENT XII

Election of President and Vice President

(SECTION 1.) The electors shall meet in their respective States and vote by ballot for President and Vice President, one of whom, at least, shall not be an inhabitant of the same State with themselves; they shall name in their ballots the person voted for as President, and in distinct ballots the person voted for as Vice President, and they shall make distinct lists of all persons voted for as President, and of all persons voted for as Vice President, and of the number of votes for each, which lists they shall sign and certify, and transmit sealed to the seat of the government of the United States, directed to the President of the Senate;—The President of the Senate shall, in the presence of the Senate and House of Representatives, open all the certificates and the votes shall then be counted;—the person having the greatest number of votes for President, shall be the President, if such number be a majority of the whole number of electors appointed; and if no person have such majority, then from the persons having the highest numbers not exceeding three on the list of those voted for as President, the House of Representatives shall choose immediately, by ballot, the President. But in choosing the President, the votes shall be taken by States, the representation from each State having one vote; a quorum for this purpose shall consist of a member or members from two-thirds of the States, and a majority of all the States shall be necessary to a choice. And if the House of Representatives shall not choose a President whenever the right of choice shall devolve upon them, before the fourth day of March next following, then the Vice President shall act as President, as in the case of the death or other constitutional disability of the President—The person having the greatest number of votes, as Vice President, shall be the Vice President, if such a number be a majority of the whole number of electors appointed, and if no person have a majority, then from the two highest numbers on the list, the Senate shall choose the Vice President; a quorum for the purpose shall consist of two-thirds of the whole number of Senators, and a majority of the whole number shall be necessary to a choice. But no person constitutionally ineligible to the office of President shall be eligible to that of Vice President of the United States.

(Proposed December 12, 1803; declared ratified September 25, 1804.)

AMENDMENT XIII

Slavery

SECTION 1. Neither slavery nor involuntary servitude, except as a punishment for crime whereof the party shall have been duly convicted, shall exist within the United States, or any place subject to their jurisdiction.

SECTION 2. Congress shall have power to enforce this article by appropriate legislation.

(Proposed January 31, 1865; ratified December 6, 1865; certified December 18, 1865.)

AMENDMENT XIV

Citizenship, Representation and Payment of Public Debt

Citizenship

SECTION 1. All persons born or naturalized in the United States and subject to the jurisdiction thereof, are citizens of the United States and of the State wherein they reside. No State shall make or enforce any law which shall abridge the privileges or immunities of citizens of the United States; nor shall any State deprive any person of life, liberty, or property, without due process of law; nor deny to any person within its jurisdiction the equal protection of the laws.

Apportionment of Representatives.

SECTION 2. Representatives shall be apportioned among the several States according to their respective numbers, counting the whole number of persons in each State, excluding Indians not taxed. But when the right to vote at any election for the choice of electors for President and Vice President of the United States, Representatives in Congress, the executive and judicial officers of a State, or the members of the Legislature thereof, is denied to any of the male inhabitants of such State, being twenty-one years of age, and citizens of the United States, or in any way abridged, except for participation in rebellion, or other crime, the basis of representation therein shall be reduced in the proportion which the number of such male citizens shall bear to the whole number of male citizens twenty-one years of age in such State.

Disqualification for Public Office

SECTION 3. No person shall be a Senator or Representative in Congress, or elector of President and Vice President, or hold any office, civil or

military, under the United States, or under any State, who, having previously taken an oath, as a member of Congress, or as an officer of the
United States, or as a member of any State Legislature, or as an executive
or judicial officer of any State, to support the Constitution of the United
States, shall have engaged in insurrection or rebellion against the same, or
given aid or comfort to the enemies thereof. But Congress may by a vote
of two-thirds of each House, remove such disability.

Public Debt, Guarantee of

SECTION 4. The validity of the public debt of the United States,
authorized by law, including debts incurred for payment of pensions and
bounties for services in suppressing insurrection or rebellion, shall not be
questioned. But neither the United States nor any State shall assume or pay
any debt or obligation incurred in aid of insurrection or rebellion against
the United States, or any claim for the loss or emancipation of any slave;
but all such debts, obligations and claims shall be held illegal and void.

Power of Congress

SECTION 5. The Congress shall have power to enforce, by appropriate
legislation, the provisions of this article.

(Proposed June 13, 1866; ratified July 9, 1868; certified July 28, 1868.)

AMENDMENT XV

Elective Franchise

Right of Citizens to Vote

SECTION 1. The right of citizens of the United States to vote shall not be
denied or abridged by the United States or by any State on account of race,
color, or previous condition of servitude.

Power of Congress

SECTION 2. The Congress shall have power to enforce this article by
appropriate legislation.

(Proposed February 26, 1869; ratified February 3, 1870; certified March 30, 1870.)

AMENDMENT XVI

Income Tax—Congress Given Power to Lay and Collect

(SECTION 1.) The Congress shall have power to lay and collect taxes on
incomes, from whatever source derived, without apportionment among

the several States, and without regard to any census or enumeration. (Proposed July 12, 1909; ratified February 3, 1913; certified February 25, 1913.)

AMENDMENT XVII

Popular Election of Senators

(SECTION 1.) The Senate of the United States shall be composed of two Senators from each State, elected by the people thereof, for six years; and each Senator shall have one vote. The electors in each State shall have the qualifications requisite for electors of the most numerous branch of the State Legislatures.

(SECTION 2.) When vacancies happen in the representation of any State in the Senate, the executive authority of such State shall issue writs of election to fill such vacancies: *Provided,* That the Legislature of any State may empower the executive thereof to make temporary appointments until the people fill the vacancies by election as the Legislature may direct.

(SECTION 3.) This amendment shall not be so construed as to affect the election or term of any Senator chosen before it becomes valid as part of the Constitution.

(Proposed May 13, 1912; ratified April 8, 1913; certified May 31, 1913.)

NOTE—The seventeenth amendment was proposed as a direct amendment of Article I, Section 3, of the Constitution.

AMENDMENT XVIII

Prohibition—States Given Concurrent Power to Enforce

SECTION 1. After one year from the ratification of this article the manufacture, sale, or transportation of intoxicating liquors within, the importation thereof into, or the exportation thereof from the United States and all territory subject to the jurisdiction thereof for beverage purposes is hereby prohibited.

SEC. 2. The Congress and the several States shall have concurrent power to enforce this article by appropriate legislation.

SEC. 3. This article shall be inoperative unless it shall have been ratified as an amendment to the Constitution by the Legislatures of the several States, as provided in the Constitution, within seven years from the date of the submission hereof to the States by the Congress.

(Proposed December 18, 1917; ratified January 16, 1919; certified January 29, 1919; effective January 29, 1920. For repeal see Amendment XXI.)

AMENDMENT XIX

Equal Suffrage

(SECTION 1.) The right of citizens of the United States to vote shall not be denied or abridged by the United States or by any State on account of sex.

(SECTION 2.) Congress shall have power to enforce this article by appropriate legislation.

(Proposed June 4, 1919; ratified August 18, 1920; certified August 26, 1920.)

AMENDMENT XX

Commencement of Congressional and Presidential Terms

End of Terms

SECTION 1. The terms of the President and Vice President shall end at noon on the 20th day of January, and the terms of Senators and Representatives at noon on the 3d day of January, of the years in which such terms would have ended if this article had not been ratified; and the terms of their successors shall then begin.

Assembling of Congress

SEC. 2. The Congress shall assemble at least once in every year, and such meeting shall begin at noon on the 3d day of January, unless they shall by law appoint a different day.

Congress Provides for Acting President

SEC. 3. If, at the time fixed for the beginning of the term of the President, the President-elect shall have died, the Vice-President-elect shall become President. If a President shall not have been chosen before the time fixed for the beginning of his term, or if the President-elect shall have failed to qualify, then the Vice-President-elect shall act as President until a President shall have qualified; and the Congress may by law provide for the case wherein neither a President-elect nor a Vice-President-elect shall have qualified, declaring who shall then act as President, or the manner in which one who is to act shall be selected, and such person shall act accordingly until a President or Vice President shall have qualified.

Congress Has Power Over Unusual Elections

SEC. 4. The Congress may by law provide for the case of the death of any of the persons from whom the House of Representatives may choose a President whenever the right of choice shall have devolved upon them, and for the case of the death of any of the persons from whom the Senate may choose a Vice President whenever the right of choice shall have devolved upon them.

Date in Effect

SEC. 5. Sections 1 and 2 shall take effect on the 15th day of October following the ratification of this article.

Conditions of Ratification

SEC. 6. This article shall be inoperative unless it shall have been ratified as an amendment to the Constitution by the Legislatures of three-fourths of the several States within seven years from the date of its submission.

(Proposed March 2, 1932; ratified January 23, 1933; certified February 6, 1933.)

AMENDMENT XXI

Repeal of Prohibition

Repeal of 18th Amendment

SECTION 1. The eighteenth article of amendment to the Constitution of the United States is hereby repealed.

Control of Interstate Liquor Transportation

SEC. 2. The transportation or importation into any State, Territory, or possession of the United States for delivery or use therein of intoxicating liquors, in violation of the laws thereof, is hereby prohibited.

Condition of Ratification

SEC. 3. This article shall be inoperative unless it shall have been ratified as an amendment to the Constitution by conventions in the several States, as provided in the Constitution, within seven years from the date of the submission hereof to the States by the Congress.

(Proposed February 20, 1933; ratified December 5, 1933; certified December 5, 1933.)

AMENDMENT XXII

Terms of Office of the President

Limitation on Number of Terms

SECTION 1. No person shall be elected to the office of the President more than twice, and no person who has held the office of President, or acted as President, for more than two years of a term to which some other person was elected President shall be elected to the office of the President more than once. But this article shall not apply to any person holding the office of President when this article was proposed by the Congress, and shall not prevent any person who may be holding the office of President, or acting as President, during the term within which this article becomes operative from holding the office of President or acting as President during the remainder of such term.

Condition of Ratification

SECTION 2. This article shall be inoperative unless it shall have been ratified as an amendment to the Constitution by the Legislatures of three-fourths of the several States within seven years from the date of its submission to the States by the Congress.

(Proposed March 24, 1947; ratified February 27, 1951; certified March 1, 1951.)

AMENDMENT XXIII

Voting Rights in the District of Columbia

(SECTION 1.) The district constituting the seat of government of the United States shall appoint in such manner as the Congress may direct:

A number of electors of President and Vice President equal to the whole number of Senators and Representatives in Congress to which the District would be entitled if it were a State, but in no event more than the least populous state; they shall be in addition to those appointed by the states, but they shall be considered, for the purposes of the election of President and Vice President, to be electors appointed by a state; and they shall meet in the District and perform such duties as provided by the twelfth article of amendment.

INDEX OF CASES

Abrams et al v. *United States* (1919), 112

American Communication Association v. *Douds* (1950), 404n.

Anderson v. *Dunn* (1821), 389

Apodaca v. *United States* (1951), 387n.

Baker et al v. *Carr et al* (1962), 273n.

Barenblatt v. *United States* (1959) 393n., 393-394

Braden v. *United States* (1962), 394n.

Brown et al v. *Board of Education* (1954), 401

Cantwell v. *Connecticut* (1940), 117n.

Chapman, In re (1897), 390n.

Civil Rights Cases (1883), 398n.

Dartmouth College v. *Woodward* (1819), 368n.

Debs v. *United States* (1919), 112n.

Dennis v. *United States* (1951), 405

Dollree Mapp v. *Ohio* (1961), 388

Elkins v. *United States* (1960), 387

Everson v. *Board of Education* (1947), 118n.

Feiner v. *New York* (1951), 405

Fletcher v. *Peck* (1810), 368n.

Frohwerk v. *United States* (1919), 112n.

Gitlow v. *New York* (1925), 110n., 113n.

Gojak v. *United States* (1962), 394n.

Guinn v. *United States* (1915), 400n.

Hague v. *Committee for Industrial Organization* (1939), 115n.

Henderson v. *United States* (1950), 401

Home Building and Loan Association v. *Blaisdell* (1934), 369

Humphrey's Executor v. *United States* (1935), 332n.

Jencks v. *United States* (1957), 383

Joint Anti-Fascist Refugee Committee v. *McGrath* (1951), 385

Kilbourn v. *Thompson* (1881), 389n.

Kovacs v. *Cooper* (1949), 115n.

Kremen v. *United States* (1957), 383

Lane v. *Wilson* (1939), 400n.

Liveright v. *United States* (1962), 394n.

Lochner v. *New York* (1905), 369

Louisiana ex rel. Francis v. *Resweber* (1947), 385

Marbury v. *Madison* (1803), 122, 123

McCollum v. *Board of Education* (1948), 118

McCulloch v. *Maryland* (1819), 84

McGrain v. *Daugherty* (1927), 390n.

McLaurin v. *Oklahoma State Regents* (1950), 401n.

Missouri ex rel. Gaines v. *Canada* (1938), 401

Missouri v. *Holland* (1920), 321n.

Near v. *Minnesota* (1931), 110n., 116n.

New Jersey v. *Wilson* (1812), 368n.

Northern Securities Co. v. *United States* (1904), 373

Palko v. *Connecticut* (1937), 384

Pierce v. *United States* (1920), 113n.

Plessy v. *Ferguson* (1896), 400

Price v. *United States* (1962), 394n.

Reynolds v. *United States* (1879), 119n.

Russell v. *United States* (1962), 394n.

Saia v. *New York* (1948), 115n.

Schaefer v. *United States* (1920), 113n.

Schenck v. *United States* (1919), 111n.

Shelton v. *United States* (1962), 394n.

Sipuel v. *University of Oklahoma* (1948), 401

Slaughter House Cases (1873), 399n.

Sturges v. *Crowninshield* (1819), 368n.

Sweatt v. *Painter* (1950), 401

Sweezy v. *New Hampshire* (1957), 390n., 391-393

Terminiello v. *Chicago* (1949), 404

Thomas v. *Collins* (1944), 113*n*.

Times Film Corporation v. *City of Chicago et al* (1961), 116*n*.

United States v. *Ballard* (1944), 119*n*.

United States v. *Curtiss-Wright Export Corporation* (1936), 321*n*.

United States v. *Rabinowitz* (1950), 386

Uphaus v. *Wyman* (1959), 392-393, 395*n*.

Watkins v. *United States* (1957), 390*n*., 391

Whitman v. *United States* (1962), 394*n*.

Wilkinson v. *United States* (1962), 394*n*.

Yates v. *United States* (1957), 113*n*., 406

Youngstown Sheet and Tube Co. v. *Sawyer* (1952), 102*n*., 308*n*.

Zorach v. *Clauson* (1952), 118

INDEX

Adams, Charles Francis, 44n.
Adams, John, 16, 18, 58-59, 61, 84, 122
Adams, John Quincy, 182
Adams, Martin Ray, 44n.
Adams, Samuel, 15, 42-43, 52
Adams, Sherman, 313, 316-317
Adams, Walter, 24n.
administrative agencies, 76, 311-317
Administrative Procedures Act, 334
Adorno, T. W., 167n.
advertising, 3, 6-7; as administrative tool, 347-348; age of, 155; brokerage and, 148; in mass society, 128-130, 139-141; politics and, 199-200
Advertising Council of America, 209
affluent society, 188
AFL-CIO, 196, 199
age differences, voting and, 223-224

agencies, federal, 76, 311-317, 327-333
agrarian life, democracy as, 30
Agriculture Department, 325, 340, 351
Alexander, Franz, 136n., 226n.
Alien and Sedition Acts, 29, 86, 110
Almond, Gabriel A., 421n.
"alphabet" agencies, 91
Altgeld, Peter, 133
ambition, restrained by federalism, 83; power and, 43
amendments, to Constitution, see Constitution, U.S.
amendments and riders, to bills, 296-298
American Bar Association, 372
American Civil Liberties Union, 114, 190, 192, 387, 408
American Legion, 191
American Medical Association, 351

American Revolution, 15, 93
American Telephone and Telegraph Co., 137
American way, controversy over, 18-19
anomy, growth of, 141-144
Anti-Federalist party, 84
Anti-Saloon League, 174, 191
apathy, voter's, 209-220, 237; futility and, 215-220, 238; nonpartisanship as, 144; public relations and, 204
Appleby, Paul H., 157, 339
Arendt, Hannah, 105, 356*n*.
aristocracy, vs. democracy, 59; protection of, 61
Arnold, Thurman, 55*n*.
Articles of Confederation, 78
Arvey, Jake, 231
Association of American Light and Power Companies, 190
atheism, communism and, 21-22
Attorney General, 315, 383; *see also* cabinet
authoritarianism, open society and, 25-27
authority, liberty and, 105-119

bail, excessive, 104
Bailey, Stephen K., 170, 179*n*.
balance of power, 60-62
Bank, first U.S., 330
bar associations, 374
Barbu, Zevedei, 167*n*.
Barenblatt case, 393-395, 406
Barkley, Alben W., 269, 340
Barlow, Joel, 44-45, 52
Barzun, Jacques, 162*n*.
Batten, Barton, Durstine and Osborn, 199
Beard, Charles A., 183
behavior, determinism or mechanism in, 135-136; in mass society, 128-129; *see also* voting behavior
behavioral science, 382; *see also* psychology
belief, freedom of, 29
Bell, Bernard Iddings, 5*n*.
Bell, Daniel, 232*n*.
"belongingness," voting and, 232
Bennett, John C., 134*n*.
Bentley, Arthur F., 155, 156*n*., 407*n*.
Benton, William, 256
Berelson, Bernard R., 210*n*., 213*n*., 221*n*., 223*n*., 226*n*., 233*n*.
Bernays, Edward L., 136*n*., 348*n*.
bicameralism, 68, 270-272
bigness, growth of, 137-139
bill of attainder, 81
Bill of Rights, 99-100, 383-385, 388; courts

and, 120; *see also* civil rights; freedom
bills, introduction of, 290-294; test votes on, 298
bipartisanship, 372, 417-418
Black, Hugo L., 113, 118, 393-394, 396, 405
Block, Herbert, 170
Blough, Roger, 311
blue laws, 119
Bode, Boyd, 422
Boorstin, Daniel, 107*n*.
Borah, William E., 264
bossism, 32; decline of, 197-199; Congressman as "tool" of, 246-247
Bowers, Claude G., 45*n*.
Braden case, 394
Brandeis, Louis D., 112, 373
Bricker, John W., 322
Brodbeck, Arthur, 142*n*., 238*n*.
brokerage process, 149; amendments and riders in, 297-298; commissions and, 333-338; committees and, 294-295; human nature and, 163; judicial process as, 407-408; vs. machine and bossism, 197-199; in mass democracy, 148; military complex and, 416; new problems and, 413; theory of, 149-162
broker politician, as legislator, 246
brokers, "age" of, 148, 155
Bryan, William Jennings, 187
Buchanan, James, 304
budget, national, growth of, 137
Burdick, Eugene, 142*n*., 238*n*.
bureaucracy, 97; "expert" and, 344-347; in New York City, 197-198; problem of, 338-347; public interest and, 327-353; size and, 137; spoils system and, 341-344; "wilderness" of, 327-328
Bureau of the Budget, 314
Burke, Edmund, 18, 55, 59, 134
Burns, James, 252*n*.
Burton, Harold, 372-373
business interests, state governments and, 95-97; *see also* private interests

cabinet, foreign policy and, 324; responsibilities of, 315-317
Calhoun, John C., 150-153
California State Employees Association, 341*n*.
Calvinism, 44-45, 135
Campbell, Angus, 218*n*., 220*n*., 221*n*., 224*n*., 225*n*., 227*n*., 231*n*.
Cannon, Joseph G., 281
capitalism, democracy as, 22-24

captive audiences, 115
Cardozo, Justice Benjamin N., 104, 361, 385, 408-409
Carney, F. M., 313n.
Carr, E. H., 35n., 136n.
Carver, Thomas Nixon, 39
Caylor, Arthur, 63n.
Central Intelligence Agency, 315, 325, 347, 351
certiorari, writ of, 375-376
Chafee, Zechariah, Jr., 111n.
Chancery court, 363
change, adaptability to, 239
checks and balances, 66-78; Calhoun and, 150; historical development of, 74-78; veto groups and, 153-154; *see also* separation of powers
Church, democracy and, 19-22; mass society and, 142-143
Church-state separation, 117-118
citizen, mass man as, 144; politician and, 205-207; role of in democratic process, 163-165; as ruler, 100-101
citizenship, crisis in, 421-422; responsibilities of, 422-423; self-interest and, 214; voting behavior and, 208-240
Civil Aeronautics Board, 331
civil law, 367
civil liberties, 100-102; extent of, 109-110; public interest and, 114; public morality and, 116-117; *see also* civil rights
civil rights, 102-105, 185, 257, 272; and civil liberties, 106-109, 119-121; courts and, 384, 387; in Constitution, 100
Civil Rights Act of 1875, 398; of 1957, 244, 257, 277, 399; of 1960, 399
civil service, spoils system and, 341-344
Civil Service Commission, 312, 330
Civil War, 30, 36, 86-87, 93, 96, 109, 183, 190, 227, 369, 397, 411; brokerage process and, 160; compromise and, 153; Supreme Court following, 123
Clark, Tom, 372-373, 393
"clear and present danger," 112-113
Clemenceau, Georges, 304
cloture, 276-278
"club," legislature as, 180, 262-267
coercion and brokerage politics, 162; majority rule and, 151
Cohen, Felix S., 357, 358n., 360n., 407n.
Cohen, Morris R., 48n., 124, 357, 381
Cold War, 21, 110, 320, 414, 418
Commerce Department, 325, 351
commissions, independent, 331-338; influencing of, 335, 351-352

committees, political party, 177-178
committees and committee system, 283-294; bills and, 290-294; investigating power of, 289; list of, 287; powers of, 285; staff assistance to, 288; testimony before, 292-293; types of, 285-287
common law, 362-364
communism, as atheism, 19-22; challenge of, 1-3; democracy and, 25-33; "objective historical laws" in, 27; "people's democracies" in, 27; religion and, 21; vs. socialism, 22-23; treason and, 102
Communist Party, dogma of, 27; Supreme Court and, 404-406
community, need for, 58
comparative cultures, 28
compromise, alternatives to, 168; basis of, 161; Calhoun's theory of, 152-153; vs. conscience, 256-258; democratic politics and, 169-171; as drift, 171; as legitimate and desirable, 168; progress and, 171; role of in democratic theories, 167-169; in Senate, 260, 265; as substitute for debate, 56; unorganized groups in, 169-170
concurrent majority, defined, 152
confederation, 78
conference committees, 286
Congress, U.S., bicameral nature of, 68; committee system in, 283-294; investigating power of, 289; lawmaking process in, 290-301; legislator's responsibility in, 242-243; list of committees, 287; party control of, 278-280; party organization in, 252; powers of, 79-80, 88-90; power structure in, 263; "purge" of, 76; seniority system in, 281-282; voting in, 298-299; *see also* legislative organization and procedure; legislative investigations
Congressional districts, 35, 272-274
Congressional Quarterly, 195-196, 252n., 261, 267n., 270n., 273n., 281n., 289n., 335n., 415n., 416n.
Congressman, average constituency of, 273; committee assignments of, 283-284; types and backgrounds of, 258-262; *see also* legislator; senators
Connecticut Compromise, 82
Connole, William R., 334
conscience, vs. compromise, 256-258; liberty of, 107
Conscience of a Conservative, The, 88
consensus, cleavage and, 234-235; diversity and, 238

consent, communist doctrine of, 27; meaning of, 421; theory of, 17
"consent engineering," 7, 136
conservatism, theory of, 60-62
Constitution, U.S., 16-17, 29, 56, 62; amendments to: First, 47, 101-102, 109-111, 116-117, 300, 393-396, 403; Fourth, 104, 386-389; Fifth, 103, 300, 390-391; Sixth, 104; Eighth, 103-104; Tenth, 79, 321; Eleventh, 374-375; Twelfth, 75; Fourteenth, 104, 110-111, 113, 117, 257, 273, 300, 369, 387-388, 402; Sixteenth, 88; Seventeenth, 75; Bill of Rights, 99-100, 120, 384-388; as "democratic battleground," 63-125; checks and balances in, 63-97; Congressional authority in, 243; on contracts, 368; "cult" of, 123-124; first ten amendments, 99-100; four principles of, 65-78; implied powers in, 84-85; limitations in, 102-103; "loose" vs. "strict" construction of, 85; need for written constitution, 65; powers of Congress, President, and States defined in, 79-82; Supreme Court and, 115-125, 396-402; unwritten vs. written, 65, 102; "worship" of, 378; *see also* Supreme Court
constitutional government, as limited government, 98
constitutionalism, democracy as, 24-25; liberal vs. conservative, 64-65
constitutional principles, 65-78
consumer goods, vs. capital goods, 26
controversy, avoidance of, 211; heritage of, 18-19; politics as, 211; withdrawal from, 138, 211
Cook, Fred J., 197n., 198n., 414, 415n.
Coolidge, Calvin, 304
Corcoran, Thomas G., 333-335
corporations, g o v e r n m e n t, 328-331; growth of, 23, 137
corruption, in regulatory commission, 351
Council of Economic Advisers, 315
county central committees, 177
courts, "due process" guarantee and, 383-396; jurisdiction of, 375-376; as moral guardian, 378-382; as political institutions, 368-370; in politics, 377-410; role of in government, 121-125, 367-370; and rule of law, 354-376; structure of, 370-371; *see also* judicial process; Supreme Court
Cralle, Richard K., 151n.
crime, punishment and, 381
criminal law, 365-367; causal factors and, 380

crisis, *see* cultural crisis; political crisis
Crossman, Richard, 6n.
Cuban invasion (1961), 323, 346-347, 418
cultural crisis, 4-5
cultural relativism, 129, 131-132
cultural universals, 28
culture, in mass society, 128-132
Cunningham, Noble E., Jr., 53
Cushing, Harry Alonzo, 43n.

Dahl, Robert A., 83n., 158n., 163-164
Darrow, Clarence, 20, 133
Darwin, Charles, 135
Daugherty, Harry, 390
Daughters of the American Revolution, 191
debate, legislative, 276-278
Debs, Eugene V., 187
decision-making, brokerage and, 155
Declaration of Independence, 17, 20, 35
defense contracts, 416
Defense Department, 324
De Grazia, Alfred, 154n.
democracy, as autocracy of people, 52; as American constitutionalism, 24-25; as "American credo," 14-19; brokerage politics and, 162; as capitalism, 22-24; vs. communism, 25-33; changes in historical meaning of, 55-56; and consent of governed, 419-423; conservative theories of, 56-62; defense of, 411; dilemma of, 27-32; "equality" ideal in, 5; failure of, 6; foreign policy and, 417-418; "freedoms" of, 28-29; internal and external crises in, 1-3; essence of, 7; law in, 356-357; liberal, 39-42; as majority rule, 35-37; mass, *see* mass democracy; mass opinion in, 6; mass society and, 130-131; as minorities rule, 149-171; "myth" of, 53; open society and, 27-32; opposition of Founding Fathers to, 16; Paine's definition of, 56; "people's," under communism, 27; as "power-less" Utopia, 53; procedural universals of, 28-29; pure, 52; reason and, 57-58; as religious faith, 19-22; vs. republic, 63-64; rhetoric of, 37-38; self-inquiry or debate in, 25; total war and, 7-8; "town-meeting" type of, 52; universals in, 28
Democracy in America, 127
Democratic Advisory Council, 179
Democratic Clubs, California, 181
democratic government, *see* democracy
Democratic National Committee, 179

Democratic party, strength of, 183; in suburbs, 231
democratic politics, new agenda of, 411-423
"democratic revolution," eighteenth century, 15
democratic theories, conflict of, 34-62; crisis in, 232-240; mass electorate and, 208-232; vs. practice, 2-3; traditional, 236-240; voter and, 232-240
depravity of man, doctrine of, 60
desegregation, 86, 121, 124, 397-402; Supreme Court and, 166
de Tocqueville, Alexis, see Tocqueville, Alexis de
Dewey, John, 44n.
Dewey, Thomas E., 221, 266
Dickinson, John, 157n.
dictatorship, rise of, 413-414; see also totalitarian society
Dirksen, Everett M., 265, 278
Dole, Robert, 273
Donovan, Robert J., 306n.
double jeopardy, 384-385
Douglas, Paul H., 230
Douglas, William O., 113, 115, 385, 394
due process clause, 103-104; court as guarantor of, 383-394; law enforcement and, 383-388; legislative investigations and, 388, 396
Dulles, J. F., 306
Durham Rule, 381

Eastland, James O., 259
economic opportunity, equality of, 18
Edward III, 363
"eggheads," liberalism and, 57
Eisenhower, Dwight D., 186, 232, 304, 313, 316-317, 334, 351, 415; concept of administration of, 305, 306; vote for, 188
Ekirch, Arthur A., 39n.
Eldersveld, Samuel J., 154n., 210n.
electoral process, in mass democracy, 146-147; see also electorate
electorate, political power and, 205-207; turnout of, 35-36, 209; see also voter; voting
Employment Act of 1946, 170
England, constitution of, 102
Enlightenment, The, 133
equality, democratic ideal of, 5; group conflict and, 158-162; hierarchy and, 58; judicial enforcement of, 401-402; liberty and, 15; of rights, 50; tyranny and, 150; under communism, 27; variety of meanings of, 17

equity, 363-364
"Era of Good Feelings," 41, 182
Espionage Act of 1917, 111
Estes, Billie Sol, 395
Eulau, Heinz, 154n., 210n.
executive agencies, rule-making powers of, 312
executive agreements, 322
executive control, 312-313
Executive Office of the President, 314-315; see also Presidency; President
ex post facto law, 81, 99

factions, responsibility and, 301; tyranny of, 40-42
Fair Deal, 186
family, as voting unit, 225-226
Farm Bureau Federation, 199
Farm Equipment Workers Union, 390-391
federal aid, to states, 91-92
Federal Bureau of Investigation, 372, 383-384
Federal Communications Commission, 76, 331-332
federal courts, 370-371; see also courts
federal departments, 315-316; rule-making powers of, 312
federal government, war power of, 89; see also Congress, U.S.; national government
federalism, 78-97; as compromise, 82-84; foreign policy and, 321-322; historical development of, 84-95; instruments of, 88; public interest and, 95-97; and states rights, 81-88
Federalist, The, 17, 40, 42, 56, 64, 68, 70-72, 77, 83, 107, 133
Federalist party, 29, 41, 84, 86, 122, 182, 357
Federal Power Commission, 76, 331-333, 367
Federal Trade Commission, 76, 331
Fiedler, Leslie A., 142n., 238n.
Fifth Amendment, 103, 300, 369, 390-391
filibuster, 277; see also cloture
First Amendment, 47, 101-102, 109-117, 300, 393-396, 403, 405; religious clause in, 116-118
Fischer, John, 160n., 220n., 325
Flanders, Ralph, 256
Fleeson, Doris, 333, 336
foreign policy, cabinet and, 324-325; challenge of, 413-415; democracy and, 7, 417-418; federalism and, 321-322; machinery of, 324-325; in nuclear era, 319-321; politics of,

325-326; President and, 319-326
Founding Fathers, 16, 52, 56, 67, 87, 97, 102, 121, 127, 133; conflict among, 106-109; overidealizing of, 29
Fourth Amendment, 104, 384, 386-387
Fourteenth Amendment, 104, 117, 257, 273, 300, 369, 384-385, 387, 402; free speech and, 110-113; see also Constitution, U.S.
Frankel, Charles, 205n.
Frankfurter, Felix, 113, 274, 374, 385n., 386-388, 392, 408
Frankl, Viktor E., 240n.
Franklin, Benjamin, 16
freedom(s), in Bill of Rights, 99-100; courts and, 390-391; defense of, 411; in democratic society, 28-29; in First Amendment, 101; law and, 355-356; natural rights and, 47; pluralistic society and, 32; protection of from majorities, 109; Supreme Court decisions on, 110-111; vs. toleration, 107
Freemasons, 41
free speech, 46-47; see also civil liberties; First Amendment
French Revolution, 86
Freneau, Philip, 45
Freud, Sigmund, 135
Friedrich, Carl J., 98n.
Fromm, Erich, 167n.
Full Employment Act, 298
Furlong, William B., 265n.
futility, voter's feeling of, 216-220

Galbraith, John Kenneth, 214
Galloway, George G., 275n.
gambling, 379
Gasset, José Ortega y, 5n.
General Accounting Office, 328
generalist, vs. specialist, 346
generalizations, voting and, 222-223
"general welfare," federalism and, 89-90
Gerry, Elbridge, 272-273
gerrymandering, 35, 273
Gibbon, Edward, 106-108
Ginger, Ray, 133
Ginsburg, Benjamin, 349n.
Glazer, Nathan, 213n.
Gleason, Gene, 197n.
Glorious Revolution (1688), 20
Goethe, Wolfgang von, 240
Golden, Harry, 293
Goldfine, Bernard S., 317
Goldman, Eric F., 303-304
Goldsmith, Oliver, 128

Goldwater, Barry, 88, 230
Gosnell, Harold Foote, 187n.
government, criticism of, 25-26; framework of, 9-10; influence on vs. control of, 174; limited, 98-121; vs. politics, 9-14; responsible, 299-301; role of courts in, 121-125
governmental power, individual liberty and, 99-105
government corporations, 328-331
grandfather clause, 400
grand jury, 100
grants-in-aid, 91
Gray, Horace M., 24n.
Great Depression, 95, 185-186
Gross, Bertram M., 278n.
group association, voting and, 226
Group Basis of Politics, The, 170
group interests, conciliation of, 235-236
group theory, in politics, 157-162
Gurin, Gerald, 218n., 220n., 221n., 225n., 227n.

habeas corpus, 100
Hague, Frank, 197
Haines, Charles G., 360n.
Halleck, Charles A., 266, 281
Hallenbeck, Wilbur C., 230n.
Hallowell, John H., 19n., 171n.
Hamilton, Alexander, 16-17, 48, 72, 84-85
Hand, Learned, 112, 114
Harbison, Winfred A., 399n.
Harlan, John M., 398, 406
harmony, quest for, 141-142
Harriman, Averill, 262
Harris, Louis, 231n.
Hartford Convention, 87
Hathorn, Guy B., 181n.
Hayden, Carl, 259
Hayes, Rutherford B., 304
Hayne, Robert Y., 87
Health, Education, and Welfare Department, 351
health insurance, 194
Hebert, F. Edward, 416
Hector, Lewis J., 335-336
Heilbroner, R. L., 350n.
Henry, Patrick, 15
hierarchy, need for, 58-60
Hobbes, Thomas, 355
Hoffa, James, 395
Hoffer, Eric, 167n.
Holmes, Oliver Wendell, 20, 111-112, 369, 373, 379, 403

Hooton, E. A., 132
Hoover, Herbert, 185
Hoover, J. Edgar, 383
Hoover Commissions, 327
Hopkins, Harry, 305, 313
Horn, Robert A., 170*n*.
House Armed Services Committee, 416
House of Representatives, 274; debate in, 276-278; leadership in, 280, 281; size of, 274
House Rules Committee, 276
House un-American Activities Committee, 393-394
Housing and Home Finance Agency, 328
Hughes, Charles Evans, 369, 373, 408
human nature, democratic theories and, 45-46, 56-57
Hume, David, 57
Humphrey, Hubert H., 179, 414
Hutcheson, Joseph, 359

idealist, as legislator, 247
"image," in public relations, 202
implied powers, 84-85
income groups, voting and, 222-225
individual, vs. entire electorate, 216; and politics, 210-213
individualism, doctrine of, 43-46
individual liberty, government power and, 99-105
industrialism, culture and, 4-5; democracy and, 30
industry, growth of, 137
influence, commissioners and, 335
information officers, 348, 350
insanity, legal, 380-381
intellectual changes, mass society and, 134-137
interest groups, 6; *see also* pressure groups; private interests
interposition, states' rights and, 86
interstate commerce, 90-91
Interstate Commerce Commission, 76, 331
investigations, Congressional, 289, 389-396
irrationality, role of, 57-58

Jackson, Andrew, 25, 123
Jackson, Robert H., 103, 115, 374, 404
Jacob, Philip E., 132*n*.
Janowitz, Morris, 154*n*., 210*n*.
Jefferson, Thomas, 15-18, 20, 23, 25, 29, 35, 42, 44, 47, 52, 70-71, 77, 110, 125, 304, 357; agrarian ideal of, 93; on Church and state, 117; defense of

majority rule by, 50
Jeffersonian democracy, 30
Jeffersonian party, 41, 85, 110, 182
Jehovah's Witnesses, 115, 119
John Birch Society, 63, 190, 260, 420
Johnson, Hiram, 251
Johnson, Lyndon, 180, 257, 266, 281*n*., 318, 334
Johnson, Dr. William Samuel, 82
Joint Chiefs of Staff, 315
Joint Economic Committee, 315
joint committees, 286
judge, as public servant, 358; selection of, 371-374
judicial decisions, theories of arriving at, 358-361
judicial process, as brokerage, 407-408; majority rule and, 408-410; nature of, 357-361
judicial review, 121-125, 408-410
justice, rules of, 41; standards of, 48
Justice Department, 351, 383

Kahn, R. L., 224*n*.
Kelley, Stanley, Jr., 201*n*., 205
Kelly, Alfred H., 399*n*.
Kelsen, Hans, 130
Kennedy, John F., 204, 257, 262, 284*n*., 285, 297, 304, 307, 318; in steel industry dispute, 309-311
Kennedy-Nixon debates, 189, 205
Key, V. O., 183*n*.
Knowland, William F., 265
Korean War, 201, 307
Krutch, Joseph Wood, 135*n*.
Ku Klux Klan, 125

Labor Department, 324, 351
labor unions, as pressure groups, 173, 192-193
laissez-faire, 51, 73, 163, 167, 192, 232, 239, 338, 369, 373; Adam Smith's theory of, 93; advertising and, 140; bureaucracy and, 340; capitalism and, 22-23
Landrum-Griffin labor bill, 367
Lane, Robert E., 154*n*., 213*n*.
Langer, William, 259
Lasswell, Harold D., 13*n*.
Latham, Earl, 156*n*., 158*n*., 162*n*., 170, 192*n*.
Lausche, Frank J., 259
law, defined, 361; duty and, 357; freedom and, 355-356; government of, 104, 243; ignorance of, 103; interpretation of, 360; man and, 243-244; quality of,

383; rule of, 66, 354-376; society and, 354-355; violation of, 103
lawmaking, 290-301; *see also* legislation; legislature
Lazarsfeld, Paul F., 210*n.*, 213*n.*, 221*n.*, 223*n.*, 226*n.*, 233*n.*
League of Nations, 303, 413
Lee, Richard Henry, 16
legal decisions, nature of, 358-361
legal heritage, court as trustee of, 379-382
legal principles, sources of, 361-367
legislation, committee system and, 284-294; debate on, 295-298; in election years, 217-218; political parties and, 250-253; *see also* legislative process
legislative districts, 272-274
legislative environment, 248-253
legislative investigations, due process and, 388-396
legislative leadership, 280-282
legislative organization and procedure, 268-301; necessity for, 274-278
legislative process, 290-301; responsibility and, 299-301
legislators, characteristics of, 261-262; conscience vs. compromise in, 256-258; defined, 245-248; dilemmas of, 253-258; lobbyist and, 244-245, 248-250; role of, 241-243; types of, 245-248, 258-261
legislatures, 241-267; evaluating of, 244-245; party control of, 278-280; seniority system in, 281-282
Levin, Murray B., 218*n.*, 222
Lewis, R. Cragin, 194
libel laws, 116
liberal democracy, theory of, 39-42
liberalism, assumptions of, 42-56; intellectualism and, 57
liberty, authority and, 105-119; civil, *see* civil liberties; equality and, 15 (*see also* equality); right to, 20-21; toleration and, 106
licensing, regulation and, 337
Liebling, A. J., 202*n.*
limited government, 98-121
Lincoln, Abraham, 35, 304; on majority rule, 37
Lincoln-Douglas debates, 154
Linton, Ralph, 28*n.*
Lippmann, Walter, 6*n.*, 34, 171, 221
Lipset, Seymour Martin, 182*n.*, 237*n.*
Lishman, Robert W., 334
lobbies and lobbying, 190; committees and, 293; expenditures on, 195-196; legislatures and, 244-245, 248-250; for Negroes, 412; power of, 251, 255;

pressure groups and, 193-194
Locke, John, 20, 47, 66
Lodge, Henry Cabot, 303
"lonely crowd," 141
Long, Earl, 202
Long, Huey, 277
Lowell, A. Lawrence, 39, 40*n.*, 147-148, 155
"loyal opposition," concept of, 54
Lubell, Samuel, 231*n.*
Luce, Robert, 271*n.*

McCarl, John R., 328
McCarthy, Joseph R., 102, 114, 120, 202, 259, 263, 289
McClellan, John B., 395
McCulloch v. *Maryland*, 84
MacIver, R. M., 48, 238
McKinley, William, 94
McNaughten Rule, 381
McPhee, William N., 210*n.*, 213*n.*, 221*n.*, 223*n.*, 226*n.*, 233*n.*
McReynolds, James C., 372-373
Madison, James, 16, 40-41, 48, 59, 64, 67, 70-71, 75, 83, 107, 133, 151, 160, 420
"Madison Avenue," 138, 199-205
Maine, Sir Henry, 155
majority, concurrent, 150-153; *see also* majority rule
majority rule, Constitution and, 75-77; decline of, 35-39; defense of, 50-56; vs. minority rights, 50-52; problem of, 39-40; vs. representative government, 55; as tyranny, 61, 83, 109, 157; usage and practices in, 75
majority tyranny, 61; federalism as bulwark against, 83; freedom and, 109; power aspirations and, 157
man, as consumer, 140; mechanistic view of, 135; *see also* mass man
Mansfield, Mike, 278
Marbury v. *Madison*, 122
Maritain, Jacques, 19*n.*
Marshall, John, 84, 122-123, 368
Martin, Joseph W., 266-267, 281
Marx, Karl, 1, 135
Mason, Alpheus Thomas, 50*n.*
Mason, George, 72
mass democracy, decision-making process in, 147-148; electoral process in, 146-147; parties and pressure groups in, 145-146; politics of, 144-148
mass electorate, 208-232
masses, ascendancy of, 5-6; democracy and, 5
mass man, as citizen, 144-145; as politician, 145; rootlessness of, 141

mass media, advertising and, 139-141
mass opinion, 6
mass society, advertising and, 140; citizenship and, 421; growth of, 127-144; politics of, 126-148, 419-420
Matthews, Donald R., 264*n.*
Mayflower Compact, 99
Mayo, Henry B., 174, 228*n.*, 253*n.*
mechanism, growth of, 134-137
Meiklejohn, Alexander, 111*n.*
merit system, vs. spoils system, 343-344
Merriam, Charles Edward, 187*n.*
Mickelson, Sig, 204*n.*
middle way, vs. extremism, 420
Mill, John Stuart, 227
Miller, Warren E., 218*n.*, 220*n.*, 221*n.*, 225*n.*, 227*n.*
Miller, William Lee, 200*n.*
Mills, C. Wright, 6*n.*, 37*n.*, 209, 237
minorities rule, challenge of, 162-171; democracy as, 149-171; growth of, 37; modern theory of, 155-162; tyranny and, 42, 150-151
Minton, Sherman, 373
misinformation, among voters, 221
missile race, 186
Monroe, James, 182
Monroe Doctrine, 320
Montesquieu, Charles de, 66
Moore, Norman B., 387*n.*
morality and moral order, belief in, 4; civil liberties and, 116; court as guardian of, 378-382; individualism and, 44-45; Supreme Court and, 124
Morgan, Arthur E., 345*n.*
Morse, Wayne, 230, 256, 277
motivation, in politics, 10-11
muckrakers, 93
Muller, Herbert, 128, 143
Murphy, Frank, 113
Myers, Francis M., 171*n.*
Myrdal, Gunnar, 378
myths, tradition and, 30

National Association for the Advancement of Colored People, 412
National Association of Manufacturers, 160, 190, 192, 199
national bank, 84
national committees, 178
national government, business pressures on, 95-97; commerce and taxing power of, 89-90; growth of, 137; powers of, 89-92; war power of, 89; *see also* federalism
National Labor Relations Board, 367
National Petroleum Council, 349

national power, growth of, 92
National Science Foundation, 328
National Security Council, 314, 325
Natural Gas Act, 332, 367
natural gas lobby, 334
"natural law," belief in, 5
natural rights, doctrine of, 44, 46-48, 98, 107
Negro, Civil Rights Act and, 398-399; constitutional protection of, 397; equality for, 400-401, 412; as second-class citizen, 218-219
Negro vote, 412
Neuberger, Richard L., 245*n.*
New Deal, 186
New Frontier, 285
New York City, politics of, 197-198
New York *World Telegram and Sun*, 199
Niebuhr, Reinhold, 19*n.*
Nixon, Richard M., 262, 267, 280, 313, 316
nonpartisanship, 53, 372, 417; apathy and, 210
Norman Conquest, 362
Notes on Virginia, 70-71
nuclear war, 320, 418
nullification, 85-86

Office of Civil and Defense Mobilization, 314
old-age pensions, 92
O'Mahoney, Joseph C., 259
open society, 25-27, 167-168; *see also* pluralistic society
organization man, 137
Orwell, George, 237
O'Sullivan, John L., 72, 75
out-party, 180

Packard, Vance, 199*n.*
Paine, Thomas, 15, 18, 20, 42, 56, 107, 110
Parker, John J., 373
parties, political, 172-190; control of legislature by, 278-280; distinguished from pressure groups, 173-176; formal structure of, 176-179; history of in America, 182-185; ideological differences between, 182-189; legislation and, 250-253; in mass democracy, 145-146; mass man and, 144; myth of democracy and, 53; pressure groups and, 173-174; rise of, 74-75
party differences, factors obscuring, 185-187
party organization, 181-182, 252-253; structure and, 177-181

patriotic symbols, 58
Pendleton Act, 342
Pennock, J. Roland, 17*n*.
"people," democracy as, 31; political power and, 206; *see also* citizen; electorate; public
Pepper, Claude, 194
perfectionism, 422
Pericles, 421
Pfiffner, J. M., 345*n*.
pluralistic society, democracy and, 423; and open society, 25; pressure groups and, 206; totalitarianism and, 32-33
political conflict, resolution of, 11-12
political heritage, 18-19
political parties, *see* parties, political
political power, 12-13, 52-54, 205-207; *see also* power
political responsibility, 53-54, 57, 171, 332
politics, courts and, 377-410; distractions from, 215; futility in, 217-218; vs. government, 9-14; Gresham's Law of, 215; group basis of, 157-159; vs. individuality, 210-213; legitimacy of, 13-14; as "masquerade," 218; motivations and techniques of, 10-11; nature of, 9; new problems of, 411-423; religion and, 211; "retreat" from, 8; power and, 12-13, 52-54, 156-157, 205-207
Populist parties, 187
pornography, 379
Port of New York Authority, 330
Post Office Department, 351
Potter, David M., 140*n*.
Pound, Roscoe, 360*n*., 407
power, American aversion to, 186; individual liberty and, 99-105; motivations for, 43; national, 92; politics and, 12-13, 52-54, 156-157, 205-207
power groups and elites, 6
power lobby, 190
powers, separation of, 66-78
precinct or ward, 177
Presidency, increased power of, 77; office and man, 302-306; power of, 309-311
President, administration and, 302-326; administrative aides to, 313-315; appointment of judges by, 371-372; cabinet officers, 315-317; as chief diplomat, 322; as Chief Executive, 311-315; as chief foreign-policy maker, 323-326; as Commander-in-Chief, 323; executive powers of, 311-315; foreign policy and, 319-326; leadership by, 317-319; powers of, 80; public speeches of, 303-305; role of, 70; and separation of powers, 317-319; as spokesman for public interest, 306-313; veto power of, 299, 317
Presidential election, vote turnout in, 35-36, 209
President's Committee on Civil Rights, 120
pressure groups, 172-174, 190-197; in mass democracy, 145-146; money and influence in, 195-197; nature of, 189-197; vs. parties, 172-176; pluralism and, 197, 250; recent changes in, 191-193; types of, 190-191
price controls, misinformation on, 221
principle, politics of, 54
Pritchett, Herman, 369*n*., 372*n*., 374, 389*n*.
privacy, invasion of, 104, 115
private interests, 190, 192; voting and, 218, 227-228
private property, democracy and, 31
procedural freedoms, 29; in pluralistic society, 32
Process of Government, The, 155
professional expert, politician as, 203
Profiles in Courage, 206*n*.
progress, vs. compromise, 171
Progressive party, 187
Prohibition amendment, 174
propaganda, 131, 136; vs. information, 348
property interests, 95-97
property rights, 31, 51
prosperity, postwar, 185
psychiatry, law and, 380-381
psychology, use of, 3, 136
public interest, bureaucracy and, 350-353; controversy over, 53-54; defined, 49; doctrine of, 48-49; free speech and, 110-114; myth of, 7; President as spokesman for, 306-313; voting and, 227-230
public-opinion polling, 55, 139
public philosophy, 171
public policy, as "equilibrium," 158
public relations, 3, 136, 138-139; as administrative tool, 347-350; rise of, 199-205
punishment, law and, 381-382
Pure Food and Drug Administration, 76
Puritanism, 45

radicalism, 420

radio and television, 139-141, 201
Randall, Clarence, 308
Randolph, John, 18
rationalizations, human interests and, 151
Rayburn, Sam, 179-180, 281*n.*, 334
real-estate lobby, 190
reason, democracy and, 57-58; faith in, 106; vs. passion, 71
Reconstruction Finance Corporation, 330, 340
redistricting, 272-274
Reed, Stanley F., 115, 385
Reed, Thomas Bracket, 275
regulation, problem of, 336-337
regulatory commissions, 331-338
relativism, mass society and, 129-130
religion, 4; freedom of, 20, 99; of legislators, 261; politics and, 211; voting behavior and, 223-227
religious toleration, 107-108
Remini, Robert V., 41*n.*
Reorganization Act, 303
representation, principle of, 42, 55, 64
representative government, 55
Representatives, House of, *see* House of Representatives
republic, vs. democracy, 63-64; Paine's definition of, 48
republican principle, 42
Republican party, 188; of California, 181; "moderation" of, 232; public relations efforts, 199-201; strength of, 183-184; in suburbia, 231
responsibility, political, 53-54, 57, 171, 332
Revolutionary tradition, 357
revolutions, postwar, 320
riders, amendments and, 296-298
Riesman, David, 132, 137-139, 213*n.*, 238
rights, in Constitution, 99-100; equality of, 50; *see also* freedom
rights of man, 46-48
Roberts Rules of Order, 274
Roche, John P., 237*n.*
Rockefeller, Nelson, 262
Roman Empire, 106-107
Roosevelt, Eleanor, 179
Roosevelt, Franklin D., 25, 76, 124, 279, 303, 313; administrative concept, 305-306
Roosevelt, Theodore, 94, 187, 303-304, 373
Rosenberg, Bernard, 220
Rosenberg, Morris, 210*n.*, 214*n.*
Rossiter, Clinton, 59*n.*, 222

Russell, Bertrand, 129, 339
Russell, Richard B., 259, 416
Rutledge, Wiley B., 113

Samish, Artie, 251
Schattschneider, E. E., 191
science, religion and, 4
search warrants, 383
secession, right of, 85-86
Securities and Exchange Commission, 76, 331
segregation, background of, 397-401; democratic politics and, 166; *see also* desegregation
self-interest, 152; citizenship and, 214; democracy and, 164, 423
Senate, U.S., as "club," 262-267; debate in, 276; internal fights in, 266; president of, 280; size of, 274
senators, backgrounds of, 259-267; stereotype of, 269; types of, 259-261
seniority, in legislative organization, 281-282
separation of powers, 66-78; courts and, 367; Presidential leadership and, 317-319
shared interests, brokerage and, 165
Sherman Anti-Trust Act, 373
Shubert, Glendon A., Jr., 353
slander, 116
Slaughter House cases, 400
slavery issue, 152
Slichter, Sumner, 414
Smathers, George, 194
Smith, Adam, 93
Smith, Alfred E., 227
Smith, Gerald L. K., 404
Smith, Howard W., 284*n.*
Smith, T. V., 161
Smith Act, 406
social changes, development of mass society and, 137-144
social Darwinism, 94
social determinism, 380
socialism, "creeping," 192
Socialist party, 187
socialized medicine, 194
social life, law and, 355
social needs, 422
social ostracism, 134
Social Security Act of 1935, 91
social security program, 92, 186
society, mass, *see* mass society
socio-economic status, voting and, 219, 222-224, 231

Socrates, 29, 354
Soviet Union, 101; Constitution of 1936, 21; cultural thaw in, 26; foreign policy and, 320; religious freedom in, 21
Speaker of the House, 280-281
speech, freedom of, 28-29, 100-117; *see also* freedom; civil liberties; First Amendment
spoils system, 341-344
stability, flexibility and, 233-234
Stalin, Joseph, 26
stare decisis, 363, 402
state central commitees, 177
state courts, judges for, 374
State Department, 324
state governments, pressures on, 95-96
states, powers prohibited to, 81-82
states' rights, 79-81; desegregation and, 87-88; secession and, 85-86
status quo, 409; defense of, 46; tolerance and, 107-108
status-striving, 11
statutory law, 365
Stedman, Murray S., Jr., 237*n.*
steel industry, Presidents' conflicts with, 103, 307-311
Stevenson, Adlai, 179, 199
Stone, Harlan F., 372
Stouffer, Samuel A., 237*n.*
subcommittees, 286
suburban community, voting behavior and, 230-232
subversive activities, postwar, 26
Supreme Court, U.S., 104, 110, 170, 367; appointments to, 372; on blue laws, 119; checks and balances, 75; Constitution and, 115-125; desegregation and, 166, 398-402; as elite of oracles, 409-410; equal rights and, 402; F.B.I. and, 383; on free speech, 100-117; on legislative investigations, 388-396; on national security, 403-407; powers of, 80-81; Presidency and, 323; redistricting and, 273; regulatory commissions and, 334; restraint of, 77; size of, 68; steel industry and, 308; *see also* courts; judicial process
Sweezy case, 391-393
Symbols, use of, 58

Taft, Robert A., 259
Taft, William Howard, 373
Taft-Hartley Act, 221, 308, 367, 404
Tammany Hall, 176, 197
Tariff Act of 1828, 41
Tariff Commission, 325

Tariff of Abominations, 41, 87
taxes, federalism and, 95
taxing power, "stretching" of, 89
Taylor, John, 16, 18, 42, 43*n.*, 44, 47, 70-71, 86, 108, 110, 123-124
Taylor, Telford, 254*n.*
Teapot Dome scandal, 390
television, anomy and, 142; growth of, 139-141; in political campaigns, 199-204
Tennessee Valley Authority, 95, 328-330
terror, in totalitarian regimes, 105
test votes, 298
third parties, role of, 187
Thomas, Norman, 187
Thompson, Big Bill, 197
Thomson, Charles, 199*n.*
Thoreau, Henry David, 106
Thurmond, Strom, 277
Tidelands Oil Bill, 277
Tocqueville, Alexis de, 127, 133, 136, 184, 237, 303, 311, 421
toleration, vs. coercion, 162; vs. liberty, 106-109; requirements of, 165-167
totalitarian state, law in, 356; pluralism and, 32-33; voting in, 146
total war, federal power and, 89
town-meeting democracy, myth of, 52
tradition, myths and, 30
Transcendalist movement, 154
treason, 101-102
Treasury Department, 324
Tresolini, Rocco J., 117*n.*, 373*n.*
trial by jury, 104
"true believers," 133, 167; as lobbyist, 249
Truman, David, 157*n.*, 159*n.*, 160*n.*
Truman, Harry S., 103, 179, 242, 262, 303-304, 307, 311, 317, 351, 373; in steel industry dispute, 308
trust-busting, 93-94
truth, quest for, 29
Turner, Julius, 252*n.*
Tussman, Joseph, 99*n.*, 422*n.*
tyranny, Calhoun's theory of, 150-151; checks and balances as protection against, 70; of majority, 61, 157; of minority, 42, 70

United Nations, U.S. ambassador to, 315
United States Bank, 330
United States Information Agency, 325, 328
United States Steel Corporation, 309-311
United States Tariff Commission, 325
universals, in democratic society, 28
unorganized groups, 169-170

Uphaus case, 392
Utt, James B., 273

values, standards of, 129-130
Vandenberg, Arthur, 417
Veblen, Thorstein, 94
Velie, Lester, 251*n*.
Veterans Administration, 328, 339
veto power, 153-154, 299, 317
Vice-President, powers and duties of, 280, 312-313, 318
Viereck, Peter, 125
Vinson, Carl, 416
Vinson, Fred M., 373, 401, 405
Virginia and Kentucky Resolutions, 86
Virginia Statute of Religious Freedom, 20-21
visceral response, voting as, 220-222
Voorhis, Jerry, 245*n*.
Vorys, John, 256
vote, nature of, 220-232
voter, alienated, 213-219; apathy or interest of 208-220; individual's importance as, 216; irrational, 233-236; misinformation among, 221; turnout of in presidential elections, 35-36, 209
voting, behavior studies of, 136; citizenship and, 208-240; compromise and, 168; in Congress, 298-299; majority rule in, 35-36; in mass democracy, 146-147; *see also* voting behavior
voting behavior, apathy and futility in, 213-220; family unit in, 225-226; group association in, 226-227; religion and, 224-227; socio-economic status and, 219, 222-225; suburban community and, 230-232; variables in, 223

Wage Stabilization Board, 307
Wagner Act, 170
Wallace, Henry, 187

war, democracy and, 7-8; nuclear, 320, 418; undeclared, 323
ward or precinct, 177
warfare state, democracy and, 415-417
war power, of national government, 89
Warren, Earl, 63, 116, 251, 372, 374, 391-392, 406
Washington, George, 304
Watkins case, 390-392
Way, H. F., 313*n*.
Ways and Means Committee, 281
wealth, gospel of, 94
Webster, Daniel, 87
Welch, Robert, 63*n*.
welfare, taxation and, 90-91
Western civilization, democracy and, 19
Westin, Alan F., 307*n*.
Whigs, 183
Whitaker, Clem, 200
White, William S., 266*n*.
White House staff, 312-313
Whyte, William H., 137*n*.
Williams, G. Mennen, 179
Wilson, Charles E., 307
Wilson, James, 18, 357
Wilson, Woodrow, 187, 303-304, 313, 373, 413
Wise, John, 45, 46*n*., 48
Wolin, Sheldon, 62
Women's Christian Temperance Union, 191
World War I, 110, 356, 413; free speech in, 111
World War II, 23, 26, 89-90, 102, 190, 227, 320, 330, 411, 413, 417, 419; defense contracts in, 229; prosperity since, 185
Wright, Silas, 41

Young, Stephen M., 269